THE HOME REPAIR BOOK

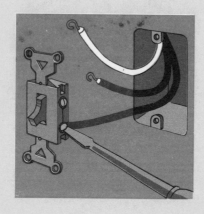

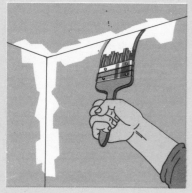

Written by
DICK DEMSKE

Illustrated by
JAMES E. BARRY

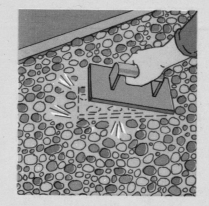

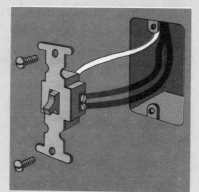

Editor-in-Chief
DONALD D. WOLF

Design and Layout
MARGOT L. WOLF

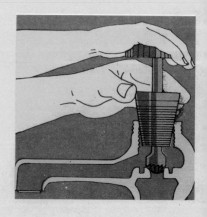

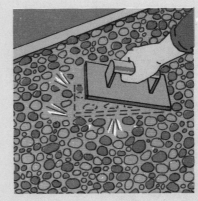

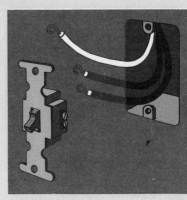

THE HOME REPAIR BOOK

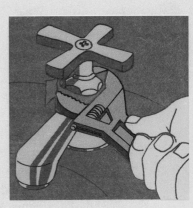

Consolidated Book Publishers

NEW YORK • CHICAGO

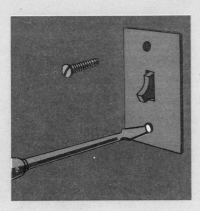

Library of Congress Catalog Card Number: 78-13807
ISBN: 0-8326-2238-9
       0-8326-2239-7 (thumb indexed)

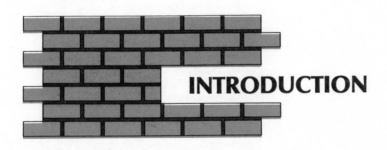

INTRODUCTION

"Do-it-yourself" has become a way of life for a generation of Americans. There are those who derive great pleasure from toiling with tools to keep their homes in tip-top condition. For most of us, however, it is a matter of expediency and economy. Expediency, because nowadays you can seldom find a neighborhood handyman-for-hire who can be called in to right the little things that constantly go wrong. Economy—well, the reasons are obvious. Often, the only way a home improvement is fiscally feasible is by performing your own labor. This is not to imply that there is not a great deal of satisfaction to be found in doing the job yourself, whatever the motivation. A job well done is its own reward.

Of course, not everybody can do every plumbing project. Not everyone can fly a jet, or scramble an egg, or drive a truck—or, for that matter, drive a nail. For this reason, we have graded the actual how-to projects according to their degree of difficulty, as determined by discussions with both professionals and home handymen. Projects deemed within the capabilities of the novice do-it-yourselfer are marked ●. Those for the more experienced and dexterous amateur are marked ▲. More difficult projects, which should be attempted by only the most accomplished do-it-yourselfer (or left to the professionals), are marked ■. Of course, only you can judge your plumbing competence, and we hope that you give careful consideration to your skills before you try any project. If you think you are up to it, so do we. Good luck.

DONALD D. WOLF

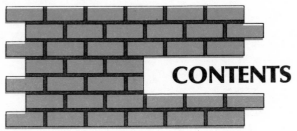

CONTENTS

part 1 PAINTING PANELING WALLPAPERING

1. COLOR AND HOW TO USE IT 15
The Color Scheme 16
Color Camouflage 18

2. PAINT SELECTION 22
Exterior Paints 22
Interior Paints 25
How Much Paint? 27

3. PAINTING TOOLS 32
Paintbrushes 33
Pad Applicators 35
Paint Rollers 35
Paint Sprayers 36
Other Tools of the Painter's Trade 38

4. LADDERS 40
Shopping for a Ladder 40
Materials 41
Ladder Codes 41
Stepladders 42
Stepladder Variations 44
Extension Ladders 45
Ladder Accessories 47
Maintenance 47
Ladder Safety 48

5. INTERIOR PAINTING 50
Preparing New Plaster and Wallboard . 50
Preparing Older Surfaces 50
Preparing Woodwork 52
Paint Application 53
Cleanup 54
Natural Finishes for Trim 54
Unusual Effects 55
Painting Tips 56

6. EXTERIOR PAINTING 58
Surface Preparation 58

Wood Surfaces 59
Metal Surfaces 60
Masonry Surfaces 60
Paint Application Methods 61
When to Paint 61
How Many Coats? 62
Putting on the Paint 63
Natural Finishes 64
Solid-Color Stains 65

7. PAINT FAILURE—CAUSES AND CURES 66
Interior Failure 66
Exterior Paint Breakdown 67
Structural Problems 70

8. WALLPAPERING 72
Wallpaper Colors and Patterns 72
Estimating Wallpaper, Trim, and Paste . 73
Vinyls 75
Foils 75
Grass Cloth, Hemp, Burlap, Cork 75
Flocks 77
Prepasted Wallpaper 77
Paperhanging Tools 77
General Preparation of Wall Surfaces . 79
Preparing the Work Area 80
Removing Selvage 81
Pattern Location 81
Hanging Wallpaper 82
Making Seams 84
Corners 85
Papering Around Doors and Windows . 86

9. PANELING 88
Types of Paneling 89
Tools Needed for the Job 90
Measuring the Room 92
Paneling in New Construction 92
Paneling in Existing Construction 93
Are the Walls Even? 94
Furring 95
Backing for Paneling 96
Panel Preparation 96
Installing the Paneling 96
Using Adhesive 97
Molding and Trim 100
Care and Maintenance 101

CONTENTS

part **2** **INTERIOR HOME REPAIRS**

1. **DO-IT-YOURSELF HOME REPAIRS** 105
   What to Look For 105
2. **BEFORE YOU BUY A HOUSE** 107
   Foundation Defects 107
   Heating Equipment 109
   Doors, Windows, Floors, Walls 109
   Household Equipment 110
3. **ROUTINE MAINTENANCE** 111
   Seasonal Checklist 111
4. **THE BASIC TOOLBOX** 114
   Nail Hammer .115
   Screwdriver 115
   Hand Drill 115
   Slip-Joint Pliers 116
   Adjustable Wrench 116
   Measuring Tools 117
   Try Square 117
   Level 117
   Handsaw 118
   Nested Saw 118
   Utility Knife 118
   Putty Knife 118
   Wood Chisel .118
   C-Clamp 119
   Force Cup 119
   Electric Drill 120
   Drill Accessories 121
5. **FLOORS AND STAIRS** 123
   Wood Floors .123
   Cracked and Split Flooring 125
   Sagging Floors 126
   Concrete Floors 127
   Tile and Sheet Flooring 128
   Stair Repairs .131
6. **WALLS AND CEILINGS** 133
   Plaster Repairs 133
   Gypsum Wallboard 133
   Wall Paneling .136
   Ceramic Tile .137
   Ceiling Tile 138
7. **DOORS AND WINDOWS** 140
   Sticking Doors 140
   Fitting a Door .141

   Window Problems 143
   Installing Glass 145
   Screen Repair 147
8. **WEATHERPROOFING AND INSULATING** 149
   Weatherstripping 149
   Insulation in Attics 151
   Insulation in Exterior Walls 152
9. **CONDENSATION PROBLEMS** 153
   When Does It Occur and Where? 153
   Moisture Sources 154
   Visible Condensation 155
   Reducing Relative Humidity 156
   Concealed Condensation 156
10. **BASEMENTS, CRAWL SPACES** 157
    What's Your Problem? 157
    Condensation Cures 158
    Condensation in New Houses 159
    Seepage Solutions 159
    Stopping Leaks 160
    Crawl Spaces 161
    Preventive Measures 162
    A Final Note of Caution 162
11. **CONTROLLING HOUSEHOLD PESTS** 163
    Pesticides and their Application 163
    Houseflies 164
    Silverfish and Firebrats 165
    Mice 165
    Rats 166
    Pesticide Safety 166
12. **SIMPLE PLUMBING REPAIRS** 167
    Repairing Water Faucets and Valves . .167
    Leaks in Pipes and Tanks 168
    Water Hammer 169
    Frozen Water Pipes 170
    Repairing Toilets 170
    Clearing Clogged Drains 173
13. **SIMPLE ELECTRICAL REPAIRS** 174
    Disconnecting Electrical Current 175
    Fuses and Circuit Breakers 175
    Appliance Cords and Plugs 176
    Lamp Repairs 177
    Doorbells and Chimes 178
14. **STORM DAMAGE** 180
    Drying and Cleaning 180
    Checking the Electrical System 181
    Electric Motors 181
    Household Mechanical Equipment . . .181
    Checking the Heating System 182

Water Supply and Sanitary Systems . .182
Odors 184
Floors, Woodwork, Doors, Walls 184
Salvaging Furniture 186

15. EMERGENCY!   189
Plumbing Emergencies 189
Furnace Failure 191
Gas Odor 191
Fire 192

part **3** EXTERIOR HOME REPAIRS

1. THE TOOLBOX   195
Tool Storage 195
Buying Tools 196
Claw Hammer 196
Screwdrivers 197
Pliers 198
Handsaws .199
Measuring Instruments 199
Utility Knife 200
Putty Knife .200
Chisels 200
Levels 201
Wrenches .201
Electric Drill 202
Other Tools 204

2. ROOFS, GUTTERS, DOWNSPOUTS   205
Making Repairs 206
Asphalt Roofing 207
Built-Up Roofings 210
Slate Roofings 210
Tile Roofings 211
Asbestos-Cement Shingles 212
Wood Shingles 213
Roof Drainage 214
Downspouts 216

3. EXTERIOR WALLS   217
Take a Calk Walk 217
Brick and Concrete Block 218
Cement and Stucco Walls 219
Siding 221

4. PROPER PAINTING PRACTICES   225
Surface Preparation 225
Primers 227
Choosing Paint 227

How to Paint 228
Painting Masonry 229
Metal Surfaces 231
Blistering 232
Chalking 233
Checking and Alligatoring 233
Cracking 234
Crawling 234
Fading 235
Bleeding 235
Wrinkling 236
Mildew and Sulfide Discoloration 236
Peeling 237

5. DOORS AND WINDOWS   238
Preventive Maintenance 238
Sticking Doors 239
Sticking Windows 242
Replacing Broken Glass 245
Screen Repair 247

6. PORCHES   249
Sagging Porch 249
Replacing Damaged Floorboards 250
Railing Repairs 251
Porch Steps 252

7. DRIVEWAYS AND SIDEWALKS   253
Minor Concrete Repairs 253
Large Cracks 254
Badly Flaking Surfaces 254
Heaved Sidewalk Sections 255
Steps in Pouring Concrete 256
Subgrade Preparation 256
Setting Forms 256
The Proper Mix 258
How Much Concrete? 259
Mixing 260
Placing the Mix 260
Striking Off and Floating 261
Edging and Grooving 261
Control Joints 262
Finishing 263
Curing 264
Blacktop Repair 264

8. PATIO REPAIRS   266
Concrete Patio Repairs 266
Brick Patios 268
Flagstone Patio Repairs 270
Patio Block 271

9. POOL CARE   272
Pool Chemicals 272

CONTENTS

Routine Cleaning 272
Pool Repairs .273
Painting 274
Winterizing 275

10. STORM!   276
The Emergency Tool Kit 276
Window Breakage 276
Roof Leaks .277
Icy Walks 278
Fallen Power Lines 278

11. IF YOU'RE BUYING…   279
Starting Your Inspection Tour 279
Above the Foundation 280
Up on the Roof 281
Should You Still Buy? 281
Professional Inspection Services 282

part 4
ELECTRICAL INSTALLATIONS AND REPAIRS

1. BASICS OF ELECTRICITY   285
The Nature of Electricity 286
Terms and Definitions 286
The Household Electrical System 287
Healthy Respect 289
Do It Yourself? 290
Electrical Codes 292
Efficient and Economical Use of Electric
Power 293

2. WHEN YOU BUY A HOUSE   294
The New House 294
Inspecting the New Home 298
Older Homes 300

3. ELECTRICAL TOOLS AND
MATERIALS   302
The Electrician's Toolbox 302
Materials 305

4. HOW TO WIRE NEW CONSTRUCTION 313
Planning 313
Mounting Boxes 314
Running the Cable 315
Thin-Wall Conduit 317
Switches 320

Three-Way Switches 321
Grounding 323
Splicing 323
Installing Lighting Fixtures 325
Hooking Up to the Hot Stuff 325
High-Voltage Lines 327
Outdoor Wiring 327

5. WIRING IN AN EXISTING HOUSE   329
Tracing the Circuits 329
Adding to Existing Circuits 330
"Roughing In" 331
Running the Wire 332
Fishing 334
Mounting the Boxes 335
Adding New Circuits 336
Surface Wiring 336
Kitchen Appliance Center 336
Adding a Subpanel 337

6. SIMPLE ELECTRICAL REPAIRS   338
Troubleshooting 338
Locating and Curing the Problem 340
Replacing Defective Receptacles and
Switches 340
Ceiling and Wall Fixtures 341
Plug and Cord Replacement 342
Lamp Repairs 346
Fluorescent Fixtures 348
Doorbells and Chimes 350

7. SMALL APPLIANCE REPAIRS   352
Look for the Obvious Things First 352
Doing It Yourself 353
Taking It Apart 354
Testing 354
Thermostats .355
Electric Toaster 355
Coffee Maker 356
Electric Frying Pan 358
Waffle Iron 359
Dry or Steam Iron 361
Electric Motors 362
Electric Fan .363
Mixer 365
Blender 365
Rotisserie Oven/Broiler 366
Electric Can Opener 367
Knife Sharpener 368
Electric Knife 368
Vacuum Cleaner 369
Hair Dryer 371

part **5** PLUMBING

1. HOW A PLUMBING SYSTEM WORKS 375
The Supply 379
Plumbing Fixtures 378
Drainage 378
Know Your Home's Plumbing System .382
Cross-Connections 382
Draining and Filling the Plumbing
System 383
Plumbing and the Law 384
2. WHEN YOU BUY A HOUSE… 385
The New Home 385
The Older Home 386
3. PLUMBING TOOLS 387
Be Prepared .387
Beyond Emergencies 389
Wrenches 389
Adjustable Wrenches 389
Pipe Wrenches 390
Pliers 392
Cutters 392
Reamers and Files 393
Threaders 394
Vises 394
Flaring Tools .395
Propane Torch 396
Tools for Working with Cast Iron Pipe . .396
4. WATER SUPPLY LINES 397
Copper Pipe .397
Working with Rigid Copper Pipe 398
Working with Flexible Copper Tubing . .399
Galvanized Pipe 401
Brass Pipe 402
Plastic Pipe 403
Pipe Fittings .406
Valves 408
Faucets 411
5. DRAINAGE PIPES AND FITTINGS 414
Cast Iron Pipe 414
Galvanized Steel Pipe 418
Copper DWV Pipe 418
Plastic DWV Pipe 418
Fixture Drain Lines 419
DWV Fittings .419

**6. SELECTING AND INSTALLING
PLUMBING AND FIXTURES** 422
Fixture Supply Lines 423
Fixture Supply Stop Valves 424
P and S Traps 425
Kitchen Faucets 426
Sink Strainers 428
Food Waste Disposers 429
Kitchen Sinks 430
Lavatory Faucets 431
Lavatories 431
Tub and Shower Fittings 433
Bathtub Drains 434
Bathtubs 435
Shower Stalls 437
Toilets 438
Bidets 442
Water Heaters 442
7. SEPTIC TANKS 445
Preventive Maintenance 446
8. WHEN THINGS GO WRONG 447
Leaky Faucets 447
Noisy Faucets 449
Leaky Valves .449
Toilet Tank Troubles 450
Clogged Toilet 454
Clogged Sink Drains 455
Clogged Lavatories 456
Clogged Bathtubs 457
Clogged Sewer 458
Sweating Pipes 459
Frozen Pipes .459
Leaking Pipes 460

part **6** HOME COMFORT (HEATING, ETC.)

1. HEATING SYSTEMS 465
Space Heating Units 466
Central Heating: Warm Air 467
Central Heating: Hot Water, Steam . . 471
Electric Heating 475
Heat Pumps .476
Solar Heating 477

CONTENTS

2. **FUELS**   480
   Comparing Fuel Costs 480
   Oil 482
   Gas 482
   Electricity 484
   Coal 484
   Wood 485
   Future Fuels 485

3. **HEATING SYSTEM CONTROLS**   487
   Thermostats 487
   Limit Controls 488
   Oil Burner Controls 488
   Stoker-Fired Coal Burner Controls . . . 489
   Other Heating System Controls 489

4. **HEATING A NEW OR REMODELED SPACE**   491
   The Capacity of Your Present Heating
   System 491
   Extending a Warm Air System 492
   Extending a Hot Water System 499
   Time for a Change? 501
   Fireplaces 501

5. **ROUTINE MAINTENANCE AND SERVICING**   503
   Routine Maintenance 503
   Burner Care 506
   Heating Problems 507

6. **KEEPING COOL**   509
   Benefits of Air Conditioning 509

   How Refrigerated Air Conditioning
   Works 510
   Central Air Conditioners 511
   Room Air Conditioning 512
   Estimating Cooling Needs 513
   Before Your Buy 514
   Shopping for a Room Air Conditioner 517
   Routine Maintenance and Simple
   Repairs 519

7. **HOW TO SAVE ON HOME COMFORT CONDITIONING**   521
   Insulation 521
   Weatherstripping and Calking 532
   Storm Sash 536
   Equipment Location 539
   Operating Economy 540
   Commonsense Dollar Savers 541

8. **OTHER COMFORT FACTORS**   544
   Humidification 544
   Dehumidification 546
   Attic Ventilation 548
   Electronic Air Cleaning 549

9. **COMFORT QUOTIENT FOR HOME BUYERS**   550
   The New House 550
   The Older Home 551

CONVERSION FACTORS 553
INDEX 561

part 1

PAINTING
PANELING
WALLPAPERING

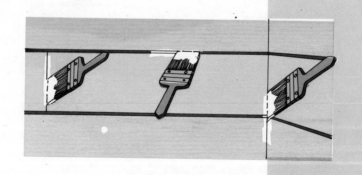

1

Color and How to Use It

APPEARANCE is usually the primary motivation for painting, and it's true that a fresh paint job on the inside or outside of a house is the easiest way to improve its looks. Protection is also important, particularly on the home's exterior. Where bare wood or metal are exposed to the weather, you can expect deterioration and decay, as well as a shabby appearance. The most economical way to provide the necessary protection is with a coat of paint. A good paint job is not cheap, but it is a worthwhile investment. A first-class paint job pays off in better looks over longer life, resulting in less cost per year.

When should you paint? Indoors, it doesn't make much difference. Many people like to brighten up their homes in the late fall in preparation for the holiday season. Others devote the whole winter to a room-by-room rejuvenation of the home. Midsummer is the only time we don't recommend—those hot days should be reserved for cooler activities. The same goes for exterior painting—not only would the hot sun cause discomfort, but also most paints cannot be satisfactorily applied in such heat. Of course, you won't paint outdoors in very cold weather, either. Spring is the favorite time for exterior painting, but early in the fall is just as good, especially if there are areas on your home that are down to bare wood. Such areas should at least be touched up, if you do not plan on painting the whole house at this time. It's a Band-Aid approach, but better than nothing.

Should you do it yourself? The question can be answered only by you, since you must realistically assess your own capabilities in the light of the job to be done. If you're afraid of heights, stay away from exterior painting above the first story. If you have a distaste for such time-consuming jobs as scraping, burning, and calking, stick to interior painting, where these measures are not required. But if you have the time and patience, you can do a highly satisfactory and satisfying job on your home. And, perhaps more important, you will be able to save from $150 to $500 on the interior, and from $350 to $1,000 on the exterior by doing the job yourself.

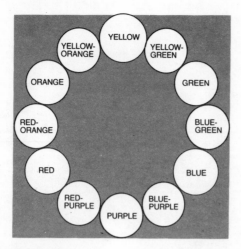

Color wheel.

Primary colors.

THE COLOR SCHEME

The basic factor in color harmony is the color wheel. An understanding of the fundamental elements of color, as illustrated by the color wheel, is very helpful in planning successful decorating schemes.

The primary colors are yellow, red, and blue. Secondary colors are combinations of the primary colors on either side. The wheel is completed by combining the primary and secondary colors and forming a third group, called the tertiary or intermediate colors.

Colors have certain psychological effects upon human beings, and these effects may be broken down into two groups. Warm colors are happy, stimulating, bright, spirited. These colors are generally on the left side of the color wheel, ranging from yellow to red. Cool colors are those that are quiet, soothing, restful, and placid. These colors are more on the right side of the wheel—mainly greens and blues.

As in music, harmony in color means the pleasant association of one tone with another. Interior decoration leans heavily upon the skillful use of these associations. There are many types of color harmony.

Monochromatic harmony is the simplest, and probably the most overlooked, form of color harmony. It is simply the use of different intensities of the same color, such as green, light green, and dark green. Tints and shades of the same color are formed by adding white or black to the original hue. This type of harmony creates an impression of sophistication by combining quiet and subdued contrast.

Analogous harmony uses colors that are next to each other on the color wheel. Two to four colors in sequence may be used. Softness and delicacy are the result.

Complementary harmony is one of the easiest ways to create a lively color scheme. Simply use the two colors that are exact opposites on the color wheel.

Split-complementary harmony gives more variety. Determine which will be your basic color, find its true complement, then use either or both adjacent colors.

Double-complementary harmony splits both ends of the true complements, and gets two sets of compléments.

Mutual complements as a color scheme utilizes five analagous colors (next to each other on the color wheel). The true complement of the middle color of this group is then used for contrast. Color planning of this type frequently achieves a bright, lively effect, with the complement of the middle color providing a dramatic contrast.

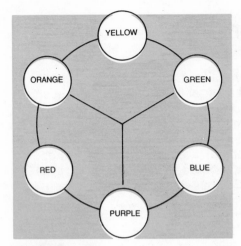

Secondary colors.

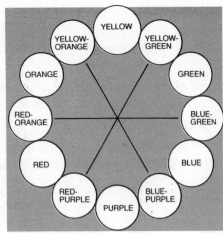

Tertiary colors.

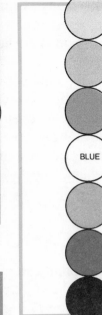

Monochromatic harmony.

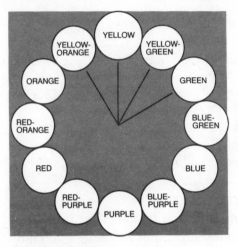

Analogous harmony.

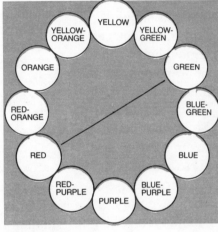

Complementary harmony.

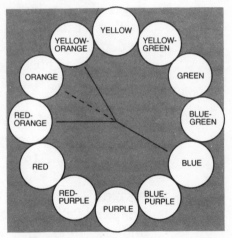

Split-complementary harmony.

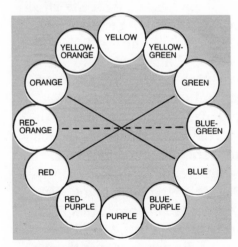

Double-complementary harmony.

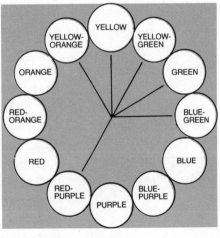

Mutual complements.

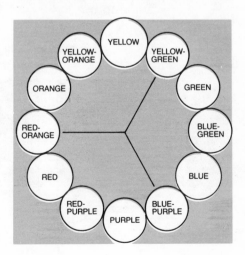

Triad harmony.

Color and How to Use It

Triad harmony is one of the most common and basic color schemes, utilizing three colors on the wheel equidistant from each other.

Obviously, there are many different ways to decorate a home—even further combinations of the color schemes discussed above. The important factors are to plan some sort of pattern, and to avoid the extremes of monotony and overdiversity.

COLOR CAMOUFLAGE

The right paint can have a magic effect in emphasizing the good points and hiding the defects of a home. Light colors reflect and tend to create a cheerful atmosphere—they are effective in making small rooms seem larger. Dark colors absorb light and, when used extensively on large surfaces, tend to be depressing. They can be used to make a large, well-lighted room seem smaller and more intimate. If a ceiling is too high, painting it a dark color may give a better sense of proportion to the room. Bright colors attract the eye and may be employed to distract attention from an unattractive feature—they may also, if improperly used, become irritating. Warm colors—reds, oranges, yellows—convey a cozy feeling and are stimulating, whereas the cool colors—blues, greens, violets—are relaxing and cooling.

Painting a too-high ceiling in a darker color makes room appear lower

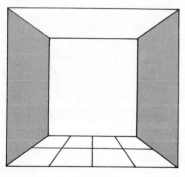 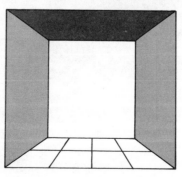

Light Reflectance of Various Colors

You may wish to make the most of the natural and artificial light within a room (such as a kitchen), or you may want to soften the glare that sometimes enters through large glass areas (such as a living room with southern exposure). Dark colors absorb light, whereas light colors reflect it, as indicated by this chart.

White	80%
Light ivory	71%
Apricot-beige	66%
Lemon yellow	65%
Ivory	59%
Light buff	56%
Peach	53%
Salmon	53%
Pale apple green	51%
Medium gray	43%
Light green	41%
Pale blue	41%
Deep rose	12%
Dark green	9%

Red is stimulating. It makes a room look smaller and dominates in large doses, but it may provide just the excitement you are looking for. Green has the opposite effect; it is smooth and tranquil. Yellow is cheerful, blue is soothing, purple is subduing and somewhat regal. White, gray, brown, and beige are neutral colors that make fine backgrounds but can be dull when used as the principal decorating schemes. These neutral colors have found a certain popularity among modern designers, however.

Decide which features of the room you feel should be accented, which you wish to minimize. A fireplace or some other feature of interest might be made the focal point of the decorating scheme; accent it by painting the surrounding wall a contrasting color. A long, narrow room may take on seemingly improved proportions if one of the end walls is painted a darker hue than the other walls, visually drawing it closer to the center of the room. Painting the walls and woodwork the same color gives a sense of spaciousness and trimness—painting the woodwork in an accenting color can complement the walls and point up some special characteristic.

A room should also be considered in terms of its function as well as its relation to neighboring rooms. An entryway, for example, should be painted in friendly, inviting tones, and in tones that will blend naturally with those of the living areas into which it leads the visitor. If you entertain formally, or enjoy dining by candlelight, dining-room colors should help to enhance the moods that are sought. And, of course, the colors on a room's walls must harmonize with the furniture and accessories of that room. If you proudly display bright

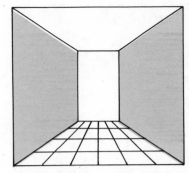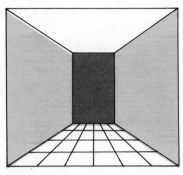

Painting one of the end walls of a long, narrow room in a darker color improves its appearance.

modern paintings on your walls, determine what wall colors will best show off the pictures without distracting attention from them. Often, a favorite drapery material or a cherished couch or other piece of furniture is the key to the decorating scheme for a given room—and, ultimately, the color scheme for the entire home.

Color Do's and Don'ts

DO

• Remember that large areas of color emphasize the color. Choose a lighter shade for such areas.

• Use light colors in a small room to increase apparent size.

• Emphasize reds and yellows in windowless rooms.

• Make use of horizontal and vertical lines for giving visual balance to rooms with high or low ceilings.

• Aim for a continuing color flow through your home—from room to room—using harmonious colors in adjoining areas.

• Paint the ceiling of a room in a deeper color than the walls if you want it to appear lower; paint it in a lighter shade for the opposite effect.

• Study color swatches in both daylight and nightlight. Colors often change under artificial lighting.

DON'T

• Use too large a pattern, or too much pattern in an area.

• Use equal proportions of colors; always use more of one color than another.

• Choose neutral or negative colors simply because they are safe and "mix well."

• Paint woodwork and trim of a small room in a color different from the background color, or the room will appear small and cluttered.

• Paint radiators, pipes, or similar projections in a color that contrasts with walls, or they will be emphasized.

• Use glossy paints on walls or ceilings of living areas, since the shiny surface creates undesirable glare.

Suggested Exterior Color Schemes

If your house has shutters, paint the trim the same color as the body of the house—or white. If not, use the trim colors suggested in the chart.

IF THE ROOF OF YOUR HOUSE IS	YOU CAN PAINT THE BODY	. . . and the trim or shutters and doors															
		Pink	Bright red	Red-orange	Tile red	Cream	Bright yellow	Light green	Dark green	Gray-green	Blue-green	Light blue	Dark blue	Blue-gray	Violet	Brown	White
GRAY	White	x	x	x	x	x	x	x	x	x	x	x	x	x	x		
	Gray	x	x	x	x		x	x	x	x	x	x	x	x	x		x
	Cream-yellow		x		x		x		x	x							x
	Pale green				x		x		x	x							x
	Dark green	x				x	x	x									x
	Putty			x	x				x	x			x	x		x	
	Dull red	x				x		x						x			x
GREEN	White	x	x	x	x	x	x	x	x	x	x	x	x	x	x		
	Gray			x		x	x	x									x
	Cream-yellow		x		x			x	x	x						x	x
	Pale green			x	x	x			x								x
	Dark green	x		x		x	x	x									x
	Beige			x					x	x	x		x	x			
	Brown	x				x	x	x									x
	Dull red					x		x		x							x
RED	White		x		x				x		x			x			
	Light gray		x		x				x								x
	Cream-yellow		x		x						x		x	x			
	Pale green		x		x												x
	Dull red					x		x		x	x						x
BROWN	White			x	x		x	x	x	x	x		x	x	x	x	
	Buff			x					x	x	x					x	
	Pink-beige			x					x	x						x	x
	Cream-yellow			x					x	x	x					x	
	Pale green								x	x						x	
	Brown			x		x	x										x
BLUE	White			x	x		x					x	x				
	Gray			x	x							x	x				x
	Cream-yellow			x	x										x	x	
	Blue			x		x	x						x				x

• Color and How to Use It

Exterior sleight of hand can also be accomplished by a coat of paint. A fresh, crisp appearance can give a formerly drab and tired-looking home a new lease on life—and a definite psychological lift to its inhabitants. But it can do even more than that—it can alter the entire physical appearance of the house.

Often, the roof color sets the tone for the rest of the house. If it is a neutral hue, the home can be brightened up by the use of a bolder, warm color such as red. Low homes can be made to look higher by emphasizing vertical lines with trim paint. Top-heavy, boxy structures benefit from color-accenting of horizontal lines such as fasciae and windowsills. Painting the upper story a darker color than the lower achieves the same effect. Split levels look better when they are not too "split." The different levels should usually be the same color. Large homes, particularly if they are well landscaped, lend themselves better to the cooler hues of the spectrum. Many vintage homes suffer from the visual weight of a profusion of gables and other projections. These should be camouflaged by painting them to match their surroundings, so that there is at least a suggestion of harmony and continuity in the home's lines.

Color is highly personal. Certain rules and color schemes can be suggested, but don't be afraid to use your own good taste and initiative. It's your house and your money. If it turns out to be a visual atrocity, you can always repaint. But chances are good that, with a little forethought and the careful selection of colors, a fresh coat of paint, both indoors and out, will do your home proud.

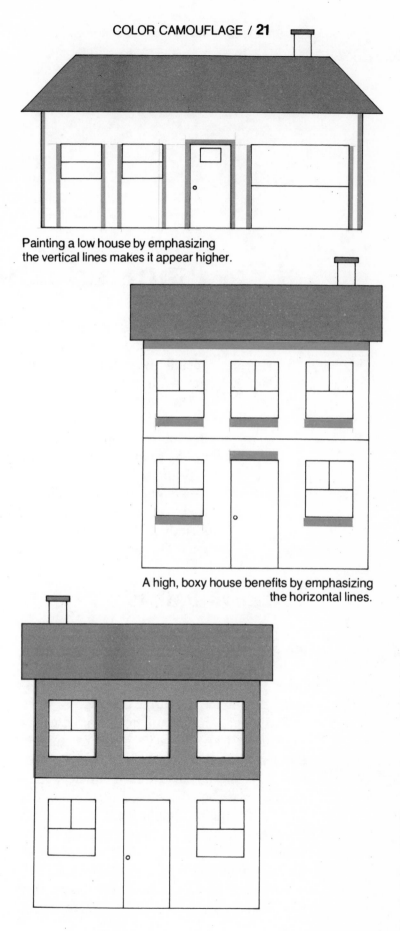

Painting a low house by emphasizing the vertical lines makes it appear higher.

A high, boxy house benefits by emphasizing the horizontal lines.

The same effect can be achieved by painting a high, boxy house in two colors.

Color and How to Use It

Paint Selection

SEEMINGLY bewildering array of paints is available—but don't be bewildered. Each type is formulated to do specific things or to act in a specific way. It is just a matter of deciding which one is best suited to the job you want it to do.

One type of paint that is never suitable is the bargain-basement special. The only thing you can be sure of with a cheap paint is that you will be doing the job over again long before you should have to. This is one area where a penny saved is wasted money—and time.

Some paints (and some applications) require the use of an undercoat first; others can be applied directly as a first, or final, coat. Manufacturers include their recommendations on the paint labels, and these should always be strictly followed. Doing it yourself doesn't necessarily mean doing it your way. Or you'll be doing it over.

EXTERIOR PAINTS

Several types of paint for house exteriors are available. Ideally, a white house paint should have a clean, highly reflective whiteness. It should remain clean and white at all times during the life of the coating.

The ideal paint should not be affected by moisture. It should be resistant to staining by rust and other residues of metal corrosion. It should also resist mildew and should not be discolored by industrial gases. The paint should wear away at an even rate, leaving a smooth adherent film, suitable for repainting after a reasonable number of years.

Although no house paint on the market has all of these desirable characteristics, many modern paints of high quality can be depended upon to provide excellent performance under most of these conditions. You should be aware of the climatic and atmospheric conditions to which house paints are subjected in your area. Through your paint dealer, you should determine the types of house paint that perform best under local conditions and the performance characteristics that are most important to your paint job.

No one type of house paint is "better" than another in every respect. Within each type, almost any quality of paint may be made, depending upon the grades of ingredients used, their relative proportions, and the care used in compounding the product. Regardless of type of paint selected, there will be greater assurance of satisfactory service if the particular paint was produced by a reputable manufacturer and sold through a reputable dealer. No type of paint formulation will guarantee a high-quality product; this can be insured only by the integrity of the maker.

Paints used on house siding are mostly based on linseed oil—that is, they have linseed oil "vehicles" to carry the pigment. These paints have a long history of satisfactory service. Many improvements have been made by modifying the linseed oils and by changing the pigmentation. Further, since no one paint can satisfy all requirements under different conditions, paints have been specialized to produce the best result for various use requirements.

For example, white paints may be self-cleaning—free-chalking—for use where siding covers the lower portion of a house; or they may be chalk-resistant for use where chalk rundown will mar brick or stone below the siding. This should be kept in mind when buying white house paint, since chalk rundown on masonry is unsightly. Another type of white paint is fume-resistant. It is used where industrial or other fumes may be present and could stain the paint. For warm, humid conditions in most latitudes, mildew-resistant paints are used to discourage mildew discoloration.

If the old paint is sound but dirty, a one-coat paint will give a gleaming new surface. Chalk-resistant, pastel-colored paints can be made from white one-coat paints. All pastel tints must be made with chalk-resistant or tint-based paints to avoid early fading. Dark-colored paints cannot be made from white paint; they are colored during manufacture. There are shingle and shake paints and clear finishes for houses sided with shingles or shakes. The choice depends on whether or not the grain pattern of the wood is to remain visible. Clear finishes need refinishing more frequently

than opaque paints, but they reveal the beauty of the wood.

All the paints mentioned above, except clear finishes, require a primer when new wood is painted. For repainting, the primer is necessary only if the old paint is in bad condition. The primer should be the one recommended for the topcoat selected.

Over the past decade or so, exterior paints have been developed in which the solvent for the vehicle is water, instead of turpentine or mineral spirits—the solvents used for linseed oil. The first of these water-thinned products were the so-called latex paints, which are emulsions of the vehicle in water. After the paint is applied, the emulsion coalesces, permitting the water to evaporate, leaving the vehicle and pigment. More recent are paints in which the linseed oil vehicle is in true water solution. The oil had to be altered to accomplish this, but such paints have the properties of both water and oil paints. The advantages of both the emulsion and the linseed-oil solution include ease of application, cleanup with water, good tint retention, and easy cleaning. Emulsion paints dry faster than do the solution paints. As repaints, emulsion paints may not adhere well to chalky surfaces. The procedure recommended by the manufacturer must be followed. It will likely call

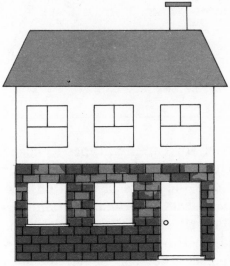

Self-cleaning paint may stain brick or other surfaces below it.

Paint Selection

What To Use And Where
(Exterior Surfaces)

Surface	House Paint (Oil or Oil-Alkyd)	Cement Powder Paint	Exterior Clear Finish	Aluminum Paint	Wood Stain	Roof Coating	Trim Paint	Porch and Deck Paint	Primer or Undercoater	Metal Primer	House Paint (Latex)	Water Repellent Preservative
MASONRY												
Asbestos Cement	X•								X		X	
Brick	X•	X		X					X		X	X
Cement & Cinder Block	X•	X		X					X		X	
Concrete/Masonry Porches And Floors								X			X	
Coal Tar Felt Roof						X						
Stucco	X•	X		X					X		X	
METAL												
Aluminum Windows	X•			X			X•			X	X•	
Steel Windows	X•			X•			X•			X	X•	
Metal Roof	X•									X	X•	
Metal Siding	X•			X•			X•			X	X•	
Copper Surfaces			X									
Galvanized Surfaces	X•			X•			X•			X	X•	
Iron Surfaces	X•			X•			X•			X	X•	
WOOD												
Clapboard	X•			X					X		X•	
Natural Wood Siding & Trim			X		X							
Shutters & Other Trim	X•						X•		X		X•	
Wood Frame Windows	X•			X			X•		X		X•	
Wood Porch Floor								X				
Wood Shingle Roof					X							X

X• Black dot indicates that a primer, sealer, or fill coat may be necessary before the finishing coat (unless surface has been previously finished).

for a primer for emulsion types to insure adhesion to chalky surfaces.

Moisture is the cause of much unsatisfactory paint service. Under certain conditions, the effects of moisture can be controlled best by using special blister-resistant paints. They may be oil- or water-base paints, and must be used as directed to obtain their maximum efficiency.

Exterior trim paints are used principally on wood trim, screen frames, shutters, and other small areas of the home. Dark, medium, and light greens are among the most popular colors. Good leveling or freedom from brush marks, rapid drying, high gloss, good color- and gloss-retention, one-coat hiding, and good durability are important properties of exterior trim paints. They are usually solvent-thinned.

Some paint manufacturers market special undercoats in a gray or other neutral color as a primer for the trim and dark-colored house paints. The regular primer for white and light-tinted house paints is also satisfactory as a primer for the dark-colored paints. This primer, generally white, may be tinted to a neutral gray or any other color with pastels in oil when used under dark-colored paints.

Exterior latex masonry paint is a standard paint for masonry. Cement-base paint may be used on nonglazed brick, stucco, cement, and cinder block. Rubber-base paint and aluminum paint with the proper vehicle may also be used.

Ordinary house or trim paints may be used for the finish coats on gutters, downspouts, and hardware or grilles. A specially recommended primer must be used on copper or galvanized steel. Use house paint, aluminum paint, or exterior enamel on steel or aluminum windows. Paint window screens with a special screen enamel.

Porch-and-deck paint may be used on both concrete and wood porches and steps. On wood, a primer coat is applied first. On concrete, an alkali-resistant primer is recommended. Rubber-base paints are excellent for use on concrete floors. Hard and glossy concrete surfaces must be etched or roughened first.

INTERIOR PAINTS

Many different kinds and formulations of paints and other finishes are available for interior use, and new ones frequently appear on the market. For a specific selection consult your paint dealer. Reputable dealers keep abreast of developments in the paint industry and stock the newest formulations. The usual interior paint job consists of painting wallboard or plaster walls and ceilings, woodwork, and wood windows and doors. For these surfaces you need to choose first between solvent-thinned paint (oil-based) and water-thinned paint (commonly called latex paint, but not necessarily latex), and then between a gloss, semigloss or flat finish. (Enamels, which are made with a varnish, resin or latex base instead of the usual linseed-oil vehicle, are included under the oil-paint grouping.)

Oil-based paints are very durable, are highly resistant to staining and damage, can withstand frequent scrubbings, and give good one-coat coverage. Many latex paints have similar properties. The main advantages of latex paint are easier application, faster drying, and simpler tool cleanup. The brushes, rollers, and other equipment can be easily cleaned with water.

Both oil-based and latex paints are available in gloss, semigloss, and flat finishes. Glossy finishes look shiny and clean easily. Flat finishes show dirt more readily but absorb light and thus reduce glare. Semigloss finishes have properties of both glossy and flat finishes.

Because enamel is durable and easy to clean, semigloss or gloss enamel is recommended for the walls of kitchens, bathrooms, and laundry rooms. For the walls of nurseries and playrooms, either oil-based or latex semigloss enamel paint is suggested. Flat paint is generally used for the walls of living rooms and other nonwork or nonplay rooms.

Ceilings are important as light-reflecting surfaces in most rooms, and they should have dull-surfaced coatings that reflect light evenly. In bathrooms and kitchens, however, semigloss finishes are generally more desirable because of their washability.

What To Use And Where
(Interior Surfaces)

	Flat Enamel	Semigloss Enamel	Gloss Enamel	Interior Varnish	Shellac-Lacquer	Wax (Liquid or Paste)	Wax (Emulsion)	Stain	Wood Sealer	Floor Varnish	Floor Paint or Enamel	Aluminum Paint	Sealer or Undercoater	Metal Primer	Latex (Wall) Flat	Latex Gloss & Semigloss
MASONRY																
Asphalt Tile							X									
Concrete Floors						X•	X•	X			X				X	
Kitchen & Bathroom Walls		X•	X•										X			X•
Linoleum							X									
New Masonry	X•	X•											X		X	X•
Old Masonry	X	X										X	X		X	X•
Plaster Walls & Ceiling	X•	X•											X		X	X•
Vinyl & Rubber Tile Floors						X	X									
Wall Board	X•	X•											X		X	X•
METAL																
Aluminum Windows	X•	X•										X		X	X•	X•
Heating Ducts	X•	X•										X		X	X•	X•
Radiators & Heating Pipes	X•	X•										X		X	X•	X•
Steel Cabinets	X•	X•												X		X•
Steel Windows	X•	X•										X		X	X•	X•
WOOD																
Floors				X	X	X•	X•	X	X•	X•						
Paneling	X•	X•	X	X	X			X	X						X•	X•
Stair Risers	X•	X•	X	X				X	X							X•
Stair Treads					X			X	X	X	X					
Trim	X•	X•	X	X	X			X					X		X•	X•
Window Sills			X													

Plaster and wallboard ceilings can be coated with flat oil paints or paints of semigloss, emulsion, or rubber-base types. If the ceiling has not been previously painted, a primer should be applied before flat or semigloss paint. On acoustic tile, use flat paint, thinned in accordance with the manufacturer's recommendation. Woodwork that is new and is to be given an opaque coating requires an undercoat. For a finishing coat, you can use semigloss, enamel, or flat oil paint. Flat oil paints are easily finger-marked and are unsatisfactory for window-sills. Emulsion and rubber-base paints are also suitable for woodwork. All these coatings can be used to refinish woods that have previously been painted, varnished, or shellacked. Before refinishing, make sure that all traces of wax have been removed and that any still glossy surface has been sanded so that the new coating can adhere firmly. Where there is to be a radical change of color, more than one coat may be required. If enamel or semigloss is to be used, an enamel undercoat should be applied first. Where a transparent coating is desired so that the grain of the wood will be visible, shellac or interior varnish, followed by wax, is usually favored. Open-grain woods require a filler. Stains can be used to add color to the wood.

When an opaque finish is desired for wood paneling, use the same treatment as for woodwork. You have the choice of flat, semigloss, emulsion, or rubber-base paints. When a transparent coating is desired, a wood filler should first be applied, if it is an open-grain wood. Over this, shellac or varnish, then wax, can be used. If it seems desirable to tone the wood without concealing its grain, apply a stain after the wood is filled. Over the stain, the varnish or shellac is added, followed by wax.

In basements and recreation rooms of many homes—and in many a living room, too—there are walls of brick, stone, or cinder block. Where it is desirable to coat these masonry surfaces to obstruct the invasion of moisture or to change their appearance, there are many products to choose from. Both old and new masonry walls may require a sealer or undercoat if they have not been painted before. Although you can use aluminum and casein paints on old masonry surfaces, it is not advisable to use them when the construction is brand-new. These coatings can be used on both new and old masonry, regardless of its age: enamel, semigloss, flat, cement-base, emulsion, rubber-base paint.

Wood floors can be coated with a floor paint or enamel, or they can be given a transparent finish with the aid of shellac, varnish, polyurethane, or one of the various types of stains produced for the purpose. All three types of wax (emulsion, liquid, paste) are suitable.

On stair treads, floor paint or enamel can be used, as well as floor varnish, stain, or shellac. Wax is inadvisable. On stair risers, which do not have to take the same wear and tear as treads, other types of paint that are suitable for woodwork can be used.

When steel windows are to be painted, they should first be coated with one of the metal primers especially devised for the purpose. Aluminum windows usually need no primer. Both types can be coated with aluminum or rubber-base paint, enamel, semigloss, or flat paint.

Heating ducts, radiators, and heating pipes also require a metal primer. On them, the same types of coatings can be used that are suitable for steel windows.

Steel cabinets call for a metal primer, too. Rubber-base paint, enamel, semigloss, or flat paint can be applied over it.

HOW MUCH PAINT?

Estimating your paint needs is a matter of simple arithmetic. Finish coats of good-quality paint normally cover about 500 square feet per gallon if the surface is in reasonably good condition. Primers usually cover about 450 square feet per gallon. For specific coverage rates, refer to the label on the paint you are purchasing.

On the outside of your home, you must also consider the kind of surface to be painted and its condition. Some soak up paint like blotters, whereas others provide excellent bases. For example, shingles fall far below the 500-square-feet-per-gallon rule, but clapboard is more receptive to paint. The following chart shows the approximate covering ability of house paint on various surfaces.

Surface	Square feet per gallon (approx.)	
	First Coat	Second Coat
Clapboard siding	500	550
Shingle siding	150	250
Asbestos shingles	180	400
Stucco	150	360
Cement block	180	240
Brick	200	400

1. Measure perimeter: 24' + 40' + 24' + 40' = 128' (A)
2. Measure foundation to eave: 10'; add 2' = 12' (B)
3. Multiply A times B: 128' × 12' = 1,536 square feet
4. Measure picture window: 7' × 10' = 70 square feet (C)
5. Deduct 4 from 3: 1,536 sq. ft.
   – 70 sq. ft.
   1,466 sq. ft.
6. Measure roof rise = 4' (D)
7. Measure roof run = 12' (E)
8. Multiply D times E: 4' × 12' = 48' per gable × 2 gable ends = 96 sq.ft. Add this to the square footage of the house: 1,466 + 96 = 1,562 sq.ft.
9. 1,562 sq.ft. ÷ 550 (the approximate coverage per gallon of clapboard siding for final coat) = approximately 3 gallons of paint for the house.

To determine paint requirements for your home's exterior, measure the perimeter of the home. Multiply this figure by the average height from foundation to eaves, plus two feet to allow for eaves, overhangs, and the like. Do not figure in the gable ends at this point, and make no allowances for windows and doors unless they exceed 50 square feet, as in the case of a large picture window, where you can subtract that square footage.

To figure square footage on the gable end of your house, measure the roof rise (vertical distance from eave to ridge) and the run (horizontal distance covered from eave to ridge). If the roof pitch (rise divided by run) is the same on both sides (or front and back) of the house, multiply rise by run to find the square footage needed to determine paint needs for the entire gable end. If the pitch is different on one side than on the other—as in the case of a house with a full shed dormer—figure rise and run separately for each side, multiply the figures for each side, and divide by two. Other unusually shaped protrusions, such as partial shed dormers, can be figured similarly—and will

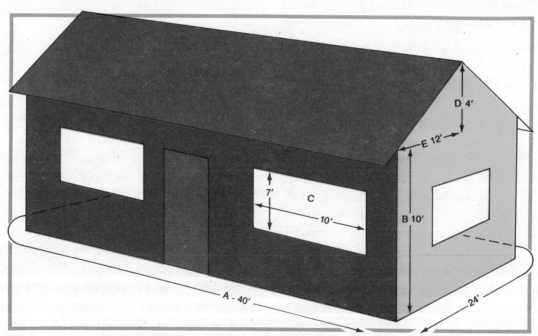

How to measure the exterior of a small house to determine paint needs.

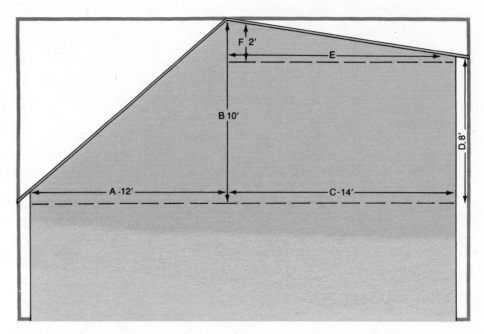

Measuring an unequal gable end of a small house to determine the paint needs:

1. Measure the roof run: 12' (A)
2. Measure the roof rise: 10' (B)
3. Multiply A times B: 10 × 12 = 120 sq.ft. As your gable is a triangle, not a rectangle, divide by 2 = 60 sq.ft.
4. As the pitch in the drawing is different on one side than on the other, measure the other side:
   Measure the run: 14' (C), multiply by the rise 8' (D) = 112 sq.ft.
5. Figure out the triangle above the rectangle you just measured: the run is 14' (E); the pitch is 2' (F). Multiply E by F and divide by 2: 14 × 2 = 28 ÷ 2 = 14 sq.ft.
6. Add 3, 4, 5: 60 + 112 + 14 = 186 sq.ft. for area of gable end.

Total Area—Four Walls and Ceiling
In Square Feet

For Rooms with Ceilings 7 Feet 6 Inches High

	3'	4'	5'	6'	7'	8'	9'	10'	11'	12'	13'	14'	15'	16'	17'	18'	19'	20'	21'	22'
3'	99	117	135	153	171	189	207	225	243	261	279	297	315	333	351	369	387	405	423	441
4'	117	136	155	174	193	212	231	250	269	288	307	326	345	364	383	402	421	440	459	478
5'	135	155	175	195	215	235	255	275	295	315	335	355	375	395	415	435	455	475	495	515
6'	153	174	195	216	237	258	279	300	321	342	363	384	405	426	447	468	489	510	531	552
7'	171	193	215	237	259	281	303	325	347	369	391	413	435	457	479	501	523	545	567	589
8'	189	212	235	258	281	304	327	350	373	396	419	442	465	488	511	534	557	580	603	626
9'	207	231	255	279	303	327	351	375	399	423	447	471	495	519	543	567	591	615	639	663
10'	225	250	275	300	325	350	375	400	425	450	475	500	525	550	575	600	625	650	675	700
11'	243	269	295	321	347	373	399	425	451	477	503	529	555	581	607	633	659	685	711	737
12'	261	288	315	342	369	396	423	450	477	504	531	558	585	612	639	666	693	720	747	774
13'	279	307	335	363	391	419	447	475	503	531	559	587	615	643	671	699	727	755	783	811
14'	297	326	355	384	413	442	471	500	529	558	587	616	645	674	703	732	761	790	819	848
15'	315	345	375	405	435	465	495	525	555	585	615	645	675	705	735	765	795	825	855	885
16'	333	364	395	426	457	488	519	550	581	612	643	674	705	736	767	798	829	860	891	922
17'	351	383	415	447	479	511	543	575	607	639	671	703	735	767	799	831	863	895	927	959
18'	369	402	435	468	501	534	567	600	633	666	699	732	765	798	831	864	897	930	963	996
19'	387	421	455	489	523	557	591	625	659	693	727	761	795	829	863	897	931	965	999	1033
20'	405	440	475	510	545	580	615	650	685	720	755	790	825	860	895	930	965	1000	1035	1070
21'	423	459	495	531	567	603	639	675	711	747	783	819	855	891	927	963	999	1035	1071	1107
22'	441	478	515	552	589	626	663	700	737	774	811	848	885	922	959	996	1033	1070	1107	1144
23'	459	497	535	573	611	649	687	725	763	801	839	877	915	953	991	1029	1067	1105	1143	1181
24'	477	516	555	594	633	672	711	750	789	828	867	906	945	984	1023	1062	1101	1140	1179	1218

(*Note:* Deduct for doors, windows, archways, etc., over 50 square feet)

Paint Selection

Total Area—Four Walls and Ceiling

In Square Feet

For Rooms with Ceilings 8 Feet High

	3'	4'	5'	6'	7'	8'	9'	10'	11'	12'	13'	14'	15'	16'	17'	18'	19'	20'	21'	22'
3'	105	124	143	162	181	200	219	238	257	276	295	314	333	352	371	390	409	428	447	466
4'	124	144	164	184	204	224	244	264	284	304	324	344	364	384	404	424	444	464	484	504
5'	143	164	185	206	227	248	269	290	311	332	353	374	395	416	437	458	479	500	521	542
6'	162	184	206	228	250	272	294	316	338	360	382	404	426	448	470	492	514	536	558	580
7'	181	204	227	250	273	296	319	342	365	388	411	434	457	480	503	526	549	572	595	618
8'	200	224	248	272	296	320	344	368	392	416	440	464	488	512	536	560	584	608	632	656
9'	219	244	269	294	319	344	369	394	419	444	469	494	519	544	569	594	619	644	669	694
10'	238	264	290	316	342	368	394	420	446	472	498	524	550	576	602	628	664	680	706	732
11'	257	284	311	338	365	392	419	446	473	500	527	554	581	608	635	662	689	716	743	770
12'	276	304	332	360	388	416	444	472	500	528	556	584	612	640	668	696	724	752	780	808
13'	295	324	353	382	411	440	469	498	527	556	585	614	643	672	701	730	759	788	817	846
14'	314	344	374	404	434	464	494	524	554	584	614	644	674	704	734	764	794	824	854	884
15'	333	364	395	426	457	488	519	550	581	612	643	674	705	736	767	798	829	860	891	922
16'	352	384	416	448	480	512	544	576	608	640	672	704	736	768	800	832	864	896	928	960
17'	371	404	437	470	503	536	569	602	635	668	701	734	767	800	833	866	899	932	965	998
18'	390	424	458	492	526	560	594	628	662	696	730	764	798	832	866	900	934	968	1002	1036
19'	409	444	479	514	549	584	619	654	689	724	759	794	829	864	899	934	969	1004	1039	1074
20'	428	464	500	536	572	608	644	680	716	752	788	824	860	896	932	968	1004	1040	1076	1112
21'	447	484	521	558	595	632	669	706	743	780	817	854	891	928	965	1002	1039	1076	1113	1150
22'	466	504	542	580	618	656	694	732	770	808	846	884	922	960	998	1036	1074	1112	1150	1188
23'	485	524	563	602	641	680	719	758	797	836	875	914	953	992	1031	1070	1109	1148	1187	1226
24'	504	544	584	624	664	704	744	784	824	864	904	944	984	1024	1064	1104	1144	1184	1224	1264

(*Note:* Deduct for doors, windows, archways, etc., over 50 square feet)

Total Area Four Walls and Ceiling

In Square Feet

For Rooms with Ceilings 9 Feet High

	3'	4'	5'	6'	7'	8'	9	10'	11'	12'	13'	14'	15'	16'	17'	18'	19'	20'	21'	22'
3'	117	138	159	180	201	222	243	264	285	306	327	348	369	390	411	432	453	474	495	516
4'	138	160	182	204	226	248	270	292	314	336	358	380	402	424	446	468	490	512	534	556
5'	159	182	205	228	251	274	297	320	343	366	389	412	435	458	481	504	527	550	573	596
6'	180	204	228	252	276	300	324	348	372	396	420	444	468	492	516	540	564	588	612	636
7'	201	226	251	276	301	326	351	376	401	426	451	476	501	526	551	576	601	626	651	676
8'	222	248	274	300	326	352	378	404	430	456	482	508	534	560	586	612	638	664	690	716
9'	243	270	297	324	351	378	405	432	459	486	513	540	567	594	621	648	675	702	729	756
10'	264	292	320	348	376	404	432	460	488	516	544	572	600	628	656	684	712	740	768	796
11'	285	314	343	372	401	430	459	488	517	546	575	604	633	662	691	720	749	778	807	836
12'	306	336	366	396	426	456	486	516	546	576	606	636	666	696	726	756	786	816	846	876
13'	327	358	389	420	451	482	513	544	575	606	637	668	699	730	761	792	823	854	885	916
14'	348	380	412	444	476	508	540	572	604	636	668	700	732	764	796	828	860	892	924	956
15'	369	402	435	468	501	534	567	600	633	666	699	732	765	798	831	864	897	930	963	996
16'	390	424	458	492	526	560	594	628	662	696	730	764	798	832	866	900	934	968	1002	1036
17'	411	446	481	516	551	586	621	656	691	726	761	796	831	866	901	936	971	1006	1041	1076
18'	432	468	504	540	576	612	648	684	720	756	792	828	864	900	936	972	1008	1044	1080	1116
19'	453	490	527	564	601	638	675	712	749	786	823	860	897	934	971	1008	1045	1082	1119	1156
20'	474	512	550	588	626	664	702	740	778	816	854	892	930	968	1006	1044	1082	1120	1158	1196
21'	495	534	573	612	651	690	729	768	807	846	885	924	963	1002	1041	1080	1119	1158	1197	1236
22'	516	556	596	636	676	716	756	796	836	876	916	956	996	1036	1076	1116	1156	1196	1236	1276
23'	537	578	619	660	701	742	783	824	865	906	947	988	1029	1070	1111	1152	1193	1234	1275	1316
24'	558	600	612	684	726	768	810	852	894	936	978	1020	1062	1104	1146	1188	1230	1272	1314	1356

(*Note:* Deduct for doors, windows, archways, etc., over 50 square feet)

Total Area—Four Walls and Ceiling
In Square Feet

For Rooms with Ceilings 10 Feet High

	3'	4'	5'	6'	7'	8'	9'	10'	11'	12'	13'	14'	15'	16'	17'	18'	19'	20'	21'	22'
3'	129	152	175	198	221	244	267	290	313	336	359	382	405	428	451	474	497	520	543	566
4'	152	176	200	224	248	272	296	320	344	368	392	416	440	464	488	512	536	560	584	608
5'	175	200	225	250	275	300	325	350	375	400	425	450	475	500	525	550	575	600	625	650
6'	198	224	250	276	302	328	354	380	406	432	458	484	510	536	562	588	614	640	666	692
7'	221	248	275	302	329	356	383	410	437	464	491	518	545	572	599	626	653	680	707	734
8'	244	272	300	328	356	384	412	440	468	496	524	552	580	608	636	664	692	720	748	776
9'	267	296	325	354	383	412	441	479	499	528	557	586	615	644	673	702	731	760	789	818
10'	290	320	350	380	410	440	470	500	530	560	590	620	650	680	710	740	770	800	830	860
11'	313	344	375	406	437	468	499	530	561	592	623	654	685	716	747	778	809	840	871	902
12'	336	368	400	432	464	496	528	560	592	624	656	688	720	752	784	816	848	880	912	944
13'	359	392	425	458	491	524	557	590	623	656	689	722	755	788	821	854	887	920	953	986
14'	382	416	450	484	518	552	586	620	654	688	722	756	790	824	858	892	926	960	994	1028
15'	405	440	475	510	545	580	615	650	685	720	755	790	825	860	895	930	965	1000	1035	1070
16'	428	464	500	536	572	608	644	680	716	752	788	824	860	896	932	968	1004	1040	1076	1112
17'	451	488	525	562	599	636	673	710	747	784	821	858	895	932	969	1006	1043	1080	1117	1154
18'	474	512	550	588	626	664	702	740	778	816	854	892	930	968	1006	1044	1082	1120	1158	1196
19'	497	536	575	614	653	692	731	770	809	848	887	926	965	1004	1043	1082	1121	1160	1199	1238
20'	520	560	600	640	680	720	760	800	840	880	920	960	1000	1040	1080	1120	1160	1200	1240	1280
21'	543	584	625	666	707	748	789	830	871	912	953	994	1035	1076	1117	1158	1199	1240	1281	1322
22'	566	608	650	692	734	776	818	860	902	944	986	1028	1070	1112	1154	1196	1238	1280	1322	1364
23'	589	632	675	718	761	804	847	890	933	976	1019	1062	1105	1148	1191	1234	1277	1320	1363	1406
24'	612	656	700	744	788	832	876	920	964	1008	1052	1096	1140	1184	1228	1272	1316	1360	1404	1448

(*Note:* Deduct for doors, windows, archways, etc., over 50 square feet)

put to use the knowledge you acquired in those seemingly fruitless hours you spent in high-school geometry class. There was a reason, after all!

Estimating interior paint needs is done in the same way, by determining square footage of walls and ceilings, then dividing the total by the coverage shown on the paint-can label. Again, do not allow for a window or door opening unless it exceeds 50 square feet. The tables show total area for four walls and ceiling of rooms at the most common heights. If the ceiling is to be painted a different color, figure it separately and de-duct the square footage from the figure given in the appropriate table.

It's always a good idea to buy an extra gallon or quart of paint to make sure that you have enough on hand when you set about doing the job—especially if you are a weekend painter. It is extremely frustrating to run out of paint with just a few more feet of wall to go; and when this happens on a Saturday evening right after the paint store has closed, the frustration is dragged out interminably. Better sufficient than sorry, and almost all paint dealers will take back unopened cans of paint.

3

Painting Tools

THE WORLD IS full of painting experts. Because painting is a relatively easy do-it-yourself task, and because many amateurs become "professionals" merely by hanging out a shingle and advertising in the classified ad sections of the local newspaper, there is a great deal of dogmatic, if misinformed, rhetoric about proper painting methods—especially the brush vs. roller vs. spray controversy.

There are still many old-timers who disdain the roller, and as for the spray gun—well, its use should be limited by law to applying pesticides to rose bushes, and never paint to a house! For these purists, only a brush can truly communicate with a surface being coated, "working in" the paint for a properly applied finish.

On the other hand, there are those who recoil in horror at the thought of picking up paint with anything other than a roller, which they regard as the greatest invention since (and an extension of) the wheel. And there are those adherents of spray painting who regard the wielders of both brush and roller as throwbacks to the age when man's use of paint was limited to decorating the walls of his cave with crude drawings of animals.

The fact is that all three methods of applying paint have distinct advantages (and disadvantages). If there is any hard-and-fast rule to follow when it comes to selecting and using these tools, it is: Use what works best for you.

COMPARISON CHART: BRUSH vs. ROLLER vs. SPRAYER				
	Small Brush	Wide Brush	Roller	Sprayer
ADVANTAGES	Maneuverability Low price Easy to use Easy to clean	Quick application Versatile Smooth finish Can cut in around trim	Speed over large surfaces Easy to use Low price	Fast, easy to use Smoothest finish Has other uses
DISADVANTAGES	Takes more time on large jobs	Requires some experience for best results	Must cut in with brush or corner roller Difficult to clean covers	Difficult to use indoors Difficult to cut in fine line Requires some experience for good results Not worthwhile for small jobs
TYPE JOBS BEST SUITED FOR	Trim, sash Cabinetwork Radiators, blinds, etc.	Walls, exteriors, large surfaces	Large unbroken surfaces Rough surfaces (stucco, block, etc.) Floors	Large exterior surfaces "Hard to paint" surfaces (wicker, stucco, blinds)
RELATIVE COST	39¢ to $5.00	99¢ to $15.00	$1.99 to $7.50	$9.95 to $1000.00 (commercial type)

PAINTBRUSHES

Quality is a very important factor in selecting a brush, regardless of the size or style needed for a particular project. A good brush will hold more paint and enable you to apply the paint more smoothly and with less effort.

All good brushes have bristles that are "flagged," a term denoting splits on the bristle end. The more "flags" the better, as they help retain paint. Hog bristle is naturally flagged; synthetic bristle is artificially flagged, or split.

Test for "bounce" by brushing bristles against the back of your hand. In a good brush, the bristles will feel elastic and springy. When the brush is gently pressed on any surface, the bristles will not fan out excessively.

Check the setting. Bristles should be solidly set to prevent any chance of fallout during painting. Jar the brush and fan the bristles. Any loose bristles will be apparent. The metal band holding the bristles is called a ferrule. Stainless steel and aluminum are generally used on better-grade brushes for greater resistance to corrosion.

Both the surface area and type of paint determine the size and style of brush to be used. Calcimine brushes with very long, tough, and elastic gray hog bristles are best for applying water-thinned paints to large areas. Enamel and varnish brushes, both flat and chisel-shaped, are best for applying oil-base paints and lacquers. The shape and length of the latter type help secure a smoother flow and prevent lap marks.

The following brush styles and sizes are recommended for most painting projects around the home:

• Flat wall brushes: Sizes vary from 3 to 6 inches in width with thicknesses of ¾ to 1½ inches and bristles from 2 to 7 inches long. They are best suited for painting large surfaces such as walls, ceilings, and floors.

Flagged bristles.

Wall brushes.

Pressing the brush on a surface to test for "bounce."

Fan brush to check loose bristles.

Flat, chisel-shaped varnish brushes.

Sash, trim, artist's brushes.

• Varnish brushes: Sizes range from 1 to 3½ inches in width, with bristles from 2 to 4½ inches long. They are ideally suited for painting baseboards, window frames, narrow boards, or enameling and varnishing furniture and small panels.

• Round sash and flat trim brushes: Sizes range from 1 to 1½ inches in width. Trellises, screens, small pipes, toys, and all

Fishtailing of brush caused by not using it properly.

Standing the brush on its tip causes the edges to bend.

Cleaning brush in thinner.

Washing brush.

Storing brush in can.

Wrapping brush in paper.

Before reuse of brush, recondition it.

Priming the brush.

small areas are best painted with sash, trim, or even small artist's brushes.

In addition to these general styles, most dealers carry special brushes for bronzing, roofing, stippling, and stenciling.

A quality brush is a fine tool and should be properly used and cared for. For example, a wide brush should never be used to paint pipes and similar surfaces. This causes the brush to "fishtail." A brush should never be left standing on its bristles. The weight causes the edge to bend and curl, ruining the fine painting tips.

Always clean a brush while it is still soft after painting. Use the thinner for the product in which the brush has been used. For example, turpentine followed by naphtha or mineral spirits should be used to remove oil-base paints in which turpentine is a recommended thinning ingredient. Alcohol or lacquer thinner are used on brushes after applying shellac or alcohol-base stains. Cleaning should be followed by washing the brush in soap and water. Latex or water-base paints can be easily removed by dissolving the excess paint in water.

Once the brush is thoroughly cleaned, it should be properly stored. Drill a hole in the brush handle, insert a wire rod through the hole, then rest the rod on a paint, coffee, or shortening can taller than the length of the bristles. Bristles should not rest on the bottom of the can.

For long-term storage, make sure that the bristles are completely dry, then wrap the brush in foil or heavy paper. Hang by the handle in an out-of-the-way place.

Before reusing the brush, work it back and forth across your fingers or palm of the hand to remove dust, dirt, or loose bristling material. If the brush is to be used in shellac, water-base, or latex paint, it should be washed in soap and water and thoroughly dried before painting.

For best results prime the brush by dipping into the paint halfway to the ferrule.

Painting Tools

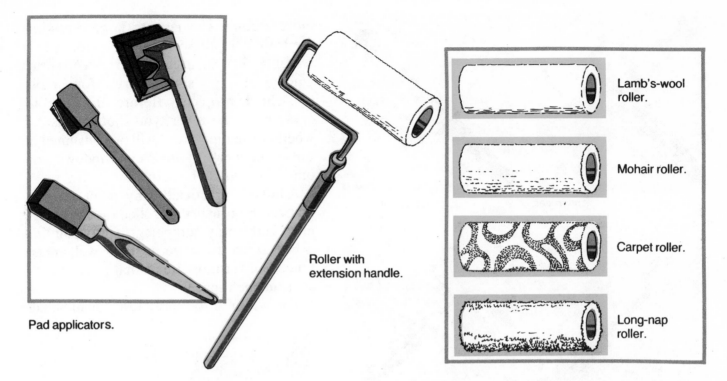

Pad applicators.

Roller with extension handle.

Lamb's-wool roller.

Mohair roller.

Carpet roller.

Long-nap roller.

Then tap lightly, five or six times, against the top edge of your paint container. The brush is now ready to use.

PAD APPLICATORS

Relatively new are pad applicators. These are similar to brushes but generally cheaper (except for throwaway brushes). On smooth surfaces, they also apply paint much faster than brushes. Made of foamed urethane for use on both interior and exterior surfaces, some of them have replaceable pads. Others are cheap enough that it is more practical to discard them after use rather than attempt to clean them.

PAINT ROLLERS

Painting with a roller is probably the easiest and quickest method for the average do-it-yourself decorator. It is important to use a roller that is suitable for the kind of paint to be applied. Lambs'-wool rollers, for ex-

ample, are excellent with oil-base paints, but they should not be used with enamels or water-thinned latex paints because these paints will cause the wool to mat, rendering the roller unusable.

Mohair rollers can be used with any type of interior flat paint, but they are especially recommended for applying enamel and for use when a smooth finish is desired. Rollers made from synthetic fibers can also be used with all types of flat paint, inside and out. If a stipple finish is desired, use a roller made of carpeting.

Another factor to consider is the length of the nap or pile, which can range from 1/16 to 1½ inches. A handy rule to remember is: the smoother the surface, the shorter the nap; the rougher the surface, the longer the nap. Use short-napped rollers for most walls, ceilings, woodwork, and smooth concrete. The longer naps are for masonry, brick, and other irregular surfaces.

For walls and ceilings the best size roller for the amateur is the 7- or 9-inch model. (Extension handles make it possible to paint ceilings without a ladder.) For finish-

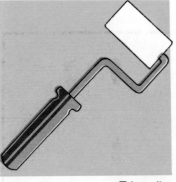

Trim roller.

Cutting-in roller.

Corner roller.

Edging roller.

ing woodwork, doors, and trim, the best choice is the 3-inch model. Smaller sizes are available for cutting in corners and for use on window frames and moldings. There are even V-edged rollers that coat both sides of a corner at the same time. To help you paint a wall without getting the paint on the ceiling there are special edging rollers.

Before applying paint with a roller, first cut in the edges of the wall with a brush or with an edging roller, taking care not to get paint on the ceiling or adjacent wall.

PAINT SPRAYERS

Since the invention of the spray gun for mass-production industrial painting, it has become increasingly popular as a practical and economical means of applying paint by professional and amateur alike.

Sizes range from the small suction-feed spray-painting attachments available with most vacuum cleaners, to large pressure-feed air compressors available for a low rental fee in most areas. Suction-feed spray equipment is satisfactory for most household projects. Before deciding to spray paint, however, you should consider whether the time saved will be consumed in the extra work of masking windows and other areas not to be painted.

Although practically any paint product that can be brushed or rolled on can be applied with spray equipment, spray painting is best suited for covering large wall areas, fences, or furniture items that can be painted in an open space.

The width of the spray fan should be ad-

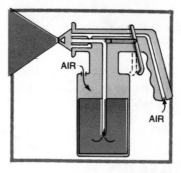

Suction-feed sprayer.

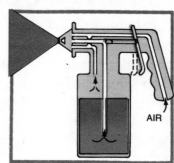

Pressure-feed sprayer.

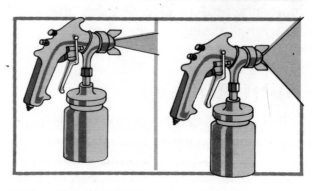

Adjust width of fan to size of article to be coated.

Painting Tools

justed to the size of the article being coated. A narrow fan is best for spraying small or narrow articles; a full-width fan should be used to spray walls.

Prepainting practice is important. The handyman should test the thickness of the paint, the size of the fan, and the motion of the spray gun before painting any surface. Excessive thickness can cause rippling of the wet film by the spraying air or lead to blistering later. On vertical and inclined surfaces, it can cause running or sagging.

The spray fan should be pointed perpendicularly to the surface being coated. The stroke or motion of the hand holding the spray gun should be started while the spray is pointed beyond the surface to be painted. This assures a smooth, even flow when you reach the surface itself.

Move the gun parallel to the surface, aiming beyond the edge of the surface and moving with an even stroke back and forth across the area. Corners and edges should be sprayed first.

Although a pressure-feed gun will handle heavier paint, the compressor unit poses a safety problem. Motors or gas engines of air-compressing outfits should be operated outside the spray area to avoid hazards from explosion and fire. The unit should also be placed in an area where it will receive a continuous supply of fresh, clean, dry air. Dust or vapor entering the air intake will decrease the efficiency of the unit and affect the results.

Regardless of the type of equipment used, every precaution should be taken by the spray operator. Skin should be protected. The area being sprayed should be well ventilated. A fire extinguisher should be available for use if needed, and all flammable liquids should be kept in safety cans.

Spray equipment should be thoroughly cleaned immediately after use. Simple cleaning can be done by spraying a suitable solvent through the equipment. A broom

Hold sprayer perpendicular to the surface to be coated.

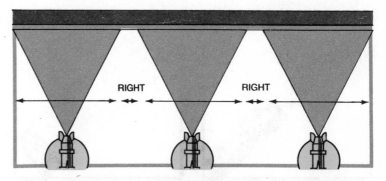

Move sprayer parallel to surface.

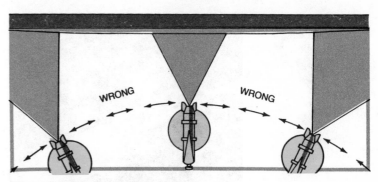

Cleaning fluid tip with broom straw.

straw can be used to unclog the fluid tip. Never use a metal wire or nail to clear air holes in the spray tip; the precision-machined openings are easily damaged.

Hook scraper.

Wall scraper.

Putty knife.

Razor-blade scraper.

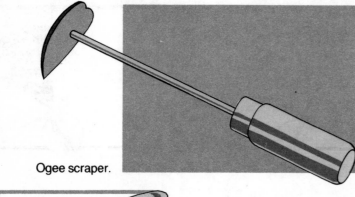

Ogee scraper.

Wire brush with handle.

Wire brush without handle.

OTHER TOOLS OF THE PAINTER'S TRADE

A variety of scrapers should be in every amateur (and professional, for that matter) painter's tool kit. Hook scrapers are good for rough exterior surfaces, and are often used with paint remover. Wall scrapers are handy for removing old paint and general scraping and cleaning. They come in various widths up to 5 inches; a 3- or 4-inch size with a stiff blade will meet most of your needs. A putty knife, similar in appearance to a narrow wall scraper, can also be used for scraping and cleaning, as well as applying and smoothing putty. An "ogee" scraper is the tool for removing old paint from crevices and recesses that can't be reached by flat scrapers. A razor-blade scraper is best for scraping paint off glass if your cutting-in is not quite perfect (and whose is?).

Wire brushes are handy for removing grime and surface dirt before applying exterior paint. Sandpaper is another important tool for smoothing surfaces. It is best used with a sanding block. When heavy sanding is required, a power belt sander may be used, followed by a finishing sander for final smoothing.

A propane torch is sometimes used to soften old paint for scraping, but this procedure entails certain obvious risks. An electric paint softener accomplishes the same end much more safely.

A calking gun is needed to seal cracks around doors, windows, corners, and other areas before exterior painting. In addition, an assortment of common tools will be helpful: hammer and nailset for driving in nails that may have come loose, a chisel for prying molding away from walls, a screwdriver for removing switch and receptacle covers, hinges, and other hardware.

Painting Tools

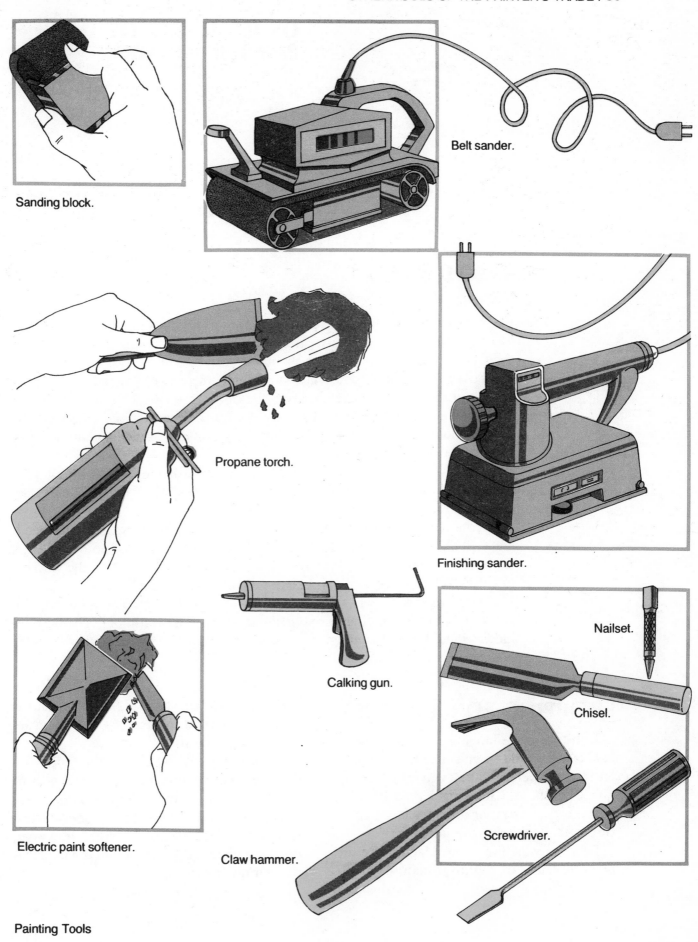

Sanding block.

Belt sander.

Propane torch.

Finishing sander.

Calking gun.

Nailset.

Chisel.

Electric paint softener.

Claw hammer.

Screwdriver.

Painting Tools

4

Ladders

O F ALL THE "tools" you need for painting, perhaps none is more important than a ladder, because it involves your personal safety. Unless you limit your paint job to the base woodwork, or are built with the reach of a pro basketball center, you will have to get "up there," whether to do the ceiling or the upper reaches of your home's exterior. Accept no substitutes for a ladder—standing on a chair is risky business and makes the job a lot more tedious, too. The range of ladder designs, types, sizes, and materials is broad enough to fit any need.

Before you make a trip to the store to buy a ladder, think about your needs. Will the ladder be used indoors or outdoors? How high will you want to climb? Who will be using it? Where will it be stored?

If you live in an apartment, a stepladder will probably meet all your needs and will be easy to handle. Its size will depend on the highest point you want to reach, bearing in mind that you should not stand higher than the step below the ladder top. Never stand on the top of a stepladder!

If you live in a house, you may need two ladders—a stepladder for indoor work and a straight ladder or extension ladder for use outdoors. The outdoor ladder should be long enough to extend a minimum of 3 feet higher than the highest area you want to reach.

SHOPPING FOR A LADDER

Don't let price alone guide you. Select a ladder according to your needs. And don't let the salesperson hurry you into making a quick purchase. Check the ladder for weak steps, loose rungs, or other weaknesses before you take it from the store.

Don't buy an unidentified ladder. Be sure that the name of the manufacturer or distributor is on the label. This information may be important in case of a quality problem or an accident.

Look for a seal affixed to the ladder indicating that it conforms to the standards of the American National Standards Institute (ANSI) or the Underwriters' Laboratories, Inc. (UL). The absence of a seal, however, does not necessarily imply that the ladder is of poor quality.

MATERIALS

Wood, aluminum, magnesium, and fiberglass are the principal materials used in the construction of ladders. Each type has its advantages and disadvantages.

Wood ladders are sturdy and bend little under loads for which they are designed. They are heavier than metal ladders, and large sizes are harder to handle. When dry, wood ladders are safe to use around electrical circuits or when you are working with power tools.

If wood ladders are used indoors, or adequately protected from moisture and sunlight when used outdoors, they will last a long time. Unprotected in the open, however, they may be attacked by wood-destroying insects, weakened by rot, or cracked and split by the action of sun and rain. Once weakened, wood may break easily and suddenly.

Metal ladders are generally a little more expensive than wood ladders of the same quality, but they last longer because they do not deteriorate from moisture and sunlight and are not susceptible to attack by insects. Aluminum and magnesium ladders are comparatively light, weighing only about two-thirds as much as those made of wood. The two metals weigh about the same, but magnesium ladders are somewhat more expensive. (Magnesium is actually a lighter metal than aluminum but not as strong; therefore, side rails and legs are constructed with thicker cross sections to provide comparable strength.) Magnesium corrodes (turns black) more than aluminum and has less impact resistance. Aluminum and magnesium ladders are not recommended for use around electrical circuits.

Fiberglass is the newest ladder material to appear on the market. It is used to make the side rails of high-grade metal stepladders and of straight and extension ladders. The result is a nonconductive ladder that is

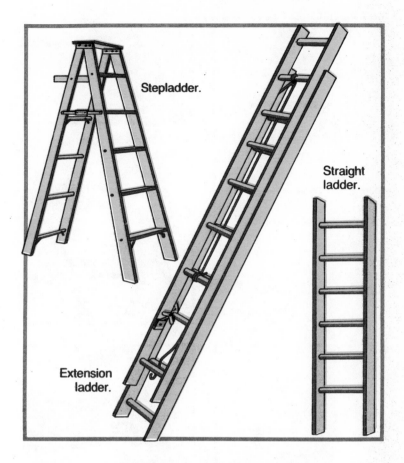

Stepladder.

Straight ladder.

Extension ladder.

light, corrosion-resistant, serviceable, and practically maintenance-free. These ladders do not dry-rot or absorb moisture, and the fiberglass side rails have greater impact resistance than wood, aluminum, or magnesium. These ladders, however, are quite expensive and are used mostly by professionals.

LADDER CODES

The stepladder and the extension ladder are the two types most commonly used around the home. Codes have been established by the American National Standards Institute to cover wood and metal stepladders and extension ladders. Any ladder you buy with an ANSI seal conforms to the code.

The code for wood ladders is a dimensional one. It covers, for example, the

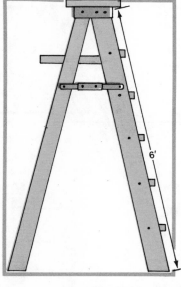

Stepladder size.

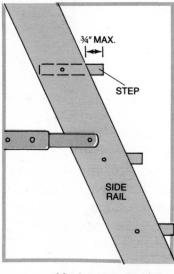

Maximum protrusion of wood steps beyond rails.

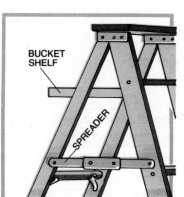

Spreader and bucket shelf.

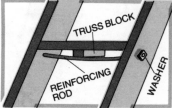

Wood stepladder metal angle brace.

Wood stepladder reinforcing rod.

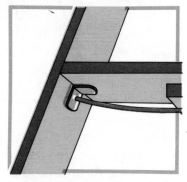

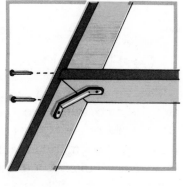

Fastening wood steps with metal angles.

Fastening wood steps in grooves.

depth and thickness of steps. Performance tests have not been developed. The code for metal ladders is based on performance. It prescribes the methods for testing the strength of ladders, with emphasis on side rails, steps, fastening hardware, and the back legs of stepladders.

STEPLADDERS

A stepladder is a self-supporting portable ladder. It is nonadjustable in length, and it has flat steps and a hinged back. Size is determined by the length of the ladder measured along the front edge of the side rails. Stepladders are useful for many indoor and outdoor jobs where the height to be reached is low and the ladder can be rested on a firm surface.

Both wood and metal stepladders are available in three categories. They are: Type I, heavy duty (250 pounds load-carrying capacity); Type II, medium duty (225 pounds); and Type III, light duty (200 pounds). These categories are accepted and widely used by the ladder industry. Look for duty rating when you purchase your new stepladder.

Steps on a wooden stepladder should be flat, parallel, and level when the ladder is open. There should not be more than 12 inches between steps, and these should be at least ¾ inch thick and at least 3½ inches deep (1 x 4 nominal size).

Each step should be braced either with metal angle braces or a metal reinforcing rod. Ends of reinforcing rods should pass through metal washers of sufficient thickness to prevent pressing into and damaging the side rails. When metal reinforcing rods are used, a wood or metal truss block should be fitted to the bottom of each step and positioned at the center between the rod and the step. The bottom step should be reinforced with metal angle braces securely attached to the step and to each side rail. Steps should not protrude more than ¾ inch beyond the front of the side rail and should have no splits, cracks, chips, knots, or other imperfections.

Steps should be fastened to the side rails with metal brackets or by grooving. At least two 6d nails (or equivalent) should be used at each end of the step, through the side rail into the step.

The metal spreader or locking device should be large and strong enough to hold the front and back sections securely in the open position. It should be resistant to rust and corrosion. The bucket shelf should be capable of holding 25 pounds and should fold completely within the ladder. Feet should be level in open position. They can be equipped with safety shoes to prevent slippage or lateral movement.

The slope in the open position should be a minimum of 3½ inches per foot of length of the front section and a minimum of 2 inches per foot of length of the back section. The width between the side rails at the top step should be no less than 12 inches and should increase toward the bottom of the ladder at a minimum rate of 1 inch per foot of length.

Metal stepladder steps should be flat, parallel, and level when the ladder is open. Steps should be corrugated, have raised patterns, be dimpled, be coated with skid-resistant materials, or otherwise treated to minimize the possibility of slipping. There should be no more than 12 inches between steps, as with wood ladders.

The depth of the step or tread should be not less than 3 inches for 225- or 250-pound capacity ladders, or 2½ inches for 200-pound capacity. Steps should have no sharp edges and should not be bent or dented. The bottom step should always be reinforced with metal angle braces.

If steps have only one fastener on each side, there should be diagonal metal braces

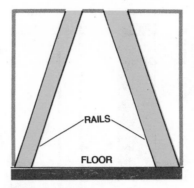

Feet should be level when ladder is open.

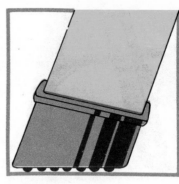

Safety shoes for wood stepladder.

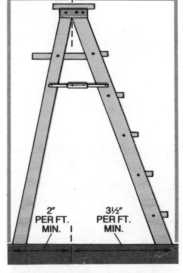

Stepladder slope when open.

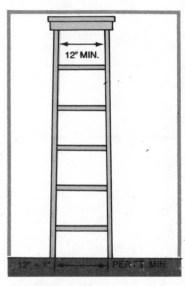

Stepladder width.

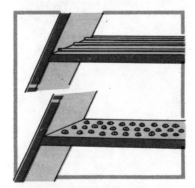

Corrugated and dimpled metal stepladder steps.

Braces on metal stepladder steps.

under both top and bottom steps. If steps have two fastenings on each side, the ladder should have diagonal metal braces under the bottom step.

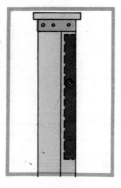

Shoes on bottom of metal stepladder rails (top left).

Folded bucket shelf (top right).

Extension trestle ladder.

Trestle ladder.

Platform ladder (left).

Testing stepladder stability.

The bucket shelf should be capable of holding 50 pounds and should fold completely within the ladder. The bottoms of the four rails should be covered for safety with insulating material, such as rubber or plastic nonslip shoes. Spreader, slope, and width specifications are the same as for wood stepladders.

Before purchasing a stepladder, test its stability by climbing to the second step from the bottom and shaking the ladder moderately back and forth while you hold onto the side rails. If the ladder feels loose, consider purchasing a heavier-duty one or one made by another manufacturer.

STEPLADDER VARIATIONS

There are three other types of ladders that are closely related to the stepladder: the platform ladder, the trestle ladder, and the extension trestle ladder. While these ladders are primarily for professional use, they may also come in handy for use around the home.

One type of platform ladder has a guardrail that lessens the danger of falling. It should have widely spaced legs to provide for good balance. Two of these ladders, used in tandem, provide a good, sturdy base for a scaffold.

Platform ladder with guardrail.

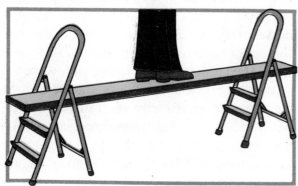

Platform ladders used to support scaffold.

overlap, the Federal Trade Commission requires that the total length and working length be clearly marked. For example: "Maximum working length 17 feet; total length of sections 20 feet."

To help you choose the right size extension ladder for your needs, the accompanying table shows the recommended relation between working height for a ladder and total length of sections. The recommended total length of sections allows for the proper overlap plus 3 feet more than the greatest working height. The extra 3 feet is the minimum required for safe use.

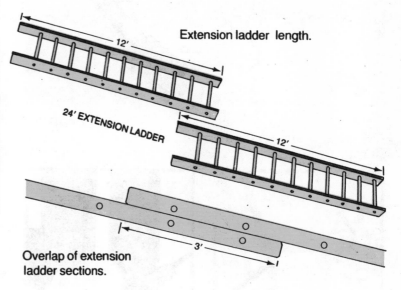

Extension ladder length.

24' EXTENSION LADDER

Overlap of extension ladder sections.

EXTENSION LADDERS

An extension ladder consists of two or more straight sections traveling in guides or brackets arranged to permit length adjustment. Its size is designated by the sum of the length of the sections, measured along the side rails.

Each section of an opened extension ladder should overlap the adjacent section by a minimum number of feet, depending on overall length. If an extension ladder is up to 36 feet in length, the overlap should be 3 feet; if total length is between 36 and 48 feet, overlap should be 4 feet. The ladder should be equipped with positive stops to ensure that it cannot be opened too far.

To eliminate confusion in identifying the length of an extension ladder because of

Recommended Lengths for Different Heights of Extension Ladders

Height You Want to Reach	Recommended Length of Sections
9½ feet	16 feet
13½ feet	20 feet
17½ feet	24 feet
21½ feet	28 feet
24½ feet	32 feet
29 feet	36 feet
33 feet	40 feet
36½ feet	44 feet

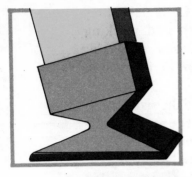

Safety boot for wood
extension ladder.

Extension ladder pulley.

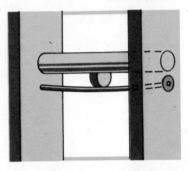

Reinforcement of bottom rung
on wood extension ladder.

Rung lock.

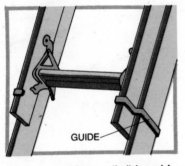

GUIDE

Side-rail slide guide.

Safety shoes for metal
extension ladder.

Metal ladder rungs: round,
round with flat surface.

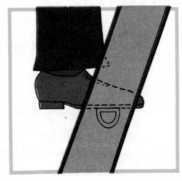

Flat surface horizontal when
ladder is at 75° angle.

Brace for metal
bottom rung.

Feet of wooden extension ladders may be equipped with safety boots or shoes, which are sometimes offered as an accessory. Pulleys should not be less than 1¼ inches outside diameter, and ropes not less than 5/16 inch diameter, with minimum breaking strength of 500 pounds. Rungs must be round and of hard wood, free from crossgrain, splits, cracks, chips, or knots. They should be not less than 1⅛ inches in diameter and spaced not more than 12 inches apart.

Although not required by standards of ANSI or UL, it is highly desirable that at least the bottom rung be reinforced with a truss rod. Safety rung locks should be resistant to or protected against rust and corrosion. Locks may be of either the spring or gravity type. Side-rail slide guides should be securely attached and placed to prevent the upper section from tipping or falling out while the ladder is being raised or lowered.

Width of wooden ladders should be not less than 12 inches between rails of the upper section. For the lower section, width should be a minimum of 14½ inches up to and including 28-foot ladders, and 16 inches for longer ladders.

Feet of metal extension ladders should have rubber, plastic, or other slip-resistant safety treads or shoes secured to foot brackets. The brackets should pivot freely to rest squarely when the ladder is inclined for use. Rungs should be round or round with flat step surface, and with a slip-resistant tread. The flat surface should be horizontal when the ladder is placed at a 75-degree angle. The top and bottom rungs should be not more than 12 inches from the ends of the side rails to provide for extra strength and stability.

Rung braces are not required by standards of ANSI or UL, but it is highly desirable that at least the bottom rung be reinforced with a metal rung brace.

The width of metal ladders varies. The upper section should be not less than 12 inches. Bottom sections are not less than 12½ inches for ladders up to 16 feet, 14 inches for ladders up to 28 feet, and 15 inches for ladders up to 40 feet. Ropes, pulleys, and safety rung locks are the same as for wooden ladders. On most aluminum extension ladders, the side rails interlock, eliminating the need for slide guides.

LADDER ACCESSORIES

A number of useful ladder accessories can add substantially to your safety and convenience. Trays are available for attachment to extension ladders to hold paint, tools, or work materials. Safety shoes should be attached to all metal ladders and to all wood ladders used in slippery or wet places. Although metal ladders are usually sold equipped with safety shoes, wear may make replacement necessary. Shoes for wood ladders are usually bought as accessory items.

Safety wall-grips of rubber or plastic strips can be attached to the tops of extension ladder side rails. These strips keep the top of a ladder from slipping on the surface against which it leans.

MAINTENANCE

Wood ladders to be used or stored outdoors should be protected with a coat or two of clear sealer, spar varnish, shellac, or

Safety rung lock on metal extension ladder.

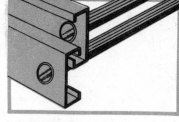

Interlocking side rails.

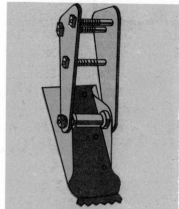

Two types of replacement safety shoes.

Tray for extension ladder.

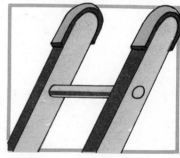

Wall grips.

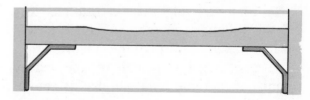

Replace worn ladder steps.

a clear wood preservative. Do not paint wood ladders since this would prevent periodic visual inspection of their condition. Linseed oil will help to rustproof metal parts such as rung locks.

Replace worn or frayed ropes on exten-

Ladders

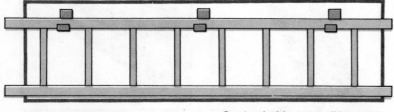

Storing ladder on wall bracket.

Wall bracket.

sion ladders. Check the condition of any ladder that has been dropped or has fallen before it is used again. Replace steps on wood stepladders when approximately one-fourth worn away.

Ladders should be stored where they will not be exposed to the elements. Wood ladders should be kept in a well-ventilated location, away from dampness and excessive heat. Store straight or extension ladders in flat racks or on wall brackets to prevent sag. If long ladders are stored horizontally, use three or more hangers for support.

LADDER SAFETY

Inspect the ladder before each use. Oil moving parts and tighten loose fasteners. Check the rope and pulley on an extension ladder for wear and breaking strength.

Set up long straight or extension ladders by the following method to avoid muscle strain or losing control of the ladder:

- Brace the lower end of the ladder against something solid so that it cannot slide.
- Grasp the uppermost rung, using both hands, then raise the top end and walk forward under the ladder, moving your hands to grasp other rungs as you proceed.
- When the ladder is erect, move it to the desired location and then lean it forward to the top resting point.

- Place ladders at the correct angle with the wall. The base of the ladder should be one-quarter of its working length away from the wall or support. If the ladder is placed at too great an angle—that is, with the base too far out—it is subject to strain that can cause it to break or slip. On the other hand, if the base of the ladder is too close to the wall, the ladder is likely to tip backward.
- Place your ladder so that it has a firm footing. The feet of either a stepladder or an extension ladder should be level. If the ground is uneven or soft under one foot, brace the ladder. If necessary, the ladder should be lashed or held in place to prevent slippage.
- Adjust the length of an extension ladder only when your eye level is below the level of the locking device so that you can see when the lock is engaged.

When using an extension or straight ladder, be sure that it is the proper length to reach the desired height. For example, in using an extension ladder to reach a roof, be sure the top of the ladder extends at least 3 feet above the roof edge. Don't climb up an extension ladder so far that you have to reach down to grasp the side rails.

Never climb higher than the step below the top of a stepladder. If you stand on the top, you can lose your balance.

Go up and down a ladder carefully, always facing the ladder. Carry your tools or other work materials in your clothing or attached to a belt. Take one step at a time.

Move the ladder to where the work can be done without reaching far to one side of the ladder. Overreaching can cause you and the ladder to fall.

Be extremely careful when using metal or wet wood ladders around electrical circuits, power tools, or appliances. Metal and wet wood conduct electricity. Always play it safe!

Brace lower end and "walk" ladder upright.

Place ladder in desired position.

Support ladder
on uneven or
unstable ground
(above and below).

VERTICAL HEIGHT

¼ VERTICAL HEIGHT

Place ladder at correct angle, neither
too far away nor too close.

Don't go so high that you have to reach down
to rails (left) and don't overreach (right).

Ladders

5

Interior Painting

Iɴ ɢᴇɴᴇʀᴀʟ, walls, ceilings, woodwork, and other surfaces to be painted should be clean, dry, and smooth. But read the label on the paint can before you start painting; it may contain additional or special instructions for preparing the surface.

PREPARING NEW PLASTER AND WALLBOARD

New plaster walls should not be painted with oil-base paint until they have been thoroughly cured—usually after about two months. Then a primer coat should be applied first.

If necessary to paint uncured plaster, apply only one coat of a latex paint or primer. Latex, or water-base, paint is not affected by the alkali in new plaster and allows water to escape while the plaster dries. Subsequent coats of paint—either oil-base or latex—can be added when the plaster is thoroughly cured.

Unpainted plaster readily picks up and absorbs dirt and is difficult to clean. The one coat of latex paint or primer will protect plaster walls.

On new wallboard or drywall, a latex primer or paint is recommended for the first coat. Solvent-thinned paints tend to cause a rough surface. After the first coat of latex paint, subsequent coats can be of either type. Clean or dust new surfaces before you apply the first coat of primer or paint.

PREPARING OLDER SURFACES

Most homes built in the past 25 to 30 years have walls and ceilings covered with wallboard, also known as gypsumboard, drywall, or plasterboard. Before painting, make minor or major repairs as necessary. Look in particular for cracks around windows and door frames, nails that have raised the surface, and just plain holes.

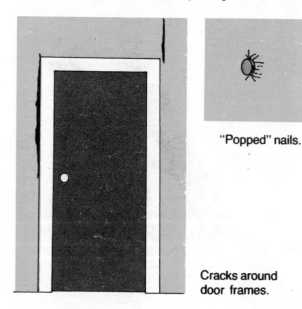

"Popped" nails.

Cracks around door frames.

Drive ringed nail near popped nail.

Use a nailset to avoid damaging wallboard.

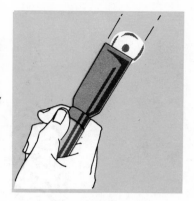

Apply spackle with a broad or putty knife.

Wood in heated homes contracts in the winter and expands in the summer, and this can cause nail "popping."

Drive popped nails back below the surface of the wallboard. Reinforce weak areas by driving a ringed drywall nail into the panel below or above a popped nail about an inch or two away. Drive the nail until it dimples the surface and no more; use a nailset to avoid banging up the wallboard and causing major damage.

Use spackle to patch the dimples and even the surface. Spackle comes in powdered or ready-mixed form. Apply it with a broad knife or putty knife, filling the area, scraping off the excess, and sanding to an even surface when dry.

Cracks can be sealed with fiberglass tape or with perforated drywall tape and joint cement. Sand the area of the crack 4 inches or so to each side when using perforated tape, then apply joint cement over the crack. Center the strip of perforated tape over the crack, pressing it flat with a broad knife. Remove excess cement, feathering the edges so they're smooth. Allow to dry, then apply another coat of joint cement a couple of inches beyond the first coat. Feather the edges and let dry overnight. You can then sand and paint. Fiberglass tape is somewhat similar in application—just follow the directions on the package you buy.

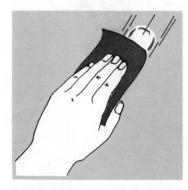

Sand even.

Sand along crack.

Apply joint cement.

Apply tape.

Apply wider coat of cement.

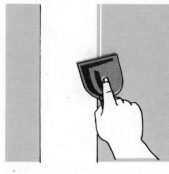

Feather edges.

Interior Painting

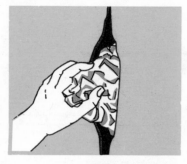

Stuff newspaper
into hole (above).

Fill with spackle (at right).

Apply final coat of spackle
to surface (below).

Chip away loose plaster.

Fill part way to surface.

Apply plaster up to
wall surface.

"Cut" surface with steel wool
to give new paint firm hold.

A hole in wallboard can be repaired by plugging it with a wad of newspaper and then using spackle to fill in until you have a flat surface that can be sanded even. It may take a couple of coats of spackle to do the job properly.

Plaster is repaired in much the same manner as wallboard. With cracks more than ¼-inch wide, chip away the loose plaster and wet down the area. Fill it half way to the surface with plaster and let it dry. Then wet it again and apply another coat to the surface of the wall. When it is dry, spackle where needed and sand.

After repairs are completed, clean the surface of dirt and grease. A dry rag or mop will remove dust and some dirt. You may have to wash the surface with a household cleanser to remove stubborn dirt or grease.

Kitchen walls and ceilings usually become covered with a film of grease (which may extend to the walls and ceilings just outside the entrances to the kitchen), and bathroom walls and ceilings may have steamed-on dirt. The grease or dirt must be removed—new paint will not adhere to it. To remove grease or dirt, wash the surface with a strong household cleanser, turpentine, or mineral spirits.

The finish on kitchen and bathroom walls and ceilings is usually a gloss or semigloss. This finish must be "cut" so that the new paint can get a firm hold. Washing with a household cleanser or turpentine will dull the gloss, but for best results, rub the surface with fine sandpaper or steel wool. After using sandpaper or steel wool, wipe the surface to remove dust.

PREPARING WOODWORK

Woodwork (windows, doors, and baseboards) usually has a glossy finish. First wash the surface to remove dirt and grease, and then sand it lightly to "cut" the finish.

After sanding, wipe the surface to remove the dust.

You can buy liquid preparations that will soften hard, glossy finishes to provide good adhesion for new paint.

If there are any bare spots in the wood, touch them up with an undercoat or with pigmented shellac before you paint.

PAINT APPLICATION

Use drop cloths or plastic sheeting to protect floors and furniture. Paint the ceiling first. Don't try to paint too wide a strip at a time. The next strip should be started and lapped into the previous one before the previous one dries.

If you are putting two coats on the ceiling, apply the second coat, and "cut in" at the junction with the walls, before you paint the walls.

Remove all electric switch and receptacle plates from the walls to avoid smearing. Use a cardboard or metal shield to avoid smearing the trim if the trim is to be another color. Or you can use masking tape if you prefer. Wipe spills up immediately.

Start painting a wall at the upper left-hand corner and work down toward the floor (left-handed persons may find it more convenient to start at the upper right-hand corner).

When using a roller, paint over a section of wall about 3 feet wide in a "W" pattern. Fill in the W with horizontal strokes of the roller. Then smooth out with vertical strokes in one direction.

Paint the woodwork last—preferably after the walls are dry.

Flush doors can be painted with a roller. On paneled doors, some parts can be painted with a roller, but other sections require a brush. (You may prefer your doors and other trim in natural color. See below.)

Interior Painting

Lap paint over previous strip of paint.

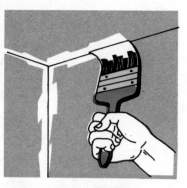
Cut in ceiling-wall joints before you paint the walls.

Remove receptacle plates.

Use a shield to protect trim.

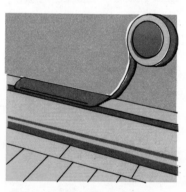
Masking tape to protect trim.

Paint a "W" pattern.

Fill in the "W", then smooth out with vertical strokes.

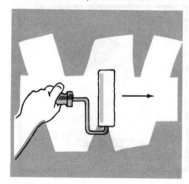

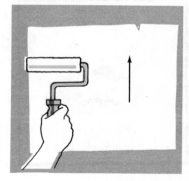

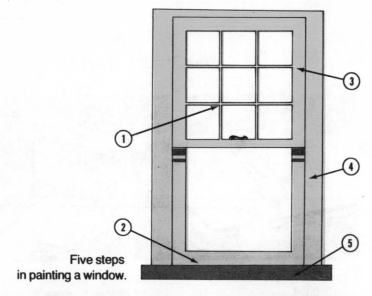

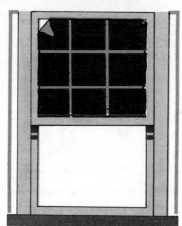

Five steps
in painting a window.

Protecting a window with
masking tape.

Protecting glass
with newspaper.

Soak brushes in
thinner (left).

Work bristles against
side of can (below left).

Squeeze brush between
fingers (below).

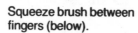

Paint the parts of a window in this order: mullions, horizontals of sash, verticals of sash, verticals of frame, horizontal frame, and sill. Windows are easier to paint and to clean afterward if the glass is masked. Both masking tape and liquid masking are available at hardware and paint stores.

A simple way to protect the glass is to cover it with a piece of wet newspaper. The moisture will paste the newspaper to the glass and also prevent paint from soaking into the absorbent paper. When you strip the paper from the glass after painting, the paint will come with it.

CLEANUP

Brushes, rollers, and other equipment should be cleaned as soon as possible after being used.

Equipment used to apply latex paint can be cleaned easily with soap and water. Rinse thoroughly.

Equipment used to apply oil-base paint may be a little harder to clean. Soak brushes in turpentine or thinner long enough to loosen the paint. Then work the bristles against the side and bottom of the container to release the paint. To release the paint in the center of the brush, squeeze or work the bristles between the thumb and forefinger. Rinse the brush in the turpentine or thinner again, and, if necessary, wash it in mild soap suds. Rinse in clear water.

NATURAL FINISHES FOR TRIM

Some doors, particularly flush doors, are attractive in their natural finish. However, they will become discolored and soiled easily unless protected. Your paint dealer can offer suggestions on how to finish and protect your doors. Many kinds of products

Draw design on textured paint.

Fill impressions with deeper color.

are now on the market, and new ones are constantly appearing.

The first step in finishing doors is to obtain the proper color tone. This is usually acquired by staining. Sometimes, however, no staining is required—the preservative finish is enough to bring out the desired color tone. With new doors, you can experiment on the trimmings or shavings to help you make a decision.

The next step is sealing. One coat of shellac is usually adequate. When the shellac is dry, the surface should be sanded smooth, wiped free of dust, and varnished. Rubbing the surface with linseed oil, as is done in furniture finishing, provides a nice soft finish but requires more work. Also, surfaces so finished collect dust more readily.

For a natural finish of other interior trim, you need to specify the desired kind and grade of wood at the time of construction. This can add substantially to the construction costs. If you already have handsome naturally finished woodwork in your home, consider yourself fortunate. And make sure you think twice, then twice more, before painting over it.

UNUSUAL EFFECTS

The beauty of paint lies in its adaptability to your decorating whims. How about textured paint to give your room a new personality? This treatment adds depth to the walls, and its rough finish blends beautifully with various decors. In addition, the heavy consistency of textured paint fills small holes and cracks, making it the perfect camouflage for old, scarred walls that would normally require replastering.

While the paint is still wet, create a random pattern by going over the surface with a special roller, a whisk broom, a comb, or other object that will make a design. Decorators often give a textured finish an individual touch by drawing stylized birds, plants, and other figures and designs. You, too, can do it. Simply draw freehand an outline of whatever you choose, using an unsharpened pencil or similar object. If you wish to make the impressions more outstanding, fill them in with a slightly deeper color when dry.

Striping is another fashionable wall treatment. Paint the walls in the chosen back-

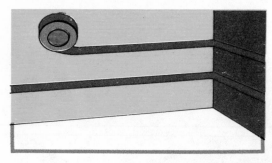

Masking walls for striping.

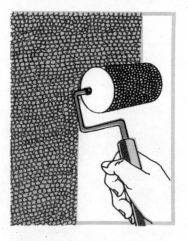

Stippling a wall.

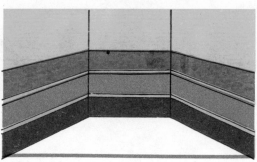

Stripe effect.

designated areas in a contrasting color. Let dry thoroughly, then remove the strips of masking tape. The walls are no longer a backdrop; they are one of the most exciting features in the room. Striped walls do wonders to increase the visual size of a small room.

Stippling the walls produces a very decorative effect and gives them dimension. Paint the walls the background color and let dry completely. Then, using a stippling roller (available in a wide assortment of design-producing sleeves), go over the dry walls in a contrasting color of your choice.

ground color and let them dry. Then, using masking tape (which must be securely fastened to the surface), mark off the areas to be striped in the desired widths. Paint these

Painting Tips

• Do the painting when the room temperature is comfortable for work—between 60 and 70 degrees F. Provide good cross-ventilation both to shorten the drying time and to remove fumes and odors.

• Check the label on the paint can for any special application and drying instructions.

• Preferably, remove all furnishings from the room. Otherwise, cover the furniture, fixtures, and floor with drop cloths or newspapers. No matter how careful you may be, you will spill, drip, or splatter some paint.

• Remove all light switch and wall plug plates. If you wish, paint the plates before you replace them after painting the room.

• Dip your brush into the paint no more than one-third the length of the bristles. This will minimize splattering and dripping.

• When using latex paint, wash your brush or roller occasionally with water. A buildup of the quick-drying paint in the nap of the roller or at the base of the bristles of the brush can cause excessive dripping.

• Wipe up spilled, splattered, or dripped paint as you go along. Paint is easier to clean up when it is wet.

• Do not let the paint dry out in the can or in brushes or rollers between jobs or during long interruptions in a job. After each job, replace the can lid securely, and clean brushes or rollers. During long interruptions in a job, also replace the can lid, and either clean brushes or rollers or suspend them in water.

Safety Tips

• Never paint in a completely closed room, and use caution when painting in a room where there is an open flame or fire. Some paints give off fumes that are flammable or dangerous to breathe or both.

• Avoid prolonged exposure to paint fumes for a day or two after painting. Such fumes can also be harmful to canaries or other pet birds.

• Use a sturdy stepladder or other support when painting high places. Be sure that the ladder is positioned firmly, with the legs fully opened and locked in position (see PAGES 42-46).

• Face the ladder when climbing up or down it, holding on with at least one hand. Lean toward the ladder when painting.

• Do not overreach when painting. Move the ladder frequently rather than risk a fall. And, to avoid spilling the paint, take the few seconds required to remove the paint can from the ladder before you move it.

• When you finish painting, dispose of used rags by putting them in a covered metal can. If left lying around, the oily rags could catch fire by spontaneous combustion.

• Store paint in a safe, but well-ventilated, place where children and pets cannot get to it. A locked cabinet is ideal if well ventilated. Unless needed for retouching, small quantities of paint may not be worth saving.

If You Have the Painting Done

You may prefer to have all or part of your painting done by a professional painter. When you hire a contractor, it is a good idea to get a signed agreement specifying:

• The specific price for the job.

• Exactly what areas or surfaces are to be painted.

• The types, brands, and quality of paints to be used and the number of coats, including primer coats, to be applied.

• The measures to be taken to protect floors, furnisnings, and other parts of the house.

• A complete cleanup guarantee.

• A completion date (allowing for possible delays—because of bad weather, for example).

Check the contractor's work with friends or neighbors who may have hired him in the past. Be sure that he is fully insured (Workmen's Compensation and Employer's Liability Insurance, Public Liability, and Property Damage Insurance). Otherwise, you could be held liable for accidents that occurred on your property.

6

Exterior Painting

SOME PEOPLE enjoy painting the house; for others it's a chore. But it must be done occasionally. One reason is for appearance. An even more important one is for protection of the wood or other surface.

When repainting is needed, delay can mean extra work when you finally do paint. Old paint that blisters, cracks, and peels must be removed before new paint can be applied.

If you wait too long, there could be costly damage. Wood rots when not fully protected. Also, moisture is allowed to reach the interior, where it can cause damage. Some metals rust when not protected; others develop a corrosive wash that stains surrounding surfaces.

On the other hand, too-frequent repainting builds up an excessively thick film that is more sensitive to the deteriorating effects of the weather. Ordinarily, every four years is often enough to repaint a house. Sheltered areas, such as eaves and porch ceilings, may not need repainting every time the body of the house is repainted; every other time may be sufficient.

Take the time and effort to do a good job when you paint. First, use good-quality paint. It will give longer and better protection. Second, prepare the surface properly. Even the best paint won't last on a poorly prepared surface. You will be wasting your time and money.

Calk joints tightly.

SURFACE PREPARATION

In general, a surface that is to be painted should be firm, smooth, and clean. With oil-base paint, it must also be dry. Latex or water-base paint can be applied to a damp surface (but not to a wet one). The paint-can label may contain additional or special instructions for preparing the surface.

Apply calking compound around windows and doors and wherever dissimilar materials abut (wood–masonry, wood–metal, wood siding–trim, etc.). Tightly calked joints help to weatherproof your house and prevent moisture seepage with its subsequent damage to paint film.

WOOD SURFACES

Wood siding preferably should not contain knots or sappy streaks. But if new siding does, clean the knots and streaks with turpentine and seal with a good knot sealer. The knot sealer will seal in oily extractives and prevent staining and cracking of the paint.

Smooth any rough spots in the wood with sandpaper or other abrasive. Dust the surface just before you paint it.

Old surfaces in good condition—just slightly faded, dirty, or chalky—may need only dusting before being repainted. Very dirty surfaces should be washed with a mild detergent and rinsed thoroughly with water. Grease or other oily matter may be removed with mineral spirits.

Remove all nail rust marks. Set nailheads below the surface, prime them, and putty the holes. Fasten loose siding with galvanized or other nonrusting nails. Fill all cracks; compounds for that purpose are available from paint and hardware stores. Sand smooth after the compound dries.

Remove all rough, loose, flaking, and blistering paint. Spot-prime the bare spots before repainting. If the cracking or blistering of the old paint extends over a large area, remove all old paint down to bare wood. Prime and repaint the old surface as you would a new wood surface. Sand or "feather" the edges of the sound paint before you repaint.

Before you repaint, be sure to correct the condition that caused the blistering, cracking, or peeling of the old paint. Otherwise, you may run into the same trouble again. It

1. Seal knots so they won't show through paint.

2. Set nailheads below surface.

3. Fill holes with putty.

4. Fill cracks in siding.

5. Spot-prime before painting.

6. Feather edges of sound paint.

may be a moisture problem. See CHAPTER 7 for causes and cures.

Old paint may be removed by sanding, scraping, or burning, or with chemical paint

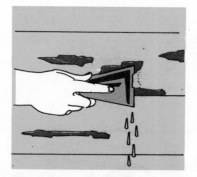

Scraping old paint from rough surfaces (above).

Sanding smooth surfaces (above right).

Using an electric paint softener (right).

remover. Scraping is the simplest but hardest method. Sanding is most effective on smooth surfaces. Chemical paint remover can be expensive for large areas. Only experienced persons should attempt burning. An electric paint softener is much safer.

Patch masonry cracks (left).

Replace crumbling mortar (below).

Wire-brushing masonry surface (below right).

METAL SURFACES

New galvanized steel surfaces (such as gutters and leaders) should weather for about 6 months before being painted. If earlier painting is necessary, first wash the surface with a vinegar solution and rinse it thoroughly. This will remove any manufacturing residue and stain inhibitors. Apply a special primer before painting.

Rust and loose paint can usually be removed from old surfaces with sandpaper or with a stiff wire brush. Chipping may be necessary in severe cases. Chemical rust removers are available.

Oil and grease may be removed with a solvent such as mineral spirits. Rinse the surface thoroughly.

MASONRY SURFACES

New concrete should weather for several months before being painted. If earlier painting is necessary, first wash the surface with a solvent such as mineral spirits to remove oil or grease. Fresh concrete may contain considerable moisture and alkali, so it is best to paint with latex paints.

Patch any cracks or other defects in masonry surfaces. Pay particular attention to mortar joints. Mortar and concrete patching compounds are available at hardware stores. Follow label directions for use.

Clean both new and old surfaces thor-

oughly before painting. Remove dirt, loose particles, and efflorescence with a wire brush. Oil and grease may be removed by washing the surface with a commercial cleanser or with a detergent and water. Loose, peeling, or heavily chalked paint may be removed by sandblasting. This is normally a professional operation.

If the old paint is just moderately chalked but is otherwise "tight" and nonflaking, coat it with a recommended sealer or conditioner before you repaint with a water-base paint. Some latex paints are modified to allow painting over slightly chalked surfaces. Follow the manufacturer's directions for use.

After cleaning the surface, wash or hose it—unless efflorescence was present.

PAINT APPLICATION METHODS

Exterior paint may be applied by brush, roller, or spray. You can paint faster with a roller than with a brush; however, a brush may give better penetration on wood surfaces. With a roller, you still need a brush for "cutting in." This means extra tools to clean after the job is finished.

Rollers work well on masonry and metal surfaces. Proper depth of the pile on the roller cover is important and varies from one surface to another. Follow the manufacturer's recommendations.

Spray-painting masonry
is the fastest method.

House painting sequence:
1-Windows, trim, doors;
2-Body of house;
3-Porches, steps.

Spraying is the fastest method. But you may not get proper penetration on wood surfaces. On masonry surfaces, voids that are difficult to fill with a brush or roller can be coated adequately by spraying. Surrounding surfaces must be well protected when spray-painting.

Paint the windows, trim, and doors before you paint the body of the house. Paint wood porches and steps last.

Read the paint-can label carefully before you start to paint. It will contain specific directions for application.

WHEN TO PAINT

New wood should be painted promptly (within two weeks) after its installation. If you find that this cannot be done, it is advantageous to protect the bare wood as soon as possible against the entrance of rain and heavy dew and mildew by brushing a paintable water-repellent preservative solution on the siding, trim, and into all joints.

Exterior Painting

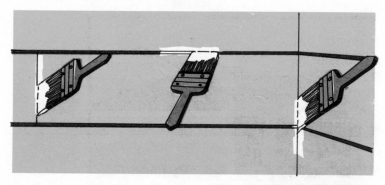

Brush into all joints.

Wood so treated should be allowed to dry for a few days prior to painting or staining.

The best time to paint is during clear, dry weather. Temperatures must be above 50 degrees F. Latex paints may be applied even though the surface to be painted is damp from condensation or rain. Solvent-thinned paints should be applied only to a dry surface.

If the outside temperature is high (70 degrees F. or higher), it is best to paint those surfaces already reached by shade. This is known as "following the sun around the house." To avoid the wrinkling and flatting of solvent-thinned paints, and water marks on latex paints, do not paint late in the day in early spring or late fall when heavy dew is common.

Do not paint in windy or dusty weather or when insects may get caught in the paint. Insects are usually the biggest problem during fall evenings. Don't try to remove insects from wet paint; brush them off after the paint dries.

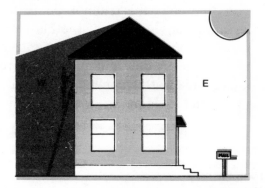

"Following the sun around the house."

HOW MANY COATS?

For the original paint job on new wood surfaces, three coats are recommended. A three-coat system will perform better and last much longer than a two-coat job. However, most original paint jobs are two-coat applications. If you plan to limit yours to two coats, be certain to apply both generously, toward the lower spreading rate of the range specified by the manufacturer on the label of the container. Again, manufacturer's instructions for use of primer and topcoat should be followed. On factory-primed sidings, the factory primer will take the place of one of the required coats.

Repaint work is best limited to a single coat of topcoat paint of a similar color. If you plan a color change, two coats of topcoat paint may be required. If bare wood is exposed, areas should be spot-primed before the topcoat paint is applied.

Use a good-quality oil-base exterior primer with solvent-thinned paint. Most manufacturers recommend use of a solvent-thinned primer with latex or water-base paint. A solvent-thinned primer may be applied to a dry surface only. Prime after you clean and repair the surface, but before you putty cracks or other defects.

Allow the primer coat to dry according to the manufacturer's label instructions. Allow longer drying time in humid weather. Apply the finish coats as soon as the primer has dried sufficiently. Allow about 48 hours' drying time between oil-base finish coats. Two coats of latex paint may be applied in one day.

On metal surfaces, prime both new metal and old metal from which the paint has been removed. Good primers usually contain zinc dust, red lead, zinc yellow, blue lead, iron oxide, or some rust-inhibiting pigment as one of the ingredients. After the primer has dried sufficiently, apply one or two finish coats of paint.

PUTTING ON THE PAINT

Stir or shake oil-base paint thoroughly before you start to paint. Stir it frequently while painting. Latex or water-base paint should not be shaken—it foams.

If you are using a gallon of paint, transfer it to a larger container or pour about half into another container. It will be easier to handle, and there will be room to dip the brush.

Dip your brush about one-third the length of the bristles. Tap off excess paint on the inside of the can; do not scrape the brush across the rim.

On windows, paint the wood dividing the glass first. Then paint the frame, trim, sill, and apron in that order. Shutters and storm sash are easier to paint if removed from the house and laid flat on supports. Wipe off dust and dirt before painting them.

On siding, start painting at a high point of the house—at a corner or under the eave. Paint from top to bottom. Complete one sidewall before starting another.

Paint along the grain of the wood. If you are painting with a brush, use long sweeping arm strokes, keeping an even pressure on the brush. Apply both sides of each brushful. End each stroke with a light lifting motion.

Apply paint to an unpainted area and work into the wet edge of the previously painted portion. When you finish an area, go over it with light, quick strokes to smooth brush marks and to recoat any thin spots.

Cleanup after painting is the same as described on PAGE 54.

1. Stir oil-base paint.

2. Pour into another container.

3. Dip your brush.

RIGHT

WRONG

4. Tap off excess paint—do not scrape bristles.

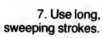
5. Start at a high point.

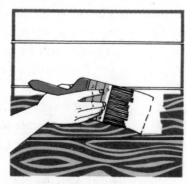

6. Paint along the grain.

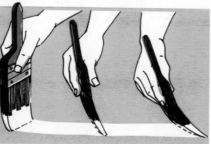

7. Use long, sweeping strokes.

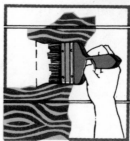

8. Work into the previously painted area.

NATURAL FINISHES

Natural finishes help to retain or enhance the natural color and grain of wood. Such finishes are most extensively used on the more attractive siding woods such as redwood, western red cedar, and Philippine mahogany but are not limited to use on these species. They are relatively easy to apply and economical to maintain. The natural-finish family includes water-repellent preservatives, bleaches, and penetrating or semitransparent stains. All are either unpigmented (clear) or pigmented very slightly, hence the term "natural finishes."

Paintable water-repellent preservatives (WRP) repel liquids such as rainwater and dew and thereby reduce the swelling and shrinking of wood. They also protect wood against mildew and decay.

The WRPs are easy to apply by brush or roller, or by dipping the wood before installation. They penetrate wood, leaving its appearance relatively unchanged except for an initial slight darkening reaction. Treatment with WRP slows the weathering process and protects against water staining as well as mildew.

Where paintable water-repellent preservative is the sole treatment to be applied to exterior wood surfaces, two coats are recommended. The best results are obtained when the first coat is applied to the back, face, edges, and ends of the wood before it is nailed into place. After installation, the second coat should be brushed over all exposed wood surfaces. As weathering progresses, the color of WRP-treated wood may lighten.

The frequency with which the water-repellent preservative needs to be renewed is dependent upon climatic conditions. In relatively dry areas, the treatment retains its effectiveness longer than in areas subject to extensive rainfall, and it may not need to be renewed for three to five years.

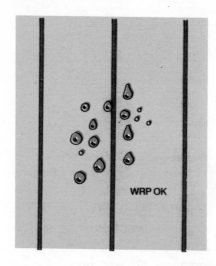

Checking to see if **WRP** is still effective.

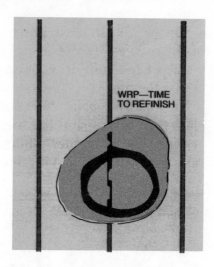

Where the treated wood is subject to frequent wetting, renewal may be required after 12 to 18 months. Successive retreatment may be extended to two years or more. Darkening of the wood or the appearance of blotchy discoloration are indications that the treatment has lost its effectiveness. This may be verified by splashing half a cup of water against the treated wood surface. If the water balls up and runs off, the treatment is still effective. If the water soaks quickly into the wood, it is time to refinish. A single recoat should suffice.

Some homeowners want their houses to have a weathered appearance sooner than natural weathering provides. This can be achieved by applying a bleach or bleaching oil. Bleaching oils are available in many paint stores. In addition to a bleaching chemical, the better bleaching oils contain

Exterior Painting

pigments to impart a grayed appearance to wood and an agent to protect the finish against mildew.

By means of chemical reaction with the wood, bleaches hasten the natural color changes brought on by weathering and eliminate the darkening that often occurs when wood weathers naturally. On new wood, two coats of bleach are recommended. The original application is often the last. Reapplication of bleach is required only if the wood begins to darken or if the bleaching becomes uneven.

Since the bleaching action is aided by moisture, together with sunlight, it is helpful to spray bleached surfaces periodically with water from the garden hose.

Semitransparent stains, sometimes called penetrating stains, contain a small amount of pigment that allows them to alter the natural color of wood but only partially obscure the grain or texture. They are generally offered in natural wood-tone colors and are available in either solvent-thinned or water-thinned types.

Two coats of penetrating stain are generally recommended on new wood, and application is best done by brush or flat applicator. Roller or spray application, followed by brushing, may be used on smooth wood and textured surfaces. Care should be taken on windy, dry days to avoid lap marks due to fast absorption.

Penetrating stains leave a flat or dull finish. They are a "breathing" type of finish, since they do not form a continuous film or coating on the surface of the wood. A penetrating stain finish is gradually worn away by the weather. When the erosion progresses to the point that portions of the wood show through, it is time to refinish. A single refinish coat is generally adequate.

SOLID-COLOR STAINS

The increasing use of textured wood sidings, an ideal surface for stains, has added to the popularity of solid-color stains. Also called heavy-bodied stains, they are made with a much higher concentration of pigment than penetrating stains. As a result, solid-color stains have higher hiding power, sufficiently high to obscure the natural color and grain of wood. They are more like paint than stain.

As a rule, only a single coat of solid-color stain is applied, but two coats provide better and longer service. Any of the conventional methods of application may be used to apply the stain to smooth wood surfaces, but brush application is best.

7

Paint Failure
—Causes and Cures

T HERE ARE FEW things more discouraging than giving your home a lovely new paint job, then watching it deteriorate before your eyes. It is especially frustrating if you've bought good paint, used good tools, and taken pains preparing the surface. What went wrong? Assuming you've followed all the instructions to the letter, how could it all crumble away in a few months, or a year? The answer is often traceable to one primary cause—moisture, a menace to the best of paint jobs.

INTERIOR FAILURE

The paint, preparation, and application have all been the best. Why do the ceilings peel, the walls blister? It will probably pay to have a plumber check for leakage somewhere in the water supply or sewage systems. Just a tiny leak can have a devastat-

Blistering, peeling wall (at left).

Scrape away all damaged paint (below left).

Install a hood and fan above range (below).

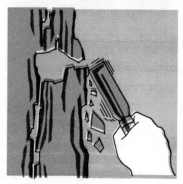

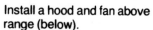
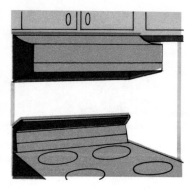

ing effect upon the surrounding walls. Moisture in the plaster causes blistering, peeling, and eventual ruination of the entire wall. If you suspect a leak behind the wall, no matter how slight, by all means have it corrected.

Ceilings, of course, can be ruined in the same manner, but many times the affected area is confined to that part of the ceiling which is underneath a toilet, tub, or washbasin. Frequent spillage of water from these sources seeps into the plaster or wallboard and causes moisture difficulties that are difficult to eradicate. Sometimes a more moisture-resistant floor overhead (ceramic tile, for example) will help, though this solution may require extensive and expensive structural modifications.

Even after you have sealed off the moisture source, the trouble may persist, because the dampness stays in the plaster or wallboard for a long time after the original soaking. This can usually be overcome by using an aluminum paint under a primer. If care is taken to scrape all affected paint from the surface, and the directions on the label of the aluminum paint are carefully followed, the problem should be solved.

Often paint cracks and peels above a kitchen range. The cure is a range hood with a fan to draw off the hot, moist vapors.

EXTERIOR PAINT BREAKDOWNS

More serious problems occur in exterior paint. There are many types of failure and as many causes.

Blistering occurs when moisture trapped in siding is drawn from the wood by exposure to the sun and pushes paint from the surface. First you must find and eliminate sources of moisture. Is there seepage or leakage from eaves, roofs, or plumbing? Is the area near a a bathroom or kitchen? Consider installing moisture-escape devices such as louvers, exhaust fans, or vents.

Scrape off old paint around the blistered area. Sanu the surface to bare wood and spot-prime with an undercoat. Seal all seams, holes, and cracks against moisture with calking compound. Apply a topcoat of quality house paint according to the directions on the label.

Chalking is normal, and even desirable, since it keeps paint clean. But when paint chalks excessively, it will not last long. The cure: be more generous with paint. Don't spread it too thin. Use two coats. Use chalk-retardant paints above masonry.

Flaking or chalking paint on masonry surfaces is caused by inadequate surface preparation. The paint flakes off in "scales" or powders and chalks off. The solution is first to remove flaking and chalking paint by wire-brushing. Seal all surface cracks against moisture with concrete patch. Apply a masonry conditioner according to the manufacturer's directions, then apply two topcoats of latex house paint or exterior masonry paint.

Cracking and alligatoring usually indicate that paint was applied in several heavy

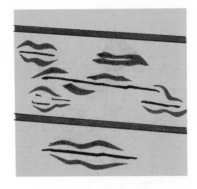

Blistered siding.

Install louvers, vents, exhaust fans.

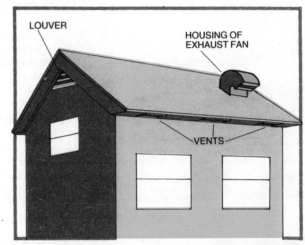

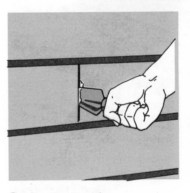

Seal seams, cracks.

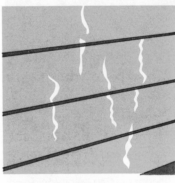

Excessive chalking.

Flaking, chalking on masonry.

Cracking and alligatoring.

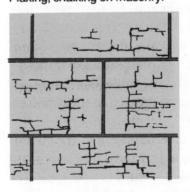

Paint Failure—Causes and Cures

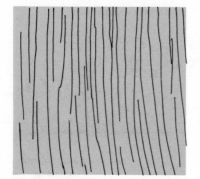

Checking.

Fill primed cracks.

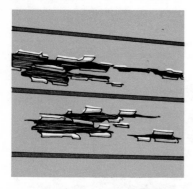

Peeling.

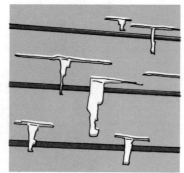

Flaking.

Topcoat peeling on overhanging horizontal surfaces.

Peeling, cracking on metal surfaces.

coats without sufficient drying time between coats, or that the undercoat used was not compatible with the finish coat. Sand the cracked or alligatored surface smooth. Then apply one coat of undercoat and one topcoat of recommended quality house paint according to label directions.

Checking is most commonly found on plywood veneer and is caused by expansion and contraction as it weathers and ages. To correct the problem, sand the surface smooth. If the cracked area is not extensive, spot-prime the exposed bare wood with an exterior undercoat. Fill primed cracks with calking compound. Apply a topcoat of recommended quality paint.

Should the problem be extensive, the best procedure is to replace the plywood. To prevent the problem on new plywood, sand the surface smooth, then apply one coat of latex wood primer and two coats of quality latex house paint according to label directions.

Peeling, like blistering, is caused when moisture trapped in siding is drawn from the wood by the sun's heat and pushes paint from the surface. The solution is to find and eliminate sources of moisture, following the same procedures as for blistering. Then scrape and repaint.

Flaking occurs when siding alternately swells and shrinks as moisture from behind it is absorbed and then dries out. The brittle paint film cracks under the strain and pulls away from the wood. Corrective measures are the same as for blistering.

Topcoat peeling is usually found on overhanging horizontal surfaces and other areas protected from the weather. It is caused by poor adhesion to the previous coat of paint because built-up salt deposits have not been washed away by rain. Sand the surface thoroughly to remove all peeling paint. Wash the sanded surface with a solution of three heaping tablespoons of trisodium phosphate to one gallon of water. Rinse well and allow to dry. Apply one coat of undercoat and one topcoat of quality house paint according to label directions.

Peeling or cracking of paint on galvanized metal gutters and downspouts indicates the use of improper metal primer or no primer at all. The paint film has little or no adhesion. Strip off all loose paint by scraper, wire brush, or power wire-brushing. It is very important that all loose paint be removed, or succeeding coats of paint will subsequently peel away too. When finishing with oil-base topcoat, prime bare spots with a metal primer. When finishing with latex topcoat, apply latex paint directly to bare galvanized areas after cleaning with a solvent and allowing the solvent to evaporate.

Fading is normal, but if it is excessive, salt air from the seashore is very often the cause. Sometimes heavy pounding of wind-driven rain or snow, followed by bright sunlight, will cause one side of the house to fade more quickly than the others. Not much can be done about it, but be sure to buy the best brand of paint, since it will invariably contain more and better pigment than cheaper types and thus hold out a bit longer.

Bleeding sometimes occurs on redwood and cedar siding and shingles. Sap runs or bleeds through paint and stains the surface. It is caused by inadequate sealing at the first paint application. If shake/shingle paints don't do the trick, the cure may be drastic. Stained areas may have to be scraped to raw wood and coated with knot sealer. If the staining material is creosote from an earlier application, the stain is blotchy rather than runny. Scraping down to bare wood is then the only cure. It's a tough one, but it can be done.

Mildew thrives on high humidity and high temperature, which stimulate fungus growth on paint film. If left on the surface and painted over, it will grow through the new coat of paint. The cure is to scrub the entire surface with a solution of one-third cup of trisodium phosphate and eight tablespoons of household bleach in four quarts of warm water. Then apply a wood undercoat. Mildew-resistant additive may be added to the undercoat if mildew conditions are severe and an oil-base topcoat is used. The additive in a finish coat should be avoided. The topcoat should be a quality mildew-resistant house paint.

Staining occurs when moisture in the siding dissolves coloring matter in the wood. Colored water escapes onto the surface through breaks in the paint film and drips from underneath overlapping boards. Stain is deposited as the water dries. The solution is first to find and eliminate sources of moisture. Then wash the stained surface with a mixture of 50 percent denatured alcohol and 50 percent clean water. Allow the surface to dry for 48 hours. Then apply two coats of quality house paint.

Excessive moisture may cause rusting of

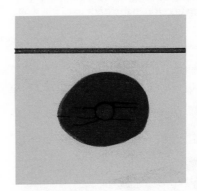

Rusting nails.

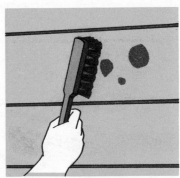

Wire-brush stained area.

Bleeding.

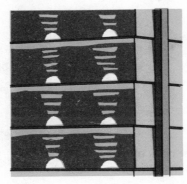

Mildew.

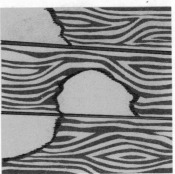

Staining.

Paint Failure—Causes and Cures

uncoated steel nails used in construction. After finding and eliminating sources of moisture, sand or wire-brush the stained paint and remove rust down to the bright

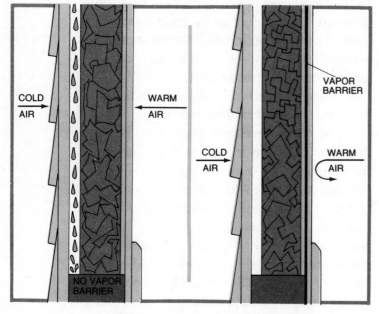

A vapor barrier protects against blistering and peeling, whereas the lack of one lets the water condensation run to the bottom of the wall.

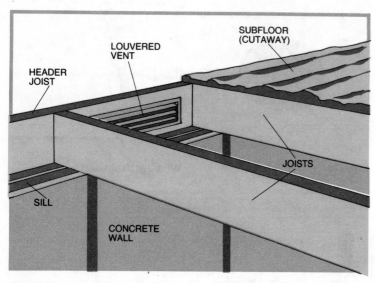

Install vent in header joist.

Install vent in place of one block of concrete-block foundation.

metal of the nailhead. Countersink the nailhead ⅛ inch below the surface of the siding. Immediately spot-prime the nailhead with undercoat. Fill the countersunk hole with calking compound or putty (see PAGES 58-61). Apply two coats of quality house paint according to label directions.

STRUCTURAL PROBLEMS

Insulated homes are certainly desirable, but they pose problems for the painter. If a home is insulated without a proper vapor barrier between the warm side of the house and the insulating material, water vapor condenses and runs between studs to the bottom of the wall, causing severe paint blistering and peeling. There is no real cure for this except to tear the walls apart and start over, which seems a bit drastic. It may be helpful to use latex paints.

Another trouble spot might be a crawl space. Moisture is often generated in these areas, then travels up through the walls, causing paint problems inside as well as out. Again, latex paint may help, but a more permanent cure may be needed.

Adequate ventilation is essential. There

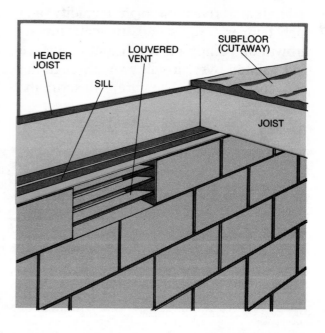

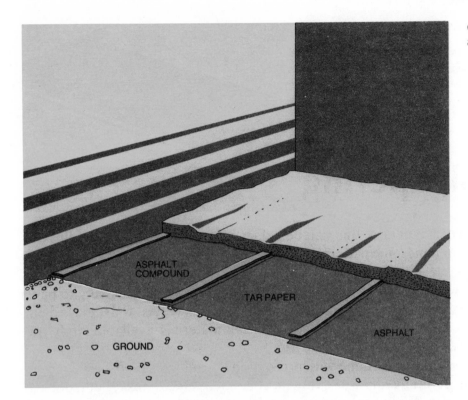

Cover ground with tar paper and spread layer of sand over it.

should be vents or louvers on at least two opposite sides of the crawl space to provide cross-ventilation. If necessary, you can install vents by cutting holes through the header joists. If the foundation is of concrete block, you can simply knock out a block to emplace a vent. Louvered vents, which can be closed off in wet or cold weather, are best. Most of them are also screened to keep out rodents and other small animals.

If dampness persists, cover the ground in the crawl space with heavy tarpaper. Overlap the joints 3 to 4 inches, and seal them with asphalt compound. Seal the tarpaper to the foundation walls with the compound. Then spread a 2-inch layer of dry sand over the tarpaper. This should solve the problem permanently.

Siding on ground-hugging houses, such as those built on concrete slabs, is sometimes in contact with the ground, drawing up moisture and causing peeling. (It also serves as an open invitation to invasion by termites.) Again, latex paint may help the

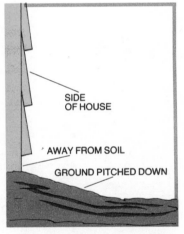

Grade soil away from house.

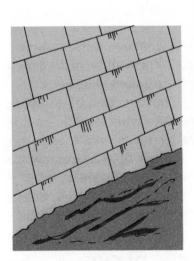

Siding in contact with ground.

peeling problem. A more permanent solution would be to regrade to eliminate the siding-ground contact. But make sure that the pitch of the soil is away from the house. Otherwise, you will be trading a headache for a migraine.

Paint Failure—Causes and Cures

8

Wallpapering

THE SPECIAL EFFECTS that can be achieved and the seemingly endless varieties of handsome patterns reflecting just about any mood make wallpaper a valuable asset in the home or apartment owner's decorating portfolio. The term wallpaper, it should be noted, does not apply exclusively to paper substances that are hung on a wall. It also includes vinyls, foils, grass cloth, fabrics, cork, and many other wallcovering materials available from your wallpaper dealer.

Wallpapering can be done with professional results by almost anyone willing to plan carefully and work slowly. It is not a difficult task, but it does require patience. Wallpaper can be purchased pretrimmed and prepasted so that all you have to do is soak it in water and apply it to the walls while wet. Hanging regular wallpaper, which must be trimmed and pasted, is not much harder to do.

The selection of wallpaper color and pattern is largely a matter of personal preference. Books and magazines about interior decorating are full of ideas regarding the use of wallpaper. In addition, many wallpaper dealers can give you valuable advice about how to achieve different effects—brightening a room or wall, visually lengthening a room, and coordinating carpet and furniture colors and styles.

The selection of wallpaper material is partly a matter of function. Vinyl wallcoverings should certainly be used in kitchens, bathrooms, hallways, or other areas where exposure to moisture and the elements could create a problem. It is extremely durable and moisture- and grease-resistant. In an entryway, durability is not a major consideration, but dramatic appearance may be. Foils, flocks, or grass cloth can be the answer to a decorating problem here. Again, your dealer can help in your choice.

WALLPAPER COLORS AND PATTERNS

The colors in a wallpaper vary slightly between different runs. If you have to reorder wallpaper, there is a good chance that the new order will not color-match the previous lot. Therefore, estimate your needs carefully and order enough wallpaper at one time to complete your entire job.

Blank stock is an unpatterned wallpaper commonly applied to a wall to provide a smooth surface for foil wallpaper and other special applications. All other wallpaper is patterned.

Some patterns—many of the vertical

stripes, for example—require little or no matching. The paper can be cut almost to the exact length required. Since only an inch or two extra length for trimming is needed on each strip, there is very little waste. The same is true of randomly patterned papers such as grass cloth or burlap.

Other patterns can involve considerable waste in installation. A clue to the amount of waste can be gained from the size of the repeat. This information is provided in the wallpaper catalog from which you make your selection. For example, the catalog may state that a certain pattern is repeated every 19 inches. Assume that the distance between the baseboard and the ceiling of the room that you want to paper is 94 inches. The 19-inch pattern will go into the 94-inch wall 5 times — with 1 inch left over for trimming. This pattern would result in very little waste.

You may find that another pattern is repeated every 18 inches. For the same wall, this pattern would repeat 6 times with 14 inches left over. The 18-inch pattern results in 14 inches of trim waste required for each strip. Unless you can find a place to use these remnants (over a window or door, for example), you will have a lot of waste.

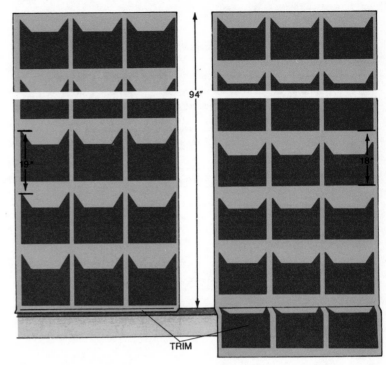

19-inch repeat on 94-inch wall.   18-inch repeat on 94-inch wall.

Papering a valance.

ESTIMATING WALLPAPER, TRIM, AND PASTE

Always plan on having some extra wallpaper; it may be needed for several reasons. A strip of wallpaper may be ruined in handling and need replacement. Other surfaces in a room (valances, for example) may be included in the job and require additional wallpaper. Future repairs may become necessary for which it is important to have wallpaper of the original batch. The same wallpaper, if bought later, may not exactly match the color of that on your wall.

The amount of wallpaper required to cover a surface depends not only on the size of the surface but on the wallpaper pattern as well. To make your estimate, you should know a few facts about wallpaper. It is sold in a variety of widths. Regardless of width, each single roll has 36 square feet of wallpaper (double rolls are also available). The length of each roll depends upon the width. The wider the roll, the shorter the length, and therefore fewer individual strips can be cut from the roll for hanging. When estimating the amount of wallpaper needed, count on about 30 square feet of coverage per roll, allowing 6 square feet for

WALLPAPER ESTIMATING CHART

Distance around room in feet	Single rolls for wall areas Height of ceiling			Number yards for borders	Single rolls for ceilings
	8 feet	9 feet	10 feet		
28	8	8	10	11	2
30	8	8	10	11	2
32	8	10	10	12	2
34	10	10	12	13	4
36	10	10	12	13	4
38	10	12	12	14	4
40	10	12	12	15	4
42	12	12	14	15	4
44	12	12	14	16	4
46	12	14	14	17	6
48	14	14	16	17	6
50	14	14	16	18	6
52	14	14	16	19	6
54	14	16	18	19	6
56	14	16	18	20	8
58	16	16	18	21	8
60	16	18	20	21	8
62	16	18	20	22	8
64	16	18	20	23	8
66	18	20	20	23	10
68	18	20	22	24	10
70	18	20	22	25	10
72	18	20	22	25	12
74	20	22	22	26	12
76	20	22	24	27	12
78	20	22	24	27	14
80	20	22	26	28	14
82	22	24	26	29	14
84	22	24	26	30	16
86	22	24	26	30	16
88	24	26	28	31	16
90	24	26	28	32	18

Note: Deduct one single roll for every two ordinary size doors and windows or every 30 square feet of wall opening.

fireplaces, make your estimate for the entire surface. Then reduce your estimate by ⅓ to ½ roll for each door, window, and fireplace, or 10 to 15 square feet each. If you estimate your needs in this way, you should have enough wallpaper to complete the job plus some left over.

You may prefer to have your wallpaper dealer estimate your needs. He is an expert. After you have selected a wallpaper pattern, he can tell you exactly how much you need if you give him sketches and measurements of the room.

The amount of paste needed for paper that is not prepasted depends on the number of rolls and the type of wallpaper you are using. Wheat paste can be used with most types; one pound of dry mix is generally enough to hang six to eight rolls of wallpaper. More dry mix may be needed than is recommended by the label instructions. Following label instructions sometimes results in a paste that is too thin.

Some dry-mix pastes contain mildew-resistant additives. These should always be used with coated vinyl wallpaper. The weight and type of backing on the vinyl determines the amount of adhesive needed. One gallon of vinyl adhesive is generally enough to hang two to four rolls of wallpaper. Ask your wallpaper dealer to recommend the amount and type of adhesive needed for your specific job.

Trim can be used as a decorative border, or to lessen the effects of any sudden change in patterns and colors between ceilings and walls. Trim is sold by the yard. Therefore, when measuring for trim, round off measurements to the next higher yard.

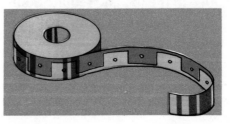

Trim.

waste (allow for greater waste if the repeat requires it). For estimating surfaces that are interrupted by doors, windows, and

Wallpapering

VINYLS

The three kinds of vinyl wallpaper commonly available are vinyl laminated to paper, vinyl laminated to cloth, and vinyl-impregnated cloth on paper backing. These vinyl wallpapers are extremely durable. They are easy to clean (scrubbable) and very resistant to damage. Most vinyl wallpapers are nonporous.

Pay close attention to labeling. Some wallpapers are vinyl-coated only. These are not particularly wear-resistant, grease-resistant, or washable. Do not confuse them with vinyl wallpapers.

Before hanging vinyl wallpapers, old paper on the wall should be removed. It is probably glued to the wall with wheat paste. Because vinyls are nonporous, moisture from the adhesive will be sealed in and cause the wheat paste to mildew. Also, sealed-in moisture can soak through old wallpaper and cause it to peel loose from the wall, taking along the vinyl that is pasted over it.

It is recommended that sizing be applied to surfaces before papering with vinyl. Sizing provides a good bonding surface. It also makes it easier to slide wallpaper strips into alignment for matching and making seams. The best sizing is a coat of the same vinyl adhesive you will use for applying the vinyl wallpaper. Be sure that any sizing you use is mildew-resistant.

Use mildew-resistant adhesives only. It is recommended that special vinyl adhesives be used. Paper-backed vinyl sometimes tends to curl back from the wall along edges at seams. Seams can then be difficult to finish. Use of vinyl adhesive prevents this problem.

Vinyl wallpaper stretches if pulled. If it is stretched while being applied, hairline cracks will appear at seams when the wallpaper shrinks as it dries. Be careful, therefore, to avoid stretching vinyl wallpaper.

Some wallpapers find that a squeegee works better than a smoothing brush for smoothing vinyl wallpaper.

FOILS

Foil wallpaper is available either with a simulated metallic finish or as aluminum laminated to paper. All foils must be handled carefully. Do not fold or wrinkle foil, because creases cannot be removed. Because of their reflective surface, foils will magnify any imperfections on the surface to which they are applied. Foils are nonporous; like vinyls, they don't "breathe."

Do not apply a cereal-based sizing to the wall; it could mildew. Sand the wall lightly with Production-grade fine sandpaper to remove texture and imperfections.

It is generally recommended that the surface first be covered with blank stock. This serves two purposes: it helps smooth the surface and it absorbs moisture from the adhesive used for the foil, thus speeding the drying process. Apply blank stock with the same adhesive used for applying the foil.

Use mildew-resistant adhesives only. It is recommended that vinyl adhesives be used because the foil seals the adhesive from the air and drying is retarded. Vinyl adhesives dry relatively fast. Wheat paste could mildew and should never be used with foil.

Some foils must be hung dry. Paste is applied to the wall and the foil is positioned on the paste. Special instructions such as these would come with the wallpaper.

GRASS CLOTH, HEMP, BURLAP, CORK

These materials are generally mounted on a paper backing. The patterns and textures are usually random and require no

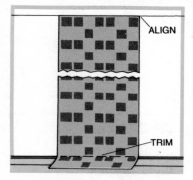

Align top end, trim only at bottom.

Align seams by pushing with the palms of your hands.

Smooth with paint roller.

Press seams with fingers.

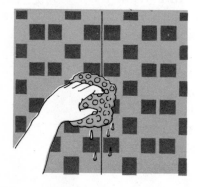

Blot seams to remove excess paste.

blank stock, you should apply sizing to the wall. Sizing provides a sealed surface that makes it easier to slide the wallpaper into place.

Be careful not to oversoak the backing—it can be weakened and allow the surface to separate. Rather than pasting several strips ahead, paste one strip and hang it before pasting the next strip.

These materials may be difficult to cut when wet. The job of trimming will be easier if you align the top end of the strip to the ceiling and do all the trimming at the bottom end of the strip. Mark it at the baseboard and cut with a scissors.

To align seams, push the wallpaper gently with the palms of your hands. Do not use a smoothing brush; the paper can be damaged by rubbing. Smooth it to the wall with a paint roller. Press seams into place with your fingers—don't use a seam roller, but firm the seams with a soft paint roller. Remove excess paste by wiping gently or blotting with a damp sponge.

In grass cloth, the color will vary slightly between rolls and even from one part of a roll to another. It is a good idea to first cut all full-length strips and arrange them for best appearance. Then stack them in this order for pasting. The edges of grass cloth are sometimes ragged. In this case, you may wish to trim ½ inch off the edges before hanging. This will make a good, sharp edge for seams. For best results, trim the edges after the grass cloth is pasted.

matching. Because of this, there is little waste. When cutting strips, you need allow only an inch or two extra length for trimming. These materials are not washable, so consider this when placing them in a much-trafficked room.

The paper backing on which these materials are mounted can be weakened from oversoaking with paste. It is recommended, therefore, that the wall first be covered with blank stock to help absorb moisture from the paste. If you decide not to use

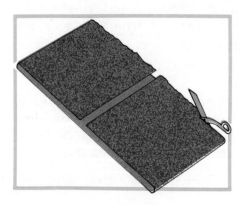

Trim edges of grass cloth.

FLOCKS

Flock is made of nylon or rayon and is available on paper, vinyl, or foil wallpapers. It presents no special preparation problems. It is fairly durable but can be damaged and flattened by rubbing and pressure. Therefore, use a paint roller or squeegee (available from your wallpaper dealer) rather than a smoothing brush to smooth it on the wall. Do not use a seam roller on seams, edges, or ends. Instead, pat down edges with a damp sponge or cloth, or use a new soft paint roller.

After hanging a strip, wipe in a downward direction with a damp sponge. Then, with a clean damp sponge, fluff up all flock with upward strokes to lay all nap in the same direction. Some small fibers will come loose during this operation, but this is no cause for concern.

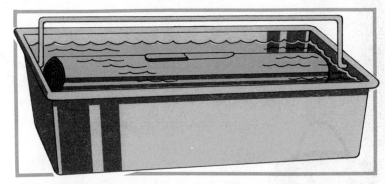

Weight paper down in water tray.

cut and soaked in water according to manufacturer's directions. Weight the paper down with a butter knife or other dull object to hold it under the water and to facilitate unrolling it. After soaking, it is ready to be hung.

No special surface preparation is required when using prepasted wallpaper—just make sure the subsurface is sound, smooth, and clean.

Wipe flock downward with damp sponge.

Wipe upward to raise nap.

PREPASTED WALLPAPER

Prepasted wallpaper, with water-soluble paste applied at the factory, is available in vinyl and paper materials. The wallpaper is

PAPERHANGING TOOLS

In order to hang wallpaper properly, you need certain tools. Some of these, like an old table or sharp razor knife, you probably already have on hand. The other items are generally inexpensive and can be purchased at your wallpaper dealer's shop. If you have a rickety old stepladder, plan on purchasing a new one (see PAGES 40-49). Nothing is more annoying, or more easily preventable, than to have your wallpapering project interrupted by broken bones resulting from a fall off a broken ladder. At best you will end up on the floor wrapped like a mummy in sticky wallpaper. Avoid accidents by planning ahead.

A pasting table or other flat, hard surface at least 6 feet long is needed for cutting and pasting wallpaper. It can be rented, or you can make one by placing a sheet of ½-inch plywood on two or three sawhorses.

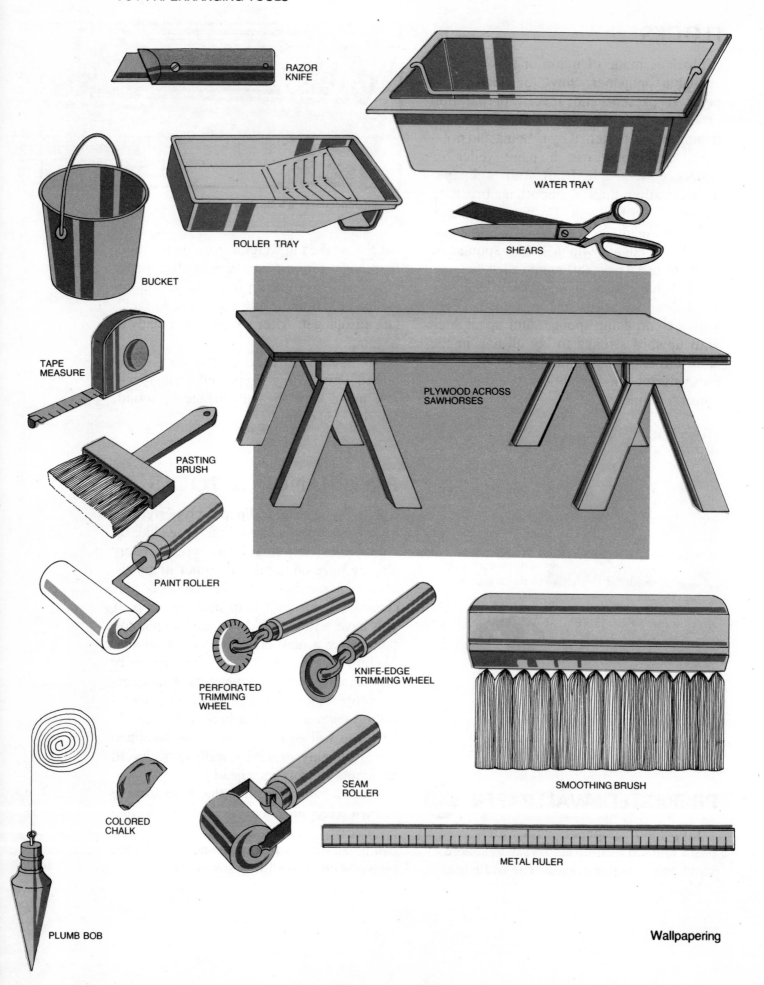

RAZOR KNIFE

WATER TRAY

ROLLER TRAY

SHEARS

BUCKET

TAPE MEASURE

PLYWOOD ACROSS SAWHORSES

PASTING BRUSH

PAINT ROLLER

PERFORATED TRIMMING WHEEL

KNIFE-EDGE TRIMMING WHEEL

SMOOTHING BRUSH

COLORED CHALK

SEAM ROLLER

METAL RULER

PLUMB BOB

Wallpapering

Two buckets, pails, or roller trays—one for paste, one for clear water—are needed. (If you're using prepasted wallpaper, just get one water tray.) A pasting brush, calcimine brush, or paint roller is necessary to apply paste if unpasted wallpaper is used.

Use a flexible metal tape rule to measure wallpaper lengths and widths, and a trimming knife to cut wallpaper. This can be either a sharp knife or a razor blade and holder. You should also have a trimming wheel to cut paper along baseboards or trim after it is installed. Two kinds, the perforated wheel and the knife-edge wheel, are available. A straightedge is essential for cutting straight lines. A long metal ruler is best, but any long, straight object will do. A chalk line will provide a true, straight, vertical guideline. You can make one with a piece of string, some colored chalk and a plumb bob or any object suitable for a weight.

A smoothing brush is used to smooth wallpaper against a wall and to remove air bubbles and wrinkles. The brush should be 12 inches wide, with bristles that are firm but soft enough not to scratch the wallpaper. (On some types of wallpaper, a soft paint roller is the preferred tool for the smoothing process.)

Shears or other heavy-duty scissors can cut wet wallpaper easier than a knife can. A seam roller makes tight joints at seams and edges. Use drop cloths to protect floors and furniture not removed from the room.

GENERAL PREPARATION OF WALL SURFACES

If old wallpaper is still in good condition, you can paper right over it. Any loose sections should be removed and the edges feathered with sandpaper. If the paper is generally loose, remove it completely with

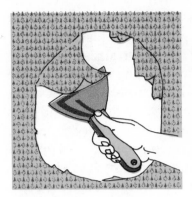
Remove loose sections of old paper.

Feather edges with sandpaper.

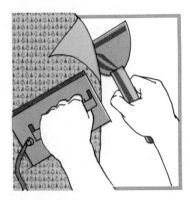
Removing old paper with steamer.

Removing old paper with chemical remover.

a rented steamer (following the renter's directions) or by soaking with wallpaper remover (following label directions). Where plaster is crumbling, scrape it away and patch with spackling compound, then sand smooth, as described on PAGES 50-52.

If you're papering over a low-gloss paint finish, dirt, grease, and wax must be removed. Following the label directions, mix a solution of trisodium phospate (TSP) to wash soiled surfaces. This provides a fine receptive surface for any adhesive.

If the surface paint is a shiny, high-gloss type, wallpaper may not stick well to it. This condition can be corrected by scrubbing with a solution of TSP or by applying a commercial deglosser. Consult a paint dealer for materials and recommendations.

If the surface is not painted, it must be sealed before applying sizing. Apply an oil-

Wallpapering

base sealer to unpainted surfaces such as new wallboard, plywood, or plaster.

It is generally advised to size surfaces before papering them. Sizing further seals the surface, preventing it from absorbing water from the wallpaper paste or glue, and thus allowing these substances to dry properly. (Vinyl adhesive should be used as sizing for nonporous wall coverings such as vinyl and foils.) Sizing also provides a roughened surface to which wallpaper paste can stick firmly.

For "breathing" wallpapers, you can use either of two sizing substances. Wallpaper paste, mixed according to manufacturer's instructions, acts as a sizing agent when applied to a surface and allowed to dry. Special wallpaper sizing is formulated specifically for this job.

Brush or roll a thin coat of sizing on the walls and allow it to dry. If the sizing turns pink in any area, it indicates a "hot spot" in the plaster; neutralize this area with a solution of zinc sulfate and water. Let dry and apply more sizing.

Take down all removable hardware that may be in your way. This includes cover plates for electrical switches and outlets and light fixtures. Since you will have to turn off the power in the room to remove the fixtures, you may find it convenient to do so only at the time you are actually papering around them.

Also remove curtain rods and brackets, drapery rods and brackets, and picture hooks. Screw holes will be difficult to find after they are covered with wallpaper. To save time and avoid having to drill new holes, place a toothpick in each hole. Remove the toothpick when papering over the hole, then push the toothpick through the paper back into the hole before going on to the next strip.

Apply sealer.   Apply sizing.

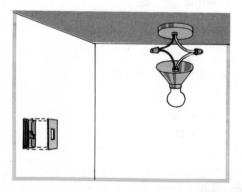

Remove wall plates, fixtures (left).

Put toothpicks in screw holes (below left).

Push toothpicks through wall paper (below).

PREPARING THE WORK AREA

A few minutes spent in organizing the paperhanging area will save time, mess, and tempers. An empty room makes the best work area. However, it is seldom practical to empty the entire room. Move out what furniture you can, and move the rest away from your work area so that you have as much room as possible for the ladder and for handling strips of pasted paper. Trying to work in a cramped space is both frustrating and irritating.

Bring all tools and supplies you will need into the work area. Set up a pasting table far enough from the surfaces to be wallpapered so as not to be in the way. Cover the pasting table with clean, plain paper such as freezer paper or brown wrapping paper. Never use newsprint to cover a pasting table; the newspaper ink is likely to soil the wallpaper.

REMOVING SELVAGE

Most wallpaper today is pretrimmed. The manufacturer has mechanically cut the edges so that strips can be butted together at a seam without the need for selvage removal. (Selvage is a narrow, unprinted strip on one or both edges of a roll of wallpaper.) A few smaller companies that produce specialty wallpapers still sell their products with the selvage intact.

The removal of selvage can be a time-consuming task. You should not be dissuaded, however, from buying a roll with these margins. The time required to remove the selvage will be well worth it if the paper is appealing.

Often, selvage strips are perforated for easy removal. In this case, simply strike the selvage sharply against a hard surface while turning the roll of wallpaper. The selvage will be torn off without damaging the patterned part of the paper.

If the selvage is not perforated, it must be cut off. It can sometimes be removed by the wallpaper dealer with a special tool. If the dealer cannot do it, you must remove it yourself. It is easiest to remove the selvage before cutting the wallpaper rolls into strips. Then, when you start hanging wallpaper, this work is out of the way.

To remove selvage, unroll some wallpaper onto your table. Align a straightedge with the selvage. Using a sharp knife, cut off the selvage. Roll the trimmed paper up so the roll looks like a scroll, one side trimmed and the other untrimmed. Repeat this process on the rest of the paper until all selvage is removed. Be careful not to damage flock surfaces by rubbing or pressing hard with the straightedge.

PATTERN LOCATION

Before cutting the first strip, determine where the pattern should end at the ceiling. This is a matter both of pattern and personal preference. Obviously, a pattern with human figures should not end with the heads cut off or just feet showing at the ceiling.

It is also important to remember that the line formed where the wall meets the ceiling is probably uneven. On painted walls, this unevenness often goes unnoticed. However, you may choose wallpaper with a pattern that forms a strong horizontal

Cut off perforated selvage and roll up trimmed paper, continuing to trim it.

Keep horizontal lines away from ceiling to make the unevenness less visible.

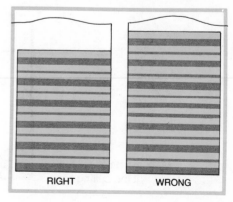

RIGHT   WRONG

Wallpapering

line. If this line is located near the ceiling line, the ceiling may appear noticeably uneven and the wallpaper poorly matched. Therefore, locate horizontal lines of a pattern as far as possible away from the ceiling line.

HANGING WALLPAPER

Follow the manufacturer's directions carefully when mixing wallpaper paste. Stir thoroughly until the mixture is entirely free of lumps. The paste should brush on smoothly, yet be thick enough to permit sliding the paper for positioning on the wall. If the manufacturer's suggested proportions result in too thin a paste, add a small amount of the dry powder to the mix.

If all four walls are to be papered, there will almost certainly be one place where the pattern cannot be matched. You should plan to locate this mismatch in the least noticeable place in the room. The best place for the mismatch is usually the least noticeable corner. However, sometimes a door opening or built-in cupboards or bookshelves can make a break in the pattern so that a mismatch will not be noticeable.

As a general rule, you should begin papering on the wall which is most noticeable and end in the corner which is least noticeable (or at another area, as noted above). After placing the first strip of wallpaper on the wall, work from right or left to the least noticeable corner. Then work from the op-

Measure and add 4 inches at top and bottom.

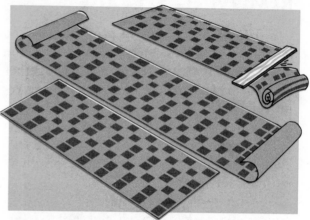
Then tear off the strip of wallpaper and tear off second strip to match first.

posite direction to the least noticeable corner or other mismatch location.

After locating where your first strip will go, hold a partially unrolled roll of wallpaper against the wall at the ceiling joint and decide where you want the pattern to "break" at the ceiling line. Mark this point lightly with a pencil and place the roll on the table. Starting at your pencil mark, measure off the distance from ceiling to baseboard.

Add about 4 inches above your ceiling mark and another 4 inches at the base for a trim margin, then tear off the strip of wallpaper, using a yardstick or other straightedge as a guide.

Lay the roll beside the first strip, unroll, and match its pattern to the pattern on the first strip. Tear the second strip off even with the first. Place it on top of the first, pattern up. Repeat this procedure with three or four more matching strips.

Mark the pattern break at the ceiling line.

Wallpapering

Apply paste to first strip.

Fold paper in on itself.

Paste and fold remainder.

Snap a chalk line on wall.

Align upper edge of strip with line.

Now turn the pile of strips over, pattern side down, and push it back to the end of your work table. Take the first strip off the pile and line it up with the edge of the table nearest you. Apply paste to about two-thirds of the top of the strip.

Now fold the section in on itself—paste to paste. Align the edges of the strip carefully, but do not crease the fold. Paste and fold the remainder of the strip—again, paste to paste.

If you are using prepasted wallpaper, simply dip the strip into the water tank. Fold the strip over as described above and proceed to the next step.

The first strip must be perfectly vertical. This is important, as this strip serves as the placement reference for the entire wall. If you are starting in a corner, measure off a distance from the wall equal to one inch less than the width of the wallpaper strip. This extra inch will allow you to trim away the excess that may not be even because of the unevenness of the corner. Place a tack near the ceiling at the point you measured.

Chalk a plumb line and suspend it from the tack, allowing the weight to swing free. When it stops moving, hold the chalked line taut; pull it out at the middle and snap it against the wall.

Open the longer folded section of the pasted strip and position it at the ceiling. Align the outer edge with your chalk guideline, then give the upper area of the strip a few strokes with the smoothing brush to hold it. (For certain types of materials, as

Stroke with smoothing brush to hold it.

Position lower end of strip, smooth with brush.

noted earlier, just press into place—do not use the smoothing brush.)

Unfold the shorter folded section and

Wallpapering

Trim at top.

Trim at bottom.

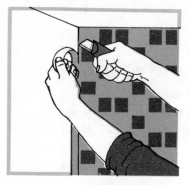
Trim at corner.

Press seams.

MAKING SEAMS

Butt joints have become almost the only method used for making seams between strips of wallpaper. They are by far the least noticeable of joints. A butt joint is made by moving the strip being hung against the strip already in place. Firmly slide the new strip tightly against the preceding one until a tiny ridge rises at the seam. As the paste dries, the wallpaper shrinks, causing the ridge to flatten.

Hairline joints are used only for blank stock, which is applied to the wall before hanging certain types of papers. A hairline joint is made by moving the strip being hung until its edge touches the edge of the strip already hung. As the paste dries, the paper shrinks, leaving a small hairline gap between the edges. This is invisible when the wallpaper is installed.

Lap joints, once common, are rarely used for seams between strips of wallpaper. They are noticeable and unattractive on an open wall. Lap joints may be used to make seams at corners. They are also used when small pieces must be joined together, such as fitting small strips in a casement window.

Do not use overlapping joints when hanging vinyl paper. Pastes made for vinyl do

guide it gently into place, keeping it on the chalk line. When this section is in position, brush from the center to the edges in sweeping strokes over the entire piece. Trim at top and bottom with a razor, a sharp knife, or, preferably, a wheel trimmer, then trim at the corner where necessary. Succeeding strips are hung in the same manner and in the same order in which they were cut.

After the strips have hung for 10 to 15 minutes, press the seams lightly with a seam roller. In the case of embossed or flock papers, seams are not rolled. With these wallpapers, a soft cloth pressed along the seams will serve the same end, while not crushing the flock or embossed pattern.

Remove any excess paste promptly from pattern, woodwork, etc. If the paper is a water-resistant type, wipe down the entire strip with a wet sponge. Use a clean, dry cloth on nonwashable paper.

Slide paper together until a ridge forms.

Paper shrinks to form tight joint.

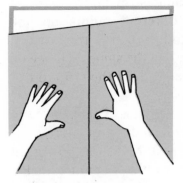
Hairline joint on blank stock.

Lap joint.

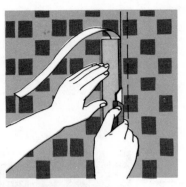
Making a double-cut seam.

not have strong adhesion for vinyl on vinyl. When hanging vinyl, use the double-cut seam method.

In this technique, a double cut is made at seams where the wallpaper strips have been overlapped. The cutting stroke must be firm enough to cut through both layers of paper. To make the cut, place a straightedge along the center of the overlap. With one stroke of the trimming knife, cut through both layers of wallpaper. Remove the trimmed strip from the top piece of wallpaper. Carefully pull the top wallpaper from the wall until the cutaway strip of the bottom strip can be removed. Then rearrange the seam, and smooth it down.

CORNERS

Special care should be taken when papering an outside corner. Do not rub on the paper where it passes around the corner. The surface of the wallpaper could be damaged.

Outside corners are more noticeable than inside corners. Mismatches are far more apparent at outside corners. Because of this, seams at or near the corner should be avoided whenever possible.

To paper around an outside corner, align the corner strip with the preceding strip. Cut a slit in the 4-inch trim margins at top and bottom and wrap the strip around the corner. Trim off the excess and let set. As

Lift top paper to remove cutaway strip below.

Smooth the seam after having it rearranged.

the paste dries, the strip will be pulled tightly against the wall.

Usually, papering inside corners results in some mismatch between strips. If the strips are carefully aligned, however, the mismatch will not be very noticeable. The correct way to paper an inside corner is to

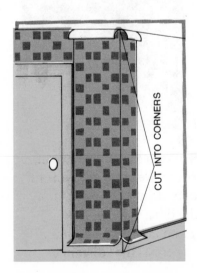
Papering an outside corner.

Wallpapering

1. Measure distance between strip and inside corner.

2. Hang first strip in corner.

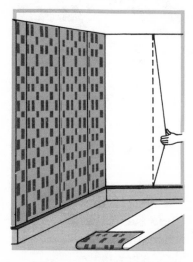

3. Measure second strip and snap chalk line

4. Hang second strip.

tween the preceding strip and the inside corner at three different points up and down the wall. Add ½ inch to the greatest distance. Measure out the same distance on a strip of wallpaper and cut the strip to this width with a straightedge.

You now have two strips. The strip cut to the measurement arrived at in the previous paragraph is hung first. Measure and record the second strip's width. Beginning at the corner, measure out and mark this distance onto the wall to be papered. Snap a chalk line at this point. Align the second strip with the line. Some mismatch may occur with this method, but it will not be very noticeable, especially with smaller patterns. Remember: this overlapped seam will have to be double-cut if you are working with vinyl material.

PAPERING AROUND DOORS AND WINDOWS

The procedure for paperhanging around doors and windows is essentially the same. The first strip to be hung around a window

1. Cut wallpaper at top corner of window.

2. Smooth paper into joint.

cut the strip into two parts and overlap them at the corner. Never simply fold a strip and then paste it into a corner. It may pull away from the corner when it dries, becoming unsightly and subject to damage.

Measure and record the distances be-is aligned with the previous strip. The new strip is then pressed against the wall until it reaches the window. Don't press the top and bottom edges, however, until all cuts around the window have been made.

Using a smoothing brush (or paint roller), gently press the wallpaper into place where the wall and vertical edge of the frame meet. Cut the wallpaper at the top corner at a 45-degree angle into the outside corner of the frame. Using the smoothing brush, smooth the paper gently into place where the wall and top horizontal edge of the window frame meet. At the bottom corner, cut a 45-degree angle into the paper toward the lower outside corner of the window frame. Gently tap the wallpaper into place where the wall and bottom horizontal edge of the frame meet. Trim excess paper from around the vertical edge of the frame. Smooth the paper to the wall.

If more than one strip is required to paper around the window, repeat this procedure with the other side. The only difference between this process and papering around doors is that you needn't trim any bottom corners on door openings.

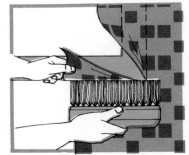

3. Cut wallpaper at bottom corner of window.

4. Press paper into place.

5. Trim excess paper around window.

Wallpapering

9
Paneling

PANELING OF WOOD and other materials is versatile, easily applied, decorative, and utilitarian. It is excellent for new construction, remodeling, and redecorating. It can be had in hundreds of combinations of materials, styles, textures, colors, and finishes that will enhance the appearance and usefulness of any room.

Paneling prices cover a wide range, from about 10¢ to $10 per square foot. Paneling usually comes in standard sheets of 4 by 8 feet or, sometimes, 4 by 7 feet. This varies, however, and some types are available in plank form with a 16-inch width and a length of 8 feet. Most types on the market today have a factory-applied finish.

Prefinished paneling is usually far easier to care for than wallpaper or a painted surface because of its durability. It won't chip, crack, or peel as most paints will over a period of years. Nor will it rip or fade like many types of wallpaper. Depending on the type of paneling used, it will retain its original appearance indefinitely and require a minimum of maintenance. An occasional wiping with a damp cloth is usually enough.

One of the most important advantages that paneling offers the economy-minded, short-on-time do-it-yourselfer is its ease of installation. Unlike paperhanging or painting, very little mess is involved. Whereas you would have to clear most of the furniture out of the room before painting or wallpapering, with paneling you just have to push the furniture out of your immediate way, then push it back as you progress.

The few tools required, basically a hammer, saw, rule, and level, are found in most homeowners' tool kits anyway, so there's no need to purchase any special devices. You may have to make a few tricky cuts with a jigsaw or compass saw, depending on the shapes involved in your room, but the installation is simple enough for any weekend handyman or woman. The matching molding available with most paneling effectively hides any small blunders that may happen during installation (even the professionals make these "miscalculations").

The consumer should be cautious when purchasing paneling and know exactly what he or she wants before throwing any hard-earned dollars into the project. Measure exactly how much you will need, keeping in mind the dimensions of the individual pieces of paneling. You most likely don't want to have a patchwork-quilt effect on your walls, which is often the result when one overestimates the dimensions of paneling sheets and thus has to fill a small space with an odd-sized piece. The paneling simply won't stretch.

After completing your measurements, buy a little more than you need in case any panels become damaged or marred during installation. Also, since paneling styles are constantly being updated and discontinued, it is a good idea to keep some spare pieces around the house for repairs or add-on pieces for future projects.

Make sure your paneling is either flame-resistant or flame-retardant. Tragedies have resulted from the use of highly flammable housing materials. Many local building codes stipulate that all paneling used in a house must meet certain minimum fire safety standards. Even if your town or city has no such ordinance, it is wise to look for safety seals when choosing any building materials. Most major paneling manufacturers so rate their products; steer clear of those that do not.

Try to deal with an established, reputable dealer when purchasing paneling. Most good businesses stand behind everything they sell and offer you helpful tips on installation. Also try to stick with the name-brand paneling manufacturers. These companies generally guarantee their products, as long as they are installed according to directions.

TYPES OF PANELING

The do-it-yourselfer is faced with a pleasant dilemma once the walls and partitions of a home or addition have been framed and the insulation is put up, or when it is time to remodel an existing room. What type of paneling will be used? With the almost endless varieties and styles available, there is bound to be a pattern that exactly fits any designing plan.

Paneling materials are divided into three basic categories: hardboard, plywood, and hardwood-plywood. Hardboard is made from cellulose-based materials pressed under extreme pressure and then cut into planks or panels. A durable finish is added on one side. It can be purchased in thicknesses of ⅛ inch and ¼ inch.

Plastic-coated hardboard panels are a popular form of prefinished wall covering. The very strong bonded plastic finish withstands plenty of punishment and is easily maintained; a damp cloth will remove just about any dirt that hasn't been ground into the finish.

This type of paneling is available in many styles, textures, and colors. Wood finishes that simulate anything from Alpine oak to sable walnut are available. The graining and coloration of these panels make it hard to distinguish them from real wood surfaces. Most come with V grooves that divide the 4-foot-wide panels seemingly into planks of uniform or random widths. One type has slots in the V grooves so that shelves can be hung without nailing or any fuss. Matching moldings and shelving are available with this paneling.

Wood-grain paneling also comes in varying textures. Distressed wood designs like

Slots in V-grooves of panels to support shelf brackets.

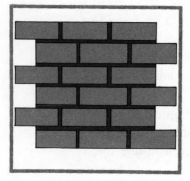

Brick-patterned
hardboard paneling.

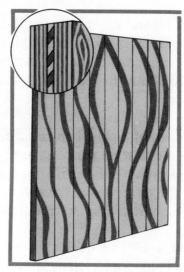

Plywood paneling.

barnsiding and intricately sculptured designs like panels from the Byzantine period are included in this category.

Designer planks come in various colors and patterns. Finishes range from high-gloss to satin-gloss. Some have mural or mosaic effects. The wide variety of patterns puts this type of paneling in solid competition with wallpaper.

"Masonry" paneling simulates brickwork, stone, and stucco. Some of these come in tilelike segments that the do-it-yourselfer can nail or glue to the wall. After fastening, a calking compound is put in the grooves to give a grout effect and hide nailheads.

Suffice it to say that, whatever you can imagine in a wall finish, it has probably been done in hardboard paneling. With all the different types, installation is usually the same (with the exception of some of the masonry patterns in which "bricks" may interlock).

Plywood paneling is made of thin layers of wood joined together with an outer veneer layer of high quality. Most of it comes prefinished. Some varieties require the installer to do the finishing, but unless you are experienced in this type of endeavor, it's better to stick with the prefinished models. The cost savings are minimal with unfinished types, and usually the factory finish will far surpass your efforts in durability and attractiveness. The panels have a more natural appearance than the hardboard wood grains, and rightly so, because they are made from actual wood.

Hardwood-plywood paneling is essentially a spin-off of the above, using specially chosen hardwood veneers. The woods range in price and quality from relatively inexpensive Philippine lauan to a very elegant (and costly) Brazilian rosewood. With the very expensive panelings, the prices are dependent on the thickness as well as the species of the wood.

There are other forms of paneling, too. Although less popular than the hardboard and plywood varieties, fiberglass paneling is attractive and versatile. It is usually textured and requires professional installation. Fire-retardant and flexible, the panels can be bent to follow the curve in a ceiling or archway. Although more expensive than most hardboard paneling, fiberglass "masonry" patterns are very realistic and offer substantial savings over actual stonework.

Solid wood paneling, somewhat the vogue in past years, has drastically declined in popularity since the advent of fine-looking, easy to handle and install, and less expensive prefinished hardboard and plywood paneling. It offers very little in the way of fire safety, compared to the newer paneling. For these reasons, solid wood paneling is not recommended for home use.

TOOLS NEEDED FOR THE JOB

You can probably do the whole paneling installation with tools you have on hand. It would be wise, though, to replace saws or hammers that have seen better days. Good tools last for many years and are inexpensive in the long run. Savings in wasted materials alone generally more than offset the slight additional cost of better-quality tools. Keep your cutting tools clean and sharp, and protect edges and faces when not in use. Store them carefully.

Use handsaws or time-saving power saws on paneling, whichever you prefer. If you use a handsaw, make sure it is the cross-cut type. A ripsaw will generally chip the face of the paneling. Keep the panel face up when cutting so that the saw cuts into the face on the downstroke. Start cutting carefully at the panel's edge and support the cut-off material during final saw strokes so that it doesn't break off.

For circular power saws, a combination hollow-ground blade is recommended. With a table saw, keep the paneling face up while cutting. If you use either a portable power saw or a radial arm saw, make sure the panel is face down while sawing. Whether you use a handsaw or a power saw, put masking tape along the line to be cut. This will help prevent edge splinters and chips.

You may need a compass or coping saw or a jigsaw (saber saw) to help you get around tricky corners and odd shapes. A level and plumb line will keep your paneling on a true line throughout the room. A drill and a chisel will be helpful for cuts within the panel's perimeter, such as one needed to accommodate a light switch. You should have a claw hammer for driving nails and a rubber mallet for pounding panels into place and setting them in adhesive. If you don't have a rubber mallet, you can make do by hitting a 2 x 4 placed over the paneling (protected by a rag) with a claw hammer. This will distribute the blow evenly without damaging the paneling.

If you're putting the paneling up with nails, use a nailset with 3d (1¼-inch) finishing nails. (Some types of paneling come supplied with color-head nails to match.) A plane may be needed to even off old door

Paneling

Crosscut handsaw.

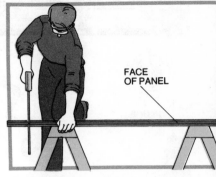

Cutting with a handsaw.

Cutting with a table saw.

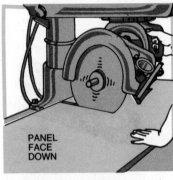

Cutting with a radial saw.

Cutting with a portable power saw.

Put masking tape along line to be cut.

Compass saw, coping saw (top).

Saber saw.

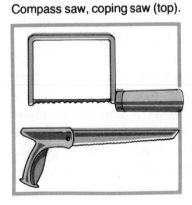

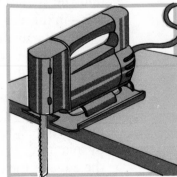

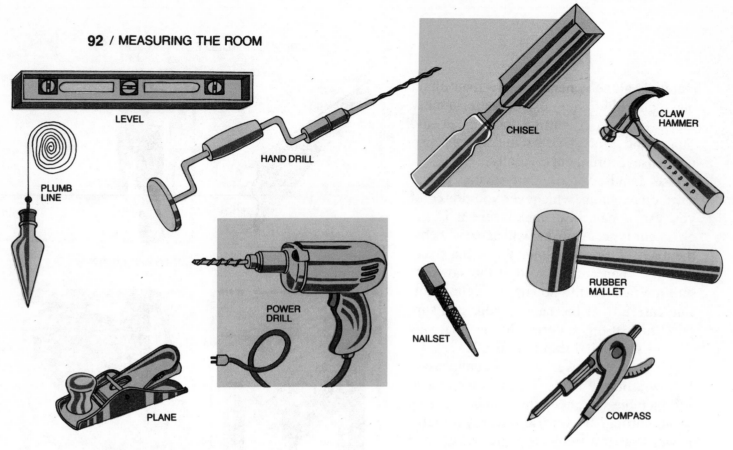

and window frames before paneling is installed over them. An art compass will be helpful in scribing out tricky or odd corners on the paneling.

MEASURING THE ROOM

Measure the length of all the walls, add these together, and the result will be the running length of paneling needed. In a room measuring 16 by 20 feet, the amount of paneling needed would be 72 lineal feet. If the paneling you have chosen comes in 4-foot widths, divide this dimension by 4 to find the number of panels required for the job—in this case, 18 panels.

Cutouts made for large openings (doorways, arches, windows) can often be used to panel under and over windows, for instance, or at stairways. You can estimate this use of otherwise wasted material by measuring carefully and, where possible, by planning to position a panel exactly at the edge of the opening.

As a double check, show your measurements and a sketch of your room layout to your dealer. He'll be glad to help and offer suggestions. Some types of paneling can be specially ordered in 10-foot lengths, suitable for older homes and apartments with very high ceilings. You may find, however, that the extra two feet will cost you substantially more than an additional 25 percent above the 8-foot panel's price. If this is the case, you might want to consider some other methods that will allow you to cover a 10-foot-high wall with 8-foot paneling. These methods are discussed later.

PANELING IN NEW CONSTRUCTION

If you're installing paneling in new construction, the preparation required is minimal and the problems that might arise are few. There are no old moldings in the way, for one thing. You have a chance to construct closets and built-ins with proportions

| Number of Panels Needed (Based on 8-Foot Ceiling Height) | | | | | | | | | | | | | | |
| Length of Room | Width of Room | | | | | | | | | | | | | |
	6'	7'	8'	9'	10'	11'	12'	13'	14'	15'	16'	17'	18'	19'	20'
8'	7	8	8	9	9	10	10	11	11	12	12	13	13	14	14
9'	8	8	9	9	10	10	11	11	12	12	13	13	14	14	15
10'	8	9	9	10	10	11	11	12	12	13	13	14	14	15	15
11'	9	9	10	10	11	11	12	12	13	13	14	14	15	15	16
12'	9	10	10	11	11	12	12	13	13	14	14	15	15	16	16
13'	10	10	11	11	12	12	13	13	14	14	15	15	16	16	17
14'	10	11	11	12	12	13	13	14	14	15	15	16	16	17	17
15'	11	11	12	12	13	13	14	14	15	15	16	16	17	17	18
16'	11	12	12	13	13	14	14	15	15	16	16	17	17	18	18
17'	12	12	13	13	14	14	15	15	16	16	17	17	18	18	19
18'	12	13	13	14	14	15	15	16	16	17	17	18	18	19	19
19'	13	13	14	14	15	15	16	16	17	17	18	18	19	19	20
20'	13	14	14	15	15	16	16	17	17	18	18	19	19	20	20

that are easy to panel around, for another. In paneling a new room, you're building out from relatively straight, true walls.

With new construction, the heavier grades of paneling can be installed directly to smooth studs without furring. Use a wood plane to smooth imperfections, or shim out low spots if studs aren't perfectly straight. Building paper, plastic sheeting, or other vapor barrier installed against studs on outside walls will protect the paneling from moisture.

PANELING IN EXISTING CONSTRUCTION

Frame walls are normally constructed of 2 x 4 studs (verticals) and plates (horizontals) at floor and ceiling, to which the wall covering material (such as lath and plaster or gypsumboard) is fastened. Studs are set every 16 inches (center to center) and at door and window openings, where they are doubled. You must locate these studs if you

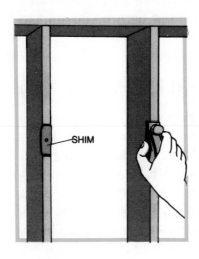

Correcting uneven stud surfaces with wood plane (at right) or shim out (at left).

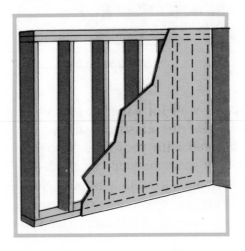

Stud finder.

Frame wall construction.

Paneling

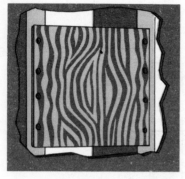

Tear out damaged plaster and build out wall.

Nail loose wallboard flat and tight.

Remove moldings with pry bar before putting up paneling.

Drive finishing nails through moldings.

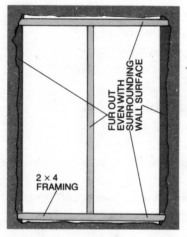

2 × 4 FRAMING

FUR OUT EVEN WITH SURROUNDING WALL SURFACE

Filling in a window opening.

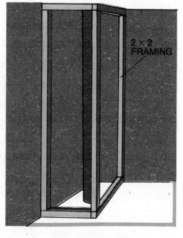

2 × 2 FRAMING

Frame around obstructions.

are furring the wall for paneling or nailing the paneling over the existing wall. To do this, tap the wall with your fist. A hollow thump means a space between studs; a solid sound indicates a stud location. Nailheads that show in baseboards or gypsumboard also indicate stud locations. Or you can purchase a magnetic stud finder in any hardware store. The wood stud won't attract the magnetic indicator, of course, but nails driven into it to attach lath or gypsumboard will.

If the existing wall is in good shape and solidly attached, you may be able to glue the new paneling directly to it or nail through the plaster or wallboard into the studs. If there is a small area of loose plaster, you can tear out that section and build it out with furring or plywood flush with the surface of the solid part of the wall. Loose wallboard can be nailed flat and tight. Paneling will hide many minor wall defects—no need to be too fussy. Just be certain that the defect won't get worse, to spoil your paneling efforts sometime in the future.

It's best to remove moldings before you put up the paneling. Do this carefully to avoid splitting, using a chisel or carpenter's pry bar. Or you can drive the narrow-headed finish nails right through the moldings with a hammer and nailset.

If you are filling in an opening, such as where you removed a door or window, build a stud framing and fur it out or cover it with wallboard or plywood to match the vertical plane of the rest of the wall.

Build a simple box frame around exposed pipes or other obstructions that you don't want to relocate. Paneling will decorate almost anything. If you're planning built-ins—closets, wall shelving, cabinets—it's best to frame them out before you start to panel.

ARE THE WALLS EVEN?

Paneling can readily be installed on any dry nonmasonry wall that is in good shape, but other methods are needed when a wall is uneven. Check walls carefully for flatness. An uneven wall may appear even when painted, but it will look very obviously out of kilter when paneled over. This is

Check for vertical and horizontal straightness of walls.

tions are noticeably large, compensatory measures will have to be taken before paneling is installed.

FURRING

One way to combat the problem of wall deviations is with furring strips. If the paneling is thick enough not to require backing (usually ¼ inch), furring is an easy and economical solution.

Furring strips may be nailed over the old wall, directly into the studs. If the existing wall is sturdy and solid, furring strips may also be fastened with adhesive. Follow label instructions for a secure bond.

Use 1 x 2 or 1 x 3 furring strips, or cut 2-inch-wide strips from sheets of ⅝-inch sheathing plywood. Space strips every 16 inches (measure from center of one strip to center of the next). Install either horizontally or vertically, following paneling manufacturer's recommendations.

especially true when the paneling utilizes straight lines in its design.

An easy way to check for wall straightness is to hold a room-height length of straight 2 x 4 lumber against the wall. If the board is flush with the wall at all points, then the wall is vertically straight in that area. Repeat this process, holding the board horizontally, to check for horizontal straightness.

There are other ways of determining vertical straightness and true perpendicularity. You can use a 2-foot carpenter's level or, better yet, a 4-foot bricklayer's level. Hold the level, lengthwise up, against the wall. As with the 2 x 4 method, if the level is flush with the wall, the wall is vertically straight in that area. If the bubble is not centered in the level, however, the wall is not perfectly plumb, or perpendicular with the ground level.

A plumb line can be used for this, too. Attach the line to the ceiling with masking tape at about two inches from the wall. With a ruler, measure the distance between wall and plumb line at different points on the line. If the distances are equal, the wall is both vertically straight and plumb.

It is very rare, even in new construction, for walls to be perfectly straight and plumb. If the walls are slightly off, paneling can usually be applied directly to them with satisfactory results. If, however, the devia-

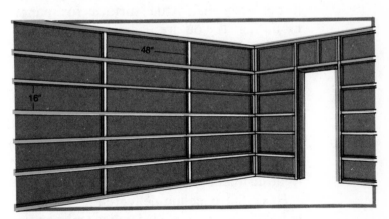

Furring strips over old wall.

Apply additional furring at doors, windows, etc. Don't skimp—use extra furring when in doubt. Where necessary, shim out furring to establish even planes, both horizontal and vertical. Pieces of shingle are ideal for shims. On an uneven wall take special pains to provide a firm, even base for the paneling.

Paneling

BACKING FOR PANELING

When using thinner paneling, you may want to use gypsumboard as a backing (the alternative would be horizontal as well as vertical furring). In addition to its being an easily installed backing surface, it can also provide an appreciable amount of sound insulation in rooms.

Other similarly strong backings, such as plywood, particleboard, and fiberboard, could also be used for these purposes. Installation for all forms of backing is essentially the same. Gypsum wallboard, however, is the cheapest and the easiest to cut and install. Simply score both faces with a razor knife and break it off, then nail it to the studs.

Special annular-ringed nails are used for attaching gypsum wallboard. Make sure the nailheads are either flush with the board's surface or beneath it, keeping it perfectly flat so that paneling can be laid flush.

Don't forget the primary reason for using the wallboard, either. It is there to provide a perfectly flat, true surface for panel mounting. If you are nailing it over a substantial deviation in either the plaster wall or exposed studs, compensate for this.

PANEL PREPARATION

Certain measures must be taken before you put the paneling on the wall to ensure its adjustment to the room's climate.

Have the paneling delivered a few days before it is to be used. Do not store or install it in a room or building that has been freshly plastered or where humidity is high.

Be sure that the room humidity is about normal before applying the paneling.

Unpack it at least 48 hours before it is to be applied and flat-stack it with narrow strips of wood between the sheets, or distribute it around the room so that air can reach all sides of each panel. This will permit balancing of the moisture content of the paneling with that of the air in the room.

If moisture or excessive humidity may be a problem during some seasons of the year, back-treat plywood and wood-base paneling as recommended by the manufacturer. A good practice is to brush-coat a water-repellent preservative containing 5 percent pentachlorophenol, followed 24 hours later with a coat of sealer—aluminum paint for wood; shellac, varnish, or similar material for hardboard.

If there are differences in grain and color of the paneling, distribute it along the wall and arrange the boards or sheets to get the most attractive combinations. Number the panels on the back or with a removable marking to identify the sequence for application.

Nail a temporary, level strip of wood at the bottom of the area that is to be paneled. The bottom end or edge of the paneling can be set on it, and you will be sure that the panels will be plumb.

INSTALLING THE PANELING

It is generally easier to start putting up the paneling in a corner or at the end of an area. This provides a good frame of refer-

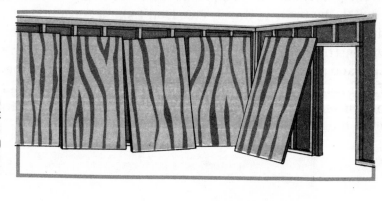
Line up paneling for best appearance (right); nail a leveling strip at bottom (far right).

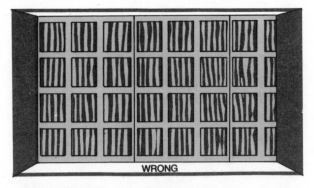

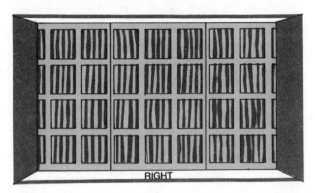

For some patterns, start in middle of wall.

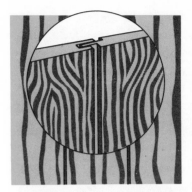

Tongue-and-groove and lapped edges make it possible to hide the nails.

Countersink nails.

Fill holes with stick putty.

ence and means that only one side will have to be cut in order to fit into the wall's width. With some panel designs, however, such as boxes or repeating motifs, it would look better to have both ends of the wall appear symmetrical. For this reason, starting the installation in the middle would be best.

Accurate marking, measuring, sawing, and fitting are necessary for a satisfactory job. Use a compass, saber, or coping saw to cut irregular lines. A block plane, a rasp, and sandpaper are helpful for fitting and smoothing the edges. Plastic wood, colored stick putty, and other patching materials can be used to repair or fill mistakes that will not be covered by the trim.

Panels grooved to represent random-width boards generally have a groove at each 16-inch interval, which is the usual spacing for studs and furring strips. Thus, nailing can be done in the grooves to hide the nailheads. Some types of paneling have tongue-and-groove or overlapped edges, which make it possible to hide the nails in the joint.

Color-coated nails that match the paneling can be used without countersinking. Otherwise, use 3d finish nails, countersink

them, and fill the holes with a matching color of stick putty. The panels should be well nailed around all edges and to intermediate support studs or furring strips.

USING ADHESIVE

Contact cement can be applied to both surfaces (paneling and furring strips or backing) at points of joining together. The cement can be applied with a brush or a serrated or saw-toothed spreader. The cement should dry to a nontacky condition before

Apply contact cement.

Press panel in place.

Paneling

Apply mastic to studs.

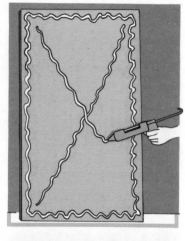

Apply mastic to back of panel.

Nail close to ceiling; molding will cover them later.

Pull away from wall and block it out with scrap wood.

Tap to make contact.

Tap at joint.

few nails at the top and bottom of each panel with the adhesive to hold the paneling snug until the adhesive dries.

If you use a mastic adhesive for paneling over a backing, run a bead with a calking gun around the edges of the panel, and then make a big "X" in the middle. Turn the panel around and stick it in place. Be sure to butt it snugly against the adjoining panel and push it firmly into contact with the wall covering material.

When the panel is in place, drive a few nails along the top edge, close enough to the ceiling so that the molding will cover them later.

Pull the panel away from the wall and block it out with a piece of scrap wood. The nails at the top will keep it from sliding out of place. When the adhesive has dried for ten minutes or so, remove the block and press the panel into place. This step is necessary for a good adhesive bond.

Using a scrap of 2 x 4 for a buffer, hammer the surface of the panel lightly to make sure the adhesive makes contact over the entire surface.

Fit all joints snugly, but not too tightly. If paneling must be forced into place, put a scrap of paneling or board over the edges and tap lightly with a hammer.

When you come to an electrical outlet, make a pocket cut in the panel with a jigsaw to expose the outlet, or drill pilot holes and make the cut with a compass saw. To locate the area to cut away, measure from the floor and front edge of the previous panel to

the panels are set in place. Position the panels accurately before joining the coated surfaces—the panels cannot be moved after the coated surfaces make contact.

Another system uses a mastic-type adhesive that is applied to the studs, furring strips, or rigid backing material. A calking gun is used to apply it to studs and furring strips. Generally, it is necessary to use a

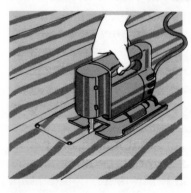

Pocket cut with saber saw for an electrical outlet.

Paneling

the outlet. Transfer these measurements to the panel and make the pocket cut. To be safe and sure, measure twice, cut once. Another method is to chalk the outer edges of the electrical box, then press the panel in place against it, transferring the chalk marks to the back of the panel. The cut is then made as above.

When you have the panel attached to the wall, you can bring the outlet plug out flush with the surface of the panel by loosening the two screws that hold it in the outlet box. Replace the outlet cover with the center screw to cover the edges of the pocket cut.

As mentioned previously, some paneling is available in 10-foot lengths. Because of the expense or difficulty in finding your choice of paneling in this length, you may opt for the 8-foot length, even if your walls are higher than 8 feet. There are a couple of tricks for horizontally butting one piece of paneling to another while still retaining a good appearance.

One involves a "shadow line." The shadow line is a stripe of black painted on the

Paint black stripe on wall and install paneling to create "shadow line."

mounting surface behind the joint of the two pieces of paneling, usually at a point 8 feet below the ceiling. Then the panels are mounted about ½ to ¾ inch away from each other so that a "shadow" separates them. The shadow-line effect is especially pleasing with wood-grain paneling, less so with soft, pastel-colored paneling.

Another method of concealing a horizontal joint is to place the 8-foot section of paneling on the lower portion of the wall. A shelf is then installed 8 feet up the wall along the entire width. Another piece of paneling is put above the shelf and no one is the wiser.

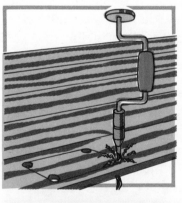  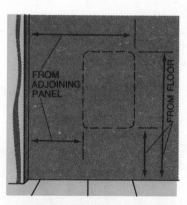

Drill pilot holes (far left).

Cut with compass saw (center).

Measuring to locate outlet (left).

  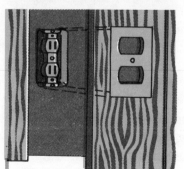

Chalk edges of electrical box (far left).

Press paneling against chalked edges (center).

Bring outlet flush with panel face (left).

Paneling

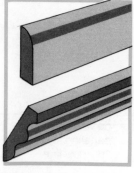

Base, ceiling moldings.

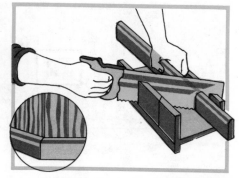

Mitering a molding.

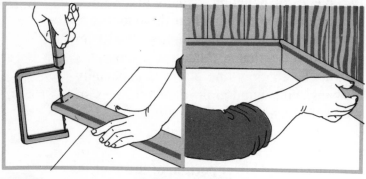

Coping a molding.

Outside corner molding (left).

Joining molding (below left).

Plastic joining molding (below).

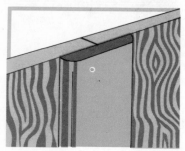
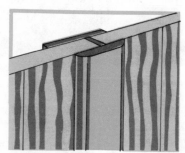

MOLDING AND TRIM

When all the panels are in place, nail molding at the ceiling line and nail on a matching baseboard molding. You can use finishing nails or nails colored to match the paneling for this job. Set colored nails flush with the surface; finishing nails should be countersunk and the holes filled with color stick putty to match the molding.

Where the moldings meet at the corners, you can either miter them (cut both at angles like a picture frame) or cope them (cut one molding to fit the curve of another). It's usually easier to miter outside corners (using a backsaw and miter box) and cope inside corners (using a coping saw).

In addition to ceiling and baseboard moldings, there are many kinds of moldings you can use to bail yourself out of tough fitting problems. Where panels meet at corners, you can use either wood or plastic moldings to make up for any slight discrepancies in fit. Outside corner moldings hide the edges of the panels and make tough wearing surfaces for the inevitable rough treatment an outside corner gets. You can butt panels together with a joining molding to hide any rough edges resulting from cutting a panel to fit a space narrower than the standard 4-foot width. With some types of plastic molding, you first put the molding on the wall with either nails or adhesive, then slide the edges of the paneling into it.

To fit paneling around windows and doorways, you should remove the trim molding and replace it to match the paneling. You can also install the paneling and nail the old molding back on. If you're really skilled, you can carefully cut the paneling to just fit up to the edge of a window or door molding, but this is a pretty tough job.

PANELING A BASEMENT

Installing paneling on a concrete or concrete-block basement wall involves a couple of extra steps, but it really is little more difficult than paneling any other room. The main difference is that you must put up furring strips (usually 1 x 2, 1 x 3, or 2 x 2 lumber) on the wall—you cannot apply the paneling directly. It is also a good idea to place insulation between the furring strips before applying the paneling, along with a vapor barrier. You may have to build a standard stud-frame wall to provide space for the insulation, depending on the type used. Your local building-supply dealer can help you with suggestions about what is best for your climate.

In many cases, especially on relatively new masonry walls, you can simply glue furring strips to the wall with special adhesive (again, consult your hardware or building-supply dealer). Glue horizontal strips along the ceiling and floor lines, then space vertical strips between them on 16-inch centers all around the room and in all corners. Check all strips with a level, and shim as necessary to plumb them.

Staple insulation between the furring strips. The store where you buy the insulation usually rents staple guns or hammers. Staple the insulation to the sides of the furring strips to leave the faces clear for applying the paneling.

If you need additional electrical outlets around the room, have the electrician install them before you start putting up the paneling. The outlet boxes should be flush with the surface of the paneling; special shallow boxes are available for this purpose. Make pocket cuts in the panels as explained above to accommodate the outlets.

To install the paneling, apply adhesive to the furring strips, rather than to the backs of the panels. Press the panels firmly into place as previously described.

To panel around basement windows, first glue a frame of furring strips around the window recess, flush with the front edge. Cut the paneling to fit up to the edge of the opening. Cut pieces of paneling to line the inside of the window recess and glue them in place. Use outside corner molding to cover exposed paneling edges.

Glue furring strips to masonry walls (right).

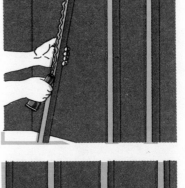

Staple insulation (below).

Shallow outlet boxes are available (below right).

Apply adhesive to furring strips (left).

Glue frame of furring strips around basement window (below left).

Apply paneling and molding (below).

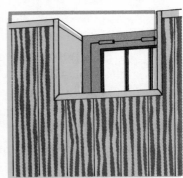

CARE AND MAINTENANCE

Wiping with a damp cloth is usually all that is needed to clean prefinished paneling when it becomes dirty. On some types, an occasional application of quality liquid wax

Paneling

Fill large scratch
with sticky putty.

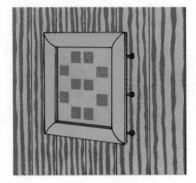

Holding picture frame
away from wall with nails.

is advised—follow the directions of both paneling and wax manufacturers.

Pencil and crayon marks and other heavily soiled areas may be cleaned with a mild soap or detergent. On plywood paneling, always wipe with the grain. After soil is removed, rinse and allow to dry thoroughly. Then (unless the manufacturer advises against it) apply a clear wax to restore the desired sheen. Cleansers that contain coarse abrasives are not recommended. Cleansers or waxes that leave deposits in the pores of wood should also not be used. On textured paneling, use heavy cloth wiping rags that will not catch on the raised areas of the design.

The finishes on modern plywood paneling are resistant to mars and scratches, but they do sometimes occur. They can generally be removed if they are in the finish only and have not penetrated into the wood. Use a clear wax on a damp cloth and rub the scratched area along the grain. You may have to wax the entire wall for a uniform appearance. But if the scratch goes through the finish and into the wood, a partial refinishing job will be required. Many scratches can be repaired with the use of a filler stick of the matching tone. If there is major damage, the services of a professional refinisher may be needed—or, if you were wise enough to purchase an extra panel or two when you first installed the walls, you might simply replace the damaged section.

Light has a tendency to mellow plywood wall paneling, except behind pictures, mirrors, and the like that are hung flat against the wall. This unevenness can be minimized by holding the picture or mirror out a bit—about a half inch—from the wall by means of nails placed in the backs of the frames. This allows light in behind the wall hanging so that the color tone mellows uniformly, leaving no sharp contrasts if the hanging is removed.

Low or fluctuating relative humidity can adversely affect any wood product. This is readily apparent when dry air causes a feeling of chilliness even when room temperature is 75 degrees or more. For your personal comfort as well as the health of the paneling, a humidity control system is recommended in high-humidity areas. With proper installation and care, your wall paneling will keep its good looks for years and years—a sound decorating investment.

part **2** INTERIOR
HOME
REPAIRS

Contents

1. DO-IT-YOURSELF HOME REPAIRS 105
2. BEFORE YOU BUY A HOUSE 107
3. ROUTINE MAINTENANCE 111
4. THE BASIC TOOLBOX 114
5. FLOORS AND STAIRS 123
6. WALLS AND CEILINGS 133
7. DOORS AND WINDOWS 140
8. WEATHERPROOFING AND INSULATING 149
9. CONDENSATION PROBLEMS 153
10. BASEMENTS, CRAWL SPACES 157
11. CONTROLLING HOUSEHOLD PESTS 163
12. SIMPLE PLUMBING REPAIRS 167
13. SIMPLE ELECTRICAL REPAIRS 174
14. STORM DAMAGE 180
15. EMERGENCY! 189

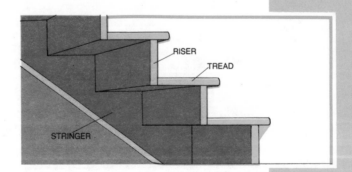

1

Do-It-Yourself Home Repairs

Y OUR HOME represents a very large and very important investment, and one that should be treated wisely and well. Both old and new houses, no matter how carefully they are built, need occasional repairs to keep them in good condition and to retard depreciation. Like anything else, a house deteriorates and declines in value if it is not properly cared for.

WHAT TO LOOK FOR

Careful attention to signs of wear can often eliminate the need for major repairs that stem from neglected minor problems. A sticking window can cause breakage of glass; faulty plumbing can cause damage to a plaster ceiling; a defective electrical fixture can cause a disastrous fire. These and similar difficulties can be avoided by proper and frequent inspections and prompt correction of the usually trivial sources of trouble. It's simply a matter of a stitch in time.

Who should make that stitch? Repairs that require specialized knowledge and skills should be performed only by qualified persons. But most repairs can be undertaken by any homeowner or apartment dweller who is handy with tools. In fact, with the virtual disappearance of the "neighborhood handyman" and the increasing reluctance of apartment "supers" to perform many minor maintenance chores, the do-it-

yourselfer is often the only one who can halt the little irritations before they develop into big—and expensive—headaches.

Of course, economics enters into it as well. The money you save by doing your own maintenance and small repairs can be

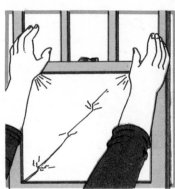
Sticking window may lead to broken glass.

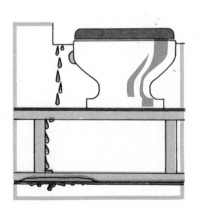
Faulty plumbing can cause damaged ceiling.

Faulty electrical fixture is dangerous.

wisely invested in home improvements to enhance the value of your house and make living in it more enjoyable and more comfortable. But this is not your only motivation, nor may it even be the major one. Pride of ownership compels a person to work hard to maintain and improve the home. This pride is considerably heightened when combined with the joy of personal accomplishment. Often a home handyperson may feel, somewhat vainly but understandably, that no one else can do the job quite the way he or she wants it done, or quite as well as he/she might do it. This may not be false reasoning, either, for certainly the tender, loving care that a do-

it-yourselfer puts into a project must count for something. Add to the joy of accomplishment the pleasure that many people experience when working with their hands. It's a fine form of relaxation, with the very practical reward of contributing something to keeping your home more comfortable, safe, and enjoyable.

Of course, not all do-it-yourselfers can do all the many chores required to keep a home in tiptop shape. Some people, whose hands may seem composed totally of thumbs, should shy away from even picking up a hammer lest they bring down the house about themselves. For them, we can only hope that they are lucky enough to find that vanishing species of neighborhood handyman. Others live in dread fear of drowning if a toilet overflows, or of electrocution every time they switch on a lamp. To them, we suggest that they post the numbers of a competent plumber and electrician next to the telephone and ring them up at the first hint of trouble.

But for the vast majority of homeowners and apartment dwellers, a regular program of inspection and maintenance will be simple and rewarding. You may be pleasantly surprised to learn how much you *can* do.

2

Before You Buy a House

WHAT FIRST APPEARS to be a bargain home may turn out to be a headache. A thorough inspection may reveal hidden defects and obvious remodeling needs.

Few people make a full-time business of checking house construction. If you have doubts about the soundness of the house you have selected, obtain an expert appraisal of the property to establish its value and point out deficiencies. In many cities there are reputable inspection firms that will examine the home and give you a detailed report. The $50 or $100 fee may be well spent. Some buyers face the expense of replacing basic equipment within the first year of ownership. If you have doubts about the wiring, plumbing, or heating plant, the owner may permit you to have it checked by an expert. You must be prepared to pay for this inspection. If the plumbing system includes a septic tank, an expert should definitely check the equipment before you purchase.

If you must call in experts, first check their reputations and beware of unscrupulous operators who may justify their fee by exaggerating flaws, which they may want to repair at inflated costs.

The age of a house should not necessarily limit your choice. Although older homes may require more repair work, many have received excellent care from previous longtime owners and compare favorably with newer structures. If it appears that repairs and improvements are needed, be sure to secure advance estimates of the cost of the work and find out who will pay for it—you or the seller.

A home inspection should be conducted in a systematic manner, beginning with the basement. Most of the common problems encountered can be fixed by the average do-it-yourselfer. Some require calling in a pro. Really major defects may lead you to decide against buying—why buy trouble?

FOUNDATION DEFECTS

If the foundation walls are solid concrete, they should be examined for cracks; if they are of unit masonry, the joints should be examined to see that no mortar is loose or has fallen out. The basement floor should be examined for cracks or signs of disintegration, and any evidence of leakage through the walls or floor should be noted.

Check joints on concrete block wall that no mortar is loose.

Make sure sill joints are tight and do not admit light, air, or moisture.

Check joists, bridging for sagging.

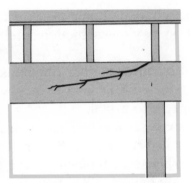

Inspect beams for cracks or shrinkage.

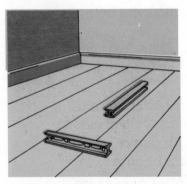

Check floors for level.

Inspect basement steps.

Check basement framing for signs of termites, rot.

Wooden stills on top of the foundation walls should be examined to see that they are sound and that there are no uncalked cracks between wall and sills to admit moisture and cold air.

If the basement has no ceiling, the joists should be examined for signs of sagging or warping. These defects often occur because the support or bridging is not adequate. Look for excessive shrinkage in the floor framing.

Girders and beams that support the first-floor joists should be examined for settlement, sagging, and, if the material is wood, shrinkage. A carpenter's level placed on the finish flooring of the first floor, both across and along the direction of the floor joists near points of support, should indicate whether column or wall footings have settled or whether there has been shrinkage in girders. Settlement, sagging, or shrinkage of floor supports may distort the shape of door frames in partitions and prevent proper closing of the doors.

Treads and stringers of basement steps should be examined to determine that they are sound and securely fastened. Basement steps should have at least one handrail that is solidly fastened. The steps should be well lighted along their entire length.

Check for signs of damage caused by termites or other destructive insects in posts, sills, joists, and other woodwork. Look also for evidence of decay from dry rot, especially in sills and at ends of joists adjoining masonry.

Make sure that all exposed water pipes are protected from freezing, especially if located under a porch or in some other unheated space. If there are floor drains in the basement or garage, see that there is sufficient water in them to maintain a seal in the traps.

HEATING EQUIPMENT

■ Because there are many types of heating systems, the details of inspection necessarily vary. The most favorable time for this inspection is in the spring when the plant is shut down for the season. If you have the heating plant inspected, try to find someone who is not also a salesman for a furnace company.

Check all radiator valves and shut-off cocks for possible leakage, and, in the case of a hot-water heating system, see that the boiler and radiators contain sufficient water. This is an indication of how well the owner has maintained the equipment. Examine the furnace or boiler to see whether grates or burners need repair or adjustment. See if there are cracks in the boiler and whether the firebox and clean-out doors fit tightly. Examine the condition of insulation on boiler, hot-water tank, pipes, and ducts to see whether new or additional covering is needed. Filters, humidifier fans,

Inspect chimney for loose mortar, smoke pipe for corrosion.

Check radiators for possible leakage.

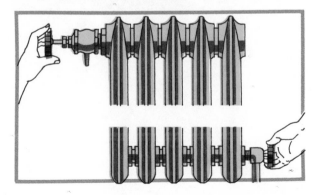

grills, and registers used with warm-air systems should also be inspected for possible defects.

Examine the chimney to see if the mortar needs pointing and whether the cement is sound around the smoke pipe where it enters the chimney. Notice whether woodwork adjoining the chimney requires fireproof covering to lessen fire hazard.

DOORS, WINDOWS, FLOORS, WALLS

Defects in the interior of a house are generally more apparent than those on the outside. A clogged drain, a leaky faucet, a sticking door or window usually attract attention, but other faults may go unnoticed unless carefully inspected. Examine all doors to see how true they hang and to find out if they stick. The lock or latch should be examined to see that the strike plate is not so far out of line that the door cannot easily be locked or latched. Raise and lower all windows to learn how they slide and whether cords or other parts need replacement. Observe how the sash fits, and see if weatherstripping is needed around the windows or doors. Notice whether there are any openings in or around the screens where insects can enter. All these little things can add up to a lot of aggravation after you have moved into the house.

If baseboards do not fit snugly to the floor, it is usually because they have

Make sure that screens fit snugly.

shrunk, but in some cases the settling of floor supports causes this condition. Creaking in a floor may be detected by bearing heavily upon various sections of it. Flooring should be examined for wear and looseness, stair treads for loose or defective coverings, and handrails for stability.

Look for cracks in the drywall or plaster, particularly over door openings, and see

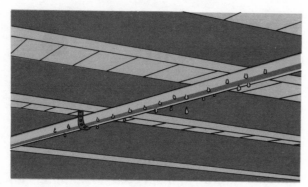

Pipes in exposed areas have to be properly insulated.

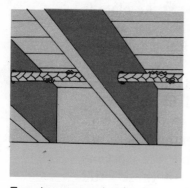

Examine exposed wiring for conditon of insulation.

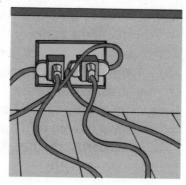

Beware of extension cords.

whether the plaster on the ceiling is cracked or loose. Other types of interior finishes such as paneling should be examined for buckling, loosening, cracking, or breakage.

HOUSEHOLD EQUIPMENT

When the structure of the house has been inspected, it is advisable to examine all equipment in which trouble could develop.

Plumbing facilities, including water-supply and drainage piping, fixtures, and equipment, should be checked to see that all parts of the system are in good condition and functioning properly. Drains and traps should be inspected for possible clogging, faucets for leaks, and flush valves or mechanisms in toilet flush tanks to see whether repairs or new parts are needed. Determine whether exposed piping is properly insulated against freezing in winter or moisture condensation during the summer. Examine all exposed wiring to see that the insulation is in good condition. If electrical appliances are included with the house, inspect the cords to see if they are in good condition. Check the operation of all appliances.

As a matter of expediency, the homeowner may frequently use an extension cord to supply an area not provided with a convenience outlet. Although this is satisfactory for temporary use, it should not continue as a substitute for a permanent outlet. Make sure there are plenty of electrical outlets.

3

Routine Maintenance

D o-it-yourself home care knows no seasons. Most homeowners make a year-round project of keeping their places in tiptop shape—after all, it's a matter of pride of possession. But some jobs are seasonal, or at least are better done at one time than another. Intended only as a general guide, this seasonal checklist will help you schedule regular maintenance around the house. Of course, much of the actual scheduling depends on the climate of the area in which you live, but the list will help to remind you when it's time to do what.

SEASONAL CHECKLIST

January

- Give yourself a few days to let the shock of the holidays wear off, then make a New Year's resolution to keep things in top shape for the next twelve months. You can start by repairing all those annoying squeaks and squeals in the floors and stairs that betrayed you every time you came tiptoeing in late at night after one of those many holiday office parties.
- And it's a good time to check out the plumbing, especially those leaky faucets that have advanced from drip-drips to roaring deluges. Some washers should do the trick. Drains that go glug-glug and pipes that go bang-bang should also be silenced, as well as the toilet tank that doesn't know enough to shut up (or off).
- As long as you are on a quiet kick, pick up a kit of household oil, stick lubri-cants, and the like and take a quick trip about the house, treating hinges, appliance doors, chairs, furniture casters, drawers, and whatever else might squeak (or stick). By now you ought to have the quietest and slickest house in the neighborhood.
- But don't let all that quiet put you to sleep—there is one more job to do. Make it a regular practice to open the faucet at the bottom of the hot-water heater and drain off any rusty water. This will help to insure long life for that hard-working appliance.

February

- Winter weather starting to get on your nerves? Perk up with a touch-up campaign, repairing and refinishing chips and nicks in furniture, cabinets, and porcelain fixtures.
- It's a good time, too, to patch any plaster cracks that have made their appearance during the cold months.
- With winter waning, this might be the

time to refinish hardwood floors that are showing signs of heavy wear worsened by wet-weather traffic.

March

● Whether the month comes in like a lion or a lamb, you know that spring can't be too far off. How about repairing and repainting the outdoor furniture so that it will be ready when those nice days finally arrive.

● Before you know it, screen time will be here. Now is your chance to make any necessary repairs—before the bugs come around.

● When the spring thaw comes, make a close check for leaks, particularly around doors and windows. Remember that April showers are on the way, and be prepared.

April

▲ Those April showers will bring May flowers—and a lush new growth of lawn. Get that lawnmower in shape, making needed mechanical repairs, sharpening the blade, and lubricating according to the manufacturer's instructions.

● Once again it's time to drain off any rusty water that has accumulated in the hot-water heater.

May

▲ Air conditioner in shape? You'll be needing it any day now, so make needed repairs and follow the manufacturer's directions for preseason maintenance (check owner's manual).

● While you are in an electrical frame of mind, how about repairing lamps, small appliances, nonworking fixtures, and faulty switches that have accumulated over the winter.

June

● Bug time, but don't let them bug you. The first line of defense is screening to keep them out, so make sure that a screen is repaired immediately after your neighbor's daughter blasts a

home-run ball through it. Also make sure that you have the proper pesticides on hand to fight off those little beasties that make it through the outer defense line (see CHAPTER 11).

● Summer water shortages are becoming increasingly common in many areas, so guard against water wastage by making sure that dripping faucets and running toilets are promptly repaired.

July

● Muggy weather can cause excessive condensation inside the house, which in turn can cause drawers, doors, and windows to stick and, in extreme cases, damage to floors, walls, and ceilings. Take corrective action as necessary.

● Don't let the hot weather make you forget that it's time to drain off the water heater again.

August

● If you have been a diligent weekend handyman all year long, you have earned a vacation this month, so head for the mountains or the shore, or just relax in your backyard with a cool drink and ponder the pitiful plight of your neighbor who has put off all his home-care projects until now.

September

● Old Man Winter may still seem to be far off, especially on those "dog days," but he is heading your way, so get ready for him. Make sure your house is weathertight, calking around doors and windows where necessary and installing weatherstripping if it is needed. Repair any damaged storm sash.

▲ Don't wait for a cold snap to get your heating system in shape. Have it cleaned (or do it yourself, but this can be a messy job). Replace filters, check boilers and humidifiers, etc. Make sure the smoke pipe between furnace and chimney is solid and not leaking or corroded. If in doubt, replace it.

October

- Don't let the World Series distract you—now you *have* to get ready for winter. Between innings, check your basement walls for cracks that could cause trouble under cold-weather pressures. At halftime of the College Game-of-the-Week, make a prewinter calk walk around the house, filling cracks and joints between various components and dissimilar materials. It will give you peace of mind come Super Bowl time.
- Time, too, to retire outdoor furniture and accessories; make sure they are properly protected during the nasty months—especially if you store them in a damp or exposed area.
- It's time again to—guess what? That's it, drain the hot-water heater. It's paying attention to regular tasks like this that means long, trouble-free life for your home and its equipment.

November

- With the chill winds starting to blow, make sure that weatherstripping around doors and windows is snugly in place.
- Turn off the water supply to outside faucets and drain these lines to avoid freezing problems.

- Holiday season is on the way, so this is a good time to fix up and paint up. Repair plaster cracks and rejuvenate rooms with a new coat of paint or a bright modern wallpaper print. This might also be the time to put down that new vinyl floor in the kitchen, or to tile the bathroom walls.

December

- It's a good idea to be prepared for wintertime emergencies, so get together a kit and be ready for the worst, while hoping for the best. Include such items as plastic sheet (in case a storm breaks a window or pokes a hole in the roof), staple gun, shovel, hammer and nails, lanterns or flashlights, calking gun, etc.
- Before you put that string of lights on the Christmas tree, check carefully to make sure that the wires are in good condition—not frayed or exposed at the sockets. And while you are at it, check out lamp and appliance cords throughout the house and make any necessary repairs, as described on PAGES 174-179.
- You've done a good year's work, so now you deserve to relax with a cup of eggnog before starting the New Year. Cheers!

The wintertime emergency arsenal.

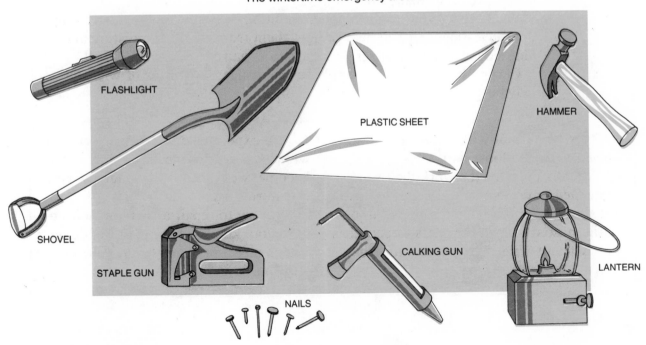

FLASHLIGHT

PLASTIC SHEET

HAMMER

SHOVEL

STAPLE GUN

NAILS

CALKING GUN

LANTERN

Routine Maintenance

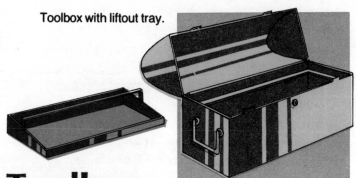
Toolbox with liftout tray.

4

The Basic Toolbox

A LL THE HOW-TO talent in the world won't help you if you don't have a proper set of tools. Don't make the mistake of going out and investing a small or large fortune in whatever the local hardware store has in stock, but—if you are new to the interior-repairs game—have on hand a few basic items. You can buy others as the need arises.

Never bargain-shop for tools. Don't settle for a lesser type or smaller size than you really need. And don't skimp on quality. A penny saved can mean dollars lost—or worse. Whatever the tool, look for a sturdy body and smooth finish. Metal surfaces should be coated for rust prevention; wood parts should be varnished, waxed, or lacquered for durability and protection against splinters.

Check all moving parts of a tool before purchase to make sure that they work smoothly and easily but are free of any play or wiggle. Look for tools that are permanently marked with the manufacturer's name or symbol as an indication of careful construction and quality materials. Some quality tools even have performance warranties.

For keeping your tools in good condition, a simple toolbox can be a prudent investment. It will help protect them from dust and moisture and provide a convenient organizer, storage space, and carrying case as well.

Certain basic safety tips apply to tool usage, regardless of what the tool may be:

- Never use a tool with a dulled cutting blade or bit or a loose part.
- Use tools only for the work they were intended to do. Never use a screwdriver to pry, chip, or pound; a wood bit to drill masonry or metal; pliers to pound or cut taut wire, or a wrench to hammer.

- Never expose pliers, screwdrivers, or wrenches to extreme heat; they could become weakened and suddenly give way during use.
- Do not try to repair a tool yourself unless you know what you are doing. Either buy a new one or take the crippled tool to an expert.

NAIL HAMMER

You need no introduction to the nail hammer—the tool for driving common or finishing nails, tacks, or staples into wood, plaster, or wallboard and for extracting nails. But you do need to consider certain important features when you buy one.

A slightly domed striking face allows you to drive nails flush without marring the surrounding surface. Curved claws, with inside edges beveled sharp, slip under a nail head to grip the shank for smooth removal. A hammer head set at a slightly acute angle to the handle helps you hit squarely. A handle may be steel or fiberglass with a rubber or plastic grip, or it may be wood. A wood handle should be firmly wedged or glued into the head.

The 16-ounce nail hammer is suitable for most uses and can be purchased for about $5 at any hardware store.

SCREWDRIVER

Another familiar tool is the screwdriver, designed to provide good turning leverage for driving and removing screws. It comes in two basic styles. The flat-tip style is for the single slot screws used in walls, woodwork, and furniture. The Phillips fits the cross-slotted screws found on many home appliances. If you don't own at least one of each, you should buy them, keeping the following points in mind.

The most generally useful flat-tip model has a wedge-shaped end about ¼ inch wide and a blade about 6 inches long. It costs about a dollar. A No. 2 Phillips with a 4-inch blade works on most cross-slotted screws and also costs about a dollar. Either style should have a large, fluted handle with a gently rounded butt end for firm, comfortable gripping. If compact storage is desirable, look for a model with a detachable, reversible blade—flat-tipped at one end and Phillips style at the other.

Assorted tip sizes and blade lengths may be a good investment if you use tools often. A flat-tip driver wider than the screw will scar the surrounding surface; a tip too narrow gives poor leverage and may damage the screw slot. Shorter blades are helpful in cramped quarters. Either prepackaged sets or three flat-tipped drivers—4, 6, and 8 inches—plus a No. 1 and No. 2 Phillips meet most household needs.

HAND DRILL

To insert long screws or bolts into or through wood, plaster, or wallboard, you first need to make neat, straight holes for

Nail hammer.

Flat-tip screwdriver.

Phillips screwdriver (above).

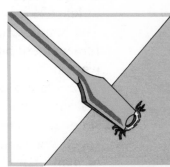

Too-wide scrwdriver
(above right).

Stubby screwdriver (right).

The Basic Toolbox

Rotary-crank drill.

Push drill.

Slip-joint pliers.

Adjustable wrench.

them. Either a rotary cranking or a push-style hand drill can do the job. Each is sold with interchangeable bits for making holes at least ¾ inch deep and up to ¼ inch wide. The handles are hollow for bit storage, and replacement bits are available at most hardware stores.

The rotary-cranking style is easy to control and versatile. By turning a crank you set gears in motion to activate the bit at any speed you want. The drill chuck holds bits of many sizes and types. However, a quality model is nearly a foot long and weighs several pounds; it is bulky to store. It costs $8 or $9.

The push drill, generally less than a foot long and under a pound in weight, can be purchased for as little as $2. Forward or downward pressure on the handle activates an inner spiral, or ratchet, that turns the bit. Some have a reverse mechanism that al-

lows a bit to be backed out of a deep hole or one in which it is stuck.

SLIP-JOINT PLIERS

With this familiar household tool you can hold bolts while tightening nuts, grip small or slippery items, straighten nails, or cut wire. To help prevent injury, use pliers to grip broken glass or other sharp objects.

For general household use, choose a pair about 6 inches long with "combination" jaws. The outer jaws should be parallel and finely grooved for holding or bending small objects. The concave inner jaws should have rugged teeth for gripping round or squarish objects up to ¾ inch across when the slip joint is in the "open" position. At the extreme inside, the jaws should serve as shears for cutting wire.

Durable pliers are made of forged steel and have a bright, reflective finish or a blue-black sheen. Handles should be easy to grasp even when the jaws are wide open and should be cross-scored or knurled for nonslip gripping. The slip-joint fastener should be impossible to loosen without special tools. Such pliers cost $3 or less.

ADJUSTABLE WRENCH

To tighten or loosen nuts or bolts or other threaded parts, you need a wrench with an adjustable jaw. It is especially useful in plumbing work.

An 8-inch model, with an angled head and a spiral midsection for adjusting the jaw, will suit most household needs. Select one with a reflective finish or a blue-black sheen, a knurled spiral for easy turning, and a jaw with exactly parallel parts for good grasp. The handle should be comfortable to grip and have a hole at the end for hanging on a peg. Such a wrench costs about $4 or $5.

The Basic Toolbox

MEASURING TOOLS

The least expensive measures are the 6-foot tapes commonly used in sewing. Yardsticks are also readily available and moderately priced and are easier to use accurately, but they are not as conveniently stored as folding rules or steel tapes on reels.

A steel tape that is rigid when extended but flexible enough to retract into a small case is especially convenient if you work without a helper. A 10-foot model with a ½-inch blade is useful for most home purposes and costs about $4. The tape is marked in inches and 1/16-inch intervals and ends in a hook that holds onto objects being measured. The case should prevent the extended tape from turning over and should have measuring marks that can be read as an extension of the tape. Many cases have a friction lock to hold the tape at a desired length.

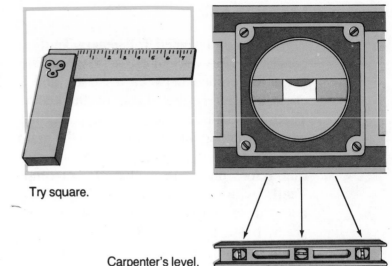

Try square.

Carpenter's level.

TRY SQUARE

The try square consists of two parts at right angles to each other: a thick wood or iron stock and a thin steel blade. Most try squares are made with the blades graduated in inches and fractions of an inch. The blade length varies from 2 to 12 inches. This tool is used for setting or checking lines or surfaces that have to be at right angles to each other. It costs about $3.

LEVEL

The level is a tool designed to determine whether a plane or surface is true horizontal or true vertical. It is a simple instrument consisting of a liquid, such as alcohol or chloroform, partially filling a glass vial or tube so that a bubble remains. The tube is mounted in a frame of aluminum or wood. Levels are equipped with one, two, or more tubes. One tube is built in the frame at right angles to another. The tube is slightly curved, causing the bubble to always seek the highest point in the tube. On the outside of the tube are two sets of graduation lines separated by a space. Leveling is accomplished when the air bubble is centered between the graduation lines.

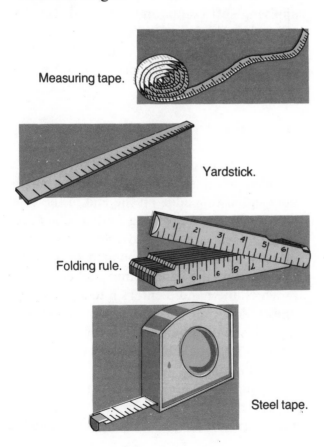

Measuring tape.

Yardstick.

Folding rule.

Steel tape.

The Basic Toolbox

HANDSAW

Handsaws designed for general cutting consist of ripsaws and crosscut saws. The major difference between a ripsaw and a crosscut saw is the shape of the teeth. Teeth with square-faced chisel-type cutting edges do a good job of cutting with the grain (called ripping), but a poor job of cutting across the grain (called crosscutting). Teeth with beveled, knife-type cutting edges do a good job of cutting across the grain, but a poor job of cutting with the grain. A quality handsaw costs $8 to $12.

NESTED SAW

For small cutting jobs, a nested saw with three interchangeable blades is a good choice. It can be stored compactly and costs about $5.

The narrow, tapered keyhole and compass blades, each about a foot long, make straight or curved cuts in wood; the compass style is particularly adapted to tight curves. The third blade has many small teeth for sawing through nails, wire, bone, or even frozen meat. The handle should be smooth hardwood or plastic with a comfortable grip and a device for securing the blades firmly.

UTILITY KNIFE

The small, sharp blade of the utility knife held firmly by a sturdy handle can save you time and effort in cutting twine, trimming carpet tile or wallpaper, and opening cartons. It is specially designed to lessen the chance of cutting accidents during handyman jobs and is an excellent safety investment for your toolbox.

Look for a utility knife with a single-edge, replaceable blade held secure by a screw at the throat of the handle. The handle should be shaped to fit your hand and hollow for the storage of extra blades. Some handles have a push-button to retract the blade or extend it for conveniently cutting different thicknesses. Such a knife costs about $2.

PUTTY KNIFE

A putty knife helps you attain a smooth finish when spreading spackling compound into chipped spots or small holes in walls, applying putty to window frames, or inserting grout between tiles. It can also be used for minor scraping of paint, plaster, or adhesive.

The thin, polished blade should have a blunt end and no sharp edges; it should be firmly attached to the handle by two rivets or eyelets. Stiffer blades are best for scraping; the more flexible ones are handy for applying soft compounds. A good style for general use has a blade about 3 inches wide, is about 7 inches long, and costs about a dollar. Narrower blades are also useful.

WOOD CHISEL

A wood chisel is a steel tool fitted with a wooden or plastic handle. It has a single beveled cutting edge on the end of the steel part, or blade. According to their construction, chisels are divided into two general classes: tang chisels, in which part of the chisel enters the handle, and socket chisels, in which the handle enters into a part of the chisel. A socket chisel is designed for striking with a wooden mallet (never a steel hammer); a tang chisel is designed for hand manipulation only.

Wood chisels are also divided into types, depending upon their weight and thickness, the shape or design of the blade, and the

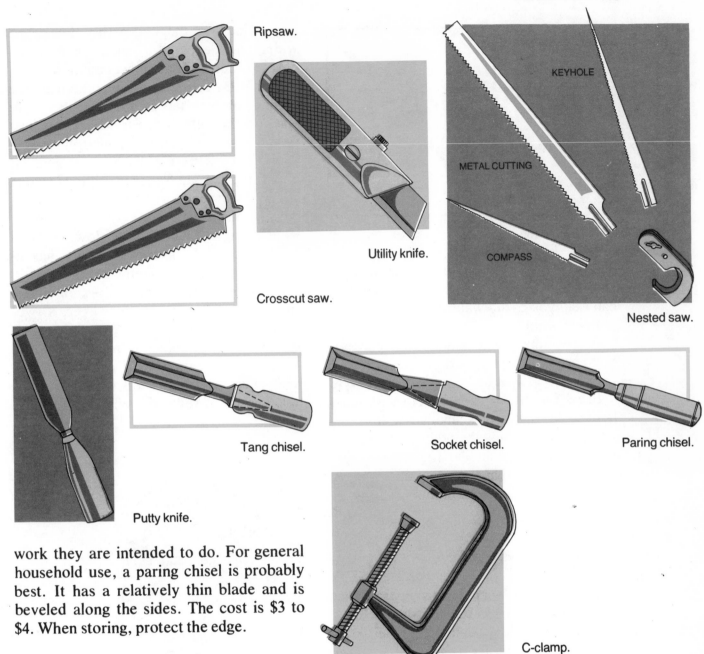

Ripsaw.

Crosscut saw.

Utility knife.

KEYHOLE

METAL CUTTING

COMPASS

Nested saw.

Putty knife.

Tang chisel.

Socket chisel.

Paring chisel.

C-clamp.

work they are intended to do. For general household use, a paring chisel is probably best. It has a relatively thin blade and is beveled along the sides. The cost is $3 to $4. When storing, protect the edge.

C-CLAMP

Named for the shape of its frame, the C-clamp holds work in place or presses two pieces together for gluing. It is handy when you use adhesive to repair furniture or objects made of metal or plastic.

A 6-inch, light-duty type with an extra-deep opening can accommodate fairly large items but adjusts by means of a screw for smaller work. A sliding handle turns the screw to tighten the clamp, and a swivel button prevents the screw end from marring the work surface. For many jobs you will need a pair. They cost $6 or $7.

FORCE CUP

Aptly called "the plumber's helper," a force cup is the well-known tool of first defense against clogged sink or bathtub drains

Bell-shaped force cup.

Ball-shaped force cup.

and overflowing toilets. By providing pressure and suction into stopped-up pipes, it can help you avoid water damage or costly plumber's bills.

Force cups are available with either a bell- or ball-shaped flexible cup screwed onto a wood handle. A ball-shaped style with a 2-foot handle is satisfactory for most households and costs about $3. It has a smaller end opening than the more conventional bell-shaped model for easier insertion in toilet discharge pipes, but it can also be conveniently used on drains.

ELECTRIC DRILL

An electric drill can do so many jobs that it is almost a must in the do-it-yourselfer's toolbox. With it you can make holes in almost any material. By using its accessories and attachments you can sand, polish, grind, buff, stir paint, and drive screws.

Depending on quality, size, gearing, and special features, a drill for home use costs from $5 to $50 or more. Your best choice is a model with the work capacity and special features you regularly use. The work capacity of a drill depends on its chuck size and rated revolutions per minute (RPM).

The chuck size is the diameter of the largest bit shank that the drill chuck can hold. Home-use sizes are ¼, ⅜, and ½

inch. Usually, the larger the chuck, the wider and deeper the holes the drill can bore; ¼-inch drills are most common.

The RPM rating is an indication of the number of gear sets in a model, its speed, and the type of work for which it is best suited. For example, a ¼-inch drill rated at about 2,000 RPM usually has one gear set and is appropriate for rapid drilling in wood and use with sanding and polishing accessories. A model with more gears has a lower RPM rating and works more slowly but can make bigger holes in hard metals or masonry without stalling or overheating.

For most jobs around a home, a single-speed drill is adequate. However, a two-speed or variable-speed model is more suitable if you intend to drill material that requires a slow speed or if you want to use many accessories. A drill with both variable speed and reverse is effective for driving and removing screws.

The trigger switch, which starts the drill,

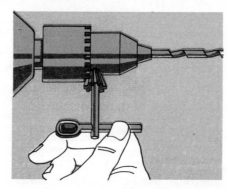

Electric drill.

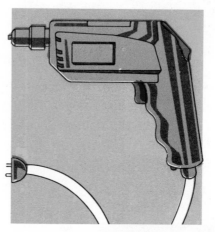

Gear-type drill chuck.

The Basic Toolbox

is on the pistol-grip handle, and many models include a switch lock for continuous operation. You activate the lock by pressing a button; the lock instantly releases if you tighten your squeeze on the trigger switch.

Variable-speed drills have trigger switches that allow you to vary bit speed from almost nothing up to maximum RPM by trigger-finger pressure. Some have controls that allow you to preset the maximum RPM for each operation.

Drills with reverse have separate reverse controls in different positions, depending on the brand. To protect the motor, allow the drill to come to a full stop before reversing direction.

The front of the drill, where bits and other accessories are inserted and removed, is called the chuck. The three-jaw gear type is the most common. Its collar is first hand-closed on the shank of a bit. Then a key is inserted into the chuck body and turned to tighten the three jaws simultaneously and with considerable force. Some models have a holder to make key loss less likely.

Some "bargain" drills have chucks that are hand-tightened by means of knurled collars. They may either offer a poor hold on bits and accessories during work or be difficult to loosen when work is finished.

Examine chuck placement as well as quality. The higher the chuck on the front of the housing, the easier the drill will be to use in corners.

DRILL ACCESSORIES

The manufacturer's catalog will contain information on the accessories available for particular drill brands and models. The common accessories that enable you to use an electric drill for many different jobs are described here.

A drill bit has a working end that makes holes and a smooth shank that is grasped by the jaws of a chuck. Although bits can be bought individually, they cost less if purchased in sets.

The twist bit, the most commonly used, cuts cylindrical holes. It has a sharp point and two spiral-shaped cutting edges that lift chips out of the hole as the bit turns. Carbon steel twist bits are suited to drilling wood and soft metals; high-speed steel bits cut wood, soft metals, and mild steel; tungsten carbide or carbide-tipped bits cut hard metals and masonry. Cutting diameters commonly range from 1/16 to ½ inch.

The spade bit cuts large cylindrical holes in wood. It has a flat, spade-shaped driving end with a pointed tip. Common cutting diameters range from ⅜ inch to 1 inch.

The wood-screw pilot bit has three widths of cutting edge. The narrowest drills a hole to give screw threads solid anchorage. The next makes a shaft for the unthreaded screw shank. The widest makes a hole, or countersink, for flat-headed

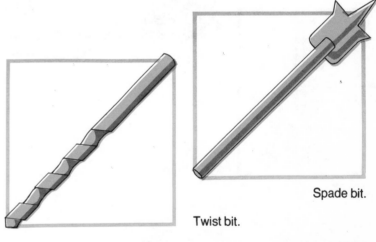

Twist bit.

Spade bit.

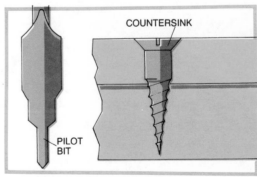

COUNTERSINK

PILOT BIT

Pilot bit.

Screw-driving bit.

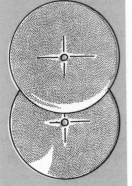

Sanding disc.

Grinding wheel.

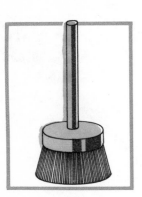

Wire brush disc.

Hole saw.

screws. A detachable stop can make shallow or deep countersinks.

The screw-driving bit attaches to drills with variable speed and reverse to drive and remove slotted and Phillips-head screws. On single- or two-speed drills, the bit must be used with a screw-driving attachment.

Polishing and sanding discs, grinding wheels, wire-brush discs, and hole saws are usually secured to a drill by an arbor that goes through the center hole of the wheel or disc and is fastened by a washer and nut or by a screw and washer. A flange keeps the wheel from slipping down the shank that fits into the drill chuck.

Discs are used with either abrasive paper for sanding or a soft bonnet for polishing. Grinding wheels are for sharpening tools or smoothing metal. Wire brushes remove paint, rust, and dirt from wood and metal. Hole saws cut round holes through boards or sheet materials by means of a rim saw blade and a centered pilot bit. Common diameters range from ½ inch to 4 inches.

The Basic Toolbox

Floors and Stairs

QUEAKS EMANATING from floors and stairs are a grudgingly accepted annoyance in most households. Few people, however, realize that, aside from their exacerbating effects on nerves, squeaks can signal the impending doom of a structure—or at least a greater problem than mere annoyance. Floor and stair squeaks are often symptoms of far more serious examples of house frame deterioration.

Squeaks caused by a sagging floor may indicate a weakness in the floor's understructure. Age, the settling of the foundation, the shifting or addition of heavy loads, and perhaps even poorly planned renovation of rooms can all create stresses to the beams and joists that support the flooring. Caught in time, many of these problems can be handled by the homeowner before they demand a thorough overhaul that would require professional help.

Often an old floor can be corrected and made like new with only some simple labor on your part. Resilient floor coverings such as linoleum, vinyl, or tile can be installed, or the existing surface material can be repaired, at relatively little cost. Concrete flooring may betray the effects of poor workmanship or corrosion—you should be familiar with the signs and know how to go about repairing the damage or stopping it in its tracks.

WOOD FLOORS

Why live with a floor that complains all the time? Elimination of squeaks and creaks can be managed with relatively little effort, the means depending on the floor's construction and whether the subflooring is accessible from below.

Most wood floors consist of two layers: a subfloor of boards or plywood and the finished floor of narrower boards—usually hardwood—tongued and grooved together and nailed into place. The subflooring is supported from underneath by wood joists normally spaced on 16-inch centers. A squeak is usually the result of a board or

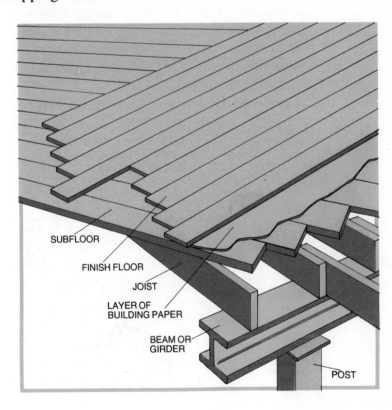

SUBFLOOR
FINISH FLOOR
JOIST
LAYER OF BUILDING PAPER
BEAM OR GIRDER
POST

Wood floor construction.

boards having separated from what is beneath. The finish floor may have pulled away from the subfloor, or the subfloor may have warped or sagged and pulled away from the joists.

It is best to make your inspection and repairs from under the floor, if this is not concealed by a ceiling or other barrier. Have someone walk around overhead so that you can pinpoint the problem. Inspect the area around the squeak. Make sure joists are level, and check between joists and subflooring for signs of warping or lifting of the floorboards.

If a squeak is detected directly over a joist, an effective method of quieting it is to drive thin wood shims between the joist and subflooring. Pieces of shingle are ideal for this. Hammer them into place over one or more joists, as necessary. Larger wedges of wood can be used if needed.

▲ When the squeak originates between joists, first install a header of 2 x 4 or 2 x 6 lumber to act as a base for the shimming. Cut the header so that it fits snugly between two joists. Tap it up firmly against the subfloor, narrow edge up, and toenail it securely in place. Now work in shims as needed between header and subfloor. This should eliminate the noise.

Another approach is to drive a screw up

Drill pilot hole through subfloor.

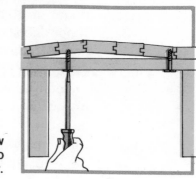

Drive screw up into finish floor.

through the subfloor and into the finish floor where the squeak is found. Use a wood screw about 1 inch long for this operation—enough to penetrate the subfloor but not the finish floor—and have someone stand on the floor overhead. It is best to drill a pilot hole to help start the screw and to avoid splitting the hardwood floor. Again, be careful not to penetrate the finish floor. Maintain the weight overhead as you drive the screw so that subfloor and finish floor will be brought together.

These methods cannot be used if the understructure is inaccessible. In that case, you will have to make the repairs from topside. You can often silence a squeak by working some talcum powder or powdered stainless lubricant into the cracks between floorboards, but this is only a temporary treatment. The best way is to nail the noisy board.

▲ Use long finishing nails for this job. Drive them in pairs, as required, along or across the board. The nails should be driven at an angle, each pair forming a V, with the points meeting under the subfloor. Drill

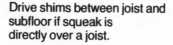

Drive shims between joist and subfloor if squeak is directly over a joist.

Install header if squeak originates between joists.

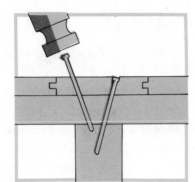

Drive in
finishing nails.

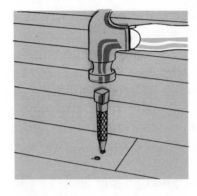

Set, fill holes
with putty.

pilot holes to avoid splitting the hardwood. Use a nailset to recess nailheads. The holes can be filled with putty or plugged with wax patching crayon. If you are doing this kind of work on a floor that is covered with linoleum or tile, about the only thing you can do is nail right through the floor covering. A lot of guesswork is involved here because the boards are unseen, so prod around with your foot to try to pinpoint the squeak as closely as possible. This will avoid having to drive too many nails. The holes in the covering can be plugged with wax crayon.

CRACKED AND SPLIT FLOORING

Floorboards become damaged for a variety of reasons, the most common of which are shrinkage and expansion because of exposure to water. When wet, the boards expand against their joints. As they dry, they return to their former size, causing cracks to appear either between the joints or along the grain of the board. New floors laid with green or wet wood also produce cracks.

You should make it a rule never to wash a wood floor with water. Rather, treat the wood with an application of any of the floor sealers available, then give it a good waxing for an easy-to-maintain protective finish. If you use a polyurethane finish on the floor, waxing is not recommended. This durable finish is maintained by simply wiping it clean with a cloth or mop.

Cracks can be filled with a variety of compounds. You can use a mixture of glue and sawdust, a wood-fiber putty, or plastic wood. The compound is pressed into the crack and then sanded and stained to the proper color. You can also fashion small wedges of hardwood to fill the crack, hammering them in tightly, then planing the excess and sanding smooth.

Splits along the grain of a board should be filled with a mixture of glue and sawdust to prevent the board from splitting further.

A warped board can sometimes be

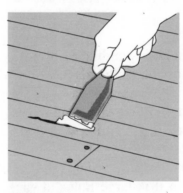

Fill cracks.

Drive wedges into cracks.

Planing a warped floorboard.

Nailing warped board flat.

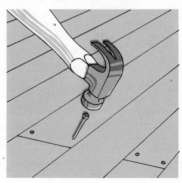

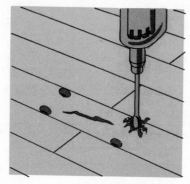

1. Drill holes in corners of damaged board.

2. Chisel out damaged section across and along its grain.

3. Remove damaged section of board.

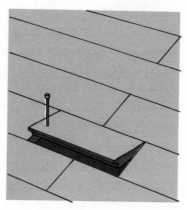

4. Nail new piece in place and countersink the nails.

SAGGING FLOORS

When a floor sags at any point or feels bouncy when you walk over it, part of the understructure is probably weak. This presents a potentially dangerous condition that should be corrected without delay. Because the condition usually is found on the lower floors of the house, thereby providing you with ready access to the understructure, you can often make the necessary repairs and adjustments yourself.

The cause of the sagging may be that the joists are spaced too far apart to provide rigid support for weakened subflooring. One or more joists may have warped or sagged. The beam that supports the joists may not be making contact all the way across.

▲Use a long straightedge and level as you inspect the subflooring, joists, and supporting beams. If a joist has warped or sagged but is otherwise sound, you can raise the floor by driving hardwood wedges between the joist and subflooring. Additional support is gained by toenailing a sturdy crosspiece between the joists under the floor.

Check to see that all joists are resting on the main beam. It often happens that a beam sags at the center—particularly if it is made of wood. Support posts may be spaced too far apart, or they may have buckled or rotted or sunk into the concrete floor. Or they may be absent altogether, in which case you will have to add one or more new posts.

■Adjustable metal posts that have a screw-type jack at the end can be used to raise the beam into position. These can be left in place as permanent supports, if needed. The base of the jack must rest on a solid cement footing. If the cement floor is less than 4 inches thick or shows signs of deterioration, you must put in a new footing.

■Because of potential damage to the frame and walls of the house, you must never at-

evened off with a good sanding or by planing. First make sure all nailheads have been recessed. If the board is a wide one, you can also try to flatten it by soaking it with water, then nailing it flat. Otherwise it will have to be replaced wth a new board.

▲To remove a badly worn or damaged section of board, first drill large holes at each end of the damaged section, The holes should not extend through the subfloor below. Drill close to the edges of the board, then carefully chisel out the damaged section across and along its grain, taking care not to harm the tongue and groove sides of the adjoining boards. Cut the replacement piece to size. Using a chisel, remove the bottom half of the groove on the replacement piece. You can now slip the new board into place, nail it down, countersink the nailheads, and plane it flush if necessary.

tempt to raise the beam more than a slight amount at a time. Put the jack post into position under the beam so that it just touches. Make sure the jack is perfectly vertical, then give the screw a half turn and stop. Wait several days to a week, then give it another half turn. Do not be in a hurry—chances are it took quite a while for the beam to sag that much, so it can wait to be straightened out. Continue a little at a time until the floor overhead is level, then either insert a chock between the existing post and the beam or leave the jack post in position permanently.

You can check the level of the floor with a long straightedge as you go along. Or you can tack a string from wall to wall across the floor above the sag. If the string is kept taut, you will be able to observe the distance between it and the floor as this distance gradually diminishes.

CONCRETE FLOORS

Smooth-finish concrete flooring is durable and normally requires little maintenance. Trouble can sometimes arise, however, generally as the result of poor workmanship. Because of its porosity, new concrete should be treated with an application of penetrating varnish or paint sealer. A paste-wax coating can be added for further protection.

Concrete sealer paints can also be applied to correct pitted and dusty concrete, two common problems. These paints come in clear form and in colors with silicone, epoxy-resin, or latex bases, the last a good choice for rooms that experience occasional dampness. It is usually necessary to apply more than one coat of paint—the first to seal and the following to fill.

■ Keep an eye out for damp spots on slab floors that have heating or water pipes imbedded in the concrete; this may indicate

Use wedge to raise subfloor.

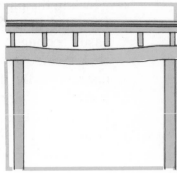
Sagging beam.

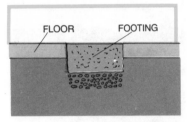
Footing for post.

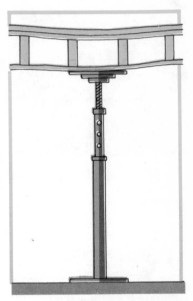
Place jack post in position.

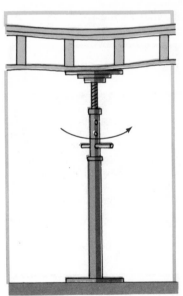
Give jack a half-turn at a time.

Check floor level with long straightedge.

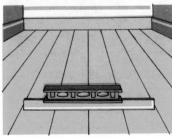

Check floor level with string tacked from wall to wall.

a leak in the pipe and the need to call in professional help. Simple cracks can be filled easily enough with patching compound, then treated as described previously. If a floor is badly damaged, however, a reinforced topping of concrete is needed. This is a job for the professionals. An unsightly floor that is still sound can be prepared to receive a covering of tile or linoleum.

1. Loosening tile with electric iron or with torch.

2. Prying up the tile.   3. Cut around tile edges.

4. Chisel tile.   5. Scrape old cement.

TILE AND SHEET FLOORING

Resilient floor coverings laid over wood and concrete are cemented in place with an adhesive such as mastic. Kept waxed and clean, they wear well, but after a time it will become necessary to replace one or more damaged tiles or deal with worn or broken sheet flooring. A seam may also come unstuck, in which case a recementing job is needed.

Finding a replacement floor tile that matches the rest is not always easy. Manufacturers of tile recommend that extra pieces be purchased with the original floor, not only to allow for wastage during installation, but to provide for just this contingency. If you are really stuck with a floor pattern, style, or color that is not available, a possible solution would be to remove several good tiles and install new ones that will create a limited pattern or decorative path encompassing the damaged area. Of course, you should first check with your dealer to see whether the tile might be available through the manufacturer. Take along a sample.

Tiles are laid butted tightly against each other, and removal of one, if not carefully done, can cause damage to others. To make the job easier, the cement and the tile can first be softened by heat. The professionals have special "hot plates" for this purpose, but you can do the job almost as effectively with a household electric iron. Set it to its hottest and put a damp cloth between it and the tile. A propane torch played over the center of the tile is a faster method, but the flame should not come in direct contact with the tile.

While the tile is still hot, work the tip of a putty knife under a raised corner or seam and carefully pry it loose. If it does not come easily—or if you are unable to use heat because of the tile's composition—you may have to cut out the tile in pieces with a

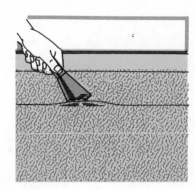

Install
new tile.

Apply adhesive
under seam.

Slit "bubble."

Work adhesive
under lifted area.

hammer and chisel, taking care not to gouge the subfloor. Begin this operation by first cutting into the seam around the tile with a sharp knife. As you remove the tile with the chisel, work from the center out to the edges; this minimizes the possibility of damage to surrounding tiles.

Sometimes, if the damaged tile is removed in one piece by the heating method, the cement is tacky enough so that you can simply press a new tile in place. Otherwise, the old cement should be scraped off to provide a smooth base, then new cement put down. Apply it evenly and sparingly to avoid its squeezing up around the edges of the tile.

On linoleum and sheet vinyl, a seam may lift because the cement was not applied properly or has been weakened by water. This can be corrected by applying fresh cement to the area beneath the flooring material and placing a heavy object on top until it dries. Work the cement in with a flexible blade, taking care not to tear the material. Wipe off the excess and allow plenty of time for drying. If there is a bubble or raised spot remote from a seam, slit the raised portion along its length with a razor or sharp knife and work the cement under the lifted areas.

You can renew worn or grubby-looking linoleum, if it is otherwise intact, by giving it a few coats of floor enamel in a color of your choice. First prepare the floor by removing all traces of wax or grease; steel wool and alcohol will help here. When it is clean and dry, apply a first coat of paint. When that is dry, give it a finish coat. You can add more colors to provide a stipple effect or to create a pattern laid out with masking tape. The floor should then be waxed to protect the enamel.

Broken linoleum can be repaired with a patch of new material. Tape the new linoleum over the damaged surface and cut through both new and old linoleum with a sharp knife. A straightedge will help guide the cut. The material is more flexible and lies flat better if it is warm. Remove the old piece and check the fit of the cut patch. Trim the surrounding linoleum so that there is a 1/16-inch gap all around—this will fill in

1. Lay new linoleum patch over damaged area; cut both at once.

2. Trim around cut area.

3. Press patch in place.

4. Tap seams flush.

over any wood or concrete floor (above grade) that is in good condition. Several types are also suitable for below-grade installation. In tile you have a choice of vinyl, cork, linoleum, rubber, vinyl asbestos, or asphalt, the last two being preferred for concrete that comes in direct contact with the ground.

Before tile can be put down, any irregularities in the floor must be corrected. Make sure nailheads do not protrude. Sand or plane smooth any raised surfaces and eliminate any existing squeaks. If it is a concrete floor, fill any cracks or gouges.

Keep in mind that resilient tiles of any composition will conform to the shape of the surface they cover. If the floor is uneven, broken, badly scarred, or pitted, you will have to lay in a hard, flat foundation for the tiles. This layer can be of hardboard or plywood, and it is fastened directly to the existing flooring. If a concrete floor is subject to persistent dampness, condensation, or leakage, correct this before proceeding any further, either by laying a waterproof barrier or pouring a new topping.

Tile can be applied successfully by the do-it-yourselfer, but the directions supplied by the manufacturer must be followed to the letter. Otherwise the results can be disappointing. Your dealer can advise you as to the number of tiles you will need to cover a given area and also give specific recommendations for the make or type of tile. When laying sheet flooring, first make a pattern of taped-together newspaper or

later when the new piece swells naturally. Apply cement and press the patch in place. The seams can be tapped flush with a mallet or a hammer and a block of wood.

Sheet flooring and tile can be applied

Fill, smooth cracks in concrete floor.

Make a pattern for sheet flooring (at right).

Trace onto sheet material (far right).

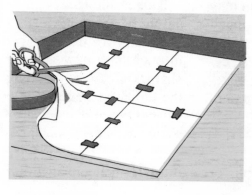

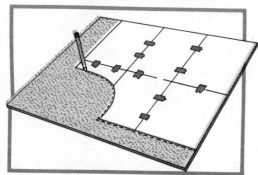

heavy wrapping paper, using small pieces to fit around corners and obstructions. Use this to trace an outline for cutting on the sheet (remembering to turn the pattern over). It is a quick, simple step that can prevent a lot of irritation.

STAIR REPAIRS

Most stairs consist of three sections: tread, riser, and stringer. On some stairs the tread rests on the riser in a simple butt joint of glue and nails; in others a dado-and-rabbet joint or simple dado is used. The stringers or side pieces serve to support the treads.

● When squeaks occur, it is because the tread or riser has worked loose at some point. If the treads are attached by butt joints (you can check this by prying off a part of the molding under the nose of the tread), you can tighten the tread by renailing it to the top of the riser. Have someone stand on the tread during the operation. Drive finishing nails at angles through the top of the tread into the center of the riser top. The holes can be filled with wood putty. If the tread is made of hardwood, you can avoid splits and bent nails by first drilling pilot holes.

▲ On a dadoed or dado-and-rabbet setup, you can avoid nailing by removing the molding and working small glued wedges into the side of the tread slot. If the underside of the stairway is accessible, apply the wedges from behind. While under there, check for any loose wedges betweeen the tread and stringer. Tighten these or replace them, as necessary.

■ Replacement of a damaged or broken tread is a job that usually calls for the services of a carpenter. However, if the wall end of the tread butts against the stringer, rather than being recessed into it, the job is considerably easier and you may wish to tackle it yourself.

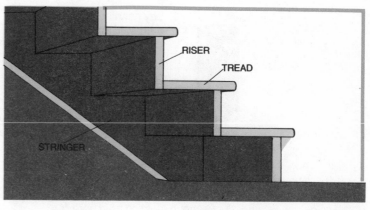

Stair construction: treads rest on a riser in simple butt joint.

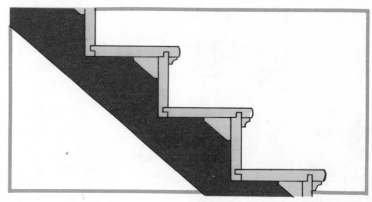

Stair construction: tread is rabbeted and dadoed.

Renail tread to riser to eliminate squeak (right).

Working wedges into rabbet, avoiding nailing (below).

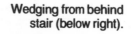

Wedging from behind stair (below right).

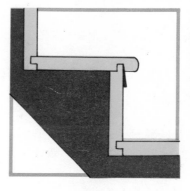

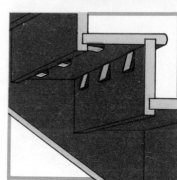

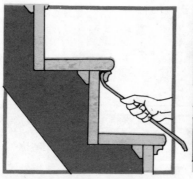

1. Remove molding from under the tread nosing.

2. Use hacksaw to loosen bottom of baluster.

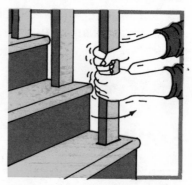

3. Twist loose top of baluster from the anchor.

4. Loosen tread from riser by prying under the nosing.

5. Use old tread as pattern for new step.

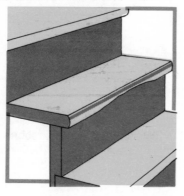

Flip tread over to other side if wear is the only problem.

First remove all molding from under the tread nosing. The feet of the balusters may be toenailed to the top of the tread or glued into slots. In such cases, use a hacksaw blade to sever the balusters as close to the tread as possible, exercising care to limit damage while cutting. The tops of the balusters are usually held in place with glue and can be separated from the anchor by twisting.

Hammer carefully under the nosing of the tread until there is a gap between the tread and riser. A pry bar may help here. Depending on the construction of the stair, you can continue prying until the tread can be worked loose by hand, or you can cut the nails that hold it with a hacksaw. The tread can now be used as a pattern for the new step. Or, if wear is the only problem, it may be possible to turn the tread over and use the other side. Fasten the tread with glue and nails; fill the nail holes with wood putty and sand smooth.

6

Walls and Ceilings

A T ONE POINT or another, every homeowner and apartment dweller is faced with the problem of correcting damage to ceilings and walls. The damage may have been caused by an external malignant force (such as little Junior perfecting his curve ball indoors, using the wall as a backstop), or it may have occurred because the house is settling (as all houses do).

Whatever the cause and wherever the blame may lie, damaged walls and ceilings detract from the beauty, as well as the value, of a home. Fortunately, most minor wall and ceiling maladies can be remedied by the layperson with a little time to spare. The tools and materials needed for these jobs are often on hand or are cheaply and easily available.

PLASTER REPAIRS

Plaster on ceilings and walls is generally applied over a lathing of wood, metal, or gypsumboard, the latter most common except in older homes. This lathing serves as a foundation for the plaster and is in turn fixed to the framework behind it.

Small cracks and holes in plaster can be filled with spackling compound, which is available in either dry or premixed form. First clear away all loose plaster and dust. Work the spackle tightly into the opening with a flexible putty knife. Trim the excess flush with the wall, wiping with the knife in alternate crisscross strokes. Give the compound plenty of time to dry, then sand the area smooth, using medium sandpaper.

GYPSUM WALLBOARD

Gypsum wallboard is a surfacing material commonly used for both walls and ceilings. Also known as plasterboard and Sheetrock (a trade name), it is made of compressed gypsum plaster between two sheets of heavy paper or cardboard. The sheets range in sizes up to 4 by 16 feet, though 4

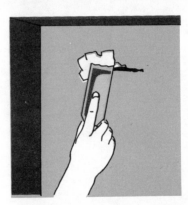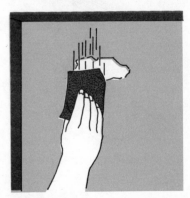

To repair small cracks in plaster, work spackle into cracks (left) and sand area smooth (right).

by 8 sheets are most favored by builders, and come in thicknesses of ⅜ and ½ inch.

Gypsum wallboard is usually nailed (or cemented and nailed) directly to the framing studs. The board is subject to dents, such as may be caused by the sharp corner of a piece of furniture. Depressions of this sort can be corrected with spackling compound or a special gypsum cement. Nail

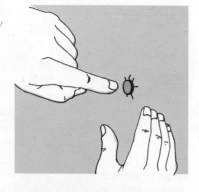

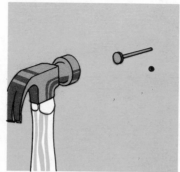

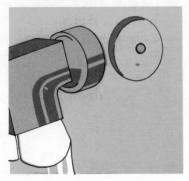

1. Popped nail (above left).

2. Drive in new nail (above right).

3. Drive nail below surface (left).

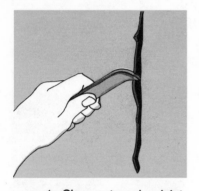

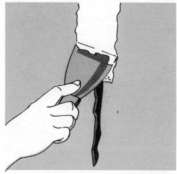

1. Clean out crack or joint.

2. Apply spackle.

3. Apply tape.

4. Apply more spackle.

5. Sand smooth after the spackle is dry.

holes can be filled in this fashion also. No preparation of the surface is necessary, and the compound can be smoothed with sandpaper when it is dry.

Settling of the house's foundation or the use of green wood for backing supports can result in a vertical warping of the wallboard. When this happens, the nails that hold the panel in place may "pop" loose. This can be corrected by removing the loosened nail and driving a single nail just above or below the old nail hole, at the same time pushing the board firmly to hold it in place. Use only a screw-type nail for the fastening, and hammer it carefully so that a shallow depression is formed around the nailhead. Patch and finish the repair with spackling compound.

The joints between panels are closed with gypsum cement and a special reinforcing tape. To close a seam that has broken open, first clean out the seam with a sharp-pointed tool (a pre-pop-top beer-can opener does a good job). Pull or scrape away remnants of the old tape, then sand the seam to prepare the surface. The area you have sanded should be slightly wider than the replacement tape.

Using a broad knife with a 4-inch blade, lay the cement smoothly and evenly into the seam and around it. Before the cement has had time to dry, apply the tape over the seam, centering it and removing all wrinkles and air bubbles with the blade of the knife. Now apply more cement over the tape. Work it on smoothly, and remove all excess. After it dries, sand it smooth. To

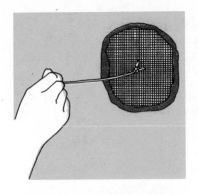

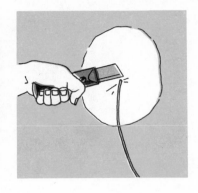

Tie string to mesh, insert in hole (far left).

Hold string, apply spackle (center).

Snip off string, finish (left).

provide a smoother finish, it may be necessary to apply another coat of cement and repeat the sanding.

Since a hole in wallboard is "bottomless" because of the absence of backing, you cannot simply work patching compound into it and expect it to hold. To repair a hole, cut a piece of wire mesh a bit larger than the hole. Tie a string near the center of the mesh and work the mesh through the hole until it covers the opening from behind. Maintain a grip on the string while applying spackle to within ⅛ inch of the surface. Give the compound a chance to set, snip off the excess string, and carefully finish off the surface.

If a large section of wallboard must be replaced, you must provide backing for the new section. Use a straightedge to draw parallel lines above and below the damaged area. With a keyhole saw, cut carefully along the lines until you encounter the studs on either side of the damage. Cut another inch of wallboard so that you are over the center line of the stud. Now cut straight down along this line on both studs. If the damaged area extends beyond the width of two studs, it is best to continue the horizontal cut to the next stud.

Measure the size of the opening and cut a new piece of board to fit. You do not have to use a saw; use a sharp knife to score the face of the board. Snap it over a straightedge or the edge of a table, then score the rear to break it off cleanly. The new section can be nailed directly to the studs, but first

you must provide horizontal backing because of the horizontal seams. Use sections of 2 x 4 or 2 x 3 lumber, sawing them to size

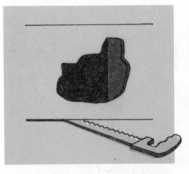

1. Cut damaged area horizontally.

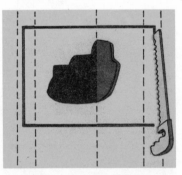

2. Cut along ends over studs.

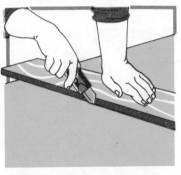

3. Score face of new board.

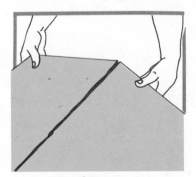

4. Snap the board.

5. Score back.

6. Provide horizontal backing.

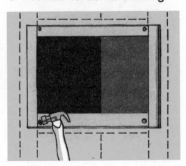

Walls and Ceilings

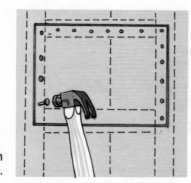

7. Nail new section in place.

so they can be toenailed to the studs. One support for the top and bottom of the replacement section will suffice. Nail the section into place and finish the seams as described above.

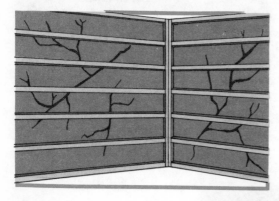

Apply furring over plaster wall.

Check furring for plumb (true vertical).

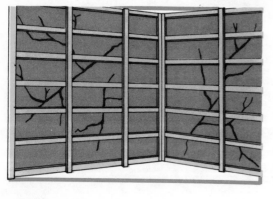

Frame for furring over uneven concrete wall.

WALL PANELING ▲

Unsightly wall surfaces can be refinished with paneling of your choice, such as wallboard, plywood, fiberboard, or hardboard, which come in various finishes and require no further covering. Or you may decide to panel a wall with wood. It all depends on the application and how much you wish to spend.

In all cases, though, you have to provide a base to support the new material. This is normally done with furring strips, lengths of 1 x 2 lumber that can be purchased at your local lumberyard.

To apply furring to a plaster wall, the strips must be placed horizontally and nailed to the wall studs. Spacing is usually 16 inches on center. Some types of paneling also require vertical furring strips where two panels meet; follow the manufacturer's recommendations in this regard. The baseboard along the bottom of the wall should be removed, as well as any molding and trim. Openings in the wall, such as windows and doors, should be surrounded by furring strips. A long straightedge board can be used to detect bulges or depressions between the wall and the furring strips. A depression can be corrected by placing wood shims behind a strip to bring it in line with the others. A bulge is handled by planing the surface of the strip. Make these checks accurately—any variances will show plainly when the paneling is in place.

On concrete walls, the furring can be nailed directly, using special masonry nails. If the surface of a masonry wall is extremely irregular along its face, you should first nail up a framework of 2 x 2 lumber, shimming where necessary to even it up. Apply the furring over this.

When working with large sheets of light, flexible paneling, it is best to nail from the center out to the sides. This will avoid any buckling problem. Adhesive may also be used—check the manufacturer's recommendations. When measuring how much paneling you need to cover the area, allow 10 percent extra for waste.

CERAMIC TILE

Ceramic tile is usually set in place with a white, waterproof tile calking used to fill the spaces around the tile. These same adhesive compounds can be used to make repairs on ceramic tile that has been cemented with portland cement, the old method of fastening.

As soon as a tile comes loose or cracks, it should be replaced. Use a chisel to cut around the damaged tile. Try not to damage the surrounding tiles. If the original fastening is cement, you will have to chisel away a part of the cement so that the replacement tile does not extend beyond the surface of the surrounding tiles.

Apply a generous bead of cement to the back of the new tile, then press it firmly into place. Wipe off all excess cement immediately. To hold the tile in place until the cement sets, support it with strips of masking tape. There should be an even space all around the tile. When the cement dries, remove the tape and fill the joints with white compound.

To cut ceramic tile to fit requires a glass cutter. Make a score along a guideline on the face of the tile, then place the tile over a nail and apply pressure on both sides to snap it clean. A file or emery cloth can be used to smooth the edge of the cut. For a curved cut, score the guideline, then make crisscross scores inside the area of the cut. Use a pliers to break out the scored section little by little.

When small, fine cracks appear in a ceramic tile the only cure is replacement. Shrinkage cracks around the wall of the tile can be filled with white plastic compound

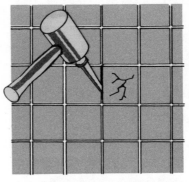
1. Chisel around damaged tile.

2. Chisel cement backing.

3. Apply cement to new tile.

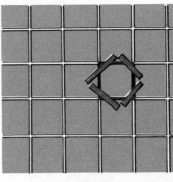
4. Support it while cement dries.

5. Fill joints with compound.

Score tile with glass cutter.

Snap over nail.

Making a curved cut.

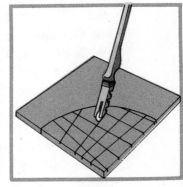

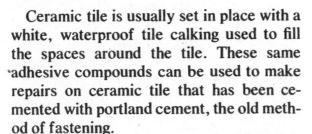

Walls and Ceilings

sold for that purpose. Correct such cracks as soon as they appear to prevent splash water or condensation from ruining the wall interior. Tile surfaces should never be cleaned with an abrasive agent. Warm water and a detergent are best (soap leaves a film on the tile).

CEILING TILE

Tiles are an excellent choice for many ceiling resurfacing jobs. Acoustical tile is especially popular, easy to work with, and can do much to brighten up a ceiling. It comes in a wide variety of patterns to suit just about any decor.

● Ceiling tile installation is begun at a room corner. However, since most rooms are slightly out of square or otherwise irregular, first find the center point of the ceiling by finding the midpoint on each of two opposite walls and stringing a line between these points; measure to the center of this line and describe a line at right angles to it. Measure from this center point to the walls to find the width of border tiles. In this way, if a tile must be cut to fit against the wall, it will be the same width at each side of the room, giving a balanced appearance.

● If an existing ceiling is level and in sound condition, ceiling tiles can be applied right over it with adhesive. Make sure the ceiling is clean and free of grease and water-soluble paint. Dab the back of each tile with adhesive in four or five spots and place it against the ceiling in approximate position, then slide it into place, spreading the adhesive. Slight depressions in the ceiling can be compensated for by applying a thicker coating of adhesive.

Where the existing ceiling is badly cracked or peeling, and in basements, attics, and other areas where the joists or rafters are exposed, the best method of installing ceiling tiles is by stapling them to furring strips. Place the first strip against the wall, nailing it securely to each joist.

The placement of the second strip depends upon the width you have determined for the border tiles. All other strips are placed on 12-inch centers (or whatever other width of tiles you may be using). Where pipes and cables are hung below the joists, a double layer of furring strips may be used to clear these obstructions. In this case, the first layer of strips may be spaced on about 24-inch centers (more or less, depending on where the obstructions fall). Pipes that are several inches below the joists should be boxed with furring strips. It is good insurance to make a sketch of your plumbing system, including the locations of valves, before enclosure so that a minimum number of tiles need be removed if you ever require access to the pipes.

The furring strips should be checked with a level and shimmed with wood wedges where necessary to provide an even, level backing for the tiles. Snap a chalk line across the furring strips as a guideline for border tiles. Measure and cut each border tile individually to assure an accurate fit. (When measuring, do not include tongues and flanges.) Cut the tiles face up with a sharp fiberboard knife. Fit the first tile in the corner, carefully aligning it with the two intersecting guidelines; staple it securely through the flanges. Install the border tiles adjacent to the corner tile, then install another border tile along each wall and begin filling in between the border tiles with full tiles, working across the ceiling. Make certain that each tile is butted tightly to and aligned properly with its neighbors before stapling. Wherever possible, light fixtures, vents, and other ceiling fittings should be positioned between furring strips so they fall in the center of a single tile, minimizing cutting and fitting. When you reach the borders on the opposite side of the room, the final tiles are face-nailed to the furring strips. A cove or crown molding at the joint between walls and ceiling conceals the nails.

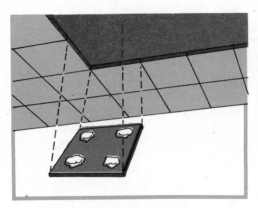

Using mastic to install ceiling tile.

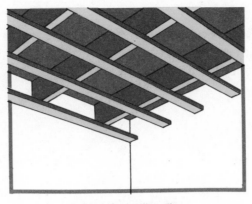

Furring for ceiling tile.

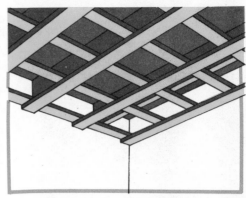

Double layer of strips to lower ceiling.

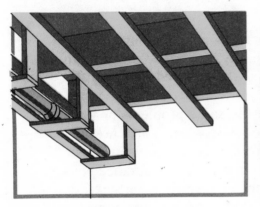

Box around obstructions.

Check furring for evenness.

Snap a chalk guideline.

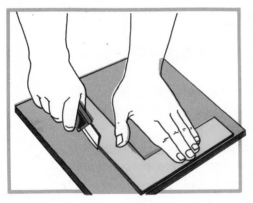

Cutting tile.

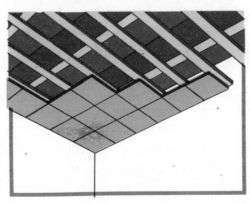

Installing tile ceiling.

Tile around ceiling fixture.

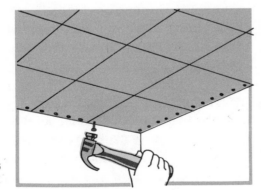

Nail final tiles to furring.

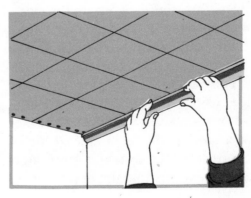

Molding to conceal nails.

Walls and Ceilings

7

Doors and Windows

STICKING DOORS result from a number of factors—improper installation, excessive or insufficient atmospheric humidity, or house settling, to name but a few. Troublesome doors can usually be repaired easily by the handyperson with the right tools.

Jammed windows are essentially caused by the same problems and are likewise easily repaired. Repairing broken windows, when done carefully and methodically, is usually an even easier chore. The cost of replacing your broken windows may even be covered by your homeowner's insurance policy. Check with your agent to make sure, but such coverage is fairly standard. If you don't have such a provision in your contract, you might consider investing in this kind of protection. The cost is nominal and often pays for itself when the first pane breaks.

STICKING DOORS

A door swells when it is damp, and then becomes difficult to open and close. Before you attempt to plane off the door rails (top and bottom) or stiles (sides), it is wise to remember that the wood will shrink as the air dries out. Think twice before planing if you suspect that this is only a seasonal problem.

The first thing to check is the condition of the hinges. Position yourself on the side of the door opposite the stops (so that it closes away from you). With the door closed, examine the spaces between the door and frame. You can run a sheet of paper around the edges to observe the hang of the door; where it binds, the door is too tight. If there is a space at the top, latch side of the rail and a corresponding space at the bottom, hinge side, it means that the upper hinge is

probably loose, and perhaps the lower one as well.

Open the door to expose the hinges. Relieve pressure on the top hinge by having someone lightly support the door by its handle, or by slipping a wedge of some sort under the bottom rail. Use a broad-bladed screwdriver to tighten all the screws. If a screw does not appear to have any purchase, the wood around the screw has deteriorated. This can be corrected.

Remove the door by knocking out first the lower, then the upper hinge pin. Use a screwdriver angled so that the head of the pin is driven up and out. Should the pin be "frozen" or stuck, remove the hinge at the jamb. Inspect the mortise and the condition of the wood. If the holes look pulpy or rotted, hammer in a small wooden plug coated with glue or stuff the spaces with toothpicks or wooden matches dipped in glue, or fill them with plastic wood. Trim, then replace the hinge and rescrew, using longer screws if possible.

The difficulty may be that the hinge plate is not recessed deeply enough in the mortise, in which case you will have to chisel the mortise deeper. Or it may be possible, if spacing at the latch stile permits, to build up the lower hinge and thus shift the door to the vertical. The shim can be any piece of cardboard of the correct thickness (a matchbook cover serves well) and it should fill the mortise completely.

When the door binds along the entire length of the latch stile, you will have to cut the mortises deeper, as required. If necessary, you can deepen the mortises on both the jamb and the door.

Shimming will help if the door tends to spring open when you try to close it. In this case, place a strip of cardboard only behind half the width of the hinge leaf. You do not have to remove the hinge for this operation. Loosen the screws so that when the door is partially closed, the hinge leaf comes away from the mortise. Slip the shim into this space and tighten the screws. Shimming at this point serves to change the angle of the door so it leans toward the outside stop.

▲ If the hinge stile is catching or binding along the stop, you can reposition the hinge leaf in its mortise to pull the door away a bit, thus curing the problem.

FITTING A DOOR ▲

Often a door binds at several points at once because it or the frame has been warped out of shape. (Cracks or stress marks on the plaster around the frame are signs that the frame is at fault.) In either case, adjusting the fit of the hinges will not do the job completely. You will have to plane or sand the door as well.

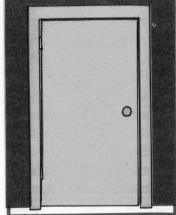

A gap between door and frame is an indication of loose hinges.

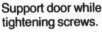

Support door while tightening screws.

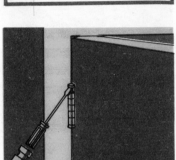

Knock out hinge pins.

Fill screw holes.

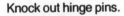

Deepen mortise.

Build up beneath lower hinge with a cardboard shim.

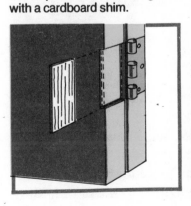

Insert shim behind half of hinge leaf.

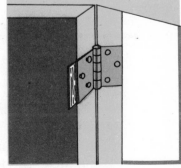

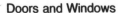

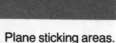

Plane sticking areas.

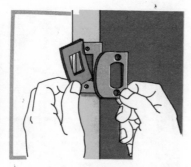

Shim behind striker plate.

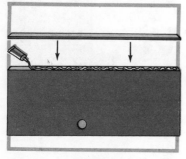

Build up door width.

Mortise for hinges.

Crayon on striker plate locates problem area.

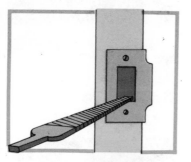

File striker plate receptacle.

Move plate, fill gaps.

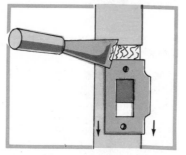
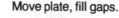

Your inspection will show where excess material has to be removed. Usually only a part of a side has to be touched up, rather than the entire length of a stile or rail. Mark

off the sticking areas while the door is closed, so that you will know how much has to be cut. Remove the door and prop it on its side against some solid support. Work the plane in smooth strokes, and do not bite too deeply at any one time. If the binding exists at the latch area of the door, it may prove simpler to plane the hinge side instead. Hinge leaves are easier to remove than the lock assembly.

When the door rubs at the top or bottom, you will have to plane one or both rails, either partially or fully. Keep in mind that you will be cutting across the grain, and if you work too roughly or use a dull tool it is easy to splinter the wood. If the amount to be removed is fractional, try a sanding block instead, but take care not to bevel the door edges.

A door sometimes becomes too narrow because of shrinkage, with the result that the latch is not able to reach the striker plate to engage it. If the distance is small, you can correct this by removing the striker plate and bringing it closer to the door with a wood or cardboard shim.

When the space to be filled is much wider, however, the best solution is to build up the width of the door by cementing and nailing a strip of wood along the hinge stile. The strip should be wide enough to close the gap and as thick as the stile. Measure to determine where the hinge leaves should be set, and chisel new mortises to receive them. The strip can be finished to match the finish on the door.

These adjustments to the door may create a problem: the door now swings freely but the latch is unable to engage the striker plate in the frame, with the result that the plate must be repositioned. To tell how much and in what direction, rub some crayon over the face of the striker plate and close the door. The resultant mark on the plate will indicate what has to be done.

If the latch is centered but falls short of

the receptacle in the plate, you might try filing the metal to bring the hole closer. Trim wood from the mortise, if required. If the entire plate has to be moved, fill the original screw holes with plugs before attempting to screw the plate in a new position. Gaps between the plate and the mortise can be filled with wood putty and touched up with paint. These same instructions apply when the plate must be moved up or down to meet the latch.

WINDOW PROBLEMS

When a wood window sash sticks or binds, it is usually because paint has worked into the sash molding or because the sash or frame has become swollen. Paint-stuck windows can sometimes be freed by tapping along both sides of the sash with a hammer and block of wood. If this does not free the window, insert the blade of a paint scraper or a broad, thin chisel between the sash and the stop molding. Tap the blade in with a hammer, then rock the tool back and forth gently to force the sash back from the molding. Repeat this at several points at each side of the sash until it can move freely. Never use a screwdriver for this job, as it will only gouge the wood.

If the sticking is severe, or if a seal forms at the bottom edge of the sash after a new paint job, the window can be pried loose from the outside without damage to the finish. A hatchet is a good tool for this, or any broad, hard metal wedge. Hammer the tool along the bottom of the sash, and pry as you go along. Once the window is free, scrape off any crusts of paint at the back face of the stop molding. Sand the molding lightly and touch up the window track.

If paint sticking is not the problem, it may be that the window has swollen permanently out of shape. Try the following

Tap gently along window to free it.

Insert chisel between sash and stop.

Pry from outside.

Scrape off paint, sand smooth.

method first: Cut a block of wood that will fit snugly into the channel between the inside and outside window stops above or below the sash. Give the block several smart raps with a hammer at both sides of the window. This should free the sash so that it can be raised (or lowered) at least partially. Repeat the procedure at the exposed channels at the bottom or top. A lubricant such as paraffin or candle wax may then be applied to the channels.

If this method fails, the sash will have to

Tap block in channel.

Repeat below raised window.

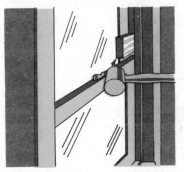

1. Remove window from tension strips.

2. Remove stop molding on windows with sash cords.

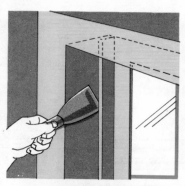

3. Disengage sash cord at both sides.

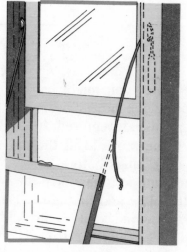

4. Keep sash from slipping past pulley.

5. Lubricate pulley.

6. Adjust tension strips.

be removed from the frame to make the necessary adjustments. (In order to remove the top sash the bottom one must be taken out first.) Most modern windows are equipped with metal tension strips fastened to the channels. With this kind it may be possible to remove the sash simply by pressing it sideways into a channel and lifting it free.

On windows that have sash cords the stop molding must be removed first. Insert a broad chisel behind the molding and twist so that the strip comes away only partially at any one point. Work carefully to avoid damaging or breaking the molding. With the strip removed, disengage the sash cord at both sides. Fasten a nail or strip of wood to the ends of the cords so that they will not slip past the pulley. Lower the weight gently and observe the action of the pulley. If it is stiff, apply a few drops of oil to the pins.

If the window has tension strips, try ad-

justing these first by turning their mounting screws. If this does not work, or if no mechanical adjustment is possible, wood can be sanded or planed from the sides of the sash to make it fit. Do not remove too much material at any one time. It is a good idea first to clean and lubricate the channels and then check the sash fit as you plane or sand. It should fit snugly without binding.

When a wood window rattles, it is because there is too much space between the sash and its stop molding. An easy way to alleviate this problem is to run a strip of metal or felt weatherstripping into the space. To make a permanent repair, remove the molding and nail it back closer to the sash.

Aluminum casement and sliding windows bind when dirt collects in the tracks. Sometimes the metal becomes pitted, impeding the window's smooth operation. Usually

Insert weatherstripping.

Renail molding.

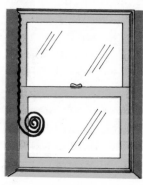

this can be corrected with a cleanup and rubbing with fine steel wool. The tracks should then be lubricated periodically with paraffin or wax. Never try to pry the window with a sharp tool, as this will distort the tracks.

When steel casement windows stick or bind, check to see that the hinges are free of rust or accumulated paint. Look for loose hinge screws or binding in the crank mechanism. Steel wool and lubricating oil will take care of the hinges. It may be necessary to open the handle assembly for cleaning and oiling.

INSTALLING GLASS

Replacing cracked or broken window glass is not difficult, but it requires some care. You will need a sharp glass cutter, prepared putty or glazing compound (more flexible than putty), and a putty knife.

Installation of the glass is normally done from the outside, so if you are repairing a second-floor window it is best to remove the sash, if that is possible. Wear heavy work gloves when removing the broken pieces of glass from the frame. Heat from a soldering gun will help soften the old putty, or a small wood chisel can be used to clean it out, but take care not to damage the frame. Extract the metal glazier's points with pliers.

The replacement glass should be cut 1/16 inch smaller all around than the frame opening. This is to allow for any irregularities that may exist in the frame.

Mark the glass with a sharpened crayon, then turn it over and lay it on a flat surface covered with a thickness of newspaper or an old blanket. A steel straightedge should be used to guide the cut. Any doubts about the glass cutter can be satisfied by first scoring a piece of the old glass; if the score mark shows signs of skipping, the cutting wheel is dull or chipped.

Remove old glass (above).

Remove old putty (above right).

Remove glazier's points (right).

Score glass (above).

Break off glass (above right).

Use slotted head of cutter for narrow pieces (right).

Make sure the glass is free of dust or grit before attempting the cut. The score mark should be begun just inside the edge of the glass farthest from you, then followed through with smooth, even pressure on the cutter. When the glass is scored, lay it over

Doors and Windows

Paint groove with linseed oil.

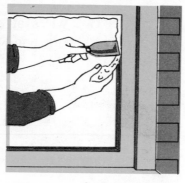
Apply bed of putty.

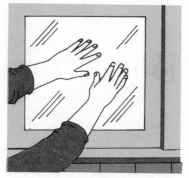
Press glass in place.

Insert glazier's points.

Smooth with putty knife.

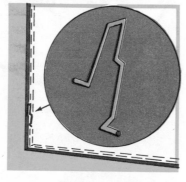
Glazing metal windows.

the straightedge and apply pressure on both sides of the score to break it cleanly. If the piece to be removed is very narrow, snap it off with the slotted head of the cutting tool.

Before the glass is installed in the frame, the groove should be painted with linseed oil in order to prevent subsequent drying out and cracking of the putty. Apply a ⅛-inch thickness of putty all around the frame. Press the glass into place, making sure it lies flat against the shoulders of the frame. Secure it with the glazier's points, pressing them in 4 to 6 inches apart on all sides.

Now roll some more putty into a "rope" about ½ inch thick. Use your fingers to press it against the wood and glass around the frame. Smooth and bevel the compound with the blade of the putty knife, making sure that you leave no breaks or separations in the seal. A coat of paint neatly finishes the job.

For metal windows the procedure varies slightly. On these the glass panes are usually secured to the frames with small metal clips buried in the compound. These have to be removed and set aside.

Lay a bead of glazing compound into the metal frame and adjust the replacement glass so that the compound meets the glass at all sides. Install the clips, then apply the final bead of compound. If there are metal strips, screw them back in place.

In numerous instances people have seriously injured themselves by walking into or putting their hands through large windows or doors. Safety and consumer agencies have been urging legislation requiring the use of less hazardous materials in such vulnerable places as sliding patio doors, storm doors, shower doors, tub enclosures, and other areas where standard glass might constitute a hazard.

Laws incorporating these recommendations have already been passed by several states. These require that "safety glazing material" be used in potentially dangerous areas such as those mentioned above. Some of the safety materials are tempered glass, laminated glass, wire glass, and acrylic plastic.

These materials may be slightly more difficult to install than regular glass, and their cost is generally higher. By installing these materials in place of standard glass panes, however, the extra cost is offset by the sense of security in knowing one's house is safe. One thing to watch out for with the rigid plastic materials such as acrylics, though, is surface mars. Whereas their lesser hardness makes them less susceptible to breakage than glass, it also increases their chances of being nicked or scratched.

SCREEN REPAIR

Keep your window and door screens in good condition by stacking them flat in a dry, well-ventilated area until ready for use. Wood frames should be tightened when necessary and given a fresh coat of paint from time to time to help preserve them.

A small hole in screening has a mysterious way of increasing in size if not patched as soon as it is discovered. If the hole is small enough, a drop or two of waterproof cement will do the job. The cement hardens into a film that covers the hole.

When dealing with larger tears, cut a patch of wire screen material that is wider than the hole by ½-inch. If you do not have extra screening around, patches in various sizes are available at any hardware store.

Unravel two wires at each side of the patch, then bend the end wires at a right angle on all four sides. Place the patch over the hole and thread the bent wires so that they pass evenly to the other side of the screen. They can now be bent back to fix the patch permanently and firmly.

An old or damaged wood screen frame can be renewed easily enough so that you do not have to go to the expense of purchasing a new one. When trouble occurs, it is usually at the frame joints.

A joint can be tightened by bracing the frame pieces with a ⅜-inch dowel. Drill a hole through the side member into the top or bottom piece. Coat the dowel with glue and hammer it into the hole, trimming or driving it flush, as the case may be.

A sagging screen door can be corrected with the use of a turnbuckle and cable, placed from one side of the door to the other. Fasten one end of the cable to the top side rail over the hinge; the other end should be screwed to the bottom of the other side rail. Tighten the turnbuckle until the door can swing freely.

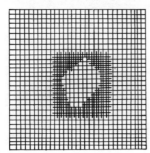

Patch a small hole in the screen with cement (left).

Place a patch over the hole if it is bigger (below left).

Fold ends under to seal permanently (below).

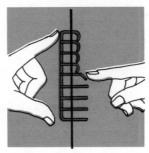

Doweling a corner joint (above).

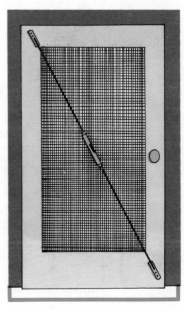

Repair for a sagging screen door using a turnbuckle and cable (right).

Doors and Windows

To replace screen wire in a wood frame, you must first remove the molding. Use a paint scraper or putty knife for this job, prying gently along the length of the molding until it comes free. Remove all staples or tacks from the frame. Cut the new screen 1 inch wider on all sides with old scissors or metal snips.

Tension must be applied to the screen when it is tacked to the frame, in order to prevent any stretching later. The best way to do this is to lay the frame across a work surface as wide as the frame (two boards across a pair of sawhorses make a good work surface). Place a board under each end of the frame, then C-clamp the sides of the frame to the work surface so that there is a slight bow formed in the middle.

Tack the new screening tautly at each end, doubling the material where you tack. Now release the C-clamps and tack the screen along the sides of the frame. Replace the molding and trim any wire that sticks out from under it.

In metal frames, a spline holds the screening in place. This must be pried out to remove the torn screening. New screening is then laid over the framing and trimmed to size, with the corners cut at 45-degree angles. The spline is then tapped back into its groove in the frame to secure the screening.

Remove screen molding.

Remove staples, tacks.

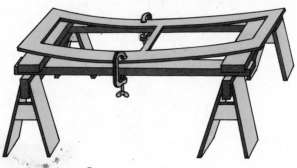
Set up screen for repair.

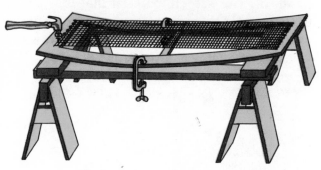
Tack new screening at each end.

Pry out spline of metal frame.

Trim screening.

Tap spline into groove.

Doors and Windows

8

Weatherproofing and Insulating

Y OUR HOUSE should be adequately ventilated even in winter, but this does not mean that unregulated drafts of cold air should be allowed to sweep through the house. In cold weather, warm air escapes around loose windows and doors and is replaced by cold outdoor air. Outdoor windiness tends to increase heat loss considerably. The result is that the output of the heating plant has to be increased to maintain the desired house temperature, and on cold windy days, if such leaks are extreme, it may be difficult to keep the house warm. In hot weather, it is just as important to keep out the heat and keep in the cool.

WEATHERSTRIPPING

Weatherstripping of doors and windows is one method of increasing comfort and reducing the consumption of fuel, whether oil or gas for heating or electricity for summer air conditioning.

Many kinds and grades of weatherstripping are available at various prices. They include metal and wood in rigid form and fabric (usually felt), rubber, and vinyl in rigid and flexible form.

The rigid types are made of strips of wood or metal to which are fastened flexible rubber strips or sponge backing. An interlocking rigid metal type is available, but use of this should be left to the professional, since it involves the removal of sash and cutting of precise grooves.

The flexible types are the best choice for the do-it-yourselfer. The felt types are the least expensive, shortest-lived of the lot. Vinyl stripping is more attractive, more ex-

pensive, and wears longer. Adhesive-backed foam rubber does not last a long time, but it may be your only choice for metal windows to which you cannot nail the material. The spring metal stripping is the most expensive, but it is also permanent.

For the bottoms of doors, special rigid weatherstripping is available. The simplest

Types of flexible weatherstripping.

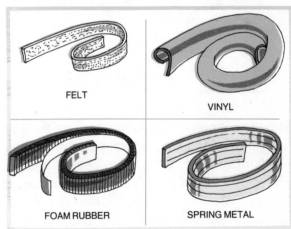

Installation of
flexible weatherstripping.

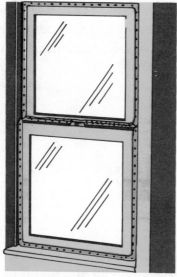

Installation of flexible
weatherstripping
on double-hung window.

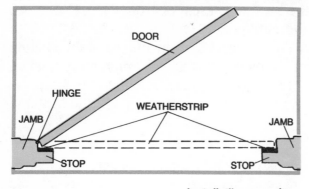

Installatiion on a door.

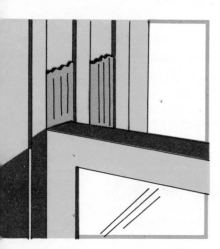

Spring-type installation
on window.

the door like a sleeve. It has a flexible vinyl facing that presses down over the top of the threshold. Yet another kind replaces the threshold entirely, and has a vinyl inset that provides a seal against the door bottom.

Flexible weatherstripping is easy to install. Most types can be cut with scissors; tin snips are needed for others. It should be fastened so that the flexible, or contact, edge presses snugly against a face of the closed window or door. Bend the stripping at corners to form a continuous seal, where possible. It should be screwed or nailed every 3 or 4 inches and at every corner.

On double-hung windows the weatherstripping should be applied in three pieces, one for each sash and a shorter length to fit where the two sashes meet. Install the sash sections in one continuous strip, nailing the sides to the window stops· and the upper and lower sections to the sill and frame. Tack the shorter piece along the top of the lower sash so that it presses against the upper sash. It may be necessary to cut the stripping to fit around the sash lock.

On doors the weatherstripping is fastened in one piece around the door stops. Its placement on the stops depends on the type of stripping used. The felt and foam types are applied to the inside face of the stops. Vinyl tubular stripping should be tacked to the side of the stop so that it presses evenly against the face of the door.

Casement windows are sealed in a similar fashion, with the stripping fastened to the stops. Channel stripping of either metal or vinyl should be used for steel windows.

Spring bronze or aluminum stripping is cut into lengths and placed on the inside of a window channel and at the jambs and frame of a door. It is of two-ply construction, one leaf of which is tacked to the wood while the other presses out against the sides of a window or door to form a draft-resisting seal.

To install on a window, raise the sash and

type is a metal or aluminum strip with a felt or vinyl sweep that is screwed to the bottom of the door. The sweep presses against the inside of the threshold when the door is closed. Another type consists of an aluminum channel that fits around the bottom of nail the strips to the sash channels with the open leaf facing the outside. Each strip should be long enough so that an inch or so of spring is still tucked under the sash when the sash is full up or down. This permits the window to be closed without having to depress the spring. A small section of spring should be tacked along the bottom face of the upper sash.

On doors, fasten the spring in three sections to the jambs and frame just inside the stops; again, the spring leaf should be facing the outside.

INSULATION IN ATTICS

Insulation in ceilings and walls is vital for keeping your home comfortable year-round. Two basic kinds of insulation are available for floors of unheated attics. Both will do the job if they are properly installed. One type is preformed mineral fiber (glass fiber or rock wool) batts or blankets. The other type is cellulose or mineral fiber in loose-fill form.

When installing insulation in attics, you don't have to stop at the ceiling joists if the attic has no flooring, but insulation should not touch the roof at the eaves. If you have a finished attic, check with an insulation specialist for the proper procedure for installing insulation.

Preformed insulation batts may be more economical than loose-fill materials in an unobstructed attic area without flooring, if they fit snugly between the joists and you do the work yourself. You can add insulation to your attic in one afternoon using batts—they can be laid out easily and there is no need to staple them down.

Once the area between the joists is fully insulated, the greatest source of heat loss in the attic is through the joists themselves, which may cover as much as 10 percent of the attic. For this reason, when adding in-

sulation batts above the level of the ceiling joists, cover joists completely if possible.

Loose-fill insulation may be better if the access to your attic is difficult or if it has a floor. If flooring is present in an otherwise unfinished attic, you may have to remove some of it temporarily to allow insulation to be blown in. Loose insulation is usually blown into the attic through flexible tubing by a small machine that puffs up the insulation as it pushes it through the tube. You may be able to rent such a machine at a large rental store. There may be some settling after the insulation is in place, so you should take that into account when measuring the depth.

The density of loose-fill insulation is extremely important in assuring the proper resistance to heat flow. The manufacturer generally specifies the number of bags of loose-fill materials needed for a specific area. If a contractor is insulating your attic, you should verify that the proper number of bags has been used.

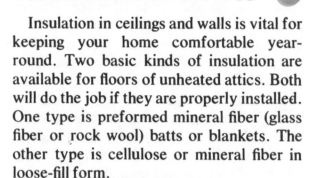

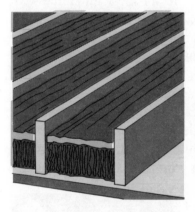

Fitting preformed insulation batts between joists (above).

Cover joists completely with insulation batts (above right).

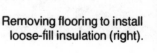

Removing flooring to install loose-fill insulation (right).

A well-insulated attic should also be well ventilated to prevent moisture accumulation. Never block ventilation ports, and always provide at least two vent openings located in such a way that air can flow in one and out the other. A good rule of thumb is to provide at least one square foot of opening for each 300 square feet of attic floor.

When inspecting your attic, you may notice interior wall spaces open to the attic, allowing cold air from the attic to fall down into the wall spaces or duct wells. These areas should be covered with insulation.

INSULATION IN EXTERIOR WALLS

● About 3 or 4 inches of insulation properly placed in the wall cavity can reduce the heat transfer through walls by as much as two-thirds. The best time to install insulation in this wall space is when the house is being built. When the wall is open, it is most economical to fill the wall space with batt insulation. Unfinished garage walls next to heated areas of the house should be insulated with batts.

■ Once a wall is finished off, it is difficult to reach the air space, and insulation has to be blown or injected into the wall through small holes drilled between the wall studs. (This can be done from the outside or the inside, depending on the ease of sealing the

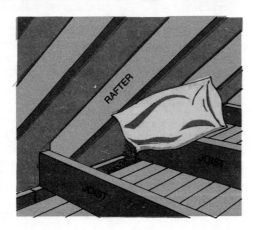

Installing wall insulation in older construction from attic.

holes and refinishing the surface.) Loose-fill materials, usually mineral fiber or cellulose, are the insulation forms best suited for this job. Although this process is much more costly than adding batt insulation during construction, it may still be a good investment if done properly. Only an experienced contractor should be employed, however, as the process can be quite complicated and poor workmanship will greatly lower the quality of the finished work.

Loose-fill wall insulation is recommended only for exterior walls with an air space at least 3 to 4 inches wide and with no existing insulation.

▲ In some older houses, access can be gained to the wall space from the attic. In this case, loose-fill insulation material can be dropped into the space from above at very low cost, making this economical in all but the mildest climates with low fuel prices. Just make sure the insulation doesn't fall all the way into the basement!

A potential problem with insulation in closed cavities in some climates is the possibility of moisture accumulation. This may be difficult to detect until moisture begins to show through the wall. If moisture problems occur, they can be minimized. The interior surface of the wall can be made vapor-resistant with a paint or covering that has low-moisture permeability. Cracks around windows and door frames, electrical outlets, and baseboards should be sealed at the surface facing the room. Outside surfaces should not be tightly sealed but allowed to "breathe."

Another potential problem that you may encounter with blown-in insulation is settling or shrinkage. Generally, this can be avoided if the insulation is properly installed. Calculating the number of bags of material needed per square foot of wall area and assuring that the full quantity has been installed is the best way to avoid this problem.

9

Condensation Problems

CONDENSATION is the change in moisture from a vapor to a liquid. In homes not properly protected, condensation caused by high humidity often results in excessive maintenance costs. Water vapor within the house, when unrestricted, can move through the wall or ceiling during the heating season to some cold surface where it condenses, collecting generally in the form of ice or frost. During warm periods the frost melts. When conditions are severe, the water from melting ice in unvented attics may drip to the ceiling below and cause damage to the interior finish. Moisture can also soak into the roof sheathing or rafters and set up conditions that could lead to decay. In walls, water from melting frost may run out between the siding laps and cause staining, or it may soak into the siding and cause paint blistering and peeling.

WHEN DOES IT OCCUR AND WHERE?

Wood and wood-base materials used for sheathing and panel siding may swell from this added moisture and result in bowing, cupping, or buckling. Thermal insulation also becomes wet and provides less resistance to heat loss.

The cost of heat loss, painting and redecorating, and excessive maintenance and repair caused by cold-weather condensation can easily be reduced or eliminated by proper construction details.

Estimates have been made that a typical family of four converts 3 gallons of water into water vapor per day. Unless excess water vapor is properly removed in some way (ventilation usually), it will either increase the humidity or condense on cold surfaces such as window glass. More serious, however, it can move in or through the construction, often condensing within the wall, roof, or floor cavities. Heating systems equipped with winter air-conditioning systems also increase the humidity.

Most new houses have from 2 to 3½ inches of insulation in the walls and 6 or more inches in the ceilings. Unfortunately, the more efficient the insulation is in retarding heat transfer, the colder the outer surfaces become and, unless moisture is restricted from entering the wall or ceiling, the greater the potential for moisture condensation. Moisture migrates toward cold surfaces and condenses or forms as frost or ice on these surfaces.

Inexpensive methods of preventing condensation problems are available. They mainly involve the proper use of vapor barriers and good ventilating practices. Naturally it is simpler, less expensive, and more effective to employ these during the construction of a house than to add them to existing homes.

Condensation takes place any time the temperature drops below the dew point (100 percent saturation of the air with water vapor at a given temperature). Commonly, under such conditions some surface accessible to the moisture in the air is cooler than the dew point, and the moisture condenses on that surface.

During cold weather, visible condensation is usually first noticed on window glass, but it may also be discovered on cold surfaces of closet and unheated bedroom walls and ceilings. Condensation may also be visible in attic spaces on rafters or roof boards near the cold cornice area, or it might form as frost. Such condensation or melting frost can result in excessive maintenance costs, such as the need for refinishing of window sash and trim, or even decay. Water from melting frost in the attic can also damage ceilings below.

Another area in which visible condensation can occur is in crawl spaces under occupied rooms. This area usually differs from those in the interior of the house and in the attic because the source of the moisture is usually from the soil or from warm moisture-laden air that enters through foundation ventilators. Moisture vapor then condenses on the cooler surfaces in the crawl space. Such conditions often occur during warm periods in late spring.

An increase in the relative humidity of the inside atmosphere increases the potential for condensation on inside surfaces. For example, when the inside temperature is 70 degrees F, surface condensation will occur on a single-thickness glass window when the outside temperature falls to -10

degrees F and the inside relative humidity is 10 percent. When the inside relative humidity is 20 percent, condensation can occur on the single glass when the outside temperature falls only to about +7 degrees F. When a storm window is added or insulated glass is used, surface condensation does not occur until the relative humidity has reached 38 percent when the outdoor temperature is -10 degrees F. These conditions apply only if storm windows are tight and there is good circulation of air on the inside surface of the window. If draperies or shades restrict circulation of air, storm windows are not tight, or lower temperatures are maintained in such areas as bedrooms, condensation occurs at a higher outside temperature.

Condensation in concealed areas, such as wall cavities, often is first revealed by stains on the siding or by paint peeling. Water vapor moving through permeable walls and ceilings is normally responsible for such damage. Water vapor also escapes from houses by constant outleakage through cracks and crevices, around doors and windows, and by ventilation, but this moisture-vapor loss is usually insufficient to eliminate condensation problems.

MOISTURE SOURCES

Moisture that is produced in or enters a home changes the relative humidity of the interior atmosphere. Ordinary household functions that generate a good share of the total amount of water vapor include dishwashing, cooking, bathing, and laundry work; add to this human respiration and evaporation from plants. Houses may also be equipped with central winter air conditioners or room humidifiers. Still another source of moisture may be from unvented or poorly vented clothes dryers.

Condensation problems can best be eliminated by specifying proper construction

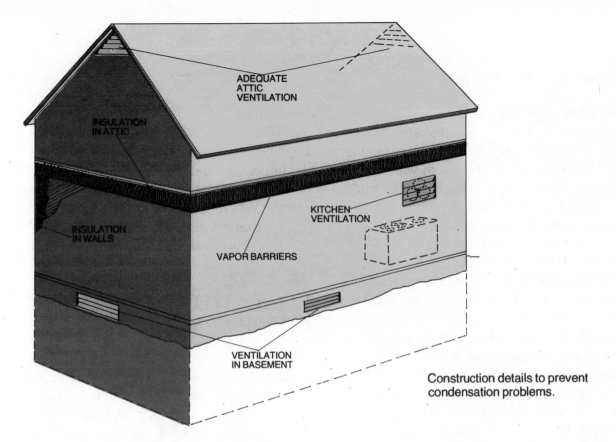

Construction details to prevent condensation problems.

details during planning of the house. Correct placement of vapor barriers, adequate insulation, the use of attic ventilation, and other good practices can be incorporated at this time. When these details have not been included in an existing house and condensation problems occur, they are often more difficult to solve. Nevertheless, there are methods to minimize such problems after the house has been built.

VISIBLE CONDENSATION

● Visible condensation on the interior glass surfaces of windows can be minimized by the use of storm windows or by replacing single-thickness glass with insulated glass. When this does not prevent condensation, however, the relative humidity in the room must be reduced. Draperies or curtains across the windows hinder rather than help. Not only do they increase surface condensation by keeping the glass surfaces colder, but they also prevent the air movement that would warm the glass surface and aid in dispersing some of the moisture.

▲ Condensation or frost on protruding nails, on the surfaces of roof boards, or

other structural members in attic areas normally indicates the escape of excessive amounts of water vapor from the heated rooms below. If a vapor barrier is not already present, place one between joists under the insulation. Make sure the vapor

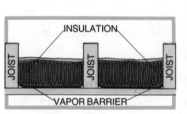

Vapor barrier between attic joists.

Make sure the vapor barrier fits tightly around ceiling fixtures.

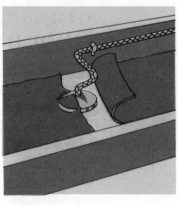

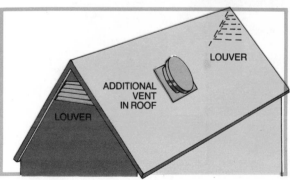

Add ventilators in attic.

barrier fits tightly around ceiling lights and exhaust fans, calking if necessary. In addition, increase both inlet and outlet ventilators. Decreasing the amount of water vapor produced in the living areas is also helpful.

▲ Surface condensation in unheated crawl spaces is usually caused by excessive moisture from the soil or from warm, humid air entering from outside the house. To eliminate this problem, place a vapor barrier over the soil; if necessary, increase the amount of ventilation (see CHAPTER 10).

● Concrete slabs without radiant heat are sometimes subjected to surface condensation in late spring when warm humid air enters the house. Because the temperature of some areas of the concrete slab or its covering is below the dew point, surface condensation can occur. Keeping the windows closed during the day, using a dehumidifier, and raising the inside temperature aid in minimizing this problem. When the concrete slab reaches normal room temperature, this inconvenience is eliminated.

REDUCING RELATIVE HUMIDITY

Reducing high relative humidities within the house to permissible levels is often necessary to minimize condensation problems. It is helpful to discontinue the use of room-sized humidifiers or reduce the output of automatic humidifiers until conditions are improved. The use of exhaust fans and dehumidifiers can also be of value in eliminating high relative humidities within the house. When possible, decreasing the activities that produce excessive moisture, as discussed previously, is sometimes helpful.

CONCEALED CONDENSATION

Concealed condensation is essentially a surface or similar condensation that takes place within a component such as a wall cavity when a condensing surface is below the dew point. In cold weather, condensation often forms as frost. Such conditions can cause staining of siding and peeling of the paint and possibly decay in severe and sustained conditions. These problems are usually not detected until spring, after the heating season has ended. The remedies should be taken care of before repainting or re-siding is attempted. Several methods may be used to correct these problems: reduce or control the relative humidity within the house; add a vapor-resistant paint coating such as aluminum paint to the interior of walls and ceilings; improve the vapor resistance of the ceiling joists; and improve attic ventilation.

10

Basements, Crawl Spaces

A LARGE PORTION of your home's usable space—as much as 50 percent in some ranch houses—is in the basement. Finished off, it becomes a family room, sewing room, den, office, or extra bedrooms. Unfortunately, many basements have dampness problems that must be cleared up before that space can be utilized.

Even if the basement is not to be finished off, such problems should be cured. Basement dampness affects comfort in the rooms overhead. It makes basement storage undesirable or impossible. And the dampness may be a warning of more serious troubles to come if it is not checked. Such a condition should never be ignored. But before corrective action can be taken, the cause of the problem must be pinpointed.

WHAT'S YOUR PROBLEM?

Almost all basement dampness problems can be traced to one of three causes: leakage, seepage, or condensation.

Leakage is usually obvious, occurring during a heavy rainfall or when snow is melting. An excessive amount of water builds up in the soil around the foundation walls, forcing its way through cracks or other defects in poured concrete walls (such as small holes around form wires), or through poor mortar joints in a concrete-block wall. If the area around the foundation has been improperly backfilled or graded, the situation is aggravated. In very wet periods, considerable flooding may result.

Seepage is evidenced by large areas of dampness on the foundation walls, rather than by water leaking through a particular spot. Usually, it will be greatest along the lower parts of the wall. Like leakage, it is caused by excessive water pressure on the outside of the basement walls. It may also be due to capillary action, which draws water from the moist soil through porous sections of the masonry.

Leakage in poured concrete (above) and concrete block walls (above right).

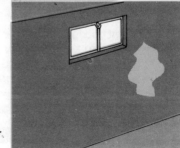

Seepage or condensation (right).

Test indicating condensation.　　Test indicating seepage.

Condensation looks very much like seepage, but here the moisture comes from air inside the basement, not from water outside (although seepage from outside may be a factor in creating the conditions for condensation). Condensation usually occurs during warm, humid weather, when the cool masonry walls seem to "sweat." It can also happen during colder months when warm air is discharged by a clothes dryer or similar appliance; moisture from this air collects on the cooler walls in the form of droplets, which may be mistaken for seepage from outside.

There is a simple test to determine whether a damp wall is the result of seepage or condensation. Tape a small mirror or a piece of sheet metal to the wall (or use a waterproof mastic if it is too wet for tape to stick). Leave it there overnight and inspect it the next day. If the surface of the mirror is fogged or the sheet metal damp, the moisture came from inside the basement,

indicating that condensation is to blame. If the surface of the patch is dry and clear while the surrounding wall is damp, seepage is the problem.

CONDENSATION CURES

If condensation is the cause of your moisture miseries, the remedy is to dry out the air in the basement as much as possible.

Adequate ventilation is essential for a dry basement. In cool, dry weather, keep the basement windows open whenever possible. On hot, humid days, keep them closed; warm, moist air may even cause mildew to form on the cooler masonry walls. If your basement has too few windows to provide needed ventilation, a small exhaust fan installed in a window or ducted to the outside will help.

Pipes that tend to sweat in hot weather should be wrapped with insulation. This is especially important if finishing off the basement ceiling is part of your plans. Otherwise, moisture dripping from the pipes will ruin your ceiling tiles or panels.

Clothes dryers should always be vented to the outside. This is a relatively easy do-it-yourself job. The vent pipe is normally run through a hole in the header joist or stringer joist (these are the joists that rest on the sills, which in turn are bolted to the top of the foundation walls). The hole can be cut either from inside the basement or, with careful measurements, from outside. Its diameter will depend on the size of the

1. Cut hole for vent of clothes dryer.

2. Insert hooded fitting through the hole.

3. Attach flexible pipe to the fitting of dryer's exhaust port.

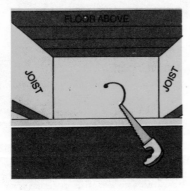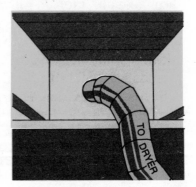

Basements, Crawl Spaces

exhaust port on your dryer. Use a saber saw or keyhole saw to cut the hole, after first drilling a ½-inch or larger pilot hole. Insert a hooded fitting through the hole from the outside, then connect the dryer's exhaust port to this fitting with flexible pipe. Both the fitting and flexible pipe can be purchased at most hardware stores.

If you do not have a clothes dryer, try to avoid hanging clothes to dry in the basement. The moisture from the wet clothes will enter the air and show up as condensation on the walls.

When basement condensation persists, an electric dehumidifier or chemical drying agents may be needed to remove moisture from the air and keep the basement dry.

CONDENSATION IN NEW HOUSES

If you are one of the fortunate few who have been able to move into brand-new houses in this time of skyrocketing costs and astronomical-interest mortgages, chances are that your condensation problems are greater than most. Condensation is at its maximum in new houses. During construction, literally tons of water are used— in concrete, mortar, plaster, wallpaper paste, tile work, and even many types of paint. This water gradually evaporates, giving a higher moisture content than normal to the air throughout the house and ending up as condensation on basement walls and windows in every room.

All the steps described above (especially providing adequate ventilation) should be employed to assist this normal drying-out process. In addition, be patient. Do not try to accelerate the process by turning up the furnace to extremely high temperatures. This will only cause uneven drying, exaggerating the effects of normal materials shrinkage and almost surely resulting in greater patch-and-repair problems later on.

SEEPAGE SOLUTIONS

If seepage is the cause of your basement dampness, a simple coat of paint may be the solution. Not just any paint, of course, but one that is resistant to water, alkali, and mildew and has good adhesion to concrete. This will provide a watertight coating that is durable and decorative.

Most such paints can be applied to both damp and uncured concrete as well as to previously painted surfaces. As with any paint job, the key to success is careful preparation.

Unpainted concrete, new or old, must be clean before application of paint. Grease, oil, and dirt should be removed with a strong cleansing agent such as trisodium phosphate. After scrubbing with a stiff-bristled brush, rinse the surface thoroughly with water to remove all residue. Allow to dry for 24 hours.

On a previously painted wall, all paint that is flaking, blistering, cracking, or chalking must be removed. This is done by scraping and brushing with a wire brush. Chemical removers can also be used. As with new concrete, the surface should then be scrubbed clean, rinsed, and allowed to dry thoroughly.

If the walls are whitewashed, scrub them with a dilute mixture of muriatic acid (10 parts water to 1 part acid). Wear rubber gloves and protective glasses or goggles for this job, and be careful not to splash any of the mixture on your skin or in your eyes. If you do, wash it off immediately with plenty of water. Again, rinse the surface thoroughly after scrubbing, and allow it to dry.

Before painting, patch large cracks and holes in the concrete, following the directions given below for plugging leaks. Hairline cracks and pores or pinholes need not be filled; the full-bodied paint will cover them.

Apply the paint with a brush or roller,

covering the surface evenly and thoroughly. Normally, a single coat does the job, but if the concrete or concrete block is very porous a second coat may be required.

■ A more serious seepage problem suggests a structural fault that will probably have to be corrected from outside the wall. You may prefer to leave this project to the professionals, since it involves excavating a trench wide enough to allow working space and deep enough to reach the problem area. The masonry surface must then be scrubbed clean before a coating of cement plaster is troweled on. This is followed by a second coating and, finally, a coating of asphalt cement or plastic sealer.

▲ Where subsoil moisture is present in excessive amounts, causing the seepage problem, drain tile should be laid around the foundation footings to carry water away from the house—another digging project. Tiles should be pitched downward ¼ inch per foot toward the drainage point. Joints between tiles should be covered with strips of tar paper to keep out dirt, and the tiles should both rest on and be covered by a layer of gravel or crushed stone.

STOPPING LEAKS

● When water is trickling through the basement wall, your first step is to plug the leak. This is best done with a quick-setting hydraulic cement that can be applied even when a crack is under pressure—that is, when water is pouring through it. Apply the cement with a trowel or wide-blade putty knife, holding it in place until the flow of water is stopped.

Such patches are usually only temporary and should be replaced when the crack is dry. For a normal dry repair, first chisel out the crack to form an inverted V-groove, about ½ inch at the surface and wider beneath so that the patching material will be locked in place. Use a cold chisel and a 1-pound ball pein or mash hammer for this job (your claw hammer should be reserved for carpentry and woodworking projects). Clean away all loose rubble and dust, and wire-brush clean. Flush with water to remove all dust particles.

Mix together 1 part cement to 2½ parts of clean sand. Add enough water to make a stiff mixture, making sure to wet all parts of

Plugging the leak with cement.

Chiseling crack.

Fill crack with patching cement.

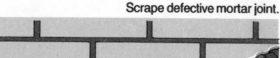

Scrape defective mortar joint.

Force mortar into joint.

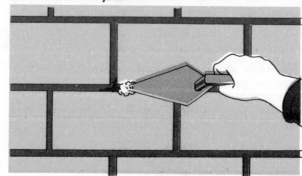

the sand-cement. Dampen the area to be patched, then force the mixture into the crack with a trowel, filling it completely. Keep the patched area slightly damp for a few days to allow the cement to cure thoroughly. If that doesn't solve your leakage problem, you will probably have to attack it from outside, as described for seepage.

■ In a concrete-block foundation wall, water may leak through a defective mortar joint between blocks. To repair this, first scrape away all loose and crumbling mortar, using a cold chisel or an old screwdriver. Clean out the joint with a wire brush and rinse with water to remove all dust particles. Make a mortar mix of 1 part masonry cement to 3 parts clean, dry sand. Add enough water to make a workable but fairly stiff mixture. Force the mortar into the joint with a trowel, striking it off flush with the surface of the block. Allow the mortar to dry thoroughly.

▲ Leaks at the wall-floor joint can similarly be corrected with cement. Even more effective is a two-part epoxy resin compound that forms a durable seal against hydrostatic pressure at this point. Once again, the area should be thoroughly cleaned before making the repair. The material is mixed immediately before use and brushed or troweled into place. Two coats are usually recommended.

▲ Leaks in concrete floors are repaired in the same way as wall leaks: undercutting, cleaning, and patching with a sand-cement mixture. However, floor leaks may be indicative of more serious problems. Your home may be in a very low, wet location or be built over a marshy area or an underground stream. In that case, a drainage tile system may have to be installed, as described above for major seepage problems.

CRAWL SPACES

Crawl spaces present some special problems because cold and dampness commonly invade these areas. Occasionally, unpleasant odors result. These conditions make living on the floor above somewhat less than ideal. The conditions are usually curable.

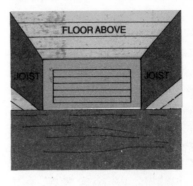
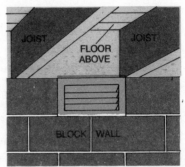

Install vent in leader joist (above).

Install vent in block wall (above right).

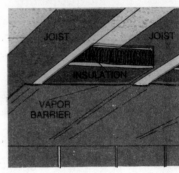

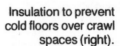

Insulation to prevent cold floors over crawl spaces (right).

Again, adequate ventilation is essential. There should be vents or louvers on at least two opposite sides of the crawl space to provide cross-ventilation. If necessary, you can install vents by cutting holes through the header joists (similar to installing a dryer vent, described above). If the foundation is of concrete block, you can simply knock out a block to emplace a vent. Louvered vents, which can be closed off in damp or cold weather, are best. Most of them are also screened to keep out rodents and other small animals.

Cold floors in rooms over crawl spaces present another problem. The best solution is to install 4-inch insulation batts between the floor joists. Staple the batts to the bottoms of the joists, forming air space between the subfloor and the insulation. (Don't block vents with the insulation.) Below the insulation, staple a vapor barrier of heavy felt paper. This will seal out any moisture. Make sure that the entire area beneath the floor is covered.

If dampness persists, cover the ground in the crawl space with tar paper. Overlap the joints 3 to 4 inches, and seal the tar paper to the foundation walls with asphalt compound. Then spread a 2-inch layer of dry sand over the tar paper. This should insure that the area above the crawl space will be cozy and dry the year round.

PREVENTIVE MEASURES

Patching holes and cracks and waterproofing basement walls solve the immediate problems of leakage and seepage, but since the ultimate cause is excess water accumulation in the ground around the foundation walls, this situation should also be corrected. This is done by making provision to divert surface water before it can come into contact with the foundation.

Check gutters and downspouts for leaks or improper pitching that may cause water to collect along the foundation wall. Gutters that are clogged with leaves and other debris may also divert water onto the ground beside the house and, eventually, into the basement. Downspouts should be connected to a storm sewer or to an underground dry well located at least 10 feet away from the foundation. Downspouts not so connected should empty onto concrete splash blocks that carry the water runoff away from the house walls.

To carry away rainwater as quickly as possible, the ground surface should slope away sharply at foundation walls, then more gradually to at least 10 feet from the walls. If such is not the case, fill in with new soil, taking special care in areas where puddles form during rainy weather. Tamp the soil firmly and sow it with good grass seed or sod rolled down evenly and firmly. If the new grading extends above basement windows, protect each one with a curved

Downspouts should carry water away from foundation.

CONCRETE SPLASH BLOCK

metal shell or concrete wall. Gravel in the bottoms of these protected areas will facilitate drainage. Hinged plastic covers may be provided to admit light but keep out rain and snow.

Where concrete walks or driveways are adjacent to the foundation wall, they should also slope away gradually. The walk-wall joint should be concave or sharply angled to keep out water. If the joints are not so protected, or if they are broken or otherwise damaged, they should be fixed.

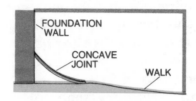
FOUNDATION WALL / CONCAVE JOINT / WALK
Walk-wall joint.

Chip away loose or damaged concrete. Scrub clean both the wall and the walk, and roughen both surfaces with a cold chisel and peining hammer. You can then apply an epoxy resin compound to the joint, as described above for basement wall-floor joints. Or you can use a mixture of 1 part cement to 2½ parts sand. Moisten the concrete surfaces, then trowel the cement-sand mixture into the joint, sloping it sharply away from the foundation wall for a minimum of 2 inches.

A FINAL NOTE OF CAUTION

If all else fails and you must call in a professional to try to solve your basement dampness problem, exercise a degree of caution and beware of "miracle cures." There are many highly reputable firms in the basement waterproofing business, but there are also some of lesser repute. Follow the usual practice of checking with the local Better Business Bureau, consumer protection groups, and other homeowners who have dealt with the firm before you sign any contract. As ever, let the buyer beware.

Basements, Crawl Spaces

11

Controlling Household Pests

Some household pests have an incredible ability to escape extinction. Cockroaches, for example, which have been on the earth millions of years longer than man, can subsist on any kind of food; they thrive in all parts of the world. Some species of cockroaches prefer man's home to other habitats. Once they enter it, they use countless instinctive tricks to keep from being evicted.

You can help control household pests by systematic housecleaning. You can rid your home of practically all pests, and keep it free of them, by a combination of continuous good housekeeping and the proper use of the right pesticide at the right time.

PESTICIDES AND THEIR APPLICATION

Pesticides may be applied in different forms and different ways to serve various purposes. Surface sprays are applied to surfaces in the home where insects are likely to crawl. The spray particles are coarse, and they dampen or wet the surfaces. When the spray dries, a thin deposit of insecticide remains. For several weeks or months, the deposit kills insects that crawl over it.

You may buy these sprays in pressurized containers, or you may buy a liquid insecticide and apply it with a household hand sprayer that produces a coarse spray.

Do not spray oil-base insecticides on asphalt-tile floors, because they may dissolve the asphalt. They may also soften and discolor some linoleums and some plastic materials; if in doubt about spraying such surfaces, test the spray on a small, inconspicuous place. If you apply an oil-base in-

secticide to the cracks in a parquet floor, apply it lightly; an excessive amount may dissolve the underlying cement, and the dissolved cement may stain the floor.

Space sprays and aerosols are designed for application into the air. They are especially effective against mosquitoes, houseflies, and other flying insects. They may also be used to penetrate the hiding places of other insects such as roaches, driving them into the open where they may be killed with a surface spray or dust.

The particles, or droplets, of a space spray are much finer than those of a surface spray, and float in the air for a time. The particles of an aerosol are fine than those of a space spray, and float in the air for a longer time.

Space sprays leave little residue, and generally should not be used as surface sprays. Aerosols are entirely too fine for surface application.

You may buy space sprays in pressurized containers; or you may buy liquid insecti-

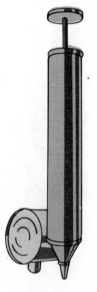

HAND SPRAYER

cide and apply it as a space spray with a household hand sprayer having a nozzle that produces very fine particles. Household aerosols are available in pressurized containers.

Some sprays sold in pressurized containers may be labeled for both surface and space applications. If you use one of these products for spraying in the kitchen or pantry, first place cooking and eating utensils, and food, where they will not be contaminated by falling particles.

Before applying a space spray or aerosol, close all windows and doors tightly. Apply the chemical into the air as directed on the container label. Some people may be allergic to the materials in space sprays or aerosols. After application, it is advisable to leave the room, close the door, and not reenter for half an hour or longer. Breathe as little as possible of the chemicals discharged in space sprays or aerosols.

Insecticidal dusts usually contain the same active ingredients as sprays. They are used for surface applications, and may be blown by a household hand duster into cracks, corners, and other places difficult to reach with sprays.

HAND DUSTER

Insecticide may be applied to surfaces in liquid, cream, or paste form with a paintbrush. This method often permits a more accurate placement of the material than does spraying or dusting. It is recommended where only spot treatments are needed. Cream or paste insecticides are usually available in stores where liquids and dusts are sold.

Poisoned bait, as the name implies, is a bait on which a pest will feed and to which a pesticide has been added. In the home, poisoned baits may be used to control rodents and some other pests. Frequently they are more hazardous to humans and pets than other forms of pesticide. If you use a poisoned bait, handle it with extreme care; follow the directions and observe all precautions on the container label.

COCKROACHES

Cockroaches seek warmth, moisture, and food. They hide during the day in sheltered, dark places in the home, and come out at night to forage. They feed on garbage as well as human food; because of this, they may transmit human diseases.

Cockroaches contaminate and spoil human food. They eat starch and glue, and thus may damage fabrics, garments, curtains, books, papers, and many other materials. Good housekeeping and the use of insecticide when necessary are the only certain means of keeping your home free of cockroaches.

Diazinon, malathion, or ronnel control all kinds of cockroaches. You can use a household surface spray or a dust. For a severe infestation, use both. Apply the spray first; then apply the dust after the spray has dried, forcing the dust into cracks and openings difficult to reach with a spray.

When treating cupboards and pantries, take everything from shelves and remove drawers so that food and utensils will not become contaminated by the insecticide. It is not necessary to treat the insides of drawers if you have thoroughly cleaned them. However, it is important to treat the sides, backs, and bottoms of drawers and the insides of cabinets.

HOUSEFLIES

Houseflies constitute about 98 percent of the flies that invade the home. They are among the filthiest of insect pests. They breed in decaying organic matter and feed indiscriminately on manure, garbage, and the food on our tables. They contaminate everything they touch and spread many human diseases.

Houseflies breed in places where garbage accumulates. Clean up these places. See that your garbage cans are equipped with tight-fitting lids. Promptly dispose of the

Controlling Household Pests

droppings of pets. Do not allow food to stand where it will attract flies.

Keep houseflies out by placing screens in your windows and doors. See that screened doors swing outward. Screens that have 14 meshes to the inch will keep out houseflies; if the screens have 16 meshes, they will also keep out many smaller insects.

If you need an insecticide to control the flies in your home, apply a household or aerosol spray. Be sure the container label says the spray is for flying insects.

SILVERFISH AND FIREBRATS

Silverfish and firebrats are slender, wingless insects ⅓ to ½ inch long. They are similar in appearance. Silverfish are shiny and silver or pearly gray; firebrats are mottled gray.

These insects are active at night, and usually hide during the day. Silverfish live and develop in damp, cool places—particularly in basements. Firebrats prefer very warm areas in the home, such as the attic in summer and the furnace in winter. Both insects crawl along pipelines and through openings in the walls or floors; they may be found in any part of the house.

Silverfish and firebrats cause damage in homes by eating foods and other materials that are high in protein, sugar, or starch. They eat cereals, moist wheat flour, any paper on which there is glue or paste, the sizing in paper (including wallpaper and bookbindings, starch in clothing, and rayon).

To control silverfish and firebrats, apply insecticide in the form of a surface spray or a dust. The results may not be immediate; but if the insecticide is properly and thoroughly applied, it will leave a residue that should be effective within a few weeks. If satisfactory control is not achieved in two or three weeks, make additional applications. If you are troubled with firebrats but not with silverfish, you may need to apply insecticide only to warm parts of the house.

Use a household spray containing chlordane, lindane, ronnel, or malathion. Apply the spray to baseboards, door and window casings, closets, and places where pipes go through walls. Some sprays have oil-solution bases; do not apply these near electric motors, gas pilot flames, or other places where they may start fires.

You can also use a dust containing not more than 6 percent of chlordane, 1 percent of lindane, or 5 percent of malathion. Apply with a hand duster, blowing it into cracks and on surfaces of the places recommended for sprays. Dusts may be applied safely to places where oil-solution sprays might start fires.

MICE

At one time or another, almost every homeowner finds mice to be a source of annoyance and damage. These little rodents usually migrate from outdoor areas into homes when the weather turns cold in the fall. They eat or contaminate human food, injure fabrics, wood, and other materials, and transmit several human diseases.

The first steps in controlling mice are to seal any holes in the walls, floors, and foundation of the house and to see that food is not left in places where mice can get to it.

If there are only a few mice in your home, they can usually be disposed of with ordinary snap traps. The traps should be placed along walls and near holes. Place them at a right angle to the wall so that the trigger mechanism will intercept the mouse's probable route of travel.

One of the best baits to use in snap traps is peanut butter smeared over the trigger surface. Other good baits are cake, flour, bacon, nut meats, cheese, and soft candies, particularly milk chocolate or gumdrops.

Where mice are so numerous that trapping is impractical, poison bait may be used. Purchase materials labeled for this purpose. Follow the directions and observe all precautions on the container label.

Care should be taken to avoid placing the materials where there is danger of contaminating food supplies. Pesticides should never be left within reach of children, irresponsible persons, pets, or livestock.

RATS

Rats destroy or pollute human food, transmit diseases, and damage property. If cornered, they are dangerous and may attack people or pets. They enter homes to find food and shelter.

The first control measure for rats is to starve them. Leave no food in open places; this includes food in unopened cardboard containers. Place garbage and refuse in tightly covered metal containers.

Remove the rats' shelter. Keep storage places orderly and clean. In the basement and storerooms, stack lumber, boxes, cartons, and other objects on racks at least one foot above the floor.

Poisoned bait is recommended as the best means of killing rats. Purchase a suitable bait, labeled for the purpose. Follow directions on the label and observe the precautions to the letter. Poisons should never be left within the reach of children, irresponsible persons, pets, or livestock.

Traps are also an effective means of killing rats in the home, but their use requires skill and much time. Traps are recommended where infestations are very small, or as a follow-up after the use of bait.

Close all holes in exterior walls. See that spaces around doors, windows, and other necessary openings are no larger than ¼ inch. If rats are a serious problem in your neighborhood, install self-closing devices on frequently used doors to the outside.

Where rats are a neighborhood problem, community action should be taken; assistance should be asked of your local board of health.

PESTICIDE SAFETY

The first rule of safety in using any pesticide is to read and follow the directions and precautions on the container label. Do this each time you use a pesticide; don't depend on your memory. Many pesticide manufacturers include leaflets of instructions with their products. Carefully read these also.

Store pesticides as directed on their labels, in closed, well-labeled containers, where children or pets cannot reach them. Do not place them near food. Do not store them under the sink, in the pantry, or in the medicine cabinet.

Always leave pesticides in their original containers. Be sure the labels remain on them. If a pesticide is marked "POISON," there will be an antidote statement on the label.

Do not dispose of surplus pesticides where they may be a hazard to fish or wildlife. Do not discard them outdoors. Do not dispose of them where they may contaminate water. If you have trash-collection service, wrap small containers in several layers of newspapers, tie securely with heavy string or cord, and place them in the trash can.

Determine the right amount of the right pesticide to use.

Be careful not to get pesticide on food, dishes, or cooking utensils.

Remove aquariums, birds, cats and dogs, and other pets and their food and water pans before applying pesticide. Keep children away from application areas.

When the label warns against breathing pesticidal mists or dusts, open windows and doors first.

Wash your face and hands with soap and water after using a pesticide.

Controlling Household Pests

12

Simple Plumbing Repairs

Every homeowner is faced at some time with the aggravating "drip . . . drip . . . drip" of a leaking faucet or the endless rush of water through a toilet that won't stop running. Trying to get a plumber to come and fix these minor (but no less maddening) problems is a tedious and expensive matter—if you are lucky enough even to find one of these artisans who wants to be bothered.

The do-it-yourselfer can save much money and avoid annoying delays by making minor plumbing repairs himself. Extensive plumbing repairs or alterations in the plumbing system usually require authorization from local officials and possibly inspection of the completed work. Unless you have considerable experience, such work should be done by a qualified or licensed plumber.

REPAIRING WATER FAUCETS AND VALVES

Water faucets and globe valves serve the same purpose: they control the flow of water. The essential difference is that faucets are used at discharge points over fixtures such as sinks, lavatories, and tubs, whereas valves are used to close off portions of the plumbing system.

Other types of valves, such as check valves, gate valves, and pressure-reducing valves, are not too common in normal home plumbing. Problems with these types of valves normally necessitate their replacement.

Faucets and globe valves are very similar in construction, and repairs are also similar. (Your faucets or valves may differ somewhat in general design from the one shown, because both faucets and valves come in a wide variety of styles depending on the manufacturer. Mixing faucets, which are found on sinks, laundry trays, and bathtubs, are actually two separate

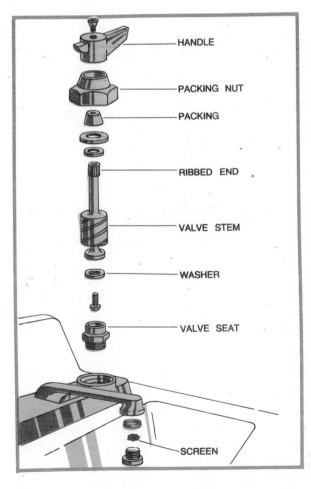

Typical faucet.

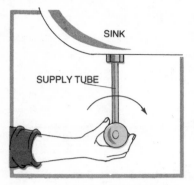

Shut off water to faucet.

Disassemble faucet.

Replace washer.

Resurface seat.

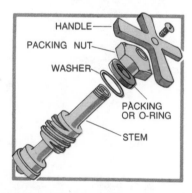

Replace O ring.

units with a common spout. Each unit is independently repaired.

If a faucet drips when closed or vibrates ("sings" or "flutters") when open, the trouble is usually a worn washer at the lower end of the spindle. If it leaks around the spine when opened, new packing or a new "O" ring is needed. To replace the washer:

1. Shut off the water at the shut-off valve nearest the particular faucet.

2. Disassemble the faucet—the handle, packing nut, packing,.and spindle, in that order. You may have to set the handle back

on the spindle and use it to unscrew and remove the spindle.

3. Remove the screw and worn washer from the spindle. Scrape all the worn washer parts from the cup and install a new washer. If you do not have the proper size washer, file down a larger one; do not use one that is too small.

4. Examine the seat on the faucet body. If it is nicked or roughed, reface it. Hardware and plumbing-supply stores carry the necessary seat-dressing tool, which is sold with directions for use. Hold the tool vertically when refacing the seat.

5. Reassemble the faucet.

To replace the packing or "O" ring, simply remove the handle, packing nut, and old packing or ring and install a new packing washer. If a packing washer is not available, you can wrap stranded graphite-asbestos wicking around the spindle. Turn the packing nut down tight against the wicking.

LEAKS IN PIPES AND TANKS

Leaks in pipes usually result from corrosion or from damage to the pipe and tubing (some acid soils also corrode metal pipe and tubing). The corrosion usually occurs, in varying degrees, along the entire length of pipe rather than at some particular point. An exception would be where dissimilar metals, such as copper and steel, are joined.

Treatment (softening) of the water may solve the problem of corrosion. Otherwise, you may have to replace the piping with a type made of material that is less subject to the corrosive action of the water. It is good practice to get a chemical analysis of the water before selecting materials for a plumbing system. Your state college or university may be equipped to make an analysis; if not, you can have it done by a private laboratory.

Pipes that are split by hard freezing must be replaced. A leak at a threaded connection can often be stopped by unscrewing the fitting and applying a pipe joint compound that will seal the joint when the connection is screwed back together.

Small leaks in a pipe can often be repaired with a rubber patch and metal clamp or sleeve. This must be considered as an emergency repair job and should be followed by permanent repair.

▲Large leaks in a pipe may require cutting out the damaged section and installing a new piece of pipe. At least one union fitting will be required unless the leak is near the end of the pipe. You can make a temporary repair with plastic tubing or rubber hose. The tubing must be strong enough to withstand the normal water pressure in the pipe. It should be slipped over the opened ends of the piping and fastened with pipe clamps or several turns of wire.

Vibration sometimes breaks solder joints in copper tubing, causing leaks. If the joint is accessible, clean and resolder it. The tubing must be dry before it can be heated to soldering temperature. Leaks in places not readily accessible usually require the services of a plumber and sometimes of both a plumber and a carpenter.

Leaks in tanks are usually caused by corrosion. Sometimes, a safety valve fails to open and the pressure that is developed causes a leak. Although a leak may occur at only one place in the tank wall, the wall may also be corroded thin in other places. Therefore, any repair should be considered temporary, and the tank should be replaced as soon as possible.

A leak can be temporarily repaired with a toggle bolt, rubber gasket, and brass washer. You may have to drill or ream the hole larger to insert the toggle bolt. Draw the bolt up tight to compress the rubber gasket against the tank wall.

Simple Plumbing Repairs

WATER HAMMER

Water hammer sometimes occurs when a faucet is closed. When the flow of water is suddenly stopped, its kinetic energy is expended against the walls of the piping. This

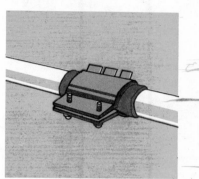

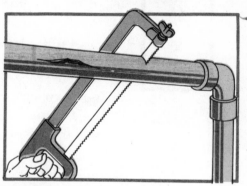

Apply pipe joint compound (above).

Repairing a small leak (above right).

Cutting away damaged section of pipe (right).

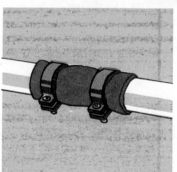

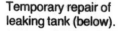

Using hose for temporary repair (left).

Resoldering a damaged joint (below left).

Temporary repair of leaking tank (below).

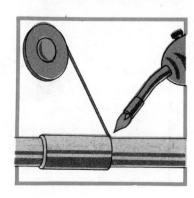

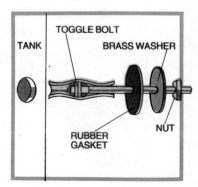

TOGGLE BOLT

TANK

BRASS WASHER

NUT

RUBBER GASKET

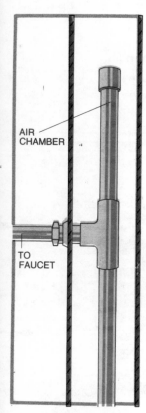

Air chamber to avoid
water hammer.

causes the piping to vibrate, and leaks or other damage may result.

Water hammer may be prevented or its severity reduced by installing an air chamber just ahead of the faucet. The air chamber may be a piece of air-filled piping or tubing, about 2 feet long, extending vertically from the pipe. It must be air-tight. Commercial devices designed to prevent water hammer are also available.

FROZEN WATER PIPES

In cold weather, water may freeze in underground pipes laid above the frostline or in pipes in unheated buildings, in open crawl spaces, or in outside walls.

When water freezes it expands. Unless a pipe can also expand, it may rupture when the water freezes. Iron pipe and steel pipe do not expand appreciably. Copper pipe stretches some, but does not resume its original dimensions when thawed; repeated freezings will cause it to fail eventually. Flexible plastic tubing may stand repeated freezings, but it is good practice to prevent it from freezing.

Pipes may be insulated to prevent freezing, but this is not a completely dependable method. Insulation does not stop the loss of heat from the pipe—it merely slows it down—and the water may freeze if it stands in the pipe long enough at below-freezing temperature. Also, if insulation becomes wet, it loses its effectiveness.

Electric heating cable can supply the continual heat needed to prevent freezing of pipes in areas of intense cold. The cable should be wrapped around the pipe and covered with insulation.

Use of electric heating cable is the best method of thawing frozen pipe, because the entire length of pipe is thawed at one time. Thawing pipe with a blowtorch or propane torch can be dangerous. The water may get so hot at the point where the torch is applied as to generate sufficient steam under pressure to rupture the pipe. Steam from the break could severely scald you.

Thawing pipe with hot water is safer than thawing with a blowtorch. One method is to cover the pipe with rags and then pour the hot water over the rags.

When thawing pipe with a torch, hot water, or similar methods, open a faucet and start thawing at that point, thus reducing the chance of the buildup of dangerous pressure. Do not allow the steam to condense and refreeze before it reaches the faucet.

REPAIRING TOILETS

Toilets vary in general design and in the design of the flushing mechanism. But they are enough alike that general repair instruc-

Wrap heating cable around pipe.

Thawing a pipe with hot water.

Thawing a pipe with a torch.

Simple Plumbing Repairs

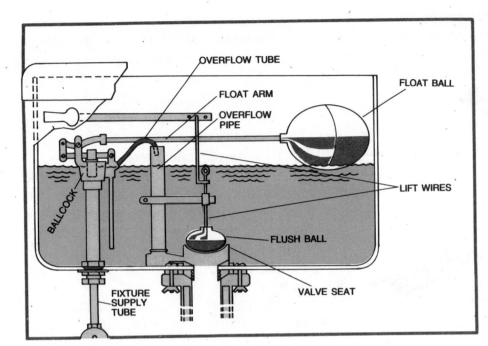

Typical toilet.

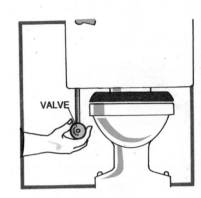

Shut off water supply to toilet.

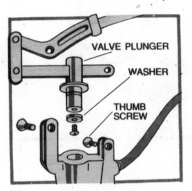

Replace washer.

tions can suffice for all designs. Parts that usually require repair are the flush valve, the intake (float) valve, and the float ball.

● The rubber ball of the flush valve may become soft or out of shape and fail to seat properly. This causes the valve to leak. Unscrew the ball and install a new one.

● The trip lever lift wire may corrode and fail to work smoothly, or the lift wire may bind in the guides. Disassemble and clean off corrosion or replace parts as necessary.

When working on the flush valve, stop the flow of water by propping up the float with a piece of wood. Be careful not to bend the float rod out of alignment.

A worn plunger washer in the intake valve will cause the valve to leak. To replace the washer:

1. Shut off the water and drain the tank.

2. Unscrew the two thumbscrews that hold the levers and push out the levers.

3. Lift out the plunger, unscrew the cup on the bottom, and insert a new washer. The washer is made of material such as rubber or leather.

4. Examine the washer seat. If nicked or roughed, it may need refacing.

If the float valve assembly is badly corroded, replace the entire assembly.

● The float ball may develop a leak and fail to rise to the proper position. (The correct water level is about 1 inch below the top of the overflow pipe, or enough to give a thorough flush.) If the ball fails to rise, the intake valve remains open and water continues to flow. A leaking float ball must be replaced. When working on the float ball, be careful to keep the rod aligned so that the ball will float freely and close the valve.

An obstruction in the toilet trap or leakage around the bottom of the toilet bowl may require removal of the bowl. Follow this procedure:

1. Shut off the water.

2. Empty the tank and bowl by flushing and sponging out the remaining water.

Simple Plumbing Repairs

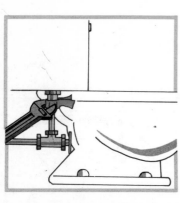

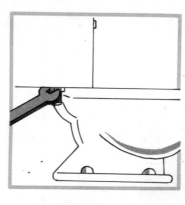

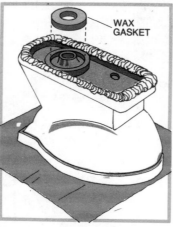

WAX GASKET

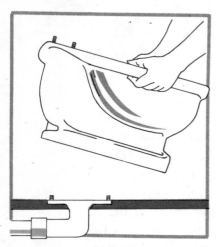

Disconnect pipe (top left).

Disconnect tank from bowl (top right).

Remove bowl (above left).

Place new wax seal (above).

Set bowl in place (left).

Level bowl (below).

3. Disconnect the water pipe to the tank.

4. Disconnect the tank from the bowl if the toilet is a two-piece unit. Set the tank where it cannot be damaged. Handle tank and bowl carefully; they are made of vitreous china or porcelain and are easily chipped or broken.

5. Remove the toilet seat.

6. Carefully pry loose the bolt covers and remove the nuts holding the bowl to the floor flange. Jar the bowl enough to break the seal at the bottom. Set the bowl upside down on something that will not chip it.

7. Remove the obstruction from the discharge opening.

8. Place a new wax seal around the bowl horn and press it into place. A wax seal (or gasket) may be obtained from hardware or plumbing-supply stores.

9. Set the bowl in place and press it down firmly. Install the nuts that hold it to the floor flange. Draw the nuts up snugly, but not too tight because the bowl may break. The bowl must be level; keep a carpenter's level on it while drawing up the bolts. If your house has settled, leaving the floor sloping, it may be necessary to use shims to make the bowl level. Next replace the bolt covers.

10. Install the tank and connect the water pipes to it. It is advisable to replace all gaskets, after cleaning mating surfaces.

11. Test for leaks by flushing a few times.

12. Install the seat and cover.

When cold water enters a toilet tank, it may chill the tank enough to cause "sweating" (condensation of atmospheric moisture on the outer surface of the tank). This can be prevented either by warming the water before it enters the tank or by insulating the tank to keep the temperature of the outer surface above the dew point temperature of the surrounding air. A tempering device that will mix a little hot water with the cold may be installed on the water-supply line to the tank to warm the water. Insulating jack-

Simple Plumbing Repairs

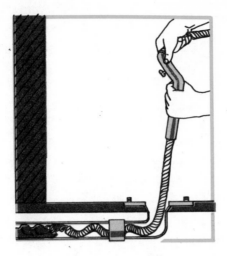

Using a clean-out auger.

Using a hose
to clear clogged drain.

"Plumber's friend"
in action.

ets or liners that fit inside toilet tanks and serve to keep the outer surface warm are available from plumbing-supply dealers.

CLEARING CLOGGED DRAINS

Drains may become clogged by objects dropped into them or by accumulations of grease, dirt, or other matter. If the obstruction is in a fixture trap, usually the trap can be removed and cleared. If the obstruction is elsewhere, other means must be used.

Cleanout augers—long, flexible steel cables commonly called snakes—may be run down drainpipes to break up obstructions or to hook onto and pull out objects. Augers are made in various lengths and diameters and are available at hardware and plumbing-supply stores. (In some cases you may have to call a plumber, who will probably have a power-driven auger.)

Small obstructions can sometimes be forced down or drawn up by use of a rubber force cup (plunger or "plumber's friend"). Water pressure from a hose may break up an obstruction or force an object on

through the pipe. Wrap rags around the hose where it enters the pipe to minimize backflow of water.

Grease and soap clinging to a pipe can sometimes be removed by flushing with hot water. Chemical cleaners may also be used. When water is added, the reaction loosens the grease and soap so that they can be flushed away. Use cold water only. Chemical cleaners should not be used in pipes that are completely stopped up, because they must be brought into direct contact with the stoppage to be effective. Handle the material with extreme care and follow directions on the container. Spills on the hands or clothing should be washed with cold water immediately. If any gets into your eyes, flush with cold water and call a doctor.

Sand, dirt, or clothing lint sometimes clog floor drains (such as are found in basement and grade-level laundry rooms). Remove the strainer and ladle out as much of the sediment as possible. You may have to carefully chip away the concrete around the strainer to free it. Flush the drain with clean water. If pressure is needed, use a garden hose. Wrap cloths around the hose where it enters the drain to prevent backflow of water. You may have to stand on this plug to keep it in place when the water is turned on. Occasional flushing of floor drains may prevent clogging.

13

Simple
Electrical Repairs

ELECTRICITY is probably the most conveniently applied form of energy for household uses. In addition to its great convenience and adaptability for various purposes, it has the advantage of safety when properly handled. There are, however, possible serious hazards to both life and property if electrical wiring and devices are incorrectly installed or utilized.

Electrical wiring and appliances are intended for specific functions and should be used only for the purposes for which they are intended. Electrical devices, particularly heat-producing appliances such as toasters, coffee makers, etc., should be moved only by means of the insulated handles provided. Current-carrying parts of wiring devices for appliances such as sockets should never be touched before current is cut off at the main switch.

It is important to avoid contact with electric wires or conductors in bathrooms, kitchens, laundries, basements, garages, or other rooms where floors may be damp. The danger of receiving electrical shocks is greatest under wet conditions because of the increased conductivity of the skin. Therefore, when your hands or other parts of your body are wet, do not touch electrical appliances, fixtures, or the connecting cords. Electric shock usually occurs when current flows from the live part of a device through the point of contact to a person's hands or body, with the return circuit being made either through wet feet or contact through a hand that is touching some grounded object, such as a radiator, stove, or heater. If current flow passes through or near the heart, the effects may be very serious.

Minor repairs to the electrical system and equipment of a house are the only ones that should be undertaken by an inexperienced home handyman. These include such tasks as replacing a blown-out fuse, replacing broken or frayed appliance cords, or overhauling a doorbell system. Unless you have considerable electrical experience, do not attempt to disturb or extend permanent wiring. Work of this nature should be done by a licensed electrician in accordance with local regulations or the provisions of the latest edition of the National Electrical Code.

DISCONNECTING ELECTRICAL CURRENT

The entire supply of electrical current may be cut off where it enters the house system by pulling or disconnecting the main switch, which is usually located in a metal box in the basement.

Each adult member of the household should be familiar with the means for disconnecting the current. The method of operation varies according to the type of design. In some equipment, a handle protrudes from the box or enclosure, and the circuit is disconnected by pulling the operating lever down; on circuit breakers or pull-out type switches, the method of opening is on the outside of the box.

FUSES AND CIRCUIT BREAKERS

The wires in each house circuit are intended to carry a certain load current and if overloaded they may become heated and cause a fire. Fuses or circuit breakers are used as safety devices to guard against this danger. When more than the rated current load is placed on the circuit wiring, the safety device operates, opening the circuit. This is called "blowing" a fuse or "tripping" a circuit breaker. Before service is restored, the cause of the blown fuse or tripped circuit breaker should first be determined. To do this, the appliance that was put on the line at the time the fuse blew should be disconnected. If the fuses on this particular branch again blow, an electrician should be called in and no further effort made to use this circuit until the trouble has been located and corrected.

If an electrical circuit is overloaded by connecting too many appliances to it at one time, a fuse may blow or a circuit breaker trip. A short circuit, which may also blow a fuse or trip a circuit breaker, may be caused by faulty electrical insulation.

Since fuses are intended to protect the wiring of a circuit, it is important when replacing them to use those of the proper rating. Branch circuits in residences are usual-

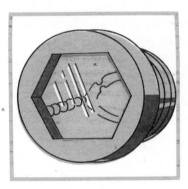
Fuse.

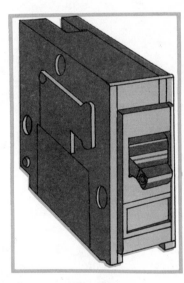
Circuit breaker.

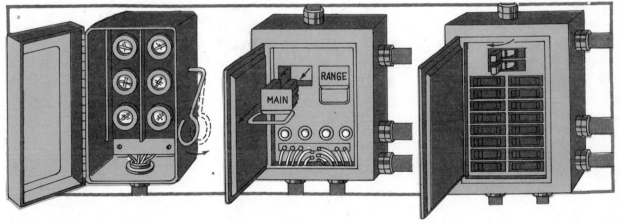
Main switch types.

Simple Electrical Repairs

ly wired with No. 14 or No. 12 wire and are intended to be protected with fuses rated 15 or 20 amperes, respectively. The 20-ampere circuits are used in kitchen, breakfast-room, and laundry-appliance circuits. The 15-ampere fuse or circuit breaker protects the usual lighting circuits. Appliances that draw heavy currents should not be connected to lighting circuits because their wires are not designed to carry heavy loads. Electric ranges and water heaters are usually installed on separate higher-voltage circuits where the rating of the fuses corresponds to the rating of the devices. Only approved fuses should be used.

Before replacing a fuse, open the switch controlling the circuit affected or the main switch, to avoid possible shock. Fuses should be replaced by those of the same rating, as fuses of higher capacity will not protect the wiring from overheating, thus defeating the safety purpose for which they were intended. The main switch need not be disconnected when resetting a circuit breaker; flip the switch. If cartridge fuses blow, call the utility company; the problem may be major.

APPLIANCE CORDS AND PLUGS

Wear and damage to appliance cords and plugs are common occurrences in the home, usually as the result of abuse rather than age. An appliance is often disconnected with a yank on the cord instead of a tug on the plug. Wires may be routed under rugs where there is much foot traffic, or around hot radiators. Or they may be casually stapled to woodwork. These are the most common causes of short circuits and nasty shocks.

You should inspect appliance cords regularly for signs of frayed, cracked, or broken insulation, and check plugs for damaged prongs and loose terminal connections. When any of these conditions exist, the cord or plug must be replaced.

It is important that the replacement match the appliance to which it is being fitted. Lamps, radios, televisions, and other low-power devices can use standard light-weight cord and any standard rubber or plastic replacement plug. Heavy-duty braided or rubber cord should be used for vacuum cleaners, power tools, outdoor extension lamps, and large appliances. Toasters, irons, hot plates, and any heating appliance should have special heat-resistant cord—any other type will invite trouble.

The most common type of plug has terminal screws to which the cord wires are attached. Yanking a cord to remove the plug from the outlet usually results in the fraying or cracking of the insulation just behind the plug or its terminal connections coming loose. If the plug and cord look intact otherwise, and prongs and insulation are in good condition, simply disconnect the cord at the terminals and pull it through the plug until you reach insulation that is intact.

Cut the cord at this point, then separate the two wires to a length of about 1½ inches. With a sharp knife, strip ½ inch of insulation from each end, taking care not to cut through the wire. Twist the wire ends so there are no loose strands. Loop each wire

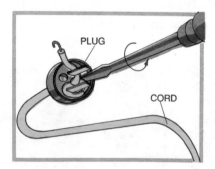

Disconnect cord from terminals.

Strip off insulation.

Simple Electrical Repairs

Twist strands of wire (far left).

Wrap around terminals (left).

around a prong and wrap the wire around the terminal screws in the same direction the screw will be tightened.

Some plugs are sealed and have the cord wires connected directly to the prongs. In this case you must cut off the plug and install a new one.

For heavy-duty plugs and cords with braided or heavy rubber insulation, cut about 3 inches off the cord's outer insulating material but leave the inside insulation for the individual wires intact. Then tie the two ends into an "Underwriters' knot," which will fit snugly into the base of the plug. This is designed to prevent wires from pulling loose from the terminals when subjected to sudden tugs, as they would be with any heavy-duty appliance that has to be moved around. Once the knot has been made and tested for fit, strip ½ inch of insulation from the wire ends and connect as described above. It is a good idea to use the Underwriters' knot on any appliance that has a plug large enough to accommodate the knot.

With light-duty cord, simple snap-on plugs may be used. These are fitted firmly over the end of the unstripped cord; movable prongs pierce the insulation to make contact with the wire, as well as to provide a firm grip.

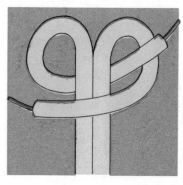 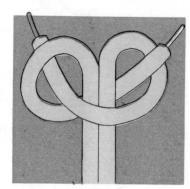

Underwriters' knot.

Snap-on plug.

LAMP REPAIRS

When a lamp fails to light and the trouble is not with the bulb or a short in the wall circuit, the cause is either the plug, the lamp

wire, or the socket. First check the plug for good contact. If it fits loosely in the wall outlet, try bending the prongs apart a bit. If the lamp does not light, check for loose wires at the plug terminals. If the plug prongs are loose or if the plug looks in any way doubtful, replace the plug, as described previously.

Sockets don't often need replacement, but if they incorporate a switching device the switch may wear with use, and the entire socket must be replaced. Unplug the lamp and remove the bulb. The socket assembly is in two major parts, a cap fixed to the lamp base and a brass shell that snaps

Press to snap off shell.

Disconnect wires.

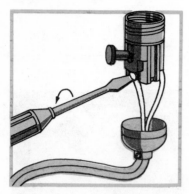

PRESS

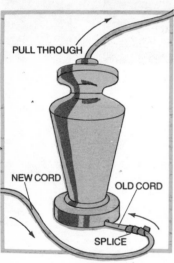

PULL THROUGH

NEW CORD

OLD CORD

SPLICE

Using old cord to bring new
cord through lamp.

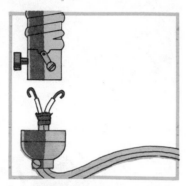

Replace switch assembly.

connect the old cord at the lamp socket and
pull gently until the new cord emerges
through the fixed socket cap. Connect to
the socket or switch and replace the shell.
Then attach a new plug.

DOORBELLS AND CHIMES

When a bell or chime refuses to sound,
the first thing you should check is the push-
button. Remove the button cover and inspect for loose connections. If all are tight,
either bridge the button terminals with a
piece of wire or paper clip or disconnect the
wires and touch the bare ends together.
(The voltage across the terminals is minimal, so do not worry about shocks.)

If the bell sounds, the trouble is in the
button and it should be replaced. If it does
not sound, you should check the power
supply, a transformer usually wired alongside or near the main fuse box. The output
terminals of the transformer can be bridged
with a screwdriver. (Never touch input terminals—these are wired to the house

into that. Inside are a combined switch and
socket plus a cardboard or fiber liner that
protects against short circuits. Snap off the
shell by pressing at the point indicated at
the base of the shell, then remove it and the
liner to gain access to the switch. Disconnect the wires and remove the switch. The
cap can be left in place and the other parts
replaced as an assembly, available in any
hardware outlet.

It is often difficult, if not downright impossible, to thread a new cord into a lamp
by probing, particularly on tall floor units.
A simple solution is to cut or disconnect the
plug of the old wire and attach one end of
the new wire to that. Make the temporary
splice as secure and slim as possible. Dis-

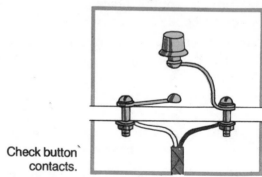

Check button
contacts.

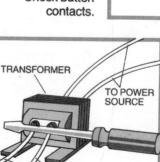

TRANSFORMER

TO POWER
SOURCE

TO BELL

Check transformer.

Simple Electrical Repairs

110-120 volt current and can give a severe shock.) If sparks appear, power is coming through and you should look elsewhere.

If voltage is not coming through the transformer, either the fuse to the circuit is blown or the transformer has burned out.

If there is power, the next thing you should check is the chime or bell. Remove the cover or housing and look for dirty or sticking parts and broken connections. Sand contact points if they appear pitted or corroded. With chimes, check for free operation of the small rods that move to strike the chime bars. Clean as required.

■When bell or chimes, pushbuttons, and power supply check out and all visible connections are tight, the trouble is in the wiring. Repair in this case is best left to the electrician.

Sand contact points on bell.

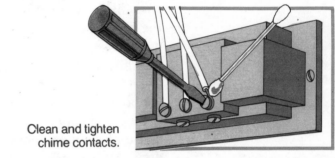

Clean and tighten chime contacts.

Simple Electrical Repairs

14

Storm Damage

HOMES AND FURNISHINGS damaged by flooding, windstorm, or tornado need prompt clean-up action. Before entering a damaged building, be sure that it is not about to collapse. Turn off gas at the meter or tank and let the house air for several minutes to remove foul odors or escaped gas. Do not smoke or use open flame until you are sure that it is safe to do so. Do not turn on an electrical system; it may have become short-circuited. After dark, use a flashlight rather than a lantern to avoid igniting escaped gas. Watch out for holes in the floor or loose boards with exposed nails.

Flooding may have swollen doors tight. When entrance must be forced because of swollen doors, accumulated mud, or bulged floors, enter by a window or other opening. Lift the pins from door hinges with a screwdriver and hammer. Be sure the door is unlocked and then carefully push it in from the outside to avoid further damage.

Loose, wet ceiling plaster is heavy and dangerous. Knock down hanging plaster before moving around in the house, and watch for loose plaster as the structure dries out.

Use even greater caution if damage resulted solely from high winds. Tornadoes may demolish some buildings and move others almost intact some distance from their foundations. Before entering or cleaning a tornado-damaged building be sure that walls, ceiling, and roof are in place and that the structure rests firmly on the foundation. Look out for broken glass and broken power lines.

Remove the window sash.

Remove the molding holding the window.

DRYING AND CLEANING

Open doors and windows to admit air that is essential to dry the house. To open swollen windows, remove the small strip that holds the lower sash. Carefully use a chisel to avoid marring woodwork. Force the sash up slightly and remove from frame by pushing it from the outside into the hands of a helper. Be careful not to break the glass.

Examine foundations and basement walls for signs of undermining. If settling or cracking has occurred, it may be necessary to dig down to the footings and reinforce or replace settled sections. Undermined footings should be reinforced with masonry or concrete, never with earth or gravel. Tilted or settled piers may need replacing. If the building is out of plumb or the floors have settled or bulged, make sure that the foundation is sound and that sills, girders, and joists are free from termite damage before renovating. If the building must be moved, call in expert help unless the structure is a simple one.

Drain and clean basements as soon as the building is safe. Pump or bail the water from the cellar and shovel out the mud while it is moist so that basement floors can dry. Remove mud from the furnace, flues, and smoke pipe.

Don't rush to move in. The house must be clean and dry before it is habitable. Drain pools of water from the premises; remove and burn or bury driftwood, rubbish, and decaying vegetation. If the house or porches rest on open foundations, be sure the structure will not collapse before removing debris from underneath.

CHECKING THE ELECTRICAL SYSTEM

Do not turn on lights or appliances until an electrician has checked the electrical system for short circuits. Wear rubber-soled shoes or boots and rubber gloves. Turn off the main switch while standing on a dry board. Use a piece of rubber, plastic, or dry wood when touching the metal handle of the switch box. Water in conduits or connection boxes and dampness on exposed wires can cause short circuits and fires. Under these conditions, a person replacing fuses may even be electrocuted, especially if standing on a wet surface.

If a sump pump is available and needed, remove all fuses except the main fuses and

Storm Damage

the one controlling the sump pump. Carefully turn on the main switch to see if the pump operates. If not, call an electrician.

ELECTRIC MOTORS

Small electric motors may be dried in an oven at not more than 150 degrees F. If you are accustomed to working with electric motors, test them after six or eight hours of drying. If there is still evidence of grounding or short-circuiting, return them to the oven for two to four hours before testing again. If you are not accustomed to working with electric motors, do not risk electric shock; have the motors tested by a technical expert.

MECHANICAL HOUSEHOLD EQUIPMENT

A competent technician should examine pump motors, refrigerators, freezers, ranges, washing machines, vacuum cleaners, food mixers, and other household equipment. They may be ruined if they are not clean, dry, and free-running before the current is turned on.

Washing machines should be thoroughly cleaned before use. Open the gear housings and clean the shafts and gears with kerosene. Wipe all parts with a clean cloth, but do not force any dirt into the bearings. Even fine grit can cause wear of moving parts. Wipe metal surfaces with a rag dampened with kerosene to remove rust and dirt stains. Coat them thinly with petrolatum or machine oil to prevent further rusting. Before using, oil the bearings and, using a soft cloth, dry surfaces exposed to hands or clothing.

The cooling systems and motors of modern refrigerators are hermetically sealed. Their construction should rule out damage

Remove mud from chimney flue.

Repair chimney mortar.

by immersion in water. In older refrigerators, the cooling unit is accessible and should be cleaned and examined.

For safety, technicians should inspect household machines and make repairs, especially of motors and power-driven appliances. It may be practical to arrange cooperative employment of electricians to collect and recondition motors in a shop.

CHECKING THE HEATING SYSTEM

Before starting a fire in a hot-air heating plant, examine the inside of the heater and wash sediment from the flues with a hose or a swab on a long stick. Often, flues can be reached through a clean-out door above the fire door. Or you may have to remove the smoke pipe and do the cleaning from that end. If the heater is jacketed, clean out all mud between the inside and outside casings, removing the outer casing if necessary. If flues or passages are choked with mud, a boiler may burst when a fire is started. Take the smoke pipe out of the chimney and reach through the thimble to remove mud from the lower part of the chimney flue so that there will be a draft for the fire. An inadequate draft may fill the house with smoke or dangerous carbon monoxide.

■ In oil-burning systems, have the storage tank examined by an experienced inspector to make sure that seams have not opened, permitting dirt or water to enter. The burner should be dismantled and all parts cleaned in kerosene and wiped dry. The air blower and fuel pump should be examined. Gear housings should be removed and the gears thoroughly cleaned with kerosene. Any remaining grit will cause undue wear. Make sure you burn kerosene-soaked rags out-of-doors. Do not wash them in an automatic washer; this may cause an explosion.

Chimneys subjected to wind or water action should be inspected promptly. Defective chimneys can cause fires and carbon monoxide gas poisoning. Disintegrated mortar in the joints between bricks should be replaced with masonry cement. If the chimney has settled badly or broken where it passes through floors or roof, it may need rebuilding. If the chimney has tilted, see if the footing has been undermined.

WATER SUPPLY AND SANITARY SYSTEMS

If your water comes from a well, cistern, or spring, ask your local health department to check it for safety and to tell you how to keep it safe. If water from a surface source must be used, take the supply from a point upstream from any inhabited area, dipping from below the surface. Avoid sources with odors, dark color, or floating material.

In an emergency, limited amounts of water may be obtained by draining a hot water tank or by melting ice cubes.

There are two general methods for disinfecting small quantities of water: boiling and chemical treatment. Boiling is the most positive way to make water bacterially safe. Certain chemicals, if applied with care, will free most waters of harmful or pathogenic organisms.

Storm Damage

The effectiveness of the disinfectant method is reduced in turbid or discolored water. First, filter such water through clean cloths or allow it to settle; draw off the clear water to be disinfected and store it in clean, tightly covered, noncorrodible containers.

A 10-minute boiling will kill any disease-causing bacteria present. The flat taste of boiled water can be improved by pouring it back and forth from one container to another, by allowing it to stand for a few hours, or by adding a small pinch of salt for each quart of water boiled.

When boiling is not practical, chlorine or iodine are commonly added to the water for disinfecting. A chlorine solution may be prepared from one of three products:

1. Common household bleach, by following the instructions on the label, or by finding the percentage of available chlorine on the label and using this table:

Available Chlorine* (percent)	Drops per quart of clear water**
1	10
4–6	2
7–10	1

*If strength is unknown, add 10 drops per quart to purify.

**Double amount for turbid or colored water.

Mix the treated water thoroughly and allow it to stand for 30 minutes. If the water does not have a slight chlorine odor, repeat the dosage and allow it to stand for an additional 15 minutes. The treated water may be made more palatable by allowing it to stand for several hours or by pouring it between two clean containers.

2. Granular calcium hypochlorite, in a ratio of 1 heaping teaspoon (¼ ounce) to 2 gallons of water, makes a chlorine solution that will disinfect water. Add 1 part of the solution to 100 parts of water or, roughly, 1 pint to each 12.5 gallons.

3. Chlorine tablets in commercially prepared form may be obtained from drugstores or sporting-goods stores. If there are no instructions on the package, use one tablet to each quart of water.

Either tincture of iodine or iodine tablets may be used to purify water. Add five drops of 2 percent United States Pharmacopeia (USP) tincture of iodine to each quart of clear water. For turbid water, add 10 drops and allow the solution to stand for at least 30 minutes.

Use commercially prepared iodine tablets according to directions or add one tablet for each quart of water. All water used for beverages, cooking, or brushing the teeth should be properly disinfected.

Test plumbing and basement drains by pouring in a bucket of water. If the water does not run out, remove the clean-out plug from the trap (a U-, P-, or S-shaped pipe found under most fixtures) and rake out mud and debris with a wire. Toilet and drain traps can be cleaned with water and a swab, or by rodding with a plumber's "snake" or a wire.

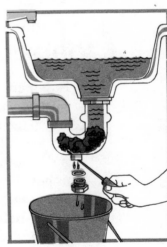

Remove clean-out plug, clean trap.

Clean toilet trap with auger.

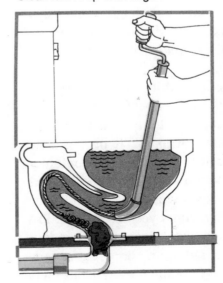

Storm Damage

▲It may be necessary to disassemble and clean check valves and other backflow preventers. In wind-damaged houses all exposed pipes should be checked for intact connections before water is turned on.

Swamped sanitary disposal installations imperil health. The domestic water supply is almost sure to become contaminated. Septic tanks, cesspools, pits, and leaching systems must be put in service at once. Local or state health departments or the United States Public Health Service can provide useful advice on cleaning, repairing, or relocating installations.

Local or state health departments have responsibility for enforcing health measures and a trained staff to help you. Problems relating to water purity, waste disposal, or rodent control should be referred to them. Also, they can help with many insect problems that are often storm-related.

Some garbage can be burned. Garbage that will not burn should be buried in a pit 4 or 5 feet deep and covered with at least 18 inches of soil. Garbage fed to pets or other animals should be cooked to prevent spread of disease.

ODORS

Basement odors, although unpleasant, are usually harmless. If ventilation does not remove them, sprinkle bleaching powder (chlorine of lime) on the floor, allow it to remain until the floor dries, and sweep it up. This powder is a good disinfectant.

But bleaching powder is caustic and poisonous. Before sprinkling it on the basement floor, read the label on the container. Follow instructions and heed precautions. Keep bleaching powder out of children's reach and away from eyes and mouth. Provide ventilation with doors and windows open while sprinkling the floor. Store powder in a closed container away from mois-

ture. Dispose of empty containers in a tightly covered refuse can.

Dry lump charcoal exposed in open containers may absorb odors from the air in enclosed spaces. But charcoal is highly combustible when moist or wet, so guard against spontaneous combustion and fire. Expose it in tin cans or other hard metal, open containers away from flammable liquids and gases, cloth, coal, firewood, or other readily combustible materials. Store charcoal in a well-ventilated place where it will be dry and clean.

FLOORS, WOODWORK, DOORS, WALLS

After the wet mud has been removed, floors may be badly buckled. Do not attempt repairs until they are fully dry. Start the heating plant as soon as it will operate, but don't use so much heat that the house becomes steamy. Dry wood as fast as you can without aggravating shrinkage or deformation. Open windows and doors wide for good ventilation, but maintain a temperature of at least 50 to 60 degrees F.

When the house is dry, some of the buckled flooring may be drawn back into place with nails. Some humps may be removed by planing or sanding. Heavily planed floors may never look well uncovered, but a smooth old floor can serve as a base for new flooring. If smooth, an old floor may be covered with a resilient, smooth surface floor covering. If the damage is too severe, new flooring may be necessary. If only the surface finish is damaged, the floor may be refinished.

Before the house is dried out, scrub woodwork with a stiff brush, plenty of water, and a detergent to remove mud and silt from corners and cracks.

Quickly drain accumulated water from partitions and exterior walls so that insula-

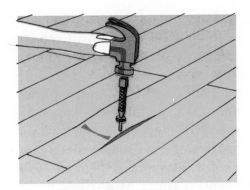

Nail down buckled floorboards.

Remove baseboard, drill holes for drainage.

Mildewed floors, woodwork, and other wooden areas may be scrubbed with a mild alkali, such as washing soda or trisodium phosphate (4 to 6 tablespoons to a gallon of water). Paint stores and grocery stores sell these products under various trade names. Rinse well with clear water and allow the wood to dry thoroughly. Then apply a mildew-resistant paint. Mildew-resistant paint contains fungicide and should not be used on playpens, cribs, or toys.

If mold has grown into the wood under paint or varnish, scrub with an abrasive cleaner, then wash with a solution containing 4 to 6 tablespoons of trisodium phosphate and 1 cup of household chlorine bleach to a gallon of water. Finally, rinse the wood well with clear water. Dry thoroughly and apply a wood preservative before repainting.

Locks should be taken apart, wiped with kerosene, and oiled. If you cannot remove them, squirt in a little machine oil through the bolt opening or the keyhole, and work the knobs to distribute the oil. Otherwise, the springs and metal casing will soon rust and need replacing. Do not use so much oil that it drips onto the woodwork and makes later painting difficult. Cleaning and oiling usually puts hinges in order.

tion and structural members can dry. Remove the baseboards and drill holes between the studs a few inches above the floor. After the insulation and frames have dried, replace the baseboards.

For a final, thorough washing of floors, use your preferred cleaning product—nonsudsing is best. Put off necessary refinishing until moisture has dried from the framing, from between walls and floors, and from the back of the trim, even though this may take months. Consult an experienced painter about refinishing. If you do the work yourself, carefully follow instructions on cans of standard brands of paints and varnishes for household use.

Use heat and ventilation to thoroughly dry mildewed wood. Badly infected wood may need to be replaced, preferably with wood that has been treated against mildew or that is naturally decay-resistant.

Squirt oil in and work lock.

Clean and oil hinges.

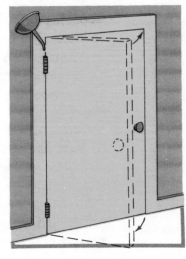

Storm Damage

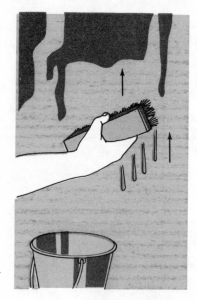

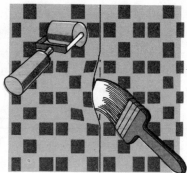

Repaste loose
wallpaper edges.

Wash walls from bottom up.

Allow the plaster to dry thoroughly before washing it. Brush off any loose surface dirt. Wash painted walls with water and mild soap or any commercial cleanser. (Professional renovators usually prefer nonsudsing products.) Use two sponges and two buckets, one for the cleaning solution and another for clear rinsing water. Start washing the wall at the bottom and work up, so that water will not run down and streak a soiled area. Water running down over a clean area can be wiped off without damage. Wash an area that you can easily reach without changing position; rinse it immediately. Then wash the next area, overlapping the first, and proceed until the wall is finished. Ceilings should be done last. Badly stained walls will need redecorating.

After walls have been cleaned and before wallpaper is replaced, paint or thoroughly spray the walls with a quaternary disinfectant, available from janitor- or dairy-supply outlets. Add 2 tablespoons of disinfectant to 2 gallons of water. This prevents mildew and may be applied on both painted walls and washable wallpapers.

Often, wallpaper is so discolored and brittle from soaking that it must be removed and the walls repapered. If the pa-

per remained dry but has been loosened by dampness, it may be possible to repaste loosened edges or sections. Use commercial wallpaper paste.

Clean wallpaper with a commercial puttylike cleaner. Some wallpapers are washable. Before washing, test a small inconspicuous spot using mild soap or detergent. Proceed as for washing a painted wall. Squeeze as much water as possible out of the cleaning and rinsing sponges and work quickly so that paper does not become soaked.

Grease spots may be removed from wallpaper with a paste made of dry-cleaning fluid with cornstarch or talcum. Allow to dry and brush off, repeating if necessary. Fumes from all dry-cleaning solvents are toxic and some are flammable. Use only with adequate ventilation, and read the precautions on the label.

SALVAGING FURNITURE

Move wooden furniture outdoors and take out as many drawers, slides, or other working parts as possible. Do not force

Remove back of furniture
to push out drawers.

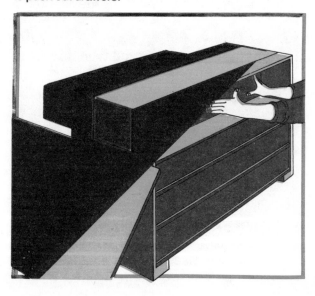

Storm Damage

stuck drawers with a screwdriver or chisel from the front. Remove the back, by cutting out if necessary, and push out the drawers. Clean away all mud and dirt, using a hose stream if necessary. Take the furniture indoors and store it where it will dry slowly. Do not leave furniture in the sun, as it will warp and twist out of shape.

▲ Some furniture, especially that made of solid wood, may be salvaged by regluing. Gluing usually requires the use of a variety of clamps. First, decide if you wish to invest in this equipment and have the time and skill to do the work. If not, consult a cabinetmaker.

■ Repairing veneered furniture is difficult and requires so many different types of tools that it is not practical to try at home. A cabinetmaker should do this job. Otherwise, the furniture may be returned to the factory for repair by the store where it was purchased. If insurance allows part value on flood-damaged furniture, it may be financially wise to apply the allowance on new articles rather than to pay for repairs to damaged items.

Furniture that has not been submerged may have developed white spots or a whitish film or cloudiness from dampness. If the whole surface is affected, try rubbing with a cloth and turpentine or camphorated oil; wipe dry at once and polish with wax or furniture polish. If color is not restored, dip 3/0 steel wool in oil (boiled, linseed, olive, mineral, lemon) and rub lightly with the grain of the wood. Wipe with a soft cloth and rewax. For deep spots, use a drop or two of ammonia on a damp cloth. Rub at once with a dry cloth, then polish. Cigarette ashes rubbed in with the fingertips are often effective in removing white spots. If all efforts to remove white blemishes fail, refinishing may be necessary.

Brush outer coverings of upholstered articles, mattresses, rugs, and carpets to remove loose mold. Do this outdoors to avoid scattering mildew spores in the house. Run a vacuum cleaner attachment over the surface. Dry the article with an electric heater, a fan, or any convenient method. Sun and air the article to prevent mold growth.

If mildew remains, sponge upholstery or mattresses lightly with thick suds of soap or detergent; wipe with a clean, damp cloth. Use little water on the fabric to avoid soaking the padding.

Another method for upholstered furniture requires wiping with a cloth wrung out of diluted alcohol (1 cup denatured alcohol to 1 cup water). Dry the article thoroughly.

With a low-pressure spray containing a fungicide, moisten mildewed surfaces thoroughly. Aerosol spraying is not effective in controlling fungi.

Be careful not to inhale mist from a spray or use near flame. Follow all precautions on the label.

In closed areas, vapors of paradichlorobenzene or paraformaldehyde will stop mold growth. If molds have grown into the article, it should be dried and fumigated by a dry-cleaning or storage company. Fumigation will kill existing mold but will not protect the article in the future.

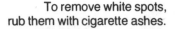
To remove white spots, rub them with cigarette ashes.

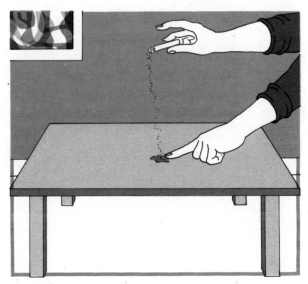

Storm Damage

Badly damaged upholstered furniture that has been submerged may need re-stuffing. Springs may need to be cleaned and oiled, and the frame may need cleaning. If you are not skilled in this work, consult a cabinetmaker or upholsterer.

Clean metal at once, especially iron. Wipe rust from iron with a kerosene-soaked cloth. Coat iron hardware lightly with petrolatum or machine oil to prevent further rusting. Use stove polish on ironwork. Wash cooking utensils thoroughly with soapy water to remove kerosene, then rub with unsalted cooking oil and heat slowly to permit oil to soak the pores of the metal for rust-resistance.

Stainless steel, nickel-copper alloy, or metals plated with nickel or chromium need only thorough washing and polishing with a fine-powdered cleanser. If the plating is broken, exposing the base metal to rust, wipe with kerosene, wash and dry the surface, then wax for rust-resistance.

Wash aluminum thoroughly and scour unpolished surfaces with soap-filled metal scouring pads. Polished or plated surfaces of aluminum should be wiped with silver polish or fine cleaning powder.

To brighten darkened insides of aluminum pans, fill with water and add ¼ cup of vinegar or 1 tablespoon of cream of tartar for each quart of water. Boil for 10 to 15 minutes, then scour with a soap-filled pad. If utensils have been submerged in flood water and are darkened both inside and out, prepare one of these acid solutions in a large container and immerse them; then proceed with the treatment described.

Copper and brass can be polished with a special polish or with salt sprinkled on a piece of lemon or on a cloth saturated with vinegar. Wash utensils after treatment.

Storm Damage

15

Emergency!

NOT EVERY HOUSEHOLD emergency poses a hazard to life, limb, and property, but when the house is plunged into darkness or the toilet bowl is overflowing and water is cascading down the stairs, it seems serious enough—and it is. You should always plan for the worst, and then hope that your planning is for naught. But if you should be called upon to administer "first aid" to a household malady, either while waiting for a repairman to wend his way to your home or as a stopgap until you can make permanent repairs yourself, it is best to "Be Prepared."

One of the basic preparations is to have an emergency toolbox ready to be whisked to the scene of the problem. For the tools you should have on hand, see PAGES 114-122. In addition, you should have a good flashlight—preferably several of them placed in strategic spots throughout the house. It's a good idea to check periodically to make sure that they are still where they are supposed to be, and that the children have not borrowed them for a backyard camping trip or to play midnight tag. Check also to make sure that they (the flashlights) are in working order. When an emergency does occur, dead batteries are an aggravation you really don't need.

Like a well-run ship, the well-run home should be ready to deal with emergencies. All family members should be acquainted with certain procedures and fixtures, such as shut-off valves and circuit breakers. When (if) something does go wrong, you can't expect to head for the family library and look for this book to tell you what to do. This is one chapter you should study in advance and be ready to put into practice as soon as it's needed. Quick action in an emergency can prevent costly damage to materials, furnishings, and equipment—and, in some situations, to the family members themselves.

● PLUMBING EMERGENCIES

Here are the most common emergencies that may occur and the action to take. The name, address, and phone number of a plumber who offers 24-hour service should be posted in a conspicuous place near your telephone.

Burst pipe or tank—Immediately cut off

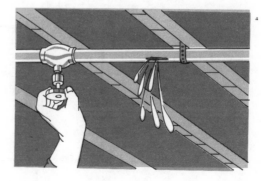

Close shutoff valve nearest leak.

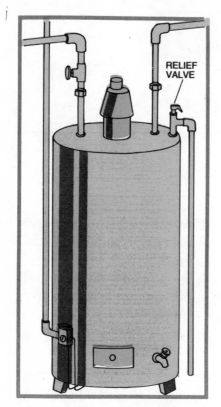

Check pressure relief
valve to find out whether
it is operative.

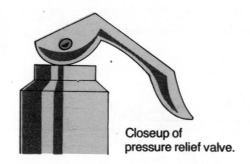

Closeup of
pressure relief valve.

Shutting down the plumbing system:
1. Turn off electricity or gas to heating units.
2. Close main valve.
3. Open faucets, flush toilets on top floor.
4. Open faucets, flush toilets on lower floors.
5. Open drain valves on heaters, etc.
6. Pour antifreeze into toilets, drains.

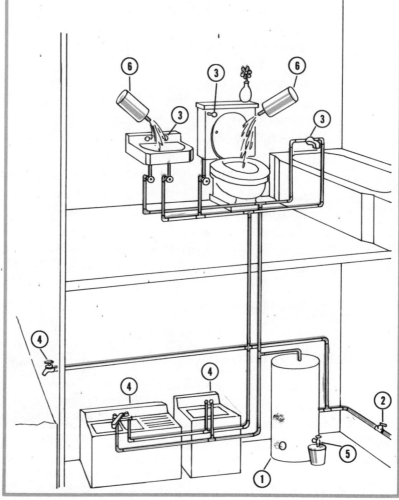

Emergency!

the flow of water by closing the shutoff valve nearest to the break. Then arrange for repair.

Toilet overflow—Do not use toilet until it is back in working order. Check for and remove stoppage in bowl outlet, or in drain line from closet to sewer or septic tank. If stoppage is due to root entry into pipe, repair of pipe at that point is recommended.

Rumbling noise in hot-water tank—This is probably a sign of overheating, which could lead to the development of explosive pressure. (Another indication of overheating is hot water backing up in the cold-water supply pipe.) Cut off the burner immediately. Be sure that the pressure-relief valve is operative. Then check (with a thermometer) the temperature of the water at the nearest outlet. If above that for which the gauge is set, check the thermostat that controls the burner cutoff. If you cannot correct the trouble, call a plumber.

Cold house—If the heating system fails (or if you close the house and turn off the heat) when there is a chance of sub-freezing weather, completely drain the plumbing system. A drain valve is usually provided for this purpose at the low point of the supply piping. A pump, storage tank, hot-water tank, toilet tank, water-treatment apparatus, and other water-system appliances or accessories should also be drained. Put antifreeze in all fixture and drain traps.

Hot-water and steam heating systems should also be drained when the house temperature may drop below freezing.

FURNACE FAILURE

When you find yourself without heat, first check the main switch. It may have been accidentally turned off (not an uncommon occurrence when it is located along a basement stairway where it may be brushed against by a person carrying a load of laun-

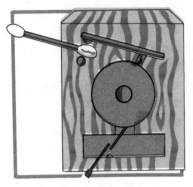
Check thermostat for dust.

Check gas valve.

dry or whatever into the basement). Also check for a blown fuse or tripped circuit breaker.

Take a look at the thermostat to see whether it has been turned down. Often, the obvious will be the cause of the problem. Remove the thermostat cover and inspect the workings for dirt or dust that may be clogging the mechanism.

Next check the fuel supply. If you have oil heat, look at the gauge atop the storage tank. If it is near the "Empty" mark, you can suspect that this is the cause of your chilly discomfort. Call for a refill. With gas heat, make sure that an intake valve has not inadvertently been shut off.

GAS ODOR

When you detect the odor of gas, get everybody out of the house—fast! Don't tarry, but if there is time, turn the furnace thermostat all the way down so that the burner doesn't come on, possibly setting off an explosion. Needless to say, don't strike a match or light up a smoke to calm your nerves. Keep everyone at a distance and call the local gas company immediately, preferably from a neighbor's phone. If this is not possible, and the gas odor is not too strong, hold a handkerchief over your nose and reenter the house to call the utility—or just dial the operator and explain your problem. Then get back outside, and don't go into the house again until the servicemen have come and repaired the leak. Above all, don't take chances!

FIRE

Fire is the dread nightmare of most homeowners and apartment dwellers, and it deserves to be. But prompt and proper action upon the discovery of a household fire can minimize the danger, at least to the inhabitants. Unfortunately, all too often a homeowner will attempt to battle a "small" blaze himself, only to lose precious minutes and have it develop into a total holocaust.

Train all members of your family to shout "Fire!" as loudly as possible at the first sign of flames or smell of smoke. They should, of course, be warned against deliberate false alarms (crying "Wolf!"), but an accidental false alarm is better than no alarm at all. Everyone in the house should be aroused and flee. Never linger to save possessions—they are not worth a life!

Next (not before) call the fire depart-

ment. As mentioned above, it is best to do this from a neighbor's house. In most cases, you need simply dial the operator. Be sure to clearly state your full address.

If the fire is confined to a small area and you have a safe and sure exit available, you can reenter the house and use an extinguisher or water to fight the blaze until the firemen arrive. But be certain you know what you are doing. Don't, to use an obvious example, throw water on a grease fire—it will only spread the flames. If there is any question of your own safety, do not try to fight the fire yourself. Homes are replaceable (and usually insured). People may be insured, but they are not replaceable.

Once again, the key to avoiding disaster is prevention. Make sure that every member of the family knows what to do in case of fire. Every room should have an alternate escape route; rooms on upper floors should have windows that are easily opened. If there are not lower roofs onto which occupants can jump, provide rope ladders or similar means of descent, and make sure that children are well acquainted with their use.

You will probably never have to put these precautions into practice. But if you do, lives will be saved.

Rope ladder for upper stories is helpful.

part **3** **EXTERIOR HOME REPAIRS**

Contents

1. THE TOOLBOX 195
2. ROOFS, GUTTERS, DOWNSPOUTS 205
3. EXTERIOR WALLS 217
4. PROPER PAINTING PRACTICES 225
5. DOORS AND WINDOWS 238
6. PORCHES 249
7. DRIVEWAYS AND SIDEWALKS 253
8. PATIO REPAIRS 266
9. POOL CARE 272
10. STORM! 276
11. IF YOU'RE BUYING 279

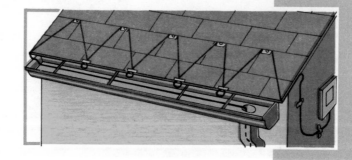

1

The Toolbox

MOST OF THE tools you'll need for working on your home's exterior are the basics with which you are probably familiar. You may already have some or all of them. But if all you have in your toolbox are a cheap hammer and screwdriver, be prepared to accumulate a few more instruments—and good ones, this time.

When you inhabit a furnished room or an apartment, your tool needs are few. But when you (and the bank) own your home, you will find that you need a small arsenal of basic tools to take care of the place. You should start picking up some of them as soon as you sign on the dotted line, watching for bargains and sales (not cheap models, but markdowns of good ones).

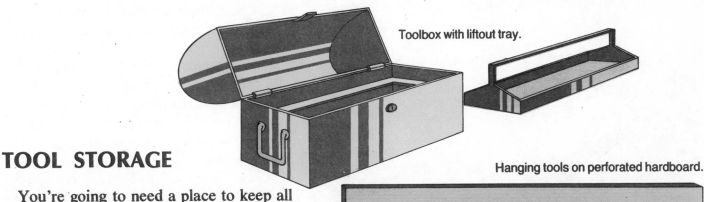

Toolbox with liftout tray.

TOOL STORAGE

You're going to need a place to keep all those shiny new tools. The kitchen "junk" drawer might be okay to start with, but you'll soon find that the screwdriver is hopelessly entangled with string when you want it most. One of the first things you should do in your new home is to make some sort of plan for tool storage. It may be only a toolbox—at first, anyway—but it should be separate, so that you know where the tools are when you need them quickly.

●A good start toward tool storage is a piece of perforated hardboard (popularly

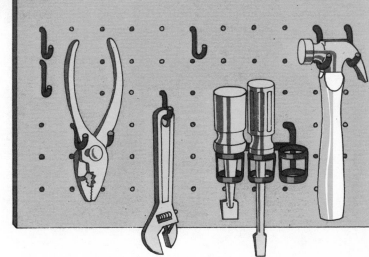

Hanging tools on perforated hardboard.

known as Pegboard, a trade name). When you buy the board, get one of the kits that contain hardware for attaching it to the wall, as well as the hooks, hangers, and assorted accessories for accommodating various tools. Hang it in the basement or garage. Later on, you'll probably want a workbench, so make sure there is room for one underneath your storage wall.

BUYING TOOLS

Does a devoted fisherman buy a cheap rod and reel? Does a dentist buy a bargain-basement drill? Of course not. The same attitude should apply to any tool. The dollar you save on a supermarket or drugstore tool can cost you many times that in time and trouble, so don't buy it. Cheap tools also often chip, break, or collapse, causing expensive damage and even injury.

Always buy quality merchandise. A good hammer is precisely tooled, properly weighted, and has maximum strength so

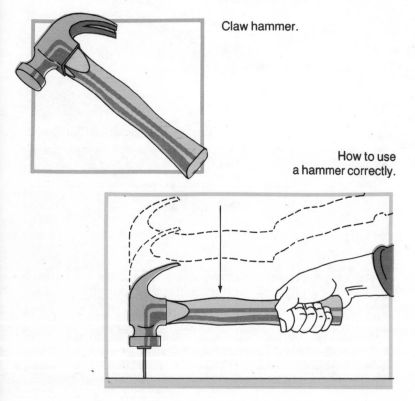

Claw hammer.

How to use a hammer correctly.

that it will drive a nail straight, true, and fast. A cheap hammer will slip off the nail, drive it crookedly, and require more strokes. Often, the head is poorly attached so that it might fly off at a crucial time and possibly even become a lethal missile. It just isn't worth it. The same applies to all tools.

When you shop, look for tools that are stamped with the manufacturer's name or symbol. Many reputable manufacturers have generous warranties, some for life! Pick up the tool and simulate its use. Does it have a tough and sturdy feel? Is the metal smooth and polished? Anything that gets rugged duty, such as a wrench or hammerhead, should be drop-forged. If there are moving parts, do they work freely and easily without wiggle or play?

CLAW HAMMER

There are many kinds of hammers: ball peen for metalwork, tack for upholstery, mason's for brickwork, to name just a few. What most laymen mean by a "hammer" is the common claw, or nail, hammer. The claw hammer is the basic hammer for jobs like whacking wood into place, but it is designed primarily for driving in or pulling out nails. The best claw hammer for general use has a 16-ounce head that is firmly attached to a wood handle, either with a solid wedge and/or glue on top, or forged in a single piece with the handle which is then covered with rubber, plastic, or leather for a firm grip. A good one costs about $8.

● To use a hammer correctly, grip it at or near the end of the handle and swing it from your shoulder. You may miss the nail at first, but keep trying (on scrap wood) until you get the "swing" of it. It's well worth the practice. An experienced carpenter can drive in large spikes this way with just a couple of blows.

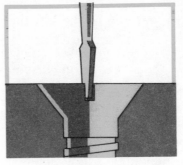

Slot screwdriver.

Phillips-head screwdriver.

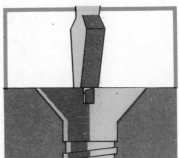

Wrong-size screwdrivers:

Blade too thin for slot (above).

Blade too thick for slot (above right).

Blade too wide for slot (right).

SCREWDRIVERS

One screwdriver is not really enough for the do-it-yourselfer's toolbox. To start with, you should have the most common one, with a flat-tipped, wedge-shaped blade ¼ inch wide and about 6 inches long. This model fits the most frequently used sizes of slotted screws, but you shouldn't use it for larger or very tiny sizes. Either the blade will be too small and slip around, or it will be too big and won't fit into the slot. Sometimes the blade will fit the slot but be wider than the screw and damage the surrounding surface. So it's best to have one with a narrow blade. For heavier work, use a screwdriver with a longer shank.

A Phillips screwdriver has an X-shaped end and is used for cross-slotted screws. One of these will do for a start, the most useful being the #2, which has a shank about 4 inches long. Buy others as needed.

A good screwdriver has a tough, tempered-steel blade and a fluted handle, usually plastic. The handle should be smooth and gently rounded at the hand. The tip of the blade is usually polished, but not necessarily the shank.

● A screwdriver is simple to use once the screw is started. Many novices try to use the screwdriver without starting the hole first. This may sometimes work in soft wood but is virtually impossible in hard wood. Use an awl, a nail, or a tool specifically designed for starting screws. Many old-timers start the screw by banging it in

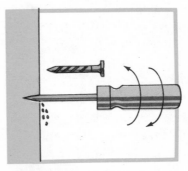

How to make a starter hole with an awl.

Screwdriver with clip to hold screws.

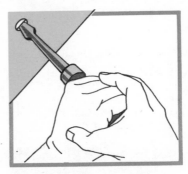

Use two hands on screwdriver.

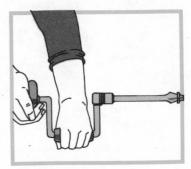

Screwdriver bit in brace.

with a hammer, but this often results in damaged and hard-to-work screw slots. It is helpful to hold the blade and screw head together in the beginning. This is not always possible, however, and some screw-

The Toolbox

drivers have metal clips over the blade that hold the screw head to the blade for use in hard-to-reach areas. Firm pressure should be applied against the screw during driving to keep the blade in place. When the wood is very hard, it is wise to predrill the entire hole (use a wood-screw pilot bit; see ELECTRIC DRILL). Special drill bits are available for this purpose, matching screw sizes. It sometimes helps to use both hands once the screw is started, one turning the handle, and the other held flat against the end of it to apply more pressure.

● It is easy to remove screws once you get them loosened. The trouble, again, is getting them started, or "broken." Don't forget that screws are driven in clockwise, and removed counterclockwise. If a screw won't budge, give it a quick twist in both directions. For larger stubborn screws, a screwdriver bit in a brace provides extra leverage.

Quality screwdrivers cost from about $1.50 for small ones to about $4 for large ones. They are often available in sets, which is fine if the set is priced less than the total of the tools inside. Check first, because this isn't always the case.

PLIERS

There are numerous types of pliers, most of them used by specialists such as electricians and electronics workers. The kind the homeowner uses most often is the slip-joint pliers. It performs numerous holding tasks—and is often the wrong tool for the job. Pliers are not really designed for tightening and loosening nuts—wrenches are. Yet this is a common household use, and it will do if you don't have the right wrench in your toolbox.

A slip-joint pliers *is* the right tool for grasping, turning, bending, or pulling bolts, wires, broken glass, and sharp or small objects. The term "slip-joint" is applied because the tool has two slots in which the center fastener pin can be located. In one slot, the pliers grip small objects, with the forward jaws tight and parallel. When the pin is in the other slot, the concave inner jaws can go around larger objects. Some pliers have cutting jaws just inside the curved portion. These are for cutting wires, small nails, etc.

When shopping for pliers, choose ones that have been drop-forged and have either a polished surface or a bluish-black sheen. The pin should be solidly fastened so that you can't remove it. The outer parallel jaws should have fine grooves or cross-hatching, the inner ones sharp, rugged teeth. Handles should be scored or tooled so that you can grip them firmly. A good pair costs about $2 to $3. Special purpose types may be more.

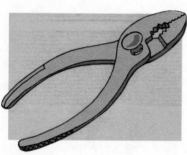
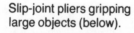

Slip-joint pliers (left).

Slip-joint pliers gripping small objects (below left).

Slip-joint pliers gripping large objects (below).

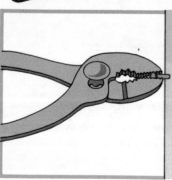
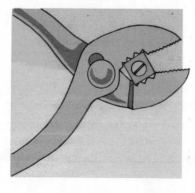

Slip-joint pliers cutting wire.

The Toolbox

HANDSAWS

Saws, too, come in a wide variety of sizes and types. The homeowner should purchase an 8- or 10-point crosscut saw for all-around work. The "8-point" means that there are eight teeth per inch. "Crosscut" means that the teeth are beveled slightly outward and knife-shaped, designed for cutting across the grain of the wood—the most common type of cut.

A ripsaw has squarish, chisellike teeth, and it cuts with the grain. Most do-it-yourselfers have little need for a ripsaw. If you must do a lot of ripping, a power saw of some kind is preferred.

A hacksaw is used for cutting metals and some plastics. It has a wide U-shaped frame with devices on each end for holding the removable, fine-toothed saw blade. A thumbscrew draws the blade taut.

A coping saw is somewhat similar in design to a hacksaw, except that the blade is much thinner and has larger teeth. A coping-saw blade can be turned to various angles for making curving cuts in wood.

Keyhole and compass saws are similar, with the keyhole blade being thinner and finer. Both are used to make curving cuts and small cuts when only one side of the work is accessible, such as in paneling, wallboard, and similar materials that are already nailed up.

When buying a saw, look for a tempered steel or chrome-nickel blade. Handles should be removable hardwood or high-

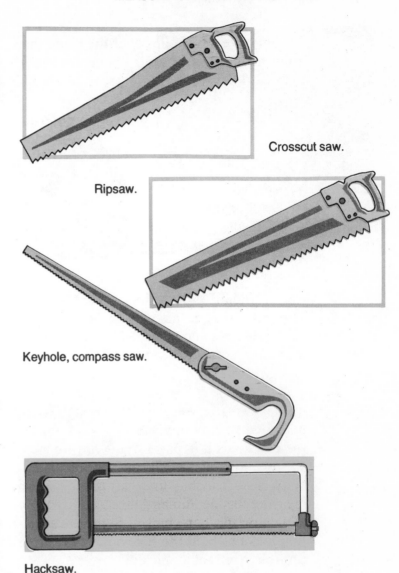

Crosscut saw.

Ripsaw.

Keyhole, compass saw.

Hacksaw.

impact plastic. Better saws have taper-ground blades, and some have a Teflon coating for rust-resistance and less binding.

Crosscut saws—good ones—cost about $10, a hacksaw about half that. Coping saws cost a little less, as do keyhole and compass saws.

MEASURING INSTRUMENTS

A 6-foot folding rule with extension is a good all-around measuring device. The readings are large and easily read, and some have red markings every 16 inches

Coping saw.

The Toolbox

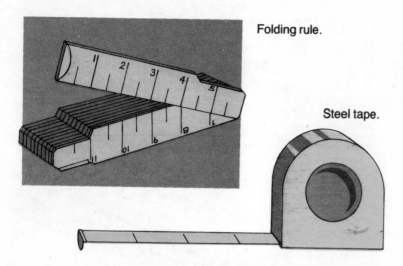

Folding rule.

Steel tape.

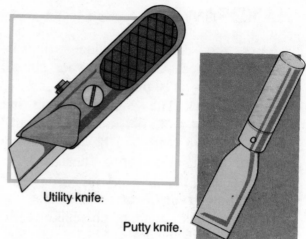

Utility knife.

Putty knife.

(the standard "centering" for framing). The extension is an extra 5-inch section that slides out and allows you to take inside measurements when working in closets, cabinets, etc.

A steel tape is flexible enough to wind up inside a small case, yet rigid enough when extended to stay in place. A small hook on the end holds it in place when you are measuring a long piece. The case usually is exactly 2 or 3 inches long, so that you can measure inside dimensions accurately by adding on the 2 or 3 inches. Some have friction locks to hold the tape open and spring returns to retract it quickly.

A good folding rule with extension costs about $5; a steel tape ½ inch wide by 10 feet costs a dollar or so less.

UTILITY KNIFE

This is an inexpensive tool that has a multitude of uses. It utilizes a razor blade, or a special blade that looks like one, to cut such things as gypsum wallboard, wallcoverings, thin woods, carpeting, rope, and string. It is also handy for opening boxes and cartons.

A good utility knife has a handle shaped to fit your palm, with space inside to store extra blades. Look for one that has a re-

tractable blade that you can withdraw for safety's sake when not in use. The retracting device also lets you extend it to various lengths to adjust for the thickness of whatever you are cutting. The knife costs about $2 to $3.

PUTTY KNIFE

This tool is used for applying and smoothing soft materials such as putty and wood filler. Those with stiffer blades can also be used as scrapers.

A good putty knife has a blade that extends well into the handle and is attached by rivets. The blade should be of hardened, tempered steel with a blunt end and no sharp edges. You will pay about $1.50 for a 1½-inch-wide putty knife, and up to $3 for a 3-inch model.

CHISELS

A wood chisel consists of a steel blade usually fitted with a wooden or plastic handle. It has a single beveled cutting edge on the end of the blade. According to construction, chisels are divided into two general classes: tang chisels, in which part of the chisel enters the handle, and socket

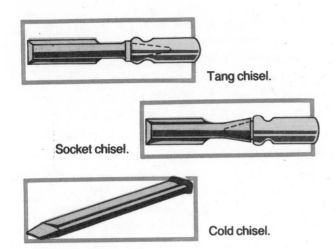

Tang chisel.

Socket chisel.

Cold chisel.

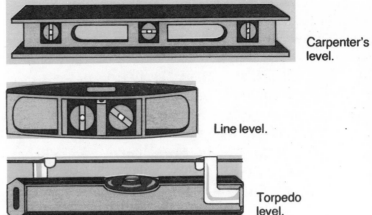

Carpenter's level.

Line level.

Torpedo level.

chisels, in which the handle enters into a part of the chisel. A socket chisel is designed for striking with a wooden mallet (never a steel hammer), whereas a tang chisel is designed for hand use only.

Wood chisels are also divided into types, depending upon their weight and thickness, the shape or design of the blade, and the work they are intended to do. For general household use, a ½-inch or ¾-inch paring chisel is probably best. It has a relatively thin blade and is beveled along the sides. The cost is $3 to $4.

Another type of chisel for your exterior-repair toolbox is the cold chisel. This is made of hardened, tempered alloy steel and is used for striking steel, concrete, stone, and other hard materials. A cold chisel is struck with a ball peen or other heavy hammer. It costs a little less than a wood chisel of the same size.

LEVELS

The carpenter's level is a tool designed to determine whether a plane or surface is true horizontal or true vertical. It is a simple instrument consisting of a liquid, such as alcohol or chloroform, partially filling a glass vial or tube so that a bubble remains. The vial is mounted in a frame of alumi-num, magnesium, or wood. Levels are usually equipped with two or more vials. One vial is built into the frame at right angles to another. The vial is slightly curved, causing the bubble always to seek the highest point in the tube. On the outside of the vial are two sets of gradation lines separated by a space. Leveling is established when the air bubble is centered between the gradation lines.

There are several other types of levels. A torpedo level is useful in tight places. It has a top-reading vial so that you can place it on a low or deep surface and tell whether it's level without bending way down to look at it. A line level hooks onto a piece of twine or string and is useful when working with concrete forms, brick, and similar jobs where lines are used.

WRENCHES

There are probably more types of wrenches than of any other tool. There are open-end and box wrenches, some with a combination of each, and some with half-boxes. (A box wrench completely encloses the nut.) There are ratchet wrenches that are turned like a crank, pipe wrenches, chain wrenches, and countless others.

Your first wrench acquisition should be

Adjustable wrench.

The Toolbox

an adjustable wrench. These come in various sizes, but one about 8 inches long, with jaw capacity up to an inch, is a good starter. This wrench has one fixed jaw, and another that is moved away from or toward the fixed jaw by means of a knurled knob.

Look for a drop-forged, alloy steel wrench with a chrome-polished or blue-black sheen. The jaws should be exactly parallel and not loose (check that by wiggling the movable jaw). Some have a locking device that holds the adjustable jaw in a constant position. A quality adjustable wrench of the recommended size costs about $5.

ELECTRIC DRILL

An electric drill can do so many jobs that it is almost a must in the do-it-yourselfer's toolbox. With it you can make holes in almost any material. By using accessories and attachments you can sand, polish, grind, buff, stir paint, and drive screws.

Depending on quality, size, gearing, and special features, a drill for home use costs from $10 to $50 or more. Your best choice will be a model with the work capacity and special features you will regularly use. The work capacity of a drill depends on its chuck size and rated revolutions per minute (RPM).

The chuck size is the diameter of the largest bit shank the drill chuck can hold. Home-use sizes are ¼, ⅜, and ½ inch. Usually, the larger the chuck, the wider and deeper the holes the drill can bore.

The RPM rating is an indication of the number of gear sets in a model, its speed, and the type of work for which it is best suited. For example, a ¼-inch drill rated about 2,000 RPM usually has one gear set and is appropriate for rapid drilling in wood and use with sanding and polishing accessories. A model with more gears would have a lower RPM rating and work more slowly but could make bigger holes in hard metals or masonry without stalling or overheating.

For most jobs around a home, a single-speed drill is adequate. However, a two-speed or variable-speed model would be more suitable if you intend to drill material (such as glass) that requires a slow speed or if you want to use many accessories. A drill with both variable speed and reverse is effective for driving and removing screws.

The trigger switch, which starts the drill, is on the pistol-grip handle, and many models include a switch lock for continuous operation. You activate the lock by pressing a button; the lock instantly releases if you tighten your squeeze on the trigger switch.

Variable-speed drills have trigger switches that allow you to vary bit speed from almost zero up to maximum RPM by trigger-finger pressure. Some have controls for presetting the maximum RPM.

Drills with reverse have separate reverse controls in different positions depending on the brand. To protect the motor, allow the drill to come to a full stop before reversing.

The front of the drill, where bits and other accessories are inserted and removed, is called the chuck. The three-jaw gear type is the most common. Its collar is first hand-closed on the shank of a bit. Then a key is inserted into the chuck body and turned to tighten the three jaws simultaneously and with considerable force. Some models have a holder to make key loss less likely.

Some bargain drills have chucks that are hand-tightened by means of knurled collars. They may either offer a poor hold on bits and accessories or be difficult to loosen when work is finished. Examine chuck placement as well as quality. The higher the chuck on the front of the housing, the easier the drill will be to use in corners.

Manufacturers' catalogs contain information on the accessories available for particular drill brands and models. The com-

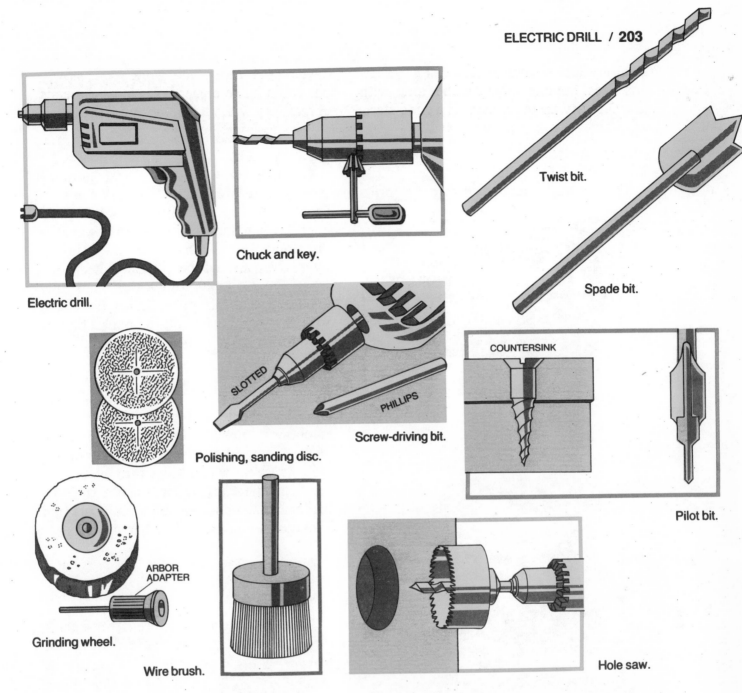

Electric drill.

Chuck and key.

Twist bit.

Spade bit.

Polishing, sanding disc.

SLOTTED

PHILLIPS

Screw-driving bit.

COUNTERSINK

Pilot bit.

Grinding wheel.

ARBOR ADAPTER

Wire brush.

Hole saw.

mon accessories that enable you to use a drill for various jobs are described here.

A drill bit has a working end that makes holes and a smooth shank that is grasped by the jaws of a chuck. Although bits can be bought individually, they cost less if purchased in sets.

The twist bit, the most commonly used, cuts cylindrical holes. It has a sharp point and two spiral-shaped cutting edges that lift chips out of the hole as the bit turns. Carbon steel twist bits are suited to drilling wood and soft metals; high-speed steel bits cut wood, soft metals, and mild steel; tungsten carbide or carbide-tipped bits cut hard metals and masonry. Cutting diameters commonly available range from $1/16$ inch to $1/2$ inch.

The spade bit cuts large cylindrical holes in wood. It has a flat, spade-shaped driving end with a pointed tip. Common cutting diameters range from $3/8$ inch to 1 inch.

The wood-screw pilot bit has three widths of cutting edge. The narrowest drills

The Toolbox

a hole to give screw threads solid anchorage. The next makes a shaft for the unthreaded screw shank. The widest makes a hole, or countersink, for flat-headed screws. A detachable stop can make shallow or deep countersinks.

The screw-driving bit attaches to drills with variable speed and reverse to drive and remove slotted and Phillips-head screws. On single- or two-speed drills, the bit must be used with a special screw-driving attachment.

Polishing and sanding discs, grinding wheels, wire-brush discs, and hole saws are usually secured to a drill by an arbor that goes through the center hole of the wheel or disc and is fastened by a washer and nut or by a screw and washer. A flange keeps the wheel from slipping down the shank that fits into the drill chuck. Some discs and wire brushes have built-in shanks that fit the drill spindle when the chuck is removed.

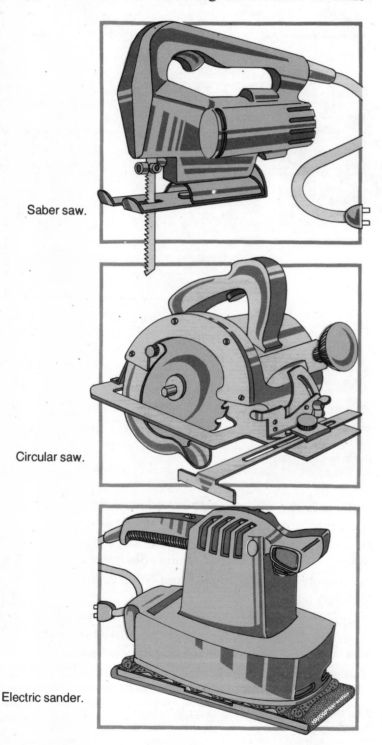

Saber saw.

Circular saw.

Electric sander.

Discs are used either with abrasive paper for sanding or a soft bonnet for polishing. Grinding wheels are for sharpening tools or smoothing metal. Wire brushes remove paint, rust, and dirt from wood and metal. Hole saws cut round holes through boards or sheet materials by means of a rim saw blade and a centered pilot bit. Common diameters range from ½ inch to 4 inches.

OTHER TOOLS

There are literally hundreds of specialized tools that you may use for specific tasks. Buy these as the need arises, as your skills increase, and as you undertake more detailed work around the house—especially if you begin making improvements as well as routine repairs. Power tools will make your work easier and the results better. The ones you will probably buy are: a saber saw, for fast cutting of curved and straight lines in wood and other materials; a circular saw, for extensive cutting of straight lines and invaluable for major jobs such as installing wood siding; and an electric sander, for smooth, speedy removal of wood, paint, or anything else removable by regular sandpaper.

2

Roofs, Gutters, Downspouts

ODERN ROOFING technology is the product of centuries of trial-and-error experimentation combined with up-to-date knowledge of roofing materials. Properly installed, today's roofs will provide years and years of virtually maintenance-free service.

Occasionally, however (especially in harsher climates), roofing materials may fall victim to the elements. Continuous exposure to intense sunlight may cause cracking in asphalt shingles. Improper drainage can result in faulty roof performance.

Thus, the choice of style and composition of roofs often depends on climatic conditions. In some tropical countries, for example, palm leaves make a perfectly adequate house roof.

In North America, where the weather ranges from tropical to arctic, many types of roofing are used. Most of the United States and Canada, however, lie in the temperate zone, and roofs are very similar in all but the extreme hot and cold zones of these countries. In practical terms, this means that most roofs are of peaked wood trusses, or rafters, covered by either plywood or wood sheathing and finished with a layer of mineral-surfaced asphalt shingles. There are other types, of course, wood shingles, slate, tile, and asbestos-cement being fairly common. Other materials such as metal, metal-bound gypsum, reinforced concrete, or concrete planks are sometimes used—mostly on flat roofs.

Roofings of various types may be and frequently are applied over old roofs, but it is usually advisable to remove the old roofing before applying an entirely new roof—particularly if one new roof has already been applied over the original. The homeowner then has the opportunity to have defective or rotted sheathing replaced, thus providing a smoother roof deck with opportunity for better nailing.

Sometimes the do-it-yourselfer prefers to leave roofing repairs to the professional. Unless the roof is low or flat, there is certainly some danger in climbing around on it. Even so, it pays to know something about roofing—if only to keep an eye on the roofer and his bill.

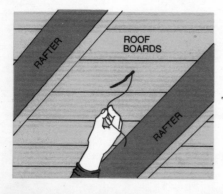

1. Locate hole from beneath and mark with wire (left).

2. Coat leak with asphalt (below left).

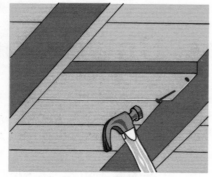

3. Nail board beneath leak (below).

MAKING REPAIRS

When a leak develops, it is important that repairs be made without unnecessary delay. If repairs are neglected over a long period, interior plaster may crack, loosen, and eventually fall. Drywall becomes soggy and crumbly, and the whole roof structure below the shingling may rot. Even small leaks often cause discoloration of wall coverings and stains on finished floors. Although it may not be possible to apply a new roof or to do extensive repair work, the do-it-yourselfer may be able to patch leaky spots until permanent repairs can be made or the old roof can be replaced.

It is often difficult to locate the point of leakage from a wet spot on the ceiling, especially if the underside of the roof is not easily accessible, because water may flow along the roof boards or rafters before dripping down. It is equally difficult to locate a hole from the top of the roof. If the attic has no ceiling, however, most holes may be found readily from the inside of the attic on a bright day. Even small holes will be plainly visible, and their location can be marked by pushing wires through to the surface.

You can make a temporary repair from underneath to hold until you can do the job properly from above. Coat the leaking area with asphalt roofing cement. Cut a 1 x 6 or similar board to fit between the rafters, and toenail it in place beneath the asphalt patch.

When making repairs on the roof, wear sneakers or rubber-soled work shoes. Avoid unnecessary walking on the roof, as this can damage the surface.

Make sure your ladder is sound before using it. Place the ladder flat on the ground and walk along the rungs from one end to the other to make sure they are all solid. Check the hooks on an extension ladder to make sure they engage fully.

To raise a long ladder, set its foot against

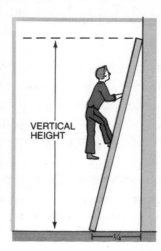

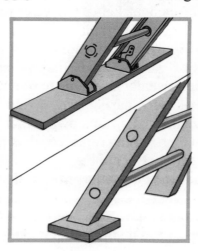

Place ladder against wall, "walk" upright. (far left).

Move foot of ladder out one-quarter of height. (center).

Use boards to level if necessary (left).

Roofs, Gutters, Downspouts

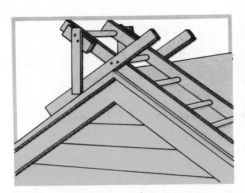

Nail braces to end of ladder and hook over roof ridge (far left).

Ladder held by rope (left).

a wall. Starting at the opposite end, lift it over your head and walk it, rung by rung, until it is upright. Then move the foot away from the wall one-quarter of the height the ladder is to reach. Make sure that the ladder rests on a firm footing. If necessary, place it on a secure board or boards to make the footing level.

Don't attempt to work on a steep roof without some additional support. One way to provide this is with a second ladder (not the one you use to get up to the roof). Nail or screw a piece of 2 x 4 to each leg of the ladder, following the angle of the roof. Nail or screw braces of 1-inch lumber or ¾-inch plywood across the joint (you will have to back these up with blocks of 2 x 4 affixed firmly to the ladder legs). Then "hook" the braced end of the ladder over the peak of the roof.

Another means of support is a strong rope tied to a ladder. Of course it must be firmly anchored or it will be worse than worthless. Tie one end to the top of a flat ladder laid across the roof and secure the other end to a stout tree or other support.

ASPHALT ROOFING

Asphalt-prepared roofings are manufactured in three forms: mineral-surfaced shingles, mineral-surfaced roll roofing, and smooth-surfaced roll roofing. Mineral-surfaced asphalt shingles and roll roofings are composed of roofing felt, made of organic

fibers saturated and coated on both sides with asphalt, then surfaced with mineral granules on the side exposed to the weather. The other side may be dusted with mica or talc. Smooth-faced roll roofing is dusted on both sides with fine mineral matter such as mica, talc, or fine sand and is usually lighter in weight than mineral-surfaced roll roofing. Mineral-surfaced asphalt shingles and roll roofing are usually available in a variety of colors; smooth-surfaced roll roofing is usually black or gray.

Mineral-surfaced asphalt shingles are made in strips of two to four (usually three) units or tabs joined together, as well as in the form of individual shingles. When laid, strip shingles furnish virtually the same pattern as individual shingles, and they have become the standard method of application today. Most shingles come in varying sizes and patterns.

The principal cause of damage to asphalt shingle roofs is the action of strong winds

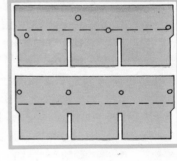

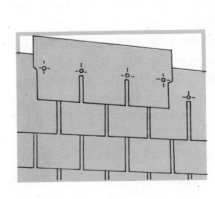

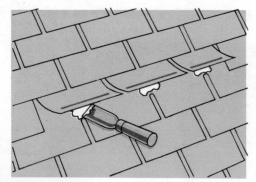

Force cement
under
shingle tabs.

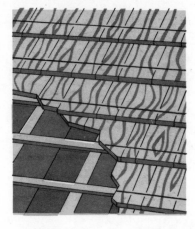

Mark wood shingles
for nailing surfaces.

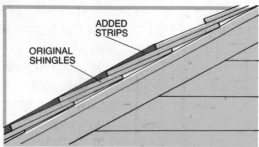

Nail beveled strips for uniform surface at
the base of the old shingle.

on shingles that have been nailed too close to the upper edges. Most shingles today are impregnated on the edges with a material that softens in the sun and seals the edges to the shingles below.

The shingles most likely to be affected by winds are those in the four to five courses near the ridge or in the area extending about 5 feet from the sloping area at the edge or rake of the roof. To fasten loose shingles correctly, use a putty knife or trowel to place a small quantity of asphalt cement under the center of each tab about one inch from the lower edge. Press the shingle down firmly after application. Too much cement will prevent the tab from lying flat. Also, be careful not to seal the lower edge completely.

Asphalt shingles are frequently applied over old wood shingles or other roofing, provided that the surface of the old covering is in reasonably good condition. If not, the old covering should be removed. A wood shingle roof is laid over intermittent wood strips, so be sure to mark the location of the strips to make sure that the new nails will strike a solid surface below. All defective or missing shingles should be replaced, and beveled strips ⅜ inch x 4 inches (the same thickness as the old wood shingles) should be nailed at the base of the old shingles to assure a uniform surface.

If the old covering is completely removed, the roof deck should be made smooth and solid, and all loose material should be swept off. Any defects in the sheathing or plywood should be corrected, and, if the old material is in very bad shape, the entire surface should be recovered with exterior plywood to form a solid new underlayment.

Mineral-surfaced roll roofings are made in various colors, both solid and blended. The mineral granules on the surface protect the asphalt coatings from the weather and increase the fire-resistant qualities of the roofing. The manufacturer's directions should be followed with respect to storing, handling, and temperatures at which roll roofing should be laid.

Minor damage to mineral-surfaced roll roofing such as nail holes or small breaks may be repaired by applying asphalt cement. To repair large breaks, the horizontal seam below the break should be opened and a strip of roofing of the type originally used slipped in under the break, allowing the strip to extend at least 6 inches beyond the break on either side. The lower edge

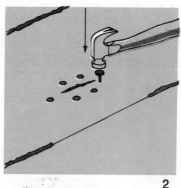
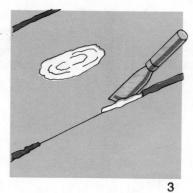

1   2   3

To repair large breaks:

1. Raise seam, slip
   in strip of roofing.
2. Nail around break.
3. Reseal seam.

should be flush with the horizontal exposed edge. Asphalt cement should be applied liberally on the upper surface of the repair strip before inserting it. After the strip has been inserted, press the edges of the roofing down firmly and nail securely with rustproof nails. Space the nails 2 inches apart about ¾ inch from the edge of the break. Apply asphalt cement to the horizontal seam and renail; cement over nails.

Leaks at the seams of roll roofing are caused principally by inadequate nailing and cementing of the roofing, by loose nails, and by buckling of the roofing at the seams. To repair leaky seams, sweep out the seams to remove accumulated dust and dirt, cut all buckles that terminate at the seams, and insert a strip of roofing in the same manner as for larger breaks.

▲ Roll roofing may be applied over old wood shingles or other roofing materials, providing that the surface of the old covering is in reasonably good condition and that it has been made smooth in the same manner as for mineral-surfaced asphalt shingles. Otherwise, the worn roofing should be removed and the roof deck prepared in the same manner as for the application of asphalt shingles. Follow the directions supplied by the manufacturer.

Although smooth-surfaced roll roofings were fairly common at one time, their use for surfacing is not recommended today. Asphalt shingles are the preferred treatment, and mineral-covered roll roofing is a less expensive second choice. Smooth-surfaced asphalt does not weather as well because the coatings are not protected from the action of sunlight by mineral granules. If you already have such a roof, however, you should know how to maintain it. Also, these roofings can be used for outbuildings and temporary structures at a lower cost than the others. Maintenance instructions, plus application materials, usually come with each package of roll roofing.

To achieve the best service, this roofing material should be recoated at regular intervals with bituminous roof coating. Seams that have opened should be recemented and any small holes in the covering filled with asphalt cement. Loose nails should be pulled, the resulting holes sealed with asphalt cement, and new nails driven.

Coating materials are usually composed of an asphaltic base and mineral fiber, thinned to heavy brushing consistency with

Cut buckled areas of
roll roofing.

Pull loose nail, fill hole
before recoating.

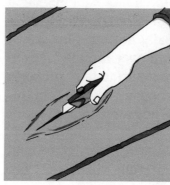

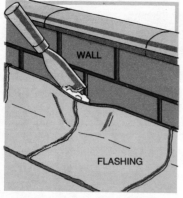
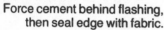
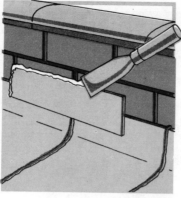

| Force cement behind flashing, then seal edge with fabric. | Prepare break in flashing with saturated flashing felt. |

a volatile solvent. Fatty acid pitch-base coatings are also available. Follow the directions of the manufacturer.

Smooth-surfaced roll roofing may be applied over other roofing, provided that the surface of the old covering is not too badly deteriorated. When this type of roofing has to be removed, it is suggested in most cases that mineral-coated roofing be applied for longer, less maintenance-prone wear.

BUILT-UP ROOFINGS

The application of built-up roofing is a specialized operation that requires particular experience and special equipment. It is therefore advisable to employ an experienced roofing concern to lay or repair this type of roofing.

Built-up roofing is used when the roof is flat or has a very low pitch. It consists of several layers of bituminous-impregnated felt, lapped and cemented together with a bitumen that is usually heated. Fine gravel or slag is then spread over the top layer to provide a weathering surface. If properly applied, built-up roofings should not require major repairs for a long time.

When a leak occurs in a built-up roof, flashings at parapet walls, skylights, and vents should be carefully inspected, be-

cause the initial failures usually occur at these locations. Bituminous flashings are made of saturated felt and flashing cement. Flashing cement should be forced behind the felt if it has separated from the wall at the upper edge, and the edge should be sealed with a strip of bituminous-saturated cotton fabric 4 inches wide, embedded in and coated with flashing cement.

A break in the flashing should be repaired by applying saturated flashing felt in pieces extending not less than 6 inches in all directions beyond the break, cementing it to the flashing and coating it with flashing cement. Sheet-metal flashings that have a ferrous-metal base, such as zinc-coated sheet iron, should be painted with corrosion-resistant paint or, if badly weathered, replaced with new flashing.

Bare spots on a built-up roof where the mineral surfacing is not properly embedded should be swept or scraped clean and a heavy coating of hot bitumen applied, and additional gravel or slag should be spread not less than 6 inches beyond the other layers. This is definitely a job for the pros.

SLATE ROOFINGS

Slate is a rigid roof material that gives good service and long life with very little need for repair. Though originally more costly, it is usually worth the extra expense. Slate is dense, nonporous rock used on roofs to produce a good-looking, highly durable covering. Only responsible and experienced slate roofers should be engaged to lay such a roof.

"Chicken ladder."

1. Remove broken slates by undercutting the nails.

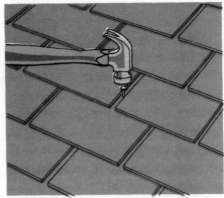

2. Insert new slate shingle and fasten it, nailing through overlying slate.

3. Insert a piece of sheet copper over the nail head.

The most frequently needed repair of slate roofs is the replacement of broken slates. When such replacement is necessary, supports such as a "chicken ladder" or ladder hooks should be used to distribute the weight of the worker. Broken slates should be removed by undercutting the nails with a hacksaw blade. A new slate shingle of the same color and size as the old one should be inserted and fastened by nailing through the vertical joint of the slates in the overlying course approximately 2 inches below the butt of the slate in the second course above. A piece of sheet copper about 3 x 8 inches should be inserted over the nail head to extend about 2 inches under the second course above the replaced shingle. The metal strip should be bent slightly before being inserted so that it will stay securely in place.

■ Very old slate roofs sometimes fail because the nails used to fasten the slates have rusted. In such cases, the entire roof covering is removed and replaced, including the felt underlay materials—obviously, a job for a roofer. The sheathing and rafters should be examined and any broken boards replaced with new material. Loose boards should be nailed in place, and before the felt is laid the sheathing should be swept clean, protruding nails driven in, and rough edges trimmed smooth.

Asphalt-saturated felt should then be applied horizontally over the entire roof deck, with the sheets lapped not less than 6 inches and over ridges and hips not less than 12 inches. The sheets should be secured along laps and exposed with large-head roofing nails spaced 6 inches apart.

All slates that are still in good condition may be salvaged and relaid. New slates should be the same size as the old ones and should match them as nearly as possible in color and texture. If an exact match is not possible, alternate the new and old so as not to leave one part old slate and the other new slate with a noticeable difference in shade.

TILE ROOFINGS

The most commonly used roofing tile consists of molded hard-burned shale or mixtures of shale and clay, but metal tile is also available. Good clay tile is hard, fairly dense, and durable and may be obtained in a variety of shapes and textures. Most roofing tile of clay is unglazed, although glazed roofing tile is sometimes used in homes.

Clay tile roofings that have been properly manufactured and applied require very little maintenance. If a tile is broken, it

Remove tile with a nail ripper.   Cement new one in place.

should be removed with a nail ripper and replaced with a new tile of the same color as the original set in roofing cement.

■Clay tile can be applied over an old roof covering provided that the covering is in reasonably good condition. The roof framing should be examined to determine whether or not the additional weight of the tile can be carried safely and, if not, additional framing or bracing should be added. A competent contractor is best consulted at this stage. Where the old roofing is left in place, all defective portions should be repaired and the surface made as smooth and solid as possible. If the old roof covering is too worn or damaged to provide a proper laying surface for the new tile, it should be removed and the sheathing or roof decking made smooth and solid.

ASBESTOS-CEMENT SHINGLES

Asbestos-cement shingles are manufactured from portland cement (see CHAPTER 7) and asbestos fiber formed in molds under high pressure. The finished product is hard, fairly tough, and durable. Asbestos-cement shingles are available in a variety of colors and textures and may be obtained in rectangular, square, and hexagonal shapes, in single or multiple units.

Asbestos-cement shingles usually require little maintenance. Occasionally, however, a shingle may become broken and need replacement. The broken shingle should be removed by cutting or drawing out the old nails with a ripper (as with slate or tile roofing). A new shingle, similar to the old one, is then inserted. The new shingle should be fastened by nailing through the vertical joint between the shingles in the overlying course approximately 2 inches below the butt-end of the shingle in the second course above. A piece of sheet copper about 3 x 8 inches should be inserted over the nail head and should extend about 2 inches under the course above. The metal should be bent slightly before insertion to hold it firmly in place (see SLATE ROOFINGS, PAGE 210).

■Asbestos-cement shingles may be applied over an old roof covering if the roof is in reasonably good condition. The framing should be inspected and, if necessary, reinforced to carry the additional weight of the new shingles safely. If the new roofing is to be laid over old wood shingles, loose shingles should be securely nailed. Warped, split, or decayed shingles should be replaced.

If the old roofing is in poor condition, it may be more economical to remove it entirely than to make the repairs necessary to provide a sound, smooth surface for the new roofing. If the old roofing is removed, loose sheathing boards should be securely nailed and defective material replaced. If

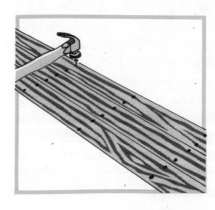

Nail loose sheathing.

the sheathing is in very bad shape, perhaps it would pay to recover the entire surface with exterior plywood.

WOOD SHINGLES

Factors that influence the service life of wood-shingle roofs are pitch and exposure of the roof, durability of the wood in the shingles (red cedar is best), preservative treatment of the shingles, and kind of nails used in fastening.

Wood shingles are usually manufactured in lengths of 16, 18, and 24 inches and in random widths varying from 2½ to 14 inches. On roofs of average pitch, shingles should be laid with about one-fourth of their length exposed. On steeper pitches, the exposure should not exceed one-third the length of the shingle.

On new roofs, wood shingles are frequently laid on open sheathing or slats to permit ventilating the underside. An open deck not only costs less but permits the shingles to dry quickly. The slats are usually 1 x 4-inch boards, spaced to accommodate the nailing of the shingles.

Hot-dipped zinc-coated nails of the proper size and shape are generally recommended for fastening wood shingles, although blued-steel nails may also be used. Longer nails are required for reroofing over old coverings than for new construction.

● Wood shingles that are cracked do not necessarily cause leaks unless the courses are not lined up properly, in which case they may admit moisture to the nail heads in the course below and cause nail failure. To stop the leak, a piece of tin or copper may be placed under the cracked shingle.

Wood shingles may be applied to old roofs as well as new. If the old roofing is in reasonably good condition, it need not be removed. Before applying the new shingles, all warped or deteriorated shingles

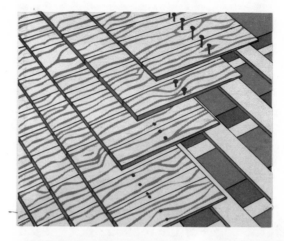

Slats for wood shingles.

1. Place copper beneath cracked shingle.

2. Cut off first row of old shingles.

3. Nail 1 x 4 in the space.

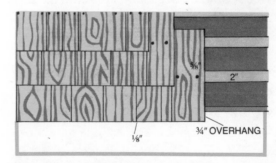

4. Space new shingles 1/8-inch apart and nail them down.

5. Use chalk line to keep shingles straight.

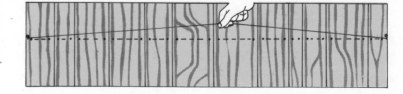

Roofs, Gutters, Downspouts

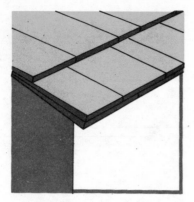
Double shingles at eaves.

should be tightly nailed or replaced. To finish the edges of the roofing, the exposed portion of the first row of old shingles along the eaves should be cut off with a sharp roofer's hatchet or saw, and a 1 x 4 wood strip nailed in the space with the outer edge flush with the eave line. Treat the edges along the gable ends in a similar manner. New shingles should be spaced approximately ⅛ inch apart to allow for expansion in wet weather. They should project between ½ and ¾ inch beyond the edge of the eaves. Each shingle should be fastened with at least two nails placed about ⅝ inch from the edges and about 2 inches under the overlap of the course above; the nails must penetrate the slats to which the original shingles are nailed. The lines of the shingles may be kept parallel to the eaves and ridges by checking the course with a chalk line.

If it becomes necessary to remove the old roofing, the deck should be prepared in the same manner as for a new roof. New shingles should be doubled at the eaves and should project from ½ to ¾ inch beyond the eaves. Courses should be properly aligned and shingles spaced and nailed as above.

ROOF DRAINAGE

Every house, regardless of what type of roofing material is employed, should be equipped with some method of carrying off and effectively dispensing with the large volumes of rainwater that can otherwise create a number of structural problems. Without such a system, water can seep into the earth around the building and cause wet basements, wood decay, peeling paint, and even termite damage. A typical rainfall drainage system includes gutters, downspouts, and leaders to bring the water to the ground and a storm sewer or drywell to absorb the water.

Most gutters today are made from galvanized steel, copper, or aluminum, although wood gutters can still be found on many older structures. In recent years, fiberglass drainage systems have been introduced, and their beneficial features (relatively light weight, ease of installation, etc.) are making them more and more attractive to home builders and renovators.

Metal gutters should be painted to avoid the corrosive, oxidizing actions of the weather. Galvanized gutters may otherwise rust once the thin zinc coating wears away, and unpainted copper gutters will stain adjoining surfaces. A thin coating of roofing cement on the inside of galvanized steel gutters will help prevent rusting.

Wood gutters should be treated with wood preservatives and then coated with exterior paint. Lining the inside of these gutters with roofing cement will further prevent decay. Small holes in wood gutters can

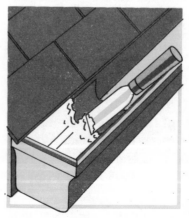
Patch wood gutters with tarpaper and asphalt cement.

Roofs, Gutters, Downspouts

be patched with pieces of tarpaper and asphalt cement.

Because water seeks its own level, a slight downward pitch to the drainage end of the gutter is necessary. If there is not enough pitch, the water will not flow effectively to the downspout. A sagging gutter will alter the pitch and, hence, reduce the flow rate. This can cause the gutter to overflow and will hasten rusting and other corrosive actions.

One way to check gutter pitch is to pour a pail of water in the end of the gutter opposite the downspout or leader end. Make note of the areas where water accumulates—it is these areas that need modification. You may need gutter hangers (available at most hardware stores for a small price) to increase the pitch or elevate a sagging length of gutter.

Leaves and other debris can impair the efficiency of a gutter. Periodic cleaning, especially after a storm, will prevent debris from accumulating. To save yourself the time involved with these cleaning operations, you may wish to install wire gutter guards. These work in much the same way that a screen door prevents insects from coming indoors, although here the idea is to prevent leaves from entering the gutters. Downspouts should be equipped with similar screens to strain out the debris and thus prevent clogging.

In the winter months, especially in areas where heavy snowfalls are common, ice and snow may pile up in the gutters instead of harmlessly sliding off the roof. The weight of accumulated snow is often enough to pull gutters loose. To avoid problems of this sort, the outside edges of the gutters should be hung lower than the edge of the roof eaves. This allows ice to slide off without taking the gutter along. If this does not prevent the buildup, it would be wise to install electric heating cables in areas where accumulation is a problem.

Roofs, Gutters, Downspouts

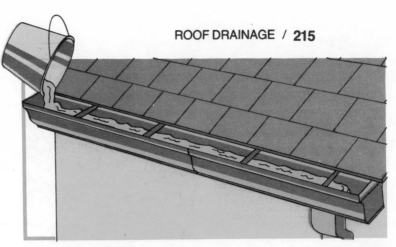

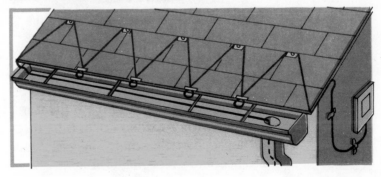

Check gutter pitch with a pail of water.

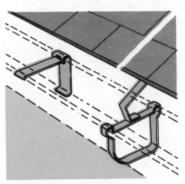

Gutter hanger.

Gutter guard.

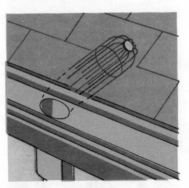

Downspout strainer.

Gutters should slant outward.

Electric heating cable for areas where ice and snow accumulation is a problem.

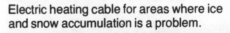

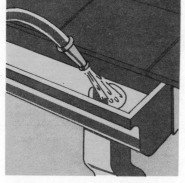
Flush downspout with garden hose once a year.

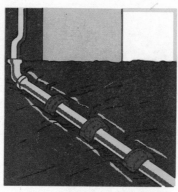
Trench, lined with clay tile, to carry away water.

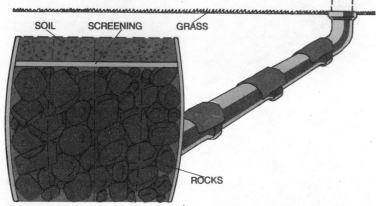

SOIL   SCREENING   GRASS

ROCKS

Simple drywell.

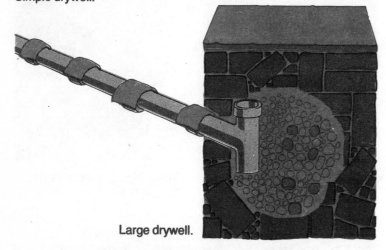

Large drywell.

DOWNSPOUTS

With a good strainer properly installed, downspouts rarely become clogged. Nonetheless, it is a good idea to flush them out once a year with a garden hose, thus forcing out small particles that could accumulate and become a clogging problem.

Many household drainage systems end with the downspout, and the water merely flows into the soil beneath it. This keeps the soil constantly damp and provides an ideal breeding ground for insects, including termites. Wood decay is accelerated by the dampness, and structural damage can occur to concrete foundations. To avoid these often costly problems, the downspout discharge should be carried a safe distance (at least 8 to 10 feet) away from the house.

This can be accomplished by digging a shallow trench of the required length (with a downgrade, of course, away from the downspout). Line the trench with clay tile, covering joints with tarpaper before backfilling. If the soil that the tile empties into is absorbent, no other efforts are required. If not, some alternate means of disposal must be found.

Never connect the drainage system to a septic tank or cesspool that handles your household sewage. Many municipalities allow rainwater runoff to flow into community sewer lines—others forbid this practice because a heavy rainfall may overflow raw sewage at the treatment plant.

If your community does not allow rain drainage into a sewer, a drywell can be constructed to handle the runoff problem. To make a simple drywell, dig a hole big enough to accommodate a large wooden barrel. Remove the top and bottom of the barrel and then place it in the hole. Fill the barrel with rocks up to approximately 5 inches from the top; cover with screening. Fill the remaining space with soil. Lead drainage tiles into the drywell.

For larger houses, or in areas where heavy rainfalls are the norm, bigger drywells may be necessary. These can be built in the same fashion as cesspools—large holes lined with masonry blocks laid without mortar. The tops of the wells should be covered with reinforced concrete set below the ground level.

3

Exterior Walls

PEOPLE COMMONLY refer to "a roof over their heads" as a euphemism for their domiciles, but the roof isn't much good without some solid walls. It didn't take primitive man long to realize that, although trees may afford some shelter from rain, they don't provide much protection against the elements and enemies—so he moved into a cave with solid walls. Today's homeowner or apartment dweller may like to roll back the walls of his "cave" to enjoy a balmy summer night, but they are quickly closed when the winds blow or a storm threatens.

As your home's first line of defense against the elements, the outside walls take quite a beating. They are exposed to extremes of heat and cold and are bombarded by rain, snow, sleet, hail, ice, the harsh rays of the sun, and foul tips off the bats of backyard big leaguers. Small wonder that—whether they be of masonry, wood, or some other material—they occasionally need some attention. Little things like loose mortar joints in brick or splits in clapboard should be repaired before they become major problems, which the ravages of the weather almost guarantee they will.

TAKE A CALK WALK

Any place where two dissimilar materials meet around the house is an open invitation to the invasion of moisture, which will almost surely lead to decay and structural weakness. Calking compound is the material used to seal these joints. It is available in any hardware store, paint supply store, or lumberyard, along with the cartridge-type calking gun. With just a little practice, any do-it-yourselfer can apply the calking in a neat strip.

Calking compound does not completely harden; it forms a tough surface "skin" while remaining soft and flexible inside. This property makes it ideal for use between materials that are constantly expanding and contracting, usually at different rates. A properly calked joint should last for many years.

Before calking, the surface should be cleaned, because the compound will not ad-

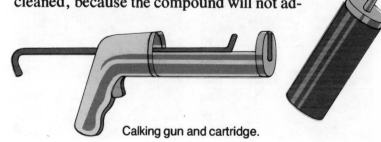
Calking gun and cartridge.

Exterior Walls

Scrape away old calking compound (left), and then apply calking (right).

When applying the compound, keep a smooth, even pressure on the gun's trigger. Run the gun along the joint in a single stroke without lifting to make a smooth, uniform bead. If you are doing the work in very cold weather, calking compound may become very stiff and difficult to handle. In this case, it is best to store the cartridge in a warm place for a few hours before using.

Calk around windows and doors and at all other places where different materials adjoin, such as where a plywood paneling abuts clapboard siding, or where shingles and brick are adjacent.

here properly where dirt or grease are present. Clean out loose dirt and debris with a wire brush. Scrape away old calking compound—it is a poor base for the new. If necessary, wash the area to be calked with a household detergent, but make sure that the surface is completely dry before applying the compound.

BRICK AND CONCRETE BLOCK

The most common problem in brick and concrete block walls is a defective mortar joint. The repair is simple. You can buy a prepared mortar mix at your hardware or building supply store. The tools required are a hammer (use either a ball peen or mash hammer—the claw hammer should be reserved for carpentry projects only), a cold chisel, a pointed trowel, and a wire brush. Chisel out loose or crumbling mortar, then clean the joint with the wire brush and wet it thoroughly. Mix the mortar, following the directions on the package. Force the mortar into the joint with the trowel, then form it with the point of the trowel to match the surrounding mortar joints. A

1. Chisel out loose mortar.

2. Wire-brush joint.

3. Trowel mortar into joint.

4. Form mortar.

Making concave joint with a dowel.

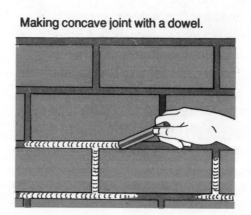

concave joint can be formed by using a dowel or a small piece of pipe to finish off the new mortar.

If a brick is loose or badly damaged, chisel out the mortar all around it, taking care not to damage the surrounding bricks. Take out the loose or damaged brick. Chisel away any remaining mortar in the opening and clean away dust and debris. Wet down the opening, then apply mortar to the sides and back. Dampen the replacement brick, coat it with mortar, and press it into place. Finish the mortar joint with a trowel.

If the mortar joints of an entire wall become porous, either because of age or because of poor original workmanship, the best solution is to apply a clear waterproofing compound (available at masonry and building supply stores) to each joint. This is a time-consuming task, but a necessary one. The alternative would be to completely remortar the wall.

On brick and other masonry walls, particularly new ones, a whitish powdery substance may develop. This is called efflorescence and is usually caused by the formation of salts in still-damp masonry. It can also be a sign of leakage. The deposit can be removed by scrubbing with a solution of one part muriatic acid to ten parts of water. Be very careful when working with this solution. Protect your skin and eyes with gloves and goggles. Work on small areas at a time, and flush frequently with clear water. Do not let the acid attack the mortar joints. If you accidentally get any of the acid on your skin, wash it off immediately.

In brick veneer walls, the brick is laid against a wood-sheathed wall behind it, attached by small metal clips. To allow proper drainage of this cavity, there are usually weep holes along the base of the wall to permit water to run off. Make sure that these holes are not blocked, either by dirt or fallen mortar, and clean them out occasionally with stiff wire or a masonry drill.

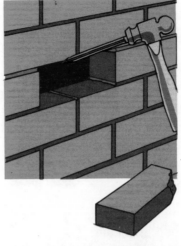

1. Remove damaged brick (above).

2. Apply mortar to cavity (above right).

3. Coat brick and place it into cavity (right).

Apply waterproofing compound to each joint (left).

Brick veneer wall (below left).

Open weep holes (below).

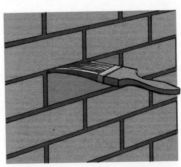
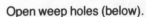

CEMENT AND STUCCO WALLS

Stucco is a material made of cement, sand, and a small quantity of lime that is applied as a finish coating over concrete or

1. Clean away crumbling stucco.

2. Chisel stucco.

3. Undercut edges.

4. Trowel on new stucco.

First application
below surface.

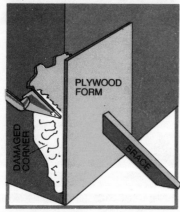

Outside corner repair,
first stage.

Outside corner repair,
second stage.

concrete block, or—less frequently—over wood or metal lathing. Cracks and gouges should be repaired quickly, to prevent their spreading due to the infiltration of water behind the coating.

First, wire-brush away the loose and crumbling material. If a larger area seems to be loose, use a cold chisel and hammer to clean off all the crumbling stucco. If in doubt, knock it out. Use the chisel to undercut around all the edges of the damaged area. Wet the area thoroughly, then apply a commercial mixture (available at your hardware store) to the area with a trowel, following the manufacturer's directions. Finish it, either rough or smooth, to match the surrounding stucco.

If the damaged area is quite deep—say 1½ inches or more—it is best to make the repair in two applications. Fill the hole with the compound to about ¼ inch from the surface. Allow the patch to dry for approximately 24 hours. Then finish it to the surface, as described above.

Outside corners are frequently damaged. The best way to get a good sharp corner repair is to do one side of the wall at a time. Prop a piece of plywood or lumber against the corner and pack in the stucco patch up to it. Allow it to dry, then move the form around to the other side of the wall and make the repair to the remaining damaged area. Make sure that the patches are allowed to dry thoroughly before removing the forms.

■Large damaged areas of stucco naturally require a bit more work. You may wish to leave such a repair to a professional, but it is still not beyond the reach of the do-it-yourselfer. You will probably have to take out all the damaged material down to the backing of lath or whatever. Wire-brush the area clean. Install new building paper against the backing, using rustproof nails. Nail a section of wire mesh against the backing. Three coats of stucco are best ap-

plied on such a repair. The first should be troweled over the mesh; scratch the surface with a scrap of the mesh to give "purchase" for the next coat. Allow it to dry thoroughly, at least 24 hours, and keep it damp during the drying period with an occasional spraying with a fine mist.

Apply the second coat to within ¼ inch of the surface, just as for a two-stage patch above. Allow it to harden for several days. Dampen the subsurface before applying the final coat. Trowel this to a smooth finish, flush with the surrounding stucco, and finish the surface to match. A whisk broom can be used to make a rough surface; a wooden trowel worked in a circular motion will give a smooth surface.

1. Install new building paper (above left).

2. Install wire mesh (above center).

3. Scratch surface of stucco patch (above right).

4. Spray during drying period (right).

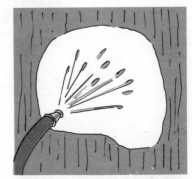

Making a rough stucco surface with a whisk broom.

Making a smooth stucco surface with a trowel.

SIDING

There is a wide variety of types, styles, and materials used as siding on frame houses. Generally, they can be broken down to shingle, clapboard, and panel types. Shingles may be of wood or asbestos cement. Clapboard, broadly speaking, may be wood, aluminum, hardboard, plastic, or steel. Paneling is most commonly plywood

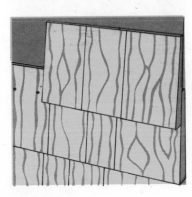

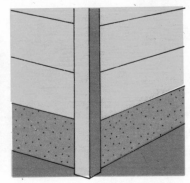

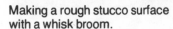

Shingle, clapboard, panel siding (from left to right).

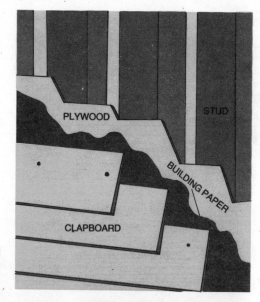

Shingle and clapboard installation.

Fill small cracks.

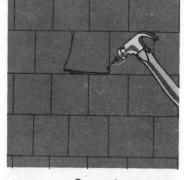

Secure loose board.

Drill pilot holes.

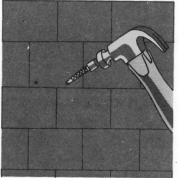

Countersink nails.

sheathing of boards, plywood, or composition material, with each course or row overlapping the one beneath it. Normally a paint job every couple of years is the only maintenance required. Faults may occasionally show up—cracks in boards or shingles, for example—or, where paint problems might exist (see PAGES 232-237), a board or shingle might become warped, blistered, or otherwise damaged.

Small cracks can be repaired by filling them with a lead-base putty. Work it into the crack with a putty knife. If a board or shingle has worked loose, secure it with galvanized or aluminum serrated nails driven along the edges. When you are repairing a material such as asbestos cement, which is very brittle, drill pilot holes for the nails before driving them. Nails can be countersunk and covered with putty. The putty is then painted over.

For wood siding split along the grain, pry up the loose portion of the board and apply a waterproof glue along the split. Press the split together and drive galvanized nails beneath the board to hold the edges together until the glue is dry. Then remove the nails and fill the holes with putty.

If a section of clapboard becomes damaged, you can replace it by first driving

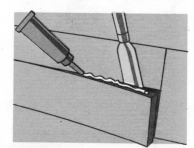

Glue split board.

or hardboard, although plastic and some other materials are available. Patterns also vary greatly. But we can generalize with regard to repairs of damaged siding. No matter what the material, clapboard and shingle siding are applied over a tarpaper-covered

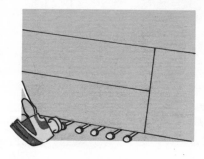

Nail to hold together.

Exterior Walls

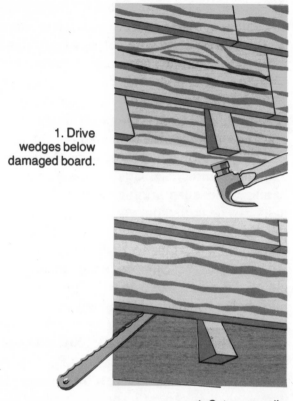

1. Drive wedges below damaged board.

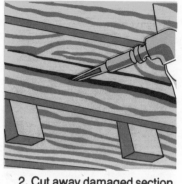

2. Cut away damaged section.

3. Put wedge under board above.

4. Cut away nails.

5. Tap new board in place.

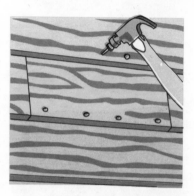

6. Nail new board in place.

wedges under the damaged section to separate it from the board below. Use a small handsaw, such as a back saw, to cut away the damaged portion. For added protection of the board below, wedge a flat piece of wood under the cut. When you have cut through the damaged board up to the board

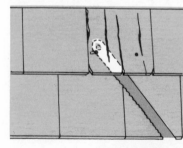

To replace a damaged shingle, cut the nails first, then remove the shingle.

Nail replacement shingle in place.

above it, move the wedges under the upper board. Then chisel away the damaged board. If the nail through the upper board passes through the damaged board, cut it away with a hacksaw blade, then remove the damaged section.

Use the damaged section of the clapboard as a pattern for cutting a replacement. Put the new board in place and tap with a hammer and a scrap of wood until it lines up with the boards on either side. Nail it approximately one inch from the bottom edge, then nail through the board above to secure the top of the replacement.

A warped shingle can sometimes simply be nailed back into place. Use serrated galvanized or aluminum nails, and use a nail set to avoid damaging the shingle while hammering. If a shingle is damaged or split and must be replaced, you must cut through the nail that holds it, which is concealed by the shingle that overlaps it above. You can do this by slipping a hacksaw blade under

Exterior Walls

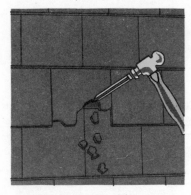

Break off damaged asbestos shingle.

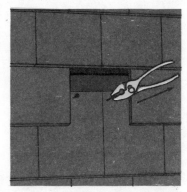

Pull out exposed nails.

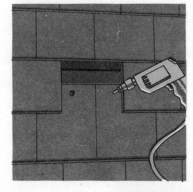

Drill nails through with electric drill.

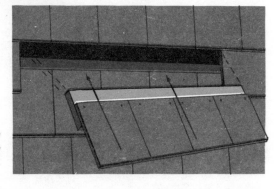

Replace shingle panel.

the shingle and cutting through the nail. Replacement shingles should be cut to fit tightly; this can be done with a utility knife. Nail through the shingle above and at the bottom of the replacement. The nails are countersunk and the holes filled with putty.

▲ Asbestos cement shingles that become cracked or otherwise damaged can be broken off piece by piece by striking them with a hammer and chisel. Just be careful not to damage the surrounding siding. Exposed nails can be pulled out with a pliers; nails of the shingle above are cut with a hacksaw. Another method is to drill them through from the outside. Slip the replacement shingle of the same size into position, and drill pilot holes for nails. Use a nail set to drive the nails home so that the hammer does not damage the asbestos shingle. Some asbestos shingles are attached to boards, usually about 4 feet in length. When one of these is damaged, it is generally best to replace the entire panel. This is done in a similar manner as replacing individual shingles.

■ When exterior paneling is used as siding, improper finishing may result in cracks or other paint problems. The latter are discussed in detail in the following chapter. Badly cracked paneling is best replaced. This can be quite a major undertaking, and one which you may prefer to leave to the professionals.

4

Proper Painting Practices

FOR SOME homeowners, painting the house's exterior is a perennial task and a year-round worry. It can be quite frustrating when you have spent large sums on the best paint money can buy and invested weeks of time in the painting process only to find a few months later that the paint is peeling, cracking, or, in general, not living up to expectations.

The source of the problem can usually be traced to faulty application and a lack of knowledge of the materials used. To save time and money, the homeowner may try to substitute one thick coat where two coats are recommended. Or, through inexperience, he or she may use the wrong primer (or no primer at all) and end up with unsatisfactory results. Mere cursory surface preparation before the paint is applied ususaly makes itself apparent after a few weeks.

Even if the proper general procedures of house painting are observed throughout the project, faulty paint performance may still occur. The problems can arise from moisture resulting from poor rainwater drainage (see PAGES 214-216) or from overall climatic conditions. Paint will generally not last long in exceptionally humid areas. In arid regions, moisture is not usually a problem—but intense sunlight can be. In areas where there is little shade and the skies are clear most of the time, the continued exposure to the sun can result in a chemical breakdown of the paint and pigment fading.

The selection and application of exterior paint, therefore, should be based on the locale, as well as the paint's properties (ease of application, expected lifetime, color, etc.). Your paint distributor should have all the information you require along these lines.

In general, when choosing paint and primer, try to stick to the established name brands. Bargain paints may give poor results, and you must accept this risk when you use them. By investing in the better (albeit more expensive) tried-and-true brands, you are almost assured of uniformly high quality.

SURFACE PREPARATION

The condition of the surface to which exterior paint is applied is just as important as the quality of the paint. The surface should be clean, and defects that would adversely affect the paint should be repaired before painting is started. These defects include cracks in the surface, exposed nail heads, crumbled putty, rotted boards, pitted or corroded metal, mold, and mildew.

If peeling or flaking of the old finish has

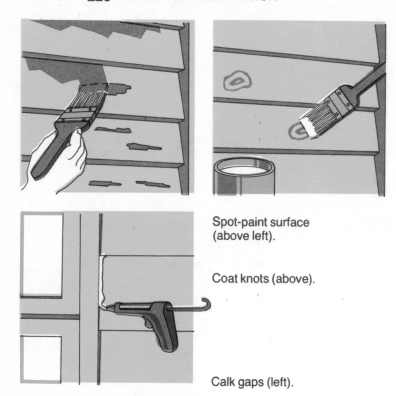

Spot-paint surface (above left).

Coat knots (above).

Calk gaps (left).

occurred, the paint should be removed and the cleaned area spot-painted. This includes building up the spot with primer and finish coats to the same level as the surrounding area. Knots should be coated with shellac or aluminum paint; decayed or split boards should be replaced (see PAGES 221-224); protruding nails should be countersunk and the holes filled with putty; as noted on PAGES 217-218 gaps between ends of siding and corner boards or small cracks around window and door casings should be filled with calking compound.

To stop rot, liquid wood preservatives that can be applied by brushing, spraying, or dipping may be obtained at hardware and paint stores. The preservatives, which are sold under many brand names, contain either pentachlorophenol, copper naphthenate, or zinc naphthenate in a light volatile oil solvent. Pentachlorophenol solutions can be harmful to plants, so don't use them around shrubbery. The copper varieties may stain paint applied over them—a coat of sealer over these preservatives is advisable before painting. The more expensive zinc naphthenates are clear and can be applied under varnish for a natural wood finish.

Two coats of any of these preservatives are advisable, but one coat will give some protection. The second coat should be applied before the first is dry. One gallon usually covers up to 400 square feet of clean, dry, unpainted wood. All three preservatives are offensive to fungi that cause rot and unpalatable to boring insects such as ants, wood wasps, and powder post beetles. These insects should not be confused with termites, which require more positive control measures.

Preservatives should be used where wood touches the ground; in joints between wood and other building materials such as masonry, brick, concrete, or metal; in places where two pieces of wood fit tightly together; and in areas where moisture collects. Gloves should be worn when using the preservatives to avoid skin irritation.

Spray hard-to-reach spots.

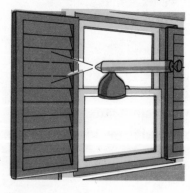

Apply preservative to doorsill.

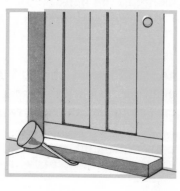

Apply preservative to garage door.

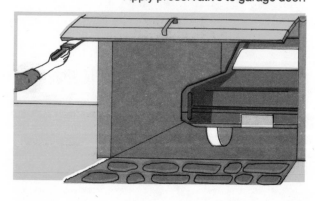

Places that are hard to reach are often the spots that need preservative most. To apply preservative to small, inaccessible joints such as in shutters or other outside blinds, use a fly sprayer, avoiding overdosage that might interfere with the movement of the slats. A bent-spout oil-can may also be used to apply preservative to the front edge and underside of a doorsill.

The bottom edge of a garage door is especially susceptible to rot and should be given a liberal coat of preservative, using a brush for an overhead door and an oilcan or absorbent pad for other types.

Badly mildewed surfaces should be washed prior to repainting with a solution of one pound of trisodium phosphate or sodium carbonate in one gallon of water. After thorough scrubbing, the areas should be rinsed with clean water and allowed to dry before painting: Commercial fungicides are available for controlling mildew on exterior painted surfaces.

PRIMERS

Primers for wood siding are of three general types: oil, fortified (made of oil and resin), and latex. The first two can be used if the house is to be painted with an oil-base paint. Only a latex primer may be used if the house is to have a latex-base top coat.

Oil primers contain oil to control wood penetration. The fortified primers are similar to oil primers, but because of the resins added to the vehicle they are faster drying and resist bleeding. The latex vehicle primers contain a little bit of oil to help develop sufficient adhesion, particularly over older surfaces.

CHOOSING PAINT

The old reliable type of paint to use is an oil base, since this type can usually cover an old finish in one coat, adheres well to most surfaces, and dries to a nice gloss. Oil-base paint will adhere only to a completely dry surface. Some oil-base paints contain mildew-resisting chemicals.

Latex paints are known by a variety of names but are always distinguished by the fact that they are water-thinned. These are very popular with the do-it-yourself public because of their quick drying, ease of clean-up, and relative lack of blistering and other problems caused by moisture. Another big plus for latex paint is that it can be applied on still-damp surfaces (after a rain or in the morning dew, for example), as compared with the waiting period required for an oil-base paint.

As a general guide, any wood siding can take an oil-base or a latex house paint. Vertical wood siding can use an oil-base, a latex, or a clear-finish paint. Wood shingles and shakes should be covered with latex and/or a clear finish. Use only latex on asbestos shingles. Downspouts can take either an oil-base or an alkyd enamel, which is a trim paint; the same is also true for metal gutters, metal windows, and doors. Use only an alkyd enamel on wood windows and doors, screens and storms, trim, cornice, and fascia. Aluminum siding and plastic siding take an oil-base house paint. The alkyd trim enamel is made from oil resins with a high proportion of fatty acids; this paint brushes on easily and retains its gloss very well. There are newer silicone alkyd trim enamels substantially more durable than the old type alkyd trim.

The clear finishes are sometimes preferred by those who want to retain the natural beauty of wood siding. No clear finish will be as durable as a pigment paint.

Stains can be used for wood shingles and rough siding and any outbuildings and fences that you plan to paint. Essentially these are heavily diluted linseed oil paints. If you are covering rough wood, stains are cheaper than paint and sometimes last twice as long.

Stir paint.

Add oil.

Pour paint back and forth.

Dip brush.

Tap brush.

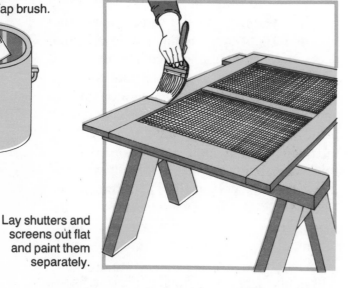

Lay shutters and screens out flat and paint them separately.

HOW TO PAINT

Once the preparation chores have been done and the proper primer has been applied according to the manufacturer's instructions, the house is ready for the top coat(s). Although paints are almost always mixed when you buy them, it is a good idea to stir them again before application. If the paint has settled (as is often the case with cans that have been around for a while), open the can and pour the surface oil into an empty, clean container. Stir up the pigment from the bottom of the original can until it is well dissolved, and then gradually pour back the oil while stirring. When all the oil has been returned to the original can, pour the paint back and forth from can to can until you are satisfied that the paint is thoroughly mixed.

When it is necessary to thin the paint, follow the manufacturer's label instructions to the letter. Paint can be ruined by the wrong oil or thinner. Add only a small amount of thinner at a time and continue stirring until it has been thoroughly absorbed into the paint.

Exterior painting should not be attempted when the temperature is below 50 degrees F. If you must paint in cool weather, be sure to stop at a time when the paint will have ample time to set before the temperature gets below 50 degrees. Don't paint in direct sunlight, as the paint will not dry properly and may develop hairline cracks.

Empty half the can into a clean receptacle. This will allow you to dip the brush without drowning it. The brush should be dipped in the paint only about 2 inches and then tapped against the side of the can to remove any excess. Do not pull the brush over the lip of the can, as this can damage the bristles of the brush.

Remove shutters, screens, and storm sash before painting; lay them out flat, and paint them separately.

Start at the highest point of the house and paint down to prevent drips and spatters from spoiling previously painted areas. If the gutters are to be the same color as the body of the house, paint them as you come to them. The trim areas (such as windows and doors) can be painted after the main

Proper Painting Practices

body of the house unless they are to be painted the same color.

Paint large areas from side to side. It does not matter if you work from left to right or the reverse so long as you follow the sun around the house. Before you move or shorten your ladder, finish an entire area of 4 to 5 square feet.

Keep your trips up and down the ladder to a minimum by taking all the necessary equipment with you. You can use a hook to hold the paint can to a rung. If you're using a roller, special trays are available for this.

Ladders are vital painting tools. If they are not used properly they are also dangerous instruments. Check out the ladder safety principles discussed on PAGES 206-207. You should never attempt to paint higher than 4 feet above the top of the ladder, nor should you stretch out farther than you can reach with both feet firmly planted on the ladder. Also, never stand on the top rung of any ladder, including a stepladder.

Most painting is done in a horizontal direction, but shingles should follow the vertical grain. Professionals often do the high trim first to prevent the ladder from marring the body surface later on. On a very high place where one trip up the ladder is all you care to take, it is possible to do both the body and trim painting at one time if you are careful.

PAINTING MASONRY

Paints for masonry wall surfaces may be divided into four types: cement-water paint, resin-emulsion paint, oil paint, and paint containing rubber in the vehicle. These paints are suitable for use on such masonry surfaces as foundations, gate posts, and fence or enclosure walls, but they should not be used on floors that are subject to abrasion. Here, a very hard-drying paint with good water-resistance and gloss-retention is recommended.

Start at highest point.

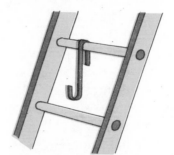
Hook for paint can.

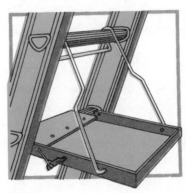
Roller tray.

Work from side to side.

Don't overreach.

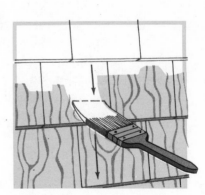
Paint shingles with grain.

Cement-water paints are water-dilutable paints in which portland cement is the binder. They are particularly suitable for application on damp, new, or open-textured masonry surfaces. These include walls that are damp at the time of painting, or that may become damp after painting as a result of structural defects; new structures (less than six months old) which normally contain water-soluble alkaline salts; and open-textured surfaces such as cinder, concrete, and lightweight aggregate block.

Close-textured surfaces that are relatively dry, such as cast concrete, asbestos-cement siding, and tile, may be painted with resin-emulsion paint or paints containing rubber in the vehicle. Walls that are dry at the time of painting, and are so constructed as to remain dry after painting, may be decorated with oil paints.

To clean a surface for the application of cement-water paint, thoroughly remove all dust, dirt, and efflorescence. Dust and dirt can be removed by brushing, followed by washing with clean water; efflorescence, old coatings of whitewash, and flaking or scaling cement-water paint are removed by brushing vigorously with a wire brush. (If efflorescence is stubborn, use methods detailed on PAGE 219.) Firmly adhering coatings of cement-water paint or cement-water paints that are "chalking" or "dusting" need not be removed, but should be brushed with a stiff-bristled brush to roughen the surface. If the old coating is organic paint, it must be completely removed. This can be done most effectively by sandblasting, normally a job for a professional.

Before applying the paint, whether initially or on a previously painted surface, masonry should be thoroughly wetted, preferably with a garden hose adjusted to produce a fine spray. A superficial dampening with a brush dipped in water is not adequate for exterior walls. Usually, wetting the walls not more than an hour before painting is sufficient. The water should be applied so that each part is sprayed three or four times for about 10 seconds, time being allowed between applications for the water to soak into the surface. If the surface dries rapidly, as it may in hot weather, it should be redampened slightly just before painting. The wall surface should be moist but not dripping wet when the paint is applied.

Cement-water paint powder should be mixed with water in accordance with the manufacturer's directions. Paints may be tinted by adding suitable amounts of coloring pigments, but, because of the difficulty of producing uniform colors by hand mixing, it is better to buy commercial brands of tinted paints that have been mill-ground in the factory.

Cement-water paint should be applied in two coats. Preferably not less than 24 hours' drying time should be allowed between coats. The first coat should be slightly moistened with water before applying the second.

Most portland cement paints cannot be satisfactorily applied with the ordinary hair-bristle paintbrush. Proper application requires a brush with relatively short, stiff fiber bristles such as fender brushes, ordinary scrub brushes, or roofers' brushes.

Although thick films are to be avoided, there is a tendency to use too much water in cement-water paint and to brush it out too

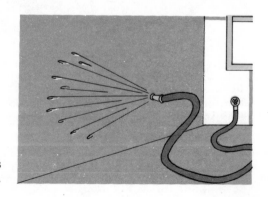

Wet masonry walls before painting.

Application of portland cement paint.

thin. Coatings applied in this manner may look well at first but generally lose their opacity and protective value much sooner than thicker films. The proper spreading rate is difficult to estimate for portland cement paint because of the differences in the textures of the masonry to be covered. On smooth masonry, one gallon of mixed paint should be sufficient to cover 100 square feet with two coats; for rough masonry, one gallon should be sufficient to apply two coats to 50 square feet of surface.

After painting, it is desirable to sprinkle the freshly painted surface two or three times a day with a fog spray, such as is used for dampening walls prior to painting; it is recommended that this be done between coats and for two days after the final coat, starting as soon as the paint has set, usually six to 12 hours after application.

METAL SURFACES

The chief reason for applying paint to exterior metalwork, particularly iron and steel, is to control and prevent corrosion. For best results, two coats of priming paint followed by two coats of top or finishing paint are recommended on new work. For repainting, a spot coat followed by a full priming coat, and then one or two finish coats, are recommended. The usual recommended spreading rate of each coat is about 600 square feet per gallon. The preparation of the surface, particularly steel, prior to painting is important. Unless the surface is properly cleaned so that the priming paint comes in direct contact with the metal, early failure of the paint film may occur.

All oil and grease should be removed first. The usual method is to wipe the surface with clean cloths and mineral spirits or carbon tetrachloride. The liquid as well as the cloths should be kept clean by frequent renewals to avoid leaving a thin, greasy film on the surface. When the oil and grease

Cleaning of metal surface with motor-driven rotary brush.

have been disposed of, rust, scale, and old paint may be cleaned from the surface with wire brushes, steel wool, or motor-driven rotary brushes.

The paint should be applied in bright, warm weather to metal surfaces that are clean and dry. Painting should not be done early in the morning when the surface to be painted is damp from dew. Ample time should be allowed for each coat of paint to dry before the next coat is applied.

Since the main function of a priming coat is to protect metal from corrosion, it should contain rust-inhibitive pigments. It can be applied by either brush or spray, but particular care should be taken to cover the surface completely with the proper thickness of paint. Two coats of primer are recommended for new work. The second coat may be tinted to a slightly different color to make sure of adequate surface coverage. Ample time should be allowed for drying before application of succeeding coats.

Two practical coatings for steel surfaces are red-lead and iron-oxide paints, red lead being used as a primer and iron oxide as a finishing material. Dull red and brown iron-oxide paints are economical for painting structural metal. They are durable and are frequently referred to as roof and barn paint.

As finish coats on iron or steel, black and dark-colored paints are more durable than light-tinted paints. Red-lead paint should not be used as a final coat, since it does not retain its color.

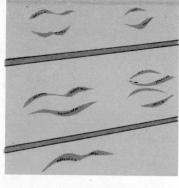
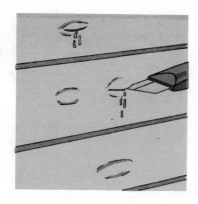

Blistering (above left).

Slit the bubbles with a razor blade.

Scrape blistered area before repainting (left).

BLISTERING

When the final coat has dried and the trim is completed, you will most likely find yourself with a satisfactory finish that will last for years with very little maintenance. Unfortunately, this is not always the case. Even with good paint and proper application, paint failures do occur, and moisture is often the culprit.

If you notice many bubbles, resembling blisters, on any outside painted surface of your house, chances are you have a blistering condition. One way to confirm this is to take a razor blade and slit a few of the bubbles. If blistered, the area beneath will feel wet, or water might actually seep out.

Blistering is caused by moisture accumulating behind the paint breaking its bond and shoving the film outward. If permitted to go too far, blistering could eventually break and lead to other more serious problems, such as peeling and cracking. To solve the problem, you must first determine where the excess moisture is coming from.

It can originate from outside or inside the house.

If blisters are localized around windows, dormers, or gutters and downspouts, then the condition is originating externally. Blisters around windows and dormers indicate that calking has probably cracked or failed, and water is penetrating beneath the paint.
●To correct this, do a thorough recalking job. Even when there is no sign of blistering, a home should be recalked before new paint is applied.

Blisters around gutters and downspouts generally indicate one of several problems: the gutters aren't pitched enough and water is overflowing during heavy rains; a gutter or downspout is damaged and leaking; or there's a damming condition (perhaps a downspout is clogged) that's causing water to back up and overflow. If you find this to be the case, repair the faulty downspout or gutter (see PAGES 214-216).

If the blistering is not localized but is found on large areas of the house, the moisture is probably coming from inside the house. The tremendous amount of moisture created in a modern home by clothes dryers, dishwashers, washing machines, sinks, showers, and cooking must get to the outside of the house one way or another. If a home isn't properly ventilated, this moisture goes through the walls but is stopped when it hits a nonporous oil-base paint film. The result is blistering.
▲There are several ways to combat internal moisture so that it won't cause paint blistering. One is to apply latex paint to the house. This is a "breathing" paint that permits the moisture to escape through the paint film. However, before you apply latex paint to the house, all the old paint must be taken off. Ordinarily latex paint can be applied right over an oil-base paint, but the old paint will continue to block moisture from getting through.
▲A better way to combat a buildup of in-

ternal moisture is to ventilate the home properly. Moisture-producing appliances such as clothes dryers should be vented to the outside. There should be adequate louvers in the attic; it is recommended that a home should have one square foot of louver for every 300 square feet of attic space.

After correcting the cause of the problem and before repainting, scrape and sand the blistered area smooth, then let it dry.

CHALKING

Under most conditions, chalking is normal and is the way in which paint ages. The paint film begins to disintegrate slowly and becomes powdery within a year or so after it has been applied. Chalking is usually desirable, since dirt and soot that settle on the house are washed off with the chalk when it rains, thus keeping the paint clean.

However, there may be abnormal or excessive chalking. This happens when paint begins to chalk too soon after it's ap-

Checking.

Alligatoring.

plied or chalking proceeds at a very rapid rate, which means that the paint will have to be renewed more often than usual.

To avoid this problem, you should not try to make a can of paint go too far. Spread it on evenly and thick enough to cover the old surface. Also, if paint is applied in rain, fog, or mist, or if there is dew on the house, it could begin to chalk excessively. Another cause of abnormal chalking is applying only one coat of paint over a surface that is too porous.

Chalk-retardant paints are available and should be used where free chalking is not desirable. They last longer, but will not stay as clean. Chalk-retardant paint is particularly recommended for painting wood surfaces that are in contact with or above masonry. It prevents chalking runoff that will stain the masonry. This product is also recommended if a home is located in an area where heavy rains prevail.

CHECKING AND ALLIGATORING

If you find tiny, interlaced cracks appearing over the paint surface, it indicates a checking condition. Alligatoring is an advanced stage of checking in which the paint surface becomes interlaced with cracked lines over a large area and literally

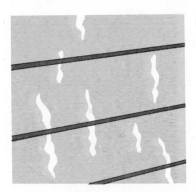
Chalking.

Chalking run-off on masonary.

Proper Painting Practices

resembles an alligator's skin. If checking is noticed, it should be repaired before it reaches the alligatoring stage, which is followed by paint flaking off.

A major cause of checking is the application of a cheap paint that contains insufficient binder. Another cause is not allowing enough drying time between two coats of paint. If the first coat is not dry before the second coat goes on, it contracts and absorbs some of the binder of the second coat, causing checks to appear.

● If you encounter checking or alligatoring on any part of the house, scrape and sand the area smooth to eliminate the damaged paint before you repaint.

CRACKING

When this condition prevails, the paint cracks all the way down to bare wood, causing the paint film to curl up at the cracked edges.

Cracking can result from several causes. There may have been excessive moisture on the surface when the paint was applied, which led to blistering or peeling and finally to cracking. An inferior paint, lacking in elastic qualities, might have been used. The paint film must have sufficient elasticity to permit it to expand and contract along with the wood, or else cracking will occur.

Cracking can also result if paint isn't properly mixed before being applied or if it isn't brushed on evenly and smoothly. In these instances, oil and solid paint particles tend to clump together and can raise globules of paint in localized areas. Upon drying, the paint cracks and begins to curl.

Cracked paint should be removed down to bare wood before repainting. Never put new paint on top of it, because the top coat will only begin to crack again as the curled edges of the old paint push upward.

You should be aware of another type of cracking condition, particularly if you have an older home that has been repainted many times with oil-base paint. It's called cross-grain cracking—cracks appear across the grain of the wood. This indicates that too many thick layers of paint film have accumulated and they are too stiff to accommodate the normal shrinking and swelling of the wood underneath. Too much paint is often worse than too little paint. When this occurs, you have only one choice: remove all the old paint down to bare wood and start over again. No more paint than is necessary to restore the desired appearance should be used for repaint jobs. Paint that is in good condition, but dirty, should be washed occasionally rather than repainted.

CRAWLING

When you begin to paint and you notice that the paint is drawing itself up into drops or globules soon after it's applied, stop!

Cracking.

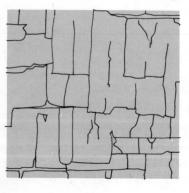

Cross-grain cracking.

Crawling.

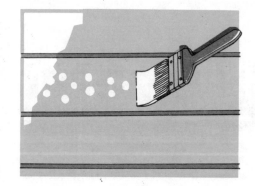

This condition is called crawling, and if you continue the globs will dry and then begin to crack.

Consider these questions, which will lead you to the cause of the crawling: Is the weather chilly or foggy? Are you using a rubber-base paint directly on top of an oil-base paint without a primer? Did you mix the paint thoroughly to distribute liquid and solid particles evenly. Did you use a paint remover on the surface before painting that left the surface greasy or waxy?

To prevent crawling, you should paint on a clear, dry day with the temperature no lower than 50 degrees. Mix the paint properly. If you must paint over a greasy or waxy surface, rub that surface with turpentine and steel wool, and then apply a bonding primer before putting on the finish coat. And don't mix paint with different kinds of bases.

FADING

All colored paint eventually fades. There are certain factors, however, that dictate whether some will experience this color failure faster than others. The paint on homes near bodies of salt water, for example, will fade much faster, because the salt air affects paints adversely.

If one side of your home is particularly subjected to heavy poundings of wind-driven rain and snow and then bright sunlight, it will fade faster than the other sides of the house. You don't have much control over salt or heavy weather conditions, but keep in mind that cheaper paints fade faster than more expensive types because they contain less or cheaper color pigments.

BLEEDING

This type of stain occurs most frequently on natural redwood or cedar siding and shingles. The soluble color or sap of the

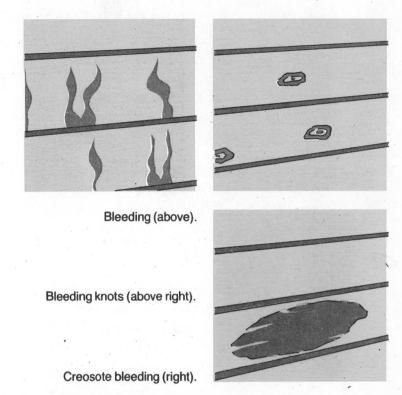

Bleeding (above).

Bleeding knots (above right).

Creosote bleeding (right).

wood begins to run (or bleed), and the siding or shingles are stained. Usually the trouble arises from inadequate sealing of the wood due to thin paint films or irregular application. This allows moisture to penetrate the wood and extract the dye.

The way to stop this action is to apply a coat of shake-shingle paint to the surface to help prevent water penetration. If the siding or shingles have a natural finish, a coat of spar varnish will help. Sometimes excessive moisture originating from inside the house is the source of trouble, in which case corrective measures should be taken to reduce this moisture (see BLISTERING, PAGE 232).

If the bleeding is caused by knots in the wood, the stained areas should be sanded or scraped clean, than coated with a knot sealer and a top coat of paint to match the surrounding surface.

An altogether different type of bleeding action can result if the siding has originally been treated with creosote or with a paint containing creosote. You can detect it by noticing staining blotches, instead of runs, coming up through the paint. It means that the creosote has dissolved and is working its way to the surface.

To combat creosote bleeding, each blotched area should be scraped and sanded down to bare wood. The wood should be painted with a clear sealer or aluminum paint primer and then with two top coats. If the blotches are extensive, it might be necessary to do this to the entire house.

WRINKLING

When paint assumes a rough, wrinkled texture, the condition is known as wrinkling. The main cause is application of too thick a coat. Never try to make one coat of

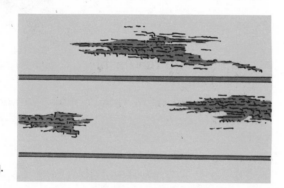
Wrinkling.

paint do the work of two, since the top surface will dry first and leave the bottom still soft. As the bottom surface attempts to dry, it can absorb the binder of the top paint and make that paint wrinkle. Wrinkling can also occur if paint is applied to a cold surface. In this case, only the top surface dries while the colder bottom surface remains soft.

MILDEW AND SULFIDE DISCOLORATION

These two conditions resemble each other. They take the form of rusty or sooty deposits on the paint surface.

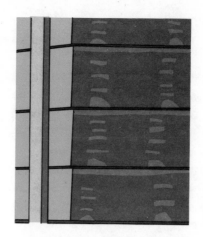
Mildew discoloration.

Mildew occurs primarily in damp climates, but it can form anywhere if a portion of the house doesn't receive sunlight. Suppose, for example, a corner is monopolized by shrubs that keep the siding in shade continuously. This spot is wide open to an attack by mildew-producing fungi.

Industrial chemicals carried in the air are the leading cause of sulfide discoloration, but this type of paint failure is not necessarily confined to those homes located in or near industrial sites. Sulfide discoloration can also occur in locations where there is rotting vegetable or animal matter, as near a stagnant beach area or swamp.

● To treat the condition, you must first determine whether it is mildew, sulfide discoloration, or just plain dirt. Dirt can be washed off with a strong detergent—mildew and sulfide discoloration cannot.

To test for mildew, apply household bleach to a spot. If the area is mildewed, the bleach will lighten it. You can get rid of fungus by scrubbing the affected area with a solution of trisodium phosphate (available in paint stores) mixed in household ammonia and water, followed by a thorough rinsing with water. Then look over the area and determine if you can get some sunlight on it. Perhaps a rearrangement of one or two shrubs will suffice.

The test for sulfide discoloration is to wash the spot with hydrogen peroxide. If the stain lightens or bleaches, a sulfide con-

Proper Painting Practices

dition exists. Hydrogen sulfide stains can be removed by a hydrogen peroxide solution, but the results are rarely worth the effort. The best solution is repainting.

When it's time to repaint and mildew or sulfide discoloration has been present, you should use a special fume- and mildew-resistant paint that will combat the condition. This type of paint contains no pigments that will discolor when exposed to hydrogen sulfide and also has a fungicide such as a phenyl mercuric compound added to it.

PEELING

Peeling can take place between the top coat of paint and the paint surface directly underneath it, or the entire paint film can peel away, exposing the bare wood. Peeling between coats is usually caused by the application of paint to a greasy or oily surface. It can also be caused by painting over an area that is too smooth or glossy, as is frequently the case under eaves where the old coat of paint was protected from normal weathering.

● Before repainting, always roughen hard glossy surfaces with sandpaper and remove loose flakes of old paint where peeling has occurred. Greasy or oily material should be removed by washing with a detergent, wiping with solvent, or sanding.

If peeling occurs between the paint film and the wood surface, it is usually the result of a moisture problem. Often, paint blisters caused by moisture break open, and the paint film flakes off. The moisture problem should be cured before painting (see BLISTERING, PAGE 232).

Peeling.

5
Doors and Windows

EXTERIOR DOORS take a lot more of a beating than do those inside the house. They are exposed to the elements, and they are operated—opened and closed—more frequently than most doors inside the house, with the possible exception of bathroom doors. They are more likely to be slammed shut by youngsters (and adults) in a hurry than are other doors. Windows, too, are subject to a lot of abuse, from the elements, and from frequency of raising and lowering or otherwise opening and closing.

Doors and windows can be the weak spots on the outside of your home. Obviously a broken window will not do its job of keeping out the elements, although its other function of letting in light will still be performed—except that you will probably have more light than you care for in such a situation. A door that does not close properly or fits poorly will also not perform as it should and will admit unwanted drafts and insects. It's just common sense to keep doors and windows in good shape.

PREVENTIVE MAINTENANCE

The old aphorism about "a stitch in time" definitely applies here. One "stitch" is to make sure that all exterior doors are hung on three hinges. Interior doors are normally hung on only two hinges, which are enough to support this weight. But exterior doors are of heavier construction, and the third hinge located midway between top and bottom hinges is necessary to support this additional weight; without a third hinge, the door is likely to bind and scrape.

It's also important to keep those hinges swinging freely by lubricating them periodically. You can use household liquid or stick lubricant or machine oil, and while you're at it, give a shot to the door-latching mechanism as well, working the doorknob back and forth as you do. For lock mechanisms, an occasional treatment with graphite should keep them working smoothly.

Windows, too, should be routinely maintained. Sash pulleys and channels should be lubricated. Hinges on casement windows

Exterior doors should be hung on three hinges.

Lubricate hinges and latches periodically.

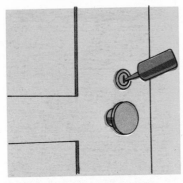

Lubricate locks with graphite.

Lubricate hinges on casement windows (below). Lubricate sash pulleys (right).

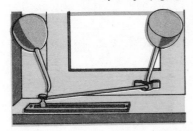

pearance of new aluminum. After cleaning the surface thoroughly with a good-quality scratchless cleanser to remove every last trace of dirt, oil, or grease, coat the surface with a rustproof finish.

STICKING DOORS

Dampness causes wood doors to swell and stick. As the air dries out, the wood shrinks and the door will once again operate freely. Therefore, planing a sticking door should be a last resort.

Check the condition of the hinges. Position yourself on the inside of the door (so that it closes away from you). With the door closed, examine the spaces between the door and frame. You can run a sheet of paper around the edges to observe the hang of the door; where it binds, the door is too tight. If there is a space at the top, latch side of the rail and a corresponding space at the bottom, hinge side, it means that the upper hinge is probably loose and perhaps the middle and lower ones as well.

Open the door to expose the hinges. Relieve pressure on the top hinge by having someone lightly support the door by its handle, or by slipping a wedge of some sort under the bottom rail. Use a screwdriver to

should be lubricated, as well as the winding mechanisms. Locks should be kept clean and lubricated so that they operate easily.

Paint on both windows and doors should be kept up, and renewed every two to three years at least on the outside. When painting windows, make sure that you don't "paint them shut." Free them as soon as the paint has dried (see page 54).

Steel window casements present other maintenance problems. Many basement windows and other window sashes are of steel. Rain, snow, sun, and constant change in temperature make them prime targets for the invasion of rust. You should keep the outside surfaces of steel windows in good shape by coating them with a rust protector. If they are already rusty, remove scale and loose rust by scraping and wire-brushing. Then apply a special primer over the cleaned surface. Follow this with a coat of rust-proofing finish.

Aluminum doesn't rust, because rust is the oxide of iron. But aluminum does oxidize, into a whitish film that dulls its surface and certainly detracts from the appearance of your home if you have aluminum windows. You can preserve the silvery ap-

Check hang of door with a sheet of paper.

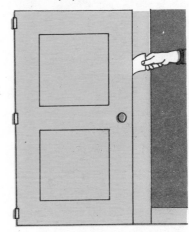

Slip wedge under door while tightening hinge screws.

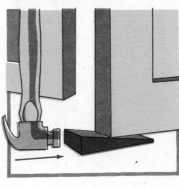

Doors and Windows

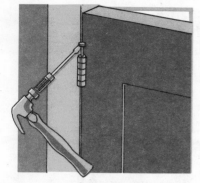

Knock out hinge pins (middle pin first, top pin last).

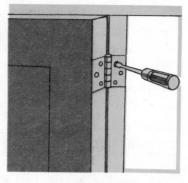

Remove hinges if pins are "frozen."

Hammer in wooden plugs.

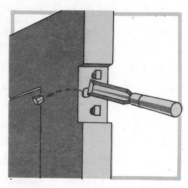

Trim plugs.

Chisel mortise deeper.

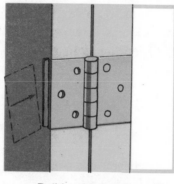

Build up hinge with a shim.

Put shim behind half the width of the hinge.

Reposition hinge leaf in its mortise.

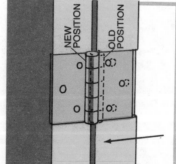

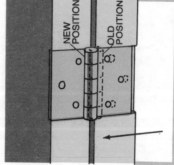

tighten all the screws. If a screw does not appear to have any purchase, the wood around the screw has deteriorated. This can be corrected.

Remove the door by knocking out first the middle then the lower and upper hinge pins. Use a screwdriver angled so that the head of the pin is driven up and out. Should the pin be "frozen," remove the hinge at the jamb. Inspect the mortise and the condition of the wood. If the holes look pulpy or rotted, hammer in a small wooden plug coated with glue or stuff the spaces with toothpicks or wooden matches dipped in glue. Trim, then replace the hinge, using longer screws if possible.

▲Sometimes the hinge plate is not recessed deeply enough in the mortise, in which case you will have to chisel the mortise deeper. Or it may be possible, if spacing at the latch stile permits, to build up the lower and middle hinges and thus shift the door to the vertical. The shim can be any piece of cardboard of the correct thickness (a matchbook cover serves well) and it should fill the mortise completely.

▲When the door binds along the entire length of the latch stile, you will have to cut the mortises deeper, as required. If necessary, you can deepen the mortises on both the jamb and the door.

●Shimming helps if the door tends to spring open when you try to close it. In this case, place a strip of cardboard behind only half the width of the hinge leaf. You need not remove the hinge for this operation. Loosen the screws so that when the door is partly closed, the hinge leaf comes away from the mortise. Slip the shim into this space and tighten the screws. Shimming at this point serves to change the angle of the door so that it leans toward the stop.

▲If the hinge stile is catching or binding along the stop, you can reposition the hinge in its mortise to pull the door away a bit.

Often a door binds at several points at once because it or the frame has been warped out of shape. (Cracks or stress marks on the interior wall around the frame are signs that the frame is at fault). In this case, adjusting the hinges will not do the job completely. You will have to plane or sand the door as well.

Careful inspection will show where excess material has to be removed. Usually only a portion of an edge has to be corrected, rather than the entire length of a stile or rail. If such is the case at the outside stile, you can probably get away without having to remove the door.

Mark off the sticking areas while the door is closed so that you know how much has to be cut. Remove the door if necessary and prop it on its edge against some solid support. Work the plane in smooth strokes and do not bite too deeply at any one time. If the binding exists at the latch area of the door it may prove simpler to plane the hinge side instead. Hinge leaves are easier to remove than the lock assembly.

▲When the door rubs at the top or bottom, you must plane one or both rails, either partially or fully. Here you are cutting across the grain, and if you work too roughly or use a dull tool it is easy to splinter the wood. If the amount to be removed is minimal, use a sanding block instead, but take care not to bevel the door edges.

▲A door sometimes becomes too narrow because of shrinkage, with the result that the latch is not able to reach the striker plate to engage it. In this case, build up the width of the door by gluing and nailing a

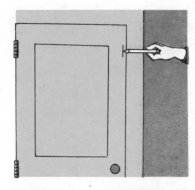

Close door, mark sticking areas.

Remove door and plane.

Plane rail.

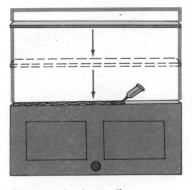

Glue wood strip to stile.

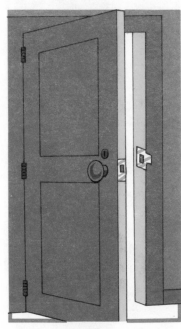

Mark striker plate, close door.

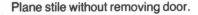

Plane stile without removing door.

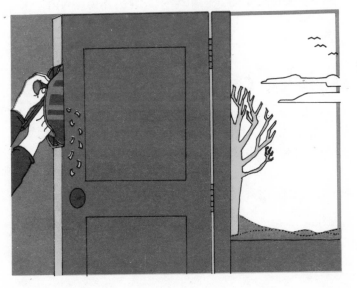

strip of wood along the hinge stile. Measure to determine where the hinge leaves should be set, and chisel new mortises to receive them. Finish the strip to match the door.

▲These adjustments may create a problem. The door now swings freely but the latch is unable to engage the striker plate in the frame, with the result that the plate must be repositioned. To tell how much and in what direction, rub some crayon over the face of the striker plate and close the door. The resultant mark on the plate will indicate what has to be done.

If the latch is centered but falls short of

the receptacle in the plate, try filing the metal to align the hole. Also trim wood from the mortise, if required. If the entire plate has to be moved, fill the original screw holes with plugs before attempting to screw the plate in a new position. Gaps between the plate and the mortise can be filled with wood putty and touched up with paint. These same instructions apply when the plate must be moved up or down to meet the latch.

● Because they are of lighter construction than standard doors, screen and combination screen-and-storm doors sometimes sag or bend out of shape, making them difficult to close. This can be corrected by the use of a turnbuckle and cable placed on either the inside or outside of the door.

The cable should be long enough to fit from one corner of the door to the corner diagonally opposite, plus enough extra for connections (either by twisting or by the use of cable clamps). Cut the cable in half. Fasten one piece of the cable to a screw eye on the top side rail over the hinges; fasten the other to the bottom of the opposite side rail. Fasten the turnbuckle between the two cables. Tighten the turnbuckle until the door is squared up and closes properly.

▲ Outside basement doors or hatchways present some special problems because they are completely exposed to the weather and serve the function of a roof as well as a door. The old wooden types should be painted every year. As they deteriorate, you can make temporary repairs by screwing 1 x 3 or 1 x 4 cleats across the boards, preferably on the inside if this is possible. Eventually, though, the entire door will have to be replaced. The best choice here is a weather-tight steel door.

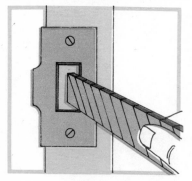

File striker plate.

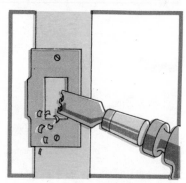

Trim wood from mortise.

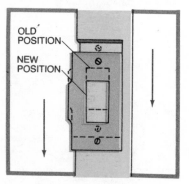

OLD POSITION
NEW POSITION

Move striker plate.

Fill depth with wood putty.

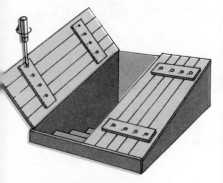

Temporary repair of basement entry door.

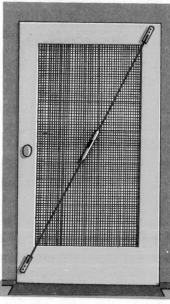

Correct sagging screen door.

STICKING WINDOWS

When a wood window sash sticks or binds, it is often because of carelessly applied paint that has worked into the sash

Tap sash with a hammer and a block to free window.

If the tapping does not help, free window with chisel.

If this still does not work, pry window up from bottom.

Sand molding and track after window is free.

molding. Paint-stuck windows can often be freed by tapping along both sides of the sash with a hammer and a block of wood. If this doesn't work, insert the blade of a paint scraper or a broad, thin chisel (never a screwdriver, which would gouge the wood) between the sash and the stop molding inside the house. Rock the tool back and forth gently to force the sash back from the molding. Repeat this at several points at each side of the sash until it moves freely.

If the window still can't be raised, or if a seal forms at the bottom edge of the sash after painting, the window can be pried loose from the outside without damage to the finish. A hatchet is a good tool for this, or any broad, hard metal wedge. Hammer the tool along the bottom of the sash and pry as you go along.

Once the window is free, scrape off any crusts of paint at the back face of the stop molding. Sand the molding lightly, touching up the window track as well.

A window may also become permanently

swollen out of shape. Try this repair first: Cut a block of wood that will fit snugly into the channel between the inner and outer window stops. Give the block several smart raps with a hammer at both sides of the window. This should free the sash so that it can be raised at least partially. Repeat the procedure at the exposed channels at the bottom. Then apply lubricant such as paraffin or candle wax to the channels.

If this method fails, the sash will have to be removed from the frame to make the necessary adjustments. The lower sash must be removed before the upper. Most newer windows are equipped with metal tension strips fastened to the channels. With some of this type, it is possible to remove the sash simply by pressing it sideways into a channel and lifting it free.

On windows with sash cords, the stop molding will have to be removed first. Insert a thin, broad chisel behind one end of the molding and twist so that the strip comes away partially at that point. Work

Hammer tapping block above window channel.

After window is raised, repeat procedure at the bottom.

Release sash from tension strips fastened to the channels.

Insert chisel behind one end of the molding.

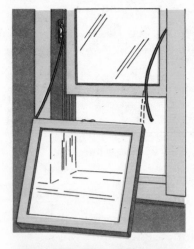

Secure sash cord.

Disengage sash cord.

Adjust tension strips.

Plane sash.

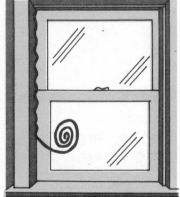

Use weatherstripping
to stop rattles.

Remove molding and nail it
back closer to the sash.

of oil to the pulley shaft (as you should be doing regularly anyway).

If the window has tension strips, try adjusting these first by turning the mounting screws. If this does not work, or if no mechanical adjustment is possible, wood can be sanded or planed from the sides of the sash to make it fit. Do not remove too much material at any one time. It is a good idea first to clean up and lubricate the channels, then check the fit of the window as you plane or sand. It should fit snugly without binding.

When a wood window rattles, there is too much space between the sash and its stop molding. An easy way to alleviate this problem is to run a strip of metal or felt weatherstripping into the space. To make a permanent repair, remove the molding and nail it back closer to the sash.

Metal sliding windows (such as aluminum storm windows) may bind when dirt collects in the tracks. Sometimes the metal becomes pitted, impeding the window's

Clean metal tracks
with steel wool.

Tighten loose
screws on hinges
of casement
windows.

carefully to avoid damaging or breaking the molding. With the strip removed, disengage the sash cord at each side. Fasten a nail or strip of wood to the ends of the cords so that they will not slip past the pulley. Lower the weight gently and observe the action of the pulley. If it is stiff, apply a few drops smooth operation. Usually this can be corrected with a cleanup and rubbing with fine steel wool. The tracks should then be lubricated periodically with paraffin or wax. Never try to pry the window with a sharp tool—this will distort the tracks.

When steel casement windows stick or bind, check to see that hinges are free of rust or accumulated paint. Look for loose hinge screws or for binding in the crank mechanism. Tighten hinges and clean with steel wool, then apply machine oil. It may be necessary to open the handle assembly for cleaning and oiling.

REPLACING BROKEN GLASS

The replacement of broken windows is the subject of frequent amusement in the funny papers, wherein the juvenile protagonist puts a baseball or football through the picture window of the neighborhood crabby old man. The humor is undeniable, but the reality isn't all that much fun.

Replacing cracked or broken window glass is not difficult, but it does require some care. You need a sharp glass cutter (if you cut the glass yourself), prepared putty or glazing compound (more flexible than putty), glazier's points, pliers, and a putty knife.

Installation of the glass is normally done from the outside, so if you are repairing a second-floor window it may be wise to remove the sash, if that is possible. Wear heavy work gloves when removing broken pieces of glass from the frame. Heat from a soldering gun will help soften the old putty, or a small wood chisel can be used to clean it out, but take care not to damage the frame. Extract the metal glazier's points with pliers.

The replacement glass should be cut ¹/₁₆ inch smaller all around than the frame

opening, to allow for any irregularities that may exist in the frame. Most hardware stores will cut glass to specified size, or you can do it yourself as follows.

Mark the glass with a sharpened crayon, then turn it over and lay it on a flat surface covered with newspaper or an old blanket. Use a steel straightedge to guide the cut. Any doubts about the condition of the glass cutter can be satisfied by first scoring a piece of the old glass: if the score mark shows signs of skipping, the cutting wheel is dull or chipped. You might as well scrap it and buy a new one—it's a lot cheaper than ruining a piece of glass.

Make sure the glass is free of dust or grit before attempting the cut. The score mark should be begun at the edge of the glass farthest from you, then followed through in a single motion with smooth, even pressure on the cutter. When the glass is scored, lay it over the straightedge or the edge of a table and apply pressure on both sides of the score to break it cleanly. If the piece to be

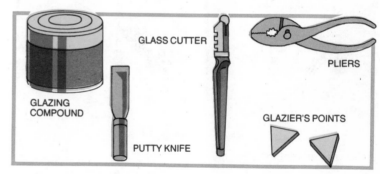

Tools to replace broken glass.

1. Score glass.

2. Break glass along score mark.

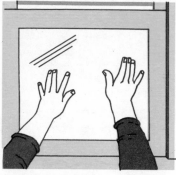

3. If the strip is narrow, break it off with glass cutter.

4. Apply bed of glazing compound before installing the glass.

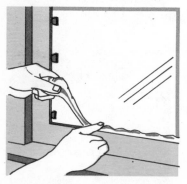

5. Press glass into frame.

6. Install glazier's points.

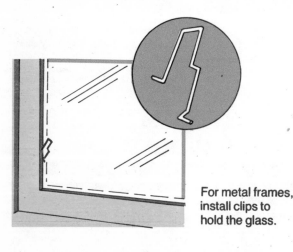

7. Press in glazing compound.

8. Smooth with putty knife.

For metal frames, install clips to hold the glass.

Insert new glass into storm window frame (left) and press gasket into place.

removed is very narrow, snap it off with the slotted head of the cutting tool.

Before installing the glass, apply a ⅛-inch bed of glazing compound around the rabbeted groove of the frame. Press the glass into place, making sure it lies flat against the shoulders of the frame. Secure it with the glazier's points, pressing them into the frame 4 to 6 inches apart on all sides.

Make a "rope" of glazing compound about ½ inch thick. Use your fingers to press it against the wood and glass around the frame. Smooth and bevel the compound with the blade of the putty knife, making sure you leave no breaks or separations in the seal. A coat of paint finishes the job.

For metal windows the procedure varies slightly. On these the glass panes are secured to the frames with small metal clips buried in the compound. These will have to be removed and set aside. Lay a bed of glazing compound into the frame and set the replacement glass firmly into this bed. Install the clips, then apply the final bed of glazing compound.

Metal storm windows normally have frames that are grooved to hold a gasket that secures the glass in place. This is removed when glass must be replaced. The new glass is inserted into the channels of the frame. The gasket is then pressed back into place.

There have been numerous instances of people seriously injuring themselves by walking through or putting their hands through large windows or doors. Safety and consumer agencies have been urging legislation requiring the use of less hazardous materials in such vulnerable places as sliding glass patio doors, storm doors, and other areas where glass might be a hazard.

Laws incorporating these recommendations have already been passed by several states, requiring that "safety glazing material" be used in potentially dangerous areas. Some of the safety materials are tempered glass, laminated glass, wire glass, and acrylic plastic.

These materials may be slightly more difficult to install than regular glass, and their cost is generally higher. By installing these materials in place of standard glass panes, however, the extra cost will be offset by the sense of security in knowing one's house is safe. One thing to watch out for with the rigid plastic materials such as acrylics is surface mars. While their lesser hardness makes them less susceptible to breakage than glass, it also increases their chances of getting nicked or scratched.

SCREEN REPAIR

Keep wood window and door screens in good condition by stacking them flat in a dry, well-ventilated area until ready for use. Frames should be tightened when necessary and given a fresh coat of paint from time to time to help preserve them.

A damaged wood screen frame can be repaired easily enough. Trouble usually occurs at the frame joints. The joint itself may be loose or the wood broken or rotted. A joint can be tightened by bracing the frame pieces with ⅜ inch dowel. Drill a hole though the side member into the top or bottom piece, or, if the corners are mitered, at an angle through both pieces. Coat the

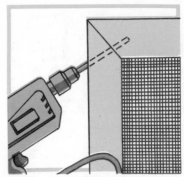
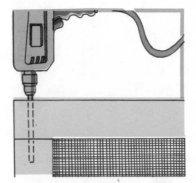

1. Drill a hole into the frame joint of the screen.

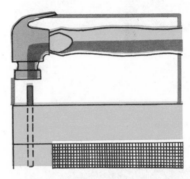
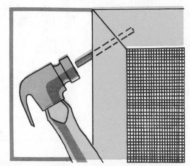

2. Drive a dowel, coated with glue, into the hole.

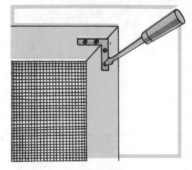
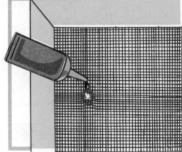

Repair of the frame joint with a flat metal angle.

A drop or two of waterproof cement will cover a small hole.

dowel with glue and hammer it into the hole, trimming or driving it flush, as the case may be. Another method is to fasten a flat metal angle over the corner joint. This type of repair is more noticeable, however.

A small hole in screening should be patched as soon as it is discovered. Otherwise, it is an invitation to tiny bugs, and it will almost surely grow rapidly in size. If the hole is small enough, a drop or two of waterproof cement will do the job. The cement hardens and covers the hole.

Doors and Windows

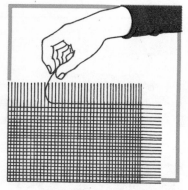

1. Unravel wires on patch.

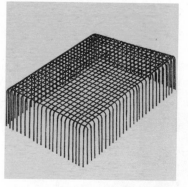

2. Bend wires.

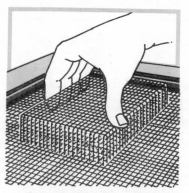

3. Insert over damaged area.

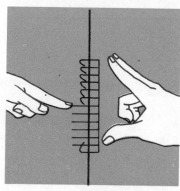

4. Bend back wires.

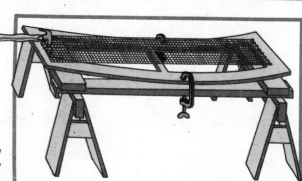

Clamp frame across sawhorses to assure tight fit.

Tack new screening tautly at each end.

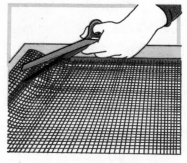

Lay new screening over metal frame.

Tap spline back into its groove.

For larger holes and tears, use a snips or heavy-duty scissors to cut a patch of wire screen material ½ inch larger than the hole. If you do not have extra screen, patches in various sizes are available at any hardware store.

Unravel two wires at each side of the patch, then bend the end wires at a right angle on all four sides. Place the patch over the hole and push the bent wires through to the other side of the screen. Then bend them back to secure the patch firmly.

When screening is badly damaged or deteriorating, replacement is necessary. To replace wire screen in a wood frame, first remove the molding. Use a paint scraper or putty knife for this job, prying gently along the length of the molding until it comes free. Remove all staples or tacks from the frame and take out the old screening. Cut the new screen 1 inch wider at all sides with scissors or snips.

To assure a tight fit, apply tension to the screen while it is being tacked to the frame. The best way to do this is to lay the frame across a pair of sawhorses or a work surface as wide as the frame. Place a cross board under each end of the frame, then C-clamp the sides of the frame to the work surface so that there is a slight bow formed in the middle.

Tack the new screening tautly at each end, doubling the material where you tack. Now release the C-clamps and tack the screen along the sides of the frame. Replace the molding and trim any wire that protrudes from under it.

In metal frames, a spline holds the screening in place. This must be pried out to remove torn screening. New screening is then laid over the framing and trimmed to size, with the corners cut at 45-degree angles. The spline is then tapped back into its groove in the frame to secure the screening.

6

Porches

Porches are things of the past. Once people began jetting around in automobiles and watching television, there was little need to pass the time waving to neighbors while rocking on the front porch. Plenty of older homes still have them, however, and their owners cherish them on balmy summer evenings when the mock-orange is in fragrant bloom.

Practically speaking, however, a porch can often be a liability rather than an asset. Most porches around today have long been exposed to the elements and often show signs of decay. Many homeowners resolve this problem by either removing or closing in their porches. To nostalgia buffs, this is heresy, but we can sympathize.

SAGGING PORCH

If a porch has a major problem, it is usually manifested by sagging. This means that one or more of the structural members has deteriorated, usually because of excess moisture. The underside of a porch is much like the crawl space of a home, except that it is not as completely enclosed and the usual moisture-preventive steps have not been taken. Use the same preventive methods on porch crawl spaces as for those under the house itself.

Staple a vapor barrier to the underside of the porch floor joists, after first making any necessary repairs to structural members (see below). Cover the ground beneath the porch with polyethylene sheeting or heavy felt paper, overlapping the seams and the house wall 3 or 4 inches and sealing all seams and the wall joint with asphalt cement. Then spread a 2-inch-thick layer of sand over the area.

You'll have to get in under the porch to take these measures, of course, which may mean removing latticework, or perhaps some of the masonry that forms the foundation of many porches. If you're lucky, it will be only latticework, because you may cause more problems than you solve by blasting through masonry.

Once inside, you may find some company. Rats, mice, cats, and other animals love

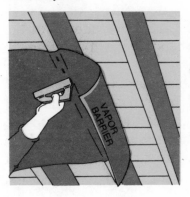

Staple vapor barrier beneath joists.

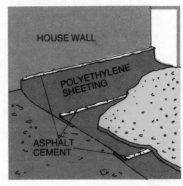

Cover ground beneath porch with sheeting.

Porches

Raise the porch flooring with a brace.

Raise the porch flooring with a jack.

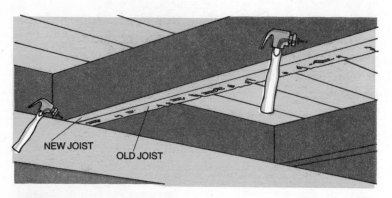

NEW JOIST

OLD JOIST

Nail new joists next to the old ones.

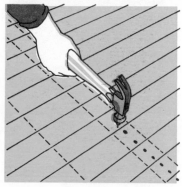

Nail floor boards to joists from above.

the cozy space under a porch. So take a flashlight—and maybe a baseball bat. Check all the wood beams and joists. Some may be obviously decayed, others less obviously so. Dig a penknife into all of the structural members to see if they are in good shape or not.

Most sag problems can be cured by running new joists next to the old ones, but first you have to get the porch up to the right level. Unlike the structural members of the main part of the house, there isn't usually much weight bearing on the joists,

so try to raise the flooring with a piece of 4 x 4 or 2 x 4, braced against a solid surface below. If that doesn't work, rented adjustable jacks should do the job.

Once the floor is level again, nail new joists next to the old, driving nails into both the old joists and the beams on each end. Afterwards, nail the floorboards down into the new joists from above.

■ If the main beams or supports of the porch are also in poor condition, you can try buttressing them as with the joists. This may not be possible, in which case you don't have much choice except to remove the porch entirely. You can build a new one if you're "into" porches, but economically it's not too wise.

REPLACING DAMAGED FLOORBOARDS

There is no reason why porch flooring shouldn't last as long as the other wood in a home. If kept painted with a good porch-and-deck paint, and if moisture doesn't collect underneath, the boards should endure. But if this painting is neglected, and moisture problems in the crawl space are also ignored, rotted floorboards are likely.

Most porch flooring is of the tongue-and-groove variety. When replacing damaged sections, it is important not to mar the surrounding boards. The section must be cut away over the nearest joists. To replace just a board or two, mark off the section of board to be removed at an exact right angle to the boards. A framing square will help here. With an electric drill or brace and bit, make large, interconnected holes inside the lines on both ends of the damaged section. With a large wood chisel, break out the damaged portion by striking along the grain.

Remove the pieces, being particularly careful not to damage the tongue or groove

1. Mark board over joists.

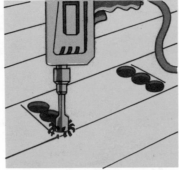

2. Drill holes.

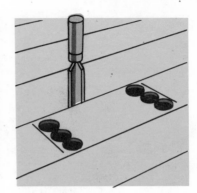

3. Chisel along grain.

of the boards on either side. Chisel out the remainder of the board on the outside of the drilled holes, making sure that you cut exactly on the line. Pull out any remaining nails and clean out all debris.

Now put a new board along the removed section, and mark carefully where the damaged section was, again at an exact right angle using the framing square. Saw along the lines and chisel off the *bottom* of the grooved edge so that the board will slip into the open space. (Leave the top portion of the grooved edge.) Slip the board into place and nail through the top with aluminum or galvanized flooring or finishing nails. Use two nails on each end, set them, and cover with wood filler.

RAILING REPAIRS ▲

Porch railings also suffer from the elements and neglect. Replacement is routine, by removing the rotted rail or baluster and replacing with a new one—if you can find a matching piece. It may be impossible to find a matching baluster for many old-fashioned railings, and a new one may have to be fabricated. You can do this yourself if you have a lathe. Otherwise, take the old one to a millworking shop and have a new one turned. The joints on exterior work are usually simple, and you should be able to knock out the deteriorated pieces with a

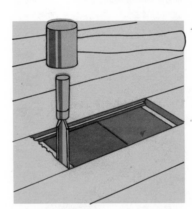

4. Chisel at ends.

5. Mark new board.

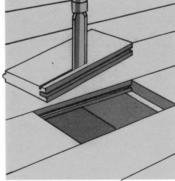

6. Remove bottom of grooved edge.

7. Fit new board into place.

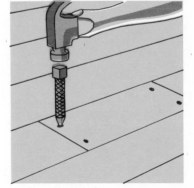

8. Nail securely.

Porches

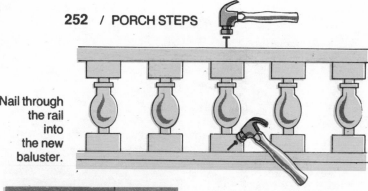

Nail through the rail into the new baluster.

hammer and replace them without complicated joinery by nailing through the rail into the baluster, or toenailing the baluster to the rail.

PORCH STEPS

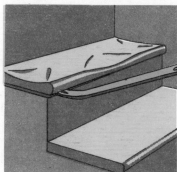

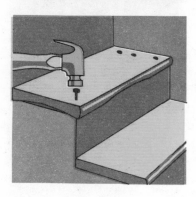

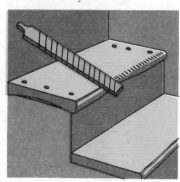

To repair porch steps:
1. Pry up worn tread (left).

2. Turn it over and nail it into place (below left).

3. Round edges of new tread with rasp and sandpaper (below).

If porch treads are simply worn down, the easiest way to repair them is to pry them up with a wrecking bar, turn them over, and nail them in place bottomside up. Outside steps are not ordinarily rabbeted or dadoed. Use aluminum or galvanized finishing nails, set the nails, and fill the holes with wood putty.

When new treads or risers are needed, take an old one to the lumberyard and try to find a match. If you can't match exactly, buy lumber of a greater width and rip to fit. (Today's dimensional lumber is slightly thinner than that of times past, but this need be of no concern, as the structural strength is essentially the same, or greater.) Rounded edges can be duplicated with a rasp and sandpaper. Apply wood preservative to new wood before nailing in place.

Porches

7

Driveways and Sidewalks

ALTHOUGH DRIVEWAYS and sidewalks can be made of a variety of materials such as brick, stone, or gravel, most are composed of concrete or blacktop (asphalt). There is no such thing as a "cement" driveway. Cement is merely a small (though very important) ingredient in a concrete mix.

Concrete is made up mostly of "aggregate" (crushed stone or other inorganic matter) and sand, mixed with cement and water. In a very real sense, cement is the "glue" that holds the mixture together. When mixed with water, it is called by the accurate and descriptive phrase "cement paste."

The cement used in concrete is portland cement, a soft, fine, grayish-green powder made from pulverized limestone and other ingredients. The term portland was applied because the concrete made from it resembled Portland stone, a widely used building material of the 19th century.

The usual concrete mix for driveways and sidewalks is roughly 10 percent portland cement, 17½ percent water, and 72½ percent sand and medium-size aggregate. Concrete mixes can vary from a lean, stiff mix of 15 percent water, 7 percent portland cement, and 78 percent sand and large, coarse aggregate to a rich, wet mix of 20 percent water, 14 percent portland cement, and 66 percent sand and small, fine aggregate. The aggregates are broken down into fine, medium, and coarse. Sand is actually a very fine aggregate, as is crushed gravel. Coarse aggregate is usually crushed stone, but it can also be gravel or blast-furnace slag.

There are quite a few important steps involved in laying long-lasting concrete, and if any of them are omitted or skimped on, the result can be flaking, scaling, or some other form of deterioration. Concrete that has been carefully mixed, placed, and cured should last several lifetimes. But even when it is perfectly constructed, a sidewalk or driveway has several natural enemies—trees, children with hammers, and frosts, to name just a few.

MINOR CONCRETE REPAIRS

The art of concrete repair has advanced greatly in the past decade or so. New repair mixes containing a vinyl or epoxy ingredient have made minor repairs quick and easy. Except for large cracks, special patching mixes are recommended rather than the standard concrete formula. Standard concrete does not adhere well to old concrete.

Patching compounds can be "feathered" to smooth edges, which makes them ideal

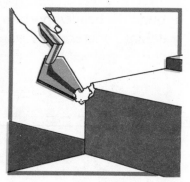

Feather edge of patch.   Repair step corner.

for repairs that need a fine edge. They can also be applied on top of old concrete without elaborate preparation. Vinyl or epoxy compounds can be used to fill in small concrete sections that have settled because of poor soil preparation or frost. These formulas are also fine for filling small cracks and holes. Chipped step corners also can be fixed with this type of patch without using forms. Application should follow the manufacturer's directions.

LARGE CRACKS

Most large holes and cracks could also be filled with these modern cement patches, but the compounds are too expensive to be used on a large scale. When a lot of crack-filling is to be done, it is just as easy and considerably cheaper to use regular concrete, first undercutting the crack to a V-shape with a chisel. (Your dentist does the

same when he puts a filling in a tooth.) This provides "tooth" for the concrete patch. A standard concrete mix is then pressed into the crack with a trowe or similar instrument. Most building supply houses sell small bags or pails of premixed concrete for this purpose. Or you can mix your own, as described later for major repair work.

BADLY FLAKING SURFACES

When the surface of concrete is badly flaked or pitted, it is probable that a poor job was done in the first place. It may be possible to save the old concrete without replacing it, but the repair could be only temporary, and eventually you might have to tear up the whole job. Before resorting to that drastic step, there are several things you can try.

● If only a small section is involved, scrape off all the flaking material with a wire brush. Be sure to get rid of any old concrete that has started to crack or deteriorate. Chip it out with a cold chisel and a mash hammer. Then cover the surface with vinyl or epoxy patching mix.

▲ If the deteriorated area is a large one, this method may prove too expensive, particularly since it isn't guranteed to last. One way to avoid a complete replacement is to use the old concrete as a base and pour a new surface on top of that. You must allow at least 2 inches of thickness for the new concrete. If there isn't room to pour another 2 inches on top of the old, you will have

Undercut crack.   Trowel in concrete.

Chip away old concrete.

Wire-brush flaking area.

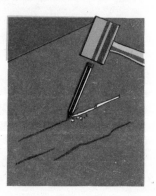

Scarify old surface by roughening it up with a sledge hammer.

to dig out 2 inches of the old concrete, in which case it is probably easier to dig up the whole thing. Most private sidewalks can be raised 2 inches without disturbing the landscape, but a driveway is another matter. Raising it that high may cause rainwater to drain into your garage, or be just enough to catch your bumper or muffler as you enter or leave. Sidewalks along the public right-of-way may be prescribed by building codes. Study the implications of a 2-inch rise in the surface before you decide to pursue that method.

Before pouring new concrete on top of the old, wire-brush the old surface and rough it up with a sledgehammer and/or an application of 20 percent muriatic acid and 80 percent water. Be sure to wear gloves and boots when working with muriatic acid, and protect your eyes. When that is done, 2-inch forms are built, as described later.

HEAVED SIDEWALK SECTIONS

A heaved-up concrete section may be caused by severe weather contrasts or by undermining tree roots. In either case, the cure for the sorry condition involves breaking up the old slab (as far as the adjacent expansion joint) and putting in a new one. If weather conditions prevent it, or if you simply don't have the time or stomach to tackle the complete repair, it will at least

help to avoid accidents if you create a slope around the heaved portion of walk. Use the patching material discussed above to smooth around the offending section as best you can. But vow to do a complete repair job in the not-too-distant future.

For the permanent repair, break up the old section using a sledgehammer or—if you can rent or borrow one—a jackhammer. Concrete was meant to last, so don't expect an easy time of it.

Once the old concrete is removed, you can determine whether or not a tree root was the cause of the problem. If so, take an axe and cut off the offending root. Any tree that is strong enough to heave concrete is strong enough to withstand the loss of one root.

If no roots are found, you can assume that Jack Frost did the dirty deed. In that case, it is wise to install wire reinforcing mesh before pouring the new section as described later in this chapter.

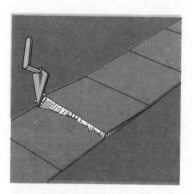
Temporary repair around heaved section.

Break up old section for the permanent repair.

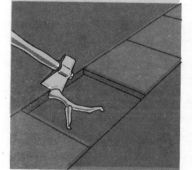
Cut off tree roots.

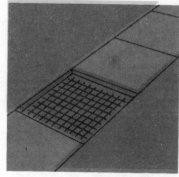
Install wire mesh.

Driveways and Sidewalks

STEPS IN POURING CONCRETE

Whether you're pouring a small new section of sidewalk or a whole new driveway, the basic techniques are the same—it's merely a matter of greater or lesser effort. Just make sure that the effort is well expended and that the job is done right. Doing it right involves the following steps:

1. Preparation of the subgrade (unless you are pouring new concrete on top of old)
2. Formwork
3. Mixing
4. Placement
5. Finishing
6. Curing

Each of these steps must be done carefully and correctly. If any one of them is done improperly, the entire job will probably be ruined, and you'll be right back where you started.

SUBGRADE PREPARATION

Concrete work can be compared to baking a cake. Getting the proper ingredients together in the right proportions is most important, but you also have to find the right pan and prepare it. The "pan" in this case is the formwork. And instead of greasing the pan, you have to prepare the ground.

Second to poor mixing, the most frequent error in concrete work is poor soil preparation. Slabs will settle, crack, and fall apart in poorly prepared or compacted soil. If that was your problem before, take a good look at the subgrade. It should be free of all organic matter such as sod, grass, roots, and soft or mucky ground. If some spots are very hard and others very soft, the concrete will surely crack from settling in the softer areas. Hard spots should be broken up, soft ones filled in and compacted.

On the other hand, do not simply remove whatever soil is under your slab and replace it with fill. If settling and cracking were not problems before, the subgrade is probably all right; as long as it is reasonably uniform and free of vegetable matter, it is better left alone. All it should need is tamping of the top portion that was disturbed by removing the old section. Undisturbed soil is better than soil that has been dug out, replaced, and poorly compacted.

If the soil is soft and highly organic, it should be dug out and replaced with fill. Remove about 4 to 6 inches of the subgrade to a depth of 8 to 10 inches below the surfaces of the adjacent sections. Be careful not to undercut the sound concrete.

Gravel, crushed stone, or blast-furnace slag can be used for fill, but sand is usually preferred for small sections because it can be leveled and compacted more easily. Rake the material, then check with a level and straightedge; it should be as level as possible. For a compactor, you can probably rent an iron tamper, or you can make your own with a 2 x 2 or 2 x 4 handle nailed to a base of ¾-inch plywood or 2 x 6 lumber. For small areas, a 2 x 4 alone will probably suffice. What you use is not as important as using it well. Make sure that you compact the soil completely. Then check it with the level, take down any high spots and fill low spots, and tamp again.

SETTING FORMS

Concrete walks and driveways are normally 4 inches thick, although you may find thinner slabs in garden walks or other walks that bear little traffic. If your driveway has any appreciable truck traffic, such as an oil delivery truck, you may want to consider a 5-inch slab. The best guideline here is to

IRON TAMPER

SELFMADE TAMPER

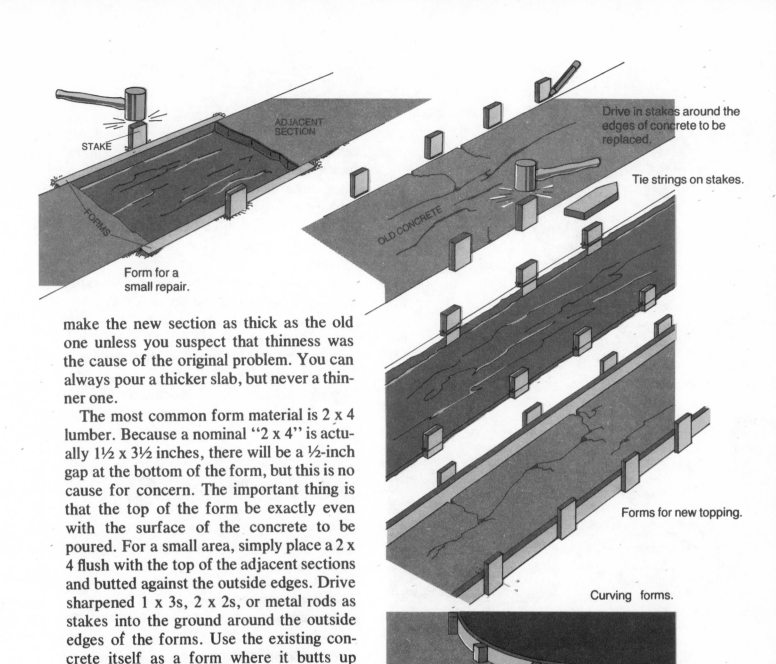

STAKE

ADJACENT SECTION

FORMS

Form for a small repair.

Drive in stakes around the edges of concrete to be replaced.

Tie strings on stakes.

OLD CONCRETE

Forms for new topping.

Curving forms.

make the new section as thick as the old one unless you suspect that thinness was the cause of the original problem. You can always pour a thicker slab, but never a thinner one.

The most common form material is 2 x 4 lumber. Because a nominal "2 x 4" is actually 1½ x 3½ inches, there will be a ½-inch gap at the bottom of the form, but this is no cause for concern. The important thing is that the top of the form be exactly even with the surface of the concrete to be poured. For a small area, simply place a 2 x 4 flush with the top of the adjacent sections and butted against the outside edges. Drive sharpened 1 x 3s, 2 x 2s, or metal rods as stakes into the ground around the outside edges of the forms. Use the existing concrete itself as a form where it butts up against the new section.

▲When replacing large pieces or an entire walk or drive, the formwork is somewhat more complicated. Assuming that the old grade was acceptable, drive in several stakes around the edges before you demolish the old work, and mark them to show the top of the walk or drive. After the old concrete has been taken out, run a string line between these marks to serve as a guide for the new forms. If there is a straight run from one section to the next, simply drive in stakes at both ends and tie the line between. Adjust the forms to that level. Line stakes should be set every 8 feet and the string pulled as taut as possible.

If the old grade wasn't correct, pour concrete to a new one. The ideal slope is ¼ inch per foot. It all depends on the terrain, though, and you can't have that type of slope on a hilly driveway. Just make sure that you don't pitch a driveway toward the garage, or a walkway toward a patio or the house. Concrete acts as a conduit for rainwater, and improper sloping is an open invitation to drainage problems.

Nail through stakes into forms.

Use double-headed nail.

Backfill under form to keep concrete from escaping.

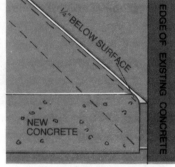

¼" BELOW SURFACE

NEW CONCRETE

EDGE OF EXISTING CONCRETE

Install isolation joints to separate floors from walls.

Use 2 x 4s for forms even though you may be pouring a 2-inch topping over old concrete. The forms must be butted firmly against the sides of the old material. Gentle curves may be formed with ¼-inch exterior plywood or one-inch lumber. Plywood, with the outside grain running vertically, or tempered hardboard are best for sharp curves.

Drive in stakes at each end of short runs and every 4 feet on long runs. Regular spacing is all right for gentle curves, but drive stakes every 1 to 2 feet for short-radius curves. For very sharp curves, you may need 2 x 4 stakes. Drive stakes tight against the outside of the forms and nail through the stakes into the forms—hold the forms with your foot while nailing. If you have difficulty doing this, set temporary stakes on the inside of the forms to hold them during nailing, and remove them when everything is nailed together and before pouring concrete. Use double-headed nails; they are easier to pull out after the forms are removed.

▲When the stakes are all in place, backfill under the forms to keep the concrete from escaping underneath. Install isolation joints, made of ¼- or ½-inch premolded fiber (available at building supply houses), at intersections such as driveway-to-walk or walk-to-house. The joint material should be ¼ inch below the surface of the surrounding concrete.

THE PROPER MIX

Since it is vital to get the right proportions in your concrete mix, take the worry out by using premixed bags on smaller jobs. Premix saves time and trouble as well as anxiety over the right proportions. On large jobs, you can accomplish the same result by ordering "readymix" from a concrete service to be delivered by cement-mixer truck.

It is less expensive, of course, to mix your own concrete. Sometimes you may find that a concrete truck cannot get to the site, and you will have to mix your own anyway. And, unless you have several willing helpers, you will not be able to handle the large loads that readymix suppliers deliver. For one or two workers, it is easier to mix smaller loads and place them in stages.

Portland cement is purchased in bags from local building and mason supply houses. Bags weigh 94 pounds in the United States and are one cubic foot in volume. In Canada, bags weigh 80 pounds each and hold about ⅞ cubic foot.

For the average concrete application, the following proportions are ideal:

  94 pounds of cement (one U.S. bag)
215 pounds of sand
295 pounds of coarse aggregate
   5 gallons of water

A regular bathroom scale is accurate enough for weighing the materials. Use a 3- to 5-gallon galvanized bucket to hold the material, but be sure to weigh the pail first and deduct its weight from the weight of the material. ("Zeroing" the scale with an empty bucket may be easier on your arithmetic.) Don't put more material in the bucket than you can readily handle—it's heavy. Put the sand and aggregate into three or four buckets of equal weight. Once you get the right weight established, mark a line on the bucket for each ingredient and return the scale to the bathroom.

A simpler, although less accurate, way to measure is by volume. To achieve the ideal mix mentioned above, use 1 part portland cement to 2¼ parts sand and 3 parts aggregate. Add 5 gallons of water for each bag of cement. Both of these one-bag formulas should yield approximately ⅙ cubic yard of concrete, enough for a typical section of sidewalk.

When buying aggregates, make sure that they are clean and free of organic matter. Don't bring in stones or sand from the beach. Order fresh, clean, dry sand and gravel or crushed stone from a dealer who specializes in such materials. The coarse aggregate should be "well graded," with a range of sizes from small to large but not too many of any one size. The maximum aggregate size for a 4-inch slab should be one inch in diameter.

In most areas of the United States and all of Canada, concrete should contain an "air-entraining" agent. This can be premixed into the cement (preferably) or be added to the water. Air-entrainment causes tiny bubbles to form inside the concrete. Hardened concrete always contains some minute particles of water, and freezing temperatures cause this water to expand. This is one of the most frequent causes of concrete scaling. The microscopic bubbles created by air-entrainment act as relief valves for the expanding concrete, and also help resist the effects of salt deicers.

HOW MUCH CONCRETE?

To estimate your concrete needs, multiply length times width in feet to get the area, then multiply again by the thickness of the slab. The usual 4-inch slab is ⅓ foot thick, so take ⅓ of the area. If, for example, you are pouring a sidewalk section 4 by 4 feet, 4 inches thick, you have:

  4 x 4 = 16 square feet of surface
16 x ⅓ = 5.3 cubic feet
Because there are 27 cubic feet in a
  cubic yard, divide your total by 27:
  5.3 cubic feet ÷ 27 = .2 cubic yard

You should always figure on a little extra for waste and spillage, so ¼ cubic yard is just about right in this example. If using premix, determine the coverage on the bag (usually ⅓ cubic yard for 45 pounds, ⅔ for 90) and buy accordingly. If you are mixing your own, figure on about 1⅓ bags of portland cement, plus 1⅓ times the other ingredients used in either of the one-bag formulas previously given. (If you want to order readymix, you'll have to have a lot more concrete work to do. Most dealers require a minimum of one cubic yard per delivery.)

You may find it easier to remember that for 4-inch slabs there are 1.23 yards of concrete for every 100 square feet. For small areas, figure .12 yards for every 10 square feet. Two-inch slabs are half of that.

Driveways and Sidewalks

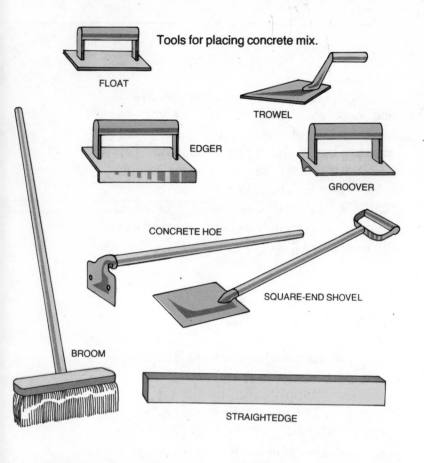

Tools for placing concrete mix.

FLOAT

TROWEL

EDGER

GROOVER

CONCRETE HOE

SQUARE-END SHOVEL

BROOM

STRAIGHTEDGE

WHEELBARROW

CHUTE

MORTAR BOX

PORTABLE MIXER

GARDEN HOSE

MIXING

Small batches of concrete can be mixed by hand on a piece of plywood. You can mix on top of existing concrete if you clean up well afterward, or in a mortar box (you may be able to rent one). For a job of any considerable size, rent a portable mixer.

Premix is dumped in a pile, then a hollow is made in the center and the label-recommended amount of water added. When mixing concrete from scratch, spread the sand out evenly on the mixing surface, then add the cement. Mix both thoroughly by turning over with a square-end shovel until they have a uniform color without streaking. Spread this mix out evenly, then add the coarse aggregate. Again turn over thoroughly. Form a hollow as with the premix.

After water has been added, use the shovel to fold all the materials over toward the center, and continue mixing until all water, cement, sand, and aggregate have been thoroughly combined.

PLACING THE MIX

When the concrete has been thoroughly mixed, or when the readymix arrives, everything should be in readiness for placing. Although job requirements may differ, most employ the following tools: concrete hoe or square-end shovel, straightedge or strike board (a straight 2 x 4 works well), float, edger, groover, trowel, broom, and garden hose. You may also need a wheelbarrow and/or chute to get the mix where you want it to go. Some sort of materials to aid the curing process should also be on hand (see CURING below). Use the hose to wet down the area before pouring concrete.

Never try to wheel concrete up a steep grade. A small grade here and there can be managed, particularly if you can get a good start. But trying to push a wheelbarrow uphill from a standing start is a heavier job than most of us can handle. If you expect difficulty in getting readymix concrete to the site, explain the problem to the dealer. He may be able to suggest a solution. If not, your only choice is machine-mixing close to the site.

Place the concrete in the forms to full depth, spading along the sides to complete filling. Try to lead the concrete as close as possible to its final position without too much dragging and shoveling. Start in one corner and continue pouring until you reach the other side. Use the shovel or concrete hoe to get as uniform coverage as possible.

When you have poured enough concrete to fill the forms, the next operations—striking off and rough-floating—should follow immediately. A prime requisite for successful finishing is that rough-floating must be completed before bleed water starts to appear on the surface of the concrete.

STRIKING OFF AND FLOATING

After placing, strike off the surface with a 2 x 4 straightedge, working it in a sawlike motion across the top of the form boards. The strike-off or "screeding" action smooths the surface while cutting off ex-

cess concrete to the proper elevation. Go over the concrete twice in this manner to take out any bumps or fill in low spots. Tilt the straightedge slightly in the direction of travel to obtain a better cutting effect.

Immediately after striking off, the surface is rough-floated to smooth it and remove irregularities. Use a wood hand float for most patchwork, but try to rent a large bull float if you are doing a big job. The float is tilted slightly away from you as you push it forward, then flattened as it is pulled back.

EDGING AND GROOVING

If you use air-entrained concrete, the finishing process can begin almost immediately after rough-floating. Even without air-entrainment, you do not have to wait long on a hot, dry, windy day. If the weather is cool and humid, however, you may be forced to wait several hours. The key to proper timing is whether or not there is water sheen on the surface. Begin when the sheen has disappeared, which happens sooner on days when quicker evaporation can be expected.

Ordinarily, the surface should be ready for finishing by the time you have finished cutting the concrete away from the forms. This is accomplished by working a pointed

Bull float.

Strike off the surface with a straightedge.

Work float forward, tilting it slightly away from you.

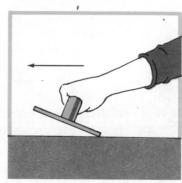

Flatten float if you pull it back.

Driveways and Sidewalks

Work trowel inside form
to cut the concrete
away from the form.

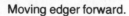

Moving edger forward.

Pulling edger back.

ward or back, the leading edge should be tilted slightly upward. Be careful not to let the edger sink too deeply into the concrete, since deep indentations may be difficult to remove with subsequent finishing.

CONTROL JOINTS

A control joint is a groove cut into the concrete to keep cracks from extending throughout an entire concrete surface. In walks and drives, control joints should be spaced at intervals equal to the width of the slab. They are desirable whenever a slab extends more than 10 feet in any direction.

Most patchwork should not require new control joints. If you're replacing only a section of concrete, control joints as such will not be needed. You will recall, though, the recommendation that any bad section be replaced up to the adjacent control joints. You will have to provide new joints to replace the ones that were lost when you removed that section. And you will, of course, need new control joints if you are replacing more than one section.

trowel along inside of the forms to a depth of about one inch.

The first finishing step is edging, which should take place as soon as the surface is stiff enough to hold the shape of the edging tool. Edging produces a neat, rounded corner to prevent chipping and other damage, which could be a problem once the forms are removed. The edger is run between the forms and the concrete, with the body of the tool held almost flat on the concrete surface. When moving the edger either for-

Use the groover and a straightedge to make control joints. The cutting edge should be deep enough to cut into the slab about one-fourth of its thickness. In most cases, that means the cut should be about an inch deep. When replacing old control joints, place the groover bit into the wet concrete where it meets the existing work. One side of the tool body should be run

Use groover to cut a control
joint into the cement.

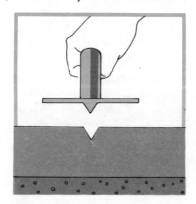

Run groover along existing
concrete edge.

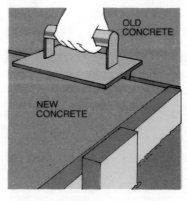

OLD
CONCRETE

NEW
CONCRETE

Use straightedge with groover
on new work.

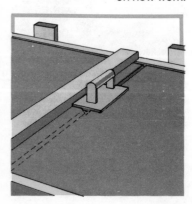

along the existing concrete while the other side runs on the new work, cutting a groove as precisely as possible between the two. Be careful not to press down too hard on the wet side so that the line goes crooked. Even pressure on the hardened side should keep the tool level.

When making control joints in completely new work, use a piece of 2 x 4 or similar board as a guide. When grooving across a sidewalk or driveway, the board should rest on, and be at right angles to, the forms. Push the groover into the concrete and move forward while applying pressure to the back of the tool. After the joint is cut, turn the tool around and pull back over the groove to provide a smooth finish.

FINISHING

After edging and grooving are completed, final floating takes place. This procedure embeds large aggregate near the surface, compacts the concrete, and removes imperfections left in the surface by previous operations. Using the wood float, work over the entire surface. Hold the float flat on the surface and use a slight sawing motion in a sweeping arc to fill in holes and smooth ridges and lumps.

Before doing anything more, compare the appearance of the finish-floated surface with that of the surrounding concrete. In many cases, this is the final step. The new surface should look slightly rough and have a nonskid texture. If it matches the old, the finishing job is done.

When the existing concrete has a glassy-smooth surface, it has no doubt been steel-troweled, and you will have to do the same to make the new surface match. Use a rectangular, steel-bladed trowel; at least two passes over the surface are necessary. If it isn't smooth enough after two, make a third. The trowel should make a ringing

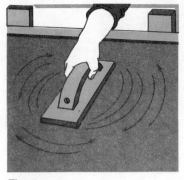
Floating.

Steel-troweling.

Brooming.

Swirling.

sound as the blade passes over the hardened surface. Don't be too concerned if the new patch doesn't exactly match the old. Even an experienced mason is hard put to accomplish that.

If there are irregularly spaced scratch marks across the old surface, it was probably "broomed." To match this, go over the floated surface with a stiff-bristled "garage" broom. If the lines on the old work are wavy, swing the broom in a similar pattern. If they are straight, work the broom over the surface in straight line. Again, don't expect a perfect match. It just isn't possible.

A swirled surface is accomplished with a hand float or trowel. Try both to see which comes closer to matching the original. With either tool, work in a fanlike, semicircular motion, applying pressure as you swing your arm in an arc over the surface. Don't move your wrist, just your arm.

Driveways and Sidewalks

Cover concrete with
wet burlap for curing.

Keep burlap moist,
sprinkling it periodically.

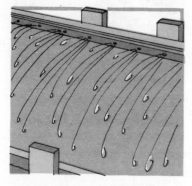

Run water continuously over
concrete from soaking hose.

"Ponding" to keep concrete
moist for small jobs.

CURING

The chemical reaction that takes place between cement and water is called hydration, a curing process that must continue for several days to a week after placing to attain maximum durability. If too much water is lost by evaporation, the chemical reaction ceases. The same is true when temperatures get below 50 degrees F. Hydration slows almost to a standstill as the temperature approaches the freezing mark.

Curing is a vital step in concrete work. It is essential to keep water in the concrete the right length of time. As soon as the finishing process is complete and the surface is hard enough so that it will not be damaged, curing should begin. In warm weather, the curing process must continue for five days. For every 10 degrees less than 70, add an extra day (six days at 60 de-

grees, seven at 50 degrees). At no time should the temperature of the concrete fall below 50 degrees. If there is a chance that this will happen, you shouldn't be laying concrete at all.

The recommended curing method for the do-it-yourselfer is to keep the concrete surface damp by covering it with wet burlap. Rinse out the burlap before use, particularly if it is new, and spread over the slab. The burlap should be checked several times a day to see that it does not dry out. Periodic sprinkling, at least daily, will keep the burlap moist.

Another method of keeping the surface wet during curing is by running a sprinkler or soaking hose continuously over the surface. Never let the surface get dry, because only partial curing will ruin the job. For small jobs, you might try "ponding"— building sand or earth dikes around the edges of the slab and filling with water. The water must be deep enough to cover the entire surface of the concrete and prevent formation of dry spots.

BLACKTOP REPAIR

The reasons for blacktop breaking up or deteriorating are similar to those for the same conditions in concrete. An additional problem with blacktop, however, is that it is easier for water, oil, etc., to get through

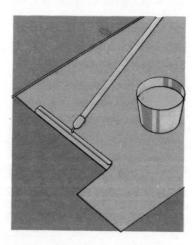

Apply sealer to
blacktop.

Driveways and Sidewalks

and attack from underneath. A good sealer applied every year or two gives added protection against such damage.

Like concrete, blacktop must not be applied when the temperature is likely to fall below 50 degrees F. No matter how badly your driveway may need patching during the winter, it will just have to wait until the birds return—and probably later.

When blacktop starts to crack and break up, the deteriorated sections should be removed. Dig out the area underneath and fill in with the old broken-up blacktop. Blacktop patch is available at reasonable cost from most building supply dealers.

Tamp down the subgrade thoroughly, and fill with gravel or other solid material if the depth is more than 2 inches. Pour in the new blacktop patch and smooth over the top with a shovel. The secret of blacktop repair is that it should be tamped down thoroughly. In this case, a metal tamper is a necessity. (You should be able to rent one.) Keep tamping until the patch is smooth and level, then run over it a few times with your car's tires. Do this as gently as possible— don't skid or "burn out" or do anything else to disturb it. Your car is merely acting as a roller.

Let the patch dry and harden for a few days. It should be as good as new. Blacktop adheres well to old blacktop. You can even apply new blacktop on top of old.

1. Dig out old blacktop.

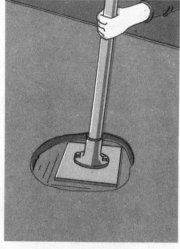

2. Tamp down subgrade.

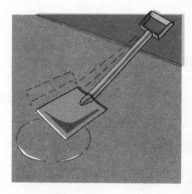

3. Smooth patch.

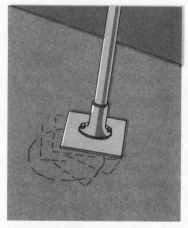

4. Tamp patch.

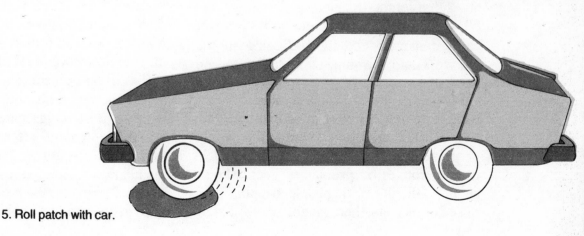

5. Roll patch with car.

Driveways and Sidewalks

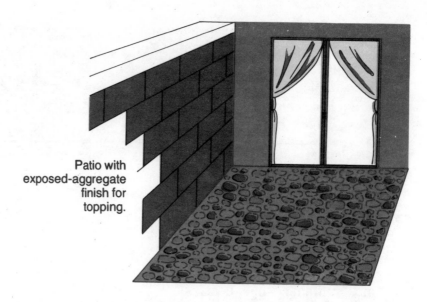

Patio with exposed-aggregate finish for topping.

8

Patio Repairs

PATIOS CAN BE built of a variety of materials. The principal ones are concrete, brick, stone, and patio block, the latter being a type of flat cinder block. Although all these materials are long-lasting when used correctly, they are subject to the same types of stresses as are driveways and sidewalks. There is also the frequent problem of poor original construction.

CONCRETE PATIO REPAIRS

Since a concrete patio is simply a concrete slab, just like a driveway or sidewalk, repair techniques are the same as those detailed in the preceding chapter. Use vinyl latex or epoxy patching mixes for small holes and cracks or wherever feathered edges are needed. For large cracks and holes, undercut the damaged portion and fill with standard concrete mix. Replace badly damaged sections by digging out the old work and forming, etc., as directed on PAGE 256.

When the entire surface needs repair, patios are much better suited to the addition of a 2-inch topping course than walks or driveways, since the additional height usually causes no problems. There should be no difficulty with people tripping over raised areas, as there might be on a side-

walk, and you don't have to worry about damaged mufflers or drainage problems, as you would for a driveway. Attached patios are ordinarily sloped away from the house and toward the lawn, where rainwater will do more good than harm.

Raising the patio height may even be beneficial. Many patios are situated below the first-floor level of the house, and often the step down is too high to begin with. But raising the patio could pose problems if the house is laid on a slab and the patio is almost at first-floor level already.

If you are considering topping the patio, an excellent and attractive way to do this is with exposed-aggregate concrete. (Exposed aggregate is often referred to as terrazzo, but true terrazzo utilizes a different installation technique and contains decorative and more expensive aggregates such as quartz, granite, or marble chips.) In an ex-

Patio Repairs

posed-aggregate finish, the aggregates in the mix are kept near the surface, and the cement paste that usually covers them is washed and brushed away. Although regular aggregates can be used, the surface is much more colorful and handsome if rounded, beach-type stones are used. An "ex-ag" surface is highly durable and slip-resistant as well as attractive.

When building a new exposed-aggregate concrete slab, many contractors do the job in two stages—a base course topped with the ex-ag course. Topping an existing patio with a layer of exposed-aggregate concrete follows the same principle.

To lay a 2-inch topping course, order or mix concrete with a low "slump" (a measure of workability). There should be a high proportion of coarse-to-fine aggregates so that the larger ones stay near the surface. With only 2 inches of concrete to lay, it is easier to keep the larger aggregates near the top than if you were starting from scratch.

The usual concrete construction techniques can be followed, except that rough-floating is done gently to keep the larger stones from being pressed down too far. When the water sheen disappears, and the concrete can bear a man's weight on a piece of one-inch lumber without indentation, it's time to expose the aggregate. Begin washing and brooming as described below, but if the stones become dislodged or overexposed, wait another 15 to 30 minutes, then try again.

Two persons are better than one for this operation. One worker washes down the surface with a fine spray from a garden hose while the other brushes the surface lightly with a stiff-bristled broom, preferably nylon. If you can't find a helper, alternately wash and broom. The combination of washing and brooming should remove all the cement paste and film from the surface of the aggregate.

Be prepared for some hard brushing, because any cement paste remaining on the surface will leave it looking dull and lifeless. A special ex-ag broom, which is attached to the hose and sprays water at the same time, is ideal for this job if you can borrow or rent one. If, in spite of your efforts, the surface looks rather grimy, give it another rubdown with a 20 percent muriatic acid solution. Follow the usual precautions when working with the acid—wear protective clothing and protect your eyes.

"Seeding" is another method by which the do-it-yourselfer can achieve an ex-

Scrub with muriatic acid solution, if brushing did not help.

Kneel on board to test hardness of concrete.

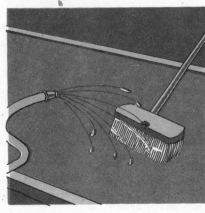

Wet and brush the surface (try to get a helper).

Patio Repairs

Ex-ag broom.

posed-aggregate finish. The topping mix is spread in the usual manner, but is leveled off ⅜ inch to ½ inch below the top of the forms. This allows room for the aggregate to be spread over the top of the concrete. The base coat is struck off and floated as usual. The aggregate stone is then spread evenly over the surface with a shovel and filled in by hand where necessary until the entire surface is covered completely with aggregate. If the first few stones start to sink to the bottom, wait another 30 minutes or so until the mix is a little stiffer.

When there is an even stone cover, tap the aggregate down into the still pliable concrete with a 2 x 4 or a wood float. Then go over the entire surface with the float, working the stones well into the mix until they are completely covered by cement paste. The surface will then look just about as it did before you started seeding.

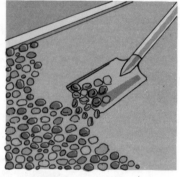

1. Level topping mix off below forms.

2. Spread aggregate stone evenly over the surface.

3. Tap the aggregate down into the concrete.

4. Go over the entire surface with the float.

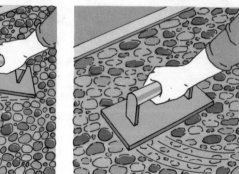

Wait about another hour, until the seeded slab can bear the weight of a man on a piece of lumber. Washing and brooming can then proceed as above.

BRICK PATIOS

Brick patios are normally built by one of two methods. The easiest both to lay and repair is the brick-in-sand patio, in which a bed of sand is put down and leveled. Sometimes cement is mixed with the base sand for a more stable bed. Then the bricks are simply set on top, with more sand being swept in later to fill the joints. Brick patios may also be put down over a mortar bed, with mortar joints between the bricks.

Although a brick-in-sand patio is more likely to heave and settle than the other type, especially over the winter months, it is simpler to repair. Any bricks that come up or sink down below the level of the others are removed. You may need an old screwdriver or other tool to dislodge the first, but the adjacent ones can be lifted out easily by hand.

If the bricks in question have settled, lay in some extra sand (any sand will do for this—even beach sand) and tamp it down well. Watering helps to settle the sand and compact it. When the bed is satisfactory, reinstall the bricks the same way they were laid before. In this type of patio, the bricks are butted as tightly as possible against one another. When all have been replaced, spread more sand over the top and work it down between the cracks with a stiff-bristled broom. Spray the patio with a hose, then sweep in more sand. It may take three or more similar applications before the brick is again locked into position so that no more sand can be worked in.

Since mortared brick patios should be set on top of a concrete base slab, heaving and settling of the brick itself should be rela-

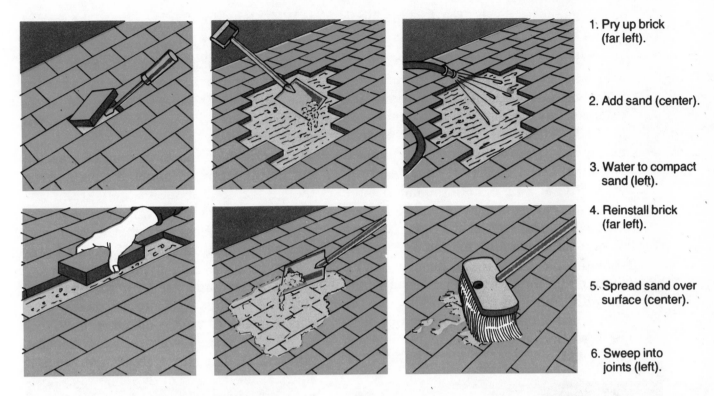

1. Pry up brick (far left).

2. Add sand (center).

3. Water to compact sand (left).

4. Reinstall brick (far left).

5. Spread sand over surface (center).

6. Sweep into joints (left).

tively rare. If a few bricks do exhibit such problems, remove them by chipping out the mortar with a brick chisel or cold chisel. You probably won't be able to remove all the mortar, but you should get enough so that you can pry up the bricks with a chisel or wrecking bar.

If the problem is settling, chip out any crumbly mortar underneath and replace with new. Lay in enough new mortar to bring the surface level with the rest. Standard or common brick is nominally 2¾ inches in depth, counting mortar, with the actual brick size 2¼ inches. But not all brick is alike, so measure what you have.

For mortar, it is easiest to purchase premixed mortar from a masonry or building supply dealer. If you mix your own, use the same proportions used for laying a new bed (see below).

▲When the brick is heaved, it is more difficult to repair. The brick and mortar must be removed and the concrete base chipped off to bring it down to the surrounding level. Then proceed as above. If tree roots have caused the heaving, remove all the concrete in the affected section, chop off the root as far back as possible, then pour new concrete. After curing, replace the brick as above.

Chip out mortar (far left).

Pry up brick (center).

Lay in new mortar (left).

Patio Repairs

When the patio is badly heaved or settled, it is probable that the concrete was poorly laid originally. In that case, all the brick will have to be removed, the concrete broken up or topped, and a whole new patio installed. Lay the slab as directed on PAGES 255-263. After thorough curing, make a mortar of 1 part masonry cement (premixed with lime) and 4½ parts of sand. Add water, a little at a time, until the mix has the consistency of soft mud. Spread a ½-inch bed over a small section at a time. After removing as much old mortar as possible from the old brick (or using new brick), "butter" the brick on both edges and one end with ½ inch of mortar and lay into the mortar bed. Continue working in this manner a section at a time until the repair is completed.

Spread mortar.

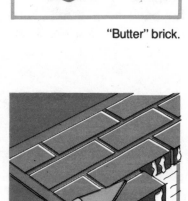

"Butter" brick.

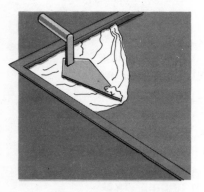

Lay brick into mortar bed.

Force mortar into joint.

Fortunately, most repair jobs to mortared brick involve only repointing or tuck-pointing crumbling mortar. Since you won't want to repeat the job in the too-near future, all weak or loose joints should be repointed along with the ones that are obviously crumbled.

●The crumbled mortar should be chiseled out to a depth of about an inch, even though the deterioration is only at the surface. The greater depth will give the mortar a better hold. Wear safety glasses or goggles when doing this type of work to prevent eye injuries from flying mortar chips.

The mortar mix used for tuck-pointing should be stiffer than normal mixes. One part masonry cement is mixed with 2¼ to 3 parts of clean sand, with less water than for normal use. The mix is about right when it slides from the trowel in a sideways position, but clings when the trowel is turned upside down. Special repointing mortar can be bought at most building supply dealers.

After dampening all the areas to be repointed, force the mortar into the joint with a trowel. Do the short joints first, then the long ones.

FLAGSTONE PATIO REPAIRS

The problems encountered with flagstone are very similar to those with brick patios. Most stone patios are laid in mortar, but plain sand is often used. Use the same repair procedures for stone as you would use for brick laid in the same way.

One difficulty may be in removing large stones. They are quite heavy, and you may need either a helper or some device to remove stones. One way to remove them without help is by placing a piece of pipe or a wood dowel or steel rod next to the stone to be removed, and lifting the stone just enough to rest a corner on the rod. A pry

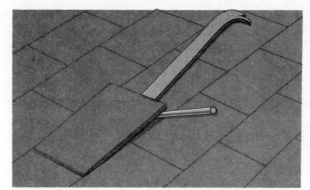

Lift at least a corner of the stone onto the rod (right).

Roll the stone out of the way (far right).

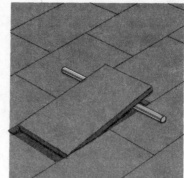

bar can help you accomplish this. The stone can then be shoved onto the rod and rolled over out of the way so that you can work beneath.

If stone has been broken badly, it may need replacement. With random shaped and colored stone, you should be able to find a replacement easily enough. The stone doesn't have to match its mates in either size or shape, although it should vaguely resemble the others. Try to select a piece that is shaped similarly to the one being replaced. It can be somewhat smaller, but not bigger. Fill in the surrounding spaces with mortar.

You'll have a tougher time finding a replacement when your patio is the more formal type, with matched rectangular stones. Color is usually not a problem, because few are exactly alike anyway, but you will have to find a piece that matches the damaged one in size. If you can't find one, have the stone dealer cut one to your specifications.

■Try to avoid having to cut stone to fit. It *can* be cut with a cold chisel and a heavy mash hammer, but that is at best an inexact science. If you must do it, score a line first on all sides with a chisel, then keep banging at it on one side and then the other until it breaks. Unfortunately, it often breaks in the wrong place, so buy a couple of pieces.

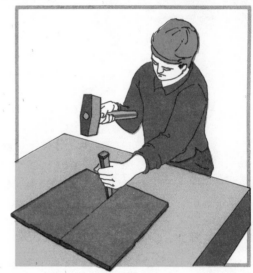

Cutting stone with a cold chisel.

Since stone comes in various thicknesses, be sure to get one that is the same as the one it is replacing—or as close as possible. If you have to choose between a slightly thicker or thinner one, choose the thinner and fill the gap with new mortar.

PATIO BLOCK

Patio block is made in standard sizes. Damaged blocks are fairly simple to replace. Procedures are the same as for brick. You shouldn't have to do any cutting; but if you do, it's easy to cut with a brick chisel and a heavy hammer.

Patio Repairs

9

Pool Care

T HE SWIMMING POOL used to be the super symbol of Hollywood success, but today you can find swimming pools in the most humble urban and suburban backyards. New methods and new materials, along with new affluence, account for this pool proliferation. Crowded public beaches accessible only by crowded highways are the determining factors that cause many families to provide their own facilities for "getting in the swim."

To insure season-long swimming fun, a certain amount of time has to be devoted to the "non-fun" aspects of swimming pools—the care and maintenance of the pool. Basically, it is a simple job if done properly and at the required intervals. When these routine tasks are neglected, trouble begins.

POOL CHEMICALS

One of the most important aspects of pool care is maintaining a proper chemical balance of the water. A glass of water coming out of the tap looks and (usually) tastes clean and clear. Put the same water in a 20 x 40-foot pool and it may look entirely different (taste is quite another matter).

That's why you shouldn't use your pool the first day you fill it up, regardless of how tempting it is and how hot the weather. The first thing you should do is turn on the filter and let it run for a day. The filter will remove the minerals and other solids that are present in most water. Any turbidity in the water should be removed, and the water should look sparkling clear after the first day.

From the very first day you fill your pool, its purity must be guarded by a chemical disinfectant. Some purifying agent, wheth-

er it be chlorine, bromine, or iodine, must be maintained in the pool water; and enough of it must remain in the water to kill disease-carrying bacteria that are brought into the water by bathers.

Chlorine is the most widely used disinfectant. Ideally it should be used at one part per million (ppm), and must have at least 0.6 ppm of "free residual chlorine." The actual ratio is really very small, since 100 percent activity is gained by only one drop of chlorine for every one million drops of water.

ROUTINE CLEANING

In addition to keeping the proper chemical balance, a few other things should be done to keep your pool clean and fresh.

Manually skimming the pool's surface is one. You'll need a standard "leaf skim-

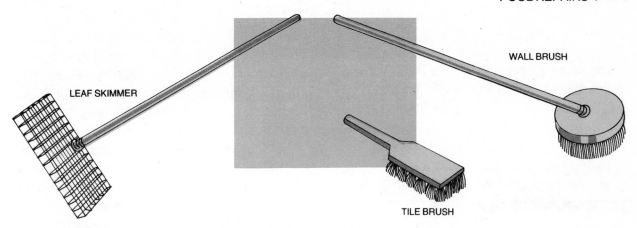

LEAF SKIMMER

WALL BRUSH

TILE BRUSH

mer," a netlike pool-cleaning tool designed especially to rid the pool's surface of leaves, bugs, debris, and other floating contaminants. Most leaf skimmers are equipped with long handles to enable you to reach the pool's center while standing on the deck.

You should also brush down walls and tile regularly. You'll need a stiff-bristled tile brush to clean near the waterline and a wall brush to clean the walls below.

Vacuuming the pool bottom is yet another chore. You'll need a special pool vacuum for this. There are many models and types. Consult your dealer as to the types best suited to your pool.

Don't forget to clean the built-in skimmer's basket and the hair-line strainer in the pump. No special equipment is needed for this. Remove the skimmer basket and the hair-line strainer from the pump. Dispose of the debris that has collected in them and replace them. This should be done as frequently as possible; daily is preferred, or even more often during the spring and fall when there is a heavy fall-out of flower petals or leaves from trees and bushes. Failure to keep the strainer clean will result in reduced circulation of the water through the pump and filter.

Clean the filter regularly. A dirty filter will result in decreased recirculation and consequent dirty water. Consult the directions of the filter manufacturer for the cor-

rect procedure for your particular filter. Most likely you should "backwash," or reverse the flow of water.

Hose the deck clean. A garden hose is all you need. This should be done during every pool-cleaning.

POOL REPAIRS

A properly designed and installed swimming pool should last many years before repairs are required, provided that normal maintenance routine is faithfully followed. Major cracks or breaks in a concrete or Gunite pool are best repaired by a professional. Minor cracks and holes can easily be filled by the do-it-yourselfer.

The pool must be drained at least below the level of the damaged area. Chip away all loose concrete from the crack and wirebrush the area clean (see PAGE 254). Butyl

Remove and clean skimmer basket.

rubber is the most easily applied material for such repairs—look for it at your hardware store in both paste and liquid form. Work the paste into the crack or hole with a putty knife, smoothing it with the surface. A waterproof liquid rubber is then applied

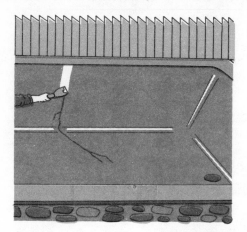

Work rubber paste into crack.

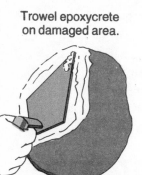

Trowel epoxycrete on damaged area.

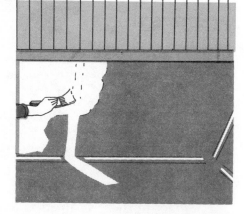

Apply liquid rubber over entire surface.

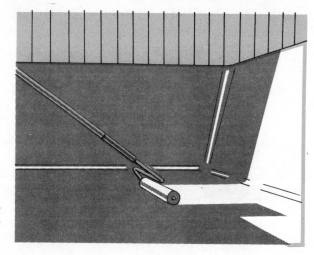

Apply all-weather sealer.

over the entire surface with a brush, roller, or spray gun. The liquid immediately forms a seamless membrane that protects the patch. It should be allowed to set for 12 to 18 hours (check label directions) and will bond perfectly to the concrete.

For larger holes and crevices, a special epoxy (again, see your hardware dealer or a swimming pool supplier) can be mixed with cement to form an impregnable, waterproof "epoxycrete." This is then troweled onto the damaged area, forming a smooth barrier to protect the surface.

As a preventive measure, you can apply an all-weather sealer to the pool walls. This will prevent cracking, powdering, chipping, or staining of the concrete caused by freezing or most chemicals. It is applied with a roller, mop, or brush at any temperature above 40 degrees. It dries to a glossy finish.

Accidental rips or cuts in a vinyl pool liner can be repaired with a special kit available at most hardware stores and pool supply dealers. Follow the manufacturer's directions.

PAINTING

Many concrete pool owners leave their pools unpainted, but paint does make a pool more attractive. The trouble with painting is that it's like the first drink for an alcoholic. You'll have to keep up the paint job once it's applied, and repainting will be necessary every few years.

There are two main points regarding pool painting. First, use alkali-resistant paints for concrete or Gunite. Second, make sure that the surface is prepared properly.

●Remove the water and repair all cracked or damaged areas to present a smooth surface throughout (see techniques described on PAGE 254). If the paint is just dull or rubbed off, a thorough scrubbing is all that is necessary. If there is peeling or

Pool Care

Plug all openings with rubber plugs.

Stuff semi-inflated tube into skimmer.

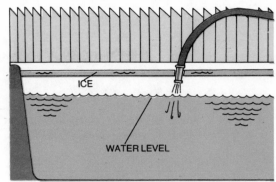

ICE

WATER LEVEL

Check water level below ice and refill if it has receded.

flaking, it may be necessary to remove the old paint completely. If so, sandblasting is the best way. You can rent the equipment, but it is probably best to have professional sandblasters do the job.

WINTERIZING

In most parts of North America, there are at least a few months of the year when the weather is too cold for swimming. It is most important to leave the water in a pool. The water inside the pool serves to brace the walls against pressures created by frozen or shifting earth on the outside walls.

Before shutting your pool down for the winter clean it thoroughly. Lower the water to below the inlet suction fitting. Remove the lights, and drain all lines at lowest points. Insert rubber plugs tightly in all openings so that no water may enter.

Fill the pool again to within two inches of the bottom of the skimmer opening. Make certain that the main drain valve is closed off. Add an extra-heavy dose of chlorine. Spread the pool cover if you are using one.

Place all removed parts in a dry, warm place and properly oil, grease, or paint where necessary. Plug all lines so that vermin or mice cannot enter the system. Remove the diving board and store it on its edge. Disconnect all electrical energy. Stuff a semi-inflated bicycle tube into the skimmer to absorb pressures created by freezing and thawing.

Check the pool from time to time. If water has receded below the ice on top, refill with a garden hose until the water meets the ice. Suspended ice can cause pool damage.

POOL "FEEDING"

To keep you and your family "in the swim" throughout the season, these simple rules are suggested by the National Swimming Pool Institute:

Don't be a know-it-all. Read carefully the directions for all chemicals you intend to add.

Don't overdose. Measure exact amounts. Pool chemicals—like medicine—should be used only in specified amounts. Too much can cause irritating side-effects.

Don't guess. Take time to learn to use a test kit. Be sure to replace reagents (test fluids) each season to assure accuracy.

Establish a routine for testing and treatment. A few minutes every day—or every other day—can make the job easy and assure you a pool in tiptop shape.

Don't work too hard. If you find that taking care of your pool is too much work, check yourself—you are doing something wrong.

10

Storm!

Even the weather forecasters have trouble predicting what will happen in a storm, so what is a poor homeowner to do? One thing he can do is to be prepared, and be aware that just about anything might happen. Forewarned is forearmed—or at least armed enough to have a fighting chance when the wind starts to howl and the snow starts to pile up.

THE EMERGENCY TOOL KIT

Undoubtedly, you keep your toolbox neatly packed and out of the way in your home workshop. But when a storm threatens, you should make up an emergency toolbox, with various tools and materials that might come in handy if an emergency arises. You should include a claw hammer and an assortment of nails, a screwdriver, pliers, and a knife. A staple gun with a good supply of staples should also be there. At least one flashlight is a must—and make sure the batteries are in good working condition. A couple of kerosene lanterns can be most helpful. A supply of candles should also be kept nearby, along with something to hold them, even if it's your collection of old Chianti bottles.

Keep a loaded calking gun nearby. A can of asphalt cement should also be in your arsenal. A couple of large sheets of poly-

ethylene (available at any hardware store) can prove invaluable. Wire and rope and several lengths of 1 x 2 or 1 x 3 lumber are other items that may come in handy, as will a roll of masking tape. Rock salt and electric heating cable provide two different methods of attacking ice buildup.

Think about the worst that might happen during a storm and try to visualize how you might cope with it. This will give a clue as to what you should have on hand. You can hope that you never have to use all these items, but the small expenditure required to be prepared is worth the peace of mind.

WINDOW BREAKAGE

When a falling tree branch smashes through a window, you probably don't want to take the time to reglaze it, and in fact it may be impossible to do so with Jack Frost nipping at your fingers. This is one place where your polyethylene sheeting will do the job—if not as well as the glass, at least enough to keep out the wind and the snow. Staple the sheeting around the window frame, doubling it at the edges for additional strength. To seal the edges, use masking tape.

If you weren't foresighted enough to lay in a supply of polyethylene, you can, of course, use other materials to cover the opening. A piece of corrugated cardboard cut to the proper dimensions and stapled or taped in place will do the job—at least until it becomes saturated with water, when you can replace it with another piece of cardboard. Even a blanket tacked over the opening is better than nothing at all, although it will shut out the light, and you may never even know when the storm has subsided.

ROOF LEAKS

When your roof springs a leak during a storm, it would be the height of idiocy to attempt a repair from the outside. Just do what you can from underneath, as outlined on PAGE 206. After the storm, it may be possible to make a temporary repair from above if the leak is close enough to the edge of the roof that you can reach it from a ladder. Do not attempt to go on the roof whenever it is wet or covered with snow or ice. Use the plastic sheeting for temporary repair. Slip the plastic under the course of shingles above the leaking area, which you can mark by inserting a piece of wire through the leak from underneath. Staple the sheeting to the roof, then calk around the edges. If the wind is blowing and threatens to lift up the patch, nail 1 x 2 strips around the exposed edges. When you later make a permanent repair the nail holes will have to be filled, but it's certainly better than having water pour through the leak.

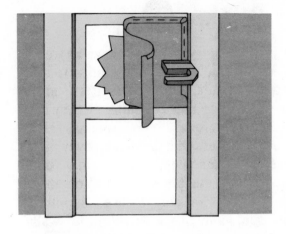
Staple sheeting over broken window.

Leakage may be caused when water from thawing snow on the roof can't run off because the gutters are frozen. The water backs up under the roof shingles and finds its way inside the house, usually causing extensive damage. You can prevent this type of damage by making sure that gutters and downspouts are kept clear so that water can flow off freely. An electric heating cable may be run along the lower edge of the roof above the gutters (see PAGE 215); it should be turned on during a storm before snow can accumulate.

Temporary roof repair: Staple sheeting over leak (right).

Calk around edges (below left).

Nail board around edges (below right).

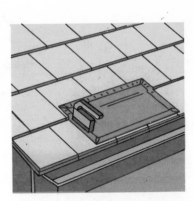

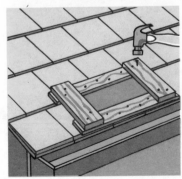

Storm!

ICY WALKS

It is elementary to keep sidewalks free of ice. An icy sidewalk is an invitation to injuries and lawsuits. Chemical melters such as rock salt will do the job, although they may cause some damage to concrete as well as corrosion to cars that are driven over them. These consequences are certainly small compared to the alternatives. You might also consider keeping a large supply of clean sand, and use it to skidproof walks and driveways. It is easy to sweep away when there is no longer a need for it.

FALLEN POWER LINES

When a tree limb comes crashing down in front of your house carrying a live power line with it, you've got a real problem. Get on the phone and report it immediately to the power company. This may take some doing, because people all over the area with similar problems will also be trying to reach the power company; but keep trying. This is a necessary first step.

Post large signs on both sides of the live wire, warning passersby:

"DANGER!
FALLEN POWER LINE!
KEEP AWAY!"

Stake these to the ground or otherwise fasten them securely and far enough away from the wire so that there is no danger. If it is dark, place kerosene lanterns near the downed line. Flares are also good for this purpose, but they must be replaced periodically. Keep the warnings posted and the lanterns or flares burning until the utility company arrives. Never attempt to move branches or other debris from the power line, or anywhere even close to it.

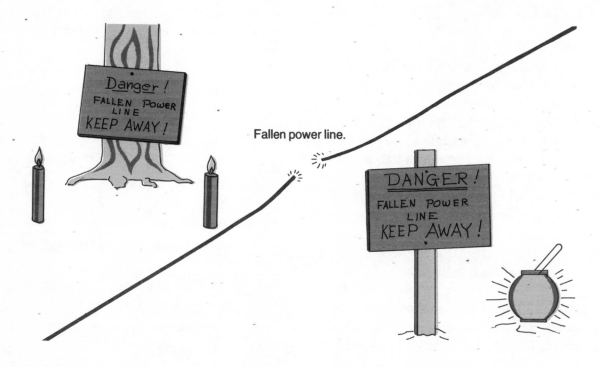

Fallen power line.

Storm!

11

If You're Buying . . .

WHEN YOU'RE buying a new home, there are many things to consider. Obviously, very important considerations are the quality of construction and the condition of the house. If it's a brand-new home, you will want to go over the specifications and make sure that all the materials are of the best quality you can afford. When the house is being built for you, one concern is the workmanship. The model always looks good, but will they build yours the same way? And will all the specifications be followed? These questions are impossible to answer when you sign on the dotted line. You simply have to trust the builder, which is worrisome. During construction, you should make frequent inspections, just to make sure your trust was well placed.

When you buy an existing home, the problems are different. The guesswork is gone—the house is there for you to examine. The workmanship is obvious in most cases. The materials are often hidden, and you have no specifications to rely on. How thick, for example, is the insulation? You can usually look at attic insulation (but not always). There is no way of determining what's behind the walls.

You will be able to determine an existing home's general condition, as well as getting a good idea of workmanship and materials, by a thorough inspection. This doesn't mean that you can anticipate every problem that may turn up if you buy, but a good inspection should give you enough information so that you can determine what shape the house is in and what major problems you can expect to encounter.

STARTING YOUR INSPECTION TOUR

A routine inspection begins at the bottom. Unless the home is built on a slab, the foundation should extend at least 6 inches above the finished ground level. Be on the lookout for large vertical cracks, which can mean that the house has settled considerably. Hairline cracks in concrete are almost always present because of the nature of the material; these are no cause for alarm. Watch out, though, for uneven or honeycombed concrete or crumbling, broken corners. These are signs of poor workmanship and could mean future—and major—problems and expenses.

If the foundation or walls are of masonry, check the joints carefully. Pick at some of the mortar with a pocketknife to see if it crumbles easily (but you'd better okay this with the homeowner first). When in doubt, ask the owner if you can drive a nail into the mortar. If the mortar is skimpy, the nail will not hold.

Also check above the foundation for the existence of metal termite shields if that is a problem in your area. Termites can undermine the house if left unchecked, although this fear is often exploited out of context by avaricious termite-inspection firms. Do look for muddy tunnels on the concrete foundation, or traces of sawdust where no sawing was done. Dig your penknife into a joist or beam to see if it encounters resistance. If it doesn't and the wood is soft or decayed inside, it is a sign of some kind of problem—possibly serious. Carpenter ants or dry rot could be the cause as well as termites, but it's trouble in any case.

If the house is built over a crawl space, look inside and check the girders and joists for signs of decay. Observe the framing and subfloor for moisture stains. Excessive dampness in the crawl space could indicate a serious problem.

The house should be on a higher eleva-

To assure drainage away from the house, it should be built on a higher elevation than the surrounding land.

tion than the surrounding land, if only slightly, to insure proper drainage. The slope from the foundation or slab should be at least ½ inch per foot, but you don't have to measure it. You can usually "eyeball" the grade to determine whether there will proper rain runoff. Also make sure that all gutters and downspouts drain either into a storm sewer or onto splash blocks and from there harmlessly onto the grass away from the house.

Before you leave the foundation area, check the basement windows. Do they fit snugly against the foundation walls? Are there adequate and free-draining wells around each one to prevent runoff into the basement?

While your mind is still attuned to concrete and masonry, look at the sidewalks and driveways. Are the surfaces level and free of flaking, large cracks, or other deterioration? Are bricks, stones, etc., well mortared, or is the mortar in need of repointing? Do driveways drain away from the garage, and walkways away from the house or flower beds? See PAGES 253-265 to determine what repairs are needed. Some are simple, some quite extensive (and expensive).

ABOVE THE FOUNDATION

Before you begin a more detailed inspection of your prospective new home, give it a "once over lightly." Silly as it may sound, see if the walls look plumb and the corners square. You don't expect a house to be so poorly built that it has a noticeable tilt, but it can and does happen. Is there a sag in the roof? It's doubtful that such major defects can exist very long without the place collapsing, but it is a possibility. Make sure.

Now go up close and examine the siding materials. For painted wood, see if the paint film is dense or opaque, or if the wood is showing through. Is the paint blistering, chalking, or alligatoring (see CHAPTER 4)? This can be repaired, of course, but an exterior paint job will cost money—and time, if you do it yourself. Check out the wood. Lap siding should be nailed evenly, with sufficient overlap and tight butt joints. Corners should be mitered or butted snugly against vertical corner boards. Shingles should have plenty of overlap. The wood should not be deteriorated.

Brick or stone veneer should be well mortared. Use the knife or nail test mentioned above. Look for rust stains on masonry or wood, a sign of cheap hardware or the wrong kind of nails. Look at the calking around doors, windows, chimneys, etc. Is it crumbling? Check the protective flashing around these openings. It should be made of noncorrosive metal. Is there proper weatherstripping? Are the sills pitched away from the house for proper drainage?

Although you may not want to go up on the roof at this time for inspection, look at downspouts and gutters. Are there obvious rust spots or debris accumulations in the gutters? These, too, can be repaired, as in CHAPTER 2, but it means more time and money. Can you see any loose roof shingles from the ground? If so, there may be a lot more trouble when you look closely.

If there are porches, see if they sag. Are there loose steps, uneven floors, deteriorated railings and floorboards? Is there a good cover of deck paint on the flooring? Again, all is fixable (see CHAPTER 6), but it's more money to be laid out, and it gives you a clue to the attitude of the seller of the house.

Is there a swimming pool? If there is an above-ground pool, do the owners plan on taking it along? If so, there will be lots of grass for you to plant, probably some grading, and maybe some landfill. A built-in pool will stay with the house, of course. Do you want it? Is the concrete in good shape,

or the vinyl liner? How about the maintenance equipment, the heater, etc. Fix-ups are discussed in CHAPTER 9, but deduct the cost from your offer.

UP ON THE ROOF

Your preliminary inspection ordinarily does not include a trip to the roof, but be sure to go up there before you put any money on the line. Take a good look, too, because roof repairs can be very costly, and a poor roof can cause lots of troubles underneath.

Check for loose shingles. If there is general deterioration, a new roof may be in order. Look carefully at the hip joints and valleys, and especially the flashing around chimneys, dormers, or valleys. Does the flashing need calking or replacement? Check the condition of chimney mortar while you're up there.

Before you descend, take a closer look at the gutters and downspouts. Are they sagging or rotted? Are there accumulations of leaves and debris in the downspouts? See PAGES 214-216 for an idea of what you're in for if repairs to roof or gutters are in order.

SHOULD YOU STILL BUY?

The fact that something is wrong with the house doesn't necessarily mean that you shouldn't buy it. There will always be a certain amount of maintenance, and just as surely there will always be some neglect, especially in an older home. Unless you suspect structural damage, the best course is to estimate the cost of repairs if done by professionals (even though you may do them yourself), and deduct that from what you intend to pay for the house. This doesn't mean that you necessarily value the house at, say, $40,000, and refuse to pay more than $35,000 because you estimate repairs at $5,000—particularly if the owner is asking $50,000. Home buying is a give-and-take proposition, and the true value is what you and the seller reluctantly finally agree on. But if you have a thorough list of defects and reliable estimates, you have a bargaining tool.

PROFESSIONAL INSPECTION SERVICES

For a fee of from $50 to $150, depending on the area and whether the inspectors are professional engineers or appraisers, you can obtain a professional consultation on the condition of your prospective home. Obviously, you can't call in an inspector every time you think you *might* want to buy a house, but if you've narrowed your choice down to one and you're very serious about buying, this service may be well worth your while.

The professional consultation can not only be a worthwhile investment for your own peace of mind, but it can also be a valuable negotiating tool. No matter how careful you are in your own inspection tour, you may miss structural flaws that only an expert can determine. The expert may also resolve any doubts you might have as to roof condition, foundation defects, etc. This is recommended particularly if the home is very old or very new. A very old home may have outlived its usefulness; a new one might not yet have exhibited the signs of decay that could already be there. Homes that have been up a few years have usually gone through the break-in period and should not yet be approaching the problems of old age.

No matter who does the inspecting, you or a professional (friends are unreliable and may look for flaws just to show you how smart they are), just make sure that it is done. Knowing *before* buying is much more satisfactory than finding out afterwards. At least you know what the problems are. It's not knowing (and probably paying too much) that hurts.

part 4 **ELECTRICAL INSTALLATIONS AND REPAIRS**

Contents

1. BASICS OF ELECTRICITY   285
2. WHEN YOU BUY A HOUSE   294
3. ELECTRICAL TOOLS AND MATERIALS   302
4. HOW TO WIRE NEW CONSTRUCTION   313
5. WIRING AN EXISTING HOUSE   329
6. SIMPLE ELECTRICAL REPAIRS   338
7. SMALL APPLIANCE REPAIRS   352

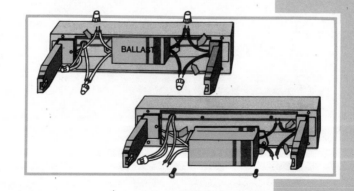

1

Basics of Electricity

ELECTRICITY is something almost everyone takes for granted. Most people alive today don't remember what life was like without it. Like the automobile, it is simply accepted as part of our heritage. But, also like the automobile, it is really quite a recent accomplishment. Some oldsters can still recall times when gas lamps were the rule. Most homes built at the beginning of the 20th century had no provision for electrical power, and there are still homes in remote areas of the United States (although fewer and fewer each year) that rely on more primitive sources of light and power. In some developing countries, electricity is a rarity outside large cities, and even there it may be available only at certain times of the day.

In spite of the gigantic strides made by electrical developers and engineers in this century, the basic nature of electricity is almost as much a puzzle today as it was to the ancient Greeks, who first observed the phenomenon of electrical energy. We know quite accurately what electricity *does*. We can accurately predict what it will do in a given set of circumstances (such as what will happen if you put your hand on an open line of 30,000 volts). But we still do not know exactly *how* electricity works or *why*.

We also know what will happen if you are accustomed to electric power and suddenly have to do without. In an all-electric house, everything stops. In wintertime you freeze, in addition to everything else. Even in a house without electric heat, the oil or gas burner probably relies on electrical controls and is shut down by a power failure. In addition, you have to work in the dark or by candlelight, do without television or radio (unless you are wise enough to have a battery-operated model on hand), blend the cake by hand, wash the clothes in the creek, and otherwise curse the darkness. The great Northeast blackout of 1965 was treated by many as a lark—but if it had lasted much longer than it did, no one would have been laughing.

THE NATURE OF ELECTRICITY

Scientists have tried to explain the nature of electricity for many years, but they usually fail to convey their enlightenment to the average layman. Simply (but mysteriously) put, electricity is the flow of energy from charged particles (the mystery remains how and why). It can come from a battery in the form of chemical energy, or from a generator, which turns water, steam, atoms or some other energy source into electrical power and creates current

Lightning: a discharge of atmospheric electricity.

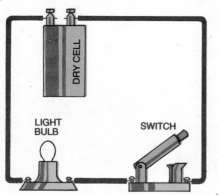

Wiring diagram with dry cell, which stores electricity.

Cutaway view of a voltaic or wet cell (at right).

Schematic of electrical wiring system of an automobile (far right).

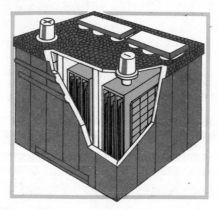

electricity. There are other forms of electric energy, such as lightning and frictional or static electricity. Static electricity means "stationary electricity" or electricity "at rest." It is electricity stored up within a body or its surface. A typical example for creating static electricity is to rub your feet on a rug; this creates an electric charge. Then, when you touch somebody or something, for instance a metal door knob, the electricity will be discharged in the form of a spark. Then there is also the companion form of electric energy, magnetism, the basic principle behind the electric motor.

For the person interested in repairing his home wiring or his electric toaster, it is far more important to know the effects of electric energy than to understand how or why it works. It is useful, however, to have some knowledge of the principles upon which the practical how-to of electricity is founded.

TERMS AND DEFINITIONS

The fundamental terms used in all electrical work are actually units of measurement. These are:

Ampere (amp)—the quantity of electric current passing through a given point in a given time.

Volt—the amount of pressure or electromotive force (EMF) that starts an electric current and keeps it moving.

Watt—the quantity of electricity being used at a given point; watt capacity is determined by multiplying amperes by volts.

Resistance—the infinitesimal loss of power caused by the material used to carry an electric charge; this resistance is usually expressed in the number of ohms.

Certain other terms are also common in residential electrical work. Among these are:

Kilowatt—1000 watts.

Kilowatt hour (KWH)—1000 watts used for one hour.

Current—electric movement or force.

Alternating current (AC)—electric force that periodically reverses its direction (see below).

Direct current (DC)—electric movement always in the same direction.

Circuit—the wire or wires through which electricity flows from the supply point to where it is used and back.

Outlet—an electric "tap" to which an electric device is plugged into a circuit.

Switch—a device for opening, closing, or modifying some element in the electric circuit.

Rheostat—a variable switch (actually a resistor) that changes the resistance and therefore the flow of power to a light or other electric device.

Service—the point of entry to the house from the electric utility; service is through the fuse box or breaker box, depending on which type is used (see "fuse" and "breaker" below).

Fuse—a screw-in device that "blows" or burns out when the circuit is overloaded (see below); a metallic element in the fuse melts at a point just below that of the wiring to prevent damage and fire in the circuit, and the blown fuse must then be replaced.

Breaker (circuit breaker)—performs the same function as a fuse, but in this case the switch on the breaker is reset instead of being replaced.

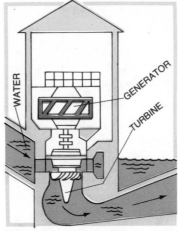

Waterpower generating electricity.

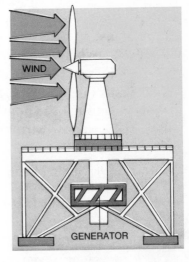

Wind power generating electricity.

Overload—a condition that results when the circuit is burdened with more wattage than the system can handle; in a properly wired circuit, this results in a blown fuse or breaker (a poorly wired circuit that is overloaded can cause melted wiring and perhaps a dangerous fire).

Cycle —the frequency at which alternating current changes direction. In the United States and many other countries, the standard frequency is 60 cycles per second; in some parts of Europe it is 50 cycles; in some industrial installations, it is 20 cycles per second (many of these are currently being phased out).

Horsepower (hp)—a rating of electrical power used on some motors and appliances; one horsepower equals 746 watts.

THE HOUSEHOLD ELECTRICAL SYSTEM

A good way to understand the household electrical system is to compare it to the plumbing system. Water is brought to the house by large underground water mains (corresponding to electrical power lines). This water is under pressure from the "water works" (power plant) so that it is forced through its outlets, such as faucets (or switches in the electrical system), which in some cases are much higher than the water main (electrical service) to the house.

When a faucet (switch) is opened, water (current) flows from the main (service) out through the tap (receptacle), delivered through the plumbing (or electrical) system by pipes (wiring). The pipes to each kitchen, bathroom and laundry area can be regarded as a circuit.

With water, the rate of flow is governed by several factors. The pressure is determined by the source, and this is roughly comparable to the voltage of the electrical system as determined by the power plant. How fast the water flows depends on the size of the pipe and its condition. A large pipe can carry more water, but this may be slowed down by corrosion or foreign material inside. The size of the pipe can be compared to the size of the wiring, and the corrosion factor to electrical resistance. Both determine the rate of flow—in this case, amperage.

When a tap is turned on, the volume of water that flows out is dependent on both the pressure from the main and the type and size of the pipes—in other words, by the voltage and the amperage. If this were measured in electrical terms, it would be called wattage.

Resistance in the electrical sense has little to do with the condition of the "pipes" (wiring), since corrosion does not affect wires in the same way that water pipes can become clogged with rust, dirt, sand, or debris. Wiring is (or should be) made of copper, and wires of the same size and type will normally offer the same degree of resistance. Copper and sometimes aluminum are used for wiring because they are good

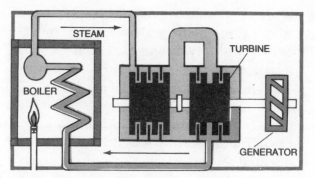

Electricity created by steam.

conductors of electricity or, conversely, have low resistance. Other metals such as nickel and tungsten are poor conductors (have high resistance). Most nonmetals have high resistance and are thus regarded as nonconductors. The most highly resistant materials such as glass and porcelain are also used in electrical work, but in a different way—they are insulators, designed to prevent electrical flow or leakage.

The plumbing-electrical analogy in terms of resistance can be demonstrated with a garden hose. Turn on the outside faucet without the hose attached and the water gushes out. Let it run into a bucket for several seconds and measure it (or visualize it if you don't actually want to perform the experiment). Now connect a large-diameter (¾-inch) hose to the faucet and observe that the amount of water coming out of the spigot is just as great (or almost so, depending on the resistance) during the same time period. Attach a smaller hose, such as ½-inch diameter, and notice that the amount of water is considerably diminished. A still smaller hose would discharge a lot less, and so on. The same situation applies to wiring. A #12 wire will allow more electricity to flow through than a #14 wire (the smaller the wire number, the heavier its gauge and the more "juice" or current it carries; see PAGES 305-306).

Another lesson to be learned at the hose faucet is that the flow of neither water nor electricity can be increased beyond a given

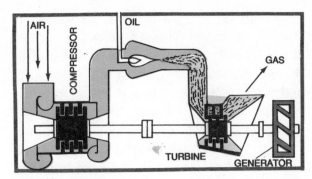

Electricity created by gas.

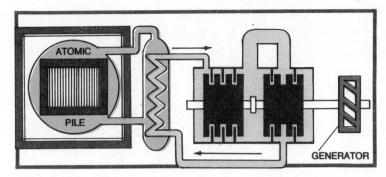

Electricity created by atomic energy.

capacity (unless through boosters of some sort). If you attach a ¾-inch hose to the end of a ½-inch hose, the water will come out at the same rate as it did at the end of the ½-inch hose before it was extended (and perhaps more slowly because of resistance). The same holds true if you splice #12 wire to #14 wire. In fact, it would not only be fruitless and expensive, but possibly dangerous as well.

Like most other analogies, the plumbing-electrical comparisons "limp" at times. For example, if two people in a house were to take a shower at the same time (in different shower stalls, that is) one might freeze and the other might be scalded because of the varying demand upon the hot- and cold-water piping. A sink faucet turned on at the same time might yield only a trickle because of the heavy demand placed on the system.

Electricity, on the other hand, does not increase and decrease in flow (except for some unusual occurrence such as a surge caused by lightning). If you run your toaster, electric broiler, and several air conditioners at the same time *on the same circuit* (which is definitely not a good idea), the circuit will be broken rather than feeding less wattage to each unit. The circuit distributes current uniformly to each appliance until it can handle no more. Then, assuming you haven't meddled with the fuses or breakers (PAGE 310), it simply breaks down because of overload. The fuse or breaker au-

tomatically interrupts the current flow and shuts the circuit down completely.

It is important to realize that household electricity (alternating current) flows only in a complete circuit. If the current is interrupted at any one point, everything else on the same circuit is shut off. (With the plumbing system, a defect in the shower head does not cause the sink to stop supplying water.) There is one more major difference between the functions of the plumbing and electrical systems. Remove a faucet and the water will pour out of the pipe. Remove a light bulb, and the flow of electricity to the socket ceases (unless you put a conductor between the two elements). The current bypasses the lamp and continues on to the rest of the circuit. You could (incorrectly) wire your house so that one missing light would interrupt the entire circuit—just like the old lights on Christmas trees, where one burned-out bulb caused the whole string to go out. But proper wiring practices and modern devices are designed to prevent that.

HEALTHY RESPECT

Make no mistake—working with electricity *can* be hazardous to your health. It is not like other do-it-yourself jobs. If you mess up while working on the plumbing, you may end up with a faucet that is leaking more than when you started to repair it; at

Basics of Electricity

worst you may flood the basement or even the house. But you are not likely to drown. There is not that margin for error with electricity. If you mess up here, it could result in fire, serious injury, or worse.

Always exercise a healthy respect when doing electrical work. Never "play around" with electricity. It's a potentially deadly game, and you must know exactly what you are doing. If you don't know, don't do it. Seek qualified advice and/or professional help.

Although there are times when you have to do electrical work in potentially dangerous situations, most of the time you can work in complete safety. The obvious but often overlooked condition is when there isn't any "juice" or current present. For example, you would never work on an appliance that was plugged in. Or would you? As obvious a precaution as it may seem, there are still people who go poking around inside an electrical gadget with the plug attached and, therefore, the power on. It seems so foolhardy that it doesn't bear warning against—but it is so basic to electrical safety that it must be said, as strongly as possible: *Pull out the plug!*

Never work on an appliance that is plugged in . . .

Disconnect appliance first.

Another type of electrical work that can be performed in complete safety is wiring that is done before being connected to the current. This does not mean that you can't do it incorrectly, but you can work without fear—at least until you hook it up. Even when you connect new work to the system, the worst that usually happens is a blown fuse or breaker. You then leave the breaker off and check out the system until you find the flaw. (Electrical wiring is explained in complete detail on PAGES 313-328.) There is nothing to fear from any electrical component that is not connected to the power source.

Even when you must work with the current on, there is nothing to fear if you are careful to take the proper precautions. Keep in mind that alternating current (as in your house) flows back and forth, and that any wire can be "hot"—and therefore off limits to your touch or any contact. If it is necessary to work around "hot" materials, keep your hands and feet dry, and never work in anything wet. It is a good extra measure of safety to stand on a wooden board whenever there is a chance of striking a live connection. Also, use insulated tools (see PAGES 303-305). It is possible to slip and touch a hot wire and not be hurt as long as your body does not form a "ground." (Grounding is explained on PAGE 323.)

DO IT YOURSELF?

Considering the danger of a good friend (electricity) turned enemy, should anyone take the chance of doing electrical work himself? There are many pros and cons to this question, but the final answer can be given only by you.

Electrical work, to be sure, should be undertaken only with complete knowledge and seriousness. It is not like brain surgery, in which years of specialized training are

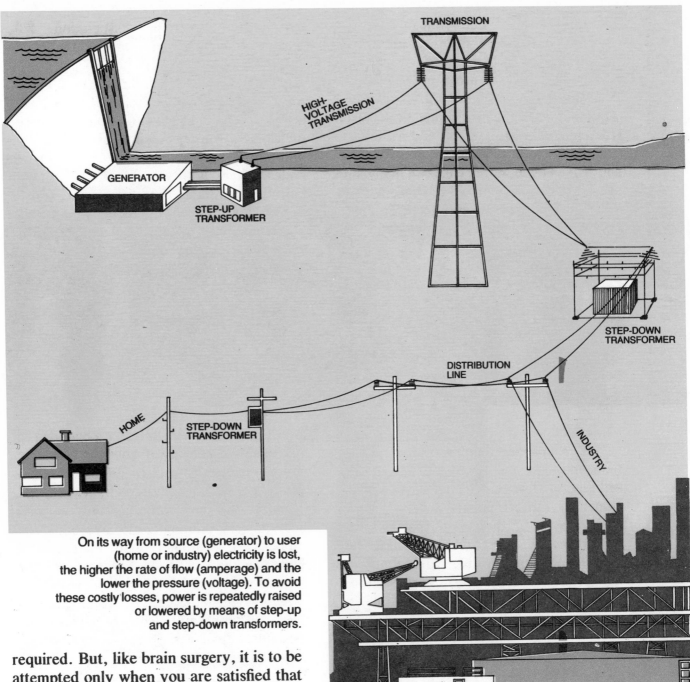

On its way from source (generator) to user (home or industry) electricity is lost, the higher the rate of flow (amperage) and the lower the pressure (voltage). To avoid these costly losses, power is repeatedly raised or lowered by means of step-up and step-down transformers.

required. But, like brain surgery, it is to be attempted only when you are satisfied that you have as much skill and knowledge of what you are doing as a neurosurgeon has for his job.

If you are naturally clumsy and can't cut a 2 x 4 without losing a finger, electrical work is not for you. If you tremble when you pull out a plug, respect your fears and steer clear of this kind of work. (Knowledge can overcome fear, but odds are poor if electricity scares the wits out of you.)

On the other hand, any person who is reasonably dexterous and can use a pliers and screwdriver should be able to learn electrical work. The theory of electricity may be a mystery, but you don't have to be a physicist or electrical engineer to strip wire or replace a motor.

Basics of Electricity

In many cases, a compromise may be in order. If you feel competent about installing wiring, but have a fear of working with "hot" electricity, you can probably find a licensed electrician who will inspect your work and make the final connection himself (for a fee, of course).

In the case of appliances, doing-it-yourself makes even more sense—in many situations. If you have an old washing machine that you feel may be close to breathing its last, why not try to fix it yourself and give it a few more months of life? If you make a mess of it, you've lost nothing, and you may have gained some valuable experience for the next time. As you gain confidence in your troubleshooting abilities, you can work on newer appliances as well, and save yourself those exorbitant service bills. But be wary of trying to fix a new appliance that is under warranty. You may void the warranty by making obvious and faulty "repairs" yourself.

One other fear should be allayed. It is often said (and even written) that do-it-yourself electrical work will void a fire or homeowner's insurance policy. Check your own policy to see if there is any such clause (unfortunately, most of these policies are nearly incomprehensible, and almost as mysterious as electricity). Very few policies actually include such a restriction.

ELECTRICAL CODES

The ultimate source of specific recommendations for electrical safety is the National Electrical Code. The Code was first published in 1895 by the National Board of Fire Underwriters. The original set of rules has been amended and added to many times, and it is wise to acquire a copy of the latest edition from your bookstore, electrical supply house, or directly from the Na-

tional Fire Protection Association, 470 Atlantic Avenue, Boston, MA 02110.

By itself, the Code is not a legal document. But many communities have adopted the National Code as a part of their local regulations. In that event, it has the force of law. Be warned, also, that some communities have adopted even more stringent codes. Check with your local municipality before attempting any large-scale work. Even if your job is a small one, it is technically covered by the local code, which should be followed. This will include inspections by building department officials. However, many homeowners do not bother with such inspections if they are just adding outlets or doing other minor work.

Local codes may cause problems. In some cases, the code forbids anyone but a licensed electrician to do any work at all. Other codes require that a licensed electrician check your work and certify that it follows regulations (which is not a bad idea in any event, especially if you are relatively new to electrical work). In still others, a fee and/or permit are required. In at least one instance, the local code not only permits homeowners unlimited leeway, but even supplies a pamphlet with instructions. Whatever the local code, follow it for your own sake.

Another general safety precaution is to use only wiring and electrical devices that meet the standards of the Underwriters' Laboratories (UL) and are so labeled. Un-

Seal of approval of the Underwriters' Laboratories.

derwriters' Laboratories tests all electrical products submitted to it by the various manufacturers. If a product does not bear the UL stamp or tag, stay away from it. You should know, however, that the UL label affirms only that the product meets *minimum* standards, and that some of the approved devices may be better designed and constructed than others.

EFFICIENT AND ECONOMICAL USE OF ELECTRIC POWER

In view of the worldwide energy crunch, it is important to make the most efficient and economical use of electric power. Electric costs have been sharply increasing over the past few years, and promise to become ever more expensive. In subsequent chapters, wattages of various appliances and other energy-eaters are noted. You will find that anything with high resistance (generally, those products that convert electricity to heat) is going to cost more in your electric bill. It is wise to use this type of power frugally. In some cases, you may want to avoid this type of power use entirely. For example, use the broiler in your gas oven to make toasted cheese sandwiches, rather than the electric broiler (assuming that natural gas is less expensive than electricity in your area).

What about electric heat? Generally, it is an expensive way to go. On the other hand, the virtue of this type of heating is that each room has its individual thermostat, and unused rooms can be reduced to minimum settings. The economics of this are tricky, depending as they do on the future costs of different types of energy. If you have rooms in your home which are used only occasionally, electric heat may be a good bet. If all your rooms are being heated most of the time, then some other form of heating will probably be more economical. When installing a heating system, ask the utility or oil dealer for estimates of future costs. Don't take them as gospel, however. These sources have their own biases, and besides that, the future is impossible to predict accurately, for them as well as you. In the final analysis, the choice must be yours, and you should make sure that you are well informed before you make it.

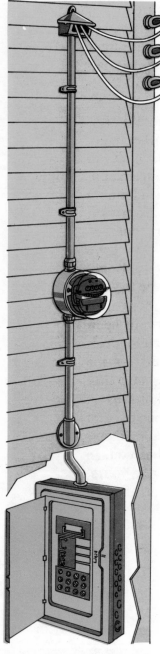

Three-wire service.

2

When You Buy a House . . .

THE ELECTRICAL system may not be the most important factor in deciding on whether or not to purchase a particular home, but it certainly rates careful consideration. An underpowered house can be an inconvenience. A poorly wired one can be a hazard.

Whether the house is old or new, overall power needs are about the same. Not too many years ago, the average home had 10 to 20 appliances. This number has risen steadily, and now there are 50 to 60 (count them—washers, dryers, dishwashers, hair dryers, toothbrushes, disposers, can openers, compactors—and on and on). All these appliances, of course, need power to run them, and there is a certain minimum capacity to look for no matter what is the age of the house. The National Electrical Code calls for at least 100 amps in a new house, and an ideal of 200 when a full range of electrical appliances is used. Older homes may be wired for considerably less, but any home with less than 60-amp service is grossly inadequate and will probably require extensive rewiring plus a new service.

The energy shortage puts the extent of future electrical power use into some question—there just might not be enough power to go around for all those appliances, and you may have to go back to manual toothbrushing. Nevertheless, it is certainly advisable to buy or build a house that is more than adequately powered for present use. No matter what happens in the future, your electric power needs are not likely to diminish greatly.

THE NEW HOUSE

Whether buying a new house from a developer or building it yourself, it makes sense to put in the most complete electrical system you can afford. The least expensive way of providing adequate housepower is to install it when the house is being constructed.

Most new homes today are built with three-wire service to the entrance panel—make sure yours is. Without three-wire service, high-wattage appliances such as electric ranges and dryers cannot be used.

(Even if you do not plan on having such appliances right away, you should have three-wire service for possible future needs. The additional cost is insignificant in terms of the overall price of the house.)

The minimum 100-amp service will provide enough wattage for lighting, an 8,000-watt range, refrigerator, roaster, ironer, and other major appliances up to a total of 10,000 watts (see table). Unless your new house is very small or you are on an extremely tight building budget, you should opt for 150- or 200-amp service. The National Electrical Code implies that 200 amps will be more than sufficient for present and foreseeable future needs in homes 3,000 square feet and under (only the most expensive new homes are larger than that).

Just because a new home has 100-amp or better service, that doesn't mean it is adequately wired. In addition to the recommended service, the individual circuits must be in the right places and of the proper size. At least 20 circuits are needed in an average-size home of six rooms. A large house should have more. The Code requires that no lamp or appliance be more than 6 feet from an outlet, which translates to an outlet every 12 feet.

The typical six-room house, illustrated on p. 18, has circuits for proper lighting and all the usual appliances, including electric range, dishwasher, garbage disposer, water heater, power tools, and central air conditioner.

The house contains five general-purpose circuits to provide lighting and outlets for most of the living areas. Circuit 1 is adequate for two bedrooms and a bath, 2 for the master bedroom and bath, and 3 takes care of the living room and the kitchen lights. Circuit 4 provides the current for the dining-room lights and outlets in the halls. Circuit 5 is for basement lighting.

The rest of the circuits are specialized. Number 6 provides outlets for most small kitchen appliances (in the kitchen work area, outlets should be spaced no more than four feet apart for convenience). Circuit 7 has more kitchen outlets and continues into the dining room, where it serves the outlets. Circuit 8 is for the dishwasher, and 9

Power Consumed by Appliances

	WATTS
Air conditioner, room type	800–1500
Blanket, electric	150–200
Blender, food	200–400
Broiler, rotisserie	1200–1650
Can opener	100–250
Clock, electric	2–3
Coffee percolator	500–1000
Dishwasher	600–1000
Dryer, clothes	4000–5000
Fan, portable	50–200
Freezer	300–500
Fryer, deep-fat	1200–1650
Frying pan	1000–1200
Garbage disposer	500–1000
Heater, portable	1000–1500
Heater, wall-type, permanent	1000–2300
Heat lamp (infra-red)	250–300
Heat pad	50–75
Hot plate (per burner)	600–1000
Iron, hand	660–1200
Ironer	1500–2000
Lamp, fluorescent	15–60
Lamp, incandescent	10 up
Mixer, food	120–250
Motor: ¼ hp	300–400
½ hp	450–600
per hp over ½	950–1000
Oven, built-in	4000–5000
Radio	40–150
Range, separate	4000–6000
Range (all burners and oven on)	8000–14000
Razor	8–12
Refrigerator	150–300
Roaster	1200–1650
Sewing machine	60–90
Stereo hi-fi	200–400
Sun lamp (ultraviolet)	275–400
Television	200–400
Toaster	500–1200
Trash compactor	500–1000
Vacuum cleaner	250–800
Waffle iron	600–1000
Washer, automatic	600–800
Washer, electric, manual	350–550
Water heater	2000–5000

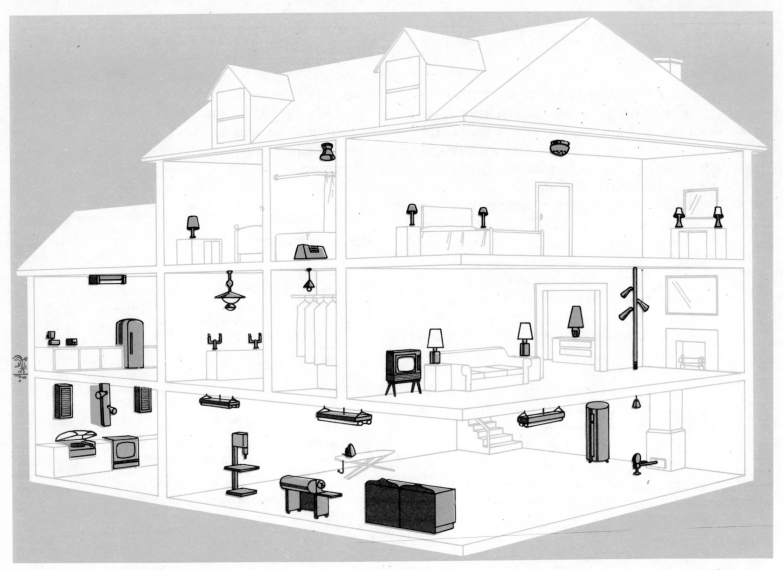

Typical house circuitry.

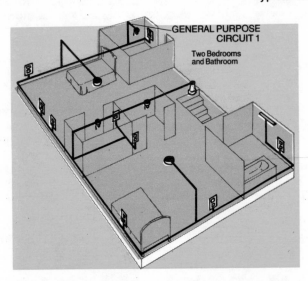

GENERAL PURPOSE
CIRCUIT 1

Two Bedrooms
and Bathroom

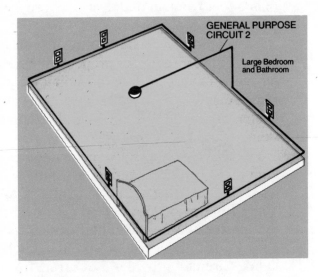

GENERAL PURPOSE
CIRCUIT 2

Large Bedroom
and Bathroom

for the disposal unit. Circuit 10 serves the laundry and basement receptacles. Circuit 11 is solely for the furnace (an oil- or gas-fired unit—an electric heating system requires several circuits of its own). Circuit 12 serves the workshop. If you have (or will have some day) central air conditioning, circuits 13 and 15 are provided for that pur-

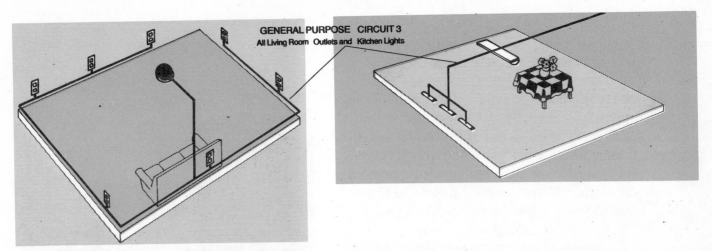

GENERAL PURPOSE CIRCUIT 3
All Living Room Outlets and Kitchen Lights

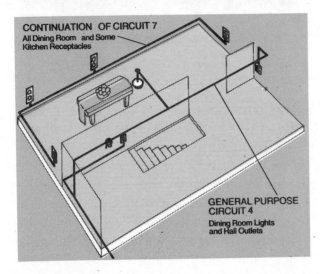

CONTINUATION OF CIRCUIT 7
All Dining Room and Some
Kitchen Receptacles

GENERAL PURPOSE
CIRCUIT 4
Dining Room Lights
and Hall Outlets

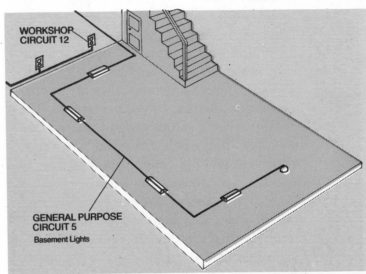

WORKSHOP
CIRCUIT 12

GENERAL PURPOSE
CIRCUIT 5
Basement Lights

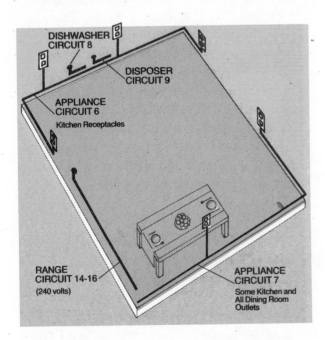

DISHWASHER
CIRCUIT 8

DISPOSER
CIRCUIT 9

APPLIANCE
CIRCUIT 6
Kitchen Receptacles

RANGE
CIRCUIT 14-16
(240 volts)

APPLIANCE
CIRCUIT 7
Some Kitchen and
All Dining Room
Outlets

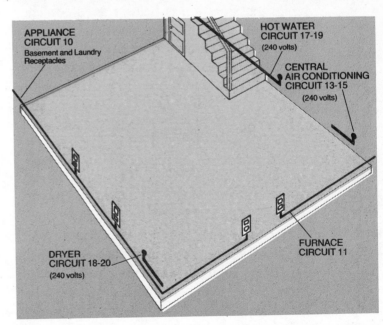

APPLIANCE
CIRCUIT 10
Basement and Laundry
Receptacles

HOT WATER
CIRCUIT 17-19
(240 volts)

CENTRAL
AIR CONDITIONING
CIRCUIT 13-15
(240 volts)

DRYER
CIRCUIT 18-20
(240 volts)

FURNACE
CIRCUIT 11

pose. Circuits 14 and 16 are for an electric range, 17 and 19 for an electric water heater, and 18 and 20 for an electric clothes dryer. (These double circuits provide 220-240 volts required by high-resistance, heat-producing appliances.)

Of course, your house may not have all these appliances, nor need all these circuits. Homes with natural gas or bottled gas may not use electric ranges, water heaters, or dryers. Those without central air conditioning don't need the two circuits reserved for that. (Room air conditioners consume a lot of current too, and if you intend to use one or more, you should plan an extra circuit or two for them.)

But what about the future? And, in fact, your present needs may be greater than our "typical" house provides—perhaps to serve additional rooms, for outdoor lighting, electric heat, pool equipment, and outbuildings. Twenty circuits should be considered a minimum; 24 are preferable. The drawings illustrate the general distribution and capabilities of electric circuits in a typical residential application, but they are not intended as an actual wiring diagram. House floor plans and room sizes differ, of course. Also, it is a good idea to split the circuits so that no room depends solely on a single circuit. In that way, if a circuit blows, you can still have light in the room while the situation is being remedied. The same holds true for the basement and for multi-story houses—for example, at least two general circuits should serve the second floor, even if there is only one room on that level.

Ideal housepower planning considers not only the number of circuits but also the capacity of each one. The general-purpose circuits (1 through 5 in the example above) can be 15-amp, with appropriate size breakers or fuses (see PAGE 310). Normally, such a circuit is adequate for 375 square feet of floor space (not including a kitchen or other high power-consuming room). Most local codes allow 15-amp general-purpose circuits.

It is better, but not essential (unless required by local code), to install 20-amp general-purpose circuits. Each such circuit will cover about 500 square feet of floor space.

Kitchen and laundry appliance circuits

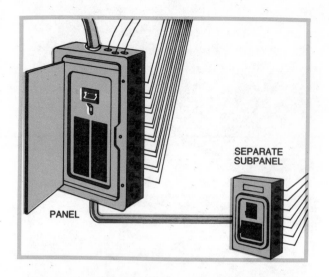

PANEL

SEPARATE SUBPANEL

such as numbers 6, 7, and 10 in our typical house should be 20 amps. No matter what the wiring pattern, there should be at least two such circuits in the kitchen and a separate one in the laundry. Electric ranges and dryers require 220-240-volt circuits with special outlets (see PAGES 305-312).

The dishwasher and garbage disposal circuits (8 and 9) are 20 amps each, and the furnace circuit (11) is 15 amps. The workshop circuit (12) requires 20 amps. The remaining circuits are doubles, usually of 25 or 30 amps each. Farms and ranches with outbuildings should have a separate subpanel (60-amp) off the main entrance panel. The circuiting from this subpanel depends on the equipment to be served, but generally, six more circuits can be run from the subpanel, with one or two three-wire double circuits for high-amperage use.

INSPECTING THE NEW HOME

If your new home is being built by a reliable contractor in a community with a strict electrical code, personal inspection of the electrical system may be a mere formality. It is always wise to check the service entrance panel to make sure that the amperage is adequate. And see that you get any extras you may have ordered, such as additional outlets, convenience switches, ceiling fixtures, or provisions for 220-240 service for a range or dryer (when you order such an extra, make sure that it—and the cost—is in writing; verbal agreements are too quickly forgotten, and you may well end up with far less than you expected). Beyond that, it should not be necessary to look at every wire and box. The certificate of occupancy furnished by the municipality is often accompanied by a certification of electrical inspection. If it isn't sent to you, the city or town should have it on file. Check with the local building department if you have any doubts.

You should be somewhat more circumspect if your new home is being built in a rural or other area where the electrical code is more lenient or virtually nonexistent, or when you are dealing with a small or little-known builder or are contracting the job yourself. If there is a model home, check the wiring and make sure that the same wiring goes into your house. When the rough wiring has been installed (before the walls are enclosed), insist on inspection by the local building authorities or, if that is not available, have it checked by a qualified electrician (other than the one who did the job, of course). Have it inspected again when the house is completed, but before you move in.

If you are buying a home that is not yet built, carefully check over the working drawings (blueprints), paying particular attention to the electrical system and specifications (see table of electrical symbols). If they do not meet with your satisfaction, tell

ELECTRICAL SYMBOLS

O	Lighting Outlet
[O]	Ceiling Lighting Outlet for recessed fixture (outline shows shape of fixture)
(wireway)	Continuous Wireway for Fluorescent Lighting on ceiling, in coves, cornices, etc. (Extend rectangle to show length of installation)
(L)	Lighting Outlet with Lamp Holder
(L)PS	Lighting Outlet with Lamp Holder and Pull Switch
(F)	Fan Outlet
(J)	Junction Box
(D)	Drop-Cord Equipped Outlet
(C)	Clock Outlet
⊕	Duplex Outlet
⊕₃	Triplex Outlet (Substitute other numbers for other variations in number of plug positions.)

⊕GR	Duplex Outlet for Grounding-Type Plugs
⊕WP	Weatherproof Outlet
Tᵥˣ	Multi-Outlet Assembly (Extend arrows to limits of installation. Use appropriate symbol to indicate type of outlet. Also indicate spacing of outlets as X inches.)
⊖-S	Combination Switch and Outlet
⊙	Floor Outlet
⊖R	Range Outlet
△DW	Special-Purpose Outlet. Use subscript letters to indicate function DW Dishwasher, CD Clothes Dryer, etc.
S	Single-Pole Switch
S₃	Three-Way Switch
S₄	Four-Way Switch
S_D	Automatic Door Switch
S_WP	Weatherproof Switch

S₂	Double-Pole Switch
S	Switch for Low-Voltage Relay Systems
MS	Master Switch for Low-Voltage Relay Systems
▣	Push Button
Buzzer	Buzzer
Bell	Bell
Combination Bell-Buzzer	Combination Bell-Buzzer
CH	Chime
D	Electric Door Opener
M	Maid's Signal Plug
□	Interconnection Box Bell-Ringing Transformer
▶	Outside Telephone
▷	Interconnecting Telephone
TV	Television Outlet
▨▨▨	Service Panel
▬	Distribution Panel
- - - -	Switch Leg Indication. Connects outlets with control points.

the builder what you want (in writing) and insist that it be done at the time the home is built. It may cost more, but it will be a lot less than doing the work later.

OLDER HOMES

A home that has been built within the past few years can be evaluated (electrically) by the same criteria as a new home. Of course, you do not have the opportunity of making improvements before construction (the ideal time), but if the housepower is adequate (100-amp service minimum) you should be able to add outlets, switches, and the like to suit your needs at relatively slight expense.

If major alterations to the existing system are required, it is a different matter. The present owner may have a clothes dryer using natural gas and cook on a gas range, whereas your preference in these appliances is for electric. New 220-240 lines will have to be run to the laundry and the kitchen. If major appliances are included with the house, check to make sure that they are in good condition and will be adequate for your needs. You may want to have the units replaced to your specifications before you buy the house—or have the purchase price reduced accordingly. The same applies to any other shortcomings you find in the electrical system (or any other part of the house, for that matter). The cost of any improvements you will have to make should be considered (by you, at least) as part of the purchase price of the house.

Try to determine whether any repairs or extensions have been made to the electrical system and, if possible, by whom. If the owner made them himself, take a closer look. He may be a perfectly competent do-it-yourselfer, and the work may be at least as good as that of a professional. Or it may

not. If you are uncertain about whether electrical alterations have been made, try the local building department to see whether a permit was obtained for such work. If that fails and you still have doubts, hire a licensed electrician to make an inspection for you.

Often, a homeowner will undertake outdoor wiring projects (lighting for a garage or patio, for example, or power for a pool filter) even though he wouldn't dream of doing indoor wiring (either because trying to "fish" wires through the walls seems too difficult or because he considers indoor wiring to be somehow more "dangerous"). If you suspect that this is the case, make certain that the job was done right, using underground cable (see PAGE 307). Check to see that outdoor outlets are heavy-duty type with watertight caps. Normal switches and receptacles are not intended for outdoor use.

As the age of the homes you are looking at increases, so does the likelihood that they are underpowered (unless a complete rewiring with a new service has been installed within the past few years). It is estimated that about 90 percent of existing homes have inadequate electrical power, so you can assume that just about any house 10 years old or more needs some electrical updating.

Clues to inadequate wiring are extension cords, flickering lights, blown fuses, a television picture that wobbles and shrinks, appliances that do not heat properly, and air conditioners that do not cool as they should. Outlets that have double and triple plug-in devices to increase the number of cords they can accommodate are sure signs of insufficient wiring.

You don't even need all these clues. Just go to the service entrance and see if there is two- or three-wire service. Open the fuse box, check the service amperage and number of circuits, and compare them with the ideals as described earlier. (The presence of the fuse box itself gives you some idea as to the age of the system; most homes built during the past decade or so have circuit breakers instead.)

If you conclude that the housepower is inadequate, you can count on having to spend up to $1,000—even more for a large house—to bring it up to today's standards. But if you are satisfied that the service is sufficient for today's (and your family's) needs, the next step is to see how that service is distributed throughout the house. Count the number of outlets, and note their locations. (Remember that the National Electrical Code requires that no lamp or appliance be more than 6 feet from a receptacle in new construction; although this does not apply to existing structures, it is a good rule of thumb in any case.) Take special notice of the kitchen—are there enough outlets above the countertop to allow you to plug in your toaster, mixer, blender, coffee maker, electric frying pan, can opener, knife sharpener, carving knife, food warmer, waffle iron, ice crusher, peanut-butter maker, and all other necessities of modern living? True, you aren't likely to be using all these items at the same time, but you may be using several at once. And it is annoying to have to keep unplugging and plugging in each time.

Check the locations of switches. They should be near the entrance to each room and at both top and bottom of stairways. There should be enough switches so that you can always light the way ahead of you. Don't be too concerned if the house has the old button-type switches rather than toggle switches. When age finally catches up with them, they can be replaced with the newer types; a new cover plate will also be re-

Outdoor outlet.

Two 3-way plugs, a sure sign of insufficient wiring.

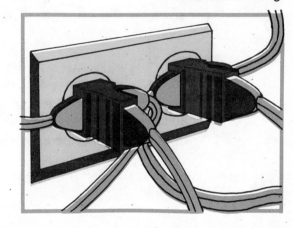

quired, but the cost is minimal, and no rewiring is involved. The same is true of old lighting fixtures; replacement is usually simple, unless you are replacing a pull-chain fixture with one controlled by a wall switch; then the job becomes more difficult. These projects will be discussed in detail in later chapters.

As you make your electrical inspection of the house under consideration, take notes of the work that you feel will be needed to bring it up to your standards. Later, figure out what these improvements will cost (including your own labor, if you plan on doing them yourself). Use these figures as a negotiating point when you discuss (or haggle) price with the owner.

3

Electrical Tools and Materials

T HE HANDYMAN who wants to do some simple electrical work probably already has most of the basic tools. A screwdriver, a common pliers, and a penknife are all that you need for many operations. As you get into bigger and more complex jobs, however, you will have to add to your tool collection. Some items are essential, some are optional but helpful.

THE ELECTRICIAN'S TOOLBOX

For anything beyond adding an outlet or repairing a lamp or appliance, you should increase your toolbox contents with the following, as needed.

A 16-ounce claw hammer is handy for driving staples, nailing outlet boxes in place, fastening hangers, and many other purposes.

A regular screwdriver is fine for occasional work, but a special electrician's screwdriver is better for extensive projects. This tool has a long, slender blade with the tip the same diameter as the shank. The blade fits snugly into the screwheads of most electrical connections, and the shape makes it easy to work with in deep-set and difficult spots. It should have an insulated handle.

A wire stripper simplifies stripping insulation off the end of wire. A jackknife can accomplish the same thing, but the

CLAW HAMMER

REGULAR SCREWDRIVER

ELECTRICIAN'S SCREWDRIVER

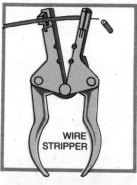

WIRE STRIPPER

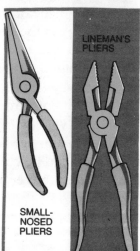

LINEMAN'S PLIERS

SMALL-NOSED PLIERS

FOLDING RULE

Electrical Tools and Materials

stripper has settings for each wire size so that it cuts the insulation without danger of damaging the wire. It is also much quicker.

A 6-foot folding rule is the best device for measuring wire runs, wall openings for boxes, and the like.

Small-nosed pliers (sometimes called needle-nose pliers) have narrow, tapered jaws to make it easy to bend wire into loops around terminals and to reach into such tight quarters as switch and outlet boxes. The better ones have insulated handles to help protect against shock.

Lineman's pliers are heavy-duty pliers used for firmly gripping cable, connectors, and the like. They also have side jaws that are used for cutting wire.

There are several varieties of multipurpose electrician's pliers. All have as their purpose the combining of as many operations as possible into one tool. The tool

usually operates as a pliers, stripper, crimper, and cutter. It may also do other jobs, depending on the model.

If you already have electricity at the work site, an electric drill makes the job go faster and easier. It's not much good, though, until service is installed. In that case, a brace and bit must be used for boring holes for wires. In either case, a ¾ inch drill bit is the most useful, although you may have occasion for using other sizes. Extension bits are particularly useful for drilling in old work.

A keyhole saw is the preferred tool for cutting out box locations in paneling and gypsum wallboard, and for any type of sawing in tight spots.

A wood chisel is useful for cutting notches in wall studs, lath, and other building materials.

A hacksaw is used for cutting the sheath-

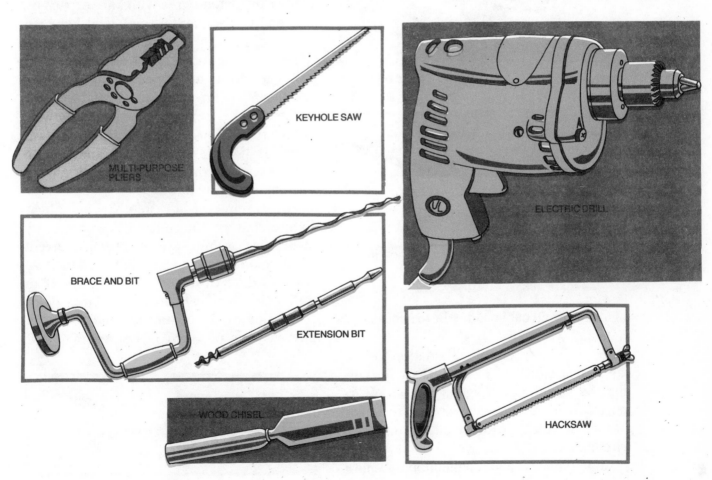

Electrical Tools and Materials

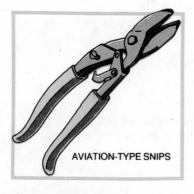

AVIATION-TYPE SNIPS

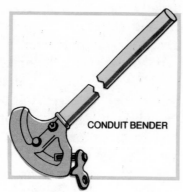

CONDUIT BENDER

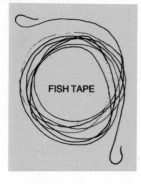

FISH TAPE

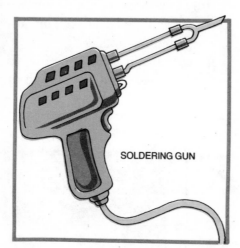

SOLDERING GUN

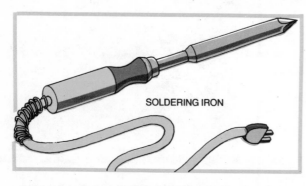

SOLDERING IRON

ing of armored cable and, where necessary, metal lath.

Metal snips (preferably "aviation" type) can be used instead of a hacksaw for cutting the sheathing on lighter gauges of armored cable. You can develop a "feel" for cutting the metal without cutting into the wire inside.

Some splices and connections require soldering; this is especially so in appliance repairs. A soldering gun or iron is required. For most applications, a soldering gun is more useful than an iron. Rosin-core wire-type solder is usually used, along with a nonacid rosin flux.

Plastic electrician's tape is used to insulate soldered joints and splices.

Fish tape is a necessity for working in construction where existing wire must be pulled through walls and ceilings, and for conduit work.

A conduit bender or "hickey" is the best tool for bending conduit (see Materials below) around corners and obstructions.

One of the most useful tools for electrical work is a simple, inexpensive device with a name that describes it perfectly: tester. There are large and somewhat complex versions, but in its simplest form the tester is a pair of insulated wires with bare prongs on one end of each and a small light between the prongs.

This tool has many applications, but basically it does one thing—it establishes whether current is flowing between two points. And it performs that function with complete safety for the user, an important consideration. It is also quick and easy to use and to interpret: when the light glows, current is passing through.

For example, if you are changing a light fixture that is controlled by a three-way switch and are not sure whether the current is on or off, put the tester between the two wires of the fixture and see if it glows. If an outlet doesn't seem to be working, place one prong of the tester into each slot; if it glows, your problem is elsewhere. Or if

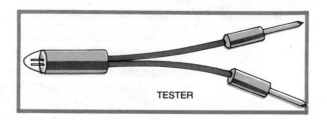

TESTER

Electrical Tools and Materials

there is trouble somewhere in a circuit and you don't know what it is, check it out from end to end with the tester until you locate the faulty switch or outlet. For the money (a dollar or so), you can't find a better buy.

MATERIALS

Each electrical project requires the use of specific materials. Many of these can be found at your hardware store. Others will have to be purchased at an electrical-supply shop.

Think of electricity and you think of wire, because that is what brings the power into your house and carries it to wherever it is used. The size of the wires in the system depends on the requirements of the National Electrical Code, local codes, and the end use intended, such as lighting, heating, or air conditioning.

Copper wires are almost universally used in home wiring. Aluminum wires enjoyed a brief popularity because of a shortage of copper, but aluminum is coming into disrepute because of its tendency to overheat under some conditions, and many local electrical codes have banned its use. Check your code before installing aluminum wire. Better yet, avoid using it.

Wire sizes are based upon the American Wire Gauge (AWG) system. Gauge (also expressed as Number or #) is determined by wire diameter; the larger the diameter, the smaller the gauge. Common sizes used for home wiring range from #0 to #18, although #00 (2/0) and #000 (3/0) may be required for service entry lines for 150- and 200-amp service. Most circuits range from #10 to #14, with #12 perhaps the most commonly used. Heavier circuits require larger wires; #16 and #18 are used for doorbell and intercom wiring.

The wire gauge is based on the total diameter, whether the wire is composed of

Electrical Tools and Materials

a single large strand or many small strands twisted together. The trend is to make the larger wires multistrand, since the large single strand is too stiff for easy handling. Multistrand is required by the National Electrical Code for wire sizes #8 and larger (that is, #6, #4, #2 and so on).

Wire is insulated with a variety of coverings. Rubber was once the most common; but it has largely been replaced by plastic, which is less likely to corrode, dry, and crack. The types of insulation most frequently used for house wiring include R (rubber, for general use, no longer manufactured, but you may find it in existing circuits); RH (heat-resistant rubber); RU (latex rubber, for general use); RW (moisture-resistant rubber, for wet locations); RHW (moisture- and heat-resistant rubber); T (thermoplastic, for general use); TW (moisture-resistant thermoplastic), and THW (moisture- and heat-resistant thermoplastic). The wire size and insulation type are usually printed on the insulation.

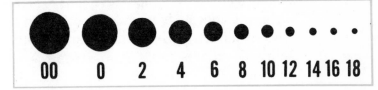

Wire sizes.

Single wire, twisted strand.

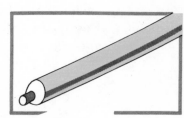

Insulated wire.

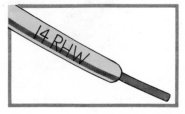

Marking on insulation.

Cable is often, but inaccurately, referred to as wire. Actually, the wires are *inside* the cable. Cable can more properly be called the wiring, since it constitutes the greater part of any wiring system.

Cable consists of two or more wires, each of which is covered with insulation, which are encased in a variety of materials depending on the type of use, size, and other variables. The wires are the actual electrical conductors; the rest is merely protection from the elements and other potential damage, as well as protection against accidental contact with the conductors.

In two-wire cable, one wire is covered with black insulation, the other with white. This color coding identifies the wires for installation—black connects to black, white to white (note exceptions on PAGE 315). The black wire is referred to as "hot," and the white as "neutral." If there are three current-carrying wires in the cable, the third is red. Don't be misled by "neutral." In alternating current, all wires carry a charge, and none is to be tampered with as long as there is "juice" to the line. New wiring also normally includes another wire, green-insulated or bare, designated "with ground" on the cable. The ground wire does not carry current, but is, as the name states, for grounding (see PAGES 320-323 for connection of this and other wires).

Cable has been classified for different uses by the National Electrical Code; the code designations are given below. Cable is

WHAT SIZE WIRE TO USE (armored or nonmetallic cable)		
#	Capacity (amps)	Use
14	15	General purpose, lighting circuits
12	20	Kitchen circuits, lower-wattage appliances, almost any household circuit
10	30	Subpanel connections, high-wattage appliances
8	40	Service wiring, electric ranges
6	55	Service wiring

Larger sizes—up to 3/0—are not normally used in household electrical systems except for main service into the house, which is not the domain of the do-it-yourselfer. Smaller sizes (#16, #18) are used for lamp cords and appliance cords.

stamped or otherwise marked with its code designation and the size and number of wires inside (and usually the brand name as well). *Type NM 12/3,* for example, is nonmetallic, sheathed (see below), and has three #12 wires inside. The number of volts and the UL approval seal (hopefully) are noted also.

Type AC flexible armored cable is made by several companies. It is often called "BX," but this is a brand name. The insulated wires are covered with a tough wrapping paper, and outside that with spiral-wrapped galvanized steel for flexibility. It can be used in any dry, interior work and is the best choice for installations where there is a potential for damage from tools after installation. Some codes require its use for all installations. Armored cable is more difficult to work with than nonmetallic sheathed cable (below).

Type NM nonmetallic sheathed cable is often called "Romex," another brand name. The insulated wires are covered by fabric, rubber, or plastic. The cable is flat or oval-shaped and is for use indoors in

Marking on cable.

dry, nonvulnerable locations. The easiest of the cables to work with, it is generally preferred by do-it-yourselfers (unless the code forbids its use). A similar cable, *Type NMC*, is waterproof and can be used in damp or wet locations.

Type USE (underground service entrance) or *UF* (underground fused) cable is usually sheathed with plastic and is primarily used outdoors. It can be run through concrete, brick walls, or other similar materials. When buying cable for this purpose, make sure its designation starts with "U" (for underground).

Type SE, service entrance cable, is used mostly for wiring up to the service and is not normally used by the average homeowner. If you do have occasion to purchase any for this use, make sure it is rated with RHW or THW insulation (rubber or thermoplastic, moisture- and heat-resistant). Type SE cable can be used for wiring 220–240 appliances, such as dryers and ranges, if allowed by local codes.

Metal conduit is not cable, but a shell through which wires are pulled. Like flexible armored cable, it provides protection for the wires. Because of its higher cost, it is not used in home wiring unless called for by codes.

Thin-wall conduit, also called electrical metallic tubing (*EMT*), may be required for outdoor installations; it can also be used indoors. It is a hollow metal tube through which wires are pulled with fish tape. This type of conduit can be bent (see PAGE 317) up to 90 degrees by means of a "hickey" (see PAGE 304). Thin-wall conduit comes in 10-foot lengths. It is relatively expensive and requires special connectors. Wires, usually Type TW for outdoor use, are pulled through it after installation. These wires are insulated but not encased in any type of cable.

Electrical boxes come in various sizes, shapes, and materials. Shallow square or

Type AC flexible armored cable.

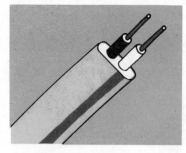
Underground cable.

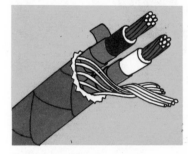
Service entrance cable.

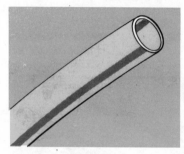
EMT thin-wall conduit.

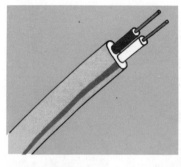
Type NM nonmetallic sheathed cable.

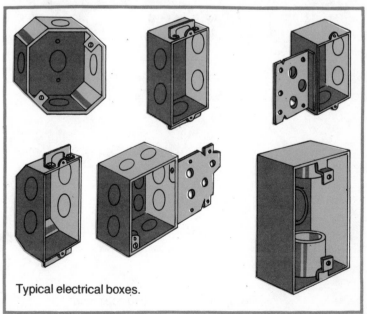
Typical electrical boxes.

Electrical Tools and Materials

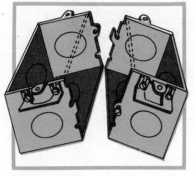

Ganging boxes.

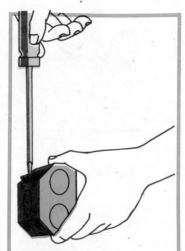

Box "knockouts."

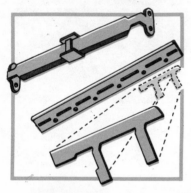

Hanger and clip.

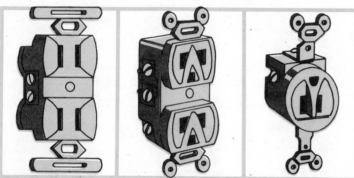

Receptables for 2-pronged and 3-pronged plugs.

octagonal boxes are used for ceiling fixtures and junctions, deeper boxes (usually rectangular) for outlet receptacles and switches. They are usually made of steel, but Bakelite or other nonmetallic substances are often used in damp locations. Shallow boxes are used for thin partitions. Wall boxes have removable sides for ganging two or more. Special waterproof boxes and connectors are needed for outside installations.

Steel boxes have "knockouts" that can be tapped or twisted out with a screwdriver tip to admit the cable. Nonmetallic boxes have integral entry holes, and most codes allow their use only in certain specific locations. Many boxes come with built-in brackets or mounting "ears" for easy nailing to framing. Other devices, such as hangers and special clips for existing walls, are used to attach boxes to ceilings and to wallboard.

Receptacles and switches are the elements that finish off the wiring system, delivering the electricity where it will be used. Receptacles provide a place to plug lamps, radios, or whatever into the system. Usually, each receptacle provides at least two outlets, accommodating plugs with two prongs or two prongs plus a third, round grounding prong. The 220–240 receptacles are larger than the 110–120 and have slanted, L-shaped or other uniquely formed slots so that only 220–240 appliances can be plugged in.

Receptables for 220-240 appliances.

Switches control the flow of current, turning it on and off to a fixture or other power user. Three-way switches allow control from two separate locations, whereas four-way switches make it possible to control the flow of current from three or more separate locations. By far the most common type of switch for residential use is the toggle (flip up, flip down), although push-buttons may be found in some older homes. When these wear, they are easily replaced with toggles. Variations of switches include mercury, or silent, switches (no "click" when turned on or off) and dimmer switches, which allow a light fixture to be illuminated through a complete range from full bright to off. Switches, as well as receptacles, can be in one box, ganged in two or more boxes, or combined in two or more boxes.

Connection devices are used to secure the cable to the boxes so that it can't slip out. Each type of cable has its own connectors. When using flexible armored cable (type AC), fiber bushings as well as connectors are needed.

Solderless connectors are often called "wire nuts." They are plastic caps with threads inside to grip the ends of stripped and twisted wires. They hold them tightly together and insulate them without splicing or taping, leaving no bare wires exposed. no bare wire exposed.

Cable is often supported by notching or drilling through the framing. Where this

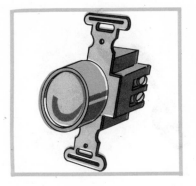

Dimmer switch.

Solderless wire connectors.

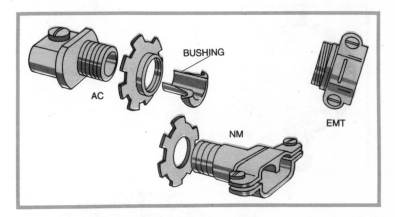

Connectors for AC, NM, and EMT cables.

Cable installed through framing.

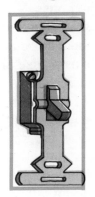

Toggle switch.

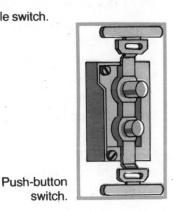

Push-button switch.

Electrical Tools and Materials

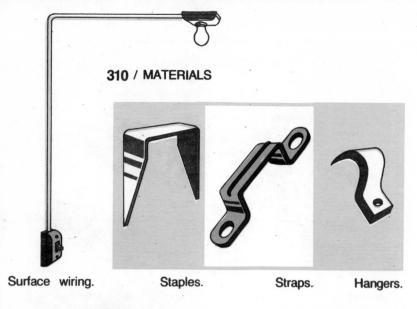

Surface wiring.   Staples.   Straps.   Hangers.

Electric meter.

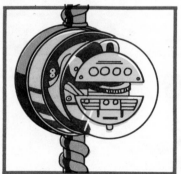

Meter dials.

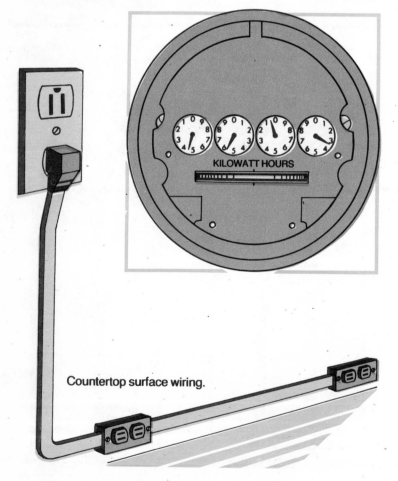

KILOWATT HOURS

Countertop surface wiring.

isn't feasible, staples, straps, or hangers are needed to hold the cable in place. See PAGES 315-319 for installation methods.

Surface wiring is insulated and then encased in a hard plastic housing. It is used with compatible surface-mounted outlets, switches, and other devices on the *outside* of the walls and ceilings. It is simple to install, but rather unsightly in the main rooms of the house. It is sometimes used on kitchen counters to provide outlets wherever needed. It is also used in workshops, garages, utility rooms, and the like. But surface wiring is prohibited by many local electrical codes.

The electric meter isn't really the do-it-yourselfer's territory, and hooking one up or tampering with it is neither wise nor allowed by codes. You should, however, know what the meter looks like and how it is read. In many ways it is similar to the automobile odometer. The dials record kilowatt hours in tens, hundreds, thousands, and so on. As soon as ten hours are clocked on the first dial, it registers on the next one—and so on. To determine how many KWH have been used since your last reading, subtract the total from the previous total as noted on your electric bill. Meters are usually installed by the power company in meter boxes hooked up by an electrician.

The breaker box or fuse box (more correctly called the "entrance panel") is where the current from the power company—after going through the meter—is routed to the various circuits of the house. The current first goes to a main fuse or breaker, then is channeled to the individual circuits. Each circuit is protected by its own fuse or breaker, which "blows" when overloaded.

Fuses come in a variety of sizes and types. A larger size must never be substituted for a smaller one. Fuses are specially designed to be the weakest link in the electrical circuit—when something goes wrong, the fuse should blow. If you put in a

Electrical Tools and Materials

larger (stronger) fuse, you run the risk of melting the wiring and causing a fire, because the circuit can become overloaded and the safety factor (the fuse) has been compromised.

Plug-type fuses are the commonly seen variety, with a threaded or "Edison" base (like a light bulb). The code prohibits use of this type of fuse in new homes because of the possibility of replacing lower-amp fuses with larger ones, as noted above. But where they are already installed, they are legal.

To change a plug-type fuse, simply unscrew it and screw in a new one (again, of the same amperage). It is a good idea to turn off the main switch before doing this; but at night this can be an overprecaution, putting the area where you are working in darkness and making it more hazardous than necessary. You can replace a fuse safely without turning off the main switch if you're careful. *Don't touch* any wires, metal, water, or any other potential ground with any part of your body. Make sure your feet are dry, and stand on a board to be doubly safe.

Time-delay fuses are similar to regular plug-type fuses except that a springlike metal strip inside allows the fuse to accept brief, temporary overloads, such as occur when starting a large motor, without blowing. This is not as unsafe as it may sound, because the circuit can take a temporary surge without danger. After the motor is running, it uses much less power and poses no danger.

A short in the circuit blows a time-delay fuse in the same way as any other fuse, and any overload more than momentary in duration will also blow the fuse. These fuses, too, are rated in amperes and must be replaced only by similarly rated fuses.

Screw-in breakers are not really fuses at all, but breakers (see below) that are screwed into a fuse box. Instead of replac-

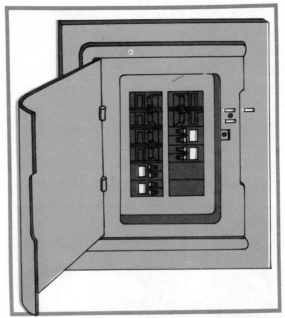

Breaker box.

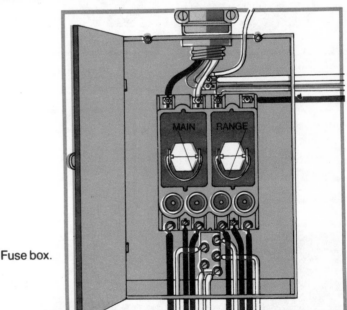

Fuse box.

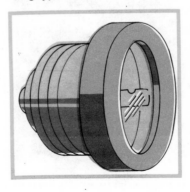

Plug-type fuse.

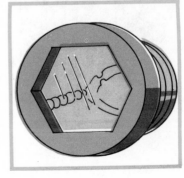

Time-delay fuse.

Electrical Tools and Materials

ing these when they blow, you simply press a reset button (or, on some types, flip a switch). A screw-in breaker is often substituted for a conventional fuse when a temporary overload frequently occurs, such as that from large power tools. The breaker should, of course, be the same amperage as the fuse it replaces.

Nontamperable fuses are designed to prevent replacement of a smaller-rated fuse

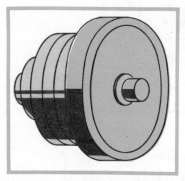

Screw-in breaker.

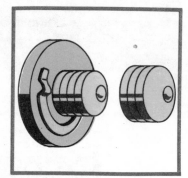

Nontamperable fuse.

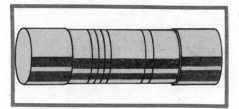

Cartridge fuse.

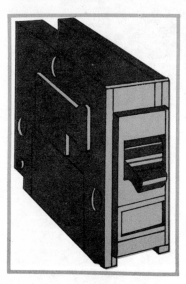

Circuit breaker.

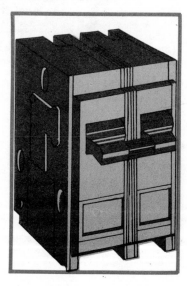

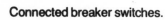
Connected breaker switches.

with a larger one. They are permitted by the code and designated "Type S." There are two parts to such a fuse: the fuse itself, which is replaceable and much like a regular fuse, and an adapter. The adapter is screwed into the standard fuse box, then the fuse is screwed into the adapter.

The difference between this and a plug-type fuse is that the adapter is rated in amps the same way the fuse is. If you remove a 15-amp fuse from a 15-amp adapter, it cannot be replaced with any other size of fuse. And once the adapter is installed, it becomes a permanent part of the fuse box and cannot be removed. (When installing a nontamperable fuse, make sure to turn it in all the way. A spring under the shoulder will not make full contact unless it is pressed very tightly against the adapter.)

Cartridge fuses are long, cylindrical fuses, similar to those used in automobiles. In residential applications, they are most frequently used in the larger sizes, such as in the main switch. When they blow, call your utility company; the problem is likely to be major.

Most new homes and older homes with new wiring utilize circuit breakers instead of fuses. They are safer in all ways and easier to "fix" when something goes wrong. An overload or short will trip the breaker the same way it blows a fuse.

Most circuit breakers are like any toggle switch. Some, however, are buttons instead of switches. To reset a toggle breaker, flick it from "off" to "on" like any other switch. With a button type, simply press. You may find that two switches are installed in one opening in the breaker box; this means that two circuits are in that opening. Only one will be tripped (hopefully) at a time, so reset that one. For 220–240 appliance circuits, two lines are joined together. Press the connector that joins the two switches to "on" to reset. The main switch is often ganged in the same way.

4

How to Wire New Construction

Wiring in new construction—whether a house, an addition, or whatever—is certainly easier than wiring in an existing structure. For one thing, new work is visible—you can see the framing and other components of the house, and there are no obstructions or built-in problems to cause undue difficulties. Cable can be run through or around the framing instead of having to be fished through walls and ceilings when you are unsure of the construction methods and of where other obstacles (such as pipes or ducts) may be located.

Professional electricians usually do new construction work in two stages—rough and finish. Cable is run through the rough framing and into the boxes; then, after the wallboard or paneling is put up, the electrician returns to install the receptacles, switches, and lighting fixtures. The amateur should follow the same procedure.

PLANNING

In planning new homes, additions, basement rooms, or even a new circuit, the same principles apply as are outlined on PAGES 294-300 regarding what to look for in a new home. You should have a good idea as to what your electrical needs are in each room. Determine how many circuits are needed and where. (To find the capacity of a circuit, multiply the voltage to the entrance panel by the capacity of the circuit—for example, a 20-amp circuit with a 120-volt service can handle 2,400 watts.)

As noted earlier, outlets for a general-purpose circuit should be placed within 6 feet of all lamps, radios, television sets, and similar power users, or at least every 12 feet. In kitchens, the receptacles should be placed every 4 feet. The optimum height for each general-purpose receptacle is about 12 inches from the floor. In kitchens, the outlets should be about 12 inches above the countertop, or about 4 feet above the floor. Equal spacing of outlets is preferred, but if you have a reasonably firm idea of where your furniture is to be placed, spacing can be varied to take this into account. Try to envision special needs, such as a television set with rotating antenna (two outlets there), room air conditioners, stereos and other appliances, perhaps all located in one corner of the family room. Extra outlets, and probably extra circuits, will be needed in that situation.

Don't forget to include outdoor recepta-

Exterior outlet.

cles for decorative lighting and power-tool use. Do you plan on an extensive display of Christmas lights, or patio amenities such as an electric fire-starter? Exterior outlets should be at least 18 inches above ground.

For both outdoor and indoor use, switches near doorways are an excellent idea. These switches can control one or more outlets in a given room or outdoor area and prevent a lot of fumbling around in the dark. In a bedroom, for example, connect a switch to one outlet for a dressing-table lamp, so that you can flick it on as you enter the room rather than stumbling all over. (This is handy even if you have a switch-controlled ceiling fixture—you won't have to light the whole room if somebody is asleep.) Connect the patio lights to an inside switch so you won't have to try to plug in a light in complete darkness. Such switches should be about 4 feet off the floor and within 6 inches of the doorway. The same holds true for halls, stairways, foyers, and other areas.

As noted on PAGES 295-297 it is a good idea to arrange lighting circuits so that at least two serve each room. In that way, a blown fuse or breaker need not plunge the entire room into darkness. If that is not feasible, it is at least minimally desirable to have more than one circuit on each floor so that there will be a light somewhere on that level in case one of the circuits fails.

If you are building a small addition with just a few outlets, you may be able to tap an underutilized existing circuit. Or you need a whole new circuit or two. Don't leave circuit planning to chance. Whether the new work is designed by an architect, a contractor, an electrician, or yourself, make sure that you have an exact plan of the electrical system and that you have discussed it thoroughly with the designer and members of your family before it is finalized. Codes are good (and mandatory) guidelines for safety and for general convenience, but each family and its needs are different. Skimping is foolish and costly in the long run. Prepare for every possible electrical use, and err on the side of too much rather than too little.

MOUNTING BOXES

If your plan has been prepared by a professional, it contains an electrical diagram with symbols for various devices (see PAGE 299). When you draw up a plan on your own, it is helpful to use symbols to indicate what type of fixture goes where.

With your plan finalized and in hand, the first step in wiring is to mount the electrical boxes. Steel boxes are usually the choice. The most convenient wall boxes for new

Typical electrical diagram.

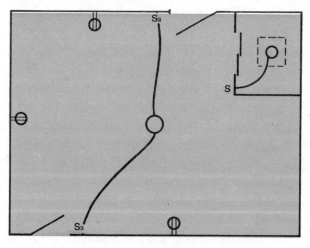

walls have "ears" or mounting brackets that are nailed to the faces of the wall studs. Other boxes are nailed to the sides of the studs through projections in the top or bottom or through holes in the boxes themselves. Your choice will be influenced by availability of various types of boxes.

The National Electric Code sets a maximum number of wires that can be installed in certain boxes, depending on cubic-inch capacity. This is not ordinarily a problem in home construction, but check the local code for any box in which a large number of wires is to be connected. For example, a 2 x 2 x 3-inch box with diagonal back edges has a 10-cubic-inch capacity and may not accept more than five #14 or four #12 wires. A wire that both enters and leaves the box is counted as one. A workable rule of thumb is that each #14 wire requires 2 cubic inches of space, whereas a #12 needs 2¼ cubic inches.

When boxes are placed between studs or joists (as is often the case for ceiling fixtures), adjustable bar hangers allow exact placement. For ganged boxes, metal or wood mounting bars between studs are needed. You should know the type and thickness of your wallcovering material before you install the boxes. When using noncombustible materials such as gypsum wallboard, the front of the box must be no more than ½ inch behind the surface of the wall. With combustible materials such as paneling, the front of the box must be flush with the finish surface.

The easiest way to remove the box knockouts where wires enter and exit is to do it before the box is nailed up. Just make sure that you knock out the right hole. The code requires that unused knockouts be refilled with metal plugs, so if you are not sure of the wiring routes, it may be better to wait until you are ready to connect the cable. This is not difficult in new work unless the working space is restricted.

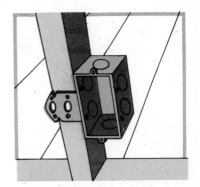

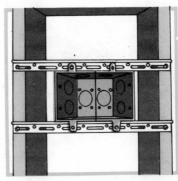

Fastening boxes to studs.   Ganged boxes on mounting bars.

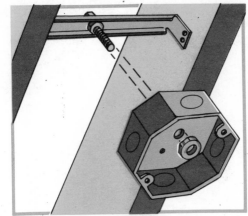

Ceiling box on bar hanger.

RUNNING THE CABLE

After all the boxes are in place, plot the circuit to determine where the *last* box will be. Start running cable from there.

When running cable, drill holes through the centers of joists and studs when cross-

Running board for cable.

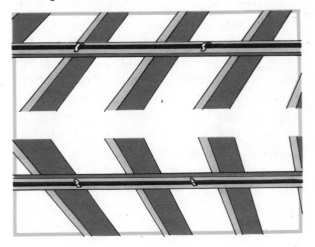

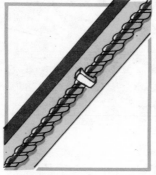

Stapling armored cable.

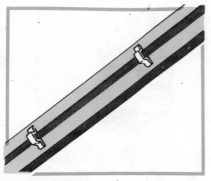

Straps on nonmetallic cable.

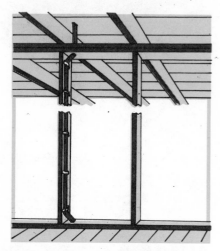

Running cable through plates.

the cable to the box during the roughing phase, then do the wire-stripping as part of the finishing. You may find it easier to strip the wire first, then connect it to the box, since you have more room to work before the cable is "tied down." Either way, leave sufficient cable inside the box to pull the wires out and connect the devices. Eight inches of cable is the general recommendation, but this is a lot of cable to stuff back in afterward, especially if the cable continues on, meaning that you will have more wires. If you strip the wires first, you can get by with less—about 5 to 6 inches of cable inside the box (check the local code on this point).

If you are using nonmetallic (Romex) cable, cut through the covering between the wires, about 4 inches back from the end, using a sharp knife or a cable stripper. Cut or tear away the wrapping (some nonmetallic cable has a ripcord down the center for the purpose). Strip away the insulation about 3/4 inch from the end of each wire. A knife will do for this, too, but a wire stripper will make a neater, faster job without danger of damaging the wire. Just

ing them. (In an unfinished basement or attic, a running board of 1 x 2 or 1 x 3 lumber can be nailed across the joists and the cable attached to that.) Use staples spaced every 4 feet or less to secure armored cable (Type AC) when running lengthwise along joists and studs; use straps every 3 feet to support nonmetallic (Type NM) cable.

To run cable from one floor to the next, drill through the sole and/or top plates. You may also find it easier and faster to run the cable up to the attic or down to the basement to get from one side of a room to another, rather than running it around the walls. It may sound obvious, but be sure to go over the headers in door and window openings and not run cable through the openings. When running armored cable, turns should be made on a minimum 12-inch radius.

Most professional electricians connect

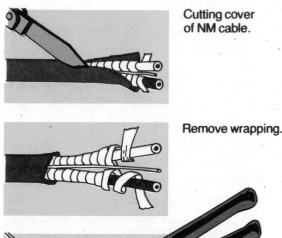

Cutting cover of NM cable.

Remove wrapping.

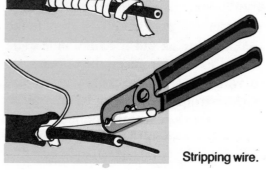

Stripping wire.

How to Wire New Construction

rotate the right size of stripper for the wire gauge over the insulation and pull the cut-away insulation off the end.

The connectors come in two pieces. Remove the locknut and slip the connector part over the cable before insertion into the box. A setscrew is turned down to hold the cable in place tightly enough so that the cable can't pull out, but not so tight as to crush it. The connector is then placed through the knockout, and the locknut is hand-tightened over the connector until both parts hug the side (or top or bottom) of the box. Final tightening is by tapping a screwdriver against the lugs of the locknut.

For armored cable (BX), use a hacksaw or snips to cut the metal covering, but be careful not to cut into the wire. Strip the wires the same as with nonmetallic cable. A fiber bushing is then placed between the metal covering and the wires so that any rough edges will not cut the insulation. The end of this bushing should project inside the connector.

THIN-WALL CONDUIT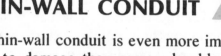

Thin-wall conduit is even more impervious to damage than armored cable. Furthermore, if rewiring is done at a later date, it is easy to pull the old wires out of the conduit and install new, larger ones. But the extra work and expense of using conduit may outweigh these benefits. The only time you must use conduit is when the local code demands it. (The National Electric Code does not insist on its use anywhere on your side of the service entrance.)

Conduit comes in 10-foot lengths in a variety of sizes, according to the number and gauge of wires it is to carry. Half-inch conduit carries four #14 or three #12 wires; ¾-inch carries five #12, four #10, or three #8. For interior work, these should be adequate for all your needs. Larger sizes go up to 2-inch, for four #1/0 or three #3/0 wires.

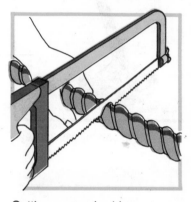

Installing connector on NM cable (above).

Tightening connector to box (above right).

Final tightening (at right).

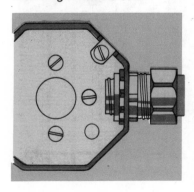
Cutting armored cable.

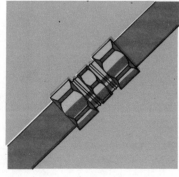
Fiber bushing in connector.

Boxes are installed in the same manner as for nonmetallic or armored cable; only steel boxes may be used. Empty conduit is then mounted in place and connected to boxes before insulated wires are inserted. For runs longer than 10 feet, pieces of conduit are joined by couplings. Cut shorter

Mounting conduit to box.

Coupling conduit.

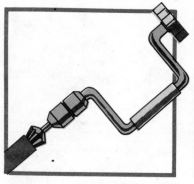

Ream-cut conduit.

Filing end of conduit.

Place hickey on conduit.

Bend conduit with hickey.

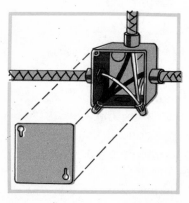

Pull box.

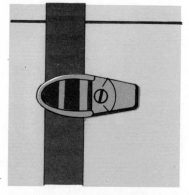

Conduit hanger.

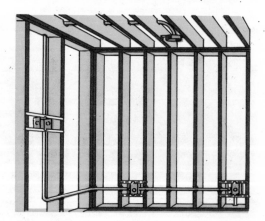

Notch studs, joists for conduit.

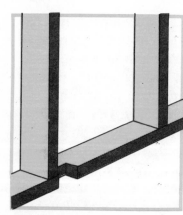

Notch plate for conduit.

lengths with a hacksaw. Ream the cut ends inside and taper with a file.

Conduit is bent with a conduit bender or "hickey" (see PAGE 304). The code forbids any bend more than 90 degrees and allows no more than four such bends in a run from one box to the next. To use the hickey, measure off the place where the bend is to begin, attach the hook of the tool on the inside of the mark, and place one foot on the straight section. Pull the pipe handle until you have the degree of bend required.

"Pull boxes" may be required to reduce the number of bends, because of junctions or simply for ease in pulling the wires through. Pull boxes are bigger than regular boxes but are installed in the same way. After the wiring is complete, the pull box is covered with a plate. Like all boxes, it must be accessible after the wallcovering is up; basement or attic locations are best.

Where conduit runs along the side of a stud or joist, it should be supported every 6 to 8 feet with a pipe strap or clamp. Where conduit runs horizontally across the wall studs or joists, cut notches to provide a channel for the conduit. You can also install conduit without notching studs, which may be preferable because it does not weaken supporting walls and it also cuts down on work. The only carpentry is a small notch in the plate; then the conduit is laid right on the rough floor. Once the conduit is in place, install furring strips (or

How to Wire New Construction

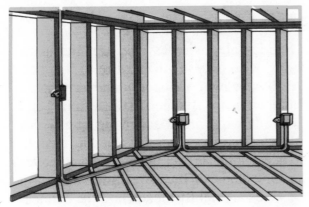

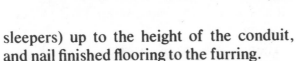

Sleepers.

Fit connector over conduit.

Tighten nut on connector.

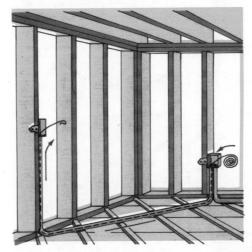

Run fish tape through conduit.

Fasten wires to fish tape.

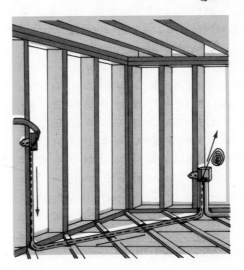

Pull tape and wires through conduit.

sleepers) up to the height of the conduit, and nail finished flooring to the furring.

When connecting conduit (which is not threaded) to boxes, fit the threadless end of the connector over the conduit and insert the connector through the box knockout; then tighten the locknut.

After conduit and boxes are installed, pull wires through the conduit into the boxes. Wires must be continuous from outlet to outlet; do not use spliced wires. Be sure that wires in the system conform to the standard color code: in a two-wire circuit, one black and one white wire; in a three-wire circuit, one black, one white, one red.

Where the run is long and several wires are to be inserted in the conduit, fish tape is needed. It comes in various lengths up to 100 feet. In straight runs, the tape moves smoothly. First run the fish tape through the conduit from one box to the next. Bend the wires around the hook on the tape. (Wrapping the end of the fish tape and the wires with electrical tape helps insure a smooth run.) Pull the tape back through the conduit until the wires appear. Cut the wires, allowing enough extra for making connections (six to eight inches), then continue on to the next box. To go through bends, work the tape back and forth until the bend is passed. Use soapstone or talcum powder as a lubricant. On short runs, wires can be pushed through without tape.

How to Wire New Construction

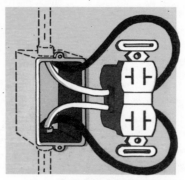

Connecting wires.

Wires that continue
beyond outlet.

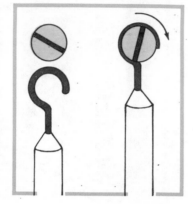

Bend wire ends.

Place under screw, tighten.

MAKING CONNECTIONS

After the wallcoverings are up, electrical connections can be made inside the boxes. If you are using armored or nonmetallic cable, the hard part of the job is done already. The important thing to remember is to connect black (hot) wires to black, and white (neutral) to white. In outlet receptacles and fixtures, black wires are connected to the brass or darker terminals, and white wires to the chrome or "white" terminals. Where the wires continue beyond the outlet, attach each of the incoming wires to one of the properly colored terminals, top or bottom, and the outgoing to the other one. Use long-nosed pliers to bend the ends of the stripped wires into a "C" shape, then wrap each end around a loosened terminal screw. Place the wires so that the screws will tighten the loop (clockwise), not loosen it.

SWITCHES

Single-pole switches interrupt the black or hot wire only. If the fixture to be operated by the switch is beyond the switch, the black wires are attached to the terminal and the white wires are attached together with a solderless connector, bypassing the switch. To use a solderless connector, place it over the bare ends of the wires and twist until the wires are tightly locked into the connector. If you have bared too much wire so that any of it is exposed, wrap it with black plastic tape.

When a switch is located beyond the fixture and is at the end of a circuit, the white wire of the fixture is attached to the white wire of the feed line. The black wire of the fixture is attached to the black wire from the switch. The black wire of the feed line is then attached to the white wire of the switch to complete the connection. To

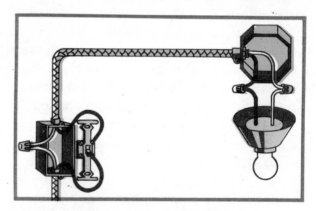

When fixture is beyond switch.

Twist connector
onto wires.

Wrap with tape
if necessary.

avoid confusion, the ends of the white wire that runs between the switch and the fixture should be painted black.

To add a switch controlling a fixture in the middle of a circuit, the white wire of the fixture is attached to both the white wires of the circuit (incoming and outgoing). The black wire of the fixture is attached to the black wire of the switch. The white wire from the switch is attached to both incoming and outgoing black wires from the circuit; the ends of this white wire should be painted black.

THREE-WAY SWITCHES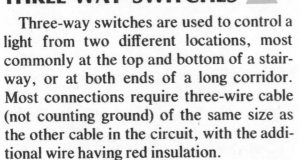

Three-way switches are used to control a light from two different locations, most commonly at the top and bottom of a stairway, or at both ends of a long corridor. Most connections require three-wire cable (not counting ground) of the same size as the other cable in the circuit, with the additional wire having red insulation.

Three-way switches have an extra light-colored terminal; just make sure that the black wire is always connected to the brass (dark) screw. When both switches are located beyond the fixture being controlled, two-wire cable is used between the fixture and the first switch. The white feed wire from the circuit is attached to the white wire of the fixture. The black feed wire goes to the black wire from the switch. The white wire from the switch goes to the black wire of the fixture (and should be painted black). At the first switch, the black feed wire is attached to the dark terminal. Three-wire cable is run between the switches. The white wire from the fixture is attached to the black wire of this cable (and is painted black). The white wire of the three-wire cable is attached to one of the light terminals on each switch, and the red wire is attached to the remaining light-colored terminal on each switch.

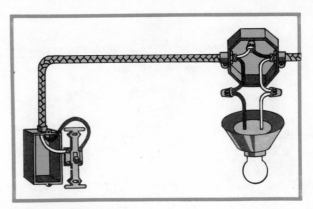

Switch at end of circuit beyond fixture.

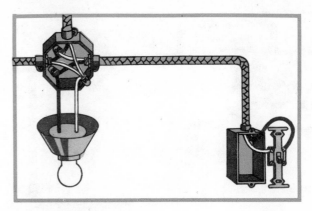

Switch controlling a fixture in middle of circuit.

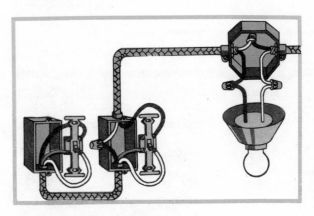

Three-way switch hookup, both switches beyond fixture.

When the circuit enters a fixture that separates the two three-way switches, three-wire cable is run from the fixture to both switches. The black feed wire is attached to the black wire from one of the switches. The red and white wires from that switch

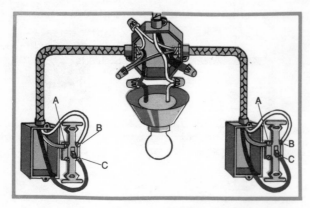

Three-way switch hookup
fixture between switches.

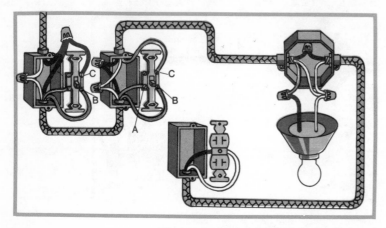

Three-way switch hookup, fixture beyond
both switches and in middle of circuit.

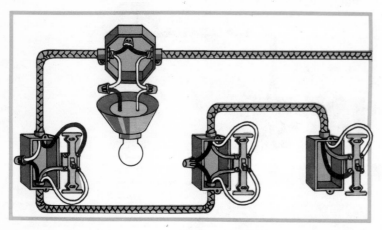

Three switches to control one fixture.

are attached to the red and white wires of the other switch. The white feed wire goes to the white wire of the fixture, and the black wire from the fixture goes to the black wire of the second switch. All white

wires from the switches must be painted black at both ends.

When two switches control a fixture that is beyond them in a circuit that continues past the fixture, four-wire (or two two-wire) cable is used between the two switches. The white feed wire from the circuit is attached to a white wire between the switches, and to the white wire in the fixture and the white wire of the line beyond the fixture; thus, it bypasses both switches. The black feed wire from the circuit is attached to a "jumper" (a short length of wire from the brass terminal of the first switch) and to the black wire leading to the second switch. The remaining two wires are connected to the two light terminals of each switch. The black wire between the switches is attached to the black wire of the three-wire cable between the second switch and the fixture, where it bypasses the fixture and is attached to the black wire of the circuit beyond. The red wire of this cable goes from a light-colored terminal on the switch to the black wire of the fixture. Thus wired, the switches control the fixture, but not the outlets beyond the fixture, which are always hot. And if it all sounds mightily confusing, it needn't be—just look at the drawings.

Controlling a light or other fixture from three separate locations requires a combination of three-way and four-way switches. As an example, consider an installation with three switches beyond the fixture. In the fixture, the hookup is white feed wire to white fixture wire, black feed wire to black wire from first (three-way) switch, and black fixture wire to white wire from the switch (paint it black). In the first switch, incoming black goes to the dark terminal. Incoming white goes to the black of the outgoing three-wire, bypassing the switch. Red and white wires of the outgoing cable are attached to the light terminals of the first switch and to one set of terminals of the middle (four-way) switch. In the second switch, incoming black bypasses, and is attached to the black of a three-wire cable leading to the third (three-way) switch. Red and white wires between the second and third switches are attached to the remaining terminals of the respective switches.

And if all that seems too simple, consider the mind-boggling possibility of a single fixture controlled from five, even ten locations! The same wiring applies—just install additional four-way switches between the three-ways at each end, hooking them up in the same way as the four-way switch in our example shown in the drawing.

In fact, while switching combinations and variations seem almost infinite, the principles remain the same and are basically simple. From the examples given here, you can figure how to wire just about any conceivable switch-controlled fixture.

GROUNDING

What comes in must go out, and, while this is a gross oversimplification, it is also true of alternating current—the neutral wire in such a system must be connected to the ground (literally, the earth). This is most commonly done by affixing a wire from the panel to the metal water pipe outside the water meter, although in rural areas a ground rod accomplishes the same purpose before the service enters the house. In addition, metal raceways, the enclosures for conductors and exposed frames of electrical equipment and appliances, must be grounded. This is to reduce the effects of high-voltage surges and lightning strikes, and to prevent shocks should exposed metal be accidentally charged. The National Electric Code is very strict in this regard, and must be complied with.

Armored cable and conduit are grounded

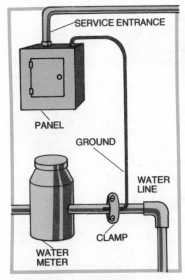

Grounding to water line.

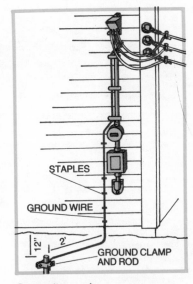

Grounding rod.

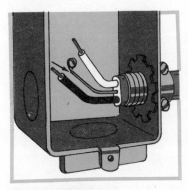

Grounding NM wire to box setscrew.

Grounding NM wire to special grounding clip.

by the metallic outside covering. Nonmetallic cable (except for older types) contain a bare or green-insulated wire, which must always be grounded to the box. A grounding setscrew is sometimes built into the box, and the ground wire is attached to this. If there is no built-in grounding screw, the ground wire is attached to special grounding clips, which are then clipped onto the edge of the box.

SPLICING

As long as there is no strain ("pull") on the wires (and this is the case when cables are securely clamped to each box), solder-

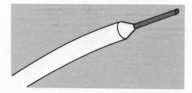

Bare wire, tapering insulation.

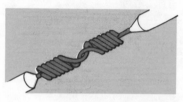

Rub with emery paper.

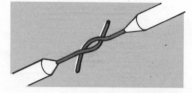

Twist wires together.

Twist several turnings.

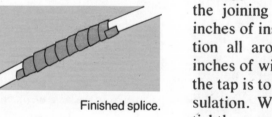

Hold soldering gun to wires.

Hold solder to wires.

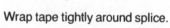

Finished splice.

Wrap tape tightly around splice.

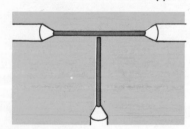

Bare wire on line to be tapped.

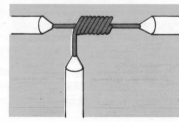

Wrap wire around tapped line.

less connectors do a safe and adequate job of connecting wires. In some cases, however, splicing may be necessary. A properly made splice can be as strong as a continuous piece of wire, but the job must be done right—otherwise, trouble will result!

Each wire is bared for about 3 inches and the insulation tapered about 20 degrees all around. Wires should be clean and shiny; if necessary, rub with emery paper. Cross the wires about 1 inch from the insulation on each side, then twist the wires tightly around each other. It should take from six to eight turnings. Hold a soldering gun or iron to the wires and heat until the wires become hot enough to melt the solder. (Be careful—too much heat will melt the insulation.) Move the solder along the wires so that it flows into every crevice, coating the wires completely. When the solder cools, cover the the splice from one end to the other with plastic electrical tape, stretching the tape tightly. Keep taping until it approximates the thickness of the insulation.

A tap splice connects the end of a wire at some point in a continuing line. It should be used only in cases where there is no pull on the tapped wire. Bare and clean the end of the joining wire, stripping away about 3 inches of insulation and tapering the insulation all around. Bare and clean about 3 inches of wire on the continuing line where the tap is to be made, again tapering the insulation. Wrap the end of the added wire tightly around the bare part of the continuing wire. Solder as described above, and wrap with tape.

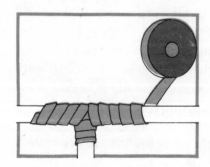

Wrap with tape.

How to Wire New Construction

INSTALLING LIGHTING FIXTURES

Lighting fixtures are prewired, and all that needs to be done in most cases is to attach the black and white wires in the fixture to the wires in the box. The usual fixture box is octagonal. Often, a threaded stud inside the box supports the fixture, or supports a strap to which the fixture is then attached. Or a strap is attached to the "ears" of the outlet box to support the fixture. Ordinarily, white wires are connected to white, and black to black; but switching arrangements may change that so that the white wires *act* like black (and, in fact, should be painted black). Switching situations are described above.

If pull-chain fixtures are used (usually in basements and garages), the chain itself is the switch, and wires are connected in the usual way—black to black and white to white. Often, this type of fixture is not prewired, so the cable wires are connected directly to the fixture.

HOOKING UP TO THE HOT STUFF ▲

With all the fixtures on the circuit installed, all that is left is the connection to the entrance panel. For this phase, an extra measure of caution is advised. Caution, however, does not have to mean fear. You can work in perfect safety by insuring that the hookup is not hot when you make the final connection.

If you are adding onto an existing circuit, plug a lamp or radio into the outlet where you plan to make the connection. If your connection is a light fixture, switch the light on. Then remove fuses or trip breakers until the current to your test facility stops. If in doubt, use your tester to make sure that the juice is off.

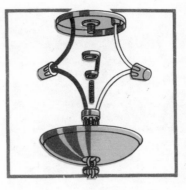
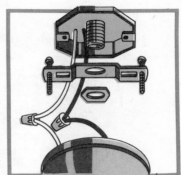
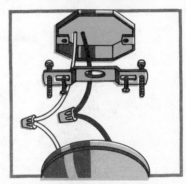
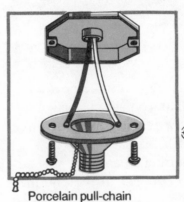

Fixture mounted to stud (above).

Fixture strap mounted to stud (above right).

Fixture strap mounted to box (right).

Porcelain pull-chain fixture, prewired.

Pull-chain light fixture, direct connection.

If you are tying a new line into a receptacle at the former end of the circuit, simply attach the cable to the two unused terminals—black to brass, white to light, of course. If the connection is in the middle of the circuit, tie into the selected receptacle with "jumpers" if the box space will allow it. This involves removing the black and white wires from either the incoming or outgoing side of the receptacle and attaching short lengths of wire (about 3 or 4 inches each of black and white) to the terminals and to both the wires that you dis-

How to Wire New Construction

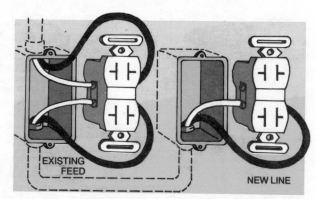

Attaching new line to end of existing circuit.

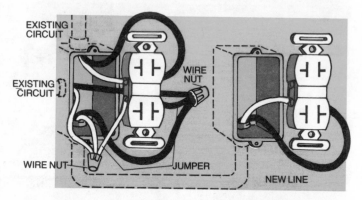

Tying into a receptacle in middle of circuit.

connected and the wires of the new addition. Make sure that you screw the solderless connectors down tightly over the three wires being joined.

When you are wiring an entirely new circuit, you have to connect to the entrance panel, which is somewhat more risky. You may prefer to have a licensed electrician take over the job at this point, inspecting

your work and then making the final hook-up. If you elect to do it yourself, just use common-sense precautions and make sure you understand every step of the job.

First, disconnect the power completely by throwing the main switch. Do this in daylight, of course, and have a flashlight on hand. The switch may be a lever outside a fuse box, a pull-out main fuse drawer, or a ganged breaker switch marked "main." (Some breakers are marked "main lighting" and may not disconnect the power to your range or dryer even after you have thrown the main switch; use the tester to make sure that there is no power in the area where you are working. To be extra safe, don't touch any wires other than those you absolutely must.)

Most breaker boxes have knockouts where no breakers are installed. Select a

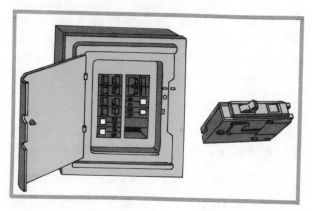

New breaker in box.

Throwing main switch.

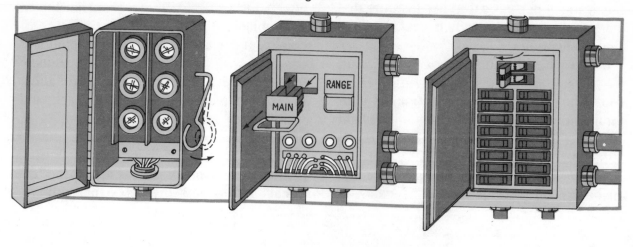

How to Wire New Construction

breaker to fit the size of circuit (and wire) you have installed, and slip it into the notches in the knockout supplied for that purpose. Use a screwdriver to punch out the hole in the panel most convenient for running in the cable. Before cutting the cable, make a trial run to the breaker and the common grounding plate to be sure you have enough wire to fit. Cut and strip the cable, attaching the black wire to the breaker terminal and the white wire to the grounding plate (where all the other white wires are connected). Do the same for the ground wire. When everything is tight, replace the panel front and reset the main switch.

Fuse boxes are wired similarly. Throw the main switch first. Where an opening exists, screw the black wire to the lug and the white and ground wires to the common plates or other connecting areas.

When there are no open circuit locations in the existing breaker box or fuse panel, you may be able to add a subpanel (see PAGE 337). You should have professional advice in determining whether your system can support a subpanel. It depends on how much wattage the entire system can carry, and a whole new system may be required. Your local utility should be able to help with this.

HIGH-VOLTAGE LINES

Old-timers often refer to high-voltage lines as "220," but most such lines today are rated at 230 or 240 volts (depending on the local utility). Some appliances (ranges and dryers, for instance) use both 120 and 240—120 for the motor and/or lights and 240 for the heating elements. It is not too important to the do-it-youself electrician whether a high-voltage line is 220, 230, 240, or even 250 volts, but you do have to know that two circuits are hooked up as one. To carry such a load, three-wire cable with #6 or #8 wire is used.

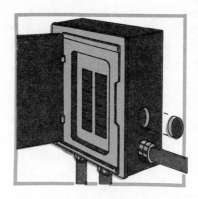
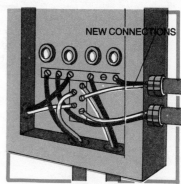

Punch out access hole (above).

Attach new circuit wires (above right).

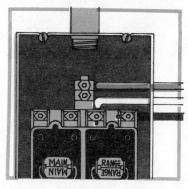

High-voltage hookup (right).

The black wire is connected to one breaker and the red to another. The white neutral wire is connected to the common ground plate or bar. Special receptacles are used for these lines, along with large square boxes where connections must be made. Large (usually 30- or 40-amp) breakers are required, two for each appliance. Before you attempt wiring a job of this sort, study the specifications that come with the appliance, and talk it over with your electrical-supply dealer to make sure that all the materials in the line are designed to handle the extra load. As always, check and comply with local codes.

OUTDOOR WIRING

The principles and techniques of outdoor wiring are not really different from interior wiring. The materials are quite another matter. Most electrical materials are made for dry areas and are not intended to be exposed to the elements. Exterior materials are made to withstand the rigors of temperature extremes: wind, water, snow, sleet and "dark of night."

Outdoor boxes have special, gasket-fitted covers and other safeguards against the elements. (The receptacles themselves are the same as the indoor ones.) Codes may vary on this point, but most above-ground wiring must be conduit. In many cases, underground wiring must be USE or UF type. It is solidly encased in plastic and is buried in a trench below the frost line. Local codes, however, may insist that all exterior wiring—above or below ground—be enclosed in conduit, in which case it is installed in the same manner as interior conduit. The same cable should be used in all instances. If, for example, you run cable underground and conduit above, use USE or UF where buried and continue it through the conduit where exposed.

To install underground wiring, dig a trench at least two feet below the ground and preferably one to two feet below the frost line. You can drill through the sidewall of the house to bring in cable to an interior junction box. Patch around the cable thoroughly after installation to prevent leakage.

It is a good idea to include some waterproof outlets on the house itself as well as at other strategic locations in the yard. All outlets should be placed above the "snow line" for your area (at least 18 inches above ground except in no-snow areas, where they can be lower).

Underground circuits should be controlled by a separate switch inside the house. The National Electrical Code recommends a Ground Fault Circuit Interrupter (GFCI), which protects not only against overloads and short circuits but current leakage as well. There are several different types of GFCI's for both indoor and outdoor locations, and the wiring instructions for each specific type are included when you buy it. Most local codes insist on a GFCI (as they should) whenever electricity is used in conjunction with a swimming pool. It is a good idea to have one with any outside hookup.

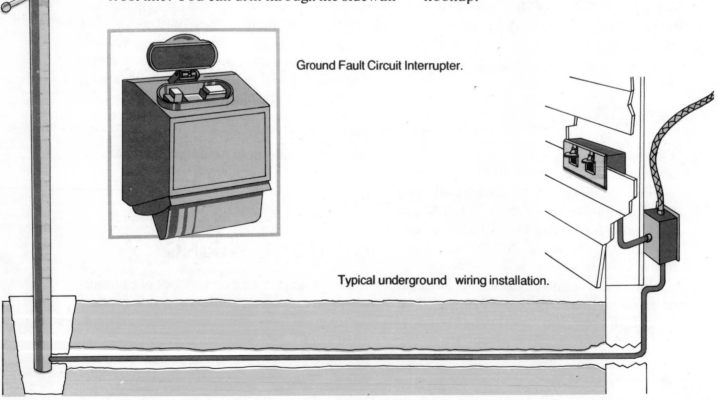

Ground Fault Circuit Interrupter.

Typical underground wiring installation.

How to Wire New Construction

5

Wiring in an Existing House

ADDING or changing wiring in an existing house is not basically different from the installation in new construction. The same principles apply, the same connecting methods are used, and most of the same materials.

What is different about "old house" wiring is the fact that it is concealed by plaster, gypsum wallboard, paneling, tile, or some other material. You cannot see exactly where the existing wires are, or what outlet is connected to what line. Even more frustrating is the fact that you don't know the framing—the exact locations of studs and joists inside walls and ceilings.

Houses built in the past 50 years or so do follow the same basic framing patterns, so you can probably assume 16-inch centers for 2 x 4 studs, 2 x 8's for most joists, etc. But you still have to find them, and you can never really assume that any house was built the way it should have been. Builders and carpenters have eccentricities like everyone else and, based on their experience, often take shortcuts that are impossible to fathom once walls are enclosed, concealing the framing.

The problems are even greater in homes built 50 or more years ago. Codes, standardization, and modern building methods were virtually nonexistent. There were few developers or large builders. Homes were put up individually (sometimes even whimsically) and often without plans. In many ways, they were built better—oak woodwork, lath-and-plaster walls, stained-glass windows, sturdy partitions. But in other ways—heating and lighting, for instance—they were primitive. In this case, any home improvement—and particularly one that involves within-the-wall work—is a real challenge.

TRACING THE CIRCUITS

It is a good idea to have a "map"—a diagram of the circuitry—of your home's wiring, whether or not you contemplate changing or adding to it. Remove a fuse or turn off a breaker, then see which ceiling fixtures go off and which outlets are out of commission. It helps to have two people on the job, but you can do it alone if you don't mind the legwork between the entrance panel and the various rooms of the house each time you shut down a circuit. (Just make sure you do it in daylight.) A tester is a big help for checking outlets—and it's easier to move around than a lamp or whatever else you might plug in as you make your inspection rounds.

If the electrician who originally wired your home was a thoughtful soul, he listed the locations of the principal circuits on the fuse or breaker box. If not, do it yourself. Make up little tags saying "kitchen," "master bedroom," "basement and office," etc., and affix them to the appropriate cables coming out of the entrance panel. Or make embossed-tape labels and fasten them to the panel below the appropriate breaker or fuse.

In addition, draw a map of each circuit noting the locations of all the outlets, and keep them handy, preferably near the entrance panel. The circuit maps should show ceiling lights, switches, outlets, and any other devices on the line. Use the symbols shown on PAGE 299.

ADDING TO EXISTING CIRCUITS

By consulting your wiring map, you can easily determine whether a given circuit has any additional capacity by adding up the wattages of all lights and/or appliances served by the line, then subtracting the total from the line's capacity. A 15-amp circuit with 120-volt service has a capacity of 1,800 watts (15 x 120 = 1,800), so if you are currently using only 1,350 watts on such a circuit, you can add fixtures or outlets to draw 450 more. If all you're planning to add is a ceiling fixture or baseboard outlet, which will be primarily for lighting, there should be no problem.

If there is extra capacity on the line, consult your map to try to determine where the circuit ends (although this may not always be obvious). If all else fails, you can remove the outlet covers to see where the

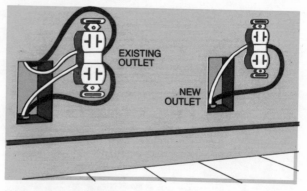

Wiring at end of circuit.

wiring ends. Here there will be only a single white and a single black wire, not incoming and outgoing pairs of each. If at all possible, this is where you should make your connections. This may mean using extra cable to get from the end of the line to where you want to add, but it is the easiest way to achieve the desired result.

It is possible that the route from the end of the circuit to your new outlet is too complicated to warrant making the connection from there. In that case, either try a different circuit or try to locate a junction box on the original line. It may be possible to tie a new junction box into the circuit, but this may be a code violation. Also, it is quite likely that cutting into the line in this way will not leave enough slack in the wires to make the necessary connections.

It is best not to extend a circuit from a switch. A switch at the end of the line controls a fixture preceding it. If you run new wiring off the switch, that switch will also turn the new outlets on and off. It may be that you don't mind this, and that starting from the switch will be so much easier as to compensate for that problem. Of course, there is a way to get around this, just as there are ways to get around most wiring situations. But this would involve not only adding to the circuit, but also rewiring between the switch and the fixture it controls, depending on what the current setup is (see PAGES 320-322). That may be more work than it is worth.

Wiring in an Existing House

"ROUGHING IN"

From your circuitry maps, try to determine whether there are likely to be any wires running through the place where the new box will be located. From the attic, basement, or crawl space, check to see whether there are plumbing pipes or heating ducts in the way. Wiring should present no great problem—you just have to be extra careful not to cause any damage when you are cutting the box opening. Pipes and ducts are another matter. It is much easier to move the new outlet (especially before you have even cut into the wall) than to move the plumbing or heating.

Wall outlets are usually placed about 12 inches from the floor, switches about 48 inches. But this need not be a hard and fast rule. If you are installing a switch in a child's room, you might want to put it at a height convenient for him or her. If all the members of your family tower above the average, install switches—and outlets, too—6 inches or so above the usual height.

Unlike new construction, in which all boxes are normally attached directly to studs, it is usually preferable to place the boxes about 4 or 5 inches from a stud. This minimizes the possibility of cutting into a concealed wire that may be running alongside the stud. Locate studs by "sounding"—tapping along the wall. A hollow sound indicates the space between two studs; a solid thump should mean a stud. If that is inconclusive, try a magnetic stud finder (available at any hardware store), moving it across the wall slowly until the needle indicates a stud location. (The magnetic needle is not, of course, attracted by the wood stud, but by lath or wallboard nails that have been driven into it.) And if that fails, drill a series of small holes directly above the baseboard, every two inches until the drill hits a stud. Normal stud spacing is 16 inches from center to center, so once you have found one it is easy to find

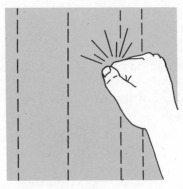
Tapping for studs.

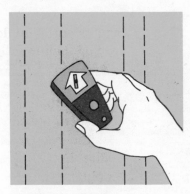
Using a stud finder.

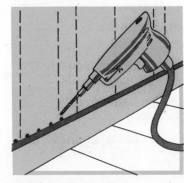
Drilling to locate studs.

Box template.

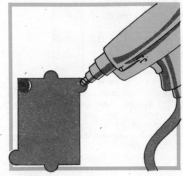
Drill holes in corner.

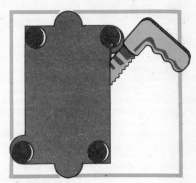
Cut opening.

others in the same wall. This spacing does not necessarily apply at corners or door openings, however, where additional studs are usually located for structural purposes.

If your walls are covered with paneling or wallboard, make a paper or cardboard template of the face of the box and trace around this onto the wall to mark the rough opening. Or trace around the box itself. Make sure your lines are level—if the box is cockeyed, so will be the outlet or switch. Drill ½-inch or ⅝-inch holes inside the marked opening in each corner, then cut the opening with a keyhole saw. (Again, watch out for hidden wires.)

If your house has plaster walls, note the approximate location of the box, then use a chisel or old screwdriver to chip away some of the plaster in the area. If you find gypsum lath behind the plaster, proceed as above, only use a fine-tooth saw (a hacksaw blade works well) to avoid damaging the plaster. If you find wood lath behind the plaster (as was used in most homes built 30 or more years ago), place the box so that you cut only halfway through the lath strips at top and bottom (the lath strips are usually 1½ inches wide). Drill and cut the opening as above, using a hacksaw or other fine-tooth blade. Then chip away a small amount (about ⅜ inch) of plaster above and

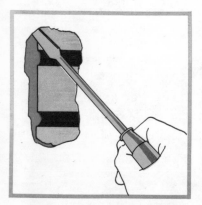

Chip away some of the plaster in the area.

Locate box halfway through top and bottom lath strips.

Cut with hacksaw or other fine-tooth blade.

Chip away plaster at top and bottom.

below the opening. This will allow you to mount the box directly to the lath.

Holes for ceiling boxes are cut in similar fashion.

RUNNING THE WIRE

At the entrance panel, shut off the power to the circuit you are tying into. Remove the cover plate at the box where the connection will be made, and remove the receptacle, switch, or fixture. Remove the locknut from the cable connector, then remove the box. You may be able to pry it loose, or you may have to chisel it out. If it is damaged, replace it later with a new one.

The trick is to find a route from the old box to the new. A straight line may be the shortest distance between two points, but in this type of work it is almost certainly not the easiest. If you are adding a wall outlet or switch at an existing outlet, the most likely route is under the floor (unless your house is built on a concrete slab). If either or both outlets are on interior partitions, drill ⅝-inch holes straight up through the subfloor and the sole plates. On an outer wall, over the foundation, bore a diagonal hole into the plate from below, using a long-shank bit or extension bit. You can now simply run cable between the two box locations (make sure you leave enough for connections at each end), pushing it up through the holes in the plates. If necessary, use a fish tape to guide the cable to the openings. In the basement, run the cable through holes drilled in the joists (if it crosses the joists) or support it with staples (for armored cable) or straps (for nonmetallic cable) if it runs lengthwise along a joist.

If you have an open attic, you can approach the job from above in much the same way. Of course, if an attic floor is in the way, you will have to lift a few floor boards to gain access to the wall plates.

Wiring in an Existing House

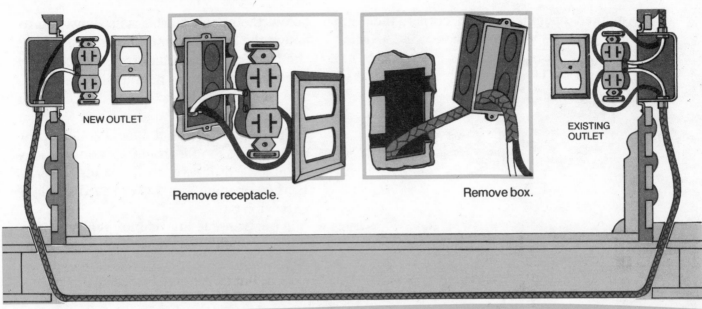

NEW OUTLET

Remove receptacle.

Remove box.

EXISTING OUTLET

Route under floor.

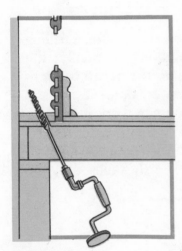

Boring up into
outside wall plate.

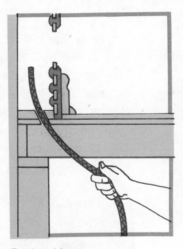

Push cable up
through holes.

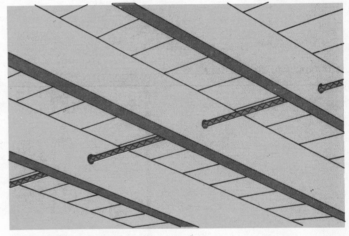

Run cable through holes
drilled in joists.

Run cable along joists.

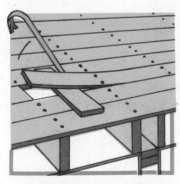

Lift attic floor boards.

Drill through top plates.

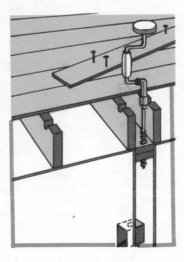

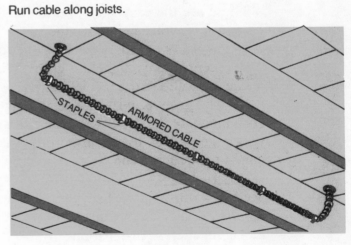

STAPLES

ARMORED CABLE

Wiring in an Existing House

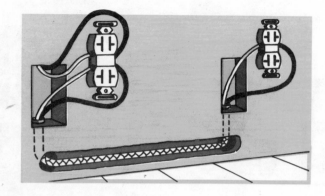

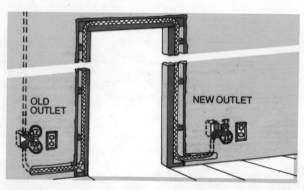

Running wire around door.

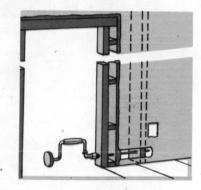

Drill from door to outlet.

Where the run must pass a doorway, remove the trim molding. Notch and groove the framing as necessary for the cable. (For such an installation, nonmetallic cable will almost certainly have to be used because of the relatively sharp bends around the door frame. Again, check the local code.) If the outlet is not too far from the door, you may be able to drill through the studs to get to the box opening, but you have to use a long extension bit.

After running the cable, replace baseboards, moldings, and the like. Some patching of plaster or wallboard may be required, but this should be minimal.

FISHING ▲

For all but the shortest runs, some fishing will probably be required. Normally, the fish tape is worked into the new box opening and back to the power source. Since it is steel and springy, you can work it through more easily than you could the cable itself.

In some cases, such as when you must go around corners, two fish tapes may be

Then simply drill holes and push the cable down to the two box openings.

Those are the easy ways, but if they are not feasible, you can remove the baseboard between the two outlets (in the same room or adjacent rooms) and cut a groove in the plaster or wallboard a few inches above the floor. The groove must be deep enough to accommodate the cable without crushing it. It is a good idea to use armored cable or conduit for such a run, so that it can withstand crushing and is less likely to be damaged by errant nails when you replace the baseboard later. Also, check code requirements for such an installation.

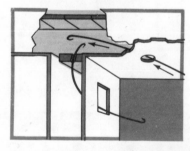

Run fish tape from both openings.

Twist to catch wires.

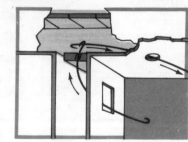

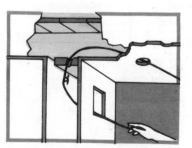

Pull tape back through.

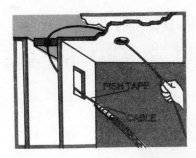

Attach cable
to fish wire.

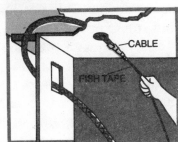

Pull through
tape and cable.

needed. One comes from the old opening, the other from the new, so two fisherfolk are required for the operation. Work both fish tapes in until they meet, then turn them slowly until the hooks engage. Slowly pull one of them back through the opening (this is not a tug of war, so decide first who does the pulling), keeping it taut enough so that the hooks stay together. Make sure that the tape being pulled through is long enough to reach between the openings.

When you have the fish tape from one opening to the other, attach the cable by bending it around the fish tape hook. To be safe, tape them together as well. Then pull fish tape and the cable back through the wall to the other box opening. (Make sure the cable is long enough to make the run, with enough left over for connections at both ends.) Detach the fish tape and you can make the connections.

MOUNTING THE BOXES

However you got it there, the cable is now at the box openings. Knock out the appropriate holes in the boxes to admit the cable, and secure the cable to the boxes with connectors, as described for new construc-

tion on PAGES 313-320 (the only difference is that the boxes are not yet attached).

If the new outlet is in a wood-lath-and-plaster wall, anchor the box to the lath with No. 5 wood screws driven through the top and bottom mounting brackets. For outlets in other types of walls, there are various special devices for mounting the boxes. Some boxes are fitted with special clamps designed specifically for such installations. There are also special metal box supports that are inserted alongside the box; they are longer than the opening is high, so they fit snugly against the inside of the wall, then projections are bent over inside the box to hold it in place. Check local hardware stores and electrical supply shops to see what is available.

The old box can be refastened as it was originally. If this is not possible (as with a box that was mounted with a bracket on the front of a stud), use one of the methods described above.

Ceiling boxes are mounted on hangers between joists. Where accessible from above, this can be done as for new con-

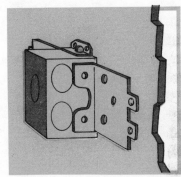

Fasten box to
wood lath (above).

Metal box supports for
wallboard (above right).

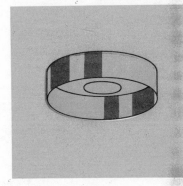

Shallow box fixture (right).

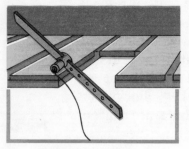
Place hanger through hole.

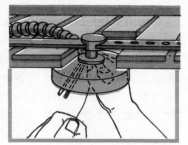
Pull wire to center hanger.

struction. When this is not possible, use a shallow-box fixture. Remove the locknut from the hanger stud, insert a length of wire through the stud, and place the hanger through the hole, holding the stud with one hand. Pull the wire with your other hand, and the hanger will center itself above the ceiling. Connect the cable to the box, then place the box over the stud and secure with the locknut.

Once the boxes are securely anchored, make the final connections as described for new construction on PAGE 320. As always, black to black (or brass terminal screws) and white to white (chrome terminal screws), except for certain switching situations. (See PAGES 320-323.)

ADDING NEW CIRCUITS ▲

Adding new circuits in old work is simply an extension of the techniques outlined above for adding to existing circuits, combined with the principles given in CHAPTER 4 for circuits in new work. Although the problems of working cable through the old work are the same—magnified, in fact, by the larger number of outlets—you may be able to simplify the circuitry. You don't have to work from an existing outlet, so you can run wires from the entrance panel along whatever route is most convenient—through the basement, for example, to the various outlets. Try to plan the outlets so that you can get from one to the other without having to do a lot of fishing.

SURFACE WIRING

If the local code and your esthetic sensitivities allow it, you can avoid most of the cutting, drilling, and fishing and add new outlets with surface wiring. Most codes do permit its use, and your sensitivities may be soothed by seeing some of the types that are available. It is not just a matter of running an exposed cable along the wall to an outlet (although that, too, qualifies as surface wiring in basement, garages, and such locations). Some types of surface wiring are concealed inside quarter-round channels that sit unobtrusively atop the baseboard, looking like part of the trim molding. Others allow you to plug in practically anywhere along the line, making them especially handy for areas such as the kitchen or workshop. There are, in fact, so many different types that only a trip to your electrical-supply store can fully acquaint you with the possibilities of this kind of wiring. But check your local code first.

Installation of surface wiring varies with the type and the manufacturer. Instructions are provided when you buy the units, and these should be followed carefully as to installation, capacities, and usage.

KITCHEN APPLIANCE CENTER

The kitchen is the place where most high-wattage appliances are used. There should be lots of convenient outlets in the kitchen work area above the countertop, with plenty of capacity to carry heavy electrical loads.

One solution to the problem raised by using several appliances at once, such as toaster, mixer, blender, electric coffee pot, electric frying pan, and the like, is to install a four-outlet appliance center. This can be done by ganging two boxes and connecting

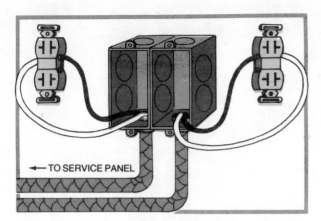
Four-outlet kitchen connection.

power company. If you have only two-wire service, chances are that you will need to have a new three-wire entrance installed. If you already have three-wire service, the odds are that you can add a subpanel. But be sure to have it checked out first.

Assuming there is sufficient housepower, there should be extra take-off lugs on your fuse box. With the main power off, run black wires from two take-off lugs to appropriate lugs on the subpanel (they should be marked to avoid confusion). One white wire is connected from the neutral strip on the main panel to the grounding strip of the subpanel. The new circuits are run from the feeder lugs on the subpanel (black wire), with the white wire connected to the neutral grounding strip.

Because of the different types of main entrance panels and subpanels, you may prefer to leave this job—or at least the final hookup—to a licensed electrician. Otherwise, get specific directions concerning capacity, wire sizes, number of outlets, hookups, etc. from your power company. Make sure to follow exactly the directions that come with the subpanel.

them to two 20-amp separate circuits. This will give you a 4,800-watt capacity at one spot, enough for four appliances at once if they are not all high-wattage gadgets—see appliance table on PAGE 295. You probably already have at least a couple of outlets that can handle one or two such appliances, so an additional four outlets should handle most needs. If you feel you will need more, run a separate circuit to a second four-outlet box.

ADDING A SUBPANEL ▲

When your entrance panel has no room for extra circuits, it is possible that you can add a subpanel to provide two, four, or even more additional circuits. The first step is to determine whether there is enough power entering the house at the service. The best source to determine that is your

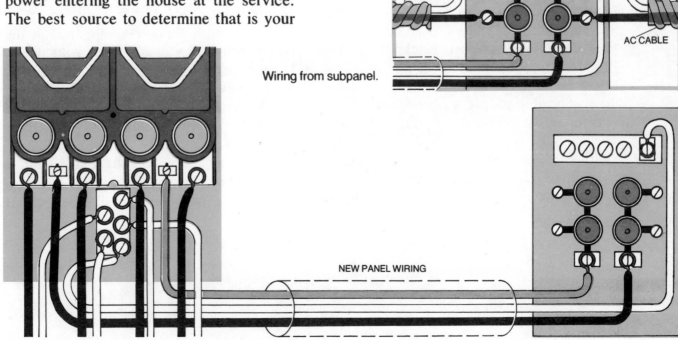

Wiring from subpanel.

NEW PANEL WIRING

6

Simple Electrical Repairs

N O MATTER how well installed your electrical system is, things will in time go wrong. Receptacles wear out (you would, too, if people were always plugging cords into you), wiring becomes damaged or insulation frayed by an overload situation or just old age, switches fail to work. Other problems crop up that have little to do with the health of the system itself. Lamp cords need replacement, overloads cause blown fuses, and doorbells become corroded by exposure to the elements.

TROUBLESHOOTING

Unfortunately, when trouble occurs, the immediate reaction is often panic—or at least *over*reaction. When the lights go out, you may think that a wire has snapped. If a lamp won't work, you conclude that it's time to throw it out.

Knowledge and preparation will help you avoid the panic button. In case the lights go out, it's a good idea to have candles (don't forget matches) and flashlights handy. A battery-operated radio is another excellent panic-soother. Those who had them during the famous Northeast blackout of the 1960's at least knew what was going on (and that, in fact, the Martians were *not* coming). Portable radios work even when the power in the house is off (but they don't help much when the radio station is also without power, which is why many stations have their own auxiliary generators). It also pays to have plenty of extra light bulbs

around, as well as extra fuses, flashlight batteries, light plugs, extension cords, and even spare receptacles and switches for emergencies.

What do you do when the entire house is plunged into darkness? First find your way to the candles and flashlights (which should be conveniently stored in a place known to all members of the family). Once you can find your way around without groping, check the lights in your neighbors' houses. If they are out too, there is undoubtedly a general power failure. A line is down somewhere, or something has happened at the power plant. If you can't see your neighbor's house, give him a call. (The phone works even when the power is off.) If there *is* a power failure, it will probably be futile to call the power company, because their lines will be jammed by similar callers.

If only the power to your house is off, it could be the main fuse, but it is more likely to be some problem with the service. It could even be downed service wires, a common occurrence during heavy storms. If that is the case, keep your distance! If a wire is down across a street or sidewalk, post a large sign on both sides, warning pedestrians and passing cars. Whatever the case, call the power company or an electrician to have it fixed. A blown main fuse could indicate a serious problem that should be investigated by a professional. A downed wire is nothing for an amateur to fool with.

Ordinarily, though, only a portion of your electrical system will be off at one time. This most likely indicates a blown fuse or a tripped breaker. It could be an indication of some problem in the line, but not necessarily. The first step is to check your entrance panel.

It is relatively simple to replace a fuse, and even simpler to flip a breaker switch (see PAGES 311-312). But fuses blow for a reason, and the trouble should be corrected before the fuse is replaced or the switch flipped.

Fuses are rated in amperes, and it is a dangerous—and unfortunately too common—practice to replace a smaller fuse with a larger one. If, for example, you find that a 15-amp fuse has blown, you may be able to restore the current by installing a 20-amp fuse. Don't do it! When an overload or short circuit exists, the fuse is *supposed* to blow. If it doesn't, and the circuit is "over-fused," the wiring may melt and cause a fire. And don't ever resort to the old penny-in-the-box substitute for a fuse. True, it may get the power flowing again. It may also burn down your house. Who says you can't do anything with 1¢ these days? Certainly not your fire department!

Often, you may replace a blown fuse with another of the same amperage (or reset a breaker) and have no further problem. The temporary aberration may have been caused by a sudden (and unusual) power surge, such as a power saw being plugged into a general-purpose circuit when you are paneling your living room. If you have obvious reason to suspect such a cause, just replace the fuse and make sure you sin no more in that regard.

But if the cause of a blown fuse or tripped breaker is a mystery, do a little detective work. Look for loose wiring on the line, or frayed insulation, or some other problem. Often, these clues will show up in the basement or other exposed area (an overload that causes insulation damage may be manifested in the exposed wiring near the entrance panel). If a thorough inspection doesn't turn up the problem, replace the fuse or flip the breaker anyway. If it doesn't blow again for some time, you probably have nothing to worry about—chalk it up as "unsolved." But if it blows again, trouble is obvious. If you can't find it yourself, call in a professional. In an older home, it may simply be a sign that you need more housepower.

With a plug-type fuse, the condition of the blown fuse is often a clue to the cause of the blow. If the copper strip in the center of the fuse is broken (actually, melted apart), the cause is most likely overload. If the glass window of the fuse is darkened—perhaps so much that you can't even see the copper strip—a short circuit is the prime suspect.

Reading a fuse; overload, at left; short circuit, at right.

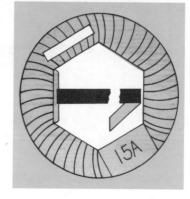 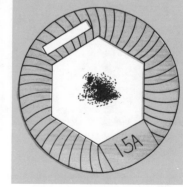

Simple Electrical Repairs

LOCATING AND CURING THE PROBLEM

In most cases, a blown fuse or breaker is caused by overload. If the stoppage occurred just after you turned on a toaster or other high-wattage appliance, you can be almost sure of it. You can verify this by computing the total wattage on the line at the time the fuse blew. (A 15-amp, 120-volt circuit has a 1,800-watt capacity; a 20-amp, 120-volt circuit has a 2,400-watt capacity.) The cure for the condition is obvious: rearrange appliances or add new circuits.

When the overload is strictly temporary, as in the case of several appliances or motors being turned on at the same time and drawing an unusually high surge of power, a time-delay fuse is a convenient and safe solution (see PAGE 311). But don't delude yourself by assuming that every overload is temporary. Make sure of the cause before deciding on a cure.

Short circuits, as noted above, blacken a fuse window. But a short is harder to determine if you have circuit breakers in your home's entrance panel. You can assume that a short is the problem if the breaker keeps tripping and your inspection and cal-

culations make you reasonably sure there is no overload. In either case (fuses or breakers), you must find the cause of the short before restoring the power to the circuit.

If the short occurs only when a certain tool or appliance is used or when a certain lamp is turned on, your detective chore is simple. You can assume that the fault is with the tool, appliance, or lamp rather than with the circuit; and the solution, obviously, is not to use that device until it has been repaired (as detailed elsewhere in this section and in the next).

If that is not the case, you should inspect the entire circuit to find the cause. Start by examining each receptacle and fixture on the circuit. Remove the plate and look inside. Are there any loose or frayed wires, or any bare wires touching other than those inside the connectors? You may have to pull the switch or receptacle out of the box to make that determination. (Remember, of course, to leave the power off.)

If, after examining all the fixtures on the line, you cannot find any crossed or loose wires, a more distressing problem may exist. In this case, it is probably best to call in a licensed electrician. You can, of course, find the problem yourself, but by the time you've torn down your walls and wiring, a professional probably would have the short located and fixed (and at a lesser overall price).

REPLACING DEFECTIVE RECEPTACLES AND SWITCHES

When, by inspection or testing, you determine that an outlet device is defective, replacement is required. To replace a switch or receptacle, turn off the power to the line by tripping the breaker or pulling the fuse. (The power may already be off because of a short circuit—but make sure.)

Remove receptable plate.

Check for loose, touching wires.

Take off the cover plate, then remove the screws holding the receptacle or switch to the box. Pull the device out all the way, and take note of all connections. If the wiring is standard as described in previous chapters, you can proceed; but if it is a complicated arrangement such as a three-way or four-way switch, make a diagram of the connections before you take them apart.

Once you have noted how the device is wired, loosen the terminal screws and remove the wires. Then install a similar device, wiring it in the same manner as the old one. Make sure you loop the wire around the terminals in a clockwise direction so that the loop is tightened as you tighten the terminal screws. Fasten the device to the box. When the new switch or receptacle is in place, fasten the cover plate. Then restore the power. If your diagnosis was correct, the problem should be solved. If not, try another tack, looking for another faulty receptacle or switch. If that fails, you must suspect an in-wall problem, which—as noted above—is probably best left to a pro.

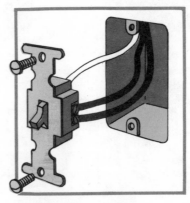

Remove screws holding receptacle or switch.

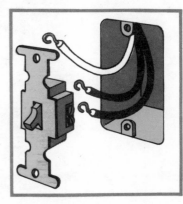

Remove wires.

Tighten wires on new receptacle or switch.

Fasten cover.

CEILING AND WALL FIXTURES

Wiring is built into most ceiling and wall fixtures and is connected to the feed wires inside the box (rather than the feed wires being connected directly to the device, as is normally the case with switches and receptacles). Solderless connectors are usually used. The fixtures are attached to the box in a variety of ways—some with screws or nuts, some by means of central nipples, studs, and/or straps.

When you suspect a problem in a fixture (or if you want to replace it with a new one for cosmetic reasons), first make sure that the power to the fixture circuit is off. Remove the knurled nut, screws, or hex nuts that hold the fixture to the box. Carefully

pull down the fixture and inspect it. Check for loose wiring and, if that is the problem, tighten the connections.

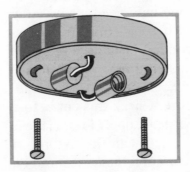

Remove nuts holding fixture.

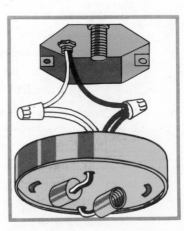

Pull down and inspect fixture.

If the wiring checks out, you can usually suspect the socket. Many fixtures have removable sockets. In that case, detach the wires and remove the socket (how this is

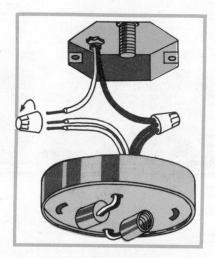

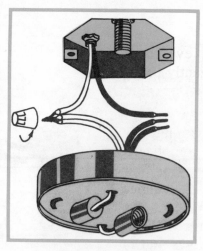

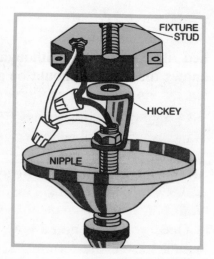

Remove wire nuts, untwist wires.

Attach wires of new fixture.

Using a hickey.

done depends on how it is attached to the fixture, which should be obvious). Take it to the hardware or electrical-supply store and purchase a new one of the same type. Install it the same as the old one.

If the socket is an integral part of the fixture, replace the entire fixture.

To replace a fixture with one just like it, remove the wire nuts and untwist the wires. Assemble the new wires and feed wires with wire nuts (black to black, white to white unless it is a complicated switch arrangement — see PAGES 320-322), and attach the fixture to the box in the same way the old fixture was attached.

If you are installing a different size or type of fixture, you may need a new strap or an extension "hickey" (not to be confused with the conduit-bending tool of the same name) to fasten a new nipple to the old one in the box, in order to accommodate the new fixture. Check this out before you leave the electrical-supply house; these parts may be included with the fixture, or you may have to buy them separately. Whatever the situation, there is a way (and a fitting) that will allow you to attach the new fixture. If in doubt, describe your problem to the electrical-supply dealer and seek his advice.

Bear in mind that if the ceiling plate of the new fixture is smaller than that of the old one, you will probably have to repaint the ceiling. The now-exposed area around the fixture is unlikely to be the same color as the surrounding ceiling because of fading and rising dirt and dust; this is especially true in a kitchen.

If, after you have installed a new socket or a new fixture, the ceiling or wall light still doesn't work, the problem is in the line itself. If wiring is visible from above (as in an attic), check it out for signs of damage. If you can't find anything amiss, it is probably an in-wall problem, and you had best seek professional help.

PLUG AND CORD REPLACEMENT

Thinner and more flexible than their heftier cousins hidden inside sturdy cable, lamp and appliance cords are subjected to a lot of abuse. They get stepped on, run over,

Cut cord beyond break.

Bare ends of wire and reinstrall plug.

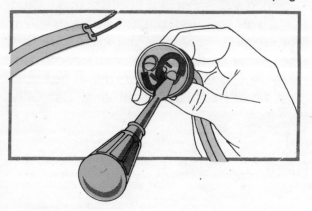

tied in knots and (although everybody knows that a cord should be gently pulled out of its wall connection by the plug) yanked about mercilessly. Small wonder that repairs and replacements are sometimes required.

A most common problem—the direct result of the type of abuse mentioned—is a cord broken at the plug. The repair is simple; just cut off the plug, bare the wires at the end of the cord, and reinstall the plug. Net loss: a few inches of cord.

But this can't always be done. Many plugs—especially on lamps and small appliances—are molded to the cord. If the wire breaks just above the plug, there is no way to rewire the plug. In this case, or if the plug itself is worn or damaged, replacement is required.

On common lamp cord (#16 or #18, two-wire) this is quick and easy—in fact, it is literally a snap. Just snip off the cord above the old plug (or above the break) and snap on a replacement—no baring of wires or tightening of screws. There are several types of such plugs. Some are slipped over the cord and a lever is pressed down, forcing pins through the insulation to make contact with the wires (all inside the plug, of course). On others, the prongs are squeezed together to make the contact in a similar fashion. But warn off the cord-jerkers; this type of connection is not intended for tugs-of-war.

Appliances (except for low-wattage ones) usually have heavier cords, and snap-on plugs will not fit. If a molded plug on such a cord must be replaced, cut the cord above the plug (or the break). Separate the wires at the end of the cord, and strip off about ⅝ inch of insulation from each. A wire stripper is the best tool for the job; if you use a knife, be careful not to cut into the wire. If the plug is not a molded type, remove the fiber insulating cover from the prongs (you can pry it loose at the edge with a screwdriver if it is a snug fit) to ex-

Molded plug.

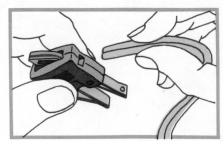
Lever-type snap-on plug.

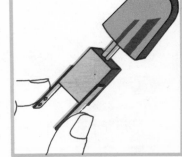

Squeeze-type plug—
slip body over cord (above).

Squeeze prongs
together (above right).

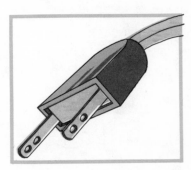

Pull body over
prongs (right).

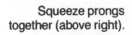
Cut cord above break (above).

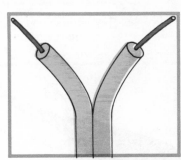

Separate, strip wires
(above right).

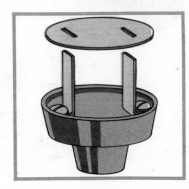

Remove fiber insulating
cover (right).

Simple Electrical Repairs

Slip plug over cord (right).

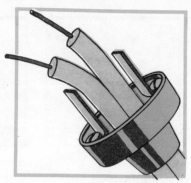

Underwriters' knot
—step 1 (below left).

Underwriters' knot
—step 2 (below right).

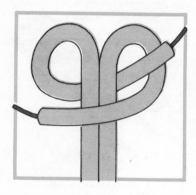

Tighten knot and pull
into plug body.

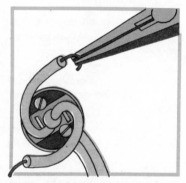

Loop ends of wires.

Tighten screws.

Tie three wires.

pose the wires. Loosen the terminal screws to release the wires, then pull off the plug. If an Underwriters' knot was tied within the plug (as it should have been), you may have difficulty pulling it off. Rather than cutting off the cord, untie the knot. That way you won't have to strip new wire (thereby shortening the cord even more), and you can retie the knot properly by following the old bends (see below).

Slip the new plug over the cord. Whether or not an Underwriters' knot was originally there, tie one inside the new plug. Separate about 3 inches of wire. Loop the black wire behind itself and the white wire. Loop the white wire over the end of the black, and bring it up through the black loop. Tighten the knot and pull it down snugly into the plug body. This will provide a strong degree of protection against cord-jerkers.

Use a small-nosed pliers to bend loops in the ends of the bared wires. Fit the wires inside the plug and place the loops clockwise around the terminal screws—black to brass, white to chrome. Tighten the screws, then place the fiber insulator over the prongs of the plug.

Replacement of a three-prong plug is similar. Tie all three wires together in a tight knot, and pull the cord until the knot is snug against the plug. Loop the green wire around the green or dark-colored screw, and fasten the other wires as above.

Many appliances have separate cords,

Connect wires to terminals.

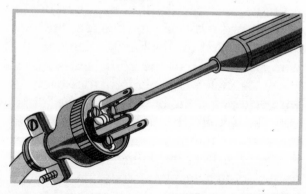

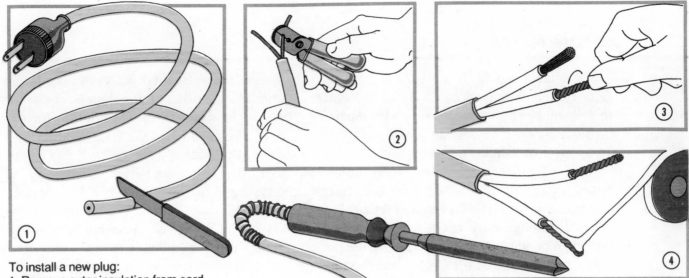

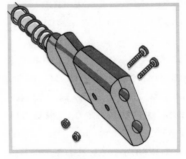

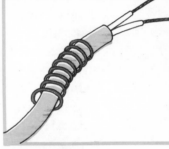

To install a new plug:
1. Remove outer insulation from cord.
2. Strip insulation from wires.
3. Twist stranded wires.
4. Heat, apply solder.

with a wall plug on one end and an appliance plug on the other. Wall plug replacement is as above. If the appliance plug (or the cord at the appliance plug) is damaged or worn, it too can be replaced.

Most new appliance plugs are riveted together and are removed by cutting the cord. If your appliance has a removable appliance plug (held together by screws or bolts) and the problem is with the cord rather than the plug, you can simply cut back the cord and reinstall the old plug. Otherwise, replace it.

To install a new plug, first use a knife to carefully remove about 2½ inches of outer insulation from the cord end. Strip off about ¾ inch of insulation from each wire, taking care not to damage the wire. Twist each stranded wire tightly, then heat with a soldering gun or iron and apply a small amount of solder to each. This will make it easier to attach the wires.

Remove the screws holding the appliance plug casing together. Insert the cord through the spring guard. Bend the wire ends into loops. Place the loops under the terminal screws so that tightening the screws (clockwise) will close the loops. Tighten the screws. Place the spring guard into one half of the casing. Attach the other half of the casing with screws or bolts.

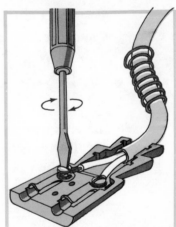

Remove appliance plug casing screws.

Insert cord through spring guard.

Bend wires.

Tighten terminal screws.

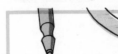

Place spring guard into casing.

Assemble casing.

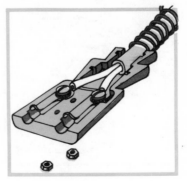

Simple Electrical Repairs

Sometimes the fault is with the cord itself. If it is damaged so far from the end that it will be shortened too much by repair, throw it away. If insulation is badly frayed, scrap it. Sometimes an extension cord is damaged by overload, if too many appliances are run off it. The wires become hot, and insulation melts. It is beyond repair.

Cord damage may not always be obvious; broken wires may be hidden by the insulation. One almost sure sign of this condition is when the lamp or appliance goes on and off as you move the cord, making temporary contact between broken wires. Replace the cord.

When a cord is to be replaced, always buy the same type and size as the original. Lamp cord is not up to the high-wattage demands of such heat-producing appliances as toasters and irons, which should be fitted with "heater" cord wrapped with asbestos

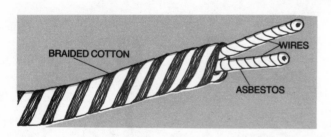

Heater cord.

layers inside a braided cotton or nylon jacket. If you are in doubt, take along the old cord when buying new at the hardware or electrical-supply store.

Terminal connectors.

Attach connectors to wires.

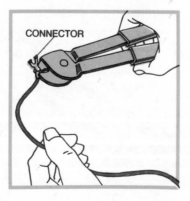

Plugs are attached to new cords as above. At the other end, it depends on what the cord is attached to. On a lamp, for example, the cord wires are fastened to terminals in the socket (see below). On appliances, the situation varies, depending on the type and the manufacturer. Many appliance cords have round connectors at the ends of the wires for fastening to terminal screws. You may be able to buy a new cord with these fittings at an electrical-supply store or from the manufacturer of the appliance. If not, you should be able to find the connectors themselves at an electrical-supply house. Attach them to the bared ends of the wires by soldering and/or crimping them on with an all-purpose tool or pliers.

LAMP REPAIRS

When a bulb breaks, it can be difficult and dangerous to remove it from the socket for replacement. Make sure the plug is pulled out before you attempt it. Wad up newspaper or a paper bag and press it down firmly on the broken bulb, then turn it counterclockwise until the bulb base is removed. If that doesn't work because the glass is broken off right down to the base, try turning it out with a needle-nose pliers (again, make sure that the plug is out). If it still won't come out, wedge a screwdriver inside the base, pressing it against the sides and turning until the base is removed.

When a lamp does not go on or flickers on and off, the obvious first thing to check is the bulb. Is it screwed all the way into the socket? Does it work in another lamp socket? If the bulb checks out all right, make sure the lamp cord is plugged all the way into the wall outlet.

Next, remove the plug and inspect the cord for signs of damage. Make repairs or replacements as detailed above. If the cord and plug are all right, the problem is in the

Wad newspapers to
remove broken bulb.

Use pliers to
remove broken bulb.

Wedge screwdriver
in base and turn.

1. Remove shade and bulb.
2. Pry off felt pad on base.
3. Remove weight.
4. Pull up tube, turn or remove
   screw to remove socket.

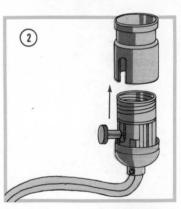
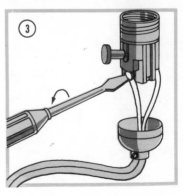

PRESS

1. Press in at button of socket,
   remove outer shell.
2. Remove socket inner shell.
3. Remove wires.

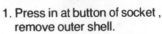
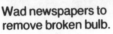

switch or socket. In either case, the fitting
should be replaced.

Lamp design and construction vary
greatly, but the wiring is basically the same.
To replace the socket on a typical lamp,
first remove the lamp shade and the bulb.
With a knife, carefully pry off the protective felt pad on the bottom of the lamp
base. If there is a weight there, remove the
nut holding it in place and remove the
weight. Lift the tube that runs through the
lamp body about 6 inches out of the top.
Turn the tube counterclockwise or loosen
the setscrew (or both, depending on the installation) to remove the tube from the
lamp socket.

Press in at the bottom of the socket's
metal outer shell and lift it straight up. Remove the insulated inner shell to expose the
wiring. Loosen the terminal screws and remove the wires. (If you are simply replac-

Simple Electrical Repairs

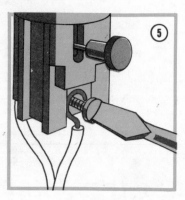

4. Pull out old cord.

5. Attach new cord.

Disassemble new socket; fit
cord through cap; attach wires.

Fasten socket cap to tube.

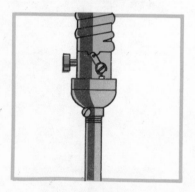

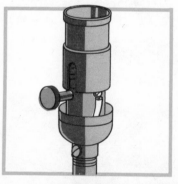

Seat socket in cap.

Place shell over socket.

Snap outer shell in place.

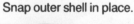

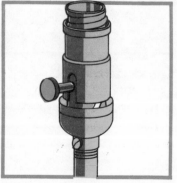

ing the cord, pull the old cord out the bottom of the lamp, thread new cord through the tube, strip the ends of the wires and attach to the terminals on the socket, and reassemble. If you are replacing the socket, read on.)

Take the old socket with you when you buy a replacement, and get one of the same type. Remove the outer shell and insulated shell from the new socket and loosen the terminal screws. Fit the cord through the socket cap, and install wires on the screws, looping them around so that, as the screws are tightened, the ends of the wires are tightened around them.

Install the socket cap on the tube, threading it on and/or tightening the setscrew. Pull the wire through the lamp bottom until the socket sits firmly in the cap. Place the insulated shell over the socket. Position the outer shell at a slight angle, then press the bottom into the cap—it should snap securely in place. Reassemble the lamp, install bulb and shade, and let there be light!

FLUORESCENT FIXTURES

Fluorescent lights give several times more illumination per watt consumed than incandescent lights. They also produce less heat, and the tubes last five to ten times longer. Because of this long life expectancy, problems that arise are often likely to be other than a burned-out tube.

Inside the fixture is a starter, a switch that opens automatically after current has flowed through it for a moment (accounting for the brief delay between the time the fixture is turned on and the time it actually lights up) and remains open. Some starters are replaceable, others (called rapid start) are built into the ballast. The ballast—wire wound around a steel core—momentarily delivers a higher voltage when the fixture is turned on, sending an arc through the gases in the tube that produce the light. It also limits the total power that can flow through

Simple Electrical Repairs

it, stabilizing the light. When something goes wrong, the tube, the ballast, and especially the starter, must be suspect.

If the tube does not light, check the fuse or circuit breaker, and the outlet, plug, and cord if the fixture is a lamp; take corrective action if indicated. If those check out, replace the starter, tube, and ballast in that order until the light works properly (below).

When a fluorescent light blinks on and off, check to make sure the tube is seated properly in the socket (see below). If the blinking persists, remove the tube and lightly sand the contacts on the tube and in the socket; then reinstall. If it still blinks, restrain the temptation to smash the offending bulb against a brick wall and, instead, replace the starter and, if necessary, the ballast of the fixture.

Sometimes the light flickers and swirls around inside a new tube. This condition is normal, and the light will become steady with use. If the problem continues, install a new starter.

A humming or buzzing noise indicates a ballast problem. Check to make sure that all ballast wire connections are tight (after first unplugging the lamp or turning off power to the fixture). If the noise persists, the ballast is worn and should be replaced.

Mild discoloration of the tube is a normal condition. If the tube becomes dark or black, it should be replaced. If a new tube becomes blackened, replace the starter. If the tube is discolored on one side only, remove it and turn it over. If discolored on one end only, remove the tube and reverse the ends.

To replace a tube, starter, or ballast, unplug the lamp or turn off the power at the entrance panel to the fixture circuit. If there is a cover plate, remove it (on lamps, the starter and ballast may be in the lamp base). To remove a replaceable starter (a small metal cylinder), give it a quarter-turn counterclockwise and pull it out. Insert a new one and turn it clockwise to lock.

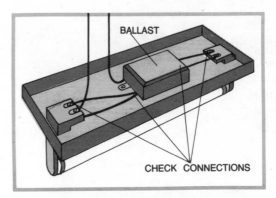

Check ballast connections.

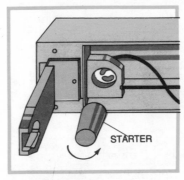

Remove starter.

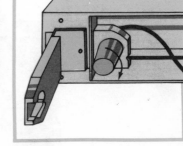

Install new starter.

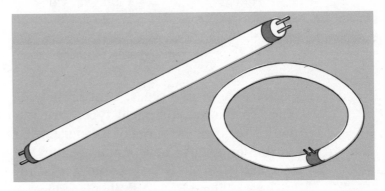

Types of fluorescent tubes.

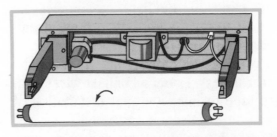

Removing straight tube.

Replacing straight tube.

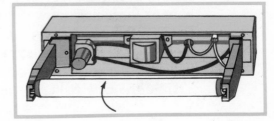

Simple Electrical Repairs

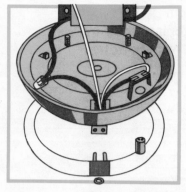

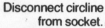

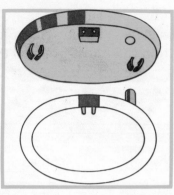

Disconnect circline from socket.

Remove circline from clips.

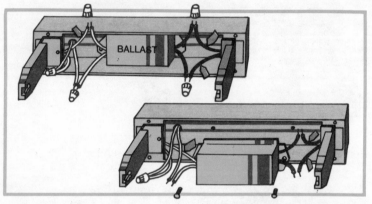

Disconnect ballast wires and remove ballast mounting screws.

Tubes are of two types: straight and circline. To remove a straight type, give it a quarter-turn and lift it out of its sockets. To reinstall or install a new one, place it in the slots and turn it to lock securely. To remove a circline tube, carefully disconnect it from the socket, then pull it out of the retaining clips on the fixture. Connect the new tube to the sockets, then press it into the retaining clips.

To replace the ballast, first remove the tube (or tubes). Label all ballast wires with coded tape to insure proper installation of the new unit. Disconnect the ballast wires from the fixture wires by removing wire nuts or loosening screws. Hold the ballast (it is relatively heavy) and remove the mounting screws or nuts; then remove the ballast.

Hold the new ballast in position and install mounting screws or nuts. Tighten. Connect all ballast wires to the fixture with wire nuts or by tightening screws (see PAGES 320-326 for use of wire nuts), making sure you match up the wires according to your coded tape. Remove the tape and install the tube.

After all repairs and replacements are made, reinstall the cover plate if there is one. Then plug in the lamp or restore power to the circuit at the service panel.

DOORBELLS AND CHIMES

Doorbells and chimes operate on low voltage, usually 10 volts for bells and up to 16 volts for chimes. A transformer is wired to the service entry to reduce the 110-120 voltage to the low level required. If you are replacing a transformer, make sure the new one is the proper size for your system (voltage should be listed on the bell or chime unit). You can work on the low-voltage side of the transformer without any danger, but the other side (between the transformer and the entry panel) is hot, and the fuse should be removed or breaker turned off when you are working there or on the transformer.

When the doorbell or chimes fail to work, first check the noise mechanism. Remove the cover and inspect for loose connections. Tighten the screws, and clean off the contacts with a cotton swab dipped in alcohol. Replace the cover.

If the bell or chimes still don't work, go to the transformer (usually in the basement either at or near the entry panel) and listen while a helper presses the push button at the door. If it hums, the problem is not there. If it is silent and the bell is also, replace the transformer with one of the same type (make sure the power is off first).

If the transformer checks out, try the push button. Remove the cover plate and check the contacts, which may become corroded by exposure to the elements. Clean the contacts with sandpaper or emery cloth, rubbing them lightly. Make sure the button touches the contacts when it is pushed in; if it doesn't, gently bend the contacts to correct the situation. Contacts that are badly bent or broken mean that a new push button is needed. They are inexpensive and easy to install; just take the wires off of the old and attach to the new.

If all else seems in order, check out the wiring. Bell wire (usually #18) is thin and easily damaged. For example, if you have recently installed ceiling tile in the basement, you may have inadvertently put a staple through the bell wire. Or your hammer may have gone astray while you were hanging a new ceiling outlet box and smashed through the bell wire without your knowing it. Any breaks in the bell wire can be spliced and covered with plastic tape.

If you suspect a problem within the walls, it is usually easier to replace the wire from the transformer to the push button or noise mechanism, or between the push button and the noise mechanism, than to try to locate the break. Attach the end of the new wire securely to the end of the old, twisting and taping them together; then pull the new wire through the wall with the old—and hope that the wires don't break. If necessary, run the bell wire along the top of a baseboard and up and around door jambs to where it must go, securing it at frequent intervals with insulated staples. The small wire is relatively unobtrusive.

If none of these corrective measures puts the sound of music back into your bell or chimes, the noise mechanism is probably defective. The best repair is replacement. Follow manufacturer's instructions for hooking up the new unit.

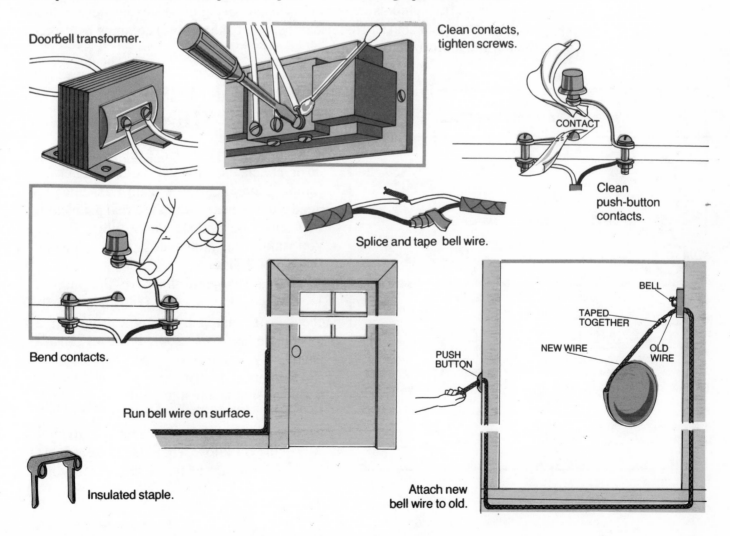

Doorbell transformer.

Clean contacts, tighten screws.

CONTACT

Clean push-button contacts.

Splice and tape bell wire.

Bend contacts.

Run bell wire on surface.

Insulated staple.

PUSH BUTTON

NEW WIRE

TAPED TOGETHER

BELL

OLD WIRE

Attach new bell wire to old.

7

Small Appliance Repairs

APPLIANCES are made by many manufacurers, and there are hundreds of types on the market. Although the wiring and operation of these vary greatly (and you should have a manufacturer's manual for each appliance), they have some basic things in common. Electrically, they can be extremely simple. Heat-producing appliances such as toasters and waffle irons are nothing more than heating elements connected to electrical power. Switches and thermostats complicate them a little, but it is relatively easy to trouble-shoot and repair them.

The other general type of small appliance has a motor that drives a fan, a mixing beater, knife blades, or whatever. These are electrically simple but can be mechanically complicated. Here again, a manufacturer's manual is needed to understand the operational idiosyncrasies of the appliance. (The table shows the symbols generally used on wiring diagrams in these manuals.) Some appliances (a rotisserie or heater, for example) combine heat-producing and motorized functions.

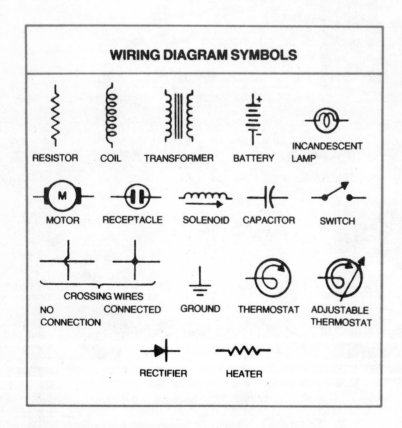

WIRING DIAGRAM SYMBOLS

RESISTOR COIL TRANSFORMER BATTERY INCANDESCENT LAMP

MOTOR RECEPTACLE SOLENOID CAPACITOR SWITCH

CROSSING WIRES
NO CONNECTION CONNECTED GROUND THERMOSTAT ADJUSTABLE THERMOSTAT

RECTIFIER HEATER

LOOK FOR THE OBVIOUS THINGS FIRST

As in any repair work, the first thing to do is check the obvious. Avoid panic and jumping to conclusions. Don't assume you need a new toaster when the real problem is that someone pulled out the plug. Before you take the appliance apart, consider these possibilities:

External Power Failure—Is the plug in? Is there power to the cord? Both are easily checked, the latter by using a tester at the receptacle (see PAGE 304). If the tester isn't handy, try a lamp or other appliance at the same outlet (just make sure the bulb is good, or that the test appliance is in working order). If that doesn't work, there is trouble either at the receptacle or in the line itself. If you know what else is on the circuit (as your circuit maps should tell you), see if there is current there. If you don't know, check the fuses or breakers to see if one of them has blown.

See PAGES 338-340 for troubleshooting blown fuses and tripped breakers. If replacing the fuse or tripping the breaker restores power to the line with no problems until you plug in or turn on the appliance in question, the problem could well be an overload. Most non-heat-producing small appliances should not cause overload unless there are other appliances on the same circuit. If you are uncertain whether the problem is overload, try the appliance on another circuit (one that you know can handle it), and see what happens. If the fuse blows again, you can be reasonably certain that the appliance has a short circuit.

Physical Damage—If an appliance has been dropped recently or has been in a fire or flood, there may be some evident damage. If fire was the culprit, there should be coverage under your insurance policy. In that case, your problems are over; the insurance company should pay to repair or, more probably, replace it.

Flooding is a different matter. This is rarely covered by insurance, except under special government-backed policies. If an appliance was caught in a flood, chances are that it should be discarded. You can possibly save it by cleaning it thoroughly and baking the electrical parts in a low oven (180 degrees F.). Check all the contacts for cleanliness, and replace any damaged insulation. Tighten all connections, lubricate moving parts, and remove all traces of rust with emery cloth or rust-removing fluids. It's worth a try, but chances of successful rehabilitation are not good.

An appliance that has been dropped should have its connections checked. See that everything lines up properly. If a plastic cover has been broken, look for tiny particles in moving parts. Dents in metal surfaces may be pressing against something inside, causing a short or moving parts to

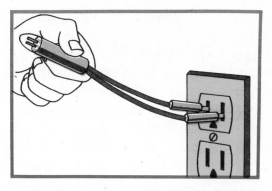

Using tester at receptacle.

jam. Parts may have to be replaced, but chances of recovery are good (unless the fall has totally demolished the appliance).

Use Your Senses—If none of the above seems to be the problem, it is time to stop, look, listen, and—most important—think. Use your senses. If you smell something burning (other than the toast), insulation may be melting. The appliance should be disconnected immediately and checked. Remove the cover and check for burned-off or smudged insulation on the wires. If anything looks questionable, replace it just to be safe.

Noise is another giveaway. A rattling noise in a motor-driven appliance may merely necessitate tightening a few screws. A grinding noise on gear-driven machines indicates worn gears or bearings. Squeaking is a sign of neglected oiling. A slipping drive belt sounds a characteristic warning—intermittent humming or flopping.

DOING IT YOURSELF

Once you've determined that the fault is in the appliance and not the circuitry, you have to ask yourself whether or not you want to try to fix it. The first thing to check is whether the appliance is still under warranty. If it is, you may void the warranty by making obvious repairs yourself.

Even if the appliance is still under warranty, however, you may find that it is easier and cheaper to fix it yourself. In spite of reforms over the past several years, war-

Small Appliance Repairs

ranties are more generous in what is not covered than what is. A brand-new machine may often be exchanged quickly at reputable stores, but if you have used it a while, the warranty may require that you pack up the appliance and send it across the country, accompanied by a rather stiff "handling charge." You may find that parts are warranted, but labor isn't. The parts cost is often minimal, whereas labor charges usually run high.

The best course is to inspect the warranty carefully when you *buy* the appliance, and avoid those that involve long and costly by-mail returns. Find out whether there is a factory-authorized repair shop in your area, which can save considerable time and money, and carefully weigh the other elements of the warranty, such as its time length and whether or not labor charges are covered.

If the warranty is intact and there is a factory-authorized repair shop in your vicinity, there is no point in trying to fix the appliance yourself. Unfortunately, problems have a way of occurring the day after the warranty expires.

You may at least elect to look for the trouble before you decide whether to fix it yourself. After you've found it, you can determine whether you can repair it or not.

TAKING IT APART

If you have saved the instructions and wiring diagram from the manufacturer, you're way ahead. Exploded views and other drawings will show you how to take apart the appliance and—more important—put it back together. Taking things apart is usually easy. If you don't have the manufacturer's instructions, make your own diagram as you go along, It will be a lot easier when it comes to the hard part: putting it all back together correctly. Always set the pieces on a newspaper or cloth in the order in which you take them apart.

Once you have the appliance housing apart, the electrical system should be evident. The first thing to check for is loose or broken wiring. On heat-producing appliances, inspect the heating element. Small appliances generally have nichrome (an alloy of nickel and chromium) coils or ribbons. These can break and are usually replaceable. If the break is near the end of the element, it is possible to stretch the element a little and reattach the unbroken section to the screw. But don't do this unless the removed section is very small. A shortened heating element will give off more, not less, heat and could be dangerous.

TESTING

Your tester will come in very handy when checking out small appliances. The neon type is best, but its leads may not reach as far as necessary, so you may also want to buy or build a test lamp using a 10- or 15-watt bulb. It works the same way as a neon tester. All it takes are a socket, a couple of lengths of #16 wire, the bulb, and alligator clips at the ends instead of prongs.

In order to use a tester, the current must be on, so be very careful not to touch any exposed wire or other electrical part while testing. Put one lead of the tester on the hot wire in the appliance, and touch the other lead at various places through the wiring to see where any electrical break occurs. Touch both sides of the switch (in closed position) if any, then both sides of the motor, heating element, thermostat, or what-

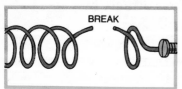

Break in heating element.

BREAK

Stretch coil slightly and reattach.

Small Appliance Repairs

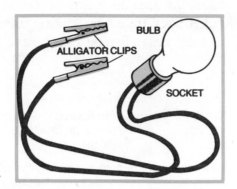

Test lamp.

ever components are in the appliance circuitry. If the light glows when the tester is on one side but not when it is touched to the other, the break is somewhere between these two points. Keep testing until you have pinpointed the outage.

THERMOSTATS

A thermostat is basically a bimetallic switch, made of two pieces of metal that expand at different temperatures. One piece is brass, which expands quickly, and the other is invar (an alloy of nickel and steel), which heats and expands much more slowly than brass. As long as it is cool, the two fused metal pieces remain in place, completing the electrical circuit. Under heat conditions, tension between the two

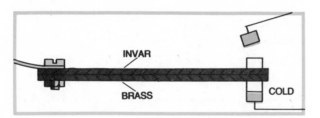

Thermostat completing circuit.

Thermostat breaking circuit.

metals expanding at different temperatures causes the fused strip to bend. When it reaches a certain preset temperature level, one end of the bimetallic strip rises far enough to lose contact with the circuit. The power is thus severed, and the appliance ceases to heat. As it cools, the metal regains its original shape until it again closes the circuit, and heating resumes. This cycle continues until the appliance is shut off.

ELECTRIC TOASTER

A toaster is a very simple mechanism, consisting of a heating element and a cord in a housing, with a timer and/or thermostat added. A two-slice automatic has one heating element in the middle and one on the

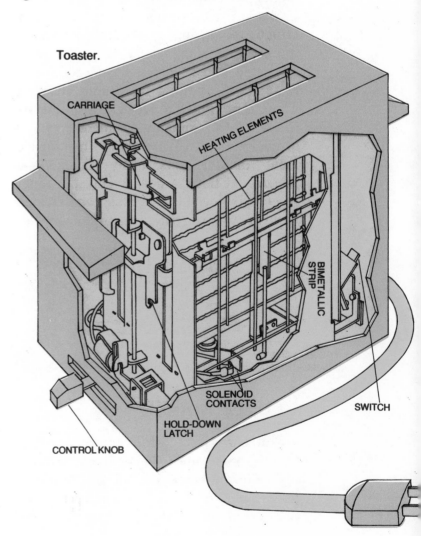

Toaster.

Small Appliance Repairs

TOASTER TROUBLESHOOTING		
Problem	**Cause**	**Cure**
NO HEAT.	No power at outlet. Defective cord. Loose connection. Switch not making contact. Elements burned out.	Check outlet, fuse; repair or replace if necessary. Repair or replace. Clean, tighten. Repair or replace. Replace.
TOAST WILL NOT STAY DOWN.	Hold-down latch not locking. Bind in toast carriage. Broken latch spring.	If bent, straighten; if binding, clear to allow free operation. Clear cause of bind. Replace.
TOAST WILL NOT POP UP.	Bind in toast carriage. Release latch binds. Broken spring.	Clear cause of bind. Clear cause of bind. Replace.

outside of each slice. Four-slice and larger models are similarly arranged.

Many toaster problems are caused by crumbs collecting in the mechanism. A thorough cleaning every few months is advisable. Most toasters have a removable plate on the bottom for crumb cleanout. There is not much to repair in an automatic toaster. Occasionally someone pokes around with a fork and ruins a heating element (and/or gets badly shocked—or worse). At times a new thermostat, timer, or cord is needed. It is easier and cheaper to buy new parts than to repair the old.

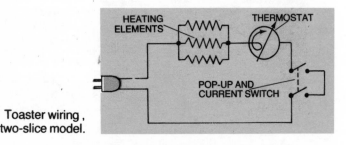

Toaster wiring, two-slice model.

COFFEE MAKER

Coffee making and drinking are sacred rituals in some homes, and keeping the coffee maker in top shape is a job of the utmost importance for the family. But the most expensive or efficiently operating pot won't

guarantee good coffee. The problems that plague kaffeeklatschers are usually the result of two causes—defective water heating or a pot that has built up flavor-killing deposits.

Defective water heating results in coffee that is too weak (flavor left in the grounds) or too hot (bitter oils extracted along with the flavor). The water should be between 175 and 190 degrees F. when it passes over the coffee. If it isn't, check the troubleshooting chart.

Deposits can be built up in the coffee pot from two main causes—hard water and improper cleaning. Hard water leaves lime deposits, and improper cleaning leaves coffee solids containing bitter oils. A regular schedule of "boiling out" the pot with baking soda will do much for the flavor. A strong vinegar solution will dissolve any lime deposits.

The percolating action of a coffee pot is not caused by boiling water, as is commonly believed, but by steam. Steam is generated under the basket stem base in the pump heater well. The steam "pumps" water up through the percolator tube in spurts. The water then splashes down over the coffee grounds, extracting the flavor. The flow is controlled by the pump check valve, a

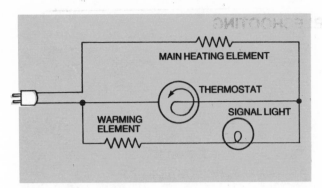

Coffee maker wiring.

Coffee maker (cutaway view) at right.

Heating element at bottom of the coffee maker.

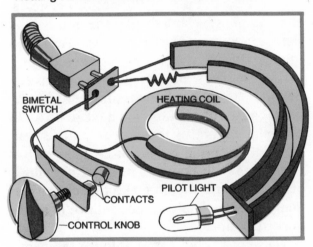

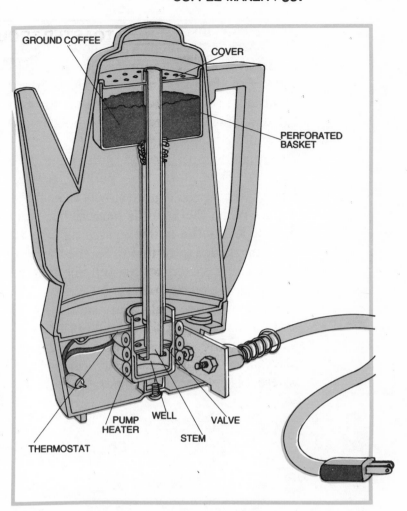

COFFEE MAKER TROUBLESHOOTING		
Problem	**Cause**	**Cure**
DOESN'T OPERATE.	No voltage at outlet.	Check outlet, fuse; repair or replace if necessary.
	Defective cord.	Repair or replace.
	Defective pump heater.	Replace.
GETS WARM BUT DOESN'T PERCOLATE.	Defective pump heater.	Replace.
	Defective thermostat.	Replace.
	Incorrect setting of thermostat.	Reset.
SLOW IN BREWING COFFEE.	Low line voltage.	Check voltage; if low, notify power company.
COFFEE TASTES BITTER.	Accumulated residue inside pot.	Clean with baking soda solution or other cleaner.
WEAK COFFEE.	Control incorrectly set.	Reset.
	Using hot water to start.	Use cold water.
	Pump valve stuck.	Clean valve; or replace if damaged.
COFFEE BOILS.	Incorrect thermostat setting.	Reset.
	Defective thermostat.	Replace.

Small Appliance Repairs

loose disc at the bottom of the stem. As water is perked up, more water flows into the well valve, where in turn it is pumped up to the top of the tube and out. It is important on all pump-type coffee percolators to keep the disc and valve seat clean, smooth, and unscratched.

Actually, most coffee pots have two heaters. One starts the perking action, while the other acts more slowly to heat the water. When the water is heated, the thermostat keeps the coffee heated as long as the plug is in. Up to that time, the thermostat remains closed so that full line voltage can reach the pump heater.

The new coffee makers are similar in operation, except that the glass "pot" sits on a heating plate, and the water heating takes place in a separate base reservoir or from where it is delivered to the pot.

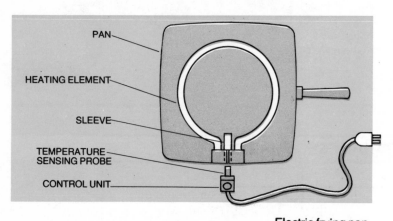

Electric frying pan.

ELECTRIC FRYING PAN

The electric frying pan is another of those basically simple appliances that contain no moving parts—it's just a heating element and a cord. There is one important distinction that should be printed clearly on the name plate—immersibility. A new user may have to check that impulsive habit of dunking the frying pan in water. Some of the electric ones can be dunked, but check the label first.

If you blunder and submerge the nonimmersible type, take off the bottom plate as soon as possible and dry off the unit with a fan or vacuum-cleaner blower. The best tool for this job is a blower-type hair dryer.

Electric pans do not go wrong easily. Second to unsanctioned immersion, the usual causes of malfunction have to do with a similar failure of the user to realize that an electric frying pan is more than just a frying pan with a cord on it. Careful reading of instructions should make this clear, but many people simply do not believe in reading instructions.

These pans cook faster at lower temperatures, and the habit-conscious user often turns the heat too high for too long. The result is sticking and burning and a difficult clean-up job. The best way to clean an electric pan is to heat several cups of water in the pan for a few minutes, then unplug the

ELECTRIC FRYING PAN TROUBLESHOOTING		
Problem	**Cause**	**Cure**
NO HEAT.	No power at outlet.	Check outlet, fuse; repair or replace if necessary.
	Defective cord.	Repair or replace.
	Broken heater element.	Replace.
	Defective thermostat.	Replace.
	Poor connection.	Clean and tighten.
NO HEAT CONTROL.	Defective thermostat.	Replace.
SHOCKS USER.	Grounded unit.	Replace defective part.
	Wire touching frame.	Locate and reinsulate or replace wire.
FOOD STICKS.	Excessive cooking temperature.	Lower thermostat setting.
	Pan is not seasoned.	Season pan; heat for half hour with shortening.

WAFFLE IRON TROUBLESHOOTING

Problem	Cause	Cure
NO HEAT.	No power at outlet.	Check outlet, fuse; repair or replace if necessary.
	Defective cord.	Repair or replace.
	Damaged heater element.	Replace.
	Broken hinge wire.	Replace.
	Defective thermostat.	Replace.
BLOWS FUSES.	Shorted cord.	Replace.
	Shorted heater element.	Replace.
	Shorted wiring.	Reinsulate.
TOO HOT.	Check thermostat setting (maximum temperature: 520° F.).	Reset thermostat, replace if faulty.
WAFFLES STICK.	Improperly seasoned grid.	Operate for half-hour with cooking oil—no batter— on grid.
	Insufficient shortening in batter.	Add more cooking oil to batter.
	Too much sugar in batter.	Correct error.
	Opening griddle too soon.	Be patient!

unit. Scrape out the residue with a wooden spoon or spatula, then wash out the inside with hot water and a mild soap.

Strong detergents, alkalies, and abrasives should be avoided. The surface of the frying pan must be seasoned; its porous surface must be sealed with fresh shortening every time such cleaners have been used on the pan.

Although it is a sturdy appliance, the electric frying pan is more susceptible to external damage than some others. Frequently, a hard blow will change the thermostat calibration. To check, note the setting at which water boils in the pan. If it is within 20 degrees either way of the 212 degrees F. setting, the calibration is close enough.

When reassembling an immersible frying pan after making repairs, take care to reseat gaskets properly. If a gasket looks worn or won't seat properly, replace it with a new one. The cost is negligible.

WAFFLE IRON

A waffle iron is electrically simple—a resistor connected to a plug. Many models have a thermostat and removable grids, so that they can be converted into a grill. The thermostat tells you when the grids are hot

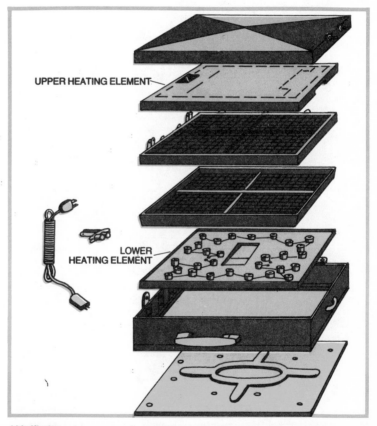

Waffle iron.

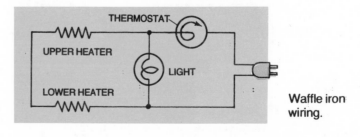

Waffle iron wiring.

enough to use, and keeps the inside at a constant temperature.

The entire electrical system is readily accessible on most models. Typically, the grids lift right out and there it is: a long coil on top and bottom, a light, and a thermostat. When the iron is hot enough, the thermostat breaks the circuit.

Visual inspection should reveal any breaks in the coil. The coil should be re-placed unless the break is within an inch of the end post; you can usually stretch it that far and reconnect without any damage. Be sure to tighten screws all the way, and never allow looseness in the coil—direct contact of the coil with the plates could be fatal. After any such reassembly, the unit should be checked with your tester for a short circuit. Put one lead on the power terminal and the other on the shell to see if any

DRY AND STEAM IRON TROUBLESHOOTING		
Problem	Cause	Cure
NO HEAT.	No power at outlet.	Check outlet, fuse; repair or replace if necessary.
	Defective cord, plug.	Repair or replace.
	Broken lead in iron.	Repair or replace.
	Loose connection.	Clean and tighten.
	Loose thermostat control knob.	Replace knob and tighten.
	Defective thermostat.	Replace.
	Defective heater element.	Replace heater if separate; replace soleplate if cast in.
INSUFFICIENT HEAT.	Low line voltage.	Check voltage at outlet; notify utility if deficient.
	Incorrect thermostat setting.	Adjust thermostat.
	Defective thermostat.	Replace.
	Loose connection.	Clean and tighten.
EXCESSIVE HEAT.	Incorrect thermostat setting.	Adjust thermostat.
	Defective thermostat.	Replace.
BLISTERS ON SOLEPLATE.	Excessive heat.	Correct condition (above); repair or replace.
WATER LEAKAGE.	Defective seam or tank weld.	Replace tank.
	Inadequate tank seal.	Reseal with proper sealer.
	Damaged gasket.	Replace gasket.
NO STEAM.	Thermostat set too low.	Set control higher.
	Valve in off position.	Turn to correct position.
	Dirty or plugged valves or holes.	Clean out.
SPITTING.	Incorrect thermostat setting.	Set thermostat higher.
	Excessive mineral deposits.	Clean out.
	Overfilling.	Drain; be more careful.
BAD SPRAY (SPRAY IRONS).	Defective plunger.	Replace.
STAINS ON CLOTHES.	Starch on soleplate.	Rub soleplate with damp cloth, polish with a dry cloth.
	Foreign matter in water.	Use distilled water.
	Sediment in tank.	Clean with vinegar.
TEARS CLOTHES.	Rough spot, nick, scratch, or burr on soleplate.	Remove with fine emery cloth, then buff or polish.
STICKS TO CLOTHES.	Dirty soleplate.	Clean.
	Excessive starch in clothes.	Iron at a lower temperature; use less starch.

power has escaped. If the light lights, look out! The old, usually round, waffle irons (such as you might have inherited as a family heirloom) are wired in parallel, so it is easy to determine if the coil is defective: one side will work and the other won't.

The waffle grids can be black or shiny or almost anything except unoiled. If a grid has been burned too badly, it requires patience and hard work to remove all the batter. But it must be removed. Don't use a detergent unless absolutely necessary. If you must use a detergent, the oil will be drawn out of the pores, and the iron must then be seasoned again, just like a new one. As an extra precaution, add a bit more cooking oil to the batter.

DRY OR STEAM IRON

Your great grandmother's old flatiron looks funny today, but modern irons aren't much different. They just heat by electricity instead of on a stove, and they look a lot more complicated then they really are. A standard iron is nothing more than a resistor taking power from the electric line as called for by a thermostat.

The dial that indicates "Permanent Press," "Wool," "Linen," etc., causes the thermostat to allow more or less heat to get to the heating element. It is important, when disassembling an iron, to mark where these indicators point. Otherwise, it may be difficult to match them up upon reassembly.

On both steam and dry irons, a common breakdown is in the cord, particularly at the plug and at the cord sleeve next to the iron. In such a case, repair or replace the plug and/or cord (see PAGES 342-346). Breaks elsewhere in the cord can be suspected where the exterior looks frayed or burned or is soft and bends too easily.

Another frequent mishap occurs when melted synthetic fabrics or cooked starch leave a sticky film on the iron soleplate.

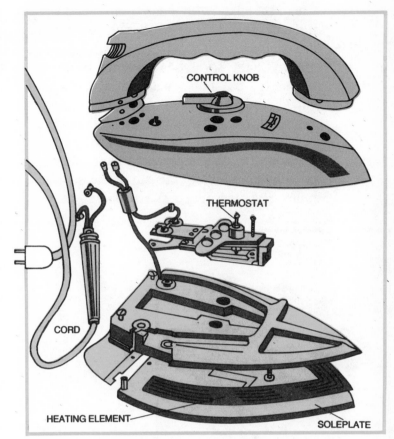

Dry iron.

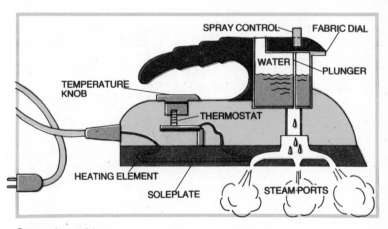

Steam (spray) iron.

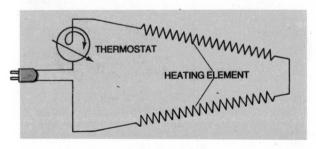

Iron wiring.

Small Appliance Repairs

Clean the plate with a damp cloth and wipe it dry. If this doesn't work, rub gently with fine steel wool or a piece of very fine emery cloth. Slight scratches will not harm the soleplate, but burrs will damage clothing and should be removed with emery cloth.

Steam irons are especially plagued by hard water, which is found in most parts of the country. The minerals in hard water accumulate and clog the small steam portholes and passages. The problem can be prevented by using a water softener or distilled water. Rain water, melted snow, or defrosted water and accumulated ice from the refrigerator are good sources of mineral-free water. If it is too late for any of these "ounces of prevention," a cure is to fill the tank with vinegar, which will dissolve the mineral deposits. Heating of the iron with the vinegar inside may be necessary, and the process may have to be repeated one or more times.

ELECTRIC MOTORS

Motor-driven appliances have either brush-type or synchronous motors. You should know something about both before attempting any repairs.

Synchronous motors are small and simple. They consist basically of two elements—a field and a rotor. The field is a U-shaped laminated frame around which are wrapped many turns of fine wire. The wire is plugged into a power source, creating a magnetic field. In an AC circuit, this field changes direction 120 times a second, causing the rotor to revolve. This motor is excellent where a constant (synchronous) speed is desired.

Brush-type motors are also called "series-wound universal motors"—universal because of their wide application. In this type, two fields are employed. Instead of the simple rotor found in the synchronous motor, there is a more complicated version of the same thing called an armature. The armature moves opposite to the field by means of a commutator, which receives its drive from the coils inside each of its bars. Impetus is given by "brushes," which push around one bar of the commutator after another, in opposition to the field. A very powerful push is thereby created.

The brushes are made of soft carbon and frequently must be replaced. Be sure to use exactly the same size brushes, or ones very

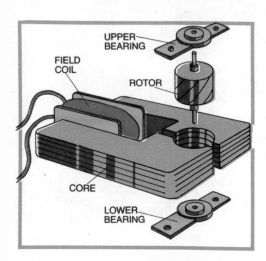

Synchronous motor.

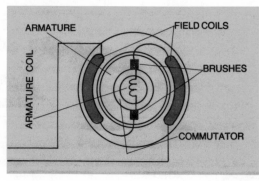

Universal motor.

Motor brush.

Sand commutator bars.

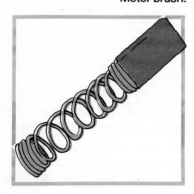

ELECTRIC FAN TROUBLESHOOTING

Problem	Cause	Cure
WON'T RUN; FAN CAN BE TURNED BY HAND.	No power. Break in cord. Defective switch.	Check outlet, fuse; repair or replace if necessary. Repair or replace. Repair or replace.
FAN WON'T TURN.	Blades hitting grille. Armature hitting stator in motor. Armature frozen, needs lubrication. Misalignment of bearings.	Straighten grille, blades. Usually indicates worn bearings, rust or foreign matter; clean, replace worn bearings. Free armature; lubricate. Realign bearings.
RUNS SLOW.	Bearings dry, gummy, or misaligned. Defective speed control.	Clean, lubricate, realign bearings. Replace.
NOISY.	Fan blades hitting obstruction. Fan blades bent. Bearings worn.	Clear obstruction. Straighten blades. Replace bearings; where this is not practical, replace motor.

similar. It is also important to know that each bar of the commutator has its own coil and is connected to the next. If the commutator bars operate unevenly, it is usually advisable and not too costly to replace the entire armature. Occasionally, sandpapering the copper bars of the commutator will temporarily restore efficiency.

ELECTRIC FAN

Basically, an electric fan is a motor with blades attached to the shaft. It may have an oscillator to move it from side to side, but it is a simple mechanism, and the problems likely to be encountered are simple also.

Don't complicate the job by taking apart more than you have to.

When disassembling a fan, remove the guard first. The fan blade assembly is attached to the motor shaft by a setscrew. The motor housing has two shells, which are held together by two or four bolts. Most fan motors are cooled by the blade motion, and there are holes in the motor housing to allow the air to enter and circulate through the motor. This also brings dust into the motor; an occasional cleaning is in order.

Possibly the most common complaint is

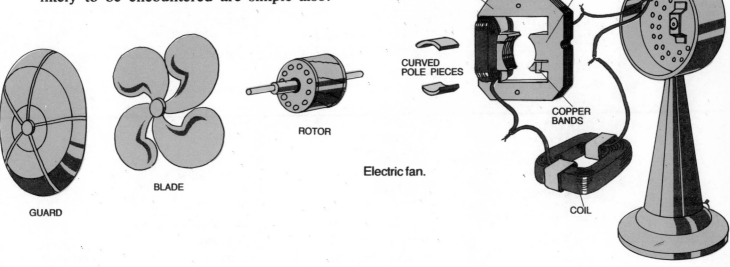

GUARD

BLADE

ROTOR

STATOR CORE

CURVED POLE PIECES

STATOR

COPPER BANDS

COIL

Electric fan.

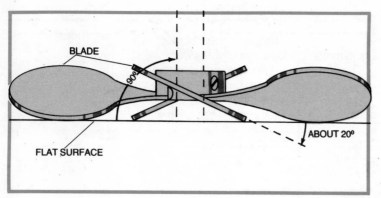

BLADE

90°

FLAT SURFACE

ABOUT 20°

Align fan blades.

noisy operation. The usual cause is unbalanced fan blades. The easiest way to align blades is to remove the entire assembly and place it, blades down, on a workbench or other flat surface. Make sure the shaft bore is absolutely perpendicular, and check to see if all blades touch the surface. If there is only a slight misalignment, bend the offending blade by hand or with pliers until it matches the others exactly. Severely bent blades can be bent back into shape in a vise. If a blade is cracked or otherwise damaged, replace the entire assembly.

If the blades appear to be perfectly straight, and there is no looseness in the oscillator mechanism, the noise trouble could well be motor bearings. The clue to this is observing how much movement there is on the shaft when the blade is wiggled by hand. There should be only a slight amount of play. If worn bearings are indicated, take the motor completely apart and replace them. On less expensive fans, this may be virtually impossible, and a new fan or motor is necessary. The relatively low cost of this type of fan justifies its replacement.

MIXER TROUBLESHOOTING		
Problem	**Cause**	**Cure**
DOESN'T WORK AT ALL.	No power at outlet. Defective cord. Worn brushes. Broken field cord. Broken armature winding. Defective switch.	Check fuse, outlet; repair or replace if necessary. Repair or replace. Replace. Replace. Replace armature. Replace.
DOESN'T RUN, BLOWS FUSES.	Bent shaft jamming armature. Defective armature or field coil. Shorted cord.	Straighten or replace shaft. Replace. Repair or replace.
MOTOR RUNS HOT.	Bind in shaft. Shorted winding in armature. Shorted field coil.	Clear bind. Replace armature. Replace.
MOTOR RUNS, BEATERS DON'T TURN.	Bent, damaged beaters. Stripped gears.	Replace. Replace.
ERRATIC OPERATION.	Worn brushes. Loose connection. Defective switch.	Replace. Replace. Clean and tighten.
SLOW SPEED, WEAK POWER.	Incorrect setting. Worn brushes. Bind in shaft.	Adjust speed control. Replace. Clear bind.
TOO NOISY.	Armature hitting field. Bent cooling fan blade. Dry gears or bearing.	Replace worn bearing. Straighten. Lubricate.

MIXER

When the beaters of an electric mixer fail to turn, it usually indicates bent or defective beaters or worn beater gears. Visual inspection should tell you whether the beaters themselves are okay. If not, they are easily replaced. Replacing gears is a little more complicated. You will have to take the mechanism apart so that the gears may be inspected. You will probably find that they are stripped, but it may be a case of plain wear and tear.

When replacing the gears, it is important to position them so that the beaters do not strike each other. Test the machine with the beaters in place before putting it back together. If they touch, adjust until they are completely independent of each other.

Another item that should be replaced in pairs is the motor brushes. Most mixers have brush caps on the outside of the motor housing so that inspection is easy. If they are worn to less than ⅛ inch from the springs, they should be replaced. Check the springs, too, to see if they have been damaged or weakened. If so, replace.

If the brushes are not smooth, clean, and curved to the surface of the commutator, you may find that the armature is defective. Before checking that, make sure that both brushes have been removed to avoid breaking them. If the trouble is in the armature, it is best to get a new one—or a new mixer.

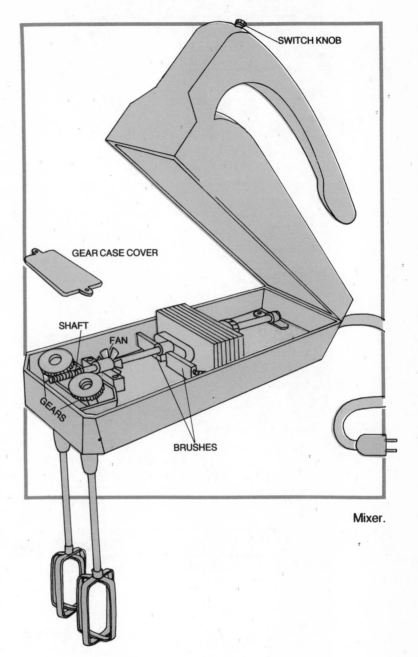

Mixer.

BLENDER

Other than dropping and breaking a blender, the usual thing that goes wrong is damage to the cutting blades. These will chip or curl back if nonblendable objects are fed into the blender. (A common misuse of a blender is to mix drinks with whole ice cubes. A blender is not an ice crusher. To use ice in most blenders, you have to crush the cubes first.) Blades are changed by holding the knife shaft with a wrench and turning the spiral nut on the blades clockwise, then removing and replacing them and retightening. Do not overtighten.

Leakage in a blender is caused by a poor seal between the jar and the bushing assembly. Sometimes the bushing can be tightened, but usually it is best to replace the gasket—a simple matter. The gasket is replaced by removing the blades, as de-

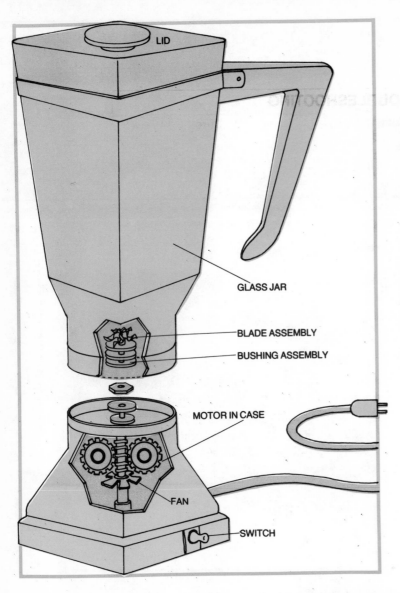

LID

GLASS JAR

BLADE ASSEMBLY

BUSHING ASSEMBLY

MOTOR IN CASE

FAN

SWITCH

scribed above, then taking off the nut and bushing. Install the new gasket, then reassemble the unit.

ROTISSERIE OVEN/BROILER

A typical rotisserie consists of a thermostatically controlled heater element, a motor to operate the spit, and a timer to stop the cooking after a preset period. Spills from overcooking are a common cause of trouble with an electric rotisserie. If a spill happens, it is much easier to clean it up right away than to bake on deposits through repeated usage.

Make sure the oven is cool and unplugged before washing. The glass, particularly, may break when wiped or washed while still warm. Dry by hand, then turn on the oven to 250 degrees and let it run for a while. This should prevent rusting. For troubleshooting chart and illustrations see opposite page.

Blender (cutaway view).

BLENDER TROUBLESHOOTING		
Problem	**Cause**	**Cure**
MOTOR WON'T RUN.	Problem at outlet.	Check fuse, outlet, wiring; repair or replace as necessary.
	Defective cord.	Repair or replace.
	Defective switch.	Repair or replace.
	Burned-out motor.	Replace armature or field coil.
	Frozen bearings.	Free; lubricate.
	Armature hitting because of worn bearing.	Replace bearing.
MOTOR RUNS, BLADE DOESN'T TURN.	Broken belt (on some models).	Replace belt.
	Incorrect placement of container.	Relocate on base.
	Defective motor coupling.	Replace.
RUNS AT HIGH SPEED ONLY.	Defective switch.	Replace.
	Open resistor.	Replace.
	Defective field coil.	Replace.
BLADE DAMAGED.	Hitting ice cubes, spoon, bones, etc.	Replace blade.
CONTAINER LEAKS.	Cracked glass jar.	Replace.
	Poor seal.	Tighten bushing or replace gasket.

ROTISSERIE TROUBLESHOOTING

Problem	Cause	Cure
WON'T OPERATE.	No power at outlet. Defective cord. Defective switch. Defective timer switch.	Check outlet, fuse; repair or replace if necessary. Repair or replace. Replace. Replace.
HEATS, BUT MOTOR DOESN'T RUN.	Defective motor. Stuck gearing. Defective motor switch.	Replace. Clean gears. Replace.
MOTOR RUNS, BUT OVEN DOESN'T HEAT.	Defective heater element. Defective heater switch.	Replace. Replace.
INCORRECT HEAT.	Defective thermostat.	Replace.

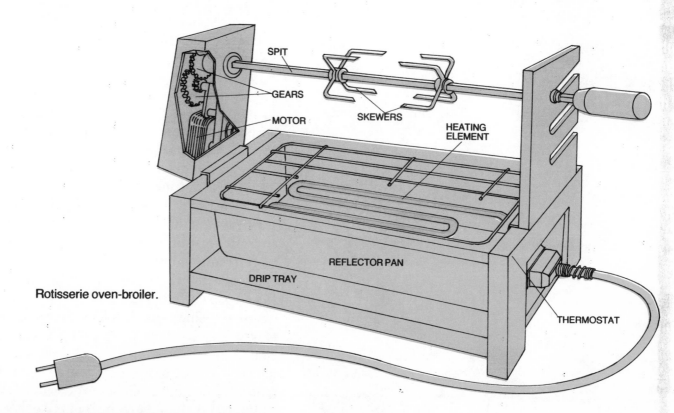

Rotisserie oven-broiler.

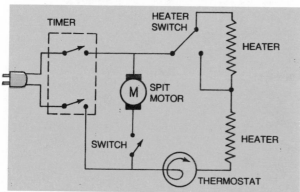

Rotisserie wiring.

ELECTRIC CAN OPENER

The electric can opener employs a synchronous motor, and not much can go wrong with the mechanism unless it is abused. The opener should be cleaned thor-

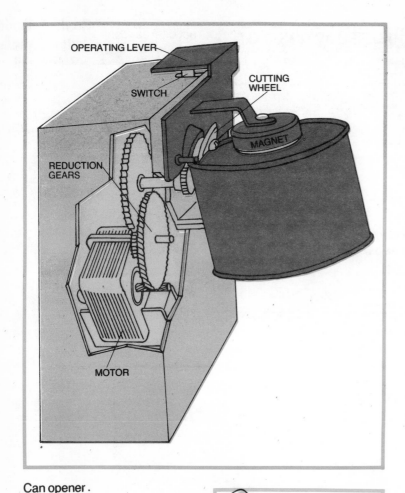

Can opener.

Cutter wheel assembly.

Electric knife.

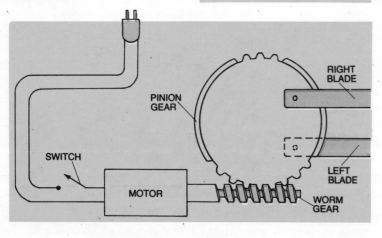

oughly and lubricated at least twice a year. (Consult the manufacturer's instructions, if you still have them.)

To clean or sharpen the cutter assembly, remove the spring tension screw and the screw in back of it. The housing can usually be removed by loosening a few screws on the bottom, without disturbing the internal workings.

Some openers have a knife-sharpening attachment. This involves extending the rotor shaft and attaching a grinding wheel. The major maintenance chore is just keeping it clean. Possible problems are the same as for the knife sharpener (below).

KNIFE SHARPENER

The electric knife sharpener is simply a universal motor, a fan for cooling, two or more small grinding wheels, and a switch. The switch is usually actuated by pressing down on a certain spot on the case, which turns the machine on. When pressure is lifted, the sharpener turns off.

The resistance caused by grinding will cause wear on the motor, so worn brushes can be a problem. Replacement is simple. Twice-a-year lubrication is recommended, and the manufacturer may suggest even more frequent intervals. This is the type of appliance that benefits from frequent use. If you use it often, your knife blades will always be sharp—a quick sharpening restores a fine edge. If you let the job go, sharpening takes more work and consequently causes more wear and tear on the motor. Use this appliance often and carefully, and it should give you many years of service.

ELECTRIC KNIFE

An electric knife is actually two knives working in opposition to each other. This creates a very fast reciprocating action that makes short work of any roast or turkey. The typical electric knife has a plastic housing in two parts. Two screws at one end hold the parts together, with lugs fitting the other ends together. The universal motor is at the far end, and a shaft runs into a gear box. In the gear box, the rotary action of the motor turns a pinion by means of a worm gear, giving motion to the blades. Each of the blades is attached to one side of the pinion gear. As one moves in one direction, the other moves opposite, creating a shearing action.

The things that go wrong with an electric knife are the same as go wrong with most motor-driven appliances. Brushes wear out, switch contacts become clogged, armatures burn out, the cord becomes worn. An electric knife usually uses a "cheater" cord, like those used to test TV sets. If your electric knife has a worn cord and you can't find a replacement, try a standard cheater cord from the local TV shop.

VACUUM CLEANER ▲

Vacuum cleaners are divided into three distinct types—upright and tank and pot. Their differences are based more on styling and customer preference than on any basic dissimilarity. All types consist of a motor-driven fan that creates suction, thereby drawing dirt from carpeting and other materials. The larger upright models have a

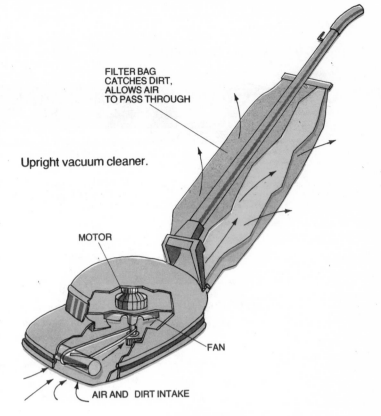

Upright vacuum cleaner.

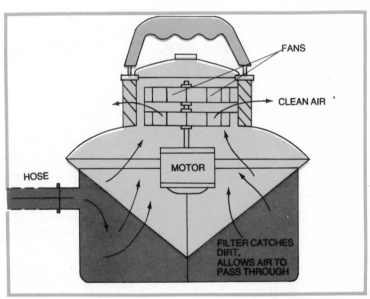

Pot-type vacuum cleaner.

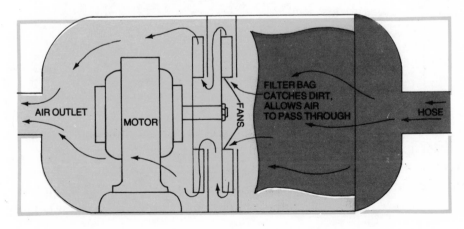

Tank-type vacuum cleaner.

Small Appliance Repairs

VACUUM CLEANER TROUBLESHOOTING

Problem	Cause	Cure
MOTOR DOESN'T RUN.	No power.	Check outlet, fuse, wiring; repair or replace if necessary.
	Defect in cord, plug.	Repair or replace.
	Defective switch.	Replace.
	Worn brushes.	Replace.
	Jammed fan.	Free; if bent or damaged, replace.
	Frozen bearings.	Clean and lubricate (if worn, replace).
MOTOR STARTS AND STOPS.	Intermittent break in cord.	Locate and repair or replace.
	Loose connection in cleaner.	Check all connections; repair.
	Defective switch.	Replace.
	Loose connection in motor.	Check motor; tighten connection.
MOTOR RUNS TOO SLOW, NO POWER.	Foreign object caught on fan or armature.	Remove object.
	Misaligned, tight motor bearings.	Realign; retighten.
	Poor brush contact.	Correct contact or replace brushes.
MOTOR RUNS TOO FAST.	Overfilled dust bag.	Replace.
	Fan loose on shaft, not turning.	Check its balance; tighten.
MOTOR SPARKS.	Dirty commutator (oil or dirt).	Clean with fine sandpaper.
	Worn brushes.	Replace.
	Incorrect brush seating.	Correct seating.
MOTOR TOO NOISY.	Foreign matter in motor.	Clean out.
	Fan damaged.	Replace.
POOR PICKUP.	Worn or damaged attachments.	Check attachments for leakage and replace as necessary.
	Incorrect nozzle adjustment for carpet nap.	Adjust for correct contact.
	Leaky hose.	Check for air leaks; repair or replace.
	Clogged hose.	Blow or push out obstruction.
	Overfilled dust bag.	Replace.
	Clogged exhaust port.	Clear.
DUST LEAKAGE.	Holes in dust bag.	Replace.
	Incorrectly installed dust bag.	Check owner's manual.
	Old, dirty dust bag.	Replace.
	Defective sealing.	Replace seal.

brush that "beats" rugs and loosens dirt. This helps them to do a better job on rugs, but the tank and pot types are generally conceded to have more versatility and drawing power.

The fan section of the housing is sealed off from the motor area so that none of the dirt gets into the motor. There is an aperture through which the dirt is sucked into a cloth or paper bag (usually disposable). The bag is of such a consistency that it allows the air to escape, yet retains the dirt.

One common reason for poor and noisy operation of a vacuum cleaner is wear of the brush bearings. The brush rotates at very high speed, and dirt is literally forced into the bearings, causing them to lose their lubrication. Frequent cleaning helps, but bearings need periodic replacement. When foreign objects such as string or paper clips are picked up the fan may become jammed, and the machine loses suction or fails to run at all. This happens often in the smaller models. The housing must be opened up (usually this is not difficult) and the offending objects removed. Occasionally, a foreign object may damage a fan blade, causing it to run very noisily. Replacement is indicated in this situation.

ward, they divide into two types, the hand-held and the hood types. Although they look radically different, their operation is almost identical. The difference is that, on the hood models, a length of plastic hose is

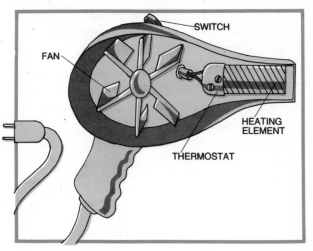

Hand-held hair dryer.

HAIR DRYER

The hair dryer has two basic parts: a motor-driven fan and a heating element. The fan blows air over the element, which gets very hot, and the warmed air flows out the nozzle. Up to this point, all dryers are pretty much the same. From the nozzle on-

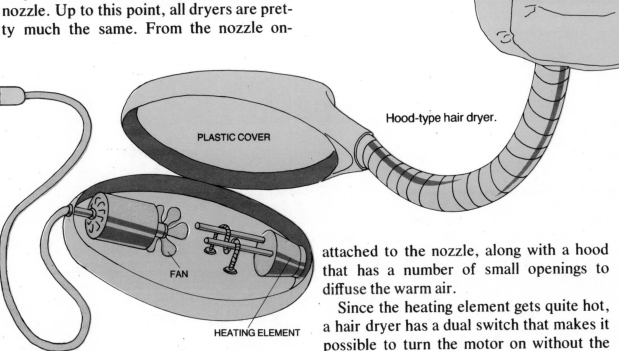

Hood-type hair dryer.

attached to the nozzle, along with a hood that has a number of small openings to diffuse the warm air.

Since the heating element gets quite hot, a hair dryer has a dual switch that makes it possible to turn the motor on without the

Small Appliance Repairs

heater, but not vice versa. There is a thermostat, too, to shut off the heating element when it gets too hot, and turn it back on when it cools sufficiently.

If neither the motor nor heater is working, it is a good bet that the trouble is in the cord assembly, at a common connection to both motor and heating element. If either one works and the other doesn't, start investigating the nonworking area and let the working one alone. When you have located the source of trouble, replacement of the malfunctioning unit is usually indicated, unless it is simply a loose connection.

On hood types, you occasionally find a leaky hose. Plastic tape does an effective job of patching.

Repairs to larger electrical appliances are better left to the professionals (except for simple mechanical replacements, such as a refrigerator door gasket). These appliances represent an investment of several hundred dollars, and it is usually worth the cost of a service call to keep them functioning properly. Also, with high voltage appliances such as an electric range or clothes dryer, there is a real danger to life and limb if repairs are improperly done. A qualified professional serviceman is your best bet in such cases.

Small Appliance Repairs

part 5 PLUMBING

Contents

1. HOW A PLUMBING SYSTEM WORKS 375
2. WHEN YOU BUY A HOUSE... 385
3. PLUMBING TOOLS 387
4. WATER SUPPLY LINES 397
5. DRAINAGE PIPES AND FITTINGS 414
6. SELECTING AND INSTALLING PLUMBING FIXTURES 422
7. SEPTIC TANKS 445
8. WHEN THINGS GO WRONG 447

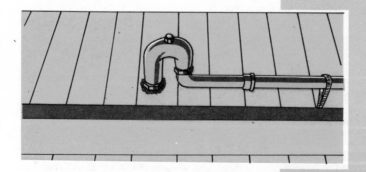

1

How a Plumbing System Works

ASK ANYONE who has spent some time in the rural areas of a developing nation, or who has participated in the "back-to-the-land" movement of start-from-scratch homesteading, what he or she missed most from the "civilized world." Chances are the answer will be indoor plumbing. Of all the amenities of twentieth-century living, this is the one thing most people would not want to do without.

Modern plumbing is something we take for granted, as well we should. Turn on a faucet and the bathtub fills with water of just the right temperature for a relaxing bath after a busy day. Flush the toilet and water comes from somewhere and goes somewhere else. The real workings of the system are out of sight—behind the walls, under the floor—and therefore out of mind. Until a problem occurs.

Suppose that bathtub drain becomes clogged, or the toilet refuses to stop running. You call the plumber, of course, and then your problems really begin to escalate.

Plumbers are busy people, and your bathroom may be awash (to say nothing of the room below) before the plumber you call can work you into his schedule. When he does come to perform his few minutes of magic, he presents a bill that makes you wonder whether indoor plumbing is really worth the aggravation—and the cost.

But it doesn't have to be that way. If you have some understanding of what is behind those walls and under the floor, you can make your own simple plumbing repairs. A knowledge of your household plumbing system will help you tackle more ambitious projects as well, such as installing a sink or even adding a new bathroom.

The household plumbing system has three distinct components: the supply (water brought into the house and piped through the system under pressure), the fixtures (lavatory, bathtub, toilet, washing machine, and other points where water is used), and the drain (water leaving the system by means of gravity).

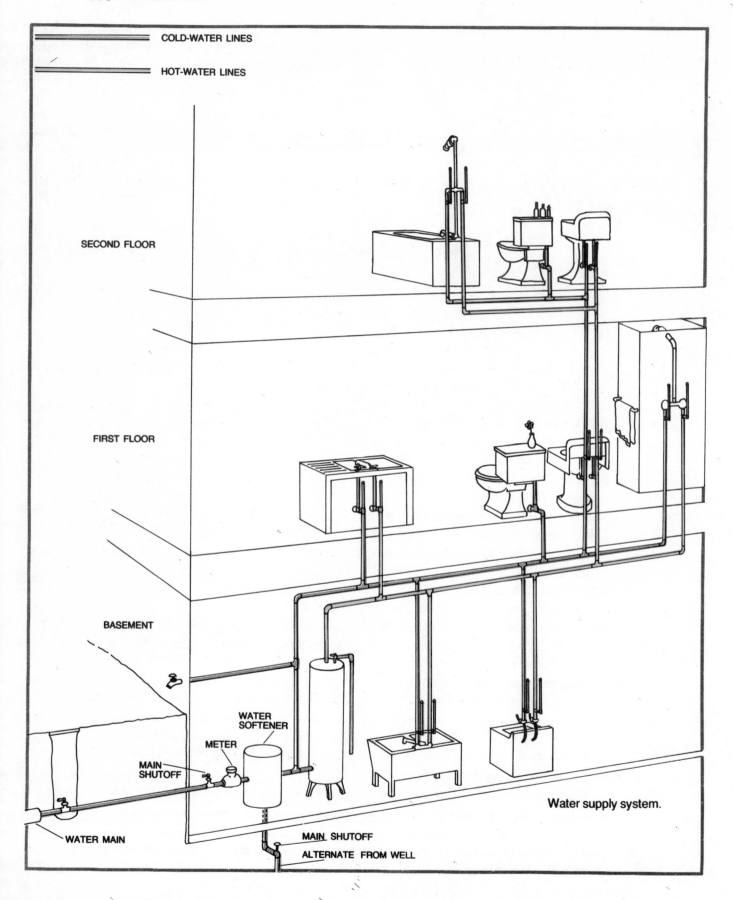

COLD-WATER LINES

HOT-WATER LINES

SECOND FLOOR

FIRST FLOOR

BASEMENT

WATER
SOFTENER

METER

MAIN
SHUTOFF

WATER MAIN

MAIN SHUTOFF

ALTERNATE FROM WELL

Water supply system.

How a Plumbing System Works

THE SUPPLY

Water for your household plumbing system may come from your own well, or it may come from a municipal or privately owned water company, which pipes it into your house. In either case, it must be in sufficient quantity to serve all outlets in the system, and it must be clear and pure for drinking.

If your home's water is supplied by a water company, the company first purifies it, then distributes it through a series of mains and branches, normally located under or near the street. Where a branch passes your house, a connection is made at the street. Near this connection, buried under the ground, a main shutoff valve is installed. This valve belongs to the water company, and it is opened or closed with a long-handled wrench called a "street key." From this valve, the water is piped into your house.

The piping enters the basement, crawl space, or utility room, where the water passes through a meter (the meter is sometimes outside the home). The meter is a very accurate measure of the amount of water your family consumes. The water company uses this measure to calculate your bill, but the meter can also be used for another purpose. If you suspect a leak somewhere in the system but are not sure, just turn off all faucets and other outlets and check the meter. If it records the passage of water, your suspicion is confirmed. Repair steps will be discussed in subsequent chapters.

Another shutoff valve is installed at the low part of the line where the piping enters the house. Like the street valve, this valve can be used to shut off all water in the house. Beyond this valve, the pipe becomes the cold-water main line. Outdoor spigots, which use only cold water, can branch off this line. If a water softener is

Typical meter inside main shutoff valve.

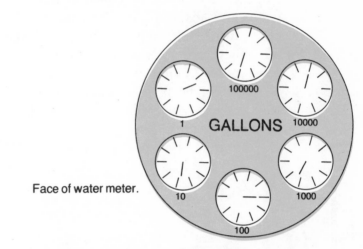

Face of water meter.

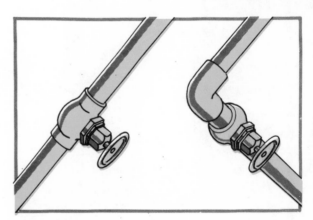

Shutoff valves in overhead lines in basement.

part of your home's system, the cold-water main line should be tied into it. After the softener, the main line is divided, with one pipe leading to the water heater, the other bypassing it. The cold-water line continues with branches to the various fixtures and appliances: boiler, tub, lavatory, sink, toilet, washer. A parallel hot-water main line

How a Plumbing System Works

from the heater also has branches to those fixtures requiring hot water (boiler and toilet need only cold water). Shutoff valves should be placed in each branch line and in main lines wherever shutoff might be required.

Every branch line that terminates in a faucet is (or should be) fitted with an air chamber or shock absorber. This is a vertical, air-filled pipe that cushions onrushing water and absorbs pressure when the faucet is turned off. Without an air chamber, an effect called "water hammer" would cause pipes to chatter and even burst. The air chamber is usually concealed within a wall, except where piping is exposed such as at basement stationary tubs.

Final delivery of the water from the

Air chamber.

AIR CHAMBER

TO FAUCET

Fixture supply lines.

TOP FITTING

TOP FITTING

FOR SINK, LAVATORY

FOR TOILET

THROUGH WALL

THROUGH FLOOR

branch lines to the individual fixtures is through fixture supply lines connecting either through the floor or through the wall. These lines should be fitted with shutoff valves for emergencies and to facilitate repairs when necessary.

PLUMBING FIXTURES

Fixtures are where it's at—where you actually use the water that is supplied in your plumbing system. Each fixture is designed to serve a specific purpose and must have certain features in order to perform its job. For example, sink and bathtub fittings must mix hot and cold water to a desired temperature, and a toilet is required to remove and replace a large quantity of water in a minimum of time. Most fixtures not only supply water for a specific use, but also provide for its removal after it has served its purpose, usually through a receptacle connected to the drainage component of the plumbing system.

DRAINAGE

Drainage must be provided to remove waste water from the fixtures to the street and public sewers or to a private disposal system such as a septic tank or cesspool. The drainage complex is subdivided into drain, waste, and vent (DWV) to best describe its functioning. Waste pipes lead from individual fixtures to a drain line, which in turn is connected to the sewer or septic tank. The system must be vented for proper flow and to allow gases to escape. For health reasons and proper functioning, the DWV system must conform to certain vital requirements:

• Pipes must be carefully and tightly fitted so that gases cannot leak out.

• Vents must carry the sewer gases to an area where they can do no harm.

• Each fixture that has a drain should be provided with a suitable water trap to prevent gases from backing up into the room (the exception is a toilet, which has a built-in trap).

• Re-vents (bypass vents for air) must be installed wherever there is a possibility of siphoning water from a fixture trap (local plumbing codes may require re-vents at all traps).

• Drainage pipes must be pitched or sloped for downward gravity flow of the water, all the way to final disposal.

Drainage system.

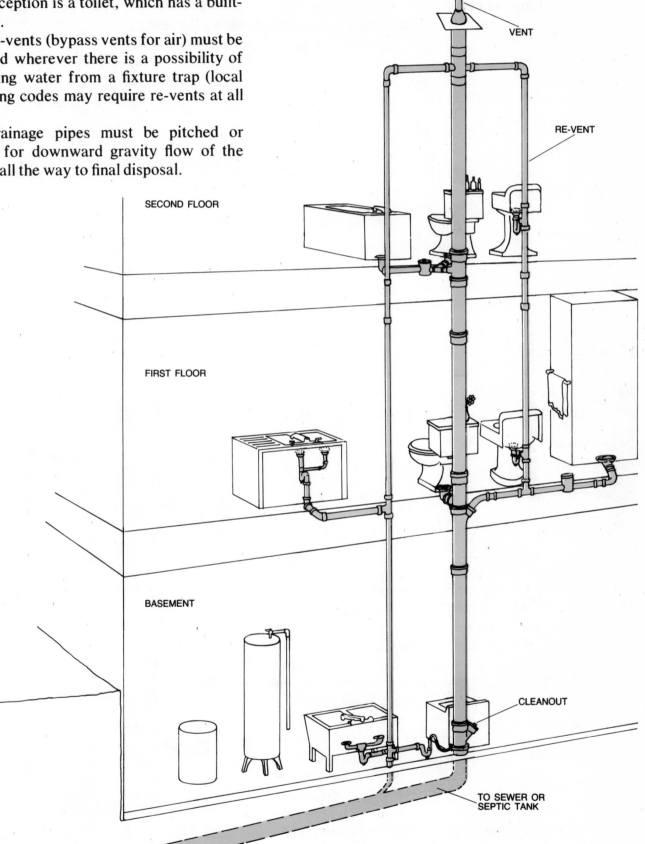

How a Plumbing System Works

Typical DWV setup for a group
of bathroom fixtures.

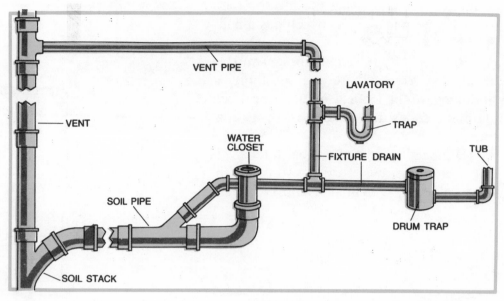

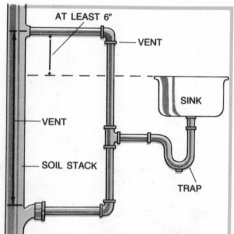

Typical DWV setup
for sink.

tinued through the roof to allow gases to escape to the outside and to admit air so that
traps will not be siphoned dry by down-
rushing water. This is the vent. Re-vents
are provided where a waste line cannot be

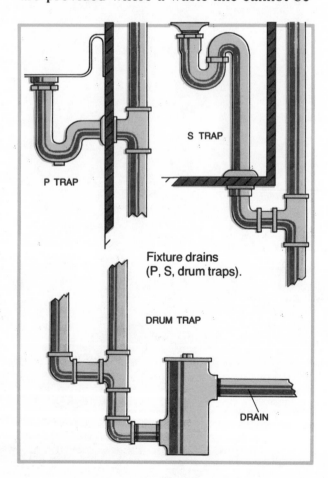

Fixture drains
(P, S, drum traps).

Just as the fixture supply provides final
delivery of water, the fixture drain is the
first step in getting rid of it after use. This is
normally where the trap is located (except,
as noted above, in toilets). The trap is a
water-filled P, S, or drum fitting that guards
against escape of gases into the house (the
gases cannot penetrate the water). From
there, the water goes into a branch drain or
waste pipe, which slopes away from the
fixture and carries the water to the soil
stack or main stack. There may also be
smaller, secondary stacks serving certain
fixtures, but toilets must always drain into
the main stack.

The upper portion of the soil stack is con-

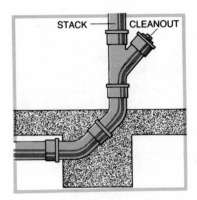

Above and below, location of cleanout plugs at the foot of stacks to allow access for clearing of obstructions.

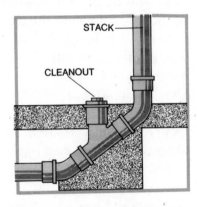

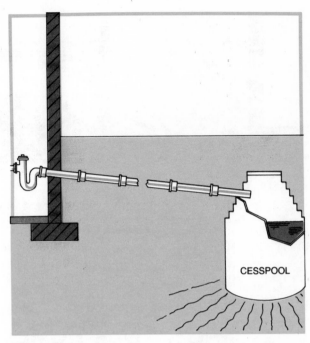

Location of cesspool.

vented directly into the stack or where the plumbing layout requires a bypass between a branch and the vent portion of the stack.

The main stack carries waste water to the building drain, which in turn carries it to the final disposal: a public sewer or your private septic tank and leaching field. At the foot of the stack, as well as at secondary stacks, there should be a cleanout plug to allow access for clearing obstructions that may clog the drain pipes. Such clogging may be caused by objects such as diapers accidentally dropped into the drainage system, or by accumulation of household wastes such as grease and disposal residue. Tree roots entering through faults in the underground drain lines can also cause clogging.

If you are not blessed with a municipal sewer system, you will need some private means of waste disposal. Cesspools are one such disposal system. Cesspools are simply holding tanks for raw house sewage. No provision is made for sewage treatment, and the waste is allowed to seep into the surrounding ground.

Because of this, cesspools are considered a health hazard. If they are installed near a water source, contamination of the water is possible. For this reason cesspools are prohibited in many areas. If you do have a cesspool, make sure it is pumped out frequently. Commercial liquefiers are available to be added to the cesspool for sewage treatment.

Septic tanks are watertight storage tanks that hold house sewage while it is decomposed by bacterial action. Unlike cesspools, septic tanks provide sewage treatment and a means for discharging the sewage with minimal health risk. The construction and installation requirements for septic tanks are closely governed by health authorities and local codes.

Sewage enters the septic tank from the house drain. Heavier solid matter falls to

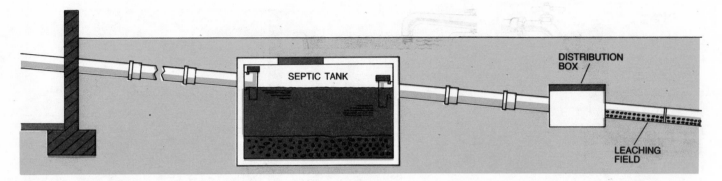

the bottom of the tank, where it is changed into a liquid state by bacterial action. Liquids are discharged from the septic tank and through distribution boxes into a leaching field or seepage pit. The liquids are then absorbed by the soil.

KNOW YOUR HOME'S PLUMBING SYSTEM

To help pinpoint problems that might occur, get to know your home's plumbing layout. Make a simple sketch of the system, showing the locations of fixtures, valves, and the like. Start where the water line enters your house. If that is in a basement or crawl space, draw the line and its cold and hot branches until they disappear into the floor overhead. Then go upstairs and note where they reappear out of the walls and are connected with the various fixtures.

Draw in the most likely routes of the piping through the walls from the basement or crawl space to the fixtures. Note the locations of all valves, so that when problems arise you need shut down only that portion of the system where the trouble is.

Note the locations of the soil stack, waste lines, and building drain in the basement or crawl space, and draw in the probable drain and waste lines that are concealed in the walls. Locate the traps and cleanout plugs. When a drain becomes clogged, this will be a big help—and at such a time you need all the help you can get.

CROSS-CONNECTIONS

A cross-connection is a physical link between the fresh water in your supply system and any waste water. Cross-connections are not always obvious and may exist

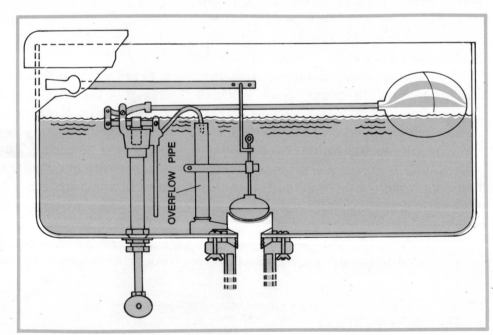

Cross-connection: toilet overflow pipe below the water level in the tank.

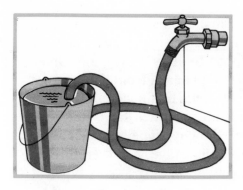

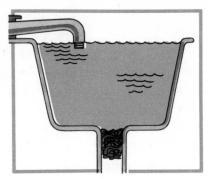

Cross-connections: far left, a connected water hose left in a bucket; left, faucet spout under water due to clogged drain.

without your being aware of them. Some examples are a faucet spout that would be under water should the drain stop; a connected water hose left in a bucket, tub, or pool; or a toilet overflow pipe below the water level in the tank. When you spot a potential cross-connection, correct it as soon as possible.

DRAINING AND FILLING THE PLUMBING SYSTEM

It may be necessary to drain the plumbing system when making certain repairs. Or you might want to drain it when leaving the home for an extended period, particularly during cold weather.

First turn off electricity or gas to water or steam heating units. Close the main shutoff valve. Starting at the highest floor and working down, open all hot- and cold-water faucets, including outdoor faucets. Flush all toilets. Open all drain valves on water-treatment equipment and the hot water heater (place buckets beneath them first). If you are draining the system to prevent freezing, pour antifreeze into all toilet bowls and drains.

To refill the system, close drain valves on water-treatment equipment and the hot water heater. Open the main shutoff valve. Close all hot- and cold-water faucets, including all outdoor faucets. Turn on electricity or gas to the hot water heater and any other heating units.

Shutting down the system:
1. Turn off electricity or gas to heating units.
2. Close main valve.
3. Open faucets, flush toilets on top floor.
4. Open faucets, flush toilets on lower floors.
5. Open drain valves on heaters, etc.
6. Pour antifreeze into toilets, drains.

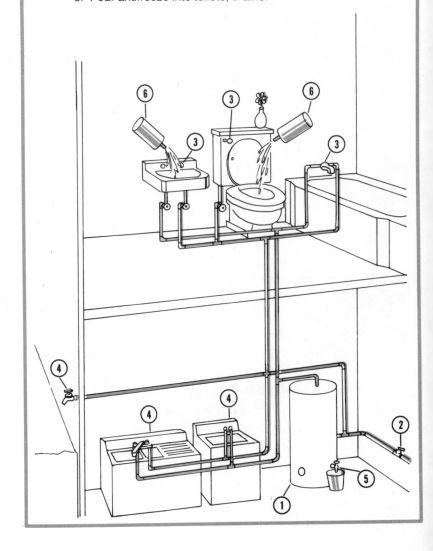

How a Plumbing System Works

PLUMBING AND THE LAW

When your sink is clogged or your toilet is overflowing, you don't stop to ask for a license to stem the tide—nor does your local building department require that you do. But when it comes to more ambitious projects—moving a bathroom or adding to your existing plumbing, for example—better check first with Town Hall (or City Hall, or County Hall if you live in an unincorporated area), for there are most likely some very stringent restrictions and regulations governing what you can do.

Plumbing codes vary from area to area. Some allow use of the most modern materials and fittings. Others adhere to tried but not necessarily true practices. Many follow the quite reasonable National Plumbing Code. In some localities, a licensed plumber must be employed for all but the simplest projects; others allow the do-it-yourselfer a free hand within limits. Almost all require inspections by municipal officials at various stages of the project. In any case, get a copy of your local plumbing code early in the planning stages of your project; read it carefully and understand it, then conform to it rigidly.

The code spells out requirements for design, materials, and workmanship, based on considerations of safety and health. It also specifies at what stages inspections must be performed by building authorities. In most cases, it calls for a pressure test of a new water-supply system, and a static-fill test of a new drainage-waste-vent system to make sure that there are no leaks.

Your local code may list certain approved materials, such as galvanized steel and copper for water-supply lines and cast iron and copper for DWV systems. Omission of a certain material from the list does not necessarily mean that it cannot be used. For example, many codes have not been updated since the days when plastics were still in the test-tube stage, and therefore do not make any mention of the many types of plastic piping that are in widespread use today. So you may decide to install economical, easy-to-work plastic water-supply and/or DWV piping even though your local code makes no reference to it, either favorable or unfavorable. But it would be wise to seek the opinion of your municipality's building department first. Building authorities have a reputation for hardheadedness, and it is not unknown for them to require the tearing down of an installation that does not conform to their codes. And remember that those codes—even though they may be outdated—are based on considerations of safety and health, yours as well as the community's. It would be better to work for changes in the code to allow the use of more modern materials rather than to attempt to circumvent it—and fail.

Modern plumbing technology recognizes the importance of the drain-waste-vent complex; for health reasons, it is the most important component of the household plumbing system. In some older installations, backup of waste water into the supply system can cause severe hazards. If you live in a home with ancient plumbing, get a copy of the plumbing code even if you have no plans to update the system, and check out your piping for possible hazards. You may have been lucky for longer than you think, but why take chances?

How a Plumbing System Works

2

When You Buy a House. . .

IT IS AN overworked but apt cliché that the purchase of a home is the largest investment that most families ever make. Steadily rising real estate values, skyrocketing building costs, and stiff mortgage interest rates make it more essential than ever that you invest your housing dollars wisely. Because the plumbing system is an integral (and expensive) part of the modern home, make sure you take a very close look at piping, fixtures, and other components before you put your signature on any home-buying contract.

THE NEW HOME

There is one major advantage, plumbing-wise, when you buy a new home. The law (or at least the local plumbing code) is on your side. Unless you are getting away from it all and building in a remote wilderness area, there are almost sure to be regulations that must be met, and inspections will be made by the municipal authorities to see that the plumbing conforms to those regulations. Almost universally, the inspection will include a check of the water-supply system under pressure and a static-fill test of the DWV system. So you can reasonably expect that the plumbing in your new home will meet minimum technical standards of performance.

But of course you may not want to settle for the minimum. Even if you are satisfied that the workmanship will be adequate, you might want to make a long-term investment in better-quality fixtures. This is especially true if you are buying a home in a development or a stock model offered by a builder. Don't be dazzled by what you see in a "model home," only to learn later when you move into your own new house that the shower is an "optional extra," along with the water heater. As when making any substantial purchase—and especially one as substantial as a house—get it all in writing. Make sure that the quality of fixtures you are buying is up to your expectations.

You should also think about future needs before the home is built. If you are buying an expandable—one of the story-and-a-half models popularly misnamed Cape Cod—you might leave the second floor unfinished, with plans to make it into a bedroom or two as the family grows. Why not have the pipes and DWV system for an upstairs bathroom "roughed-in" and capped off before the walls are enclosed. It is far easier and much less expensive to have this done during the original building than when plaster and wallboard have been installed. The same is true—even more so—if you plan to finish your new home's basement as a family recreation room, with an adjacent bathroom or powder room. Digging up a concrete floor to install new drainage piping is a costly proposition. It is far better to install these pipes before the concrete floor is poured and cap them off until they are needed.

If your new home will depend on a septic waste-disposal system, you can get a good idea of how efficient it will be by performing a percolation test. This will indicate how well the soil will absorb the liquid runoff from the tank; the more porous the soil, the better the system will function and the less the size of absorption area required. Sometimes such a test will be required by local health authorities, but if this is not the case, you should do it yourself, or have it done.

Dig a number of holes (a half dozen or so) at least 4 inches in diameter and 36 inches deep spaced throughout the area where the absorption bed will be located (see PAGE 445). Place about 2 inches of gravel in the bottom of each hole, and then pour about 12 inches of water on top of the gravel. Allow to stand for at least four hours (overnight is better), then refill the holes with water to a level of 6 inches above the gravel. (If the original water level has not fallen well below the 6-inch mark, you'd better forget about putting a septic tank in that location.) After another four-hour wait, take measurements to learn how long it takes the water remaining in the hole to drop 1 inch. This is called the percolation rate. When you have this information, check local building codes to find how large an absorption field is needed to match the percolation rate. (A percolation rate of more than 60 minutes is not suitable for a septic-tank disposal system.)

THE OLDER HOME

Although much of the plumbing in an existing house is out of sight, you can still learn a lot about the system by checking out what you can see. Start in the basement or crawl space, if possible, to find out the type of piping used. If it is an old home with the original iron or steel pipes, chances are that they will have to be replaced in the not-too-distant future. If you see some sections of new pipe in old runs, or sections of copper pipe along with galvanized pipe, that is a clue that trouble has already begun.

Check the pressure in the lines by turning on the kitchen faucets, then those in the bathroom. Or, in a two-story house, open all the faucets in an upstairs bathroom, then flush the toilet for good measure. If the water slows to a trickle, there is a problem. Corrosion inside the old pipes might be impeding the flow of water, meaning that an entirely new system may be needed.

Check out all the faucets in the house to make sure that they flow freely. Watch out for rusty water—another indication of corrosion within the pipes. Note the drainage from all fixtures. If it is sluggish, try freeing it with drain cleaner, a plumber's friend or snake (see PAGES 454-455), or ask the owner to do it. That may cure the problem, but if it doesn't, watch out. Replacing a badly corroded drainage system can cost thousands. If the house has a septic-tank disposal system, rather than being connected to a municipal sewer system, be especially wary of sluggish drains. They could mean that the entire system will have to be replaced. At the very least, this is an indication that it is time for a tank cleaning (see PAGE 446)—and that the home's present owner is guilty of neglect.

Inspect all fixtures and fittings to determine which will have to be replaced for cosmetic reasons or because they are worn or damaged. A leaky faucet is usually easy to repair (but why didn't the owner do it before he showed you the house?). A faucet on which the chrome finish is worn away is a relic that will have to be replaced. Badly worn or chipped sinks and lavatories, too, will require replacement. A cracked toilet tank is probably beyond anything but a temporary repair.

Check the type, capacity, and recovery rate (see PAGE 442) of the water heater. Make sure that it is large enough to meet your family's needs. Try to determine its age—you might ask the owner to show you the guarantee. If it is still under guarantee, make sure that you get the guarantee if you should decide to buy.

3

Plumbing Tools

I F YOU HAVE ever tried to loosen a screw with a pocketknife, or ruined a brass nut by mangling it with pliers, you know the importance of using the right tool for the job. Plumbing, just like any other trade, requires the use of specific tools—some of them designed for only a single function. You should be familiar with these so that, when the time comes, you will know what to use where.

That does not mean that you should head for the hardware store with a blank check in your wallet. Not at all. Other than a few tools that you should have on hand for emergencies, you should buy tools only as you need them. Too many do-it-yourselfers look on the hardware store as a child looks at the candy store—they want everything in sight. As a result, their workshops become displays of seldom-if-ever-used tools that would be more suitable for plumbing an interplanetary rocket than a household system. Resist the impulse to buy.

BE PREPARED

The wise homeowner is prepared for plumbing problems before they occur. You don't know when the sink will become clogged or the toilet will overflow, and you will want to be able to react quickly to such household crises. How you should react is detailed on PAGES 447-460. But you should have an emergency toolbox on hand that you can rush to the scene of the accident.

You probably already have many of the tools needed for such a toolbox. For leaky faucets, these will be screwdrivers (including Phillips-head, if your faucet handles are held on by this type of screw), an adjustable wrench, locking pliers, electrician's tape, and a supply of faucet washers in assorted sizes (you can buy such an assortment at any hardware store). You might also want to purchase a seat-dressing tool

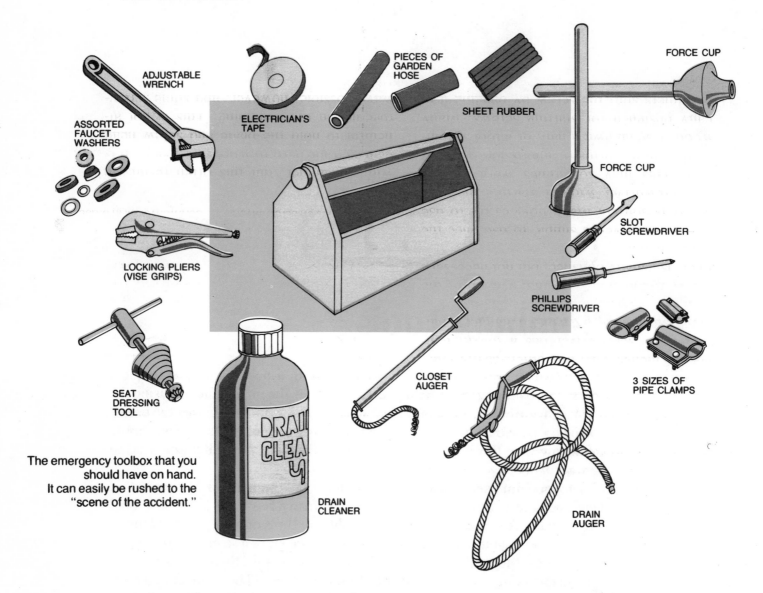

ADJUSTABLE WRENCH

ASSORTED FAUCET WASHERS

ELECTRICIAN'S TAPE

PIECES OF GARDEN HOSE

SHEET RUBBER

FORCE CUP

FORCE CUP

SLOT SCREWDRIVER

LOCKING PLIERS (VISE GRIPS)

PHILLIPS SCREWDRIVER

SEAT DRESSING TOOL

CLOSET AUGER

3 SIZES OF PIPE CLAMPS

The emergency toolbox that you should have on hand. It can easily be rushed to the "scene of the accident."

DRAIN CLEANER

DRAIN AUGER

(cost: about a dollar) in case a new washer doesn't stop the leak.

To attack clogged drains, keep drain cleaner—either liquid or dry type—near the kitchen sink. If the cleaner doesn't do the job, you should have the familiar "plumber's friend" or force cup—a rubber suction cup on the end of a wood handle. One type has a flat bottom and is intended primarily for sinks. The ball-type plunger, with a rounded bottom rather than a flat opening, is especially effective for unclogging toilets. On most of these the rounded bottom can be turned up for use in unclogging sinks. A drain auger or "snake"—spring steel or coiled wire with a small metal handle—will be needed to remove some particularly stubborn obstructions in drainage pipes. A closet auger is specially designed for unclogging toilets; a drain auger can also be used, but care must be taken not to damage the vitreous china finish.

You may never have occasion to use them, but it's a good idea to have a couple of pipe clamps of various sizes (⅜-inch, ½-inch, ¾-inch), along with some small pieces of sheet rubber or short lengths of garden hose. If a pipe ever springs a leak these items will let you make a quick, although temporary, repair.

Plumbing Tools

With your emergency toolbox packed and ready, you should be able to handle most common plumbing problems.

BEYOND EMERGENCIES

As you become more familiar with your household plumbing system, you may wish to undertake projects more ambitious than simple repairs—installing new fixtures, perhaps, or even adding a bathroom. Your collection of tools will grow apace. Just remember to buy them only as you need them.

The type of piping in your plumbing system will determine many of the tools you buy. Supply piping may be copper with soldered joints, galvanized steel with threaded joints, or plastic with bonded joints (see PAGES 397-405). Each type calls for a separate set of tools. Similarly, drainage pipe—copper, galvanized steel, cast iron, plastic (PAGES 414-421)—requires still other tools.

WRENCHES

Wrenches are basic to the plumber's craft. They can be divided into two broad classifications: fixed and adjustable. Fixed wrenches (open-end and box) are of a specific size and cannot be adjusted. When you buy fixed wrenches, get a quality set of graduated sizes. For working in tight places, special thin open-end wrenches, called closet spud wrenches, are particularly helpful.

Packing nut socket wrenches come in various sizes to fit tub and shower faucet assemblies. Hexagonal in shape and with a hollow core, this type of wrench fits over the faucet stem to remove the valve packing nuts and stem assembly. Since these parts are made of brass, ordinary wrenches should not be used on them. Application of

Open-end wrench.

Box wrench.

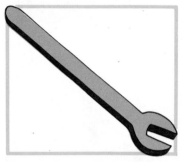
Closet spud wrench.

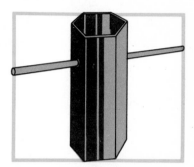
Packing nut socket wrench.

too much pressure will bend or break the fittings, which are very difficult to replace since they are inside the wall. It is far cheaper to buy and use the right wrench for the job than to have to tear apart the wall.

ADJUSTABLE WRENCHES

These are wrenches that can be adjusted to fit nuts and bolts of various sizes within the limitations of the individual wrench. There are many different types of adjustable wrenches.

The adjustable open-end wrench is used

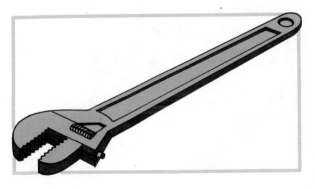
Adjustable open-end wrench.

Plumbing Tools

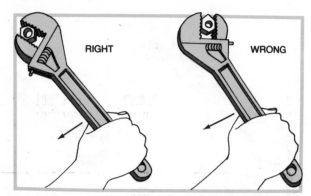

Right and wrong way to use
adjustable open-end wrench.

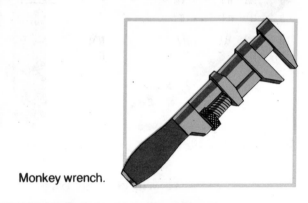

Monkey wrench.

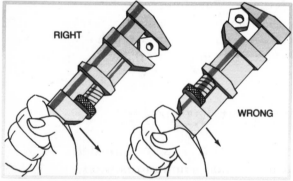

Right and wrong way
to use monkey wrench.

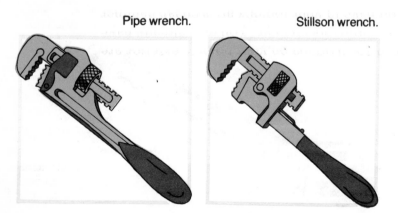

Pipe wrench.　　　　Stillson wrench.

on square or hexagonal nuts and for working on the interior parts of many types of faucets and valves. They come in many sizes according to the length of the tool; the jaws of the larger wrenches also open more widely. For most minor plumbing jobs, a 12-inch wrench is your best choice. A 6-inch wrench is also handy for smaller work.

Place the wrench on the nut so that you pull the handle toward the side with the adjustable jaw. This will prevent the jaw from opening and slipping off the nut. Be sure that the nut is all the way into the throat of the jaws, and that the jaws are adjusted to fit snugly around the nut. Otherwise, you may damage the nut or valve.

A monkey wrench is used for the same purposes and in the same way as the adjustable open-end wrench. Force is applied to the back of the handle—the side of the wrench opposite the jaw opening.

PIPE WRENCHES

These are adjustable wrenches designed to grip round surfaces. There are several types, although the term "pipe wrench" is also used in a narrower sense to designate one particular type. This type of wrench has hardened steel jaws that provide excellent bite and grip. It is often called a Stillson wrench, which is only a slight misnomer. The main difference between a pipe wrench and a Stillson wrench is that the latter has a separate housing in which the adjusting nut operates. In both types, the movable jaw is pivoted to permit a gripping action on the work. Both are used for working with steel or iron pipe.

Pipe wrenches come in many sizes. For small pipe work, a 6-inch or 8-inch length is best. For pipes in the ½-inch to 1½-inch range, a 12-inch or 14-inch wrench should be used. For pipe up to 2 inches, the wrench should be 18 inches long.

Two wrenches are needed in most applications, unless the work is held in a vise. One is used to hold the pipe, the other turns the fitting. Pipe wrenches work in one direction only, so they are placed on the work in opposing directions. Adjust the jaws so that the bite on the work is taken at about the center of the jaws. Always turn the wrench in the direction of the opening of the jaws, applying force to the back of the handle. As pressure on the handle is increased, the grip of the wrench on the work is tightened.

The serrated jaws of pipe wrenches bite into the pipe or fitting and always leave marks. They should not be used for tightening or loosening nuts, which would be damaged by the jaws. Nor should they be used on tubing or chrome-finished pipe that is easily marred.

A strap wrench is best for working with brass, aluminum, lead, soft metal, or plastic pipe. It consists of a handle and a heavy webbed strap that loops around the pipe in the opposite direction to that in which the pipe is to be rotated. The strap is then passed through a slot in the handle and drawn up tightly. As the handle is pulled the strap tightens further, gripping the pipe and turning it.

A chain wrench is used on large-diameter pipe, such as cast-iron drain pipe. It consists of a forged steel handle to which is attached a length of heavy sprocket chain. When looped around the pipe, the chain grips the pipe on its entire outer circumference. The tool works in one direction only, but the handle can be backed partly around the work and a fresh hold taken without freeing the chain—somewhat like a ratchet wrench.

The basin wrench is a specialized tool with a long handle and jaws that adjust to various working positions. It is used to remove or tighten nuts on faucets and spray attachments in hard-to-reach spots under sinks and lavatories.

Plumbing Tools

Use of two pipe wrenches.

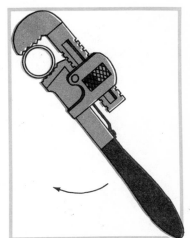
Fitting wrench on pipe.

Strap wrench.

Basin wrench.

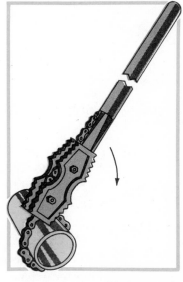
Chain wrench.

Slip-joint pliers.

Water-pump pliers.

Locking pliers.

Channel-lock pliers.

PLIERS

Pliers are probably the most misunderstood and misused of all tools. They are used as substitutes for hammers, wrenches, bottle openers, and who knows what else. When properly applied they can perform many holding and gripping operations. But they should never be used to grip pipe or turn nuts—they can mark or dent a pipe but not hold it, and it takes only a few turns to damage a nut. In addition to the "garden variety" household pliers, there are several specialized types.

Water-pump pliers came in with the machine age, and were originally designed for tightening or removing water-pump packing nuts. One jaw is adjustable to several different positions. The inner surface of the jaws consists of a series of deep grooves adapted to grasping cylindrical objects.

Channel-lock pliers are similar to water-pump pliers, but the jaw-opening adjust-ment is different. Lands (raised areas) on one jaw fit into grooves on the other. Channel-lock pliers are less likely to slip from the adjustment setting than water-pump pliers, but they they are less effective than a wrench and should be used only where it is impossible to fit a wrench.

Locking pliers are very useful when working with small-diameter pipe. They can be clasped on an object and they will stay by themselves, leaving your hands free for other work. The jaw opening is adjusted by turning a thumbscrew at the end of one handle; the tool is then clamped on the pipe or other object and locked in position by squeezing the handles together. Some types include a release lever; others must be pulled apart to release. Locking pliers should not be used on nuts, bolts, or tube fittings, since the teeth in the jaws are likely to damage the surface to which they are clamped.

CUTTERS

A hacksaw can be used to cut pipe and tubing, but it is difficult to obtain a straight, clean cut this way. It is also hard work—especially sawing through steel pipe. A pipe cutter will spare your muscles while doing the job cleanly, accurately, and quickly.

Most pipe cutters have a cutting wheel on one jaw and two rollers on the other. Place the cutter over the pipe (which should be clamped in a vise) and tighten the handle

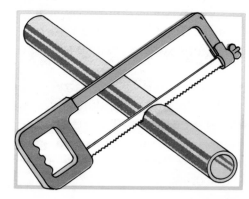
Hacksaw.

Plumbing Tools

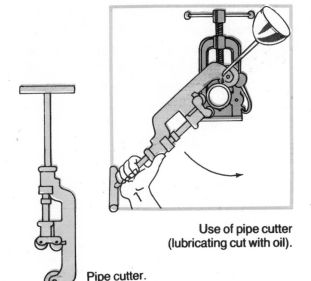

Pipe cutter.

Use of pipe cutter
(lubricating cut with oil).

pipe with thread-cutting oil until the pipe is cut through.

Use a tube cutter on copper tubing. This tool is similar to a pipe cutter, but smaller and lighter. A vise is not ordinarily used in this operation, since both tubing and cutter can be hand-held. Do not tighten the cutter too fast or you are likely to flatten the tubing. No cutting oils are required during this operation.

REAMERS AND FILES

Both inside and outside edges of pipe and tubing often become burred when cut. Burrs on the outside may interfere with threading of the pipe or joining tubing; they can also cause nasty cuts when you work with the pipe. Burrs on the inside edge obstruct the flow of water within the pipe. Remove burrs from the outside edge of pipe with a flat file. A spiral-type reamer is best for removing the burrs inside the pipe or tubing.

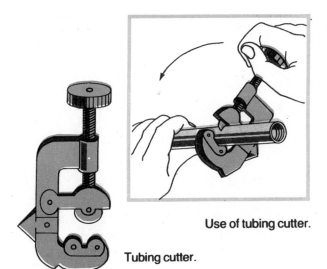

Tubing cutter.

Use of tubing cutter.

down snugly. Turn the cutter around the pipe, tightening the handle as you do. Frequently lubricate both cutting wheel and

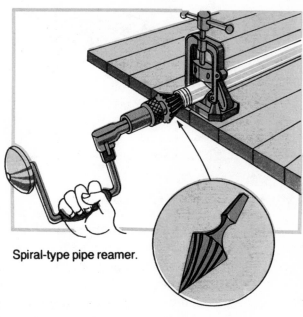

Spiral-type pipe reamer.

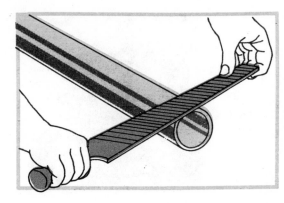

Filing burrs from end of cut pipe.

Plumbing Tools

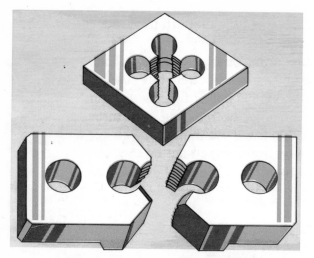

Split type and solid type
pipe-threading dies.

Cutting threads.

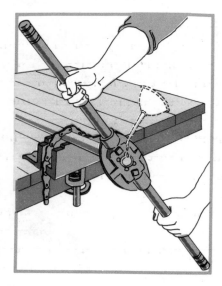

Two-handled
die stock.

THREADERS

At most plumbing-supply shops and many hardware stores, you can buy steel or iron pipe cut and threaded to order. For a large project, or a complex one where each piece must be individually measured, you may prefer to thread your own. You will need dies in the pipe size you are using. The dies are held in a die stock with a long handle or handles to turn the tool on the pipe.

When cutting threads, the pipe must be held securely in a vise. Turn the die stock onto the pipe to start, then make a quarter turn at a time, backing off slightly and lubricating with cutting oil at each step. Continue in this manner until the full length of thread is cut. Length of threads for various pipe sizes are given below.

Pipe (inside diameter)—inches	Length of thread (inches)
¼	⅝
⅜	⅝
½	13/16
¾	13/16
1	1
1¼	1
1½	1
2	1¼
2½	1½
3	1⅝

When the thread is cut, back the die stock off the pipe. Wipe the thread clean.

VISES

Plumbers, too, have their vises. But they differ somewhat from ordinary bench or machinist's vises in that they are fitted with serrated jaws to grip pipe and prevent it from turning. Like other tools discussed here, there are several types and sizes of vises. Make sure you select one large enough to accommodate all the sizes of pipe you will be working with.

The yoke vise is favored by most plumb-

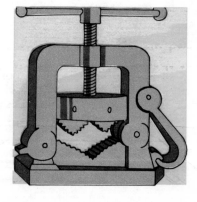

Yoke vise.

Plumbing Tools

Chain vise.

Combination vise.

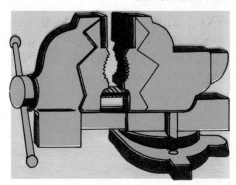

FLARING TOOLS

Many valves and other fittings to which tubing is attached are of the "flare" type, requiring that the tubing be flared or turned outward in a sort of bell shape at the end for joining. There are various types of tools for this job. Most consist of a split die block with holes for different sizes of tubing, a clamp to lock the tubing in the block, and a yoke with a compressor screw that fits over the block. A cone at the base of the screw forms a 45-degree flare or bell shape on the end of the tubing. The sleeve nut of the fitting is first slipped on the tubing, then the tubing is clamped in the die block and the compressor screw is tightened to form the flare. It is then backed off and the tubing is released from the block.

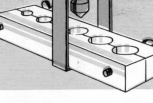

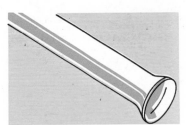

Flaring tool.

Flared tubing.

ers for general pipe work. It is usually bolted to a bench or a portable stand. Its V-shaped jaws grip the pipe both top and bottom. The upper jaw is on a hinged yoke, which is raised to admit the work and is then brought down and locked by turning an adjusting handle at the top.

The chain vise is often used by plumbers when "roughing in" new systems, since it is easy to transport and set up under a variety of conditions. It has a fixed lower V-shaped jaw with teeth on which the pipe is laid, and a bicycle-type chain fastened to one side. When the pipe is positioned, the chain is brought over it and locked in a slot on the other side, securing the pipe.

The combination vise is basically a machinist's vise, fitted with integral jaws (sometimes removable) for holding pipe. It can be used in a pinch, but is not recommended for heavy-duty work.

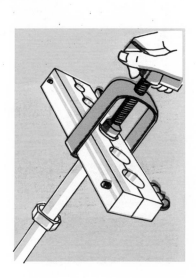

Using the
flaring tool.

Plumbing Tools

Propane
torch.

PROPANE TORCH

When making solder connections in copper plumbing lines, a propane torch is the best tool for the do-it-yourselfer to use. It is easier to handle than the larger blowtorch, and also much safer. When the propane is exhausted, the soldering head is simply transferred to a fresh tank. Some newer types require only the addition of oxygen pellets to recharge the supply tank. Use of the propane torch is discussed in detail on PAGE 398.

TOOLS FOR WORKING WITH CAST-IRON PIPE

Cast-iron drainage pipe can be cut with a hacksaw or a cold chisel and hammer. Use a heavy ball pein hammer or a short-handled sledge for this job—never a claw hammer, which is intended for carpentry only.

To assemble cast-iron pipe, you will need a yarning iron to drive oakum into the joints, along with a blowtorch and melting pot to melt lead and a cast-iron ladle for pouring the hot lead into the joints. Other specialized tools include a joint runner (for horizontal pipe joints), and inside and outside calking irons for forming the lead in the joints. The use of these tools is explained on PAGES 414-419.

As with many other traditional materials, new and simpler methods of installation have been developed for cast-iron pipe. Although it is not available everywhere, you may be able to find "hubless" pipe (see PAGE 414) for your DWV lines and save yourself a lot of work, as well as the cost of several tools. Although hubless pipe is cut the same way as regular cast-iron pipe, the only tool you need for assembly is a wrench.

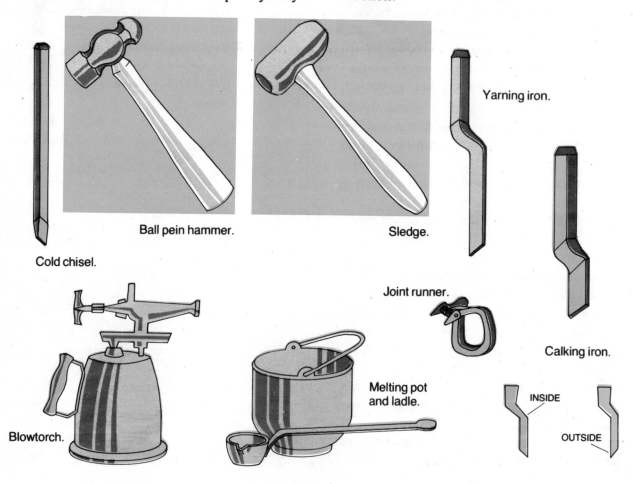

Cold chisel.

Ball pein hammer.

Sledge.

Yarning iron.

Joint runner.

Calking iron.

Blowtorch.

Melting pot and ladle.

INSIDE

OUTSIDE

Plumbing Tools

4

Water Supply Lines

TO MANY PEOPLE, plumbing means a bewildering maze of pipes, elbows, valves, and other fittings scattered below the joists in the basement until they disappear into the floor overhead. Pipes and fittings are, of course, basic to plumbing—they deliver the water to where it is used, and that is what it's all about. But there need be no bewilderment. Anyone who is reasonably handy with tools can quickly learn the rudiments of working with pipe.

Copper and galvanized steel water-supply lines are most commonly found in residential installations. Where codes permit, new types of plastic pipe are increasing in favor, especially with the do-it-yourselfer. In some situations, brass pipe is desirable or may be required—this is the most expensive but most durable of all. Each type of piping requires the use of special tools.

COPPER PIPE

Copper piping (and tubing) is corrosion-resistant, allows relatively unimpeded flow of water, and is comparatively easy to work with. It comes in two types: rigid (hard-temper) and flexible (soft-temper). Rigid is often used where appearance is a factor; exposed, as in a basement, the straight lines of piping have a more workmanlike look. Flexible is used for underground lines, such as the main house supply, and is also favored for remodeling work where the pipe must be fitted inside existing walls.

The sizes of copper pipe or tubing are nominal outside dimensions. For main, branch, and supply lines, ¾-, ½-, and ⅜-inch are most commonly used, although the line from the street main may be larger.

Wall thickness of copper pipe varies. The heaviest, Type K, available in both rigid and flexible, is used primarily for commercial and industrial installations. Type L, both rigid and flexible, is thinner and lighter than K and is usually used in residential water lines. Type M, available in rigid only, is the thinnest and is sometimes used for light water-supply lines. Some plumbing codes do not permit the use of Type M; make sure to check your code and follow its restrictions. Types K and L are sold in 12- and 20-foot lengths (rigid) and 30-, 60-, and 100-foot coils (flexible). Type M is sold in 12- and 20-foot lengths only.

Nominal Size	Outside Diameter	Inside Diameter		
(inches)	(inches)	(inches)		
		Type K	Type L	Type M
3/8	.500	.402	.430	.450
1/2	.625	.527	.545	.569
3/4	.875	.745	.785	.811
1	1.125	.995	1.025	1.055
1 1/4	1.375	1.245	1.265	1.291
1 1/2	1.625	1.485	1.505	1.527

Solder is used to assemble rigid copper pipe and fittings. Properly done, this type of "sweated joint" makes a permanent, trouble-free installation. Flexible copper tubing is easier to install. It can be bent around corners without the need for fittings, and this also makes it simple to compensate for measuring or layout inaccuracies. For joining flexible tubing, soldered, flare-type, or compression fittings can be used. With the flare type, the end of the tubing must first be flared to a bell shape. Compression fittings use brass ferrules and nuts; they need only be tightened and are very easy to assemble.

WORKING WITH RIGID COPPER PIPE

To measure the length of rigid copper pipe, use the face-to-face method. Measure the exact distance between the two fittings that the pipe will join. Then add the depths of the soldering hubs in the fittings.

Face-to-face method of measuring when using solder fittings.

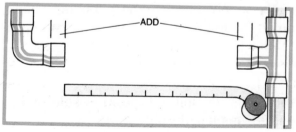

A tubing cutter produces the best results when cutting rigid copper pipe (see PAGE 393). You can also cut it with a hack saw, but then the pipe should be held in a jig to ensure a square cut. You can build a simple wooden jig by cutting a shallow V-groove

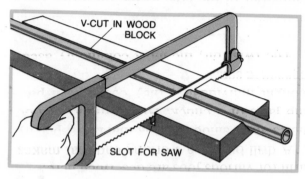

Jig for cutting pipe with hacksaw.

along the length of a 2 x 4 about 2 feet long. Near one end, cut a slot across the 2 x 4 at a right angle to the groove. Hold the tubing in the groove and guide the hacksaw in the slot. Use a fine-toothed hacksaw blade. After cutting, ream the pipe to remove burrs.

Rub the end of the pipe and the inside of the fitting to be soldered with steel wool or fine emery cloth. Clean surfaces are essential when soldering. Make sure that there are no dents in the end of the tubing and that it is perfectly round; otherwise it will not seat properly in the fitting.

Apply a thin coat of noncorrosive flux or soldering paste to the end of the pipe and the inside of the fitting. Place the fitting over the pipe up to its hub and rotate it a few times to spread the flux evenly. Wipe excess flux from around the fitting.

Heat the fitting with the flame of a propane torch. When the flux begins to bubble out around the fitting, remove the torch and apply the end of the solder to the edge of the fitting. Capillary action will draw the solder into the space between the pipe and the fitting, filling and sealing the joint. A properly soldered joint will show a line of solder completely around the edge of the fitting. Do not hold the flame on the joint

Water Supply Lines

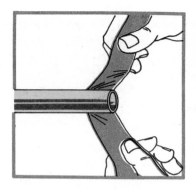

Rub pipe with emery cloth.

Apply flux.

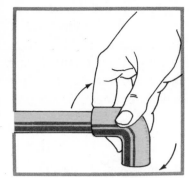

Rotate fitting to spread flux.

Heat the fitting.

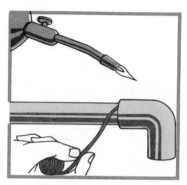

Apply solder.

Soldered joint, showing bead.

once it has been filled. Excess solder should be wiped away with a rag.

Do not move the pipe or fitting while the solder is cooling. This could weaken or break the seal. It takes less than a minute for the solder to cool and harden.

When making other soldered connections to the same fitting (such as a coupling or elbow), wrap wet rags around the completed joint to prevent the hardened solder from melting.

If a soldered joint in a water line must be disconnected to repair a leak or to add new pipe or fittings, the water must first be drained from the entire line. Wrap other connections in the same fitting with wet rags to keep them from melting, then heat the leaking joint until the solder runs and you can pull out the pipe. Wipe off the old solder and clean the pipe and the fitting with steel wool or emery cloth before resoldering.

Wrap soldered joint in rags when doing another joint on fitting.

WORKING WITH FLEXIBLE COPPER TUBING

You can cut flexible copper tubing with either a cutter or a hacksaw, but be careful not to dent or flatten the tubing.

It is softer than rigid pipe, and thus easier to damage. Flexible tubing can be bent as necessary in water-supply lines, eliminating the need for many fittings. It is best to bend it around some sort of form—even your knee—but be careful not to kink the tubing.

For more uniform bends, use a bending spring. These are available in various sizes to fit the tubing. Just slip the spring over the tubing and bend by hand to the desired form. Then slide the spring off the tubing.

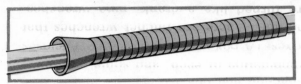

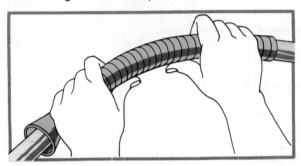

Slip bending spring over tubing.

Bend tubing to desired shape.

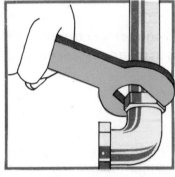

Start flare fitting nut by hand.

Finish tightening with wrench, but do not overtighten.

Hand-tightening compression fitting to align it properly.

Slip nut and ferrule over pipe.

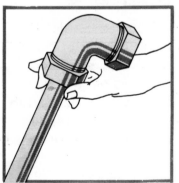

When you use soldered fittings with flexible tubing, measuring and joining are the same as with rigid pipe. With flared fittings, measure face-to-face between the fittings, then add approximately 3/16 inch at each end (slightly less for ½-inch or smaller tubing). After cutting, file off all burrs—the tubing must be perfectly smooth for flaring.

Before flaring the tubing, remove the nut from the fitting and slip it over the tubing. Loosen the die block clamp screw of the flaring tool and insert the tubing in the appropriate hole, with its end extending approximately ⅛ inch outside the block. Tighten the clamp screw to hold the tubing firmly. Slide the yoke over the end of the die block and turn the feed screw clockwise until the flaring cone forces the end of the tubing against the chamber of the die block, forming a bell-shaped flare (see PAGE 394). Back out the feed screw, slide the yoke off the die block, and loosen the clamp screw to remove the flared tube.

Thread the nut onto the fitting by hand. When you are sure it is correctly aligned, tighten (but make sure not to overtighten) with an open-end or adjustable open-end wrench. The flared end of the tubing will seat against the cupped end of the fitting, forming a tight seal.

To measure tubing length when working with compression fittings, again use the face-to-face method. The add-on factor here is the distance the tubing will penetrate the fitting, usually ¼ to ⅜ inch.

Compression fittings have a ferrule held in place by a nut. Remove the nut and slip it over the tubing. Slip the ferrule over the tubing so that the tubing extends through the ferrule ⅛ inch or so. Place the tubing into the fitting, pushing it in as far as it will go. Thread the nut onto the fitting, hand-tightening it to make sure that it is properly aligned. Finish tightening with an open-end or adjustable wrench, but do not overtighten.

GALVANIZED PIPE

Although it has given way to copper in popularity over the past few decades, tough, durable galvanized steel pipe is still widely used. It is sold in sizes from ⅛ inch up to 6 inches (the approximate inside diameter). For residential water-supply piping, ⅜-, ½-, ¾-, and 1-inch pipe are most common. Main lines may be 1-inch or ¾-inch, branches ¾-inch or ½-inch, and fixture-supply pipe ½-inch or ⅜-inch.

GALVANIZED STEEL PIPE SIZES			
Nominal Size	Outside Diameter	Inside Diameter	Threads per Inch
(inches)	(inches)	(inches)	
⅜	0.675	0.493	18
½	0.840	0.622	14
¾	1.050	0.824	14
1	1.315	1.049	11 ½
1 ¼	1.660	1.380	11 ½
1 ½	1.900	1.610	11 ½
2	2.375	2.067	11 ½

Steel pipe is more economical than copper, but it is more difficult to work with because of its rigidity and because of the threading that is required for joining. It may corrode when exposed to some kinds kinds of water—in such areas, the local plumbing code will probably specify the use of some other type of pipe. It should not be buried in the ground or embedded in concrete.

When working with galvanized pipe, careful measuring is vital. Allowance must be made for the threads that join the pipe to the fittings. The face-to-face method of measuring is usually used. Measure the exact distance between the fittings to which the pipe will run. Then add the extra length of threading that will penetrate the fittings.

Pipe Size (inches)	Pipe Screwed into Fitting (inches)
⅜	½
½	½
¾	½
1	⅝
1 ¼	⅝
1 ½	⅝
2	¾

Remember that this length must be doubled for threading into fittings at both ends of the pipe.

You may be able to measure the entire job in this manner, then order the pipe cut to exact length and threaded at a hardware or plumbing-supply store. For a larger job

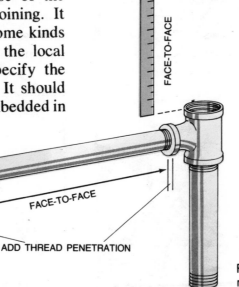

Face-to-face method of measuring galvanized pipe.

where it may be difficult to measure the entire layout, you may elect to perform these operations yourself. You will need a vise, a pipe cutter, a reamer, and stock and dies of the appropriate size or sizes to thread the pipe (see PAGE 392). When cutting and threading, frequently apply cutting oil to both cutter or dies and pipe. After threads are cut and dies are removed, wipe off surplus oil and all metal chips from the threads, and ream the inside of the pipe.

To ensure watertight connections, pipe joint compound or a special Teflon tape is applied to the threads before they are joined to the fittings. To connect a fitting, secure the pipe in a vise or, if the pipe is already in position, hold it with a wrench. (Never attempt to tighten a fitting with only a single wrench—you may loosen a connection elsewhere in the line.) Start the fitting by hand, making sure that the threads are aligned properly and not crossed. Tighten the fitting with a pipe wrench, then wipe off excess compound.

Applying joint compound.

Applying Teflon tape.

Start fitting by hand.

Tighten with pipe wrench.

If pipe is already in place, hold with wrench while tightening fitting with another wrench.

BRASS PIPE

Where water is highly corrosive, brass pipe may be used—or even required by code—for the water-supply system. Brass is worked similarly to galvanized steel pipe, with threaded joints. However, a standard pipe wrench should not be used since it will mar the brass finish. The strap wrench is the preferred tool for assembling brass pipe.

Brass pipe can be attached to copper or plastic piping (and vice versa), but if brass and galvanized steel are used in the same system, a dielectric connector should be used to join the two metals. Otherwise, corrosive action may result.

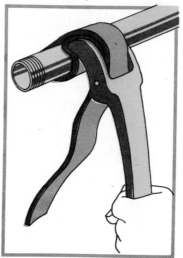

Use of strap wrench on brass pipe.

PLASTIC PIPE

Where local plumbing codes have caught up with the plastics industry, plastic pipe is an excellent choice for water-supply lines. Just make sure that you check the code for your community before deciding to use plastic pipe.

Plastic pipe is easiest of all for the do-it-yourselfer to install. It is lightweight and, more important, will not rust, rot, or corrode and offers practically no resistance to water flow. Some types can be cut with a sharp knife; all can be cut with a hacksaw or other saw. Joining is with compression-type fittings or a solvent (which solvent depends on the type of plastic). The latter method is simpler, but measuring is critical; the solvent is unforgiving of mistakes, and if you go wrong, you have to cut the fitting out of the line and throw it away. (You *may* be able to salvage it in some cases, as explained later.)

Of the many different types of plastic pipe that are manufactured, three are most commonly used by the do-it-yourself plumber. All can be installed underground as well as inside the house, but only one can be used for hot-water lines. Whichever type you select, make sure that it bears the seal of the National Sanitation Foundation if the water it will carry is to be used for drinking. Sizes are generally the same as for copper pipe.

Chlorinated polyvinyl chloride (CPVC) plastic pipe can be used for both hot and cold water-supply lines. It comes in rigid and semirigid lengths from 10 feet to 30 feet. CPVC solvent is used for solvent-welded joints.

Polyvinyl chloride (PVC) pipe is for use only in cold-water lines—heat will soften the plastic. It is available in the same lengths as CPVC pipe. PVC solvent is used to weld joints.

Polyethylene (PE) pipe is flexible and comes in coils of varying lengths. Wall thicknesses also vary. PE is especially useful for lines bringing water from the water main of a well into the house. It should not be used for hot-water lines. In addition to compression fittings and solvent welding, PE can also be joined by clamping it over serrated fittings.

When working with plastic pipe, again measure face-to-face and add the length that the pipe will be inserted into (or over, in the case of clamped-on PE pipe) the

Cutting plastic pipe with saw, pipe held in vise.

Cleaning out inside of pipe with a knife.

fitting. Never use a rotary pipe or tubing cutter on plastic pipe. Flexible PE pipe can be cut with a sharp knife. Semirigid and rigid PVC and CPVC are best cut with a hacksaw or other handsaw, or even a power saw, using a fine-tooth blade. You can use a jig to ensure square cuts when cutting with a saw. You can build a simple one as described previously for cutting rigid copper pipe. The plastic pipe can also be held in a vise, but first wrap it with cloth or tape to prevent surface damage. After cutting, remove burrs from inside the pipe with a pocketknife.

Solvent is the most commonly used

Wiping outside
with emery paper.

Cleaning inside of fitting
with emery paper.

erously to the outside of the pipe, and apply a thinner coat to the inside of the fitting socket. Press the fitting onto the pipe and give it a quarter turn to distribute the solvent evenly. Make sure that the pipe and fitting are properly aligned. There should be a continuous bead showing around the fitting; if the bead is uneven or if there is none, the joint may leak. But don't apply too much solvent either; this could clog the line and slow or block the flow of water.

method of connecting plastic pipe and fittings. Just make sure you get the proper solvent for the type of pipe you are using. Some solvents come with a special cleaner that is applied first. Otherwise, use emery cloth to clean both the inside of the fitting and the outside of the pipe before joining.

Work on only one joint at a time—the solvent is very quick-setting. Use the brush supplied with the solvent or any nonsynthetic bristle brush. Apply the solvent gen-

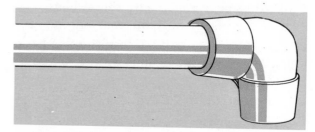

Continuous bead showing around fitting.

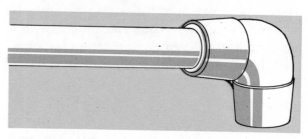

Uneven bead showing.

Apply solvent to pipe.

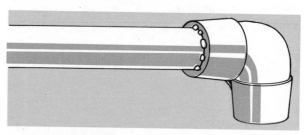

No bead showing.

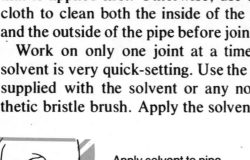

Give fitting a quarter
turn on pipe.

Apply solvent to fitting.

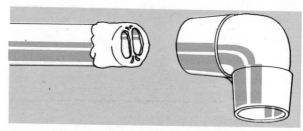

Too much solvent could clog the line.

Hold the pipe and fitting tightly together until the curing process begins (about 15 seconds). Wipe off excess solvent. Do not move the joint until the solvent weld has set (less than a minute). Wait two hours before testing the line under pressure.

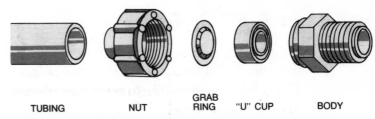

TUBING   NUT   GRAB RING   "U" CUP   BODY

Compression fitting for plastic pipe.

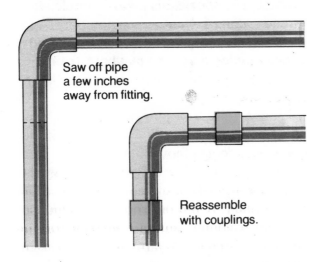

Saw off pipe a few inches away from fitting.

Reassemble with couplings.

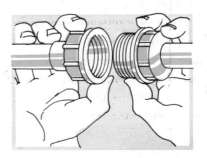

Tighten fitting by hand, not wrench.

Once set, a solvent-welded joint is permanent. If the joint has to be broken for any reason, you may be able to salvage the fitting by sawing off the pipe a few inches away on each side, then reassembling the line with couplings.

To use a clamp-on fitting with PE pipe, first slip the clamp over the pipe, then force

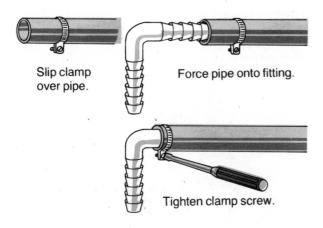

Slip clamp over pipe.

Force pipe onto fitting.

Tighten clamp screw.

the pipe over the serrations on the fitting. Slide the clamp up near the end of the pipe (over the fitting) and tighten the clamp screw.

Water Supply Lines

Another type of plastic pipe fitting that doesn't require solvent is the compression fitting. To use, clean and smooth the pipe with emery paper the same as for solvent connections. Insert the pipe in the fitting, which has a special nut that is hand-tightened to make a watertight joint. A grab ring holds the pipe, while a U-cup collar inside the fitting is forced against the pipe by water passing through the line—the higher the water pressure, the tighter the seal.

On many fixtures, piping is exposed for a short distance between where the supply line comes out of the floor or wall and where it is attached to the fixture. Chrome-plated fixture-supply lines are generally installed here. They are available in both rigid and flexible types and have appropriate connectors at both ends, depending on the type of piping and the fixture it serves. A fixture-supply line should be installed in conjunction with a valve (supply stop) to control the flow of water to the fixture—but this is not always the case, especially in older plumbing systems (see PAGES 423-424).

Typical fixture supply line for soldered pipe, wall to sink or lavatory connection (at right top) and for threaded pipe, floor to toilet connection (at right).

PIPE FITTINGS

Everybody knows that a straight line is the shortest distance between two points. But it is rarely possible to run a line of piping from the water main straight to the outlet (faucet or whatever). For this purpose, a wide variety of fittings is used.

Each kind of pipe—copper, threaded steel and brass, plastic—has its own fittings, but there are certain similarities among all. Fittings are ordered according to the size of pipe on which they will be used: a ½-inch coupling joins two lengths of ½-inch pipe; a ¾-to-½ reducer is used between those two sizes of pipe. Following are the most commonly used fittings.

Couplings connect pipes of the same diameter when those pipes will not normally have to be disconnected. Reducing couplings connect pipes of different diameters when they will not normally have to be disconnected. They may step down only one size (1 inch to ¾ inch, for example) or several sizes (such as 1 ¼ inch to ½ inch).

Unions connect pipes—usually of the same size—that may have to be disconnected at some time (for example, pipes leading into and out of the water heater, which may require replacement). Unions consist of three parts. Two of these have matching ground joints and are attached to each of the pipes to be joined; the third part is a large nut that draws the pipes together.

Nipples are short lengths of threaded pipe, saving you the trouble of cutting and threading when only a small extension is needed. The shortest is a close nipple, with threads along its entire length. Short nipples have ½ inch or so between the threads. Other nipples may be anywhere from 2 to 24 inches long, and even longer in the larger sizes of pipe.

Elbows (ells, Ls) join two pieces of pipe at an angle of either 90 degrees or 45 degrees. Reducing elbows join pipes of different sizes at an angle of 90 or 45 degrees. Street elbows for threaded pipe have an inside thread (female) on one end and an outside thread (male) on the other end to connect to another fitting, such as a coupling or a union.

Tees join two pipes to a third at a 90-degree angle. Reducing tees join three pipes of two or three different sizes. There are various combinations of reducing tees; for example: ¾-¾-½-inch, ¾-½-¾-inch, ¾-½-½ inch, 1-¾-½-inch.

Cross tees join four pipes at 90-degree angles to one another. Reducing crosses also come in various size combinations, the same as reducing tees.

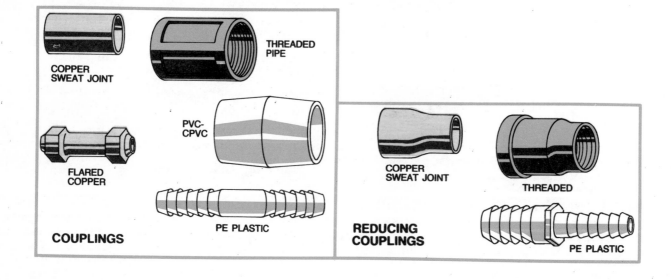

COPPER SWEAT JOINT

THREADED PIPE

FLARED COPPER

PVC-CPVC

PE PLASTIC

COUPLINGS

COPPER SWEAT JOINT

THREADED

PE PLASTIC

REDUCING COUPLINGS

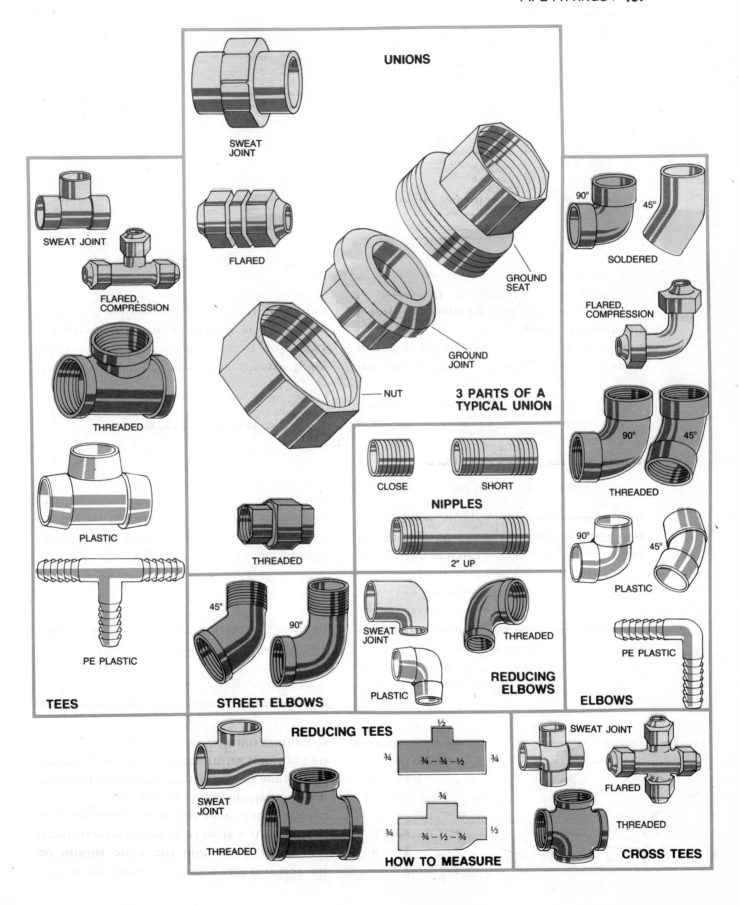

UNIONS

SWEAT
JOINT

FLARED

GROUND
SEAT

GROUND
JOINT

NUT

3 PARTS OF A
TYPICAL UNION

THREADED

SWEAT JOINT

FLARED,
COMPRESSION

THREADED

PLASTIC

PE PLASTIC

TEES

SOLDERED

FLARED,
COMPRESSION

THREADED

PLASTIC

PE PLASTIC

ELBOWS

90°   45°

90°   45°

90°   45°

CLOSE   SHORT

NIPPLES

2" UP

45°   90°

STREET ELBOWS

SWEAT
JOINT   THREADED

PLASTIC

**REDUCING
ELBOWS**

REDUCING TEES

SWEAT
JOINT

THREADED

½

¾   ¾ – ¾ – ½   ¾

¾

¾   ¾ – ½ – ¾   ½

HOW TO MEASURE

SWEAT JOINT

FLARED

THREADED

CROSS TEES

Water Supply Lines

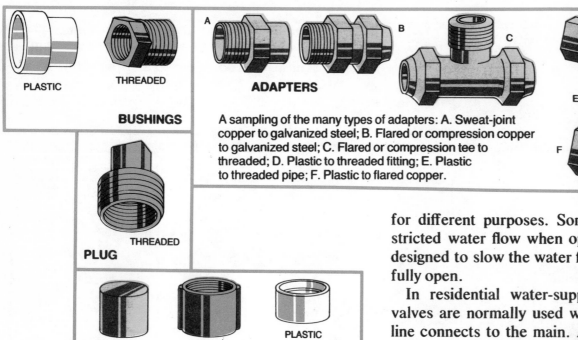

PLASTIC   THREADED

BUSHINGS

ADAPTERS

A sampling of the many types of adapters: A. Sweat-joint
copper to galvanized steel; B. Flared or compression copper
to galvanized steel; C. Flared or compression tee to
threaded; D. Plastic to threaded fitting; E. Plastic
to threaded pipe; F. Plastic to flared copper.

THREADED

PLUG

SWEAT JOINT   THREADED   PLASTIC

CAPS

Bushings are inserted into a coupling or
other fitting to reduce the size.

Adapters are used to join pipes of different materials; for example, sweat-jointed
copper or solvent-welded plastic to threaded galvanized steel.

Plugs seal off the female end of fittings.
Caps close off the end of a pipe.

VALVES

Wherever a water line may have to be
shut off at times for repair or replacement
of fixtures, a valve should be located in the
line. Valves used in residential plumbing
are usually of cast bronze, although some
plastic valves are made for use with plastic
piping. The brass valves can be used in
either copper or galvanized steel water
lines without the need of any special connectors, except where the water is highly
corrosive. Then a dielectric fitting should
be used to join the different metals.

There are many different types of valves

for different purposes. Some allow unrestricted water flow when open; others are
designed to slow the water flow even when
fully open.

In residential water-supply lines, gate
valves are normally used where the house
line connects to the main. A gate valve is
intended to completely shut off or open a
water line, but not to control flow. A wedge
is moved to close the waterway. When the
valve is open the flow of water is virtually
unrestricted. Dirt or other foreign matter in
the valve seat may prevent full closing, or
the seat or wedge may wear out in time. If
this happens, the valve should be replaced.

Globe valves are the most commonly
used types for residential water-supply
lines. They can withstand frequent opening
and closing and relatively high water pressure. The design of the globe valve constricts the waterway, so they are also used
to control the volume of flow.

A globe valve contains two chambers
separated by a partition. Water flowing
through must change course several times,
thus slowing it down. Turning the handle of
the valve increases or decreases the opening of the passage. It is fairly easy for the
do-it-yourselfer to repair a globe valve
when something goes wrong (see PAGE
449).

Angle valves are similar to globe valves,
but the ports are at right angles to each other. Since the 90-degree change of direction
constricts water flow, the internal design of
an angle valve does not include the globe

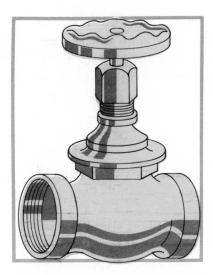

Gate valve.

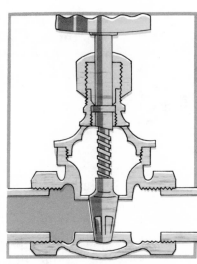

Cutaway: gate valve closed.

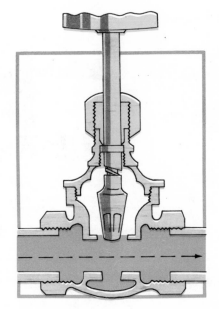

Cutaway: gate valve open.

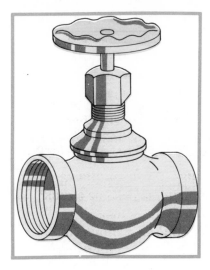

Globe valve.

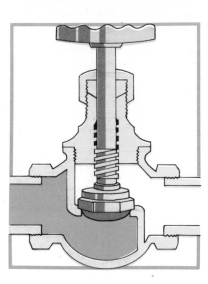

Cutaway: globe valve closed.

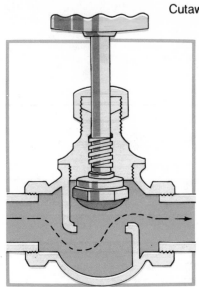

Cutaway: globe valve open.

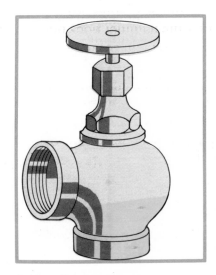

Angle valve

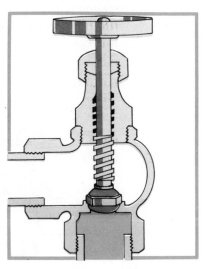

Cutaway: angle valve closed.

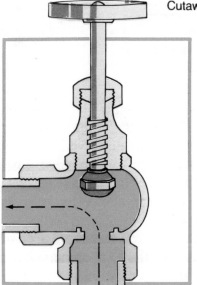

Cutaway: angle valve open.

Water Supply Lines

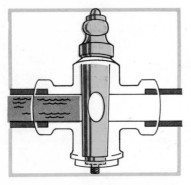
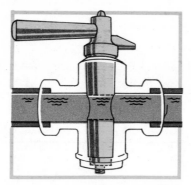

Cutaway: ground key valve closed (left), open (right).

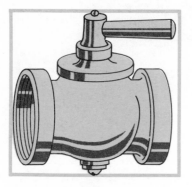
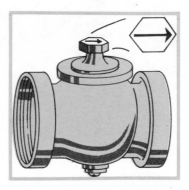

Ground key valve with handle in open position.

Ground key valve with control nut.

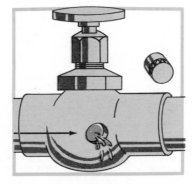

Bleeder valve.

Remove plug to drain.

valve's partition. The water changes direction only once; thus, despite its external shape, the angle valve allows a less restricted flow than a globe valve. Installed where supply lines must make a right-angle turn, angle valves eliminate the need for an elbow.

Ground key valves are used mostly in gas lines, but they are sometimes found in water lines. A tapered ground plug inside the valve seats into a matched ground body. A hole through the plug allows the water to pass through, although somewhat restricting the flow because it is smaller than the piping. A lever or nut controls the on-off action; a quarter turn opens or closes the line. On handle types, the position of the handle indicates whether open or shut; when the handle parallels the water line, the valve is open. On nut types, an arrow usually indicates the direction of water flow.

Drainable or bleeder valves should be installed to control the flow of water to outside connections, such as the faucet to which you attach your garden hose. The workings of this type of valve are similar to the globe valve, but it includes a cap or screw on the side. When the water to the outside is turned off for the winter, this cap or screw is removed to drain water remaining in the line to prevent freezing and possible bursting of the pipe. Drainable valves must be installed with the drain opening on the nonpressure (outer) side of the valve seat.

Pressure flush valves are sometimes used to allow replacing of the water in a toilet bowl directly from the supply line, without the need for a toilet tank. Because they require relatively large-diameter lines, they are rarely used in residential plumbing installations, where they would monopolize the water flow when the toilet was flushed. However, they may be found in some apartment bathrooms as well as commercial and industrial plumbing systems.

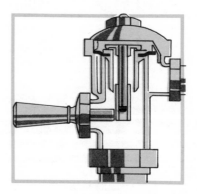

Pressure flush valve.

Water Supply Lines

A pressure flush valve consists of two chambers—upper and lower—separated by a rubber diaphragm, which is held in place by equal water pressure on both sides. When the valve handle is activated, water in the upper chamber is released, and pressure in the lower chamber forces the diaphragm up into the head of the valve. Water then rushes through the valve into the toilet bowl until the valve closes automatically after a set interval.

Check valves allow water to flow in one direction only, operating automatically to prevent backflow. Some plumbing codes require the installation of a check valve in a cold-water line between the meter and the water heater. Check valves are also used to prevent water pumped to an overhead tank (such as in a hot-water heating system) from flowing back when the pump stops. The most common type of check valve has a swinging gate that opens in only one direction to allow water through; pressure from the opposite direction forces it shut.

Temperature-pressure relief valves are installed on water-heating equipment (hot-water heater, boiler). They are important safety devices; if all other shutoff systems fail, they will release steam that has built up inside the tank, relieving it of the danger of explosion.

FAUCETS

Faucets are at the end of most water-supply lines (except those to toilets, washers, and certain other appliances). Two basic types are found in most residential systems: compression and noncompression.

Compression faucets regulate water flow by means of a lever, T, cross, ball, or other type of handle that turns a threaded spindle. When the spindle is all the way down, a washer or disc on its lower end is pressed against a smoothly ground seat, closing off the flow opening. When the spindle is

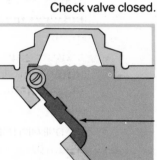

Check valve open.

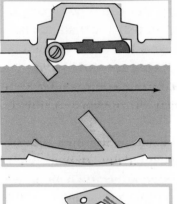

Check valve closed.

Temperature-pressure relief valve.

Simple compression-type faucet.

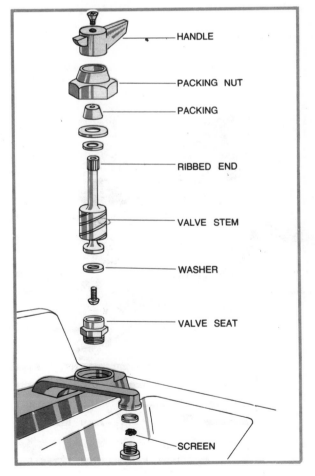

HANDLE

PACKING NUT

PACKING

RIBBED END

VALVE STEM

WASHER

VALVE SEAT

SCREEN

raised off the seat, water can flow through, its rate of flow regulated by the distance between the spindle and the seat. A mixer-type compression faucet is actually two individual faucets—one controlling hot water and the other cold—that share a single spout.

If the washer and seat do not make a firm contact at all points, the faucet will leak. This usually is a sign of a worn washer, which can easily be replaced. Many faucets have removable seats that can be replaced when they are worn. Seats that are not removable can be reground if they become worn, nicked, or damaged. All these repairs are detailed on PAGES 447-449.

A noncompression faucet has a single lever or knob that mixes hot and cold water. How this is done varies according to the manufacturer. One type utilizes a ball that is rotated within the faucet to regulate both water and flow. Another type has a

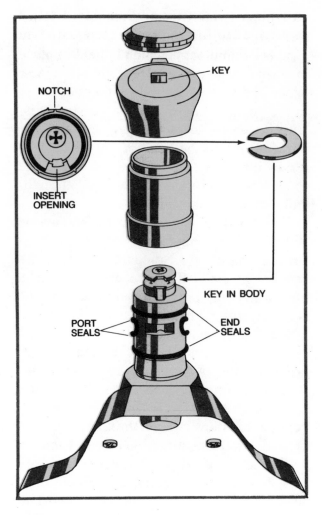

Typical cartridge-type noncompression faucet.

Ball-type noncompression faucet.

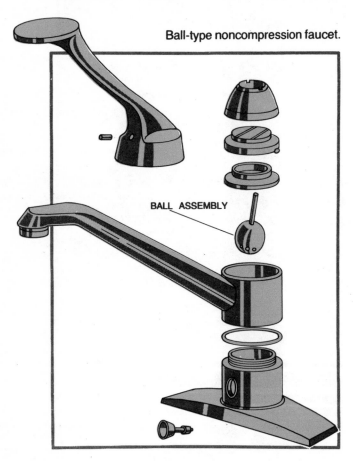

Hose faucet.

cartridge at the top of the faucet with several ports to regulate the water. Repairs of noncompression faucets usually involve replacement of part or all of the mixture and flow control. Since they vary greatly in design, always save the manufacturer's in-

Water Supply Lines

structions (which usually include detailed diagrams) for future repair reference when you install noncompression faucets.

Hose faucets are heavy brass units made for outdoor installation, but with the water-flow valves located inside the building, controlled by elongated stems. Sometimes called frostproof faucets, they eliminate the need for inside shutoff valves.

In older plumbing systems, other types of faucets are sometimes found. The Fuller ball faucet has a hard rubber or composition ball fastened to a shaft with an eccentric end. When the faucet handle is closed, the ball is drawn tightly against the opening, shutting off the water flow.

A ground key faucet is similar to a ground key valve. A tapered cylindrical brass plunger fits snugly into a sleeve in the body of the faucet. The plunger has a hole or slot running horizontally through it, corresponding to a similarly shaped opening in the faucet body. A handle turns the plunger; when the handle is parallel to the faucet body, the openings are in line and water passes through.

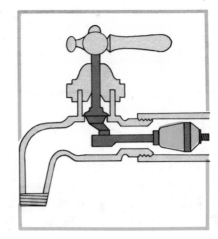

Fuller ball faucet.

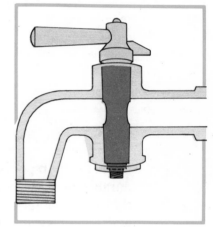

Ground key faucet.

Water Supply Lines

5

Drainage Pipes and Fittings

G ETTING rid of water and waste is even more important—for health and
sanitary reasons—than bringing water into the home fixtures. Drain-
waste-vent systems are closely governed by plumbing codes. Before making
any additions or alterations to the DWV system in your home, be sure to
check the local plumbing code. Materials used for DWV lines include cast
iron, galvanized steel, copper, and some types of plastic.

CAST-IRON PIPE

Cast-iron pipe is extremely strong and
durable, and is generally considered to be
the best material for residential drain-
waste-vent systems. It can be used above
or below ground and is resistant to just
about all corrosive materials. It comes in
2-, 3-, and 4-inch diameters (inside), and 5-
and 10-foot lengths.

The most common type of cast iron pipe
has a hub or "bell" at one end and a beaded
"spigot" at the other for connecting to
fittings and other lengths of pipe. A relatively new type of cast iron pipe eliminates
this hub; both ends are straight, and connections are made by means of a neoprene
sleeve inside a metal sleeve, which is tightened over the pipes and fittings.

When measuring hubless pipe, measure
tight—the ends of joining pipes or pipes
and fittings butt together. When measuring
standard cast iron pipe, allow additional
length for fitting into the bell or hub. Hub
allowances are 2¼ inches for 2-inch pipe,
2½ inches for 3-inch pipe, and 3 inches for
4-inch pipe. When pieces of pipe less than 5
feet long are needed, use double-hub pipe,
which has a hub on each end. When the
pipe is cut, each piece will still have a hub,
which is necessary for joining (the spigot
bead is not). With standard bell-and-spigot

Bell-and-spigot pipe.

Hubless pipe.

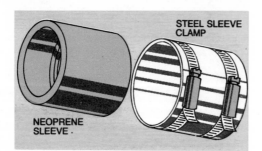

STEEL SLEEVE
CLAMP

Hubless
pipe
connector.

NEOPRENE
SLEEVE

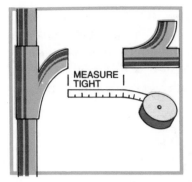

Measuring hubless pipe.

2. Make hacksaw cut.

3. Break pipe with chisel.

Measuring bell-and-spigot pipe.

To join two lengths of hubless pipe, or a pipe and a fitting, slip the neoprene sleeve over one pipe, and the metal sleeve (usually stainless steel) over that. Fit the other pipe or fitting into the neoprene sleeve until both

Double-hub pipe.

1. Slip sleeve over hubless pipe.

pipe, the leftover spigot end would be useless; and would have to be discarded.

Mark the line of cut around the pipe with a chalk line. Make sure it is straight—square ends are especially important when you are using hubless pipe. Make a 1/16-inch-deep cut all around the pipe with a hacksaw. Place the pipe across a piece of 2 x 4 laid flat on the floor or the ground. Using a cold chisel and hammer, strike lightly all around the scored line. Continue striking around the pipe, hitting the chisel harder each time, until the piece needed breaks off cleanly at the cut.

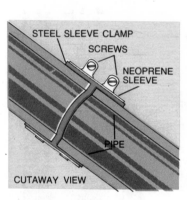

STEEL SLEEVE CLAMP
SCREWS
NEOPRENE SLEEVE
PIPE
CUTAWAY VIEW

2. Fit pipes together.

3. Tighten with torque wrench.

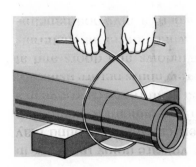

1. Mark chalk line around pipe.

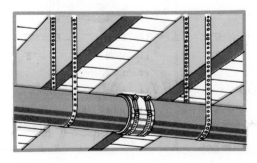

Supporting horizontal runs.

Drainage Pipes and Fittings

pipes butt against the separator ring inside the sleeve. Then tighten the clamp screws on the metal outer sleeve. Tightening pressure is critical, and a torque wrench should be used to ensure that the clamps are tightened to the manufacturer's specifications (60 inch-pounds is the normal torque). Horizontal runs of hubless pipe should be supported near all joints.

Joining bell-and-spigot cast-iron pipes and fittings is quite a bit more complex. Molten lead is poured into the joint and tamped to seal connections. The ends of pieces to be joined must be clean and dry. Moisture will cause the molten lead to fly out of the joint, and serious injury may result. Wear safety goggles and heavy gloves when pouring lead, and keep out of range even though the joint appears dry.

When erecting a vertical drain line, posi-

tion each piece with the bell end up. Place the spigot end of the next higher section into the bell to its full depth, and temporarily secure it in position with wood or other bracing. Check with a level or plumb bob to

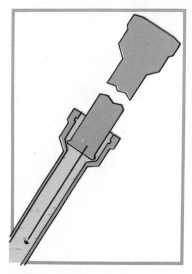

Positioning bell-and-spigot pipe.

Pouring a joint safely.

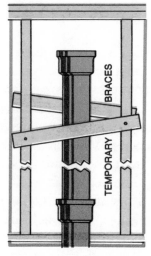

Temporary bracing.

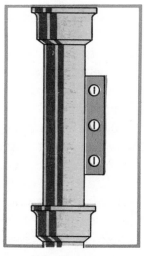

Check with a level.

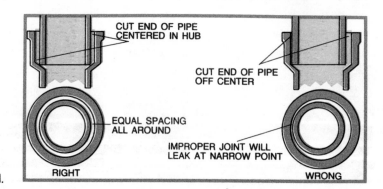

Center spigot in bell.

make sure that the two sections to be joined are perfectly plumb (vertical). Also make certain that the spigot end is centered in the bell; otherwise, a faulty joint will be the result.

Pack oakum around the pipe inside the bell. Oakum comes in rope form. For 4-inch pipe, about 5 feet are needed for a joint; for 3-inch pipe, 4½ feet; for 2-inch, 3 feet. Wrap oakum completely around the pipe and drive it to the bottom of the hub with a yarning iron, compressing it firmly to make a solid bed for the lead and prevent its leaking into the pipe. Continue wrapping, packing, and compressing until the joint is filled to within 1 inch or ¾ inch from the top of the bell. (Check your local plumbing code on this point; some codes require 1 inch of lead in a joint, others only ¾ inch.)

Make sure that the oakum is securely packed down, as, when lead is poured, projecting strands would cause minute ducts to form in the joint, causing leakage.

For small pours, you can use a blowtorch to melt lead in the melting pot. If the line will require several pours, use a plumber's furnace—but use it with caution. In fact, caution is the watchword during all phases of the leaded-joint procedure.

Light the furnace and place the lead in the pot. If your local code requires 1 inch of lead in the joint, use 1 pound of lead for each inch of pipe diameter. If it requires ¾ inch, use 3 pounds for 4-inch pipe, 2¼ pounds for 3-inch pipe, and 1½ pounds for 2-inch pipe.

Heat the ladle by placing it next to the melting pot; dipping a cold ladle into hot lead could cause the lead to spit out of the pot. When the lead is molten, ladle it out and pour it evenly into the hub around the joint, continuing in a single pour until the lead is about ⅛ inch above the top of the hub.

When the lead cools, pack it against the

Wrap oakum.

Packing oakum.

Heat with blowtorch.

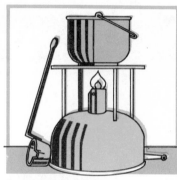
Plumber's furnace.

Ladle lead.

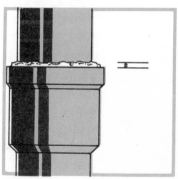
Fill joint.

Packing with outside calking iron.

Packing with inside calking iron.

Drainage Pipes and Fittings

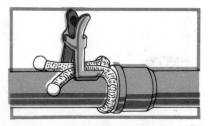
Wrap joint runner around pipe.

Horizontal pour of lead.

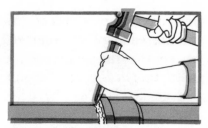
Cut off surplus lead.

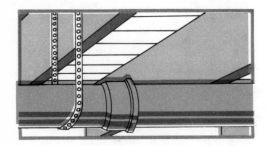
Support should be provided near all joints.

hub by tapping all around with an outside calking iron, tamping it firmly to make an airtight and watertight seal. Similarly, use an inside calking iron to pack the lead against the pipe.

When making a horizontal leaded joint, an asbestos joint runner must be wrapped around the pipe, to prevent the lead from running out of the hub as it is poured. Center the spigot in the hub and pack in oakum as above. Place the joint runner around the pipe, fitting it as tightly as possible just above the hub, with the runner's clamp at the top of the pipe to form a channel for pouring. Tap the runner snugly against the hub.

Make the joint with a single pour, letting the lead overflow the runner. When the lead has cooled, remove the joint runner. Cut off surplus lead with a cold chisel and hammer, then calk the joint with outside and inside irons as above.

Support should be provided near all joints in a horizontal drainage line.

GALVANIZED STEEL PIPE

Threaded galvanized steel pipe is often used in conjunction with cast-iron pipe for branch drains and vent lines of 2 inches or less. It is cut, threaded, and assembled the same as steel water-supply pipe (see PAGE 401). Never bury steel pipe under the ground.

COPPER DWV PIPE

Copper DWV pipe has thinner walls than copper water-supply pipe, since it does not normally have to withstand pressure. For most copper DWV pipe systems, 1½-, 2-, and 3-inch (inside diameter) pipe is used. It comes in 20-foot lengths. Only soldered fittings are used for copper DWV lines. The pipe is cut and joined the same as rigid copper pipe, described on PAGE 398.

PLASTIC DWV PIPE

Plastic DWV pipe is freeze-proof, rust-proof, and corrosion-proof and resists acids and alkalies. It is also economical, lightweight, and very easy to install, even for amateur plumbers. No special tools and only minimal skills (such as the ability to measure accurately) are needed.

That's the good news. The bad news is that many plumbing codes have not yet caught up with the good news, so make sure you check out the code in your municipality before you install plastic DWV pipe.

The materials used for residential DWV pipe are polyvinyl chloride (PVC), which is light in color, and acrylonitrile butadiene styrene (ABS), which is black. Some codes may allow only one or the other. Solvent-welded joints are used in DWV runs, and each type of pipe has its own solvent. If you are joining PVC pipe with ABS fittings (or vice versa), a special solvent must be used.

Both PVC and ABS DWV pipe come in 1½-, 2-, 3-inch, and larger sizes. The dimensions refer to nominal inside diameter; the outside diameter of the thicker-walled ABS pipe is greater than that of PVC. Both types are usually stocked in 10-foot lengths.

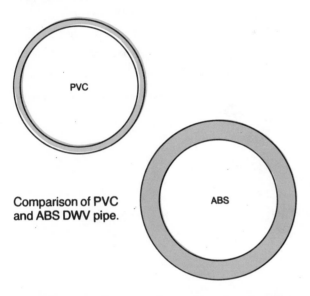

Comparison of PVC and ABS DWV pipe.

Measure lines using the face-to-face method (the distance between the two fittings) and adding the amount the pipe will penetrate the fittings. Both types of plastic DWV pipe are easily cut with a handsaw. Solvent-welding is the same as described for plastic water-supply pipe on PAGE 403.

Sawing plastic pipe.

FIXTURE DRAIN LINES

Exposed drainage lines for such fixtures as sinks, lavatories, and some types of bathtubs are usually of chrome-plated brass

Fixture drain.

for appearance. A P or S trap (see PAGE 380) is normally located in this line. Fixture drains are fitted with slip nuts for fastening.

DWV FITTINGS

Fittings for use with galvanized steel DWV pipe are the same as those for galvanized water-supply pipe (in larger sizes, of course), as described on PAGE 401. For cast-iron, copper, and plastic DWV pipe, the variety of fittings available to get the line where it has to go is even greater than that available for their water-supply counterparts.

Couplings or sleeves connect copper or plastic pipes. (Cast-iron pipe connections are detailed earlier in this chapter.)

Bends correspond to elbows in water-

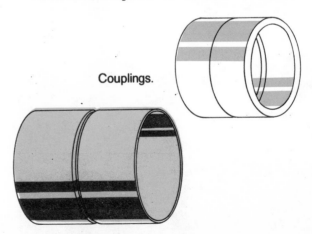

Couplings.

supply lines. A ¼ bend joins two pipes at a 90-degree angle; a ⅛ bend joins two pipes at a 45-degree angle. There are also reducing bends, double bends (somewhat like tees), long bends (also called closet bends and designed for connecting to toilets), and sweeps, which are gently curving bends.

There are tees, reducing tees, long tees, and short tees. There are also Ys, double Ys, reducing Ys, even TYs and double TYs. And P traps and running traps. Crosses. Tapped fittings for connecting cast iron with galvanized steel branches. Offsets to get the pipe past obstructions. Cleanout plugs.

In fact, there are fittings to handle just about any conceivable DWV situation. The most commonly used are shown here. The illustration also shows how reducing tees and Ys are measured.

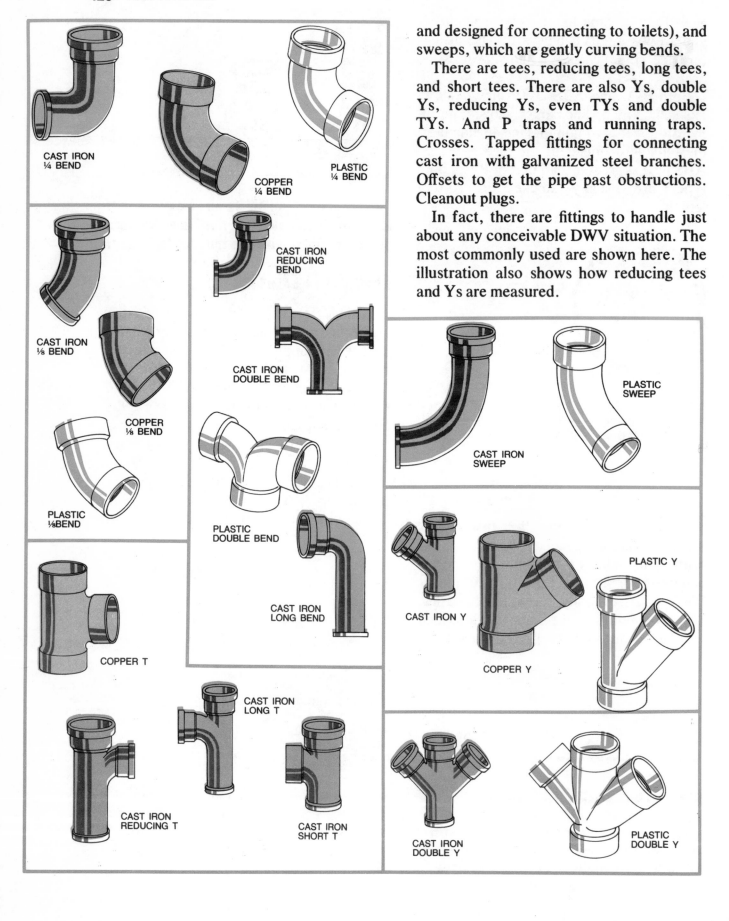

CAST IRON ¼ BEND

COPPER ¼ BEND

PLASTIC ¼ BEND

CAST IRON ⅛ BEND

COPPER ⅛ BEND

PLASTIC ⅛ BEND

CAST IRON REDUCING BEND

CAST IRON DOUBLE BEND

PLASTIC DOUBLE BEND

CAST IRON LONG BEND

COPPER T

CAST IRON REDUCING T

CAST IRON LONG T

CAST IRON SHORT T

CAST IRON SWEEP

PLASTIC SWEEP

CAST IRON Y

COPPER Y

PLASTIC Y

CAST IRON DOUBLE Y

PLASTIC DOUBLE Y

Drainage Pipes and Fittings

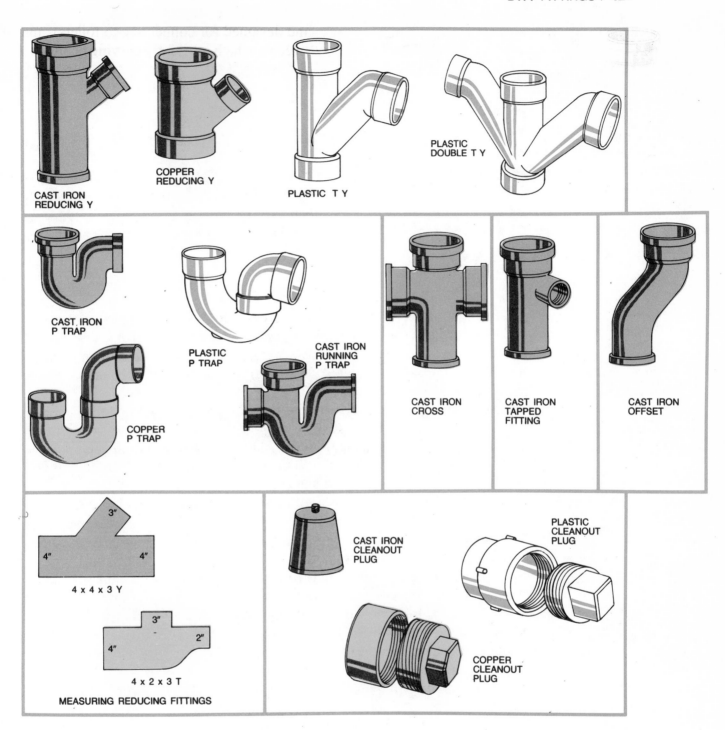

CAST IRON
REDUCING Y

COPPER
REDUCING Y

PLASTIC T Y

PLASTIC
DOUBLE T Y

CAST IRON
P TRAP

PLASTIC
P TRAP

CAST IRON
RUNNING
P TRAP

COPPER
P TRAP

CAST IRON
CROSS

CAST IRON
TAPPED
FITTING

CAST IRON
OFFSET

3"

4"   4"

4 x 4 x 3 Y

3"

4"   2"

4 x 2 x 3 T

MEASURING REDUCING FITTINGS

CAST IRON
CLEANOUT
PLUG

PLASTIC
CLEANOUT
PLUG

COPPER
CLEANOUT
PLUG

Drainage Pipes and Fittings

6

Selecting and Installing Plumbing Fittings and Fixtures

Y OU CAN BUY plumbing fixtures at bargain-basement prices—but don't.
They are generally poor investments and wear out much more quickly
than higher-priced ones. That doesn't mean you should automatically go for
top-of-the-line platinum-plated faucets and a marble bathtub, but do avoid
the cheapies.

Quality fittings and fixtures are built to take a lot of abuse and to last a long
time, which they do. Fittings such as faucets become worn by frequent usage, as does any mechanical device. Often, worn parts can be replaced
(PAGES 447-461) and the fitting will be as good as new. But eventually it will
have to be discarded and a new one installed.

Sinks, lavatories, bathtubs, and toilets (except for the flush mechanisms)
are less prone to wear and might well last the lifetime of a house, unless they
become damaged (severely chipped porcelain in a kitchen sink, for example,
or a cracked and leaking toilet tank). But they are frequently replaced for
cosmetic reasons, as a major part of a general updating of a kitchen or bathroom. Modern fixtures are "decorator-designed" in styles and colors that
make them an integral part of a room—particularly a bathroom—motif.
There is also a trend to design such fixtures as tubs and toilets to fit people,
rather than making people fit the fixtures, and this may be another reason for
installing new ones.

Just about any plumbing fitting or fixture you may buy, from a faucet to a
bathtub, will include specific installation instructions, since these vary from
unit to unit and manufacturer to manufacturer. These instructions should be
read and followed carefully. Some general guidelines for selection and installation are given here.

Unless you are undertaking a major remodeling—a bathroom, for example, in which you are rearranging toilet, tub, and lavatory locations—new
fixtures should be as close in size as possible to the old ones to minimize
structural and piping changes. Measure carefully, not only the space available, but also the supply-pipe sizes. When replacing smaller fittings such as
faucets, it is best to take the old one along when buying the new one.

FIXTURE SUPPLY LINES

Fixture supply lines carry water from the piping within the wall or beneath the floor to the faucet, toilet, or other point of use. They are either rigid or flexible, and are chrome-plated for appearance since they are often exposed. They may be replaced at the same time new fixtures are installed. They may also develop leaks or become damaged, necessitating replacement.

To replace a fixture supply line (or any other fitting or fixture), the water must first be shut off. If there is a supply stop valve where the water line comes out of the wall or floor, turn it off. If there is not, turn off the water at the nearest valve you can find in the supply line (probably in the basement or crawl space) or, if necessary, turn off the main valve, shutting off all water in the house (it's best to warn the family before you do this).

If the supply line is feeding a faucet, open the faucet to drain out as much water as you can. If it is to a toilet, flush the toilet to remove the water from the tank. Place a bucket or basin beneath the connection to catch the water remaining in the line when you remove it.

Use an open-end or adjustable wrench to loosen the nuts holding the old line at top and bottom (on sinks and lavatories, you may need a basin wrench to loosen the upper nuts; and if you intend to salvage the nuts, wrap them first with tape to prevent damage or marring by the wrench jaws). Unscrew the nuts and pull out the old line.

If there is no stop valve below the fixture supply, you might want to install one now (see below). Otherwise, simply install the new line. Fixture supply lines are formed at one end to fit either faucet connections or toilet connections. The lower end is plain. Use a tubing cutter to cut the new line at the lower end so that it is the same length as

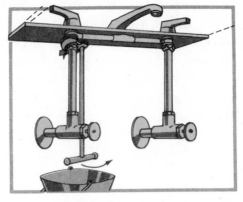

1. Loosen upper nut.

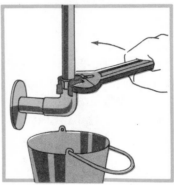

2. Loosen lower nut.

3. Cut tubing to fit.

4. Bend if necessary.

FAUCET SHANK

5. Place upper end over opening.

6. Fit lower end.

7. Tighten with wrench.

the old one. (For a completely new installation, measure from stop valve to faucet connection; if this is not a perfectly straight line, use a flexible fixture supply line and bend gently to fit.)

The lower end is connected to the supply stop by a flared joint or a compression fitting. For a flared joint, slip the lower nut over the tubing (the upper nut should already be on the tubing). Clamp the tubing in a flaring tool and form the bell-shaped flare (see FLARING TOOL, PAGE 395). Remove the tubing from the tool.

Place the formed upper end of the fixture supply line squarely over the faucet or toilet connection and hand-tighten the nut. If the line has a compression fitting at the lower end, place the nut over the tubing and slip the sleeve over the end. Fit the flare or the compression nut to the supply stop valve and hand-tighten the nut. Tighten both nuts with a wrench, after wrapping them with tape to protect against damage. Do not overtighten—this can weaken the joint and may even break the connection. Turn on the water to test the connections. If they leak, tighten the nuts a bit more.

FIXTURE SUPPLY STOP VALVES

When a supply stop becomes too worn to do its job of controlling the flow of water to a fixture, it should be replaced. The procedure is the same whether it is an angle valve connected to a wall supply pipe or a straight valve connected to a pipe coming through the floor.

First turn off the water at a valve below the supply stop valve, usually in the basement or crawl space. If no other valve can be found in the supply line, turn off the main valve where the water line enters the house. Open the faucet or flush the toilet above the supply stop, and place a bucket

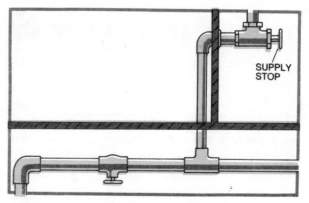

SUPPLY STOP

1. Turn off water in line behind stop.

2. Remove supply line.

or basin below the valve to catch water remaining in the line. Wrap tape around the nut holding the supply line to the stop and loosen the nut with a wrench. Remove the supply line from the stop.

If the old stop valve is soldered to a copper water-supply pipe, water remaining in the pipe must be drained before the stop can be disconnected. You can do this at some previous point in the supply line (a faucet that is on the same branch on the floor below, for example). Or you can disassemble the old valve and let the water flow out into a bucket. Then use a propane torch to heat the joint and melt the solder; pull off the old valve.

The new valve must be disassembled before being soldered onto the pipe, so that it will not be damaged by the heat. Clean the end of the pipe with steel wool or emery cloth; also rub the inside of the stop fitting. Apply flux and solder the fitting to the pipe, as described under Working with Rigid

3. Disassemble old valve.

4. Heat and remove.

5. Disassemble and attach new valve; clean off pipe.

6. Attach supply line.

7. Check flare.

8. Tighten nut.

9. Threaded pipe installation.

Copper Pipe on PAGE 398. Allow to cool and reassemble the valve. Attach the fixture supply to the new stop valve before turning on the water.

It is not necessary to disassemble the old supply stop if it is connected to a flexible copper supply pipe with a compression or flared fitting. Just make sure that you buy a replacement stop valve with the same type of fitting. Keep a bucket in place below the valve as you loosen the nut holding it to the pipe; let the water drain out the end of the pipe. If the joint is flared, check the flare on the pipe to make sure it is perfectly round. If it is bent, re-flare the end of the pipe (see Working with Flexible Copper Tubing, (PAGE 399). Start the nut onto the new stop by hand; finish tightening with an open-end or adjustable wrench after wrapping tape around the nut.

If the water pipe is galvanized steel, use a wrench to remove the old stop valve. Clean off the pipe threads with a rag and apply

new pipe joint compound or Teflon tape to the threads (PAGE 402). Screw on the new stop valve, starting it by hand to make sure the threads are aligned, then tightening it with a wrench.

P and S TRAPS

The fixture drain immediately below sinks and lavatories usually includes a P or an S trap, sometimes formed by one or more J bends (you have to know your alphabet to be a plumber). When these fittings corrode or leaks develop at the joints, they have to be replaced.

Place a bucket or basin below the trap to catch water that remains in the fitting. Remove the slip nuts at both ends, using a large adjustable wrench or a channel-lock pliers. Pull off the trap.

Remove the nut and washer from the new fitting and slide them (nut first) over the sink tailpiece (the part of the drain ex-

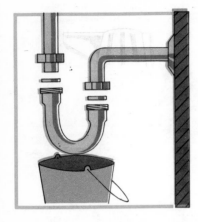

Remove old J bend (shown on a P trap).

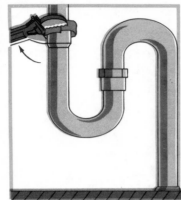

Install new J bend (shown on an S trap; procedure is the same for either one).

tending through the bottom). Slide the new trap over the tailpiece and fit the other end onto the outflow pipe. Hand-tighten the nuts at both ends, then wrap tape around the nuts and finish tightening with an adjustable wrench or channel-lock pliers.

KITCHEN FAUCETS

Most modern kitchen sink faucets are mixer types. They can have either an exposed deck (the deck is the section that connects the various components of the faucet), also called top-mount, or a concealed deck, or bottom-mount. On almost all types, the hot- and cold-water supply lines are on 8-inch centers—that is, 8 inches from the center of one pipe to the center of

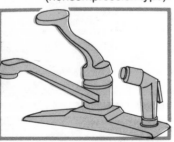

Exposed deck faucet (noncompression type).

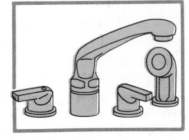

Concealed deck faucet (compression type).

the other. Noncompression (single-control) faucets are similar to compression (individual hot and cold controls). Thus, there is usually no problem in substituting one type for another. Some adjustment may be necessary in the fixture supply line—if it is too long for the new installation, it can be bent slightly to fit; if it is too short, it will have to be replaced.

To remove the old faucet, first shut off the water, either at the supply stop valves or at some other valves in the hot- and cold-water supply lines. If necessary, turn off the main valve. Open the faucet to drain out as much water as you can. With a basin wrench, remove the nuts holding the supply lines to the faucet. Then remove the hex nuts holding the fixture to the sink. On an exposed-deck type, these are beneath the sink and are best reached with a basin wrench. On a concealed-deck faucet, the nuts are normally above the sink counter, usually concealed by caps of some sort. Unscrew (or raise) the caps and remove the nuts with an adjustable wrench. If the old faucet has a spray hose attachment, remove the nut holding the hose to the faucet. The old faucet can now be removed.

Wipe off the top of the sink counter where the new faucet is to be installed. Most exposed-deck faucets have a built-in gasket on the bottom; if yours does not, spread a bead of plumber's putty (available at hardware and plumbing supply stores) around the perimeter where the new faucet is to be placed. For concealed-deck faucets, rubber washers are supplied to seal around the parts that penetrate the counter.

Remove the spray hose from the new faucet (if it has one) and set the faucet in position. Tighten the nuts on the faucet shanks (from above or below, depending on the type), then reconnect the supply lines. Pass the spray hose through the guide sleeve in the sink top and attach it to the faucet connection. Turn on the water to

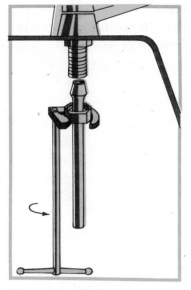

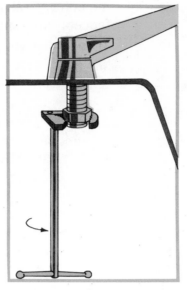

Remove
holding nuts
(exposed deck).

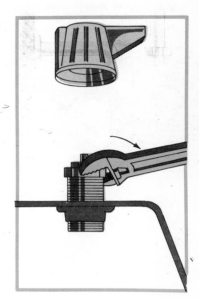

Remove supply line nuts.

Remove
holding nuts
(concealed deck).

Remove spray hose (far left).
Connect supply lines (left).

Connect spray hose.

Slip-nut connection.

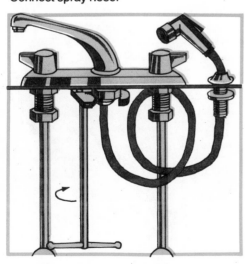

Wall-mount mixer faucet.

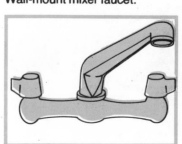

Selecting and Installing Plumbing Fittings and Fixtures

Single faucet, male.   Single faucet, female.

check the installation. If there is leakage at any joints, tightening will usually correct the problem.

On some kitchen sinks, usually vintage models, the backsplash is an integral part, and the faucets are mounted in the vertical section. In such installations, the supply pipes come directly out of the wall. Mixer-type faucets for such wall mounts are also on 8-inch centers. To replace these, first shut off the water at the nearest valves (probably in the basement or crawl space).

Then use a basin wrench to remove the slip nuts behind the backsplash that hold the faucet shanks. Remove the old faucet, set the new one in place (with washers over the shanks) and fasten with the slip nuts.

If your home and its plumbing are really of an early era, it is possible that the kitchen sink has single faucets coming out of the backsplash. These can usually be replaced by unscrewing them from the supply pipes and screwing new ones in place (after first turning off the water supply, of course). However, check the old faucet before buying a new one; some have male (outside) threads, others female (inside), and the replacement must be of the same gender.

SINK STRAINERS

Many kitchen sinks—especially those of higher quality—have built-in strainers (rather than the lift-out kind) to trap waste and debris before it can enter the drain. The strainer also contains a mechanism to open

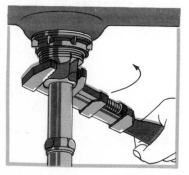

To replace sink strainer:

1. Remove slip nut.   2. Loosen large nut.

3. Apply putty around opening.

4. Insert new strainer.   5. Washers, large nut.

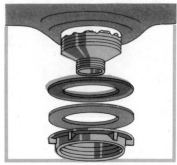

6. Tighten nut.

and close the drain, and this may become damaged. Then it must be replaced.

The strainer is normally secured by a large nut locked underneath the sink; the nut has a series of lugs on its surface. To remove the old strainer, first remove the fixture drain by loosening the slip nut with an adjustable wrench or a channel-lock pliers (as always, tape the nut first to prevent it from being marred or damaged). Then use a screwdriver and hammer to tap the lugs in a counter-clockwise direction, loosening the nut that holds the strainer. Finish removing the nut by hand. Lift the strainer out from the top of the sink.

Thoroughly clean the area all around the sink opening. Apply a bead of plumber's putty approximately ⅛-inch thick all around the opening. Remove the nut and washers from the new strainer and insert it through the opening. From beneath the sink, place the washers over the threads, then screw on the large nut, hand-tightening it. Have an assistant hold the strainer

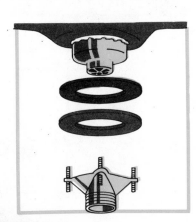

7. Place retainer over body of retainer-type strainer.

8. Tighten retainer.

from above while you tighten the nut by tapping the lugs with a screwdriver and hammer. Wipe off excess putty and connect the fixture drain to complete the installation.

Another type of replacement strainer is held in place by a retainer, making it a one-person installation. Remove the old strainer and clean around the opening as above. Apply a bead of putty around the opening. Remove the screws that hold the retainer to the new strainer body. Insert the body through the opening in the sink. Place the washer on the retainer and, from the underside of the sink, place the retainer over the strainer body. Tighten the screws on the retainer, taking a turn or two on each one, then moving to the others so that all are tightened evenly. Remove excess putty, then connect the fixture drain to the strainer.

FOOD WASTE DISPOSERS

Waste disposal units built into the kitchen sink are more popular than ever—and with good reason. What better way to get rid of food waste before it becomes smelly garbage? Although some early models sounded like a division of Patton tanks rumbling through the kitchen, and sometimes spat out or choked on large bones and other materials that they found indigestible, today's generation of disposers is quiet, efficient, and generally trouble-free.

There are two basic types: batch feed and continuous feed. Batch-feed disposers are filled with a certain level of waste, then activated by placing a cover on top. Because the cover must be in place for the machine to operate, it is considered safer; you can't accidentally dispose of your fingers by carelessly putting them into the unit.

Despite this, continuous-feed models are the more popular. They are activated by a switch separate from the unit and operate

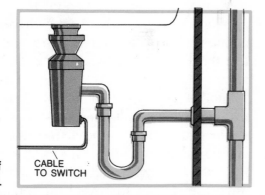

Typical plumbing of food waste disposer.

CABLE TO SWITCH

continuously as waste is being fed. Thus, they are faster. But they, too, should be covered when in operation, not only to keep out forgetful fingers, but also to prevent waste from being splashed out—especially hard bone fragments.

Installation of a disposal unit is not difficult. Most types are mounted somewhat like the strainer-with-retainer described above, although each manufacturer has his own variation on the theme. The plumbing usually consists of altering the drainage trap to meet the unit (see P and S Traps, above). Wiring should be done by a licensed electrician, following the manufacturer's instructions.

KITCHEN SINKS

"Everything *but* the kitchen sink," goes the old cliché, but sometimes a kitchen sink needs replacement too. It may become damaged and disfigured by nicks and scratches. Or you may want a larger unit, or a sparkling new one to complement a kitchen remodeling. In any event, your choice is broad.

Most of today's kitchen sinks are made of cast iron or formed steel covered with porcelain enamel, or of stainless steel. They come in many configurations. There are single-well, double-well and triple-well, the latter with a narrow and shallow depression between two large bowls. There are shallow-well and deep-well. There are shal-

low- and deep-well combinations, and large and small combinations. Whatever turns you on . . .

Sinks are usually held in place by metal clips screwed to the underside of the counter. Most cast iron and steel units are flush-mount—that is, they are flush with the surface of the counter and are framed with a metal rim. Calking beneath the rim prevents leakage. Stainless steel sinks are usually self-rimming, with a lip all around that rests on the countertop and no further frame needed. This type is somewhat easier to keep clean since there is only a single

Clips for mounting.

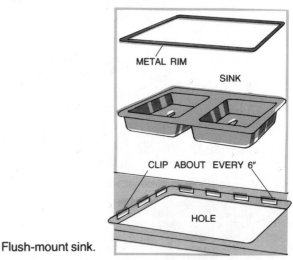

METAL RIM

SINK

CLIP ABOUT EVERY 6"

HOLE

Flush-mount sink.

Self-rimming sink.

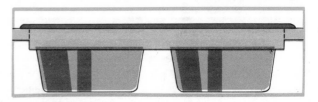

seam to trap dirt, rather than two as with a flush-mount sink.

Installation of faucets, supply lines, strainers, and traps is detailed above.

LAVATORY FAUCETS

Mixer-type compression and noncompression faucets for bathroom lavatories are similar in design and installation to kitchen sink faucets, as described earlier, except that most of them have the connections on 4-inch centers, rather than 8-inch. Many such units also include pop-up drains, controlled by a plunger or a lever on the faucet deck. The plunger or lever is attached beneath the lavatory to an adjustable lift rod that moves another rod leading to a fitting in the drain, controlling the opening-closing motion of the drain plug.

The pop-up drain is installed at the same time as the new faucet. Remove the old faucet as described under Kitchen Sink Faucets. Disconnect and remove the trap below the lavatory. Loosen the nut that holds the old drain in place and lift out the drain. Wipe the lavatory clean around the drain opening and where the faucet will be installed.

Remove the lift rod from the plunger. Set the new faucet in place, with the plunger placed through the hole between the water

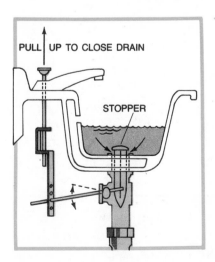

PULL UP TO CLOSE DRAIN

STOPPER

Pop-up mechanism.

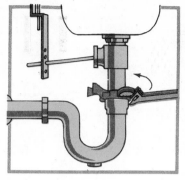

Remove trap.

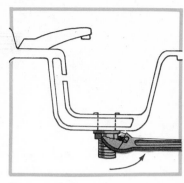

Remove drain.

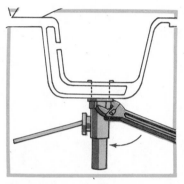

Tighten nut on drain sleeve.

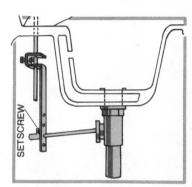

SET SCREW

Fasten lift rod.

supply holes in the lavatory. Tighten the nuts around the faucet shanks and connect the supply lines, just as for a kitchen sink faucet.

Apply a bead of plumber's putty around the drain opening. Set the drain sleeve in place and secure it by tightening the slip nut from beneath the lavatory. Fasten the pop-up drain body, following manufacturer's directions. Fasten the lift rod to the plunger, adjusting it as necessary so that the plunger or lever works freely without hitting the faucet deck.

LAVATORIES

When it is time to replace your bathroom lavatory because it is dingy or damaged or as part of a general remodeling, your choice is even wider than with the kitchen sink. The trend is toward larger basins built into vanity counters, and if space permits you may wish to plan such a unit. The basin it-

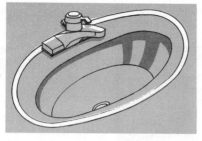
Flush-mount lavatory.

Self-rimming lavatory.

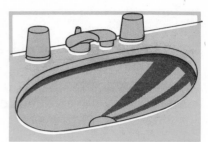
Under-counter lavatory.

self may be round or square, oval or rectangular, trapezoidal or triangular (for fitting into tight corners in tiny baths or powder rooms). It can be shallow or deep, with near-vertical or gradually sloping sides. It can be of porcelain-enameled cast iron or

formed steel or of vitreous china. Increasingly popular is the molded plastic one-piece lavatory, with integral countertop.

There are various types of lavatories for building into countertops. The flush-mount is held in place by metal angles or clips screwed to the underside of the counter; a metal frame set in a bed of sealant surrounds the lavatory. This type of lavatory is relatively inexpensive, and installation is quite easy. But dirt tends to collect between the frame and the basin and between the frame and the countertop.

The self-rimming lavatory projects above the countertop; it is installed in a sealant bed and requires no framing rim. Because there is only a single seam around the perimeter, it is fairly easy to keep clean.

Notch studs.

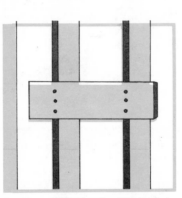
Fasten backer board.

The under-counter lavatory is mounted beneath an opening in the countertop, held in place by metal angles. Fittings for this type are located in the countertop rather than in the lavatory itself. Sealant is applied between the basin and the underside of the counter, but this area is likely to be a dirt collector.

Where available space does not allow the construction of a vanity counter around the lavatory, a wall-hung unit is the usual choice. Some types include one or more legs for support, others are simply cantilevered from the wall. Both kinds require behind-wall backing. If you are replacing an old fixture that had such backing, you can fasten the new unit to that.

In new construction, cut ¾-inch-deep x 7¼-inch-long notches in the wall studs behind where the lavatory is to be hung, with the tops of the notches at lavatory height

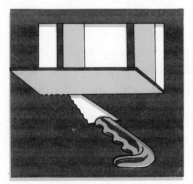
Cutting through wallboard.

Fasten brackets.

Hang lavatory.

(normally 31 inches from the floor—but there is no rule saying that you can't make it lower to accommodate the children, or higher for a family of basketball players). Clean out the wood with a sharp chisel, then use 10d nails to firmly fasten a 1 x 8 board to the notches across the studs before installing wallboard.

If you are installing a wall-hung lavatory in an existing room where there is no backing, you will have to cut through the plaster or wallboard, notch the studs as explained above and fasten the backer board. Then patch up the wall.

With the backing and the wall covering in place, heavy-duty brackets are fastened through the wallboard to the 1 x 8 board. The lavatory is then hung on these brackets. If the unit has legs, these are normally adjustable so that they rest firmly on the floor.

Installation of lavatory faucet and drain fittings is as described above.

TUB AND SHOWER FITTINGS

If you have an old-fashioned (or new-fangled) free-standing tub in your bathroom—the claw-footed off-the-floor model that is enjoying something of a renaissance in a number of exotic variations such as giant seashells—replacement of fittings is easy. The plumbing is exposed; just follow the same procedures as for replacing a kitchen sink faucet.

With the far more common built-in tub, it's a different story. Much of the plumbing is concealed within the wall. Although you may be able to replace parts of some faucets in such an installation, replacement of the complete unit means opening up the wall.

But before you tear down the wall, look at the other side. Often, the builder provides an access panel or door behind the

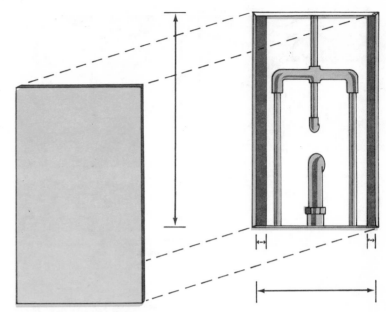

Typical access panel.

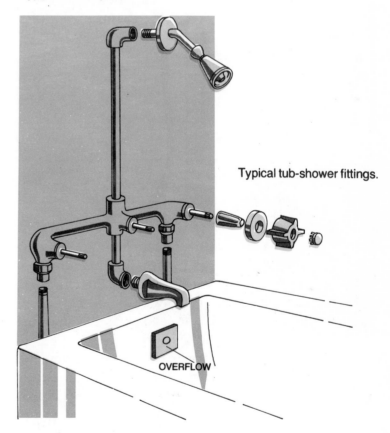

Typical tub-shower fittings.

plumbing end of the tub, in a closet or a hallway on the other side. Many building codes mandate such a panel or door. If you find no such access, it will probably be preferable for you to cut through the wallboard outside the bathroom, rather than in-

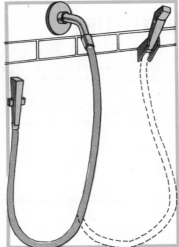

Shower-head replacement.

Hand shower replacing regular head.

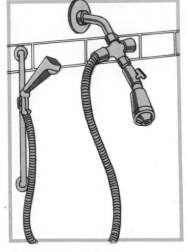

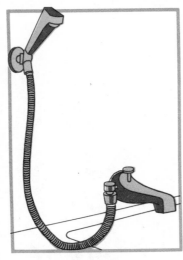

Adapter between head and hand shower.

Hand shower on diverter faucet.

head with tape and loosen it with an open-end or adjustable wrench or a channel-lock pliers. Remove the old head, start the nut on the new head by hand, then tighten it with a wrench to complete the installation.

Flexible hand showers are a convenience item that can easily be installed on an existing shower. The unit delivers the water where you want it. It can be raised or lowered, wall-hung or hand-held. Kids like it because it allows them to put the shower at their height. It is helpful for personal hygiene and localized body bathing, and provides a controlled spray whether showering or bathing. For mothers (and dads) it simplifies the bathing of infants and children. It can even be used to speed up bathroom clean-up chores.

A hand shower can be installed in place of the original shower head, simply by unscrewing the head and substituting the new unit. A special adapter can also be installed above the existing shower head that allows the installation of the flexible unit while retaining the existing fixed shower. Or the flexible shower unit can be installed on a special diverter faucet in a bath where there is no provision for a shower. A variety of accessories is available to hold the unit on the wall. Installation follows normal plumbing procedures.

side. You can then reach the faucet and its supply lines, the diverter (for directing water to the shower head rather than through the tub faucet, usually a part of the faucet body), and the line leading to the shower. Replacement of these fittings is similar to that of other fittings described previously. After completing the plumbing, either patch up the wallboard or, if the area is in a closet or other inconspicuous place, you might elect to cover the hole with a piece of ¼-inch plywood, screwed to the flanking studs, so that you can remove it easily for future servicing.

Shower heads can be replaced with minimal effort. Wrap the retaining nut on the

BATHTUB DRAINS

There is nothing so simple that it can't be complicated by progress. In years of yore, a rubber stopper was used to keep the water in the bathtub; when the bather was cleansed and relaxed, the stopper was removed and the water whooshed away down the drain. When the stopper became too worn to do its job properly, it was replaced by a new one, available at any hardware store. And no plumbing knowledge was needed for the job.

Then came progress, in the form of trip-lever and pop-up bath drains. True, these solved the sometime problem of misplacing the rubber stopper. And they probably are more esthetically pleasing. But they are mechanical devices, and the moving parts are subject to wear. When they wear to the point of nonfunctioning, they must be replaced. And this is somewhat more difficult than replacing a rubber stopper.

Although the design of these drains varies greatly according to manufacturer, basically they include a handle or lever that activates a lift rod (adjustable to fit any size tub) to raise or lower a plug, opening or closing the drain. Often, a trip-lever or pop-up drain is installed in conjunction with a drum trap (see PAGE 380).

Except on free-standing tubs, drain replacement must be done through an access panel behind the tub wall. If there is no such opening, you will have to make one (see Tub Faucets, above). Follow manufacturer's installation instructions.

Trip-lever drain.

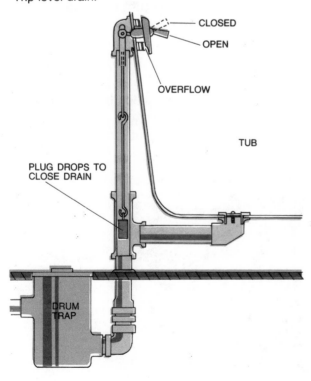

CLOSED

OPEN

OVERFLOW

TUB

PLUG DROPS TO
CLOSE DRAIN

DRUM TRAP

BATHTUBS

About a decade ago, a highly critical study of bathroom and fixture design was published by a professor of architecture at Cornell University. To the complete amazement of the publishing world, it became a runaway best seller, with over 100,000 copies being snapped up by people who, apparently, were less than completely satisfied with their present bathrooms.

Plumbing fixture manufacturers have been slower than the reading public to accept the innovative ideas expressed in this study, but there have been some changes, most notably in the concept and design of bathtubs. Among other things, it seems that bathing is becoming a gregarious experience. Coming onto the market are tubs large enough to enable couples to bathe together, and there is at least one that is a room-sized 5 x 7 feet—large enough to accommodate the entire family. Even the traditional one-person tubs are available with seats, shelves for soap and shampoo, and nonskid safety surfaces—features that were not generally offered 10 years ago.

Shared bathing notwithstanding, the most commonly installed tub remains the rectangular model, usually enclosed on three sides by a tiled or similar water-resistant wall. Corner tubs are also quite common; these are installed with one long side and one end against a wall, the others exposed. Square tubs are also popular, although these take up more space than the rectangular. Small square tubs are also available, but these are suitable only for children's bathing. Adults can use them for showering, or for kneeling baths taken with a flexible hand shower.

Tub sizes vary greatly. In addition to the 5 x 7-foot family-sized pool noted above, the more common rectangular tubs are generally 4 to 6 feet long and from 30 to 37 inches wide. These are outside dimensions;

Installation in new construction.

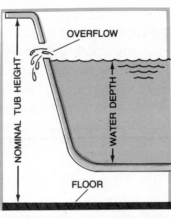

OVERFLOW

NOMINAL TUB HEIGHT

WATER DEPTH

FLOOR

Tub depth.

occupants. The height is measured from floor to rim, so the figure may be deceptive. Water depth is determined by the distance from the floor of the tub to the overflow outlet; this is the significant inside dimension. If you are a deep-soaker, take this into account when selecting a bathtub.

Those big old tubs were made of cast iron with a porcelain-enamel finish, and this is still a preferred material for more contemporary configurations. Such units are rugged, rigid, and heavy, weighing as much as 500 pounds. Add a few hundred pounds of water and another 200 (more or less) pounds of bather, along with a few ounces of bubble bath, and you have quite a load. Just make sure that your floor structure is up to supporting all this weight.

the actual bathing area depends on the width of the tub rim. Square tubs (not always perfectly square) may be from 36 to 48 inches. Tub height is normally 12 to 16 inches; the lower the height, the easier the tub is to get in and out of—a significant factor in a home with elderly or handicapped

Considerably lighter—and cheaper—are formed-steel bathtubs, also with a porcelain-enamel finish. They generally hit the scales at about 100 pounds, making them better suited for upper-story installations (easier to get up the stairs) and for remodeling, since they are more easily jockeyed into position and do not normally require additional floor bracing.

When buying a steel tub, make sure it has a sound-deadening undercoating to hold down the noise level when the shower is being used. Also, look for a one-piece tub. On some steel tubs, the apron is fabricated separately and welded in place before enameling; the welded seam may be visible.

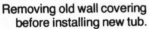

Removing old wall covering
before installing new tub.

Support for tub flanges.

Positioning tub.

Calk wall-tub joint.

Install tub-shower unit.

Lightest of all are fiberglass-reinforced polyester (FRP) bathtubs, often called simply fiberglass tubs. The surface is a smooth and attractive gel coat that is easy to keep clean but is not as durable as porcelain. Abrasive cleaners should never be used on the surface of a fiberglass tub—they will damage the finish.

One-piece FRP tub-showers combine bathtubs and shower wall surrounds. The troublesome tub-wall joint is eliminated. The units come in a wide variety of sizes and designs, many including molded-in soap dishes, grab bars, and seats.

After your new bathtub has been delivered, treat it with care. Uncrate it gently, making sure that your tools do not slip and scratch or chip the tub finish. If the tub must be set on end or edge for any reason, place pads or a folded blanket underneath. Do not stand on the tub during installation or, if you must, first remove your shoes.

In new construction, supply and drain lines are roughed-in while the wall framing is still exposed. The tub is then set in place before the floor and wall coverings are applied. Finally, the fittings are installed.

To install a replacement tub in an existing bathroom, remove the old fittings and pull out the old tub, trying to avoid damaging the walls. If the new tub is the same size as the old one, completely remove the wall covering from the end wall where the plumbing is located—this will make it easier to fit the new tub in place (this step is not necessary if you are installing a corner tub that is exposed on two sides). If the new tub is higher than the old one, cut the wall covering on all walls to the height of the new tub. (If the wall niche is longer than the new tub, this step is not necessary on the wall that will be built out to meet the tub. If the tub is longer than the niche, of course, a wall will have to be moved.)

For steel or FRP tubs, support must be provided for the flanges along the wall sides (the stronger cast-iron tubs do not normally have such flanges). Use 8d common nails to fasten 1 x 4 boards to the wall studs, with their tops perfectly level and at the height of the flanges. You will probably need assistance to tilt the tub into position and lower it onto the 1 x 4s. Anchor the tub as recommended by the manufacturer.

After having made all necessary adjustments to the existing plumbing so that it fits the new installation, re-cover the walls, calking at the wall-tub area to make a watertight joint. Install the fittings as previously described.

When replacing an existing bathtub with a new one-piece FRP tub-shower unit, remove the wall covering on all three sides of the niche from floor to ceiling. (If the new unit is shorter than the old tub, remove the wall covering from one end and the back wall only, then build wall framing at the other end to meet the new unit.) Set the tub-shower in place and make sure that it is level. Fasten to wall studs, as directed by the manufacturer of the unit. Apply wallboard above the tub surround (usually about 73 inches high), calking between the FRP unit and the wallboard to assure a watertight joint.

SHOWER STALLS

One way to ease the morning main-bathroom crunch is to install a shower in a second bathroom that may not have enough room for a full-sized tub. A shower stall should also be considered for a big old bathroom that is not equipped with a shower in the tub. Or you might want to install one in a laundry room or utility room near the back door, where the kids can clean up after a session in the mud without having to traipse through the house.

There are many prefabricated shower-stall units from which to choose. Some are free-standing, but most require the support of stud framing. You may be able to place one in a corner of the room, then build a wall along the third side.

Most modern units are made of fiberglass-reinforced polyester. They may come knocked-down (floor, three walls, doors) requiring assembly, or as one-piece molded units. (The one-piece units are easier to install, but make sure that you can get it through the door and into position without having to tear out too many walls of your house.)

The FRP shower stalls come in a wide range of sizes; 30 x 36 inches is generally considered the minimum for adults. Soap dishes and the like are usually molded in, and some larger one-piece stalls even have integral seats so that you can laze while lathering.

Installation instructions are provided by the manufacturer. Plumbing procedures are similar to those for bathtubs.

TOILETS

The aforementioned bathroom study published by a Cornell University professor was especially critical of toilet design, stating that it forced the user into uncomfortable and unnatural positions and suggesting that it might be responsible for various back disorders. A radically different low-slung design was presented, which was widely hailed by the medical profession. But change comes slowly in the plumbing industry, and slowest of all to toilets. In many respects, today's fixtures are close cousins to the pioneering models of a century ago when mankind was first emerging from the outhouse era.

This is not to suggest that there have been no improvements—far from it. But many of them are out of sight, and thus out of mind for most people, to whom toilets are not high on lists of things to think about. You *should* think about them, however, when it is time to shop for a new unit for your bathroom.

Most residential toilets consist of a bowl and a tank that serves as a reservoir for the water used to flush the bowl. (In some apartments and many commercial installations where there are large water-supply pipes capable of introducing ample water for flushing action directly into the bowl, the tank may be eliminated.) Both tank and bowl are made of vitreous china. They may be separate pieces, or they may be joined as an integral unit. The mechanism inside the tank performs an important part of the flushing cycle, but even more important is the design of the toilet bowl. A poorly functioning flush mechanism is easy to replace (see CHAPTER 8), but replacing a poorly functioning toilet is quite a bit more difficult, not to mention expensive.

A good toilet should flush quietly, completely, and efficiently. It should also provide a large water-surface area to prevent bowl contamination. The federal government has established minimum exposed-surface-area standards and minimum trapway (discharge passageway) diameters for each of the four basic bowl designs: washdown, reverse trap, siphon jet, and siphon vortex.

Washdown bowl.

Reverse trap.

Siphon jet.

Siphon vortex.

The washdown toilet bowl flushes by a simple wash-out action, discharging into a trapway at the front. It is easily recognized by the characteristic bulge on the front exterior. It has a large exposed surface at the inside front, which, since it is not protected by water, is subject to fouling, staining, and contamination. The trapway is often irregular in shape because of the exterior design and method of manufacture, so it is more subject to clogging than other types. It is the least expensive, but also the least efficient and the noisiest. It is no longer accepted by many municipal codes, so make sure to check your local code before installing a washdown toilet. Better yet, unless you are really tight for the bucks, avoid this type altogether.

The reverse trap toilet is flushed by creating a siphon action in the trapway, located at the rear of the bowl, pulling the waste from the bowl. There is a larger exposed water surface than in the washdown type, reducing fouling and staining of the bowl interior. Because the trapway is usually round, it is less likely to clog. Moderately noisy but efficient, it is somewhat more expensive than the washdown.

Still more expensive—and more efficient—is the siphon jet toilet, an improved version of the reverse trap. A built-in jet of water starts the flushing action. It has a larger exposed water surface, with most of the bowl interior covered by water. The trapway is also larger, making flushing action quieter and less likely to clog.

At the top of the line in price, efficiency, and quietness is the siphon vortex toilet. Flushing is started by a whirlpool-like action. There are almost no dry surfaces on the interior of the bowl.

Most types of toilets are available with either round or elongated bowls. The compact round types are designed for use where space is at a premium. The elongated bowls are generally considered to be more comfortable and, since they provide a larg-er interior water surface, are more sanitary and easier to keep clean.

Wall-hung (off-the-floor) toilets keep the floor unobstructed for easier cleaning. Discharge is through the wall rather than the floor. (Some floor-mounted toilets also discharge through the wall, making them easier to install in homes built on concrete slabs.) Off-the-floor toilets require the support of special metal carriers installed inside the wall. In new construction, this is no problem, but in an existing bathroom the wall covering must be removed to mount the carriers as well as to change the drainage lines when changing from a floor-mount to a wall-hung toilet.

Some manufacturers offer special designs to fit particular situations. One model, for example, has a unique upward discharge action, making it possible to install the toilet in a basement without having to chop up the concrete floor. Another has a triangular tank for corner installation, permitting even a small closet to be transformed into an additional powder room.

Specialized designs, such as the upward discharge or off-the-floor models, require specialized installation techniques, and manufacturer's directions should be followed carefully. But installation of floor-mounted toilets is generally standardized and requires no great plumbing expertise beyond that already acquired as a do-it-yourselfer.

As with all other fixture replacement projects, turn off the water supply before removing an old toilet, either at the fixture supply stop valve or at some other valve in the supply piping. Then flush the toilet, holding down the handle until most of the water drains from the tank. Lift off the tank top and sop up the small amount of water remaining in the tank with rags or a sponge.

Disconnect the supply line at the bottom of the tank (first wrapping the nut with tape to avoid damage if you intend to use the same supply line to the new toilet). If the

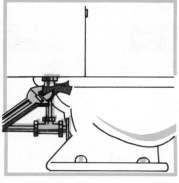

Disconnect supply.

Remove tank bolts.

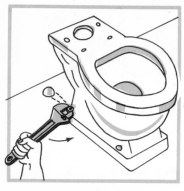

Pry off caps and remove nuts.

Twist and lift bowl.

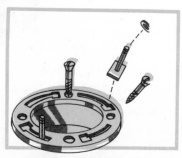

Remove bolts from flange.

Scrape flange clean.

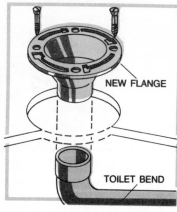

NEW FLANGE

TOILET BEND

Install new flange.

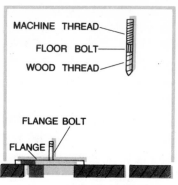

MACHINE THREAD

FLOOR BOLT

WOOD THREAD

FLANGE BOLT

FLANGE

Install floor bolts.

tank is a separate piece, remove the bolts that hold it to the bowl and lift it off. Some tanks are mounted on wall brackets or screwed to the wall; in that case, disconnect the tank first from the bowl, then from the wall and lift it off.

Toilet bowls are usually held to the floor by two or four bolts, which are concealed beneath caps of ceramic or plastic material. Pry off the caps with a putty knife and remove the nuts, using a wrench. Twist the bowl slightly to free it from its seal, then lift it straight up (do not tilt the bowl, since there is likely to be some water remaining in the trapway that might spill out).

There is no obvious use for a discarded toilet tank. However, you can still find old toilet bowls recycled to serve as planters on the lawns of homes and in front of some plumbing supply shops. If your esthetic senses move you in that flowery direction, so be it. Otherwise, junk your old toilet. (If it is in good operating condition and not badly cracked, you may even be able to sell it for a few dollars.)

Remove the hold-down bolts from the floor flange around the drain opening. With a putty knife, scrape the old wax gasket or other material from the flange, then wipe it clean. Insert two new hold-down bolts in the flange slots.

If the old flange appears damaged, or if it is a new installation (rather than a replace-

WAX GASKET

Putty the bottom of bowl.

Selecting and Installing Plumbing Fittings and Fixtures

ment), fit a new floor flange into the waste-pipe opening. Screw the flange to the floor, first making sure that the slots for the hold-down bolts are aligned with the holes in the bowl base. Insert hold-down bolts in the flange slots.

Some toilets are secured by only these two bolts; others require two more toward the front. Mark the location of the front bolts, using the bowl itself as a guide. Drive hanger bolts (one end has a wood thread, the other a machine thread to accept a nut) into the floor at these locations, making sure that they are perfectly vertical.

Set the new bowl upside down on pads or a blanket on the floor. Place a new wax gasket around the outlet, and apply a bead of plumber's putty completely around the base rim. Lift the bowl and align it over the bolts, then lower it gently and as straight as possible into position, with the discharge opening over the floor flange opening. Press down on top center of the bowl and twist it very slightly to settle the ring of putty into the floor. Use a carpenter's level to check that the bowl is perfectly level, and shim with wood wedges if necessary (but be sure you don't lift the bowl too much and break the putty seal, or the seal around the discharge opening).

If the toilet is a two-piece unit with a separate tank, place a large rubber washer on the tank outlet. Carefully set the tank atop the bowl. Tighten the nuts that hold the tank to the bowl, taking a few turns on one nut, then the other, and alternating this way so that it is tightened evenly—but not over-tightened. Using the tank as a guide, align the bowl with the wall (do the same if the toilet is a one-piece unit). Place washers over the flange and floor bolts and tighten with a wrench—again, do not overtighten. Place a small amount of putty inside the bolt caps and place them over the exposed bolt ends.

Install flush mechanism in tank (see

Set bowl.

Twist to set.

Check that it is level.

Place washer on tank outlet.

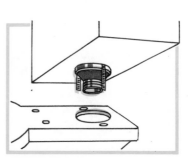

Set tank.

Set bolt caps.

Tighten floor flange nuts.

Install seat.

PAGE 450). Connect the fixture supply line, as described earlier. Install a new toilet seat, inserting the hinge bolts through the holes in the bowl, slipping washers over the bolts and tightening (once again, not too tight) the nuts. Place the tank top on the tank and turn on the water to complete the installation.

BIDETS

Long a standard in European and Latin American bathrooms, the bidet is gaining acceptance in this country—but slowly. The major barrier to widespread usage seems to be that most Americans (if they have ever even seen one) simply do not know what it is. It looks very much like a toilet. It is usually located next to the toilet (since the bidet is frequently used after using the toilet). Therefore . . . Tales of tourists treating the bidet as an auxiliary toilet are legion.

But the bidet is much more closely related to the shower than to the toilet. It is designed for cleaning the perineal areas of the body—the ultimate in personal hygiene. Many medical authorities believe that this washing practice helps prevent skin infections and irritations in the genitourinary area. Certainly, the thermal effect and soothing action created by water under pressure striking the body is also advantageous in the care of postoperative patients and elderly people.

The user sits astride the bowl of the bidet facing the controls, which regulate both water volume and temperature. Water enters the bidet either through an upward spray in the bowl or through a flushing rim that helps maintain bowl cleanliness. A stopper retains water in the bowl if desired.

The bidet is also useful as a footbath or for any other function that a low-set bowl might perform. There need be no hesitancy about using it for these various purposes; the flushing rim washes down the bowl to keep it sanitary, and the vitreous china can simply be wiped clean.

Installation of a bidet does not require extensive plumbing. Generally, it is connected to water-supply and drain lines much the same as a bathtub or shower. Follow manufacturer's directions for individual units.

WATER HEATERS

You may not think of the water heater in your plumbing system as a fixture. In fact, you may not think of it at all—until you have to. The other fixtures (except for the toilet) could not do their jobs without it. The chilly charm of a cold wake-up shower would quickly pall (even turn blue) on a wintry morning. And all the cold power you might muster won't put a sparkle in your crystal. Hot water is here to stay, as is the water heater (few of us would want to return to the Saturday night ritual of heating kettles of water on the wood or coal stove for the weekly bath).

The modern water heater will last, on the average, 8 to 15 years before needing to be retired. When you notice a puddle of water on the floor beneath it, it's time for replacement. When the storage tank was simply a galvanized steel cylinder, it was possible to

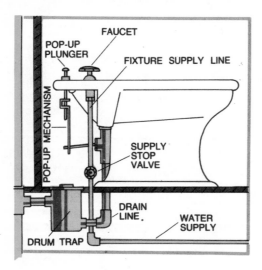

Typical bidet plumbing.

FAUCET
POP-UP PLUNGER
FIXTURE SUPPLY LINE
POP-UP MECHANISM
SUPPLY STOP VALVE
DRAIN LINE
WATER SUPPLY
DRUM TRAP

plug small leaks. But today's far more efficient models are surrounded by insulation and enclosed by a metal sheathing, making repairs impractical if not impossible, and certainly not worth the time and effort.

Another reason for replacing a water heater might be its limited capacity. The 30-gallon storage tank that might have been perfectly adequate for the young couple with two small infants is woefully overtaxed when the family grows and the infants become two-shower-a-day teenagers. New appliances such as clothes washers and dishwashers also put new strains on the water heater.

What size heater to buy is not simply a matter of storage-tank capacities, which are most commonly 30-, 40-, and 50-gallon, along with some larger sizes. Another important factor is the recovery rate: the number of gallons of water the heater can raise 100 degrees F. in one hour. The recovery rate depends on the type of heating element and the fuel used. Oil-fired heaters have a very rapid recovery rate; electric heaters are generally the slowest, and natural gas and LP gas are between. But heater design also affects the speed of recovery.

The amount of water you can draw from the heater per hour equals the recovery rate plus approximately 70 percent of its storage capacity. A 30-gallon heater with a 40-gph (gallons per hour) recovery rate would deliver a maximum 61 gallons of hot water in the first hour (40 plus 70 percent of 30—21—equals 61)—less after that as the stored water has been diminished.

As a rule of thumb, a family of two requires first-hour water delivery of 45 gallons. Add five gallons per person up to six persons; over that, add five gallons for every two persons. Add an extra 10 percent if you have a clothes washer and dishwasher.

Using the above figures, determine your family's needs and the size heater to install, based on capacity and recovery rate. Then

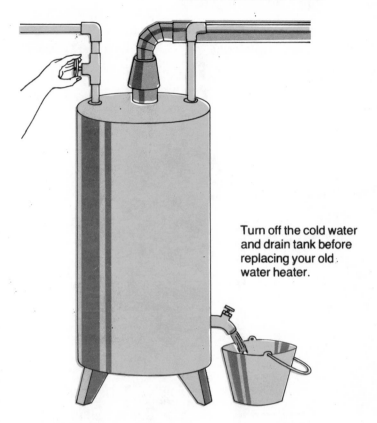

Turn off the cold water and drain tank before replacing your old water heater.

consider one more factor—the local availability and price of each of the fuels, as well as the initial cost of the unit. Then make the decision on what to buy.

For most residential installations, a glass-lined steel tank is the best choice. It will give many years of service—high-quality tanks are fully guaranteed for as much as 10 years, an indication of their durability. If you live in an area where the water is extremely corrosive, you might opt for a considerably more expensive copper tank.

If you are replacing a water heater with a new one using a different fuel, you may wish to leave the job to a professional—especially if you are switching to electricity. If you do it yourself, make sure you follow manufacturer's directions to the letter.

If the new heater is to use the same fuel as the old, the job is considerably easier. Turn off the fuel supply to the heater. Turn off the cold-water supply, either at a valve directly above the heater or, if necessary, at the main valve. Open hot-water faucets upstairs to drain water from the lines, and

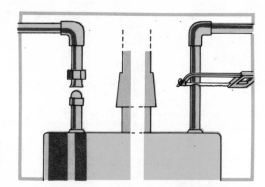

Disconnect at union, or
saw pipes if
if there is no union.

Remove stack.

RELIEF
VALVE

Install relief valve.

Replace stack.

drain the heater through the tap at its bottom, either using a bucket brigade or attaching a hose to the tap and leading it to the stationary tubs or out a window.

While it is draining, you can disconnect the pipes leading to the heater. If there are unions in the lines, simply disconnect them. If there are not, you will have to saw through the pipes. An oil- or gas-fired heater will also have a stack leading to the chimney; remove this by lifting it off the top of the heater. Pull out the old heater.

You may have to adjust the piping to fit the new heater. Use new pipes and fittings of the same material as the rest of the water-supply system; how-to details are given on PAGES 406-407. Make the final connection with a union fitting.

A temperature-pressure relief valve (PAGE 411) must be installed on the new heater; a tapped hole is provided at the top. Just thread in the valve, then attach a length of pipe to the valve leading to a nearby drain or simply ending about 4 inches above the floor.

Connect the fuel line to the heater. For an oil- or gas-fired heater, inspect the galvanized stack pipe. If it shows signs of corrosion, replace it with a new pipe of the same size (most hardware stores carry this pipe). Install the stack between the chimney and the heater. Then light the burner.

To help your new water heater attain a ripe old age, give it a little attention every month. Open the tap at the bottom and drain off any accumulated sediment into a bucket. While you are at it, check the relief valve by lifting it up. If water comes out the pipe, it is doing its job.

7

Septic Tanks

A SEPTIC waste system consists of three basic elements: a drainage line that carries waste and water from the house, a tank into which it is discharged, and an absorption field where liquids drain away into the ground.

The drainage line is similar to that which leads to a municipal sewer system; it is pitched away from the house, in this case to the tank, which is usually made of reinforced concrete. The purpose of the tank is to collect sewage and liquefy the solid matter contained in it through the dissolving action of bacteria in the waste. The liquid then flows from the tank to the absorption field, which is usually a series of perforated pipes through which the outflow seeps into the surrounding ground.

Solids remaining in the tank settle to the bottom, where further bacterial action separates them into a sludge (which remains on the bottom) and a scum (which rises to the top). The scum gradually breaks down into liquid and flows out into the absorption field.

Many septic disposal systems include a distribution box between the tank and the absorption field to regulate and equalize the liquid discharge through all the outflow pipes. Like the rest of the system, it is buried out of sight, but it is usually close enough to the surface to allow access to the cover. This is a useful checkpoint, where you can monitor the quality of the outflow liquid to make sure that the system is functioning properly.

Another important accessory is a grease trap to keep grease, fats, detergents, and similar materials out of the septic tank, where they would rapidly build up as solids on the bottom, because they refuse to succumb to the bacterial action in the tank. The grease trap is normally located right at the kitchen sink or just outside the house near the sink.

Rain water, surface water, and runoff from around the house foundation can upset the balance of the septic system if they drain into the tank or inundate the absorption field. If the terrain is such that this could pose a problem, a seepage pit should be provided at least 20 feet away from the absorption field to catch such drainage. The seepage pit can be simply a large-diameter vitrified-clay or concrete pipe covered with a manhole and set into the ground on a bed of coarse gravel. Drainpipes from gutters and other water collectors empty into the pit, and the water seeps through the gravel into the ground.

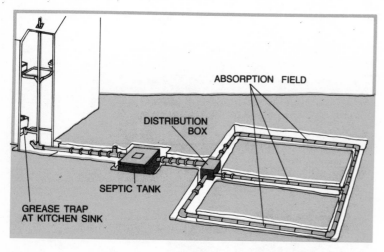

Typical septic waste disposal system.

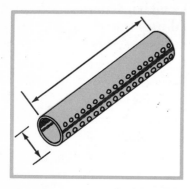

Outflow pipe.

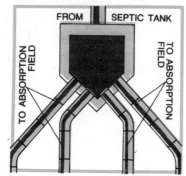

Distribution box.

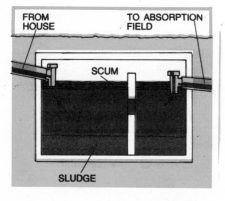

Septic tank.

Seepage pit.

PREVENTIVE MAINTENANCE

To function properly, the septic tank must maintain a delicate balance of sludge, liquid, and scum. If a heavy layer of sludge builds up, it may overflow into the absorption field, clogging the outflow pipes. Then the whole system backs up, with toilets re- fusing to flush, sinks and bathtubs refusing to drain, and other similar unpleasant- nesses. If the sludge overflow completely clogs the outflow lines, raw sewage may be forced to the surface. At that stage, about all you can do is dig up your yard and start all over again with a new system.

Obviously, things should never be allowed to reach that stage. You should pe- riodically check the distribution box to make sure that the effluent (the liquid out- flow) is free of particles of sludge. Do this every four months or so—and more fre- quently if sluggishly draining fixtures cause you to suspect trouble.

The tank itself should be inspected annu- ally. If you have a regular service contract with a septic-tank maintenance firm, they should do this; just make sure that they do. It will mean digging to expose the tank opening and measuring the levels of sludge, liquid, and scum. This is done with a spe- cial device; the rule of thumb is that the combined depths of sludge and scum should not exceed one-third of that of the liquid. When it does, the tank should be cleaned out. This job is best left to the professionals with their special equipment.

If possible, plan ahead so that the tank is cleaned in the spring rather than in the fall. During the cold winter weather, bacterial action is slowed and undigested solids can accumulate at a rapid rate. Normally, such cleaning is necessary only every three years or so, but this depends on a number of factors such as tank capacity, porosity of the soil in the absorption field, and the number of persons in the household. You can help prolong the period between clean- ings by having your family practice miserly water usage: shorter showers, shallower baths, less frequent toilet flushing, more concentrated laundering. Make sure that you don't neglect those leaking faucets and running toilets that can quickly overfill the septic system. Immediate repairs of such water wasters are in order (see CHAPTER 8).

8

When Things Go Wrong

NO MATTER how superbly designed and installed the plumbing system of your home may be, or how well made and expensive the fixtures, things will go wrong occasionally. It is, after all, one of the most frequently used mechanical systems in the home, with moving parts performing under constant pressure, so that wear is inevitable. Fortunately, when problems do arise, they usually can be set right again with a minimum of grief. Just tote your emergency toolbox (CHAPTER 3) to the trouble spot and apply a bit of your newfound plumbing expertise.

LEAKY FAUCETS

The ceaseless "drip . . . drip . . . drip" of a leaky faucet is a close cousin to the ancient water torture, causing daytime aggravation and nighttime insomnia. More than that, it is water—and therefore dollars—down the drain. Your water bill doesn't distinguish between what you use for drinking, cooking, washing, laundering, and the like and that which trickles away without serving you in any way. Dripping water can also stain a sink or lavatory and eventually wear away the finish of the fixture, too. It's better to make the repair as soon as the problem is noticed.

First shut off the water supply at the supply stop in the line below the faucet. If there is no supply stop, turn off the water at some point farther back in the line. If necessary, turn off the valve where the water enters your house.

On some faucets, the handle covers the packing nut. It must be removed to give ac-

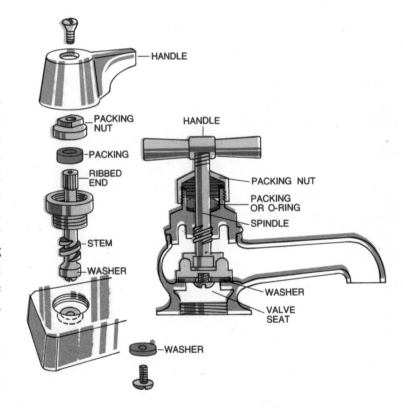

cess to the nut. On other faucets, the packing nut is exposed. In the latter case, wrap the nut with tape or rags to protect the chrome finish. Remove the packing nut by

1. Remove packing nut.

2. Remove stem.

WASHER

3. Remove old washer.

4. Replace washer.

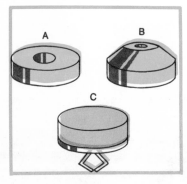

A   B

C

5. Types of washers.

6. File damaged rim.

7. Use of seat-grinder.

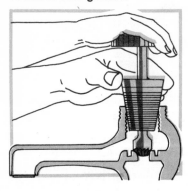

8. O-ring or packing replacement.

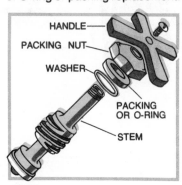

HANDLE

PACKING NUT

WASHER

PACKING OR O-RING

STEM

9. Recessed bath faucet removal.

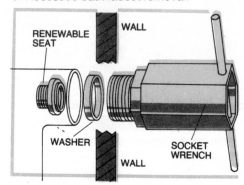

RENEWABLE SEAT

WALL

WASHER

SOCKET WRENCH

WALL

turning it counterclockwise with an open-end wrench or monkey wrench.

Remove the faucet stem or spindle (you may have to replace the handle to turn it out). Check the washer at its lower end. If the washer appears worn or damaged, carefully remove the screw that holds it in place and take out the washer (if necessary, apply penetrating oil to loosen the screw). Replace with a new washer of the correct size. If the rim around the stem bottom is intact, use either a Type A or a Type B washer. If the rim is damaged, file it away completely and install a Type C washer.

Shine a flashlight down inside the faucet body and check the seat to make sure it is smooth and free of nicks. If the seat is damaged or rough, grind it down with a dressing tool. There are various types of such tools (all inexpensive), and all are used in much the same way. Clamp the tool on the faucet (some types of dressing tools are held in place by the packing nut or bonnet) and turn the stem by the T-handle; a fluted grinder at the lower end of the stem reconditions the seat.

On many faucets, badly worn seats can be replaced. Remove the old one (usually an Allen wrench does the job), and screw a new one of the correct size in its place.

With the seat reconditioned and a new washer in place, reassemble the faucet. If a leak continues around the stem, remove the handle and packing nut or bonnet and examine the O-ring or packing around the stem. If it is worn away or damaged, replace with the proper new parts.

On some types of bath faucets, the bonnet holding the stem in place is recessed in the wall. You will need a socket wrench with an extension to remove it for repair and replacement of the washer. Otherwise, the procedure is the same as above.

The design and construction of noncompression (single-control mixer) faucets vary greatly, and so do their repair procedures. Most manufacturers of these faucets include repair instructions along with installation instructions. The best advice is to file away this repair sheet for future reference.

Most problems with noncompression faucets occur when parts wear out. Replacement of the old parts is the only real remedy.

NOISY FAUCETS

A faucet that squeals or chatters when you turn it on or off is just as annoying as a leaky one. Take it apart as above, and make sure that the faucet washer is tightly screwed to the stem. If the washer is worn, replace it, even though the faucet may not be leaking. If the stem (after being screwed back into the faucet) can be moved up and down, the threads are probably worn and the stem should be replaced. Occasionally, a design deficiency will cause faucets to chatter and whistle. A new faucet is the only cure (see PAGE 431).

LEAKY VALVES

The various types of valves are described on PAGES 408-411. With gate and globe valves, the commonest problem is leakage around the stem. To repair, first shut off the water at another valve between the leaking

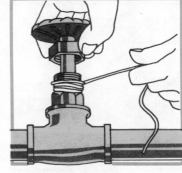

1. Loosen packing nut.   2. New packing.

unit and the water source, or at the main house intake. With an adjustable or open-end wrench, loosen the packing nut. Hold a bucket beneath the valve to catch the water remaining in the line, then remove the packing nut. Remove the old packing and wrap new packing around the stem, then replace the packing nut.

When a gate valve does not do its job of regulating or closing off the flow of water through a line, it usually indicates either an obstruction or damage in the valve seat that prevents the valve wedge from closing properly. It may also mean wear of either the wedge or the seat. Whatever the cause, the entire valve should be replaced.

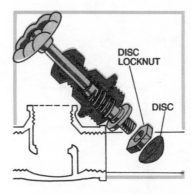

DISC LOCKNUT

DISC

3. Replace disc.

Globe valve repairs are similar to faucet repairs. After removing the packing nut, screw the stem out of the valve body. Inspect the disc or washer at the bottom of the stem. If it is worn or damaged, unscrew

4. Unfasten nut on ground key valve.

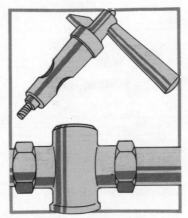

5. Remove plunger.

6. Smear grinding compound on plunger.

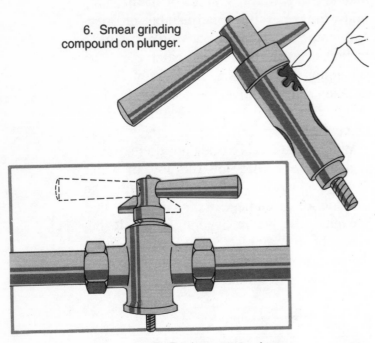

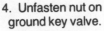

7. Replace, rotate plunger back and forth.

the locknut that holds it in place and replace it with a new one.

Ground key valves may become grooved or worn by tiny particles in the water rubbing against the metal, allowing the water to leak through. The surfaces must be repolished. Shut off the water supply and unfasten the nut or screw at the bottom of the valve that holds the plunger in place. Pull out the plunger. Smear a small amount of valve-grinding compound on the sides of the plunger and replace it in its sleeve. Rotate the plunger back and forth to wear the two surfaces smooth, forming a leakproof joint. Remove the plunger and wipe it clean. Wipe clean the inside of the sleeve, then reassemble the valve. If the parts are too badly worn to respond to this treatment, replace the valve.

TOILET TANK TROUBLES

The flush mechanism inside a toilet tank may seem to the uninitiated as mysterious and complex as the workings of a space-vehicle computer, but it is really quite simple. Basically, it is made up of two assemblies; a ballcock, which regulates the filling of the tank, and a flush valve, which releases water from the tank to the toilet bowl and then shuts off this flow. Individual

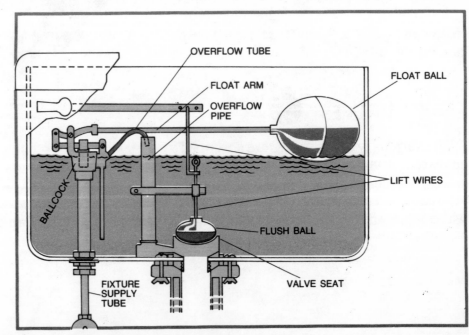

Cross section of toilet tank.

parts of each assembly may wear out and need replacement; sooner or later the entire assembly or assemblies will have to be replaced.

Sometimes when a toilet is flushed, a fine spray of water shoots up against the top of the tank, often leaking out around the cover. Check the overflow tube on the ballcock to see if it has a hole or is split. If so, replace the tube (usually plastic). There could also be a faulty or damaged connection between the overflow tube and the ballcock. If this is the case, correct the connection.

If the toilet tank overfills, check for a worn washer on the bottom of the ballcock plunger stem and replace if necessary. Also, check to make sure that the operating levers are moving freely. If they are frozen tight and you cannot free them, replace the entire ballcock assembly.

When the toilet will not stop running, with water going through the overflow tube, pull up on the float arm (the metal rod between the ballcock and the float ball) to see if this stops the flow. If it does, unscrew the float ball and shake it to tell if there is water inside. If water is present, the float ball has sprung a leak and should be replaced. If the float ball checks out, bend the float arm down slightly to lower the ball. This should stop the water from running. If the flow still persists, turn off the water supply, remove the valve plunger, and replace the washer.

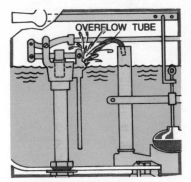

Leak at overflow tube; water spurting out.

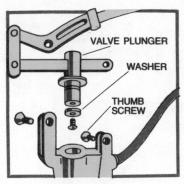

Leak at plunger stem; replace washer.

If that doesn't stop the leak, the ballcock should be replaced.

Replacing a ballcock is no more difficult than replacing any of its parts, except possibly the float and float rod. First empty the water from the toilet tank. Shut off the water at the supply stop, at some other valve in the line, or at the main house inlet, and then flush the toilet. Place a pail or basin under the supply connection to catch the water that remains in the tank. Unscrew the fixture supply tube and the locknut from the ballcock shank and remove the old assembly.

Remove the locknut from the new ballcock and place the shank through the opening in the tank, with the large rubber washer inside the tank. Tighten the locknut over the shank, then fasten the supply line. Connect the overflow tube to the ballcock and place the other end into the overflow pipe

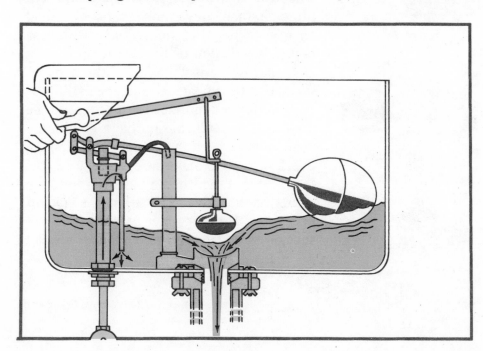

Cross section showing flushing action.

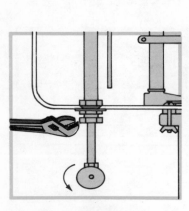

1. Remove fixture supply tube.

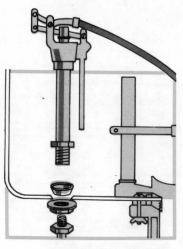

2. Remove old ballcock.

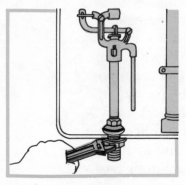

3. Install new ballcock.

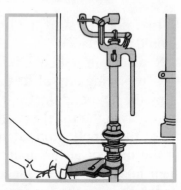

4. Refasten supply line.

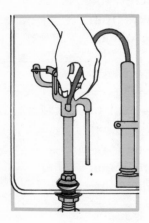

5. Connect overflow tube.

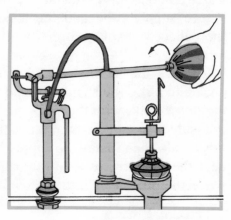

6. Fasten float ball.

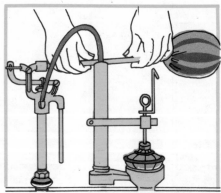

7. Bend arm if necessary.

of the flush valve assembly. Screw the float arm into the ballcock assembly and fasten the float ball at the end of the arm. Check to make sure that all connections are tight, then turn on the water, allowing the tank to fill. It may be necessary to adjust the float arm by bending it slightly to permit the tank to fill properly and to keep the arm clear of the overflow pipe and other parts of the mechanism. Be careful, and use both hands when bending the arm; do not damage the threads at either the ballcock end or the float ball end.

Another type of ballcock eliminates the need for the float ball and float arm, thus

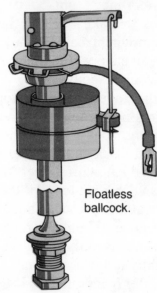

Floatless ballcock.

also eliminating the sources of a lot of toilet troubles. This device works on a different principle than conventional ballcocks (fluid energy), filling the tank faster with less noise. Installation of the floatless ballcock is similar to the installation of the conventional unit (less float arm and float ball).

If the toilet continues to run because the tank fails to refill, the problem is with the flush valve. Check the stopper guide on the overflow pipe to make sure it is aligned correctly so that the stopper ball drops into the center of the valve seat; adjust the guide if necessary. If the stopper ball still does not seat properly, it may be damaged; inspect

1. Replace stopper ball.

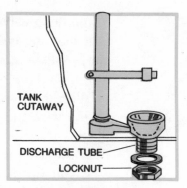

TANK CUTAWAY

DISCHARGE TUBE

LOCKNUT

2. Insert discharge tube.

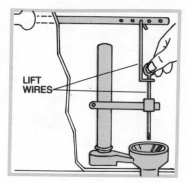

LIFT WIRES

3. Install lift wires.

and replace if necessary. Also check the valve seat, cleaning the surface with very fine steel wool. If it is nicked or otherwise damaged, replace it.

To replace the flush valve, first shut off the water and empty the tank as above. Remove the old flush valve, lift wires or chain, washer and locknut holding the valve seat in place. Insert the discharge tube of the new valve assembly through the tank bottom. With the overflow pipe positioned, tighten the locknut to lock the discharge tube in place. Center the guide arm on the overflow pipe over the valve seat and tighten it in place. Install lift wires through the guide and the trip arm and screw the flush ball onto the lower lift wire, aligning it to drop into the exact center of the flush valve seat. (Some flush valves use a chain in place of the lower lift wire; no guide is needed with this type.)

The toilet tank serves as a reservoir for the large amount of water needed for flushing action—more than could be delivered quickly through the ½-inch or even ¾-inch water lines normally used in residential plumbing systems. In some commercial and public buildings and apartment houses, where toilets are located near a main water supply line, such a reservoir is not needed. The much greater capacity of the pipe can deliver enough water directly. Here, a different type of flush valve, usually lever-actuated, is used to regulate the flow. When

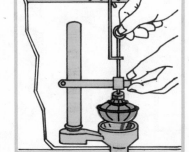

4. Install flush ball.

problems arise, such as continual running of water into the toilet bowl, the fault is somewhere within the flush valve.

The construction and operation of flush valves vary greatly, depending on the manufacturer, but most have certain similarities. When troubleshooting such a valve, first shut off the water supply. Some types have a cutoff on the valve body—usually a large screw. Otherwise, close a stop valve in the supply line.

Wrap tape around the cap at the top of

5. Remove cap from flush mechanism.

6. Lift out inside cover and valve.

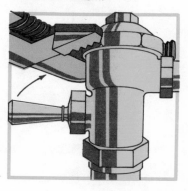

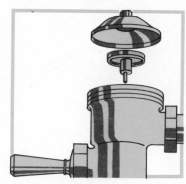

7. Unscrew disc ring.

8. Insert new washer.

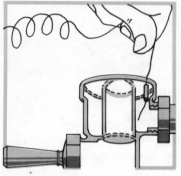

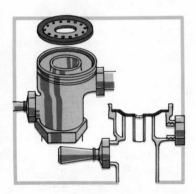

9. Run wire through bypass.

10. Insert new diaphragm.

the disc ring that holds it in place and pry out the old washer. Insert a new washer and replace the disc ring, screwing it down firmly, but not too tightly.

With the inside cover and valve out, run a fine wire through the bypass hole in the flush valve body. If this is clogged, the water flow into the bowl will not shut off.

Clean the surface of the seat on which the washer rests. Sediment that has collected on the seat may prevent the valve from closing tightly. If the seat is worn or damaged, it should be reground or replaced (see Leaky Faucets, above).

If leakage persists, the rubber diaphragm inside the valve body may be worn or damaged. Unscrew the disc to remove the old diaphragm and replace it, making sure to insert the new diaphragm with the cup down. Screw the disc back in place.

CLOGGED TOILET

When you flush the toilet and the water level in the bowl rises rather than recedes, head for the emergency toolbox fast! The plumber's friend is your first line of defense. Place the plunger over the discharge opening in the toilet bowl and work it vigor-

the valve to protect the finish, and remove the cap with an open-end or adjustable wrench—do not use a pipe wrench! Lift out the inside cover and valve. Inspect the washer on the valve for signs of wear or damage. If it needs replacement, unscrew

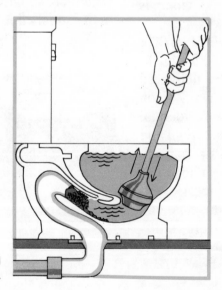

Use of plunger (right) and working auger into trap (far right).

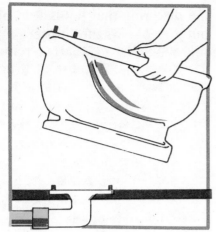

Remove the toilet from the floor and turn it upside down.

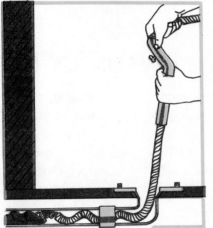

Work auger into drain or waste line and get the obstruction out.

ously up and down. This should clear the stoppage.

If the plumber's friend doesn't do the job, try the snake, or auger. A closet auger, designed to get the auger wire right down to the blockage, is preferred. You can use a drain auger if that's all you have on hand, but be careful not to scratch the inside of the toilet bowl.

Work the snake into the trap and crank it in one direction until it becomes tight. Pull it back; often it will bring the obstruction up with it. If it doesn't, try again, cranking the snake until it pushes through and clears the stoppage.

If all else fails, bail out as much water as possible from the bowl, and soak up the rest with rags. Remove the toilet from the floor (see PAGE 441), turn it upside down (placing it on old newspapers), and work

the obstruction out through the discharge opening. If it has already passed into the waste line and is stuck there, work it out with the snake.

To reposition the toilet, follow the instructions for setting a new toilet as given on PAGE 441. Use a new wax gasket around the opening, and apply fresh putty around the rim. When the toilet is reset and the floor mopped clean, it might be a good idea to assemble the family and lecture them on what a toilet is for—and what it is not for (it is definitely not to be used as a garbage disposal).

CLOGGED SINK DRAINS

This is another annoyance that you often bring on yourself (or other members of the family do) by removing the outlet strainer and allowing food wastes, grease, and other "indigestible" matter to run into the sink drain.

If the drain is not completely clogged, try running scalding water into it for several minutes. That may clear the stoppage. If it doesn't, try a dry or liquid chemical drain cleaner, following the manufacturer's instructions. (Do not use pure lye.) If this clears the drain, flush it with hot water for several minutes.

If the chemical doesn't work or if the drain is completely clogged, try using the plumber's friend. Remove the strainer from the drain and make sure there is enough water in the sink to cover the plunger, providing a good seal. Work the plunger up and down until the drain is cleared and water runs out normally.

Some plumbers prefer a force pump rather than the plumber's friend or plunger for unclogging sink drains. The force pump must be positioned squarely over the drain and covered with enough water to make a

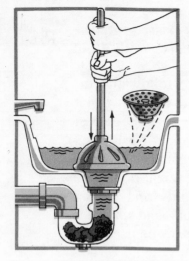

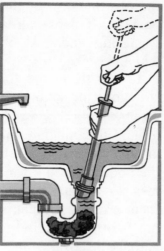

Use of plunger.

Use of force pump.

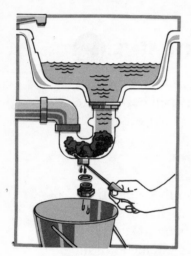

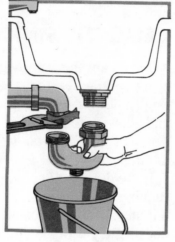

Remove cleanout plug.

Remove trap.

Use auger in drain line,
rotate it, and work it in some more.

the job, check the trap below the sink. If there is a cleanout plug, place a pail below it to catch the water, then remove the plug. Try to clear away the obstruction. If that doesn't work, or if there is no cleanout plug, loosen the slip nuts and remove the trap. If the stoppage is in the trap, remove it. If not, use the drain auger, feeding it into the drain line. Rotate the auger, then work it in some more. Rotate it again and repeat the procedure until the obstruction is cleared. Reassemble the trap, then run scalding water down the drain for several minutes.

CLOGGED LAVATORIES

When a lavatory with a pop-up drain stopper becomes clogged, first twist the stopper to disengage it, then lift it out. Often, accumulated hair, grease, and the like are caught on the stopper, causing clogging. Clean it off. With the stopper out, use a length of wire with one end bent into a hook to fish out debris that may be stuck between the discharge outlet and the trap.

If clogging persists, follow the measures

Remove stopper.

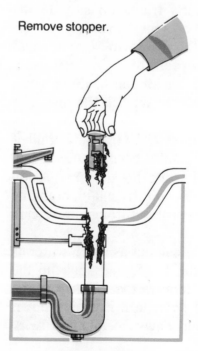

firm seal. Then pump the handle to clear away the obstruction by air pressure. If a plumber's friend or force pump doesn't do work, you will have to get at the obstruction by removing the trap. If the bathroom is on the first floor, the tub may have a P or S trap that is accessible from the basement or crawl space. In this case, loosen the slip nuts, take off the trap and clear the line with an auger, as under CLOGGED SINK DRAINS above. (For location of the traps, see PAGE 380.)

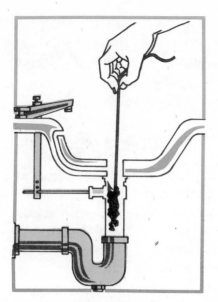

Use wire to fish out debris.

Plug up overflow and use plunger.

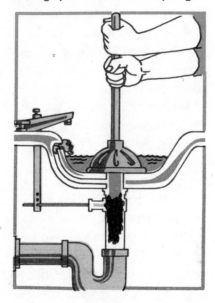

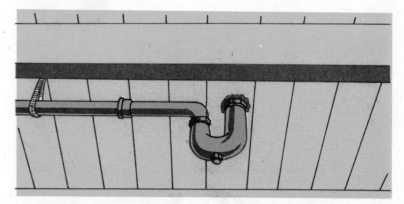

Location of pipes in basement.

prescribed for sink drains. Plug up the overflow outlet with rags before using the plumber's friend; otherwise it cannot make an airtight seal and will not work effectively.

CLOGGED BATHTUBS

If scalding water, chemicals, and the plumber's friend (remember to plug the tub overflow with a wet cloth or rags) don't

Many second-floor and some first-floor bathtubs are fitted with drum traps, usually located near the bathtub drain with an access cover flush with the floor. If the tub is recessed into a wall niche, the trap may be on the other side of the wall—in a closet, perhaps, or beneath a kitchen cabinet. Or it might be within the wall itself; builders often leave an access panel in the wall next to a recessed bathtub, which is easily removed to service all the tub plumbing.

Make sure the tub is empty before opening the drum trap; bail the water out if necessary. Use an open-end wrench (never a pipe wrench) to remove the drum trap access cover. Work the drain auger in the line between the tub and the trap—the obstruction may be found there. If not, work the auger in the outflow line from the trap until the stoppage is cleared. Check the rubber gasket before replacing the trap cover; if it is in poor condition, install a new one. Then replace the cover on the trap. Run hot water into the drain for several minutes.

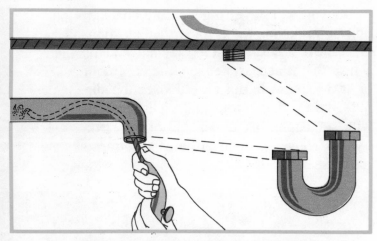

Remove debris through trap in basement.

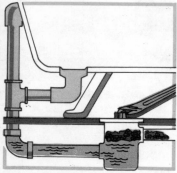

Remove drum-trap cover.

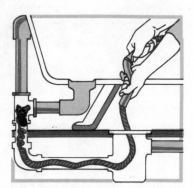

Work auger toward tub.

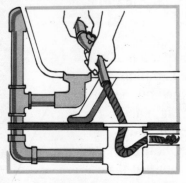

Work auger in drain line.

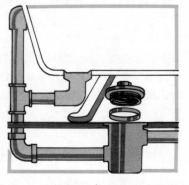

Replace rubber gasket.

Some plumbing systems, particularly those in older installations, do not include a bathtub trap, or have it placed beneath the floor where it is inaccessible. If you can't find a trap, and the clogging resists all your

efforts to work it loose, you are probably best off calling in a professional. It will likely be less painful than ripping up the floors in search of the problem.

CLOGGED SEWER

When drainage problems are noted at several or all fixtures in the house, the obstruction is most likely in the main sewer line, rather than at individual fixtures. Blockage in a sewer line may be caused by collected waste or foreign matter at some point in the underground pipe or by surrounding tree roots that have taken over. Roots will enter fine cracks in certain pipe materials and continue to grow inside the pipe until they form an almost solid mass. This can take place at a single point, or along a great length of an older pipe.

Start at the basement cleanout plug, placing a bucket below the plug. Use a wrench to loosen the plug, just enough to allow water to flow out into the bucket. When all has drained out remove the plug.

Remove the nozzle from your garden hose. Without turning on the water, work the hose into the cleanout opening until it reaches the obstruction. Stuff rags into the opening around the hose so that it is tightly sealed. Have a helper slowly turn on the water as you hold the hose tightly against the stoppage. As the obstruction begins to

1. Loosen drain plug.

2. Work garden hose
to obstruction.

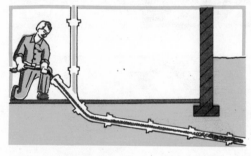

3. Plug opening with rags
and turn on hose.

4. Drain auger at work.

5. Electric auger at work.

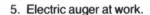

give way, increase the water pressure until it clears. If there is no movement, turn off the water and remove the hose.

Try turning a drain auger into the drain opening until it hits the obstruction; turn

the handle and work the auger back and forth until the blockage is cleared. Run the hose into the drain to wash away the debris.

If the problem persists, it is likely that tree roots have penetrated the sewer line. You may want to call in professionals to handle the problem. Or you can rent an electric auger fitted with sharp blades for cutting through roots. Follow dealer's instructions for use of such a machine. When the stoppage has been cleared, use the hose to rinse out the drain before replacing the cleanout plug.

SWEATING PIPES

Exposed pipes that "sweat" during hot weather can be cured of this affliction by wrapping them with insulation. You can use asbestos or fiberglass insulation or a special thick insulating tape made for this purpose. Make sure to insulate the pipes before you finish off a basement. Sweating pipes will cause unsightly damage to the ceiling.

FROZEN PIPES

Frozen water pipes may burst, or the joints may be forced open. They should be thawed as quickly as possible, but exercise caution when doing so.

Open the faucets in the frozen line. The safest way to melt the ice is to wrap cloth or burlap around the pipe, then pour boiling water over the cloth. Keep it saturated with hot water until the water in the lines is flowing freely.

Don't use a blowtorch or propane torch to thaw a frozen pipe unless the pipe is in an absolutely safe location—away from flammable walls or other materials. If you use a torch, move it along the pipe rather than concentrating on a single spot. Work

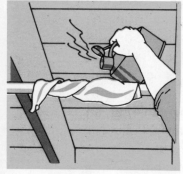

Wrap with burlap and
pour water.

Use of
Blowtorch.

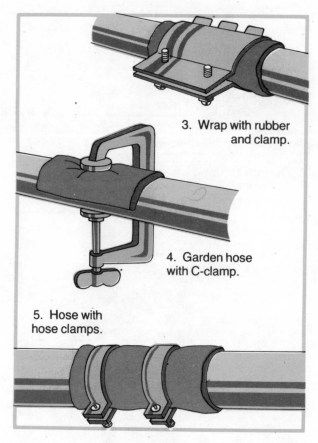

3. Wrap with rubber
   and clamp.

4. Garden hose
   with C-clamp.

5. Hose with
   hose clamps.

toward an open faucet, not away from it, so
that steam generated within the pipe can escape.

LEAKING PIPES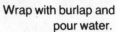

When a pipe springs a leak, the first thing
to do is turn off the water—fast! If there is
not a shutoff nearby, turn off the main intake valve. If it is impossible to shut off the
water because of a worn or damaged valve
or for some other reason, you can stop water from flowing through a copper pipe by

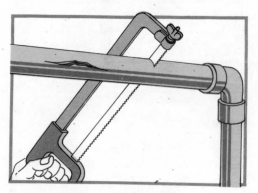

6. Cut out damaged section
   of pipe with cutter or hacksaw.

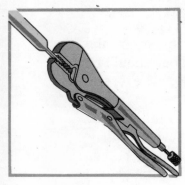

1. Crimp pipe.

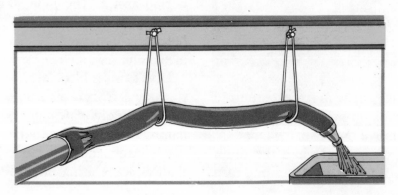

2. Use hose to divert flow.

crimping the pipe below the leak or break; a vise-grip pliers is the best tool for this. Of course, you will have to replace this section of pipe later, but at least your house won't float away before you can make permanent repairs. If a pipe breaks or a connection comes loose and water is pouring out the end of a pipe, you can also place a garden hose over the end of the pipe to direct water flow into a bathtub, stationary tub, or even out a window until you can stanch the flow.

For a temporary repair of a damaged pipe, wrap a piece of sheet rubber firmly around the leaky section and clamp it tightly (special clamps for this are available in various pipe sizes). Or you can cut a section of garden hose, slit it, and place it over the leak, holding it there with a C-clamp. If the pipe is actually broken, you can rejoin the two sections with a short piece of garden hose, securing it with hose clamps on each end.

To make a permanent repair, cut out the

7. Fit a coupling to one end.

8. Reattach with union.

damaged section of pipe with a cutter or hacksaw. Fit a coupling to one of the remaining ends, cut a short piece of pipe to fit the cutout section, and attach it to the other end with a union (see PAGES 406-407).

When a leaky pipe is inside a wall, you would have to break through the wall to repair it. It's much easier to disconnect it from the supply line and the fixture it serves and run a new line through the wall next to the old one.

part **6**
HOME COMFORT (HEATING, ETC.)

Contents

1. HEATING SYSTEMS 465
2. FUELS 480
3. HEATING SYSTEM CONTROLS 487
4. HEATING A NEW OR REMODELED SPACE 491
5. ROUTINE MAINTENANCE AND SERVICING 503
6. KEEPING COOL 509
7. HOW TO SAVE ON HOME COMFORT CONDITIONING 521
8. OTHER COMFORT FACTORS 544
9. COMFORT QUOTIENT FOR HOME BUYERS 550

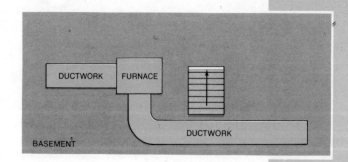

1

Heating Systems

THE HEATING SYSTEM is something of a mystery to most homeowners. Of course, they are painfully aware of it when they groan over the monthly fuel bills, and even more so when they awaken on the coldest morning of the year to discover that the furnace went to sleep right after they did and the thermostat has frosted over. But beyond that, it's just a maze of pipes coming out of a strange box in the basement or the utility room. A necessary evil—and just hope that it keeps on cooking!

It needn't be that way. We certainly don't recommend that the average do-it-yourselfer should design and install his own heating system. That is very definitely a job for the reputable professional contractor or the most knowledgeable and experienced amateur. The professional should also be called on to inspect the system annually. But there are many things that you can do to help your heating system operate more dependably, more efficiently, and more economically. And before you can do that, you must first understand just how it operates.

It seems likely that man has been conscious of his cold-weather comfort ever since he started fooling around with fire (probably quite accidentally) untold millennia ago. That wondrous discovery led to "space heaters" on the floors of caves and later in pits dug into the earthen floors of crude huts and in braziers in the homes and palaces of kings, pharaohs, and the just plain wealthy and powerful. Sometime around the first century A.D., the Romans conceived the idea of central heating, building subterranean fires to warm floors and, hopefully, the rooms above. At about the same time, the Chinese invented a system by which heat from central ovens was directed through pipes to the various rooms of a dwelling. Sound familiar?

Surprisingly, the idea of central heating was slow to gain widespread acceptance—about 1,900 years. Although increasingly sophisticated central-heating equipment has been installed in most American homes built over the past 50 years or so, the idea is only now catching on in many other parts of the world, including Europe, Australia, southern Africa—and China, where it all began!

But we don't mean to put down space heating. It is a perfectly good concept and has a very important place as supplementary heating and in such installations as homes in very warm climates (where it may be needed only to "take off the chill" on some of the cooler nights), and summer cottages and ski chalets that are not intended as full-time residences.

Pot-bellied stove.

Circulator heater.

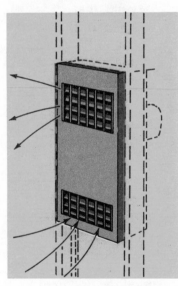

Grilles in doors and walls
to allow circulation of air.

Vertical wall heater.

SPACE HEATING UNITS

Space heaters, also called area heaters, are installed in the room or area to be heated. They include stoves, circulator heaters, and "pipeless" heaters.

Stoves are one of the simplest heating devices and also among the dirtiest (after the open fire). They also require more attention and heat less uniformly than most others. But they are relatively inexpensive. Most of them burn wood or coal and heat by radiation. If more than one stove is used, more than one chimney may be needed. Stoves are suitable for a backwoods hunting lodge or similar installation; otherwise, they are not very satisfactory.

Circulator heaters heat by convection, passing heat from an outer jacket. They are available for burning wood, coal, oil, or gas. With proper arrangement of rooms and doors, a circulator heater can heat four or five small rooms, but the heating may not be uniform. A small fan to aid circulation will increase efficiency. The distance from the heater to the center of each room to be heated, measured through the door opening, should not be more than about 18 feet. Doors must be left open, or grilles or louvers provided at top and bottom of doors or walls to allow circulation of air.

Pipeless furnaces can provide adequate

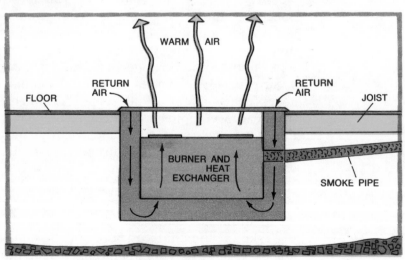

Diagram shows the working
of a floor heater.

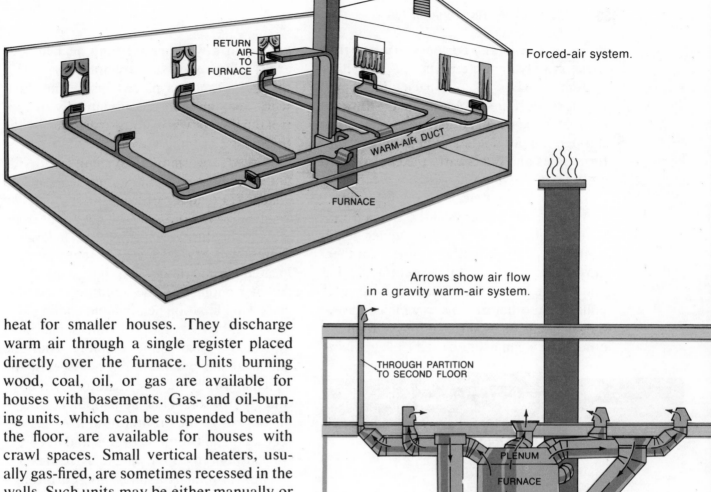

RETURN AIR TO FURNACE

WARM-AIR DUCT

FURNACE

Forced-air system.

Arrows show air flow in a gravity warm-air system.

THROUGH PARTITION TO SECOND FLOOR

PLENUM

FURNACE

heat for smaller houses. They discharge warm air through a single register placed directly over the furnace. Units burning wood, coal, oil, or gas are available for houses with basements. Gas- and oil-burning units, which can be suspended beneath the floor, are available for houses with crawl spaces. Small vertical heaters, usually gas-fired, are sometimes recessed in the walls. Such units may be either manually or thermostatically controlled. Heater vents are exhausted through the walls or carried up through the partitions to discharge burned gases through a common vent extending through the roof. Such a unit is often the choice for an extension built onto a house where the existing heating system is not up to carrying the additional load.

CENTRAL HEATING: WARM AIR

Gravity warm-air heating is typified by the big round furnace in the middle of the basement with an octupus-like network of large pipes to carry heat to the various rooms of the house. It works on the principle that warm air rises and cold air settles. Cold-air return grilles strategically located at such points as the bases of stairways and beneath large window areas collect the cool

air and duct it to the bottom of the furnace. It then passes through the heating chamber into the plenum above, where it is directed through the pipes to the various room registers located in floors or baseboards.

Gravity warm-air heating systems kept many generations of Americans in comparative cold-weather comfort. But they were inefficient, sometimes erratic, and often dirty; and the low-hanging pipes, which had to be pitched upward toward the heat outlets, virtually proscribed the use of the basement for anything other than doing the laundry at the stationary tubs and similar chores. Today, gravity warm-air systems are rarely installed, although they are still found in many homes built up to 20 or so years ago.

Forced warm-air systems are more efficient and generally cost less to install than their gravity counterparts. A forced-air system consists of a furnace, ducts, and registers. A fan or blower in the furnace circulates the warm air to the various rooms through supply ducts and heat outlets. Return grilles and ducts carry the cooled room air back to the furnace, where it is reheated and then recirculated.

A forced-air system can be divided into several different sections or zones, each operating independently with its own thermostat and all served by the central heating unit. Zones are often used in split-level houses and other designs in which one section is likely to retain heat longer than another. They can also be used to keep living areas warm while conserving heat in such areas as bedrooms that are not in use during the day. Dampers placed inside the ductwork open and close automatically to control the flow of warm air as called for by the thermostat.

Forced warm-air systems provide uniform heat and respond rapidly to changes in outdoor temperatures. They can be installed in houses with or without basements—the furnace need not be below the rooms to be heated, nor need it be centrally located. Some units can be adapted for summer cooling by the addition of cooling coils. Combination heating and cooling systems can be installed, with the same ducts utilized for year-round comfort. And the ducts are up out of the way beneath the joists, allowing the basement to be used for other purposes. This development was a major spur to the proliferation of basement recreation and rumpus rooms and even extra bedrooms over the past few decades.

The warm air is usually filtered through inexpensive replaceable or washable filters. Electronic air cleaners can sometimes be installed in existing forced-air systems and are available on many furnaces for new installations. These remove pollen, fine dust, and other irritants that pass through ordinary filters and are especially helpful for persons with respiratory ailments. The more expensive units feature automatic washing and drying of the cleaner.

A humidifier may be added to the heating system to add moisture to the house air and avoid the discomfort and other disadvantages of a too-dry environment.

Warm-air supply outlets are best placed along outside walls; by heating these naturally colder areas, they are more likely to keep a uniform temperature throughout the entire room. The outlets should be low in the wall, preferably in the baseboard, where air cannot blow directly on the room's occupants. Floor registers tend to collect dust

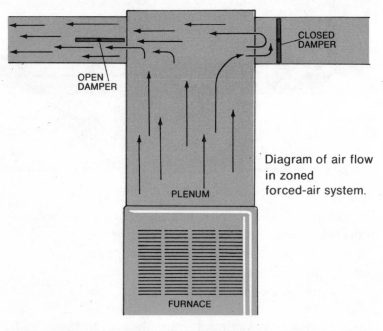

Diagram of air flow in zoned forced-air system.

CLOSED DAMPER

OPEN DAMPER

PLENUM

FURNACE

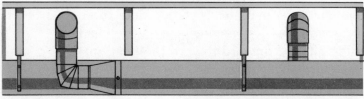

Location of ducts, run beneath joists, for a forced warm-air system.

Air filter.

Baseboard outlet.

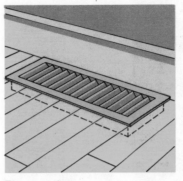

Floor outlet.

High wall outlet.

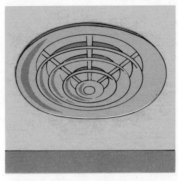

Ceiling diffuser.

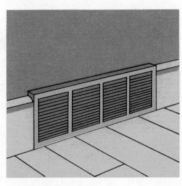

Baseboard return.

Floor return.

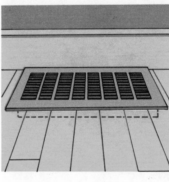

and debris, but they may have to be used when installing a new system in an old house.

High wall or ceiling outlets are sometimes used when the system is designed primarily for cooling. However, satisfactory cooling as well as heating can be obtained with low wall or baseboard outlets by increasing the air volume and velocity and by properly directing the flow by adjusting register fins or louvers.

Ceiling diffusers that discharge air downward may cause drafts; those that discharge air across the ceiling may cause smudging. However, these may be the only choices in a finished basement room that is heated by the main furnace.

Most installations have a cold-air return in each room except for smaller areas such as bathrooms. When supply outlets are along outside walls, return grilles should be along inside partitions in the baseboard or floor. When supply outlets are along inside walls, as was customary with earlier forced-air systems, return grilles should be along outside walls.

Smaller homes with perimeter-type heating systems (outlets on outside walls) may have just a single, centrally located return. In two-level or split-level homes, return grilles should be on each level. Returns should be situated in natural cold-air traps, such as hallways and at the bottoms of stairways.

In houses with crawl spaces instead of basements, horizontal oil- or gas-burning

Location of return grille in cold-air trap.

Horizontal furnace installation in crawl space.

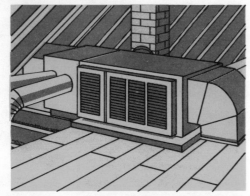

Horizontal furnace installation in attic.

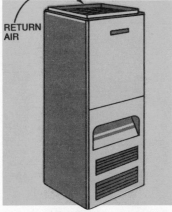

RETURN AIR

Counterflow furnace.

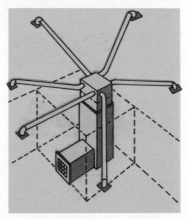

Upflow-type vertical furnace.

furnaces may be installed in the crawl space or suspended from ceiling joists in a utility room or attached garage. A gas unit of this type can also be installed in an attic. Adequate space should be allowed for servicing furnaces in crawl spaces or attics, and furnaces and ducts installed in attics should be heavily insulated to prevent excessive heat loss in these naturally cold areas.

The entire crawl space is sometimes used as an air supply plenum or chamber. Warm air from an upright furnace or a suspended horizontal furnace is forced through a central duct into the crawl space, from where it enters the rooms above through perimeter outlets, or through a series of slots in the floor adjacent to the outside walls. With tight, well-insulated crawl space walls, this system can provide comfortable, uniform temperatures throughout the house.

Vertical oil or gas furnaces designed for installation in a closet or wall recess are popular for smaller houses. A counterflow type discharges the warm air at the bottom to warm the floor level. Some types provide discharge grilles into several rooms from a centrally located furnace. Upflow-type vertical furnaces may discharge the warm air through attic ducts and ceiling diffusers. Return air is usually pulled directly into the furnace from a wall grille, rather than through return ducts. Because of this, these furnaces are less expensive, but also heat less evenly.

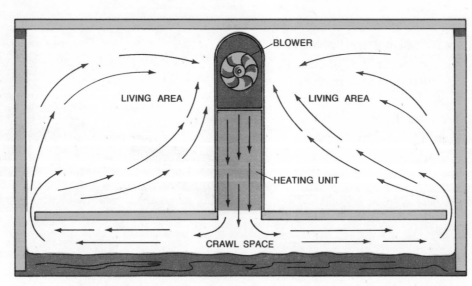

BLOWER

LIVING AREA

LIVING AREA

HEATING UNIT

Crawl space plenum system (arrows show flow of warm air)

CRAWL SPACE

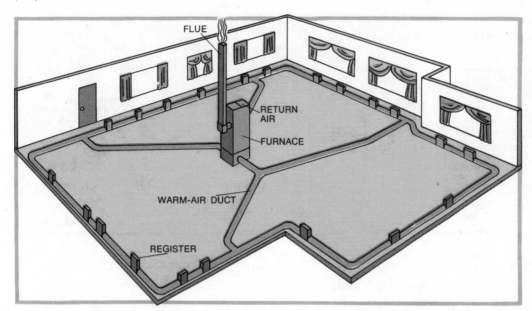

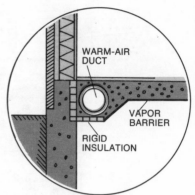

Perimeter loop system.

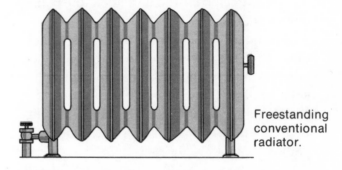

Freestanding conventional radiator.

Houses built on concrete slabs may be heated by a "perimeter loop." A counter-flow furnace circulates warm air through ducts cast around the outer edge of the slab. The warm ducts heat the floor, and the warm air is discharged through floor registers to heat the various rooms. To prevent excessive heat loss in such a system, the edge of the slab should be insulated from the outer walls and separated from the ground by a vapor barrier.

CENTRAL HEATING: HOT WATER, STEAM

Hot-water and steam heating systems are similar. Each consists of a boiler, pipes, and room-heating units (radiators or convectors). Hot water or steam, generated in the boiler, is circulated through the pipes to the room units, where the heat is transferred to the room air.

Boilers are made of cast iron or steel and are designed to burn gas, oil, or coal (which may yet make a comeback). Cast iron boilers are more resistant to corrosion than steel units. Water is the corrosive culprit, but its effect can be lessened with chemi-

cals. Proper water treatment can greatly prolong the life of steel boiler tubes. Consult an expert on this; water composition varies greatly in different parts of the country.

When you buy a boiler, make sure that it is "certified." Certified cast iron boilers are stamped "IBR" (Institute of Boiler and Radiator Manufacturers); steel boilers should be stamped "SBI" (Steel Boiler Institute). Most boilers are rated for both hot water and steam—check the nameplate. It's best to seek the advice of a reputable contractor when selecting a boiler.

Conventional radiators are set on the floor or mounted on the wall. More modern types are recessed in the wall. Recessed radiators should be backed with 1-inch insulation board, a sheet of reflective insulation, or both.

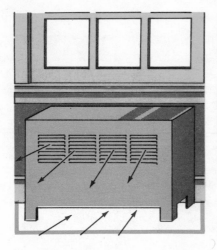

Radiator cabinet (left), baseboard radiator (above), cabinet convector (right).

Radiators may be partially or fully enclosed by a cabinet. A full cabinet must have openings at top and bottom for air circulation. Preferred radiator location is under a window.

Baseboard radiators are hollow or finned units that resemble and take the place of conventional wood baseboards along outside walls. They provide uniform heat throughout a well-insulated room, with little temperature variation between floor and ceiling.

Convectors usually consist of finned tubes enclosed in a cabinet or baseboard unit with openings at top and bottom. Hot water or steam is circulated through the tubes. Air enters at the bottom of the enclosure, is heated by the tubes, and exits at the top. Some larger units include fans for forced air circulation. With this type of convector, summer cooling can be provided by adding a chiller and the necessary controls. Convectors are installed against an outside wall or recessed in a wall.

In a gravity hot-water heating system, the boiler must be located in the basement or crawl space, below the radiators. The supply line from the boiler to the radiators must have sufficient pitch or rise to induce circulation of the heated water. After the water gives off its heat in the radiators or convectors, it returns to the boiler through a separate return pipe line.

Because water expands when heated, an expansion tank must be provided in the system. In an "open" system, the tank is located above the highest radiator or convector and has an overflow pipe extending through the roof, thus exposing the water to the air. In a "closed" system, the expansion tank may be placed anywhere, but usually near the boiler. Half the tank is filled with air, which compresses when the heated water expands. Since the water is under pressure, the boiling point is raised. Higher temperatures can therefore be maintained without steam forming in the radiators, and smaller radiators can be used. There is little difference in fuel requirements between an open and a closed system.

Gravity systems require large supply and return mains; consequently, response to temperature changes is relatively slow because of the large volume of water in the pipes. Forced hot-water systems are considerably more efficient. A small booster or circulating pump forces the hot water through the pipes to the room radiators or convectors.

A one-pipe forced hot-water system utilizes a single pipe or main for both supply and return. It makes a complete circuit from the boiler through the system and back to the boiler. Two risers extend from the main to each room radiator or convector. In a two-pipe system, there are two

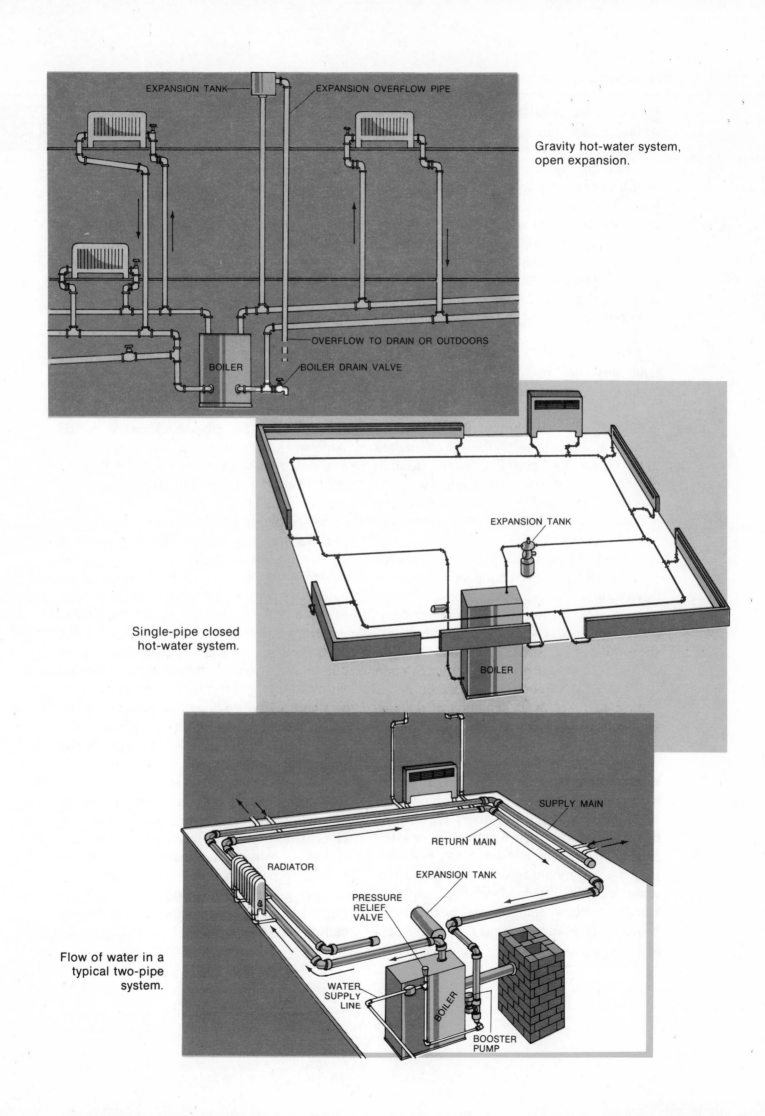

Gravity hot-water system, open expansion.

EXPANSION TANK

EXPANSION OVERFLOW PIPE

OVERFLOW TO DRAIN OR OUTDOORS

BOILER DRAIN VALVE

BOILER

Single-pipe closed hot-water system.

EXPANSION TANK

BOILER

Flow of water in a typical two-pipe system.

SUPPLY MAIN

RETURN MAIN

RADIATOR

EXPANSION TANK

PRESSURE RELIEF VALVE

WATER SUPPLY LINE

BOILER

BOOSTER PUMP

mains. One carries the heated water to the room-heating units; the other returns the cooled water to the boiler.

A one-pipe system is more economical to install since, as its name implies, it requires less pipe. However, in a one-pipe system, cooled water from each radiator mixes with the hot water flowing through the main, and each succeeding radiator receives cooler water. Allowance must be made for this in sizing the radiators—larger ones may be required at points farther along in the system.

As with gravity systems, an expansion tank must be provided, either above the highest point in the system (open) or near the boiler (closed).

Heating coils may be installed in the boiler or in a separate water heater connected to the boiler of a forced hot-water system to provide hot water for household use year-round. A qualified and reputable heating engineer should be consulted about the design of such a system.

A single boiler can supply hot water for several different circulation zones so that temperatures of individual rooms or areas of the house can be controlled independently. Remote areas such as a garage, workshop, or even a small greenhouse can be supplied with controlled heat. Valves open and close to direct the hot water in response to thermostat demands in the various zones of the house.

Gas- and oil-fired boilers for forced hot-water systems are compact and can be installed in an out-of-the-way corner of the basement or in a closet, utility room, or other space on the first floor. Electrically heated systems are even more compact; the heat exchanger, expansion tank, and controls may be mounted on a wall. Some systems include thermostatically controlled electric heating components in the baseboard units, eliminating the need for a central heating unit. Such a system may be a

single loop installation circulating water by means of a pump, or it may be composed of individual sealed units filled with antifreeze solution. The sealed units depend on gravity flow of the solution in the unit. Each unit may have a thermostat, or several units may be controlled from one thermostat.

Steam heating systems are similar in concept and design to hot-water systems, but they are generally less popular for residential installations because they are less responsive to rapid changes in heat demands. In a one-pipe steam system, steam is generated in the boiler and delivered through a large main to pipes connecting to individual radiators. Here it gives off heat and condenses to water which drains through the same pipes back to the boiler. Air that may be in the radiators or pipes is exhausted through vents on the radiators, which emit the air but close on contact with steam.

A two-pipe steam heating system delivers the steam from the boiler through a supply line to radiators or convectors in the rooms, where it gives off heat and condenses to water. A separate pipe line from the lower end of each heat outlet drains the water to the return line that carries it back to the boiler. A trap at each radiator or convector prevents steam from returning with the water. Usually piping is arranged so that gravity provides the impetus for the water to return to the boiler. Where sufficient drop cannot be provided, as in a house without a basement, a condensation pump is installed for this purpose.

Radiant-panel heating is another method of heating with forced hot water or steam. (It is also a method of heating with electricity.) Hot water or steam is circulated through pipes concealed in the floor, wall, or ceiling. Heat is transmitted through the pipes to the surface of the floor, wall, or ceiling and from there to the room by radiation and convection. No outlets are re-

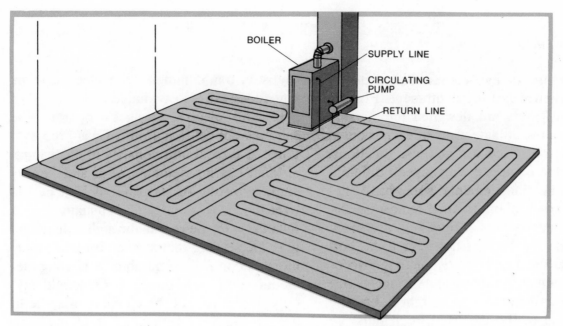

BOILER
SUPPLY LINE
CIRCULATING
PUMP
RETURN LINE

Radiant-panel heating.

quired — the floor, walls, or ceiling, in effect, act as radiators.

With radiant-panel heating, rooms are usually more comfortable at lower air temperatures than with other heating systems at higher air temperatures because temperatures are generally uniform throughout the room. This uniformity reduces body heat loss of the room's occupants and increases body comfort.

Underfloor radiant-panel heating systems are difficult to design, and the job should be left to a qualified engineer. A carpeted or bare wood floor, for example, might be very comfortable whereas a vinyl-covered kitchen floor or ceramic-tiled bathroom floor in the same system might be too hot, especially for bare feet. Panel heating in exterior walls requires adequate insulation behind to minimize heat loss. Ceiling panels, too, must be properly insulated unless you want to heat the space above the ceiling, as in a two-story house.

ELECTRIC HEATING

Electricity for house heating was first adopted in low-cost power areas such as the Tennessee Valley and the Pacific Northwest. A decade or so ago, improved equipment and techniques made electricity very competitive with flame fuels for heat-

ing in other parts of the country as well, and "all-electric" homes were highly touted. Convenience, cleanliness, even heat, safety, low maintenance cost, lack of noise or fumes, space saving, individual room temperature control, and many other advantages made it seem that electric heating was an idea whose time had come.

Then the "energy crunch" suddenly appeared. Utility companies, especially in the Northeast, that had been encouraging electric heat installations with lower rates for greater electrical usage, suddenly reversed these policies and penalized the electric heat users with higher rates. Owners of modestly sized all-electric homes in such areas as New England and New York found $300 and $400 monthly bills in their mailboxes. And that was several years before the record-breaking cold spells 1977–1978. Needless to say, electric heating systems rapidly declined in popularity.

Today, the cost of electricity in many areas proscribes the installation of new electric heating systems. Many utilities refuse to service such installations. (The same is true of gas-fired systems in some regions.) Still, hope must spring, and we hope and trust that solutions will be found to the energy problem, making it possible to more widely enjoy the many benefits of electric home heating systems.

There are many types and designs of electric house heating equipment. Electric baseboard units are designed for installation along the outside walls of each room in place of the baseboard at these locations. They come equipped with several different types of heating elements; some have supplementary sections with thermostats and convenience outlets. Provisions are made for wiring the heaters from the back, bottom, and ends and for connecting two or more sections. As many units as necessary may be assembled and installed, but the safe limits of the electric circuit must be considered. A 20-ampere house circuit with a 120-volt service can handle 2,400 watts. Most heaters consume between 1,000 and 2,500 watts (check the nameplate for this information). Make sure that your home's electrical system is adequate for this load (220-240 volt service is normally required).

Electric heating cable can be installed in new plastered ceilings or in new plaster over existing ceilings. The cable is laid back and forth, with spacing dependent on the heat-loss factor in the room to be heated.

Gypsum board panels with electric cable embedded are also available.

Central electric furnaces operate the same as conventional oil- or gas-fired systems. A typical unit consists of electric resistance heating elements, a fan, and thermostatic controls. Air is warmed as it passes over the heating coils and is usually forced by a fan into the rooms through a duct system. Depending on the need for heat, thermostats control the number of heating elements operating at one time. On a mild day, only one or two of the elements may be in use. During very cold weather, all the heating elements may come on to maintain the house temperature.

Electric heating units may be installed in the floor of a room and covered with a grille. These are usually used in front of hard-to-heat areas such as under floor-length picture windows and glass doors where it is impossible to install baseboard heaters. Heating is by convection from resistance heating elements.

Radiant and convection heating panels, equipped with various types of heating elements, are available for recessed or surface wall mounting. In the convection-type heater, warmed air is circulated either by gravity or by an electric fan. One or more of these wall units are installed in each room according to the heat requirements. Some have self-contained thermostats; others are controlled by wall thermostats. A grille should cover the front of the unit to prevent contact with the heating element.

Electric baseboard unit; partly cutaway view showing fins and wiring (left).

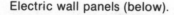

Heating cable in ceiling panels (below left).

Electric wall panels (below).

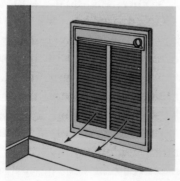

HEAT PUMPS

The heat pump is a single unit that both heats and cools. It works on the same principle as does a refrigerator. In a refrigerator, heat is taken out of the stored food and cabinet and expelled into the surrounding air. The heat pump extracts heat from the

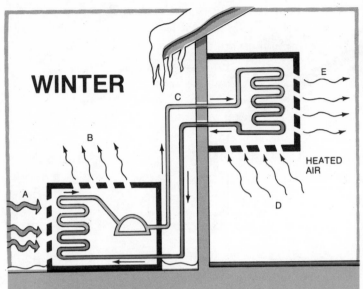

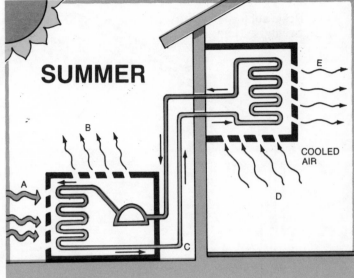

Heat-pump system.

A. Outside cold air.
B. Colder air expelled.
C. Heat extracted from outdoor air pumped inside.
D. Room air drawn in.
E. Warm air into room.

A. Outside warm air.
B. Warmer air expelled.
C. Cooled refrigerant pumped inside.
D. Room air drawn in.
E. Cold air into room.

outside air to warm a room or the entire house. A variation obtains heat from water in a well or pumped through a coil of pipes buried in the earth. As the heat is removed, the air or water is returned outside. Supplementary resistance heaters are usually used in conjunction with heat pumps to help heat the house during extremely cold weather.

In summer, the operation is reversed. Heat is removed from the air inside the house and discharged to the outside.

Heat pumps came on the market in a big way in the 1950's, and for a while it appeared that they were going to revolutionize home heating/cooling. Although the initial cost of a heat pump is higher than most other types of heating systems, it is efficient and clean and — except in colder climates — generally less expensive to operate. But problems plagued the devices. The units were noisy and vibrated excessively. Breakdowns were common and repairs expensive. The state of the art was not sufficiently advanced to make pumps that

could stand the wide range of temperatures encountered in year-round use. As a result, heat pumps virtually disappeared from the national market, maintaining sales only in the deep South.

A few years ago, a new generation of heat pumps appeared. The bugs had been eliminated, and the manufacturers were much more cautious in their marketing. Slowly the pumps have been making their way north, their progress helped by skyrocketing fuel costs and acute gas and oil shortages. Comparative figures invite dispute, but it would seem that in the long run the heat pump may well be more economical than other systems even in a cold climate. In any event, it is enjoying increasing popularity.

SOLAR HEATING

Somewhere on the horizon, as dazzling as a desert sunset, is the prospect of solar

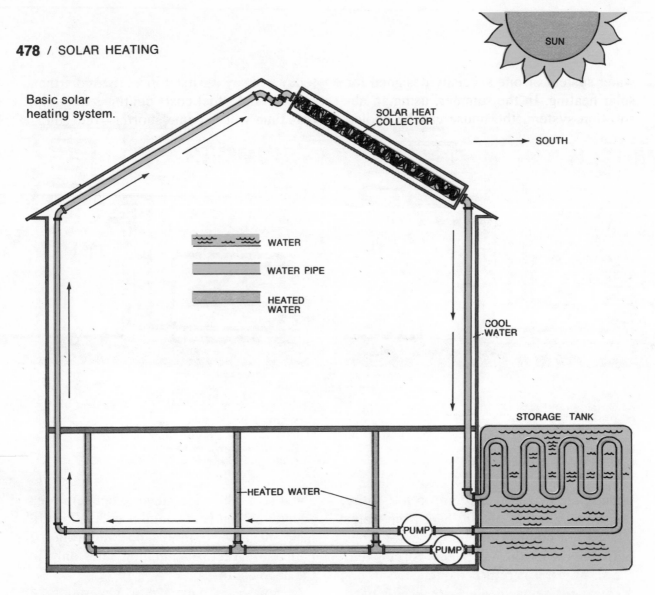

Basic solar heating system.

SUN

SOLAR HEAT COLLECTOR

SOUTH

WATER

WATER PIPE

HEATED WATER

COOL WATER

STORAGE TANK

HEATED WATER

PUMP

PUMP

heating. Scientists tell us that the amount of solar radiation striking the roof of a typical house in a single year is ten times greater than the house's annual heating demands. How to harness this radiation to provide heating and cooling inside the house had intrigued men for centuries. Although the technology in the field is still somewhat limited, the sense of urgency inspired by the energy crisis has led to some intense experimentation and innovative installations. Builders in various parts of the country have begun to offer solar-heated houses. But the systems currently available are, for the most part, prohibitively expensive for the average homeowner.

The parts of a solar heating system are relatively simple. A large, usually flat, pan-

el is placed on the roof of the house, in a wall, or on the ground next to the house. The collector should be about half the size of the roof. It faces south and is tilted at approximately 45 degrees in the northern United States, flatter farther south.

As the sun's rays hit the collector, they heat either air or a water-antifreeze mixture that takes the heat into a storage tank. The tank, which is usually filled with water, must be fairly large—about 2,000-gallon capacity. The tank can also be filled with rocks to store the heat; in that case an even larger tank is required, and air, rather than water, brings the heat from the collector to the tank. The storage tank then serves as a source of heat for the distribution system, either a slightly modified forced-air or hot-water system or one specially designed for solar heating. In the summer, using an absorption system, the house can be cooled using the same heat.

There are many variations to the system. The walls and floors of the house itself may serve to store the heat, then warm the rooms by radiation. The Pueblo Indians used such a system to cope with the hot days and bitter cold nights in the Southwest. They built their dwellings with thick adobe walls that collected and stored the sun's heat, then radiated it to the inside to take away the chill of the night.

Another approach is to have solar cells in the roof, which react chemically when exposed to solar radiation, generating electricity which is then stored in batteries and used to power conventional heating (and cooling) systems. Although still in the early experimental stages, this type of application could be a breakthrough that might make solar heat economically feasible for residential use.

A solar heating system is rarely intended to fulfill all the heating needs of a house. The storage tank usually carries enough heat to get through a few overcast days and nights. After that, a conventional system must carry the heating load. Despite that, and despite its high initial cost, it is estimated that a solar heating system as available today will pay for itself in a little more than ten years. As fuel costs continue to go up, that time will become shorter—the "fuel" costs of a solar heating system will never rise.

If solar heating for residences gains widespread favor, it will require some rethinking of local zoning ordinances. At present, few such laws would protect the owner of a solar-heated house from a neighbor's erecting a building or planting trees that would block the sun from his collectors, rendering his heating system useless. That would be the ultimate "spite fence," but neighbors have been known to do such things.

Many companies have jumped into the budding solar energy field, not all of them of unquestionable character. Since the technology is new and not widely known, it is inevitable that some fast-buck hustlers and outright crooks have come on the scene, making exaggerated promises of performance and economy in pushing "solar heat" on homeowners whose sales resistance has been greatly weakened by the shockingly high costs of conventional heating fuels. As ever, let the buyer beware. If you wish to explore the possibilities of using the sun to help heat your house, deal only with reputable and knowledgeable manufacturers and contractors—who, at this stage, are still few and far between.

Heating Systems

2

Fuels

O VER THE CENTURIES, man has burned a number of fuels to keep himself warm, among them animal fat, wood, dried manure, peat, charcoal, bones, coke, coal, oil, and gas. The latter two are most widely used today, and it wasn't too long ago that you could depend on lively arguments between proponents of each fuel whenever the subject came up at a gathering of homeowners — which was "cleaner," which was more economical, which was all-around "better." Today these same homeowners are more likely to sympathize with each other about the astronomical fuel costs and the shrinking availability of both oil and gas in many areas. And the diehard who has clung to his coal furnace may laugh at both of them as he ponders his wisdom in the warmth of a home heated with a fuel that is in relative abundance.

Modern heating equipment is generally efficient when used with the fuel for which it was designed. But even with modern equipment, some fuels cost more than others to do the same job. Although cost comparisons vary widely according to geographical area and fuel availability, it is possible to set some general guidelines for determining which fuel will be most economical. Electricity, although not a fuel, must also be considered because of its increasing popularity for heating homes.

COMPARING FUEL COSTS

A few terms must be understood to make the comparisons. As a basic unit of measurement, a Btu (British thermal unit) is defined as the quantity of heat required to raise the temperature of one gram of water one degree Fahrenheit. (As this country is approaching the metric age, we should inform you that a calorie is the quantity of heat required to raise the temperature of one gram of water one degree Centigrade; one Btu is the equivalent of 252 calories.) A therm is 100,000 Btu's.

The therms of heat per dollar should not be the sole consideration in selecting a heating fuel. Installation cost, the efficiency with which each unit converts fuel into useful heat, and the insulation level of the house should also be considered. For example, electrically heated houses usually have twice the insulation thickness (a one-time expense), particularly in the ceiling and floor, and therefore may require considerably less heat input than houses heated with fuel-burning systems. To compare costs properly, efficiency of combustion and heat value of the fuel must be known.

Heating units vary in efficiency depending upon type, method of operation, condition, and location. Gas- and oil-fired steam and hot-water boilers of current design, operated under favorable conditions, have 70 to 80 percent efficiency. Forced warm-air furnaces with gas burners or atomizing oil burners generally provide about 80 percent efficiency in converting the fuel to heat. Oil-fired furnaces with the less expensive pot-type burners usually develop not over 70 percent efficiency. Stoker-fired coal furnaces range from 60 to 75 percent efficiency. Electricity is rated at 100 percent efficiency because there is no chimney and usually no ductwork through which heat may be lost. Proponents of other fuels point out that this is "in-house" efficiency and does not take into account the use of other fuel at the electrical powerhouse that went into generating the electricity. But for our purposes, the in-house figure is valid, although conservationists may think otherwise.

You can figure the comparative costs of various fuels and electricity based on local prices by using the table on this page. The efficiency of electricity, oil, gas, and coal is taken as 100, 75, 75, and 65 percent respectively. The efficiencies may actually be higher (except for electricity) or lower, depending upon conditions, but these values are reasonable.

The heat values in the table are taken as 3,413 Btu per kilowatt hour (kwh) of electricity for resistance heating; 139,000 Btu per gallon of No. 2 fuel oil (the grade most commonly used for home heating); 1,050 Btu per cubic foot of natural gas; 92,000 Btu per gallon of propane (LP) gas; and 13,000 Btu per pound of coal.

More Btu's of heat per kilowatt hour can generally be obtained with a heat pump installation than with resistance heating units. The difference varies depending on outside temperature and other factors. In warm climates, heat pumps may need only about half as much electricity as resistance heaters. In the very cold climates of the northerly states, the heat pump may use as much electric energy as is required for resistance heating.

For the person in the market for a new heating system, fuel cost comparisons are at best a vague, albeit important, guideline. As anyone who has had to pay fuel bills during the past three or four winters is painfully aware, prices can fluctuate (invariably upward) wildly over the course of a heating season. Relative costs provide a good take-off point, but perhaps a more vital consideration is the likelihood of continued availability of the fuel. At the present time, new electric and gas heating installations are barred by some utility companies. This situation is likely to ease, but what the future holds is uncertain. Check out the conditions and prospects in your region before making any decision on heating fuel.

Fuel	Quantity to supply one therm of heat	Multiply values in column 2 by local costs per	Comparative costs per therm of heat
Electricity	29.3 kwh	kwh	_____
Fuel oil	.96 gal.	gal.	_____
Natural gas	127 cu. ft.	cu. ft.	_____
LP gas (propane)	1.45 gal.	gal.	_____
Coal	11.8 lbs. (.006 ton)	ton	_____

Fuels

OIL

Oil in one form or another has been used as a heating fuel for a very long time. Around the turn of the century, the technology had advanced as far as the kerosene heaters that were providing cold-weather comfort for households throughout the United States. Then, in the early 1920's, the first automatic oil burner heralded a new era of comfort control, allowing the home's occupants to select the desired temperature by the mere touch of a thermostat. Those early automatic burners were remarkably sophisticated, and the basic design, with modifications, is still in widespread use today.

Oil requires no handling and little space for storing—often the storage tank is buried in the ground. It leaves no ash and burns "clean"—the combustion chamber is sealed off from the heat exchanger so that combustion by-products cannot enter the distribution system.

Two grades of fuel oil are used for home heating. No. 1 is lighter and somewhat more expensive than the far more common No. 2, which has higher heat value per gallon. The nameplate or instruction booklet that comes with the oil burner indicates what grade of fuel is to be used. In general, No. 1 is used in pot-type burners and No. 2 in gun- and rotary-type burners.

There are two kinds of oil burners: vaporizing and atomizing. Vaporizing burners premix the oil vapor with air. The pot-type vaporizing burner consists of a pot containing a pool of oil. An automatic or handset valve regulates the amount of oil in the pot. Heat from the flame vaporizes the oil. In some heaters, a pilot flame or electric arc ignites the oil pot when heat is required; in earlier models, the oil is ignited manually and burns at any set fuel rate between high and low fire until shut off. There are few moving parts, and operation is quiet. Some pot-type burners do not even require electric power.

Atomizing burners are of two general types: gun (pressure) and rotary. The gun burner is by far the more popular for residential heating applications. It has a pump that forces oil through an atomizing nozzle. A fan blows air into the oil fog, and an electric spark ignites the mixture, which burns in a refractory-lined firepot. This is the type of oil burner used in most modern residential oil heating installations.

The future of oil as a heating fuel is wrapped up in national, international, and industrial politics. Boycotts, embargos, depletion allowances, offshore and onshore drilling rights, supertanker economics—these and other murky matters will determine the availability, as well as the affordability, of heating oil in the years ahead.

GAS

Three kinds of gas—natural, manufactured, and bottled—are used for residential heating. Bottled gas (usually propane) is referred to as LPG (liquefied petroleum gas) or simply LP. It has been gaining in popularity as a heating fuel, especially in rural areas where other fuels are less readily available. Different gases have different heat values when burned. A burner adjusted for one type of gas must be readjusted when another gas is used.

The room thermostat controls a valve that feeds the gas to the burner. A pilot light is needed for combustion. The pilot may be lighted at the beginning of the heating season and shut off when the crocuses and rosebuds appear. It may also be kept burning year-round, helping to prevent condensation during nonheating seasons that will hasten corrosion of metal parts of the furnace. However, this latter practice is now being discouraged by energy conservationists, who claim that the cumulative waste of

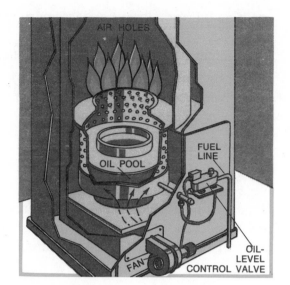

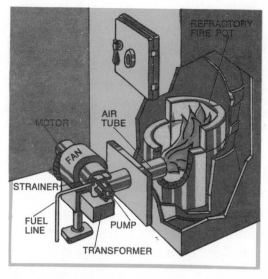

Pot-type vaporizing oil burner (far left).

Gun-type atomizing oil burner (left).

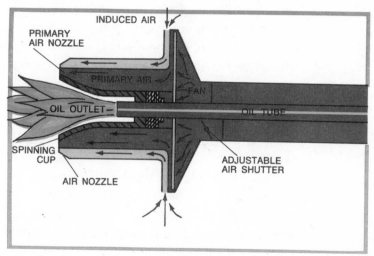

Rotary-type atomizing oil burner.

gas resources by year-round pilot burning is horrendous.

The pilot light should be equipped with a safety thermostat to prevent the gas valve from opening if the pilot goes out; no gas can then escape into the house. (Pilot lights of all gas-burning appliances—water heaters, clothes dryers, ranges—should be equipped with similar safety devices.)

Conversion gas burners may be used in boilers and furnaces designed for other fuels if they have adequate heating surfaces and are properly gas-tight. All gas burners should be installed by competent, experienced heating contractors, closely following manufacturer's directions. Gas-burning equipment should bear the seal of the American Gas Association.

Gas-burning furnaces must be vented to the outside. Keep chimneys and smoke-pipes free from leaks. Connect electrical controls for gas-burning equipment to a separate switch so that the circuit can be quickly shut down in case of trouble. Gas burners should be cleaned, inspected, and properly adjusted annually. Gas is a clean, trouble-free, and safe fuel, but it does have dangerous and explosive potential if used incorrectly or carelessly. Even the most painstaking safeguards can be compromised by foolishness. Don't be foolish.

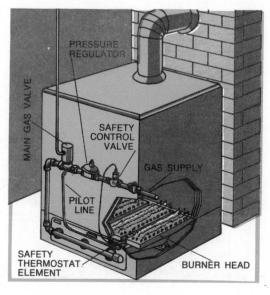

Gas burner, room thermostat controlled.

Fuels

Bottled gas is heavier than air. If it leaks into the basement, it will accumulate at the lowest point and create a hazard. When using bottled gas, make sure that the safety control valve is so placed that it shuts off the gas to the pilot light as well as the burner when the pilot goes out.

ELECTRICITY

Electric heating offers convenience, cleanliness, evenness of heat, safety, and freedom from odors and fumes. It also offers, in many regions, ridiculously high electric bills because of a power shortage that has prompted many utility companies to refuse service to new electric heating installations. Some of these utilities are even encouraging users of electric heat to switch to competitive fuels — the same homeowners that they were wooing a few years back with promises of low-cost "all-electric" living.

Nevertheless, electric heating continues to be popular in those areas where the power crunch is not so acute, and presumably it will return to other areas when the energy situation gets sorted out, as it must.

Houses that are heated electrically must be well insulated and weatherstripped. Windows should be double- or triple-glazed, and walls, floors, and ceilings should be vapor-sealed. The required insulation, weatherproofing, and vapor barriers can easily be provided in new homes but may be difficult to add to older houses. No chimney is needed for electric heat.

The heating equipment should be only large enough to handle the heat load. Over-sized equipment costs more both initially and in operation and requires heavier wiring than does properly sized equipment.

COAL

Coal has a somewhat spotty history as a heating fuel. Its combustible qualities were known to the early Greeks, yet through the centuries it was seldom used. In coal-rich England, burning coal was made a capital offense in the 14th century, and at least one man was executed for transgressing the law. Queen Elizabeth I changed all that, and London effectively became one big smudgepot — but its residents (at least those who could afford shelter and coal) were snug and warm, if somewhat sooty.

From early in this century until the

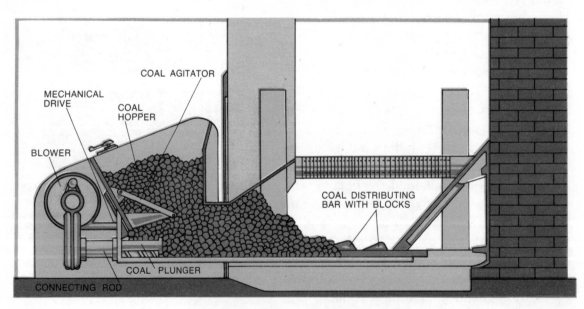

Coal stoker fire burner.

1940's, coal was the staple fuel throughout much of the United States, and the coal bin was a space-consuming fixture in many basements. Homeowners whose driveways were not adequate to bear the weight of the delivery truck would have the coal (usually in quantities of one or two tons) dumped in the street, from where it became a family project to move it by shovel and wheelbarrow to the "coal window" outside the basement bin. Several generations of Americans developed their muscles in this way. Who needed health spas?

Gas and oil shoved coal far into the background as a residential heating fuel during the post-World War II building boom. But the sudden and critical fuel shortage of a few years ago catapulted coal into prominence again, at least as an alternative to be considered. Although few people actually converted from gas, oil, or electricity to coal as a heating fuel, those who still heated with coal furnaces had their day and most have decided to stick with coal "for the duration" until they see what the future fuel situation will be. Since the nation's coal reserves are quite extensive, it is just possible that coal may be the fuel of the future, at least the immediate future, as well as that of the past.

Two kinds of coal are used for home heating: anthracite (hard) and bituminous (soft). Anthracite coal sizes are standardized, bituminous are not. Heat value of different sizes of coal varies little, but certain sizes are better suited for burning in firepots of given sizes and depths. If you burn coal, your supplier can advise you on this.

Both anthracite and bituminous coal are used in stoker firing (stokers automatically feed the coal to the furnace, relieving the homeowner of the tedious shovel-wielding that plagued his grandfather morning and night). Stokers may be installed at the front, side, or rear of a furnace or boiler. Space must be allowed for servicing the stoker and for cleaning the furnace. Furnaces and boilers with horizontal heating surfaces require frequent cleaning, because fly ash (a fine, powdery substance) collects on these surfaces. Follow manufacturer's directions for operating stokers.

Although coal furnaces of recent manufacture are considerably improved over earlier models, they still create dirt and grime, which can be transmitted throughout the house. Still, they must be considered as an alternative if crunch comes to crash in the energy situation.

WOOD

Wood, probably man's first heating fuel, deserves at least passing mention, although its use today is usually limited to rustic cabin stoves and home fireplaces, which are intended primarily for aesthetics and only secondarily as supplemental sources of warmth. The use of wood requires more labor and more storage space than do other fuels. And, unless you can chop your own, wood costs are, like other fuels, almost out of sight, especially in such unforested areas as New York City, Chicago, Los Angeles, and other major urban centers. On the plus side, wood fires are easy to start, burn with little smoke, and leave little ash.

Most well-seasoned hardwoods have about half the heat value per pound as that of good coal. A cord (equivalent to a stack of cut firewood 4 by 4 by 8 feet, or 128 cubic feet) of hickory, oak, beech, sugar maple, or rock elm weighs roughly two tons and has about the same heat value as a ton of good coal.

FUTURE FUELS

Although it is unlikely that new heating fuels will be discovered in the immediate future, the pressures created by the rapid depletion of natural resources and by international politics will spur developments along this line. Much research has already been done in solar heating (see CHAPTER 1). Many other areas have been explored as well. Some may bear fruit.

One potentially fruitful experiment literally grew on trees. The town of Brookhaven, New York, collected hundreds of thousands of cubic yards of leaves for its Composting Center. As any good green-thumber knows, the center of a compost pile generates a lot of heat as the organic material decomposes. Brookhaven decided to utilize this heat by running a copper pipe through the pile and into a large greenhouse on the site. The results have been "gratifying," although town officials don't recommend that you throw away your present heating unit and depend on the leaves of autumn to offset the cold of winter — at least not yet.

Although a lot of the ideas that have been put forward for sources of heat fall into the crackpot category, many of them warrant further study. Tapping the wind as a producer of energy — and, consequently, heat — is certainly not new, but it is coming under fresh scrutiny by universities, utilities, industry, private individuals, and the federal government. Several experimental facilities have already been built, and results are being carefully studied. In the New Mexico desert, a 170-foot-high vertical axis wind turbine, resembling an upside-down eggbeater, is being tested by the Federal Energy Research and Development Administration. If it checks out, the device will generate electric power that can be utilized for residential heating.

Not only the wind above but the heat below are prospects for heating your home. Several miles beneath the earth's surface are magmas, or steam chambers, which scientists are looking at with renewed interest as heat sources. In Reykjavík, Iceland, where the chambers are relatively close to the surface, most of the city's heating needs are supplied by these subterranean sources.

Some farther-out suggestions for future fuel sources seem somewhat further away as well. These include the conversion of old tires into fuel oil and the recovery of gas from garbage and (back to the basics) manure. Although all these schemes are technologically feasible, their implementation seems economically prohibitive at present. Tomorrow? Who can say?

For now, the most promising possibility seems to be the sun. With the heavy emphasis being given to solar heat research projects, advances will almost surely be made that will bring the cost of installing this type of residential heating within the reach of the average homeowner — and then the choice will be much more attractive.

Beyond that? Nuclear fuel is almost certainly in the offing, although nobody can say at this time exactly when. There are well over 200 nuclear generating plants already in operation or under construction in this country, but the true capabilities and limitations of nuclear power are yet to be fully evaluated. Most likely, the benefits of nuclear power will be utilized in terms of more readily available power for the home heating system; but a more direct method of nuclear heating may yet be devised.

Such exotic thoughts of future fuels won't keep you and your family warm next winter. If you are in the market for a new heating system, your fuel choices are still among gas, oil, electricity, and possibly coal, with a consideration given to that friendly old sun as a supplementary source of warmth.

3

Heating System Controls

OUR PRIMITIVE forebears may have discovered fire as a source of heat, but controlling it was something else. They knew that rubbing two sticks together turned on the heat, and they soon learned that water carried from the nearby stream in a brontosaurus-skin bucket would douse it. But the idea that someone might simply turn a dial pointer to 60 or 65 or 70 or whatever and then sit back while the heating system delivered that exact degree of heat would have been totally incomprehensible to them—as it was to most people until quite recently. Remember this the next time you adjust your heating system's thermostat.

THERMOSTATS

In its simplest form, a thermostat is a bimetallic switch, made of two pieces of dissimilar metals that expand at different temperatures. One piece is usually brass, which expands quickly when heated, and the other may be invar (an alloy of nickel and steel), which heats and expands much more slowly. The two fused metal pieces remain in place when cool, completing an electrical circuit. Under heat conditions, tension between the two metals expanding at different temperatures causes the fused strip to bend. When it reaches a temperature level indicated by the thermostat's selector dial, one end of the bimetallic strip rises far enough to lose contact with the circuit. The power is thus severed, and the furnace burner or electric heat current is shut off. As it cools, the metal regains its

original shape until it again closes the circuit, and heating resumes.

Since the thermostat (or thermostats, in the case of a zoned system) controls the

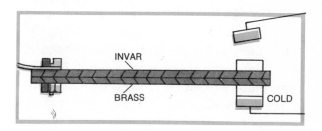

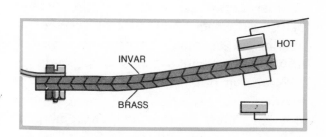

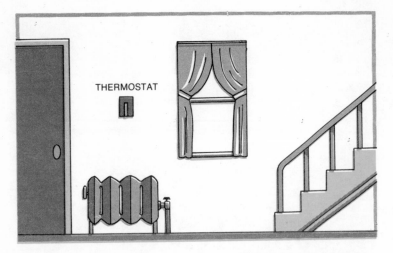

Bad thermostat location.

house temperature, common sense dictates that it must be properly located. This usually means on an inside wall and away from cold walls or doors that open to the outside. Other locations to avoid are the foot of an open stairway (too much draft), above a heat register, lamp, or television set (excessive heat will negate its function), or where it will be affected by direct heat from the sun. If you suspect a thermostat's accuracy, it's a good idea to check it against a good thermometer.

LIMIT CONTROLS

Although the thermostat is the most recognizable control in a modern heating system, each type of heating plant requires special controls. No matter what the system, there should be a high-limit control to prevent overheating. These are usually provided, or at least recommended, by the manufacturer.

The high-limit control, which is usually another thermostat, shuts down the system before a furnace, boiler, or other type of heating unit becomes dangerously or wastefully hot. In steam systems, it responds to pressure; in other systems, it responds to temperature.

A high-limit control is often combined with fan or pump controls in forced-air or forced hot-water systems. These may be set to start the fan or the pump circulating when the furnace or boiler warms up and to stop it when the heating plant cools down. They are ordinarily set just high enough to reach, without surpassing, the desired temperature and can be adjusted to suit weather conditions.

Forced-air systems can be set for continuous air circulation (CAC). The fan or blower will run continuously at a slow speed, while the burner responds to temperature changes inside the house. This minimizes temperature fluctuations and provides a more even warmth for maximum year-round comfort.

OIL BURNER CONTROLS

The controls for an oil burner allow electricity to pass through the motor and ignition transformer and shut them off in the proper order. They also stop the motor if the oil does not ignite or if the flame goes out for any reason. This is accomplished by means of another thermostat built into the relay. The sensing element of the stack control is inserted into the smokepipe near the furnace or boiler. Some heating units are equipped with electric eye (cadmium sulfide) flame detectors, which are used in place of the stack control.

Without the protection of the stack thermostat or electric eye, a gun- or rotary-type burner could flood the basement with oil if

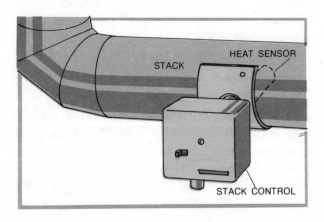

Heating System Controls

it failed to ignite—and the occasional horror stories that one reads in the newspapers about oil being mistakenly delivered to the wrong address testify to the fact that this is a slimy mess to be avoided at whatever cost. With the stack or eye control, the relay allows the motor to run only a short time if the oil fails to ignite; then it opens the motor circuit and keeps it open until it is manually reset. If the trouble persists, it will again shut down the system. By then, you should get the clue.

STOKER-FIRED COAL BURNER CONTROLS

The control system for a coal stoker is much like that for an oil burner. However, an automatic timer is usually included to operate the stoker for a few minutes every half hour or so to keep the fire alive during cool (not cold) weather when little heat is required.

A stack thermostat need not be used, but it is advisable in the event that a power failure might allow an untended fire to go out. Otherwise, the stoker will fill the cold firepot with coal when the power comes on again. An electric eye can also monitor this. In a stoker-control setup for a forced-air system, the furnace thermostat can act as high-limit and fan control.

OTHER HEATING SYSTEM CONTROLS

In some forced hot-water systems, especially those that also provide domestic hot water, a mixing valve is used. The water temperature of the boiler is maintained at some high fixed value, such as 200 degrees Fahrenheit. Only a portion of this high-temperature water is circulated through the heating system. Some of the water flowing through the radiators or convectors by-

passes the boiler. The amount of hot water admitted is controlled by a differential thermostat operating in the range between outdoor and indoor temperatures. This installation is more expensive than the more commonly used control systems, but it responds almost immediately to demands made upon it. Although it cannot anticipate temperature changes (even the computers do poorly at that), it is to a measure regulated by outside temperatures, which change earlier than those indoors.

The flow of hot air or hot water to various parts of the house can be separately controlled. This zoning—maintaining rooms or sections of the house at different desired temperatures—can be used for such purposes as maintaining sleeping quarters at lower temperatures than living areas. Fuel savings help to offset the initial higher cost of these more elaborate control systems. Once again, the advice of a competent and reputable professional is strongly recommended when mapping out a zoning system for your house.

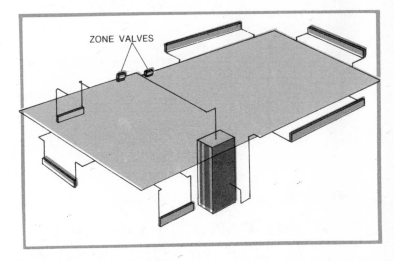

Two-zone hot-water system.

Controls for **gas burners** and **electric heating units** are integral parts of the units themselves. They have been detailed in the preceding chapters: HEATING SYSTEMS, and FUELS.

4

Heating a New or Remodeled Space

SOONER OR LATER, most families seem to outgrow the confines of the old homestead. Children graduate from the playpen, so a playroom is needed if the rest of the house is to be spared the noise and havoc that accompany preteen and adolescent years. More bedrooms are also needed to accommodate the burgeoning family. Perhaps the family life-style and fortunes have changed, and the need is simply for more room. Not too long ago, the solution would probably be to "pick up and move up," but the skyrocketing cost of housing and high mortgage interest rates make this less attractive these days. Besides, there are other good reasons for staying put: friends, familiarity, and maybe just because it's a nice neighborhood. So more and more people are finding new space within their present homes, or adding on to them, rather than "movin' on."

Many housing styles—most notably the story-and-a-half "Cape Cod" and some split-level and "raised ranch" designs—make allowances for expansion within the existing walls. An attic may be finished, or an upper or lower level, providing one or several new rooms. Or a garage or basement may be converted to living space, assuming they are dry and weatherproof. More ambitious projects might include raising the roof to gain second- or third-floor space, or knocking out the walls to enlarge a room or add a whole new wing. Whatever your expansion plans may be, a method of heating the new space should figure in the early stages.

THE CAPACITY OF YOUR PRESENT HEATING SYSTEM

Perhaps the furnace that presently heats your home is adequate to heat the new space as well. Sometimes a contractor installs a furnace with additional capacity, especially in a house designed with expansion in mind. But this is definitely not always the case, and if you try to overburden a furnace that is already working at peak capacity, you are asking for trouble—and will surely get it. At best, the heat will be uneven, not only in the new space but throughout the system. Eventually, overworked burners will succumb to early demise.

A "heat loss calculation" should be made

of your home, including the planned expansion space, to determine whether the existing furnace is up to carrying an increased load. This involves some complicated formulas and, unless you are a graduate physicist or a mathematical marvel, is better left to the slide-rule savants. Most fuel oil companies and utilities can supply you with the information you need. Or you can contact a reputable heating contractor for advice on your present system's capacity.

If the new space is within the existing walls of the house or if only a small room extension is added, perhaps only a minor relocation of ductwork or piping and heat supply outlets will be needed. You can probably do this work yourself. If your house is uninsulated or underinsulated, you may be able to, in effect, increase the present system's capacity by adequately insulating both new and old areas (see PAGES 521-531). By helping the furnace do its job more efficiently, you will also be adding to its capabilities, perhaps enough to offset the additional burden of the new space.

EXTENDING A WARM-AIR SYSTEM

If you are sure that the existing furnace can "take the heat" of the additional load, it is not very difficult to extend the ductwork or pipes to new outlets. Tools you'll need are an "aircraft" snips, an old screwdriver or cold chisel, a ball peen or tinsmith's hammer, a drill, and a keyhole saw. A tin snips will also come in handy. Always be very careful when working with sheet metal—it can cut like a razor, and even worse because of jagged edges that are almost unavoidable when cutting. It is recommended that you exercise that ounce of caution by wearing a heavy, long-sleeved shirt and work gloves whenever you might come in contact with the sharp metal edges.

If you have a gravity warm-air heating system, you must locate a spot on the plenum—the "bonnet" on top of the furnace—where you can "tap in." For heat runs to the first and second floors, 8-inch or 9-inch pipes are usually used; 24-inch lengths in these sizes, with one end crimped so that it can be fitted into the other end of an adjoining section, are available at many hardware stores or at heating supply outlets (although you may have to shop around, since some of the latter sell only to contractors). Using

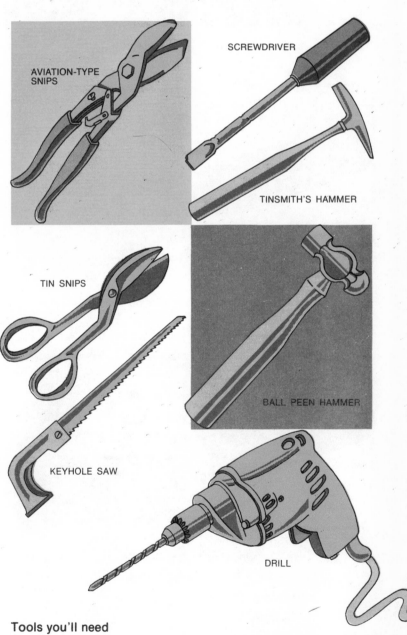

AVIATION-TYPE SNIPS

SCREWDRIVER

TINSMITH'S HAMMER

TIN SNIPS

BALL PEEN HAMMER

KEYHOLE SAW

DRILL

Tools you'll need

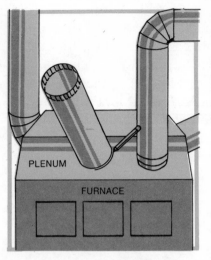

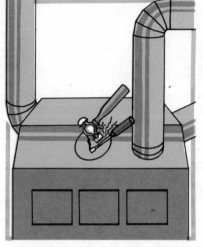

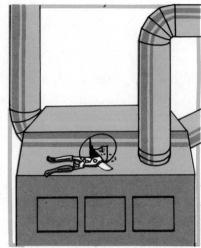

1. Draw an outline on the plenum.

2. Make a gash in the metal.

3. Cut out with aircraft snips.

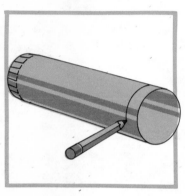

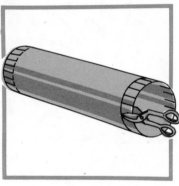

4. Draw a pencil line around the pipe.

5. Make snips-cuts into the line.

6. Bend out every other tab to a 90-degree angle.

7. Fit the unbent tabs inside the hole.

snips into the gash and cut out the hole following the marked line. (There are three basic configurations of aircraft snips, called "right-hand," "left-hand," and "center-cut." Right-hand cut in a counterclockwise direction and are generally favored for most usage. Left-hand cut in the clockwise direction and are used primarily when obstacles prevent the use of right-hand snips; southpaws often prefer to do most cutting with left-hand snips. Center-cuts are a compromise, and are perfectly suited for most do-it-yourself purposes—why buy three, if one will do? But they are not satisfactory for cutting holes of less than 6-inch diameter.)

A length of pipe—or in some cases, an elbow, depending on where the heat run is going—is then connected into this hole. Make a pencil mark all around the pipe or elbow approximately ¾ inch in from the uncrimped end. Use the aircraft snips or tin snips to make cuts approximately ¾ inch apart in to this line, all around the pipe. Bend out every other tab to a 90-degree angle, taking care not to cut yourself in the process. Fit the unbent tabs inside the hole in the plenum, then reach through the pipe and bend them over inside to lock the pipe in place. It's not really necessary, but you can further anchor it by drilling holes

the pipe section as a template, draw an outline on the plenum with pencil or crayon. Inside the outline, make a gash by striking an old screwdriver or cold chisel with a hammer. Insert the point of an aircraft

Heating a New or Remodeled Space

through a few of the outer tabs and the plenum and driving in sheet-metal screws.

A damper should be installed inside the pipe near the furnace, so that you can control the flow of hot air through the run, helping to balance the entire system. Dampers are available at heating supply outlets and many hardware stores, or you can make your own by cutting a circle of sheet metal to a diameter about ⅜ inch less than that of the pipe. Various types of handles are available; attach one to the edge of the damper, then place the damper inside the pipe, with the handle inserted through a hole drilled in the pipe.

Additional pipes and elbows are then added to lead the run to its outlet, with the crimped end of one length fitting into the uncrimped end of the next. Elbows are usually made in four sections and are adjustable from 90 degrees to straight, so you should have no trouble getting the run where you want it to go. One or two sheet-metal screws at each joint will hold it all together. Pipe runs should be pitched upward (this is gravity heat, remember). Long runs can be supported by wire loops nailed to the joists at intervals of approximately 4 feet.

For first-floor installations, the pipe enters a fitting that is attached to a wall or floor register. For upper-floor rooms, the pipe must connect with a duct or riser that carries the heat through a first-floor partition to the higher levels. If you have a house that was designed for expansion, a thoughtful contractor may have installed such a riser—unconnected to the furnace—when the house was being built. It takes only a few minutes and costs just a few dollars at that stage, before the walls are enclosed, but it saves a lot of grief for you at this stage. If you are not so fortunate, you have a real job on your hands. But with patience, it can be done.

First, you must find a location for the ris-

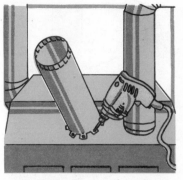

8. Secure with metal screws.

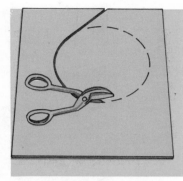

9. Cut sheet metal damper

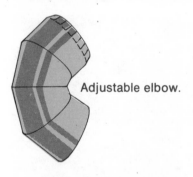

10. Attach handle.

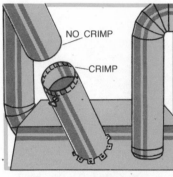

11. Fit pipes together.

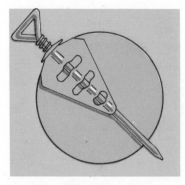

Adjustable elbow.

12. Pitch pipe runs upward; support them with wire loops.

13. Connect pipe to first-floor registers (right).

14. Riser connection for upper floors (below).

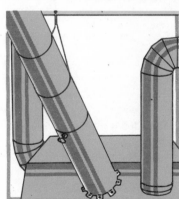

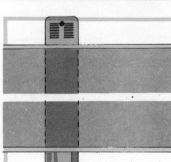

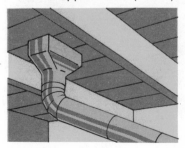

Heating a New or Remodeled Space

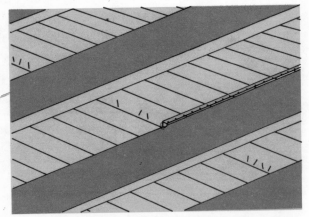

15. Measure carefully to find the partition. (Note nails penetrating the subfloor.)

16. Saw out subfloor and floor plate (above).

17. Cut out top plate from attic (above right).

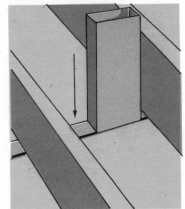

18. Slide in the riser through the cut-out (right).

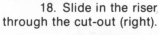

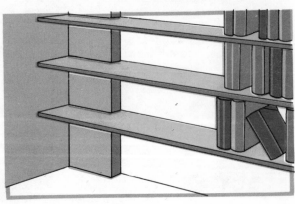

er. It must run between the studs of a partition, as close to the furnace as possible, and preferably to a point where it can be connected to a register in the upper-floor room. Otherwise, horizontal ducts will be needed beneath the second floor, cutting down the flow of heat. Wall registers are normally preferred, but it may be better to install a floor register than to have the heat turn so many corners. Stay away from stud channels that are crossed by electrical wiring or contain outlets or switches. You can check this by looking on the first floor, and by observing where wires disappear from the basement into the floor above.

Carefully measure on the first floor and in the basement to find the partition; you can usually corroborate your figurings by noting nails penetrating the subfloor where the partition plate is fastened. If you are unsure, remove the shoe molding along the partition and drill or drive nails through the subfloor, then note their locations in the basement. Drill pilot holes from below and saw out the subfloor and the plate to make room for the riser (usually $3\frac{1}{4}\times 10$ or $3\frac{1}{4}\times 12$ inches).

With a flashlight, carefully inspect the between-studs wall cavity to make sure that no wires run across it. If there are wires, shift the riser location—that is a lot easier than trying to move the wires. If the passageway is clear, proceed to the second floor to continue the operation.

Again, carefully measure and cut an

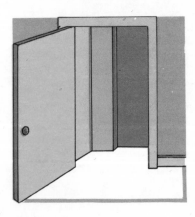

Riser cleverly concealed as part of a bookshelf (far left).

Riser run unobtrusively through a closet (left).

Heating a New or Remodeled Space

opening in the top plate of the first-floor partition to match that cut in the basement. Now slide the riser down through the cut-out (or up from the basement), hook up the basement piping, and use duct or pipe as necessary to lead from the riser to a wall or floor register.

You may be able to shortcut this somewhat tedious operation if there is a closet or utility room on the first floor through which you can unobtrusively run the riser without having to work inside the walls. Or if you run into insoluble problems trying to run the riser inside the walls—perhaps you simply can't find an open space uncluttered with wiring or pipes—you may prefer to run it outside the wall in a corner of a first-floor room and box around it, or conceal it as part of a built-in bookshelf or cabinet.

A gravity system is not very effective for heating a basement room. It operates on the principle of hot air going up, but you want the heat to go down in a basement room. At best, you may be able to heat the upper reaches of the room, but the floor will almost surely remain too cold for comfort.

Ductwork for a forced-air system is usually "stepped down" in width as each individual heat run or branch line (usually 4- to 6-inch pipe) is "taken off." To add to such a run without stepping down (which would require new ductwork), cut a hole in the side of the duct, using aircraft snips as described earlier. To divert air to your new takeoff, you can install a small baffle inside

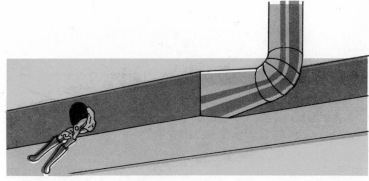

1. Cut a hole in the side of the duct.

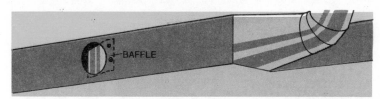

2 Install a small baffle inside the duct.

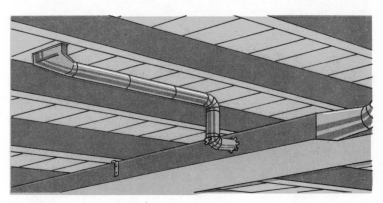

3. Lead the run to a first-floor outlet.

the duct. This is simply a bent piece of metal shaped to catch the air flow and is held in place by sheet-metal screws. With the baffle in place, attach a piece of pipe or an elbow to the hole in the duct by dovetailing the end as above. Install a damper, then lead the run to a first-floor outlet (usually on

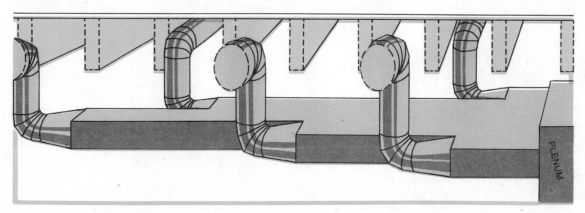

"Stepped-down" ductwork.

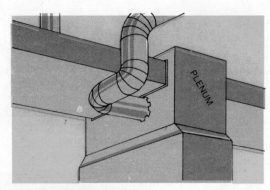

Cut into plenum to run pipe to a first- or second-floor heat outlet.

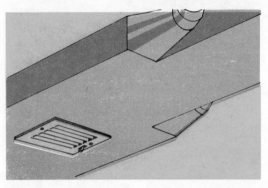

Basement outlet in duct.

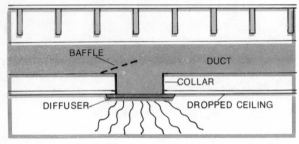

Collars to tie heat outlet to new ceiling.

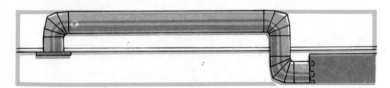

New heat run for basement room.

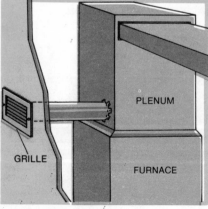

Heat run off plenum.

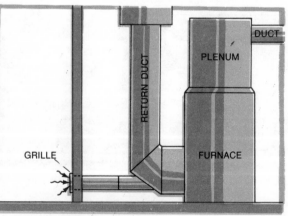

Basement cold-air return.

the outer wall) or to a riser leading to the second floor. The methods of installation are the same as for a gravity system.

You may also be able to cut into the plenum of a forced-air furnace to run pipe to a first- or second-floor heat outlet. As above, a baffle may be needed to divert the flow of air toward the new run. This is especially necessary when a main duct line runs off the same side of the plenum.

A forced-air system offers several possibilities for heating a basement room. If the ductwork passes through the area to be heated, you can install a register or registers by cutting into the bottom or side of the duct and fastening with sheet-metal screws. Some types of registers will divert the heated air when they are opened; others may require a baffle inside the duct. If the ductwork is to be boxed in as part of the basement finishing, you can have short collars made at a sheet-metal shop to bring the registers level with the surface of the new ceiling.

Where ductwork does not run through the new living space but is off to one side of the basement, a new heat run can be tapped into the side or (where accessible) the top of the duct. Pipe is then run between the joists to a ceiling register, or down through or behind a partition to a wall outlet. Again, a baffle may be needed inside the duct.

You may also tap directly into the plenum to heat the basement room, especially

Heating a New or Remodeled Space

if it is adjacent to the furnace. You may be able to run a short collar from the plenum to a wall register in the room to provide comfortable heating.

Since a forced-air heating system depends on the circulation of air by means of a fan, it follows that, when you increase its output of heated air by adding new outlets, you must increase its air intake by adding new cold-air returns. In the basement, this is relatively simple. Just place a grille at floor level and pipe it to the cold-air drop or return plenum on the furnace — the part that feeds cold air to the blower compartment. It's also a relatively simple operation to cut a return opening into the floor of a first-floor room and duct or pipe it to the return drop. You may prefer to place the return grille in a wall or partition. This is a little more difficult but well within the capabilities of most do-it-yourselfers.

First, pry away the shoe molding with a chisel or other tool. Find wall studs by tapping on the wall (a hollow sound indicates a wall cavity; a solid thump means a stud) or, if your ear is not that finely attuned, with a magnetic stud finder (the magnet does not react to the wood stud, of course, but to the nails that hold wallboard or lath to the stud). Check both in the room and in the basement to make sure that no wires are in the way — you don't want a shocking experience when you cut through the floor. Place the grille against the baseboard between studs, and mark the baseboard at the ends of the grille. Set the grille aside, and drill ¾-inch starter holes through the floor just inside the lines. With a keyhole saw, cut away the baseboard just inside the lines.

Mark on the wall 1 inch inside of the cutaway baseboard, up to 1 inch less than the

5. Cut the baseboard away with a keyhole saw (right).

6. Mark wall inside the cutaway baseboard (far right).

Heating a New or Remodeled Space

1. Pry away base shoe molding (right).

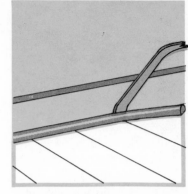

2. Locate stud by tapping (below left), or with a stud finder (below right).

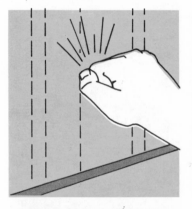
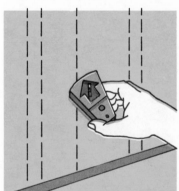

3. Mark baseboard for location of grille.

4. Drill starter holes through the floor.

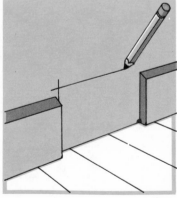
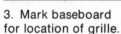

7. Drill starter holes through the floor.

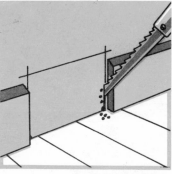

8. Cut away floor plate and wall.

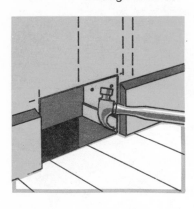

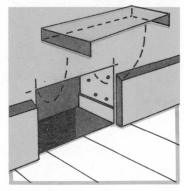

9. You might have to nail blocks to studs **(above)**.

10. Cap off wall opening **(above right)**.

11. Now you can attach the grille **(right)**.

height of the grille, and mark a horizontal line at that point. Drill starter holes inside the lines at an angle through the floor. Use a keyhole saw to cut through the floor plate and the subfloor and to cut the opening in the wall. You will probably have to nail blocks of 2×4 or 1-inch lumber to the studs to provide backing for the screws that hold the grille. You will also have to cap off the opening to prevent air from being drawn down through the wall cavity rather than from the room. Cut a piece of sheet metal about 1 inch wider (4½ inches for a 2×4

wall) and 2 inches longer than the opening. Notch the back corners and bend down a 1-inch flange in the back and at each end. Insert into the wall opening, flush with the top, and nail through the end flanges into the studs or blocks. Then attach the grille. Cut the shoe molding to fit flush with the grille and nail it back in place.

In the basement, you can use the space between the joists below the new opening to duct the return air to the return drop or to a return line. Simply close off the joist space with hardboard or other material nailed across the bottom. At the duct, cut a hole in the top to admit the return air. Cap off the ends of the joist runs with sheet metal or wood headers to keep the system closed.

It is considerably more difficult to cut a return in an upper-floor room, although it can be done if there is no floor installed. Wall plates must be cut away to allow the passage of air, and caps installed between joists to direct the air where you want it to go. If a floor has already been put down, you may prefer to cut a return somewhere near the foot of the stairs on the first floor to draw the cooled air from upstairs and direct it to the furnace. While this may result in a drafty staircase, it is a compromise that generally does the job.

Basement connection of cold-air return.

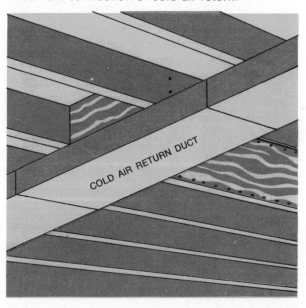

Closed returns are not as important with a gravity system. Chances are the existing returns will provide sufficient air to supply the new outlets. If not, a new return can be cut into the first floor as above.

EXTENDING A HOT-WATER SYSTEM

As with a warm-air system, the first consideration is the capacity of the system. If you are satisfied that it is up to the extra duty, it is not too difficult to tap into the piping.

On a one-pipe system, with a single main circling the basement and returning to the boiler, you can simply tap into the main to supply additional radiators or convectors on the first floor and above.

Copper pipe is generally used for hot-water systems. Decide where the main can best be tapped, as near to the new outlet as possible. Turn off the water at a shutoff valve somewhere behind the point to be tapped and, if possible, drain the line. (Unfortunately, drainage valves are not always located where you want them. In that case, you might drill a small hole at the point where the tap will be made and let the water trickle into a bucket, rather than come at you in a torrent when you cut through the line.)

Cut through the pipe with a hacksaw or tubing cutter, removing a section large enough to allow the insertion of a tee fitting of the same size as that used to feed other branches in the line. File off any burrs on the cut ends of the pipe. Clean the outside ends of the pipe and the inside of the tee with steel wool or emery cloth.

Copper pipe is assembled by "sweating" the joints—heating them and running in solder to seal and secure them. First apply a coat of soldering flux to both the pipe and the inside of the tee. Place the tee on the pipe and twist slightly to spread the flux

Heating a New or Remodeled Space

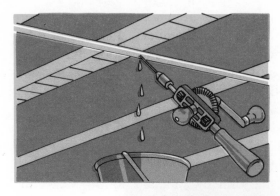
1. Drill a small hole into the pipe to drain the water.

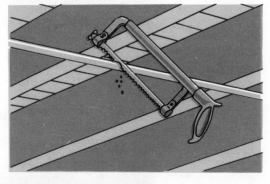
2. Cut through the pipe with a hacksaw.

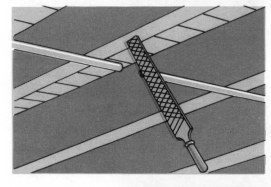
3. File off any burrs on the cut ends.

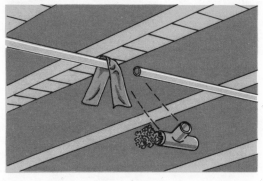
4. Clean ends with steel wool or emery cloth.

5. Apply flux.   6. Twist fitting to spread flux.

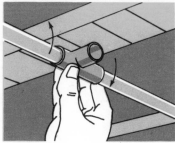

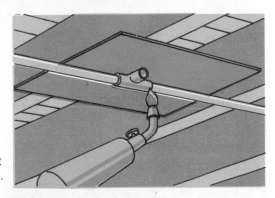

Aluminum fin clusters.

evenly. If you are sweating a joint near wood structural members, such as joists or subflooring, protect the wood from the flame of the propane torch by placing asbestos sheeting over the area. Heat the fitting at the joint until the flux begins to bubble out of the joint. Back off the torch and hold a strip of solder to the heated joint; it should flow around evenly and be drawn into the joint by capillary action. Wipe off excess solder and allow to harden—this should take less than a minute. Attach pipe and other fittings as necessary to reach the new radiator or convector. The pipe can simply be brought up through the floor to

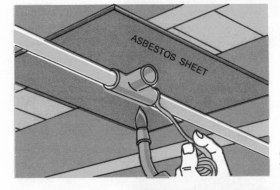

7. Apply heat with a torch.

8. Hold solder to the heated joint.

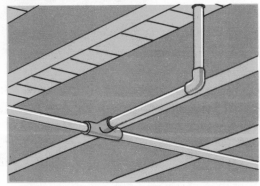

9. Bring pipe up to first-floor outlet.

reach a first-floor outlet. For a second-floor outlet, you will have to drill a hole slightly larger than the pipe through the subflooring and floor plate, and another from the upper floor through the top plate, to allow the pipe to be brought up inside a first-floor partition. This may require lifting some floorboards on the second floor. Make sure you do this operation early in the framing stage of your project—it will be a lot easier then than as an afterthought.

A one-pipe system requires that the outlets be several inches above the main for proper functioning. For this reason, radiators or convectors are not usually practical for heating basement rooms in such a system. Aluminum fins can be installed in clusters over the main to radiate heat into a basement, however. They are fastened in place with sheet-metal screws, clamps, or tabs. If the room is finished, they can be concealed behind perforated sheet metal or similar material that will allow the passage of heat.

Tapping into a two-pipe system for additional outlets is done similarly, except that both supply and return lines must be provided. With this system, radiators or convectors need not be above the main line, so they can be used in the basement as well as the upper floors. The return outlet must be above the boiler water line, however, so the units must be installed high enough on the wall to allow this. Heat fins can also be used with this system—on the hot-water line, of course.

Extending a steam heating system is generally done the same way as with hot water. Because of the more exacting design re-

Heating a New or Remodeled Space

quired of such a system, however, it is recommended that this work be left to a qualified contractor.

TIME FOR A CHANGE?

There is always the possibility that your present heating system, in the opinion of the experts and by your own reckoning, just isn't adequate to heat the new living space. If your present furnace is a monstrous relic with an insatiable thirst for fuel as it clanks and sputters its way through old age, this might well be the time to start from scratch with a modern, efficient unit that has enough capacity to heat the new rooms as well as the existing ones. You might also opt for a completely new ductwork system that will add considerably to basement headroom in addition to the space you will gain by replacing the old colossus with a compact modern furnace. Although this may seem like an expensive way out, you may be better off lumping all the expenses together, rather than having to replace the furnace in a few years anyway while living with less than satisfactory heating in the new room or rooms.

If the existing furnace is doing its job well, but simply can't be called upon for additional service, there are other solutions. One is to install a second, smaller furnace, with its own system of ductwork and pipes to heat the new area, and possibly even one or two adjacent rooms to take some of the load off the existing furnace. You can often find used furnaces in perfectly good condition, units that have been replaced by larger-capacity furnaces to serve the same purpose that you need to serve. But be wary. Buy such a unit only from a reputable contractor who will back it up with some kind of guarantee. Or, if you are thinking of buying a used furnace from an individual, have it checked out by an ex-

pert—your fuel oil dealer or a representative of the local utility—before you lay out the cash. Don't buy trouble.

Perhaps the simplest solution to heating your new room is an individual space heater. A gas heating unit installed in an outside wall can provide even, quiet heat for a room. Just make certain that it is vented to the outside. Never use an unvented gas heater; such an installation is extremely hazardous and is prohibited in many parts of the country. A properly vented heater is perfectly safe.

Electric baseboard heaters are another way to provide heat for the new room. Many types are available (see PAGE 476). Most come with specific installation instructions that should be diligently followed. Installed along outside walls, the electric units combine warm air with radiant heating. But before investing in electric baseboards, make sure that your electrical system has the capacity to accommodate them. Check with a licensed electrician or your utility company. If extensive rewiring is needed, you may be better off with some other type of heating.

FIREPLACES

A fireplace is not really intended as a primary source of heat in a room. In fact, it can actually cause a heat loss if there is a considerable difference between indoor and outdoor temperatures. A fire in the fireplace generates a considerable flow of air up through the chimney. The source of this air is generally the furnace-heated air in the rest of the house. With a properly designed and dampered chimney, however, this need not be the case, and a fireplace can be a good source of supplemental heat in the new room. In milder climates, where it is only necessary to "take the chill off" at night, a fireplace may handle the job more

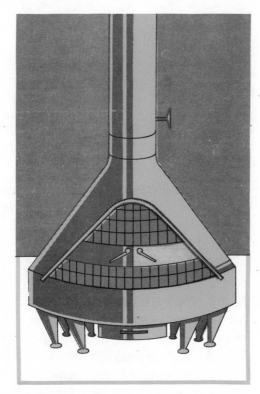

Freestanding prefabricated fireplace.

Prefabricated in-wall fireplace.

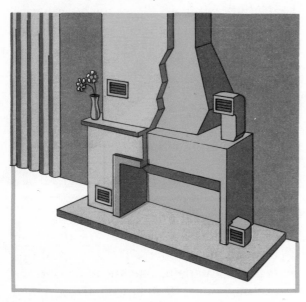

than adequately. And, of course, there is the psychological warmth of that crackling fire and the glowing embers.

You are not likely to find a masonry fireplace built into an attic, basement, or garage that you are finishing, although you may want to plan such a unit as an integral part of a new addition. But it is not difficult to install a modern, freestanding, prefabricated fireplace. These come in all sizes, shapes, and colors, in both wood-burning and realistic "gas-log" models. Some units are also available for building into a wall. These have the appearance of a conventional fireplace but do not require the heavy concrete foundation of a masonry unit. They can be framed in with wood or any other common building material.

A prefab fireplace can sometimes be vented through the existing chimney, but check local building codes and a competent engineer on this point. You can also install a prefabricated chimney, but again check local ordinances, which often set restrictions on use of certain types of chimney materials.

Installation of a prefabricated fireplace and chimney is a job that requires no special skills beyond those of most home handymen. The chimney must be run above the roof to the height dictated by the local code, usually a minimum of 2 feet above the ridge, or 3 feet above a flat roof. If working at heights—even the height of a ranch house roof—is not for you, hire a contractor. Otherwise, you can do the entire project yourself. Just how it is done will depend on the type of fireplace and chimney you select. Again, follow manufacturer's directions to the letter.

5

Routine Maintenance and Servicing

A MODERN heating system is quite a mechanical marvel. But, as with all marvelous mechanisms, things can sometimes go wrong. When they do, you may be able to set them right yourself, but if it's more than a simple fixit, you will probably be better off calling in a qualified serviceman.

If you heat with oil and have a delivery contract, you may also have a service contract to cover emergencies and, possibly, annual checkups and maintenance as well. Most gas utilities have emergency crews ready to cope with problems. If such services are not available in your area, have the name and phone number of a competent service contractor noted near your telephone. If electricity provides your heat, find a good electrician. It is wise to have these professionals in to check over your system even if nothing is wrong. It will be money well spent — they will know something about your heating system and, more important, they will know you. You won't just be some stranger calling on them to come out in the middle of a cold, snowy night to turn your heat back on.

Of course, it is better to avoid having to call on them at all. The "ounce of prevention" will lessen the likelihood of emergencies arising. That ounce is in the form of routine maintenance, most of which you *can* do yourself.

ROUTINE MAINTENANCE

A forced-air heating system sends out hot air to the rooms of the house and draws cooled air back to be reheated and recirculated. It also draws back household dirt, dust, and lint. To prevent these impurities from being recirculated as well, one or more filters are located either in the cold-air drop or inside the blower compartment. By the very nature of their work, these filters will become clogged if they are not regularly maintained. If this is allowed to happen, the cooled air will not pass through into the furnace heat exchanger, and the system will become "starved" for air. Uneven and certainly unsatisfactory heating will be the result, as well as an unnecessarily high consumption of fuel.

Air filters should be cleaned or replaced every 30 to 60 days during the heating season. The most common type are disposable, costing a few dollars at most. You can check them by taking them out of their compartments and holding them up to a light; if little or no light shines through, they are past due for replacement. If a disposable filter appears to have more useful life in it, you can vacuum-clean it, or tap it, intake side down, onto newspapers spread on the floor to remove most of the accumulated dirt. Then reposition it until time for replacement. Arrows on the edges of the filter indicate the direction of air flow. It is important that this positioning be observed;

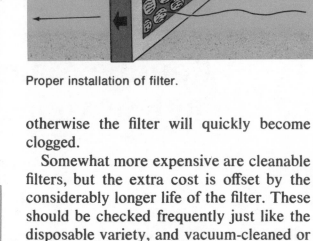

Proper installation of filter.

otherwise the filter will quickly become clogged.

Somewhat more expensive are cleanable filters, but the extra cost is offset by the considerably longer life of the filter. These should be checked frequently just like the disposable variety, and vacuum-cleaned or washed with soap and water, following manufacturer's directions for the particular type.

Dirt can interfere with your forced-air heating system in other ways as well. Clean the fan blade or blower that moves the air at least once a year. It tends to accumulate dirt that might pass through the filter (especially if the filter itself is allowed to become dirty) or be drawn through the

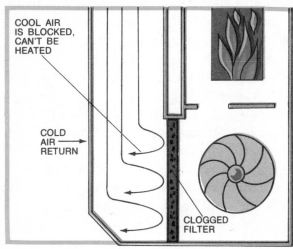

COOL AIR IS BLOCKED, CAN'T BE HEATED

COLD AIR RETURN

CLOGGED FILTER

Clogged filter.

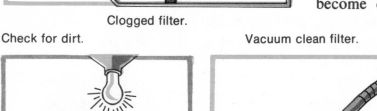

Check for dirt.   Vacuum clean filter.   Tap out dirt.

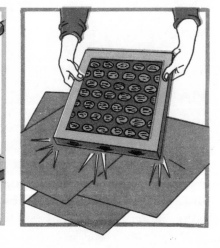

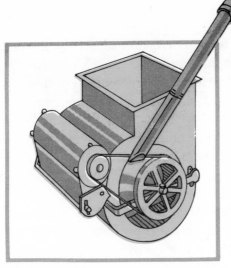

Clean the blower.

Oil the blower.

Check belt tension.

openings around the blower compartment door. To function properly, it must be clean.

While you are cleaning the blower and its compartment, oil the blower and motor ports (unless they have sealed bearings). A few drops are usually sufficient—don't over-lubricate. On belt-drive blowers, check belt tension at the same time. It should deflect easily but not sloppily as you squeeze it gently. If a belt is too taut, it will cause undue wear. A too-loose belt may lead to slippage, also causing wear and possibly damage to the motor, as well as erratic operation of the fan.

Registers and diffusers should be vacuum-cleaned every few weeks, along with return grilles. This applies to gravity as well as forced-air systems. Make sure there is a clear path for warm air coming out of the registers, unobstructed by curtains or furniture.

With a hot-water system, you must bleed the air from the lines periodically. With time, a certain amount of air will find its way into the pipes in the system, eventually settling in the radiators at the upper levels of the house. Where there is air, it keeps out the hot water. There is usually a small valve at the top of each radiator. At least once a year, or more often if a radiator seems to

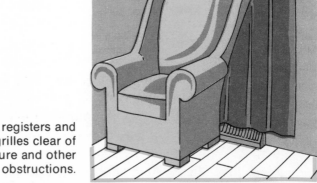

Keep registers and grilles clear of furniture and other obstructions.

Clean registers.

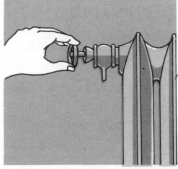

Bleed radiators.

have trouble heating up, hold a bucket under this valve and open it, keeping it open until water starts to flow out. Be careful— that water will be hot! Shut the valve when the water flows steadily without sputtering.

Other routine maintenance on a hot-water system is usually best left to a profes-

Routine Maintenance and Servicing

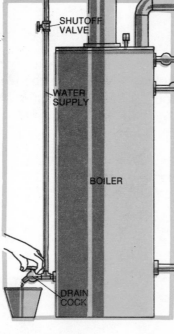
Drain boiler.

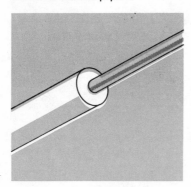
Insulate steam pipes.

sional serviceman. Once a year, usually shortly before the heating season begins, have him check the pump operation, check the operation of the flow control valve, check for piping leaks and valve operation, oil the pump motor, and drain and flush the boiler. On most systems, you can probably perform this last operation yourself—ask the serviceman to show you how.

With steam heat, have the serviceman give the system an annual checkup. You can help the system by insulating steam pipes that run through areas you don't want to heat. Every two to three weeks during the heating season, open the valve at the bottom of the boiler and drain off a bucket of water. This will keep sediment from settling on the bottom of the boiler. Sediment that is allowed to remain there will actually insulate the boiler from the flame in the burner and result in a lot of heat (and fuel dollars) going up the chimney rather than being converted into comfort for your home.

BURNER CARE

An oil burner should be checked by the serviceman every year to insure clean, satisfactory, economical (as much as possible in these days when no fuel is really eco-

nomical) heat. Have him clean the burner and adjust the fuel-to-air ratio for maximum efficiency. He should clean the heating elements and surfaces and make sure that there are no oil leaks. Oil filters and the burner nozzle should be changed, and the oil pump checked. And make sure he checks all electrical connections, especially on safety devices.

There are several tests that you might ask the serviceman to perform to check on the oil furnace's efficiency. A draft test will indicate whether excessive heat is being lost up the chimney or if there is insufficient draft for proper combustion of the oil. A smoke test will show whether the oil is being burned cleanly and completely. A CO_2 test will also show how completely your oil (and your dollars) are being burned. A stack temperature test will show if stack gases are too hot or not hot enough for efficiency as well as safety. All these tests require the use of special equipment; make sure that your serviceman has such equipment and uses it.

A gas furnace (bottled, LP, or natural) requires less frequent maintenance—every three years should do it. Have the serviceman check the operation of the main gas valve, the pressure regulator, and the safety control valve. The primary air supply nozzle should be adjusted for proper combustion. A draft test and stack temperature test, as described for oil furnaces, should also be performed.

If you heat with coal, adjust and clean the stoker at the end of each heating season, following the manufacturer's directions. Clean the burner of all coal, ash, and clinkers (a messy but necessary job). Oil the inside of the coal screw and hopper to prevent rust.

With an electric furnace, very little maintenance is required. Check the manufacturer's directions that came with the unit, and follow those recommendations.

When the serviceman tells you (as he inevitably will) that major repairs are required, you will face the question of whether to repair or replace. Get several estimates on both courses—the larger the job, the more estimates. Check around with friends and neighbors to compare heating costs. If yours seem to be far above the norm, it may be time to scrap the old and start anew. When you have narrowed your choice of contractors, ask each one how many years he thinks it will take before the amount you save by having the new system equals what you will have to pay for it. Bear in mind that fuel costs will almost surely continue to go up—doesn't everything? Then weigh all these factors and make your decision.

HEATING PROBLEMS

You may first perceive it as a noticeable chill while you are viewing a hot cops-and-robbers chase on television, or when you get out of bed some frigid morning with icicles forming on every breath you take. You glance at the thermostat—it is set for 65 degrees, but the temperature is in the low 40's. The furnace is out! Your first impulse might be to chuck it all and migrate to the perpetual warmth of Pago Pago. Or you might consider a more practical, if far less appealing, solution like moving the family into the cozy confines of your mother-in-law's house "for the duration." As you button up your overcoat and chug-a-lug a cup of steaming coffee, it probably occurs to you that you should call the serviceman. But before you put those numbed fingers to work dialing the telephone, wait . . .

First check the main burner switch. If the furnace is in the basement, the switch may be located on the staircase wall. It is not uncommon for a person to brush against it while carrying a load of laundry up or down the steps, shutting off the system. If the house is warm and the weather outside not too blustery cold, it may be some time before the furnace stoppage is noted. Make sure the switch is on, then make sure that the fuse or circuit breaker that services the furnace line is not blown or tripped. If necessary, replace the fuse with one of the same rating, or reset the breaker. If the circuit again blows, the problem is electrical. Call the serviceman.

If that checks out, consider the fuel supply. If you heat with oil, look at the gauge on top of the oil tank, or wherever it is located if you have an underground tank. Should the gauge read Empty or close to it, call your dealer for an immediate refill. If coal supplies your heat, a quick glance at the bin will tell you if you are out—and you have no one to blame but yourself. The same is true of bottled gas. If gas for your furnace is piped in, that should not be a problem unless there is a severe gas shortage in your area—and then you should hear about it through the news media. You may

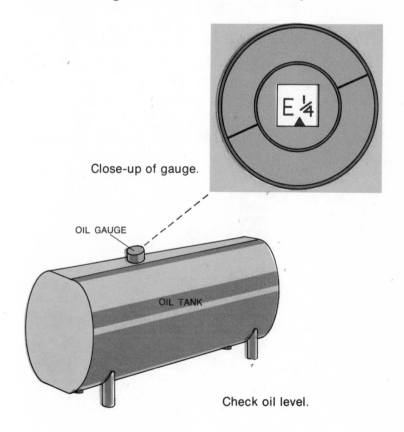

Close-up of gauge.

OIL GAUGE

OIL TANK

Check oil level.

Routine Maintenance and Servicing

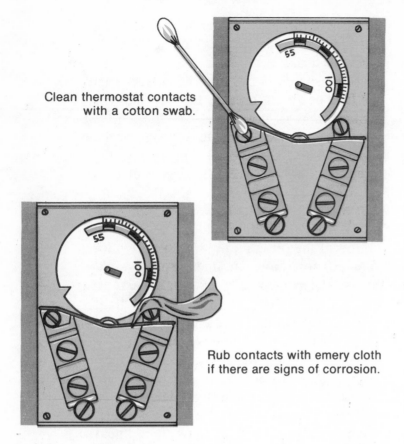

Clean thermostat contacts with a cotton swab.

Rub contacts with emery cloth if there are signs of corrosion.

look dirty, clean them with a cotton swab dipped in alcohol. If there are any signs of corrosion, rub the contacts with a piece of very fine emery cloth. Turn the thermostat to its highest setting to see if the furnace burner comes on. If not, it's probably time to call the serviceman (hopefully, those fingers of yours are still operative and not frostbitten by this time).

Not all furnace problems are signaled by a total shutdown. Some that are scarcely noticeable at first may be harbingers of troubles to come. A burner that incessantly repeats the on-off cycle may indicate a clogged filter. If your inspection acquits the filter, call in the serviceman. A blower that just won't quit when it should could be another indication of a clogged filter, or it could mean that the return grilles are blocked by furniture or some other obstacles. Check out these possibilities before calling for help.

A noisy blower might be quieted by tightening the blades or correcting the belt tension. Or it may be thirsty for oil. But if you can't spot an obvious cause, call the serviceman. If you smell gas or a combustion odor, immediately shut down the heating system and call the utility or oil company. The message should be clear—other than for regular maintenance and simple repairs, the heating system is not really amateur territory. But you sure have to know what to expect from it and from the professionals on whom you call for help.

have forgotten to pay your bill. Gas companies have been known to shut off residential fuel supplies for such oversights, although recent court decisions have generally been averse to such practices.

The electrical circuit checks out and you have a fuel supply. Next take a look at the thermostat. This seemingly mystical device is simply a form of switch that is activated by temperature changes. Remove the cover and inspect the switch contacts. If they

6

Keeping Cool

MAN HAS BEEN looking for ways to keep cool for almost as long as he has been seeking warmth. The picture of Cleopatra lounging in her barge surrounded by slaves waving huge fans to waft the cooling breezes of the Nile in her direction is a familiar one. And, indeed, it was an effective method of air conditioning—for Cleopatra, if not for the slaves.

But it has only been over the past 20 or so years that air conditioners as we know them today have come into widespread popularity. If summer daytime temperatures in your region normally rise to the 80's or above, you probably think of an air conditioner as a necessity rather than the luxury it was considered a few decades ago. It is somewhat ironic that the power shortages that have become commonplace in recent years are felt most acutely in the hottest weather, caused by the use of air conditioners when they are most needed and resulting (sometimes) in the shutting down of those very cooling units. But we can hope that solutions will be found for these problems and that hot-weather comfort will continue to be a pleasant reality.

Of course, in many regions an air conditioner is not really needed. There are other alternatives to cool a home. You may be able to reach an acceptable warm-weather comfort level by installing an exhaust fan in the attic to remove hot air and circulate cooler air through the house. Adding, or improving, insulation is another help to year-round comfort. Installing an awning or planting trees to block out heat-causing sunlight is effective, especially where excessive heat and humidity are only an occasional problem. Even if you do opt for air conditioning, these steps should be taken to help you get the most out of the unit you choose.

BENEFITS OF AIR CONDITIONING

The benefits of air conditioning are many. In addition to lowering temperatures inside the home, an air conditioner reduces the humidity level that causes the "clammy" hot-weather discomfort. It also re-moves dust and pollen from the air, providing a more healthful and comfortable environment for the family. On somewhat cooler days when heat isn't a problem, the unit can be used to circulate air throughout the room or the entire house, or to exhaust smoke, odors, or stale air.

There are various methods of air condi-

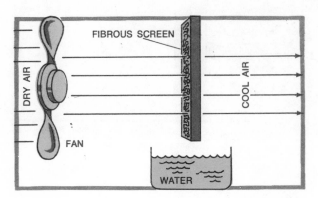

Cooling by evaporation.

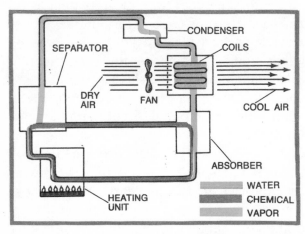

Cooling by absorption.

tioning. Cooling by evaporation is probably the simplest and oldest. Air cooled by evaporated water is circulated by a fan. However, this type of cooling is satisfactory only in very dry areas—otherwise the cooled air is likely to be damp and muggy, perhaps making you feel even more uncomfortable than without such a system.

An absorption system of cooling works somewhat like a coffee percolator, heating a mixture of water and chemicals so that it rises from the bottom to the top of the system. Here, the coolant fluid is separated and the chemicals flow back to an absorber, where they are cooled. The water rises as a vapor to the highest point in the system, where it enters a condenser and is cooled to return to liquid state. It then flows over cooling coils in a vacuum system that causes it to become a vapor again, chilling

the coils. A fan blows air passing over the coils throughout the house. Such a system is fairly effective but quite unwieldy and expensive for home installations.

By far the most common and popular type of air conditioning for today's homes is a refrigerated unit.

HOW REFRIGERATED AIR CONDITIONING WORKS

In its simplest form, an air conditioner is a heat-transfer mechanism. It removes heat from where it is not wanted (indoors) and disposes of it at a convenient location (outdoors). Basically, an air conditioner, a refrigerator, and a home freezer all operate on the same principle and use equipment that is closely related.

A complete air-conditioning system, whether it is a small window unit or a large central unit, includes an evaporator or cooling coil, a compressor, a condenser coil, a capillary tube, a blower fan for circulating air, and a power unit for operating the compresser and blower. Since air conditioners work on the principle of removing heat, a refrigerant is needed. The refrigerant or coolant is Freon, a chemical that boils at

Refrigerated cooling.

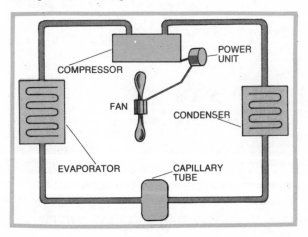

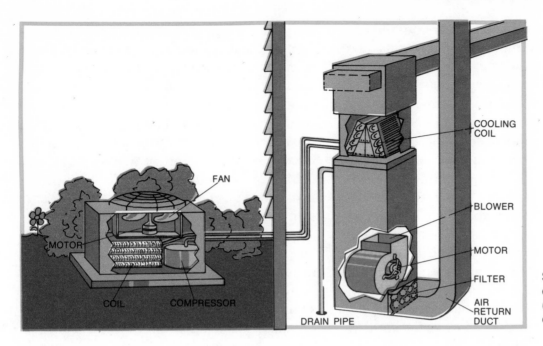

FAN

MOTOR

COIL   COMPRESSOR

DRAIN PIPE

COOLING COIL

BLOWER

MOTOR

FILTER

AIR RETURN DUCT

Split central air-conditioning system (compressor and condenser coils are outside the house).

from 20 to 40 degrees below zero. Normally, Freon is a gas, but when stored under pressure in a tightly sealed chamber, it becomes a liquid. When pressure is released suddenly, the Freon begins to boil, and the evaporation taking place inside the chamber causes the sides of the container to become "ice" cold. If the evaporation takes place inside a coil and the coil is exposed to warm room air, the intense cold begins absorbing the heat from the air.

The components of an air conditioner work together to absorb heat inside an area. The blower fan draws warm air from the room and passes it over the evaporator coils on the inside, cooling the air, and then returns it to the room. Dehumidifying the air takes place when the moisture in the warm air begins cooling. The moisture left on the evaporator or cooling coils is eventually picked up by the fan and vaporized. The result is not only cooler air, but drier air. Before the cooled air from the evaporator is passed back into the room, it goes through a filter that removes dirt, pollen, dust, and other undesirable foreign matter.

Since the Freon must be used over and over again, it is cycled through a compressor. This works like a pump, compressing the Freon gas, thereby raising its temperature to about 210 degrees. The hot gas is then routed outside to the condenser coils, where it is cooled by outside air and the blower fan. Once the heat is removed from the compressed gas, it turns to a liquid state and is ready to begin the same cycle again.

The compressed gas is further aided in the cycle by flowing through a capillary tube of much smaller size than the coil. The restriction in the capillary tube meters the Freon in its flow to the evaporator.

Armed with basic knowledge of how an air conditioner functions, the next step is to determine the type that suits your needs. There are many brands on the market today, and each manufacturer offers a number of models, types, and installation variations.

CENTRAL AIR CONDITIONERS

Central air conditioners are usually year-round units, cooling the house in the summer and heating in winter. These units have

Keeping Cool

the compressor and condenser coils outside the house and the evaporator coils and heating unit inside. A central unit is usually connected with a duct system (like a warm-air heating system) to distribute the air uniformly throughout the house.

The most popular form of central air conditioning is called a split system. It is designed to work in conjunction with existing warm-air furnaces using the present ductwork and furnace blower as integral parts of the cooling system, serving as the air distribution network. The condensing unit for the system often sits on an outdoor cement slab adjacent to the house, but it can also be placed in the garage, on the roof, in the remote recesses of the yard, or even in the wall of the home.

A thermostat is conveniently located inside to control temperatures. You can set the temperature during both summer and winter for total comfort. A simple switch changes it from cooling to heating.

Cooling coils absorb heat and excessive moisture from the air that is circulating through the duct system of your home. The cooled air is then recirculated throughout the house. The cooling coils can be readily adapted to forced-air heating units presently using an upflow furnace, downflow furnace, or horizontal furnace.

Central air conditioning can also be adapted for use with steam, hot water, or central electric heating systems. If your home is heated with any of these, however, ductwork must be installed to distribute cool air throughout the house.

A central air conditioning system will provide even temperatures for your family twelve months of the year. Hot spots or cold spots are eliminated with a properly installed system. Humidity is kept at a constant level, making for less frequent colds and relief for sinus sufferers. Airborne dust and dirt are also greatly reduced, keeping the entire house cleaner.

Although central air conditioning might sound like the greatest thing since sliced bread, it does have some shortcomings, primarily economic. The cost of a central system can run high, especially if ductwork must be added. The ideal time to install this system is when the house is in the construction stage. The installation is not for amateurs, but rather for qualified contractors. Homes located in regions with mild climates would not reap the full benefits of central air conditioning.

ROOM AIR CONDITIONING

For most homeowners, there are many advantages to installing a room air conditioner rather than a central air-conditioning system. A central system may be excessively expensive to install if you live in an older house, or unnecessarily expensive in a climate where air conditioning is needed only occasionally for short periods. Window air-conditioning units have become common in households across the country because of their compact styling, portability, and ease of installation. Another important advantage is the substantially lower cost of maintenance. Window units can be installed in one or two rooms, or in the case of modern, lightweight models, moved from room to room wherever they are needed.

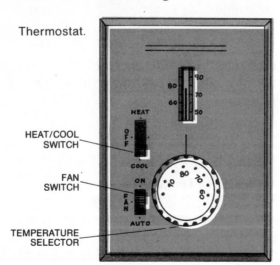

Thermostat.

HEAT/COOL SWITCH

FAN SWITCH

TEMPERATURE SELECTOR

HEAT

OFF

COOL

ON

FAN

AUTO

Keeping Cool

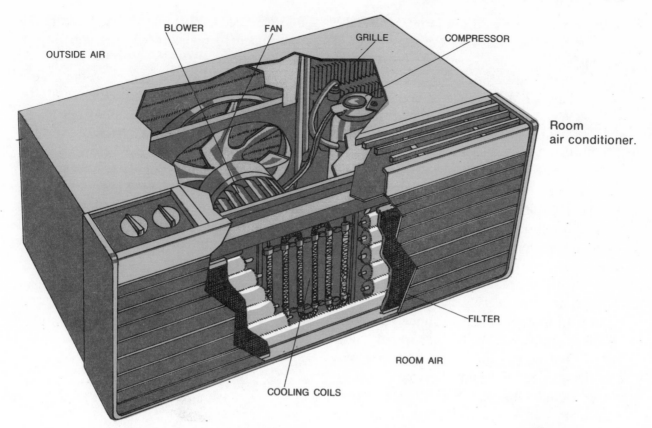

OUTSIDE AIR   BLOWER   FAN   GRILLE   COMPRESSOR

Room air conditioner.

FILTER

ROOM AIR

COOLING COILS

Although room air conditioners differ in cabinet styling, weight, and component placement, they all basically function the same way, performing four jobs to make you comfortable on a hot, humid day. They cool the air, remove moisture from the air, filter out dust, and circulate the air inside a room or several rooms.

The operation of a room air conditioner is basically the same as a central unit. Although smaller, the components are much the same and do the same jobs. The evaporator section of the room unit projects into the room, and the condenser-compressor compartment extends to the outside of the house.

ESTIMATING COOLING NEEDS

Before you select a room air conditioner for your home, it is important to determine the cooling capacity needed. If the cooling

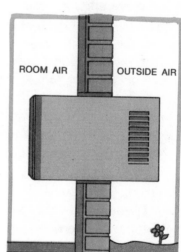

ROOM AIR   OUTSIDE AIR

Typical through-wall installation.

capacity of a unit is too small for the room where you plan to use it, it will not do an adequate job of cooling and dehumidifying. If it is too large for the room, it will probably cost more and not dehumidify properly. You can arrive at a cooling capacity estimate in several ways.

A salesman at a reputable air conditioner dealer can make an estimate for you if you

Keeping Cool

give him accurate information. Usually, the answers to the following questions are all he needs:

- What are the height, width, and length of the area to be cooled?
- What are the number and sizes of windows and the directions they face?
- Where is the space to be cooled located in the house?
- Does the longest side of the room face north, east, south, or west?

Some dealers offer free home surveys. Just make sure, as always, that you deal only with reputable and knowledgeable people and not merely hard-sell artists. If you plan to cool several connected rooms, professional advice will be especially valuable. One large room air conditioner may be all you need if air flow between rooms is free enough, but in other homes two or more smaller units in separate rooms may be more efficient and economical. Another way to determine your cooling needs is to use the Cooling Load Estimate Form for Room Air Conditioners developed by the Association of Home Appliance Manufacturers (AHAM). If you are good with figures and prefer doing such calculations yourself, you may wish to go this route. The form is free and can be obtained by writing to AHAM, 20 North Wacker Drive, Chicago, Illinois 60606.

If you don't care to be quite that precise, you can make a reasonably good estimate of your cooling needs by following a fairly simple method. Find the volume of the room by multiplying the width, length, and height in feet. Multiply this number by 10 if the roof or attic is well insulated or if another room is above. If the room has many windows or an uninsulated roof, multiply instead by 18. Now multiply by 16 if the longest wall faces north, by 17 if it faces east, by 18 if it faces south, by 19 if it faces west. Divide this result by 60 to find your

cooling needs. This answer is stated in the units used to measure cooling capacity in air conditioners: Btu/h.

If you plan to cool several rooms, do a calculation for each room, then add the answers to find your total cooling needs.

You can make a quick check of your figures by consulting the list below. It compares space to be cooled with "average" cooling capacity needed. These, of course, are "ballpark" figures, since other variables enter into your calculations, but they will give an indication of approximate needs.

Space to be cooled	Cooling needed (Btu/h)
medium-size bedroom	5,000–6,000
medium-size living room	8,000–12,000
several connected rooms	15,000–20,000
medium-size house	24,000 or more

BEFORE YOU BUY

Room air conditioners come in a number of styles. One consideration is whether a unit is to be mounted in a window or through a wall. Some models are sold with adapters and can be mounted in several ways.

If a unit is to be window-mounted, its shape and dimensions will be determined by the shape and dimensions of the window. If the unit doesn't fit properly, an airtight installation is difficult to achieve. If you don't have an airtight installation, the conditioner will never cool up to its capacity.

Double-hung windows, in which the sash slides up and down, accept conventional air conditioners that are box-shaped and wider than they are high. When such a unit is installed, the bottom sash rests on the top of the conditioner. Panels supplied with the air conditioner fill in side spaces.

Casement windows, which swing out and

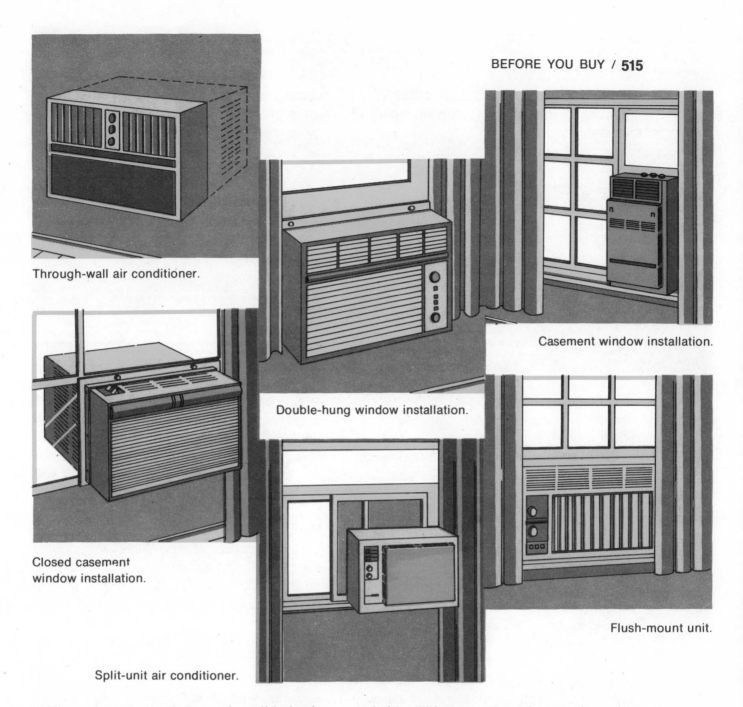

Through-wall air conditioner.

Double-hung window installation.

Casement window installation.

Closed casement window installation.

Flush-mount unit.

Split-unit air conditioner.

in like a door, and windows that slide horizontally usually require tall, narrow conditioners. Such conditioners are installed in windows left completely or partly open; fit of these is critical.

For closed casement windows, a specially shaped conditioner is available that has a small front and is deep from front to back. It is installed by removing one or two small panes of glass and inserting the unit in the opening.

For both sash and sliding windows, U-shaped, split-unit conditioners are also available. This type allows installation with a minimum of open window space that must be sealed by panels or other devices.

In some areas local laws or building regulations require that a conditioner must not project more than a certain distance from the outside of a building wall. Check to see if such rules apply to your home. If they do, ask your dealer about air conditioners designed with a minimal overhang.

Another special type fits almost flush with the window in which it is placed. You may consider this type of unit more attrac-

Keeping Cool

Poor interior location.

Poor exterior location.

tive because drapes can be pulled across the front to conceal it when it is not operating.

Location of the air conditioner is an important consideration. A window that faces north is best because it is shaded most of the day. The unit should not be installed in a window where outdoor airflow will be blocked by a nearby building or dense bushes. Inside, avoid room corners or places where large pieces of furniture could hinder air circulation.

The electric motors in air conditioners are designed with different volt and ampere ratings to fit different home wiring systems. Motors may operate on 115 volts, 210 volts, or 230 volts, and they draw currents ranging from less than 7.5 to over 25 amperes

To find the conditioner best suited for your home, you must know the electrical capacity of your wiring in volts and amperes, the codes in your area with regard to connecting air conditioners to home wiring, and the electrical load on the wiring. A conditioner that draws more current than the wiring will safely carry can cause blown fuses or a fire hazard. If your wiring is inadequate for the conditioner you want to buy, you have only two choices: buy a smaller

air conditioner or install higher-capacity wiring in your home.

Circuits in most homes and apartments supply electricity at about 115 volts and 15 amperes. Kitchens and laundry rooms may have circuits that supply 20 amperes. Before you buy a conditioner, find out the amperage of the outlet where the unit will be located. One way to do this is to check your house or apartment fuse box and read the amperes from the appropriate fuse or circuit breaker. If you have any doubts about the amperage or voltage of the outlet, consult a licensed electrician or public utility representative.

In most of the United States, air conditioners that draw 7.5 amperes or less at 115 volts may be connected to household circuits. In some areas and buildings, air conditioners with ratings up to 12 amperes may be plugged into 115-volt, single-outlet circuits, but nowhere should units drawing more than 12 amperes be connected to 15-ampere, 115-volt circuits. Few houses or apartments are equipped with single-outlet, 115-volt circuits. Installing them should be left to a licensed electrician and can cost anywhere from $25 to $125, depending on the capacity of the existing building wiring and the location of the outlet. Only if you have considerable wiring experience should you attempt the job yourself. Some localities require that only a licensed electrician do such work, or at least that all work be inspected by a licensed electrician—a good idea in any case.

To find the electrical rating allowable for a conditioner connected to your home wiring, contact the city or county engineer's office, a licensed electrician, or the electric utility company. You can also consult a local air conditioner dealer. Some offer a free home survey to determine any electrical changes that should be made to install various air conditioners. Again, consult only a reputable dealer.

If you live in an apartment, check with the building manager before you purchase a room air conditioner. Many buildings have strict rules about the maximum amperage allowed for air conditioners.

Even if you follow your local electrical code to the letter, it is possible to overload a circuit's current-carrying capacity if you plug other appliances into it in addition to the air conditioner. The combined load would result in tripped breakers or blown fuses, or even an electrical fire if the circuit is improperly wired or fused. To avoid this situation you must determine the circuit's load. You can check the load yourself if you know all the appliances and lights that are already on the circuit to which you plan to connect the air conditioner. Add the wattages of the appliances and the lights usually functioning and divide by 115 volts. The answer is the ampere load on the circuit without the conditioner. Then add the ampere rating of the conditioner to get your projected total load.

If the total is more than 12 amperes on a 15-ampere circuit, or more than 16 amperes on a 20-ampere circuit, you should install the conditioner on a circuit with fewer appliances or buy two small-amperage conditioners rather than one large one and put them on two different circuits. Another alternative is to have an electrician install another circuit.

If you are considering buying a 210- or 230-volt air conditioner, consult a qualified electrician or the local power company about the actual voltage delivered to your home. It may be anywhere from less than 200 volts to more than 240 volts.

SHOPPING FOR A ROOM AIR CONDITIONER

When shopping for an air conditioner, compare the efficiency of the units you are considering. With the spiraling costs of energy today, operating costs of the unit are a point to be reckoned with before laying out your hard-earned money. An air conditioner that operates more efficiently uses less electricity.

The initials EER stand for Energy Efficiency Ratio, something to check very closely when selecting an air conditioner. A unit's EER is computed by dividing the Btu/h by the watts of power used (both stated on a plate on the machine). The higher the resulting figure, the more efficient the air conditioner. The EER does not relate to cooling capacity, only efficiency. Two units with different EERs can provide an equal cooling capacity. Both will cool the room satisfactorily, but in so doing one will use less electricity. A conditioner that achieves an EER rating of 8 to 9 will ease your electric bills substantially during its lifetime.

There are certain practical and convenience features to look for in a room air conditioner. In this respect, shop for an air conditioner much the same as any appliance and treat your purchase as the investment it is.

Check to make sure the unit has been properly certified. A seal of approval, such as that of Underwriters' Laboratories, Inc., should be attached guaranteeing that it has

Keeping Cool

AHAM certification.

Seal of the
Underwriters' Laboratories.

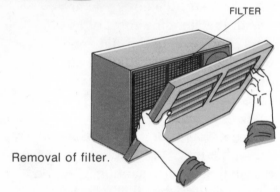

BTU hr COOLING CAPACITY
AMPERES and WATTS RATING

AHAM
CERTIFIED

ASSOCIATION OF HOME
APPLIANCE MANUFACTURERS'
Room Air Conditioner Standard CN 1

FILTER

Removal of filter.

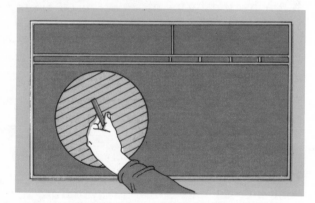

Adjusting the front grille to direct air flow.

met certain standards of electrical safety. Ratings for amperes, watts, and Btu/h should be indicated and a seal attached saying "AHAM-certified."

The warranty should state clearly how many years of free repair parts and labor you are buying with the unit. Be sure the warranty will be honored at a local authorized service shop. Check to see if additional in-home service contracts are available.

The unit's filter should be easy to remove and reinstall and either simple to clean or inexpensive to replace. Have the dealer demonstrate filter care.

The front of the unit should be both practical and good-looking. The front grille should be adjustable to direct air flow to the desired area. The grille "cleanability" should also be considered. Common features on a typical air conditioner include a thermostat to regulate room temperature, fan settings for additional cooling, and opening vents for bringing outside air into a room. Some models also feature heat controls for regulating heat on cool days, or fan-only settings to circulate fresh air. Have the dealer explain and demonstrate the use of all controls.

As with any major purchase, shop around. Consider the dealer's reputation in the community, experience in the business, and ability to deliver, install, and service what he sells. Friends, neighbors, or your local Better Business Bureau can possibly advise you.

Unit controls.

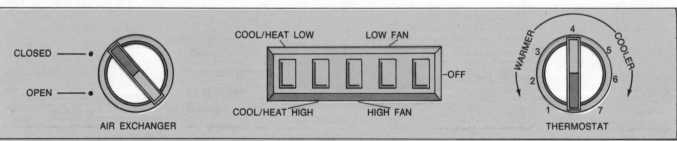

AIR EXCHANGER CONTROL   **MASTER CONTROL**   **THERMOSTAT CONTROL**

Keeping Cool

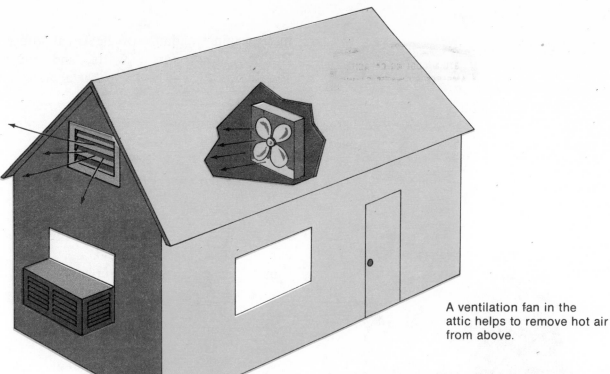

A ventilation fan in the attic helps to remove hot air from above.

Collect as much literature on the product as you can, and study it carefully, comparing different styles and models. Take your time and consider all possibilities before you reach for your wallet.

ROUTINE MAINTENANCE AND SIMPLE REPAIRS

Proper care and usage will greatly increase your satisfaction and the cooling you get from your room air conditioner, not to mention prolong its life. The best guide to a unit's use and care is your owner's manual. Keep it handy and consult it often.

The thermostat should generally be left alone once you have found a comfortable temperature. However, you should set the thermostat at a slightly higher temperature if you plan to be away for several hours. The reverse is true if you are entertaining a number of guests. People generate heat, so the thermostat will probably need to be set at a slightly lower temperature.

Grilles should be adjusted so that cool air flows up, out, and away from the nearest wall to blanket the whole room. Fans should be set at high speed in hot weather to take full advantage of the conditioner's cooling capacity. During periods of cool, moist weather, low speed should be used for less cooling and more moisture removal.

The workload of your air conditioner will be greatly reduced if all windows and doors in the room to be cooled are kept closed. Shades or drapes should be pulled across the windows during the day. A ventilation fan in the attic to remove hot air from above will also help.

Cleaning and protection of certain conditioner parts are necessary occasionally to insure efficient, trouble-free cooling and to prevent service calls and repairs. Be sure to unplug the conditioner before performing any maintenance chores.

The filter should be cleaned or changed at least once a month to prevent dirt from collecting on the cooling coils and decreasing cooling efficiency. If the filter is reusable, it can be removed, washed in soap and water, and replaced damp on the unit. If you change filters, make sure the replacement is of the same material, quality, and thickness as the original.

Cooling coils on the outside of the unit should be protected in winter by a dust-proof cover. This will keep out wind-blown dirt and help prevent rusting caused by rain or snow conditions. Be sure to remove the

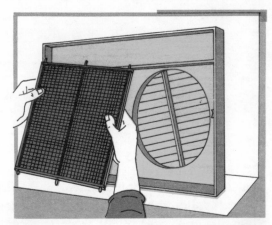

Installation of a new filter.

Protect outside coils in winter with a dustproof cover.

Vacuum clean the cooling coils.

cover before using the conditioner the following summer.

When something goes wrong, be sure you really need a serviceman before you call him. Check first to see if there is a simple solution.

If the conditioner won't run, check to make sure the plug is firmly in its electrical outlet. It's not only embarrassing to have a serviceman jiggle the cord to solve your problem—it's expensive. A blown fuse or a tripped circuit breaker could also cause a shutoff. Check these and replace a blown fuse or reset a tripped breaker. If the problem repeats, call the serviceman.

When a conditioner does not provide enough cooling, it sometimes indicates a clogged or dirty filter. Clean or replace the filter and vacuum-clean the cooling coils. Check the vents and window mounting to be sure no cool air is escaping.

If the unit still doesn't cool the room properly, call the local electric utility company to find out if there is temporary low voltage in your area. If there is, the efficiency of your conditioner may be lessened until voltage returns to normal. In this case a repairman would not be able to help. You might be better off shutting down the unit and suffering through the heat, rather than having it operate at the reduced voltage, which could damage the mechanism. Outside temperature can play tricks with your conditioner, too. If it is less than 70 degrees outside, water can drip inside the room. The solution to this problem is either to turn the unit completely off or to use the fan-only setting.

It takes some careful thought and planning to design an air-conditioning system perfect for your personal needs. And it takes proper care and maintenance to keep it keeping you cool. But it's worth a little sweat to save a lot, as you will appreciate when you are relaxing inside your cool house during the dog days of summer.

Keeping Cool

7

How to Save on Home Comfort Conditioning

HOMEOWNERS around the country are faced with a serious problem—conserving energy and money without sacrificing on comfort in the home. Although the problem is serious, the solutions are fairly simple. There are several energy-saving steps the average do-it-yourselfer can take without having a garage full of tools or laying out big bucks.

We all know that heating and cooling the home is taking a bigger and bigger bite out of the personal budget each year, and it probably won't get better. A few energy conservation steps can ease those monthly bills as well as add resale value to the home. With the dwindling natural resources of our country, the nation as a whole will also benefit.

INSULATION

It's an interesting fact that most homes, built in the days when energy was plentiful and cheap, don't have enough insulation, and some don't have any at all. The expression "better late than never" surely applies here.

No matter where you live, insulation is a hidden but most important part of your house. During the heating season, insulation keeps warmth indoors where it belongs, and your family is comfortable and snug. Insulation is equally important in hot weather, since it helps keep the extreme heat of the sun from penetrating. And, in air-conditioned homes, insulation eases the task of the cooling system.

A properly insulated house costs far less to heat and cool than its noninsulated twin. Less fuel is burned, and at the same time a higher level of comfort is experienced. By the same token, air conditioners that work less use less electricity. It can truthfully be said that insulation pays for itself over and over again.

An insulated home is also a far more pleasant place in which to live. Indoor temperatures can be kept more constant. Inside surfaces of walls, floors, and ceilings, insulated from outdoor extremes, are closer to room air temperature and therefore conducive to comfort and well-being. Annoying drafts are minimized or eliminated, and the whole living area stays comfortable in the coldest, or hottest, weather.

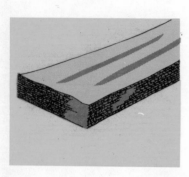

Batt.

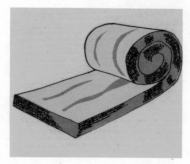

Blanket.

Loose fill
insulation.

In the heating season alone, adequate insulation in the attic floor generally saves up to 30 percent on fuel bills and can save up to 50 percent. In an air-conditioned home, summer savings are comparable.

The most common kinds of insulation for the home are mineral fiber, cellulose fiber, plastic foam, and aluminum foil sheets. These types can be divided into categories according to how they are installed.

Mineral fiber insulation is purchased in batts or blankets and is the most widely used type. Mineral fiber, whether fiberglass or rock wool, is used to insulate unfinished attic floors, attic rafters, and the underside of floors. Batts come precut in widths of either 15 or 23 inches and in lengths of 4 or 8 feet. Blankets are purchased in the same widths and are cut to the desired length. All mineral fiber insulation can be bought with or without a vapor barrier backing and is fire- and moisture-resistant. Installation of this type is very easy.

Loose fill insulation comes in glass fiber, rock wool, cellulose fiber, vermiculite, and perlite. Basically, this type is used only for unfinished attic floors and is best suited for areas that are irregular or have many obstructions. If a vapor barrier is needed, it must be bought and installed separately with this type. Cellulose fiber is chemically treated to be fire- and moisture-resistant but has not yet been proven to be heat-resistant. This means that the insulation could break down in a hot attic. Check to be sure that bags indicate that the material meets federal specifications. Because this type of insulation is simply poured into place, installation is no problem.

Glass fiber, rock wool, and cellulose fiber can also be blown into place. Generally used for attic floors and finished frame walls, this type has the same physical properties as poured-in loose fill. Because it consists of smaller tufts, cellulose fiber gets into small nooks and corners more consistently than rock wool or glass fiber when blown into closed spaces such as walls or joist spaces. Professional installation is required with this insulation.

Ureaformaldehyde can also be used for unfinished attic floors or finished frame walls. Foamed in place, it may have higher insulating value than blown-in materials, but it is more expensive. The quality of application to date has been very inconsistent, so choose a qualified contractor who will guarantee his work.

Regardless of the type of material from which insulation is manufactured or the physical form in which it is applied to the house, the principle remains the same. Between the fibers are tiny air spaces. There are untold numbers of these in each piece of insulation, and each one is a tiny insulator in its own right. The cumulative effect is what does the job. By creating an extremely effective barrier to the passage of heat, the insulation isolates the house from exterior weather influences.

Your money's worth in insulation is mea-

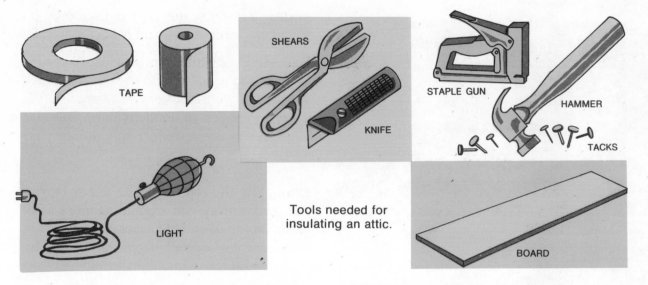

Tools needed for insulating an attic.

sured in R-Value. R-Value is a number that tells how much resistance the insulation presents to heat flowing through it. The higher the R-Value, the better the insulation. One brand of insulation might be slightly thicker or thinner than another, but if they're marked with the same R-Value they'll resist heat flow equally well. If you have a choice of insulating materials, simply price the same R-Value for both and get the better buy. Pay more only for more R-Value. The R-Value is marked on the outside of the package.

Insulating the attic floor, where savings generally will be greatest, usually can be done by the homeowner himself. The amount of insulation needed depends entirely upon how much insulation, if any, is

Measure present insulation in floor.

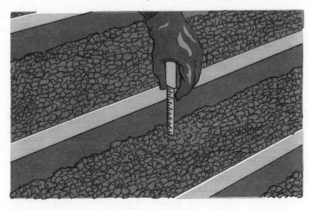

already there. To find out, go up into the attic and measure the depth with a tape measure or yardstick.

If there is 6 inches or more, no additional insulation is needed. Insulation with an R-Value of R-11 should be used in attics with between 2 and 6 inches of insulation already in place. If there is no insulation at all present, new insulation should have an R-Value of R-22. If you can't get into your attic or don't want to do the work yourself, call a reputable contractor and get an estimate for the needed R-Value. These amounts will make certain that your home meets current Federal Housing Administration standards for new houses.

Amounts greater than these may be necessary if your climate is substantially colder or warmer than average or a high amount of attic insulation will have to partially compensate for poorly insulated walls.

A minimum of tools and experience are needed to insulate an attic properly. Besides the insulation, the materials needed are: tape (2 inches wide), staple gun or hammer and tacks, heavy-duty shears or knife to cut insulation, and temporary lighting and flooring.

Some simple safety steps should be taken when working in the attic with insulation of any type. Provide good lighting (it's dark up

Use board to form walkway on joists.

Watch out for nails!

What the well-dressed insulator will wear: gloves, breathing mask, long-sleeved clothing.

resulting water vapor can wet the insulation, robbing it of its insulating qualities. Excessive moisture can also cause rotting in the wood used to build the house. Added ventilation will remove water vapor before it gets a chance to condense and will also increase summer comfort by cooling your attic.

If you are installing batt or blanket insulation, buy the type with the vapor barrier attached (unless you are adding more insulation on top of existing insulation, in which case no vapor barrier should be used). Install it with the vapor barrier side toward the living space.

For loose fill insulation, lay down polyethylene sheets between the joists before pouring in, or blowing in, the insulation.

The actual job of insulating an attic is quite simple. If batts or blankets with vapor barrier attached are used, merely lay the insulation between joists or trusses. Loose fill insulation is poured between the joists up to the top of the joists. Use a rake or board to level it. Fill all the nooks and crannies, but don't cover recessed light fixtures or exhaust fans. The National Electrical Code requires that insulation be kept at least 3 inches away from light fixtures.

Extra precautions must be taken not to cover any vents that would block the flow of air into the attic. The space between the chimney and the wood framing should be filled with noncombustible material, preferably unfaced batts or blankets.

While insulating the attic, it's a good idea to check for roof leaks by looking for water stains or marks. If you find leakage, make repairs before you insulate. Wet insulation is ineffective and can damage the structure of the home.

Insulating a finished or partially finished attic is a little harder because some parts are inaccessible. A contractor can do a complete job, and in some cases this is the best course. If you can get into the unfin-

there!). Lay boards or plywood sheets down over the tops of the joists or trusses to form a walkway. Be careful of roofing nails protruding through the roof sheathing. If you use glass fiber or mineral wool, wear gloves, a breathing mask, and long-sleeved clothing. Because most insulation comes wrapped in a compressed state, it should be kept wrapped until ready for use.

A vapor barrier is usually necessary when insulation is installed. This is a material that will block moisture and not absorb it. If warm, moist air from inside the house is allowed to pass through the wall covering and meet the cool dry air from outside, the

Polyethylene sheet as vapor barrier.

Lay batts or blankets in place.

Pour in loose fill insulation.

Level loose fill insulation.

Do not cover fixtures.

Do not cover vents.

Noncombustible material should be used for insulation around chimneys.

Check for roof leaks.

How to Save on Home Comfort Conditioning

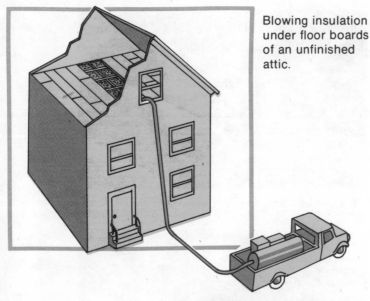

Blowing insulation under floor boards of an unfinished attic.

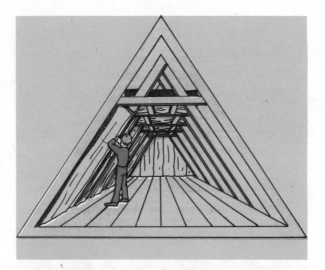

Insulating rafters, end walls, and collar beams.

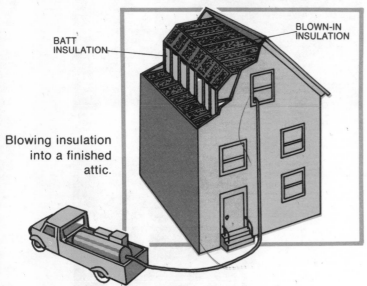

BATT INSULATION

BLOWN-IN INSULATION

Blowing insulation into a finished attic.

ished parts of the attic to do the work, you can do the job yourself.

Insulating an attic that is unfinished but has a floor is usually a job for a contractor. Assuming there is less than 4 inches of insulation under the floor, insulation can be blown under the floor boards. If there is more than 4 inches, the job is not economical.

The do-it-yourselfer can insulate the rafters, end walls, and collar beams of an unfinished, floored attic. This is the best way if you are planning to finish the attic. Batts or blankets are installed between the rafters

and collar beams, and between the studs on the end walls. At ceiling height, 2×4 beams must be installed between each roof rafter, if the attic doesn't already have them. This gives a ventilation space above the insulation and forms the roof of the attic. Between the collar beams, add insulation with an R-Value of at least R-22. Rafters and end walls require insulation thick enough to fill up the rafter and stud space. Insulation for the rafters should be R-19, and the end walls should have at least R-11 insulation.

The homeowner with a completely finished attic is more limited as to what he can do himself. Insulating an attic without tearing down the finished walls is almost always a job for a competent contractor. A contractor will blow insulation into the open joist spaces above the attic ceiling, between the rafters, and into the floor of the outer attic space, then install batts in the knee walls. If you want the outer attic spaces heated for storage or any other purpose, have the contractor install batts between the outer attic rafters instead of insulating the outer floors and knee walls. Insulating this type of attic is not worth considering unless there is less than 4 inches of insulation already installed.

How to Save on Home Comfort Conditioning

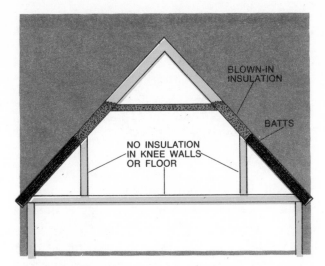

Insulating the outer spaces of an attic.

Installing insulation in the attic ceiling.

You can insulate wherever you can get into unfinished spaces. Installing insulation in the attic ceiling is the same as installing it in an unfinished, floored attic. If you want to insulate the outer attic spaces, install batts between the rafters and the studs in the small triangular end walls. If there is no existing insulation, use R-22 for the ceiling and R-11 for the end walls.

The next step toward easing your energy bills and adding to the comfort of your home is to insulate the walls. This depends on what type of walls you have and how much, if any, insulation is already there.

To find out what's inside the wall, turn off the principal electric switch or a circuit breaker or fuse for a convenient outlet or switch box on an outside wall. Remove the cover plate and the electrical box (usually nailed to a framing member) to get a look inside the wall cavity. You'll be able to see or feel any insulation that's in the wall stud cavity space. If you are in doubt as to the amount of insulation, or whether it will be adequate, your best bet is to call an insulation contractor.

Most frame houses have a wood structure—usually 2×4s—even though they may have brick or stone on the outside. If you have this type of walls, you should

consider insulating them if they are not already insulated. A contractor can fill them with insulation and cut energy waste by about two-thirds. This job is not for the do-it-yourselfer.

The contractor will measure the area you want insulated to determine how much material he will need and to estimate the cost. To install the insulation, the contractor must be able to get at all the spaces in the wall. For each space, he must drill a hole, usually in the outside wall, after removing the finish layer (usually clapboard or shingle). This amounts to a lot of holes, but once the job is complete, a good contractor will leave no traces behind.

If you have brick veneer on the outside, the procedure is much the same, except

Check for insulation in walls.

How to Save on Home Comfort Conditioning

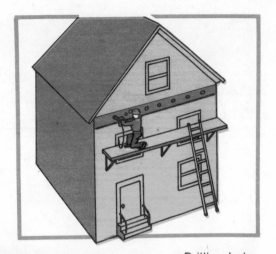

Drilling holes into the outside wall.

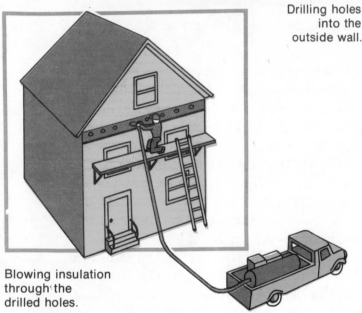

Blowing insulation through the drilled holes.

add an R-Value of 8 for rock wool, 10 for cellulose fiber, or 11.5 for ureaformaldehyde in a standard wood-frame wall. You should agree with the contractor on what the R-Value is before the job begins. Next, check a bag of the type of insulation he intends to use (there will only be bags of mineral fiber or cellulose fiber—there's no good way to check quantity with foam). On it will be a table indicating how many square feet of wall space that bag is meant to fill while giving your house the desired R-Value. The information may be in different forms (number of square feet per bag or number of bags per 1,000 square feet), so you may have to do some simple arithmetic to interpret the number correctly. Knowing this and the area of the walls to be insulated, you should be able to figure out about how many bags should be installed to give you the desired R-Value.

This number should be agreed on between you and the contractor before the job is begun. While the job is in progress be sure the correct amount is being used. There's nothing wrong with having the contractor save the empty bags so you can count them. Four or five bags more or less than the amount you agreed on is an acceptable difference from the estimate.

Some houses have structural brick or masonry walls without a wooden frame behind. Insulating this type of wall is more complicated than frame walls but may be worthwhile if there is no insulation already there. Call a contractor to get an estimate and find out what's involved.

If you are adding a room or have unfinished walls, the job of insulating them is relatively simple. If stud spacing is standard (16 inches, center to center), push blankets or batts into the space between the studs until they touch the sheathing or siding. Be sure to place them so that the vapor barrier faces inward. Fit flanges tightly against the sides of the studs and begin sta-

that it may be cheaper to do the job from the inside.

Once the holes have been made in the walls, the contractor will blow the insulation material under air pressure through a big flexible hose into the area to be filled. If the contractor uses foam-type insulation, he'll pump the foam into the wall spaces with a flexible hose and an applicator. With either method, each space will be completely filled, and the siding replaced.

Before you sign an agreement with the contractor, define what you're buying and make sure it's spelled out in the contract. Insulation material properly installed will pling at the top with a heavy-duty stapler. Space staples about 6 to 12 inches apart. To fill a stud space that is less than standard, cut the insulation lengthwise about an inch wider than the space and then staple normally.

To help prevent condensation in insulated walls, seal any openings that could afford a path to moisture, especially around the window and door frames. Painting the interior walls with a low-permeability paint, such as high-gloss enamel, will also help in this respect. Discuss this matter with a paint dealer before purchasing paint.

If you live in a climate where your heating bills are big enough to be a major hassle, it's a good idea to insulate the underside of your house. It won't save much on air conditioning, but it certainly will save on heating expenses.

If your house (or part of it) sits on top of a crawl space that can be tightly sealed off from the outside air in the winter, the cheapest and best place to insulate is around the outside walls and on the ground inside the space. This should be considered only if there is no existing insulation and if the crawl space is big enough to allow plenty of room to do the work.

First cover the earth inside the crawl space with a layer of 6-mil polyethylene plastic, sealing it to the walls and at seams with 2-inch-wide duct tape or masking tape.

Install batt or blanket insulation (R-11) around the walls of the crawl space, fastening it to the sills by nailing through $\frac{1}{4} \times 1\frac{1}{2}$-inch strips of lattice. Cut the insulation long enough to allow it to overlap the floor by 2 feet. When all the insulation is in place, secure it by laying 2×4s along the wall-floor bend. Force insulation against the header joists and the end joists to insure a good weather seal.

Even with a plastic vapor barrier on the floor, the air in the crawl space will be too damp if fresh air doesn't get in. This will mean that the new insulation will be wet and won't keep the house as warm. It will also mean that wooden framing members will be wet, and they'll rot. Proper ventilation will prevent both of these problems.

If the crawl space is part of the forced-air heating system, seal it as tightly as possible—the air moving through it from the furnace is enough ventilation in winter. If the crawl space has vents, keep them shut in winter, open in summer. If there are no vents, run the blower on the furnace three or four times during the summer to keep the air in the crawl space from getting too damp, preventing wetting the insulation.

All other crawl spaces should have vents that can be opened in summer to clear out the damp air and closed very tightly in winter to make the most of your new insulation. A word of caution: Your furnace may

Insulating a new wall.

Insulating a crawl space.

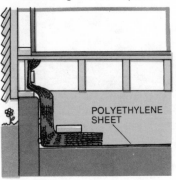

POLYETHYLENE SHEET

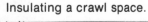

Seal all openings around windows and door frames.

How to Save on Home Comfort Conditioning

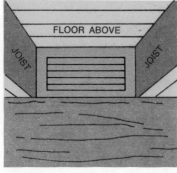

Install vent in header joist.

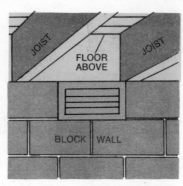

Install vent in block wall.

Staple chicken wire below joists.

Slide batts or blankets on top of the wire.

Check walls for dampness from the ground outside.

Seal cracks with epoxy patching compound.

get its combustion air from the crawl space. If so, some of the vents should be left open year-round. Check with your fuel oil dealer or gas utility if you are not sure.

Insulating crawl spaces should not be done if you live in Alaska, Minnesota, or northern Maine. The extreme frost penetration in these areas can cause heaving of the foundation if the insulation method described here is used. Residents of these areas should contact local building code officials or government agencies for advice.

Insulating the floor of your house is a good idea if you have a crawl space that you can't seal off in winter, or if you have a garage, porch, or other cold unheated space with heated rooms above it. Install batts or blankets, preferably with foil facing, of R-11 rating between the floor joists. Staple wire mesh or chicken wire to the bottom of the joists, and slide the batts or blankets in on top of the wire, leaving an air space between the vapor barrier and the floor.

Check your floor joist spacing—this method will work best with standard 16- or 24-inch joist spacing. If you have irregular spacing there will be more cutting and fitting and some waste of material.

If you have a basement that you use as a living or work space and that has air outlets, radiators, or baseboard units to heat it, you may find that it will pay to add a layer of insulation to the inside of the wall. You only need to insulate the parts of the walls that are above the ground down to about 2 feet below ground level.

Before insulating, check to see whether moisture is coming through the walls from the ground outside. If it is and your walls are damp, eliminate the cause of dampness to prevent the insulation you're about to install from becoming wet and ineffective.

If the dampness is caused by water seeping through cracks in the foundation walls, seal these cracks with an epoxy patching compound, available at most hardware stores. Follow manufacturer's directions for application. If seepage covers a large area, it may indicate a more serious problem of excessive water pressure against the outside of the foundation. The solution here may involve digging down outside the foundation and applying bituminous coatings to the outside of the walls, and laying drain tiles to carry ground water to a drywell or other location away from the house. It's hard labor that you will probably want to leave to an experienced contractor.

Install a framework of 2×3 studs along the walls to be insulated. The bottom plate of the frame should be nailed to the floor with concrete nails, and the top plate nailed to the joists above. Studs should be placed 16 or 24 inches apart between the top and bottom plates.

Batt or blanket insulation rated R-7 should be cut into sections long enough to extend from the top plate to about 2 feet below the ground line. Staple the sections into place between the studs, with the vapor barrier toward the living space. Only in very cold northern climates will there be added benefits by installing the insulation the full height of the wall.

To finish the basement, install wallboard or paneling over the new insulation and furring. Add molding at the top plate and baseboard at the bottom for a basement that's fit for a king—a comfortable king at that!

As in insulating a crawl space, residents of Alaska, Minnesota, and northern Maine should check local practices before insulating basement walls.

In recent years the family of insulation products has grown to include merchandise for such specialized requirements as sound control, window sealing, and insulating suspended ceilings. Insulation can now be purchased for any purpose, leaving the homeowner no excuse for not wrapping his home with a warm blanket of insulation and saving on fuel bills at the same time.

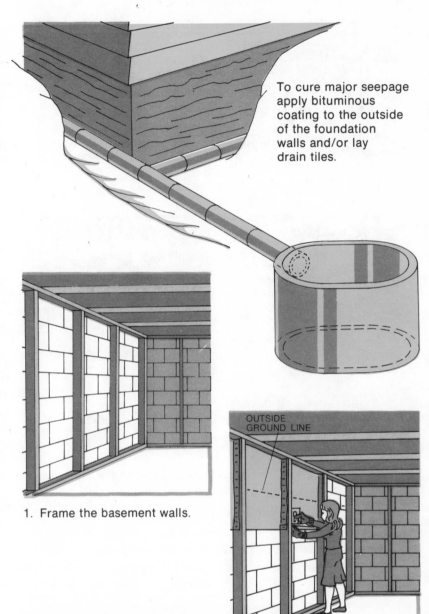

To cure major seepage apply bituminous coating to the outside of the foundation walls and/or lay drain tiles.

1. Frame the basement walls.

2. Staple insulation to studs.

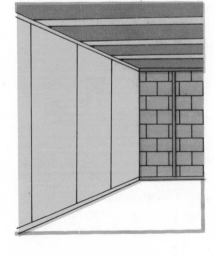

3. Install wallboard over framing.

How to Save on Home Comfort Conditioning

Calk around windows.

Calk around faucets.

Calk around chimney.

Calk between house and porch.

WEATHERSTRIPPING AND CALKING

In a well-insulated house the largest source of heat loss is air leaks, especially around windows and doors. Good weatherstripping and calking of exterior window and door frames will not only reduce the heat loss in winter and heat gain in summer, but will reduce uncomfortable drafts as well.

Weatherstripping and calking a home are generally worthwhile and economical projects in all climates. The average homeowner can seal his home against the elements for a minimal cost and almost without working up a sweat. Materials are available at most hardware stores.

Calking should be applied wherever two different materials or parts of the house meet. The best way to approach this job is to load up the calking gun and make a thorough examination of the outside of the house, looking for any areas where outside air could leak in.

Common problem areas are around windows and doors, where water faucets, pipes, or wires penetrate the outside house surface, around the chimney, and between the main body of the house and porches.

Calking compound is available in a variety of types and prices to fit anyone's budget. Decide on the type best suited for your needs and the easiest to work with.

Oil- or resin-base calk is readily available and will bond to most surfaces, including wood, masonry, and metal. This type is not the most durable, but it costs the least.

Latex, butyl, or polyvinyl-based calk is also readily available and will bond to most surfaces. It is more durable but more expensive than oil- or resin-based calk.

Elastomeric calks are the most durable and also the most expensive. These include silicones, polysulfides, and polyurethanes. The instructions provided on the labels should be followed.

To fill extra-wide cracks or as a backup for elastomeric calks, use oakum, calking cotton, sponge rubber, or glass fiber.

Lead-based calk is not recommended, because it is toxic. Many states prohibit its use.

Calking a house usually requires the use of a ladder to do the job right. Be sure you use it safely. Carry the calking gun in a sling

Carry calking gun in a sling when climbing (left) and don't overreach (right).

How to Save on Home Comfort Conditioning

so that you can use both hands climbing the ladder, and don't try to reach for that extra little bit — get down and move the ladder.

Estimating the number of cartridges of calking compound required is difficult, since the number will vary greatly with the size of the cracks to be filled. If possible, it's best to start with a half dozen cartridges and then purchase more as the job continues and you need more.

Before applying calking compound, clean the area to be sealed of paint build-up, dirt, or deteriorated calk, using solvent and a putty knife or other scraping tool.

Drawing a good bead of calk with the gun will take a little practice. First attempts may be a bit messy, but don't get discouraged. Make sure the bead overlaps both sides for a tight seal. Sometimes a wide bead is necessary to do the job right.

Fill extra-wide cracks like those at the sills (where the house meets the foundation) with oakum, glass fiber insulation strips, or similar material, then finish the job with calk.

Calking compound also comes in rope form. This type is forced into cracks with the fingers and is especially good for extra long cracks.

Weatherstripping is another project the homeowner can do to keep the winter chill from entering his domain and to ease high energy costs. A minimum of tools, skills, and cash is required to properly seal doors and windows in a home.

Three types of weatherstripping are commonly used to seal windows. All are readily available at hardware stores or building supply outlets.

Thin spring metal is installed in the channel of a window so that it is virtually invisible when installed. Although somewhat difficult to install, it is very durable.

Rolled vinyl weatherstripping is available with or without a metal backing. It is visible when installed. This type is durable and easy to install.

Foam rubber with adhesive backing is the easiest of all to install, but it breaks down and wears rather quickly. It is not as effective a sealer as metal strips or rolled vinyl and should never be used where friction occurs.

Weatherstripping is purchased either by the running foot or in kit form for each window. In either case, measurements of all windows must be taken to find the total length of weatherstripping needed for the job. Measure the total distance around the

Various kinds of weatherstripping.

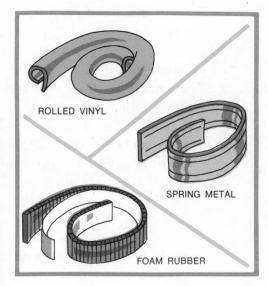

ROLLED VINYL

SPRING METAL

FOAM RUBBER

Clean area before calking.

Fill wide cracks before calking.

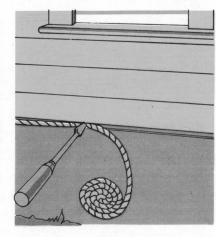

How to Save on Home Comfort Conditioning

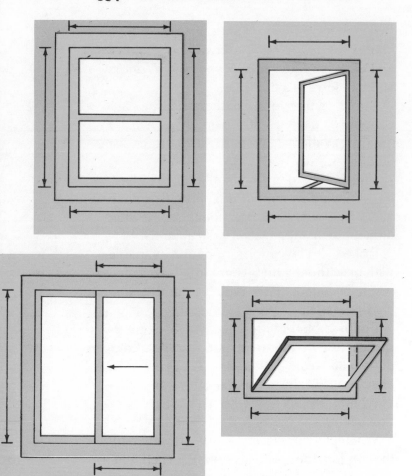

Measuring windows for weatherstripping: double-hung window (top left), casement window (top right), hopper- or awning window (above right), sliding window (above left).

edges of the moving parts of each window to be sealed. Be sure to allow for waste. If a window kit is purchased, be sure the kit is intended for the correct type and size of the window.

Thin spring metal is installed by moving the sash to the open position and sliding a strip in between the sash and the channel. It is then tacked in place into the window casing. Do not cover the pulleys in the upper channel.

Strips should also be installed the full width of the sash on the bottom of the lower sash bottom rail and the top of the upper sash top rail.

Then attach a strip the full width of the window to the upper sash bottom rail. Countersink the nails slightly so they won't catch on the lower sash top rail.

Nail vinyl strips on double-hung windows so that when the window closes the vinyl will seal any possible air leaks. A sliding window is much the same and can be treated as a double-hung window turned on its side. Casement and tilting windows should be weatherstripped with the vinyl nailed to the window casing so that, as the window shuts, it compresses the roll.

Install adhesive-backed foam, on all types of windows, only where there is no friction. On double-hung windows, this is only on the bottom and top rails. Other

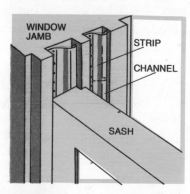

1. Installing spring metal in side channels.

WINDOW JAMB

STRIP

CHANNEL

SASH

2. Installing spring metal on top and bottom of sash.

BOTTOM RAIL

STRIP

3. Installing spring metal between sash.

How to Save on Home Comfort Conditioning

types of windows can use foam strips in other places.

You can weatherstrip your doors even if you're not an experienced handyman. There are several types of weatherstripping for doors, each with its own level of effectiveness. Select the type best suited for your needs.

Foam rubber with either an adhesive or a wood backing can be purchased for the sides and top of a door. Both types are installed on the door jamb to prevent air leaks when the door is closed. They are easy to install, but not very durable.

Rolled vinyl with an aluminum backing is installed much the same as foam to reduce drafts. It is also very easy to install and is much more durable than foam.

The third type of weatherstripping designed for use on the sides and top of a door is spring metal. This is the best type for do-it-yourselfers to use when sealing doors. It is easy to install and extremely durable. After installation in the door jamb, a screwdriver should be used to lift the outer edge for a positive seal.

Accomplished handymen and carpenters can install fitted interlocking channels, the best weather seal available for doors. This technique for sealing doors uses two metal channels, called J-Strips, that interlock when the door is closed, all but eliminating air leaks around the door.

Door sweeps that fit either on the outside or inside of the door are easy to install and are useful for flat thresholds. A drawback is that the sweep will drag on the carpet or rug when the door is opened or closed. Check the supplied instructions for proper installation.

If you feel courageous enough to remove the door, door shoes can be installed. These are useful for wooden thresholds that are not worn, and they are very durable. Remove the door by knocking out the hinge pins with a hammer and screwdriver. If the

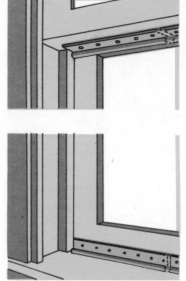

Installing adhesive-backed foam rubber.

Installing vinyl strips on double-hung window.

Installing foam rubber weatherstripping on door jamb (right)

Installing rolled vinyl weatherstripping on door (below).

Installing interlocking channels on a door (below right).

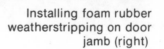

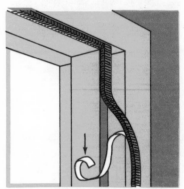

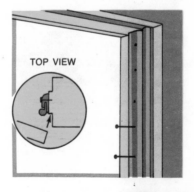

TOP VIEW

TOP VIEW

Door sweeps, outside or inside, are easy to install.

How to Save on Home Comfort Conditioning

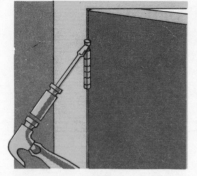

1. Knock out hinge pins.

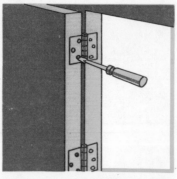

2. Unscrew hinges.

3. Plane bottom of door.

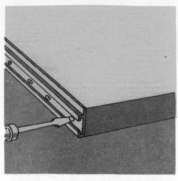

4. Screw on door shoe.

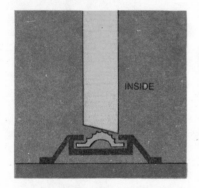

Installing a vinyl threshold after having removed door.

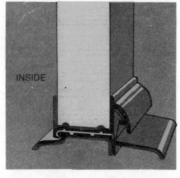

An interlocking threshold is a very good weather seal.

pins are jammed and can't be removed, unscrew the hinges from the door jamb to take off the door. The shoe is installed by removing a small amount of wood from the bottom of the door with a plane, then screwing the shoe into place.

A vinyl bulb threshold to seal the bottom of the door also requires the removal of the door. If there is no threshold, or the wooden one is worn, this is the best kind to use. A vinyl bulb, similar to the door shoe, is installed on the threshold, and the bottom of the door is beveled with a plane to seal against the vinyl with the door shut. The vinyl will eventually wear out but can be replaced.

An interlocking threshold much like the metal channels for the sides and top of a door can be purchased. Although this type is an exceptionally good weather seal, it is very difficult to install, and the job should be done only by a skilled carpenter.

STORM SASH

Windows and doors can be big energy wasters. This is because doors and windows that open have cracks all around them allowing air to pass through the joints and around window and door frames if they are not tightly sealed. Another reason is that glass itself is a highly heat-conductive material.

Storm windows and doors cut heat loss (or heat gain) at these points about in half. Insulating glass (two panes of glass sealed together at the edges) has approximately the same effect. Triple glazing (insulating glass plus a storm window) is even more effective and often is used in extremely cold climates.

According to the National Bureau of Standards, an investment in storm windows will pay for itself in a decade, including interest costs at 6 percent, and thereafter return an annual dividend of 13 percent. This is based on a climate where winter temperatures are similar to those of Washington, D.C. In regions of the country where snow lies on the ground all winter, payback will occur in less than 7 years, the NBS says. And with fuel costs rising rapidly, this time period will shrink considerably.

There are basically three kinds of storm windows, each providing about the same effectiveness. The more expensive ones are more attractive and convenient, but not more effective.

Plastic sheeting, available in hardware stores, makes effective storm sash. At a cost of only about 50 cents per window, no home located in a cold region should go without at least this type of storm sash. Because of the low price, this type is also ideal for people who rent homes.

Measure the width of your larger windows to determine the width of the plastic rolls to buy. Measure the length of your windows to see how many linear feet and therefore how many rolls or the kit size you need to buy.

Attach to the inside or outside of the frame so that the plastic will block airflow that leaks around the movable parts of the window. If you attach the plastic to the outside, use 1/4×11/4-inch wood slats and tacks around the edges. If you decide to attach it to the inside, masking tape will work.

Inside installation is easier and provides greater protection to the plastic. Outside installation is more difficult, especially on a two-story house, and the plastic is more likely to be damaged by the elements.

Be sure to install tightly and securely, and remove all excess. Besides looking better, a clean installation will make the plastic less susceptible to deterioration during the course of the winter.

Storm window suppliers will build single-pane aluminum storm windows to your measurements that you can install yourself. Cost is about $10 to $20 per window. This type of storm sash is taken down at the end of winter.

Determine how you want the windows to fit in the frame. Your measurements will be the outside measurements of the storm window. Be as accurate as possible, then allow 1/8 inch along each edge for clearance. You'll be responsible for any errors in measurement, so do a good job.

When the windows are delivered, check the actual size against your order. A poor window fit will mean possible air leakage.

Install the windows and fix in place with movable clips so that you can take them down easily. The side of the aluminum frame that touches the window frame should have a permanently installed weatherstrip or gasket to seal the crack between the window and the single-pane storm window frames.

Single-pane storm windows built to your specification.

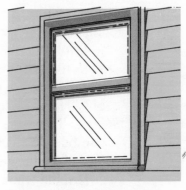
Triple-track combination storm window.

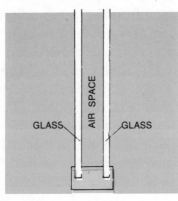
Insulating glass prevents heat loss or gain (right).

Plastic sheeting attached to the outside of the window (center).

Plastic sheeting attached to the inside of the window (far right).

GLASS   AIR SPACE   GLASS

How to Save on Home Comfort Conditioning

Drill drainage holes, if your units don't have them already.

Single-pane storm windows aren't as expensive as the double-track or triple-track combination windows. The disadvantage of the single-pane windows is that they can't be opened easily once they are installed.

A mill finish (plain aluminum) will oxidize quickly and degrade appearance. Windows with an anodized or baked enamel finish look better.

Triple-track combination (windows and screen) storm windows are designed for installation over double-hung windows only. They cost about $30 to $45 per window. They are permanently installed and can be opened any time with a screen slid into place for ventilation.

Double-track combination units are also

Corner joints should be strong and airtight.

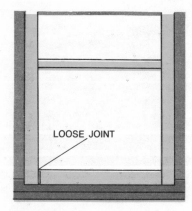

LOOSE JOINT

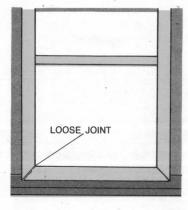

LOOSE JOINT

available at a lower cost. Both kinds are sold almost everywhere, and can be bought with or without the cost of installation.

You can save a few dollars (10 to 15 percent) by installing the windows yourself, but in most cases it is better to have the supplier install the windows for you, even though it costs a bit more.

When the windows are installed, make sure that both the window sashes and screen sash move smoothly and seal tightly when closed. Poor installation can cause misalignment.

Be sure there is a tightly calked seal around the edge of the storm window. Leaks can hurt the performance of storm windows considerably.

Most combination units come with two or three small holes (or other types of vents) drilled through the frame where it meets the window sill. This is to keep winter condensation from collecting on the sill and causing rot. Keep these holes clear, or drill them yourself if your units don't already have them.

The quality of construction affects the strength and performance of storm windows. Corners are a good place to check construction. They should be strong and airtight. Normally, overlapped corner joints are better than mitered. If you can see through the joints, they will leak air.

Storm windows are supposed to reduce air leakage around windows. The depth of the metal grooves (sash tracks) at the sides of the window and the weatherstripping quality make a big difference in how well storm windows can do this. Compare several types before deciding.

Combination (windows and screen) storm doors are designed for installation over exterior doors. They are sold just about everywhere, with or without the cost of installation. In most cases, it is easier to have the supplier install the doors.

Before the installer leaves, be sure the

doors operate smoothly and close tightly. Check for cracks around the jamb, and make sure the seal is as airtight as possible. Also, remove and replace the exchangeable panels (window and screen) to make sure they fit properly and with a weathertight seal.

The same rules apply to judging the quality of storm doors as apply to storm windows. Corner joints, weatherstripping, and hardware quality should be checked.

Storm doors of wood or steel can also be purchased within the same price range as the aluminum variety. They have the same quality differences and should be similarly evaluated. The choice between doors of similar quality but different materials is primarily up to your own taste.

EQUIPMENT LOCATION

Often, the location of heating and cooling equipment is only casually considered when it is being installed, and then "out of sight, out of mind" may be the deciding factor. This can cause problems. In addition to forcing the units to work overtime to do their job, poor circulation of heated (or cooled) air and higher fuel bills will be the consequence.

Even though the advent of forced-air systems allowed the positioning of the furnace and blower at almost any location, the most efficient place remains near the center of the house. This location enables the blower to distribute heated air through the network of ducts more evenly, reducing hot spots or cold spots. Keep this in mind when building a home or adding a new room.

Air conditioners can also be installed in places that are not advantageous to maximum efficiency. The part of the conditioner that is on the outside of the house should not be in direct sunlight all day. Heat from the sun will overload the unit's cooling ca-

Good location for condenser of air conditioner.

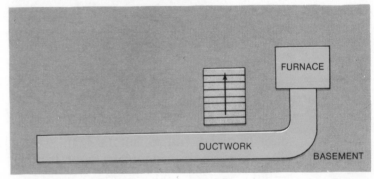

Poor furnace location.

Good furnace location.

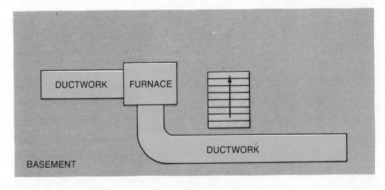

pacity, causing it to work harder than necessary to cool the house. If shade from buildings, trees, etc., is not available, build a small awning to shade the condenser unit from the sun. The condenser should not be placed where tall grass, dirt, or leaves can collect on the coils or obstruct air flow, reducing the air conditioner's ability to do its job.

How to Save on Home Comfort Conditioning

If you've ever waited for what seemed like hours for hot water to come out of the shower or bathroom faucet, you already know the benefits of having a centrally located hot-water heater.

OPERATING ECONOMY

A periodic checkup and maintenance of heating and cooling equipment can reduce fuel consumption by about 10 percent. Finding a good heating/cooling specialist and sticking with him is a good way to ensure that your equipment stays in top fuel-saving condition.

Check out the people you contact with the Better Business Bureau and other homeowners in your area. Once you're confident you're in touch with a reputable outfit, a service contract is the best arrangement to make. For an annual fee, this provides a periodic tune-up of your heating/cooling system and insures you against repairs of most components.

There are some service jobs you can do yourself and save even more money. Study any manuals you might have concerning the equipment or have a serviceman show you how to do certain routine maintenance chores before you start tinkering.

An oil-burning furnace should be cleaned and adjusted each year for maximum efficiency. Check for oil leaks in the system, and change the oil and air filters annually.

There are also several tests servicemen can use to check oil furnace efficiency (see PAGES 503-508). If you suspect a problem, call a serviceman immediately.

Coal furnaces should also be serviced at the end of each heating season. Adjust and clean the stoker, clean the burner of all coal, ash, and clinkers, and oil the inside of the coal screw and hopper to prevent rust.

Furnaces that use bottled, LP, or natural gas should be attended to every three years.

Valves and nozzles should be cleaned and adjusted for best operation.

Hot-water heating systems should be checked yearly by a serviceman. Once or twice a year open the valve at each radiator to rid the system of trapped air. If you are in doubt as to how to do this, consult your serviceman.

Forced hot-air heating systems have air filters that should be cleaned or replaced every 30 to 60 days during the heating season. Ask your serviceman how to do this, buy a supply of filters, and stick to a schedule. You can save a lot of fuel this way.

The blower fan and all registers should also be cleaned periodically on forced-air systems. Dirt at either of these locations will greatly reduce the unit's capacity.

The best preventive medicine for steam heat systems is to drain a bucket of water from the boiler every three weeks during the heating season. This will keep the sediment off the bottom of the boiler. If the sediment is allowed to remain, it will actually insulate the boiler from the flame in the burner.

In addition to the checks and adjustments a serviceman can do, the filters in a whole-house air conditioner should be replaced often. If the filters are cleaned or replaced every 30 to 60 days you will save far more money in fuel than the cost of the filters.

A water heater is another piece of equipment that should not be overlooked in your maintenance schedule. Every three months,

Replacing central air conditioner filter.

How to Save on Home Comfort Conditioning

Seal air escape routes between attic and the rest of the house.

Drain water from the heater tank.

drain a bucket of water from the spigot at the bottom of the heater tank. A real energy waster is a water heater that is set too high. If you have a dishwasher, 140 degrees is high enough. If not, 120 degrees is plenty. Depending on the type of fuel used, this simple setback will save $5 to $45 a year.

COMMON SENSE DOLLAR SAVERS

Keep doors and windows firmly shut and locked to cut down heat loss in winter and heat gain in summer. Check your window and door latches to see whether they fit tightly and, if necessary, adjust the latches and plug any air leaks. You don't really need to open windows in winter—you usually get enough fresh air just from normal air leakage even if your house is well calked and weatherstripped.

Seal any openings between the attic and the rest of the house where air might escape, such as spaces around loosely fitting attic stairway doors or pull-down stairways, penetrations of the ceiling for lights or a fan, and vents, pipes, etc. It may not seem like much, but it adds up!

If you can't get inside your crawl space, you can still create some barriers against wind and cold by planting shrubs around the foundation. You can also tar-paper the

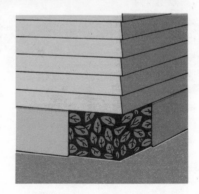

Protect foundation with shrubs (above) or tarpaper (right), if you can't get inside your crawl space to insulate it.

outside walls and rake leaves against the foundation, covering them with a weighted tarpaulin. The same holds true of a basement foundation.

A good way to keep your house cool in the summer is to keep the sun out. Large shade trees on the east and west sides will help tremendously. Awnings and sunshades will also help keep the inside of your home cool. Anything that stops the sun

How to Save on Home Comfort Conditioning

A good way to keep your house cool is to keep the sun out.

before it gets in through the glass is seven times as good at keeping you cool as blinds and curtains on the inside.

All leaky faucets should be fixed, particularly the hot ones. One leaky faucet can waste up to 6,000 gallons of water a year.

FIX LEAKY FAUCETS:

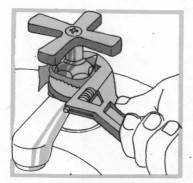

1. Remove packing nut.

2. Remove stem.

3. Remove old washer.

4. Replace washer.

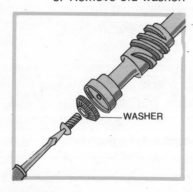

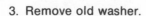
WASHER

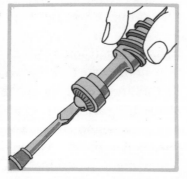

You can also save by turning the hot-water heater down when you'll be away from home for a weekend or more. Always use full loads in the dishwasher and clothes washer, and use warm wash and cold rinse. Take showers—they use less hot water than baths. You should use cold water to run the garbage disposal. In general, every time you use cold water instead of hot, you save.

You can notice a substantial savings in fuel costs by lowering your thermostat. For an investment of about $80 you can install a clock thermostat, which will automatically turn the heat down at night and up in the morning.

If your house was not insulated when it was built, but is now, your furnace may be too big. In general, that means that it is inefficient and would use less fuel if it were smaller. Wait for one of the coldest nights of the year, and set your thermostat at 70 degrees. Once the house temperature reaches 70 degrees, if the furnace burner runs less than 40 minutes during the next hour (time it only when it's running), your furnace is too big. A furnace that is too big turns on and off much more often than it should, and that wastes energy. Depending on the type of fuel burner, a serviceman may be able to cut down the size of your burner without replacing it.

Don't overheat rooms and don't heat or cool rooms you're not using. It's important that no room in your house get more heat than it needs, and that you should be able to turn down the heating or cooling in areas of your home that you don't use. Most heating systems have valves or dampers to regulate the amount of heat room by room. If you have hot spots in your home and can't solve the problem yourself, call a serviceman.

Closing off unused rooms is just as important in saving on air conditioning as it is for heating. Keep lights off during the day — most of the electricity they use makes heat,

How to Save on Home Comfort Conditioning

not light. You can also reduce the load on your air-conditioning system by not running heat-generating appliances like the dishwasher during the hot part of the day.

If you have central air conditioning, you may want to look into the air economizer, a system that turns off the part of the conditioner that uses a lot of electricity and circulates outside air through the house when it's cooler out than it is in. Ask your dealer if he can install one on your central system.

When adding a room, consider adding a room-size heat pump. A heat pump runs on electricity and is just like an air conditioner, except that it can run in reverse. It gets more heat out of a dollar's worth of electricity than the resistance heaters in baseboard units and electric furnaces.

The last energy-saving tip is probably the most obvious, but usually not considered — lighting. Plan your lighting sensibly and reduce lighting where possible, concentrat-

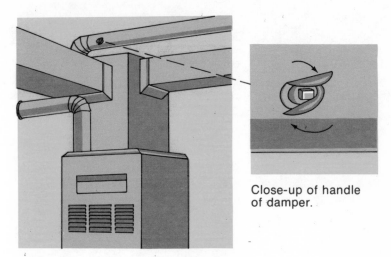

Close-up of handle of damper.

Adjust the heating system to regulate the amount of heat for each room.

ing it in work areas or reading areas where it is really needed. Fluorescent bulbs should be used rather than incandescent. A 25-watt fluorescent bulb gives off as much light as a 100-watt incandescent bulb but costs one-fourth as much to light.

How to Save on Home Comfort Conditioning

8

Other Comfort Factors

"I T'S NOT THE HEAT, IT'S THE HUMIDITY." How many times have you heard this old saw from some sage trying to explain why you feel like a parboiled dishrag as you perspire your way through an August day? He is right, of course. Humidity and the lack of it play a very important role in your comfort. There may not be much you can do about the outside humidity, short of surrounding yourself with it in the form of a swimming pool or a cool lake, but you can control it in your house—a vital factor in comfort conditioning.

HUMIDIFICATION

As the cool, dry air of winter is heated in your home, it becomes even drier. On a cold day, the air inside a home without proper humidification may actually be twice as dry as hot desert air. Just as with desert travelers, throats become parched and sore. Lung irritations, sinus problems, and colds

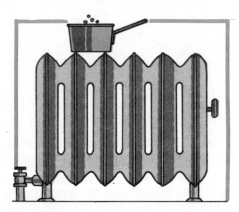

Humidification in the good old times.

result. Plants wither, furniture dries up and comes apart at glued joints, and even rugs and draperies become brittle. To add insult to misery, temperatures must be kept high—much higher than the energy-conserving recommended 65 degrees—to provide comfort. By adding moisture to the air in the proper proportions, you can lower the thermostat 10 degrees or more, be perfectly comfortable, and save many dollars as well. For every degree over 70 degrees F. that you heat your house, at least 3 percent more fuel is consumed, so that 10 degrees can mean a 30 percent or greater fuel saving!

In the "good old days," humidification meant putting a tin can filled with water atop the stove or radiator. And it worked. Today, more sophisticated devices are generally employed, but if you live in an old house or apartment without proper humidification, by all means use the tin-can method. Better an unsightly tin can than unhealthful discomfort.

Most modern warm-air furnaces include some kind of humidifier. If yours does not, it is a relatively simple and inexpensive installation, and one that will quickly pay for itself in reduced fuel bills, not to mention increased comfort. Many such units can also be used in conjunction with other heating systems (hot water, steam).

There are two basic types of humidifiers: evaporator and atomizer. In evaporator types, warm air moving over water in the unit picks up moisture, which is then circulated throughout the house. The simpler types consist of a water-filled pan inside the furnace plenum, but most now include a motor and fan assembly to draw the air through the humidifier and push it back into the ductwork. A supply pipe from the house cold-water plumbing system carries water to the humidifer, and a humidistat can be set to a desired humidity level, which is then automatically maintained.

Atomizer-type humidifiers are placed in the cold-air returns of warm-air furnaces. They break up water into tiny particles that are absorbed by air passing through. Some types can also be placed at a distance from the furnace—in a utility room or cabinet— and rigged to provide access to household air. If properly located, such units can effectively humidify the entire house.

Installation procedures for both types of humidifiers vary greatly, and manufacturer's instructions should be scrupulously followed.

Many warm-air furnaces, particularly earlier or smaller models, are equipped with evaporative-plate humidifiers, which work by capillary action. These are not as efficient as the powered units and are subject to frequent clogging by mineral deposits. If you have such a unit, keep it regularly ser-

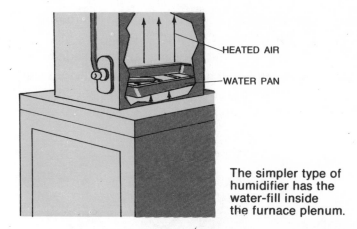

The simpler type of humidifier has the water-fill inside the furnace plenum.

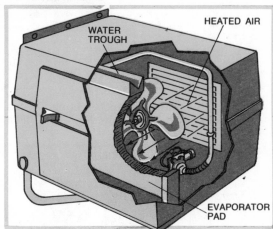

Power humidifier.

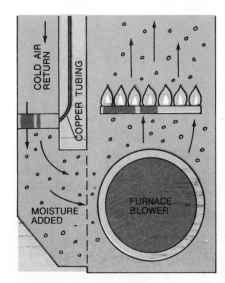

Atomizer-type humidifier.

Evaporative-plate humidifier (pan with plates, one being replaced).

viced according to the service manual (if you have one), and replace the plates as they become clogged and corroded. And consider installing a more efficient (and therefore more economical in the long run) power humidifier.

Sure signs of excess humidity: moisture on walls and windows, sweating pipes and mildew in the basement.

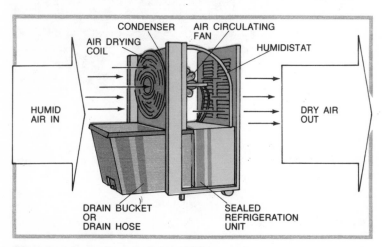

Diagram shows how a dehumidifier works.

Portable dehumidifier.

DEHUMIDIFICATION

It's a matter of famine or feast—your home's air may need to be humidified, but it may also be too humid. You have "buttoned it up" so securely with vapor barriers that there is no way for inside water vapor to get out. Cooking, bathing, washing, and even breathing by the house occupants cause excessive humidity. Physical discomfort is noticed because the natural rate of evaporation from the skin is slowed down by the ambient humidity. Moisture forms on windows and walls. In the summertime, plumbing pipes sweat, and bread turns moldy. Mildew forms on walls and other surfaces, and paint deteriorates. Don't despair—dehumidify!

A portable dehumidifier is built somewhat like an air conditioner but is designed to dry air rather than cool it. It consists of a refrigerated air-drying coil, a condenser, a fan, and a humidistat, all housed in a cabinet that may be designed as a piece of furniture so that it can fit unobtrusively in any room. The fan draws moisture-laden air over the coil; the cold coil causes the moisture to condense, and it is carried off through a drain or collected in a bucket as the air passes through. The collection bucket must be emptied regularly; if there is a drain hose, it should be connected to a

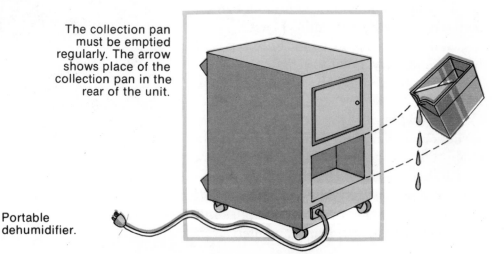

The collection pan must be emptied regularly. The arrow shows place of the collection pan in the rear of the unit.

Other Comfort Factors

drainage pipe or led to a basement drain or other drain opening.

The minimum water-removal capacity of a dehumidifier in a house or apartment in the "average" temperate summer climate is roughly one pint per day for every hundred square feet of floor space. If the space includes a laundry, bath, or kitchen, figure an additional 50 percent over the minimum. A specially hot and muggy climate, a large and active family, or a house with many doors and windows may double these requirements.

All dehumidifiers are equipped with three-prong plugs for connecting to three-hole, grounded electrical outlets. Such an outlet protects you from shock or burn if the unit malfunctions. This is especially important for a dehumidifier because it may be operated on a damp floor that could conduct electricity, and because it collects water, which could spill and cause an electrical accident. Don't commit the grievous error of snapping off the third prong from the plug so that it fits into a two-hole outlet. Water, metal, and electricity can be a lethal mix. If you have no three-hole grounded outlet, have an electrician convert a two-hole outlet. Three-prong adapters are a poor substitute.

Always read the owner's manual and follow its directions. Place the dehumidifier at

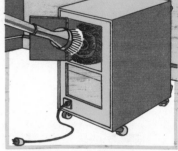

Proper location for a dehumidifier.

Vacuum clean the grilles regularly.

Clean the coils with a soft brush once each season.

least 6 inches from the nearest wall where air can flow freely to and from all sides. Avoid placing it in a room corner or near a large piece of furniture. Close all doors and windows in the area to be dehumidified. For the first few days of operation, set the humidistat (if the unit has one) to "drier" or "extra dry." This aids moisture removal from furnishings as well as room air. After the area has generally dried out, adjust the humidistat to your particular comfort level.

Dehumidifiers need little upkeep, other than regular cleaning. Always disconnect the power cord before cleaning or emptying the collection bucket. Be sure the area, the unit, and you are dry before reconnecting the cord. Regularly dust the grilles or louvers with a soft brush or the dusting attachment of a vacuum cleaner. Every few weeks, wash the inside of the water container with a sponge or soft cloth and a mild

Three-prong plug and three-hole outlet.

Other Comfort Factors

detergent to discourage the growth of mold, mildew, or bacteria. On cool days, check the cold coils for frosting. If you find any, turn off the unit until the frost has melted. At least once each season, remove all dust and lint from the coils with a soft brush.

Circulating air through the house by means of an attic fan.

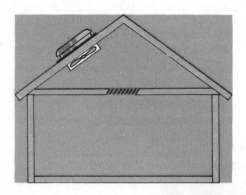

Roof fan.

Ceiling fan.

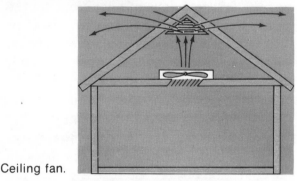

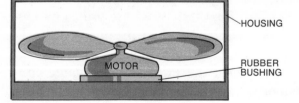

HOUSING

MOTOR

RUBBER BUSHING

Fan mounting for quiet operation.

ATTIC VENTILATION

Circulating air through the house by means of a fan in the attic won't reduce summertime temperatures, but it will give the effect of doing so by helping to evaporate body perspiration. At night, it will replace hot indoor air with cooler, drier outdoor air and, coupled with open windows in strategic locations, will move cool air throughout the entire house. It cannot, however, be used in conjunction with a dehumidifier, which requires a relatively sealed environment to function properly.

There are two basic types of attic fans. One type is mounted in a gable end or in the roof and draws air through a louver in the ceiling below, exhausting it to the outdoors. The rest of the attic is sealed to ensure proper circulation. The other type is mounted in the ceiling, usually in a central location such as a hallway. It draws air up into the attic, where it passes outdoors through louvers, usually located in the gable ends. The louvers must be large enough to permit free passage of the air.

The fan's capacity to do the job is determined by the cubic feet of air it can move per minute. Figure the cubic feet of living space in your house (not including closets, basement, or garage). In most areas of the country, the fan should be able to move approximately two-thirds of this total every minute. In warmer southern areas, it should be able to handle the entire volume once a minute. Check the rating of a fan before you buy.

Quiet operation is an important consideration. Make sure the fan you buy is mounted on rubber bushings or felt sound absorbers or is isolated from its housing by springs. Actual installation will depend on the type and the manufacturer's specific directions, which should be followed to the letter. That way, if something goes wrong, you have only him to blame.

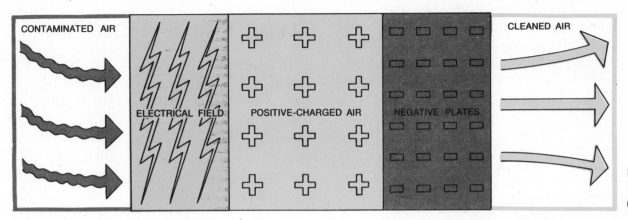

CONTAMINATED AIR

ELECTRICAL FIELD

POSITIVE-CHARGED AIR

NEGATIVE PLATES

CLEANED AIR

Electronic air cleaning (schematic).

ELECTRONIC AIR CLEANING

Even in the cleanest of homes, the air is filled with billions of undesirable particles, most of them so tiny that they are invisible to the human eye. Outdoor air continually enters the home, bringing with it airborne soil particles, particulate wastes (industrial wastes, automobile and airplane exhaust), pollen, and mold spores. Inside the house, dust and other particles are generated from mattresses, pillows, blankets, carpets, fabrics, food such as flour, cooking smoke and grease, animals, and tobacco smoke.

Put them all together and they spell misery, particularly for persons who are especially sensitive to such irritants as dust, pollen, and cigarette smoke. They also cause discoloration and staining of paint and wallpaper and leave greasy deposits on glass, windows, and mirrors.

The filter in a warm-air furnace will remove some of these contaminants. But if you live in an area where air pollution is a serious problem, or if members of your family are especially susceptible to respiratory problems, an electronic air cleaner can be installed as part of the air system of your total home comfort conditioning. Such a unit removes the contaminant particles by electrostatic precipitation—the same principle used at large industrial stacks as required by many local clean-air ordinances.

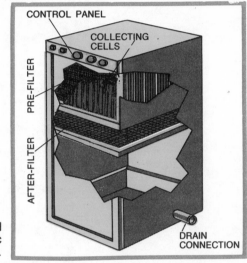

CONTROL PANEL

COLLECTING CELLS

PRE-FILTER

AFTER-FILTER

DRAIN CONNECTION

Self-contained electrostatic air cleaner.

The air particles are passed through a powerful electrical field, where they are positively charged. They then pass through a series of negatively charged plates, where they are trapped until they are purified of contaminants. The air is then recirculated.

Electronic air cleaners are available either as self-contained units, which can be placed wherever they are most needed, or as units designed for installation in the ductwork of a central system. Once again, the actual installation will depend on the type you choose, and manufacturer's directions must be followed.

Maintenance is simple. Usually, all you need do is clean the collector plates at intervals as recommended by the manufacturer. In some units, this can be done without even having to remove the plates.

Other Comfort Factors

9

Comfort Quotient for Home Buyers

You've heard it said many times: "Buying a home is the biggest financial investment of your lifetime." For most families, that is true. So before you invest, you will want to know what you are getting for that hard-earned 30 years of payments. You certainly don't want to move into that brand-spanking new ranch, or golden oldie Victorian gingerbread fantasy, or that genuine George-Washington-slept-here colonial, and then turn blue from nose to toes with the first chill night because the heating system is inadequate, incompetent, or nonexistent. When you are shopping for a home, structural soundness is a most important consideration; the heating system is not far behind.

THE NEW HOUSE

If you are having a house built, you have the luxury of time to consider what type of heating system will best suit your needs and what type of fuel will be most plentiful and most economical (although there may be some long-range international political prognostications and not a little guesswork involved in making the latter choice). Study PAGES 465-486, then, armed with this knowledge, get at least three estimates from reputable heating contractors, making sure that they understand exactly what you want. Get everything in writing before signing on the dotted line with the one you final-ly select. Insist on quality equipment, and see that you get it.

Central air conditioning is most easily and economically installed when the house is being built, so if that figures in your plans, now is the time to do it. Even if, for financial reasons, the central air conditioning must wait awhile, it will be relatively inexpensive at this stage to provide ductwork for future installation.

If you are thinking of buying a new house that is already built or in which the heating system is already installed, make sure that there are heat outlets in all rooms (except the attic and basement). Many building codes require this, but check it anyway.

Warm-air furnaces should also have cold-air returns in all but the smallest rooms. If the house has an attic that may be finished at a later date, are there risers in the walls that can be hooked up simply and inexpensively to the existing furnace? And is the furnace of adequate capacity to handle future as well as present needs? Is the heating plant of first-rate quality—a known brand and not a cheapie Brand X? It may be difficult for you to answer some of these questions. If you have serious doubts, call in a professional engineer for his opinion—it will be money well spent.

If you are looking at the house during cold weather, turn up the thermostat to at least 60 degrees (the builder or real estate broker probably has it set at the minimum of 55 to keep pipes from freezing and to prevent other cold damage). Wait for the furnace to do its work, then check all the rooms to see that they are evenly heated. A particularly cold room may mean only that a damper needs adjustment—or it may mean that the system is inadequate or poorly designed and can't do the job it should.

Check the insulation. Just about every new home will have at least some insulation—but where, how much, and how effective? If the house is in the early building stages, you can insist on having insulation of the proper R-Value (see PAGE 523) installed in walls and ceiling or roof. If walls are already enclosed, at least check out the

insulation in the attic to make sure it is adequate.

Storm windows or double-glazed windows may come with the house—or they may not. In the latter case, these will probably be among your first acquisitions after, or even before, you move in. You may be strapped for cash, but they should figure into your budget.

THE OLDER HOME

You can't always judge the condition of a furnace or boiler by its age. Some old furnaces, usually coal burners converted to oil or gas, are still cooking away at 40 or even 50 years. Still, it is reasonable to assume that after 12 to 15 years a heating plant becomes weary, and repairs if not replacement are in the offing. If in doubt about the heating system, consult an engineer.

Be suspicious if there are signs of neglect—a sooty combustion chamber, for example, or dirty filters. While these may entail only simple repairs and adjustments, they are an indication of how poorly the system has been cared for.

Check to see if there are heat outlets in all rooms. In older homes, this is not always the case. If there are rooms—a finished attic, for example, or a pantry that has been converted to a small bathroom—how will they be heated? There are many ways, of course (see PAGES 490-502), but they all cost money, which may be in short supply immediately after you buy a house.

Don't be timid about asking the owner of a house you are considering buying to let you see the previous year's heating bills. Take into account whether that winter was unusually cold or uncommonly mild—that

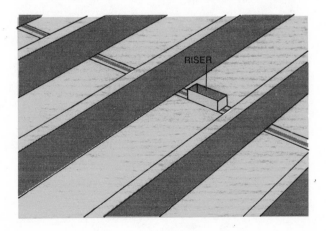

Risers make future heating hookups much easier.

Comfort Quotient for Home Buyers

will, of course, be reflected in the bills. And even if it's midsummer, don't be afraid to ask that the thermostat be turned up so that you can actually see—and hear, and possibly smell—the system in operation. This is what the professional engineer would do as part of a total house inspection. At a cost of anywhere from $50 to $125, his services may well be worth it if you have questions about a house you are seriously considering buying.

Many older homes are completely uninsulated; others may have only minimal insulation in the attic. Today's fuel costs almost mandate insulation, which will pay for itself in a few years (see PAGES 521-531). Still, it means another immediate cash outlay, which must figure into your "what-can-I-afford" calculations before you make that hard decision to buy the house.

If there are no storm windows, add more bucks to the comfort cost of buying the house. If there are storms, check them out closely. Old, wood-framed storm windows may become rotten and have to be replaced. Even if they are in good condition, they have to be painted (annually is best) and, unless you have the house sealed for year-round comfort conditioning with summer air conditioning, put up in the fall and taken down in the spring. Double- or triple-track aluminum types mean one less home maintenance chore. But make sure they are in good condition too.

If one or more room air conditioners are included with the house, make sure that they are in working order—even if it is a sub-zero day. And do some quick calculations, using the formulas given on PAGE 514, to see if the air conditioner ratings are right for the rooms they are expected to cool. Replacement of a faulty or wrongly sized room air conditioner is only a small factor in the overall price of a house. But why should you pay for something that doesn't work or doesn't work as it should? When you are buying a home, you need to save as many dollars as you can.

CONVERSION FACTORS

There are two systems of measurement used in the world today—the metric system, based on the centimeter, gram, and second, and the imperial or United States system, based on the foot, pound, and second. The conversion factors listed below are used to change from one unit to another. Figures with the units given in the first column are multiplied by the numbers in the third column to obtain figures with units shown in the middle column. For example, to determine the number of cubic inches in 2 U.S. dry barrels multiply 7,056.0 (from the third column) by 2 (the number of U.S. dry barrels). Thus, 2 U.S. dry barrels equal 14,112.0 cubic inches.

Many of the numbers in the right column are written in scientific notation—a method used to simplify the arithmetic involved in multiplying large numbers. If a number in any part of the problem is not in scientific notation already, it may be put in scientific notation. This is done as follows: 1) Move the decimal place either to the left or right until the number is between 1 and 10, dropping insignificant zeros to the right of the decimal point. 2) For each decimal point moved to the left in the step above, multiply the new number by 10^1. This means for each decimal place moved to the left, the exponent (the small superscript to the right) of the 10 is increased by 1. Thus 1,000,000 is written as 1×10^6. 3) For each decimal place moved to the right multiply the resultant number by 10^{-1}. Thus 0.000001 is written as 1×10^{-6}. Numbers not in scientific notation are imagined to be multiplied by 10^0, e.g., 2 may be thought of as 2×10^0.

To multiply two numbers written in scientific notation the following steps are taken: 1) Multiply the left halves of the problem's two factors as usual (That is, the half to the left of the multiplication sign for scientific notation). 2) Add the exponents of the tens appearing on the right half of each factor. (A negative and a positive number added result in subtraction; two negative numbers added always result in another negative number.) Note: the tens are not added; only one ten appears in the final answer. Thus, when 2×10^6 is multiplied by 4×10^4, the answer is 8×10^{10}. After the multiplication is performed, the decimal place in the left half should be moved so the answer is a number between 1 and 10, with the exponent adjusted accordingly. For example: $(2 \times 10^6)(12 \times 10^{-4})$; and, $(3 \times 10^{-4})(4.02 \times 10^{-9}) = 12.06 \times 10^{-13} = 1.206 \times 10^{-12}$.

To Convert	Into	Multiply by
A		
acre	sq chain (Gunter's)	10.0
acre	rods	160.0
acre	sq links (Gunter's)	1×10^5
acre	hectare or sq hectometer	0.4047
acres	sq feet	43,560.0
acres	sq meters	4,047.0
acres	sq miles	1.562×10^{-3}
acres	sq yards	4,840.0
acre-feet	cu feet	43,560.0
acre-feet	gallons	3.259×10^5
ampere-hours	coulombs	3,600.0
ampere-hours	faradays	0.03731
ampere-turns	gilberts	1.257
angstrom unit	inch	$3,937 \times 10^{-9}$
angstrom unit	meter	1×10^{-10}
angstrom unit	micron	1×10^{-4}
astronomical unit	kilometers	1.495×10^8
atmospheres	ton/sq inch	0.007348
atmospheres	cms of mercury	76.0
atmospheres	ft of water (at 4° C)	33.90
atmospheres	in of mercury (at 0° C)	29.92
atmospheres	kgs/sq cm	1.0333
atmospheres	kgs/sq meter	10,332.0
atmospheres	pounds/sq in	14.70
atmospheres	tons/sq ft	1.058
B		
barrels (U.S., dry)	cu inches	7,056.0
barrels (U.S., dry)	quarts (dry)	105.0
barrels (U.S., liquid)	gallons	31.5
barrels (oil)	gallons (oil)	42.0
bars	atmospheres	0.9869
bars	dynes/sq cm	1×10^6
bars	kgs/sq meter	1.020×10^4
bars	pounds/sq ft	2,089.0
bars	pounds/sq in	14.50
bolt (U.S. cloth)	meters	36.576
Btu	ergs	1.0550×10^{10}
Btu	foot-lbs	778.3
Btu	gram-calories	252.0
Btu	horsepower-hrs	3.931×10^{-4}
Btu	joules	1,054.8
Btu	kilogram-calories	0.2520
Btu	kilogram-meters	107.5
Btu	kilowatt-hrs	2.928×10^{-4}
Btu/hr	foot-pounds/sec	0.2162
Btu/hr	gram-cal/sec	0.0700
Btu/hr	horsepower-hrs	3.929×10^{-4}
Btu/hr	watts	0.2931
Btu/min	foot-lbs/sec	12.96
Btu/min	horsepower	0.02356
Btu/min	kilowatts	0.01757
Btu/min	watts	17.57
Btu/sq ft/min	watts/sq in	0.1221
bucket (British dry)	cubic cm	1.818×10^4
bushels	cu ft	1.2445
bushels	cu in.	2,150.4
bushels	cu meters	0.03524
bushels	liters	35.24
bushels	pecks	4.0
bushels	pints (dry)	64.0
bushels	quarts (dry)	32.0
C		
calories, gram (mean)	Btu (mean)	3.9685×10^{-3}
candle/sq cm	lamberts	3.142
candle/sq inch	lamberts	0.4870
centares (centiares)	sq meters	1.0
centigrade	Fahrenheit	$(C° \times 9/5) + 32$
centigrams	grams	0.01
centiliter	ounce fluid (U.S.)	0.3382
centiliter	cubic inch	0.6103
centiliter	drams	2.705
centiliters	liters	0.01
centimeters	feet	3.281×10^{-2}
centimeters	inches	0.3937
centimeters	kilometers	1×10^{-5}
centimeters	meters	0.01
centimeters	miles	6.214×10^{-6}
centimeters	millimeters	10.0
centimeters	mils	393.7
centimeters	yards	1.094×10^{-2}
centimeter-dynes	cm-grams	1.020×10^{-3}
centimeter-dynes	meter-kgs	1.020×10^{-8}
centimeter-dynes	pound-feet	7.376×10^{-8}
centimeter-grams	cm-dynes	980.7
centimeter-grams	meter-kgs	1×10^{-5}
centimeter-grams	pound-feet	7.233×10^{-5}
centimeters of mercury	atmospheres	0.01316
centimeters of mercury	feet of water	0.4461
centimeters of mercury	kgs/sq meter	136.0
centimeters of mercury	pounds/sq ft	27.85
centimeters of mercury	pounds/sq in	0.1934
centimeters/sec	feet/min	1.1969
centimeters/sec	feet/sec	0.03281
centimeters/sec	kilometers/hr	0.036
centimeters/sec	knots	0.1943
centimeters/sec	meters/min	0.6

To Convert	Into	Multiply by
centimeters/sec	miles/hr	0.02237
centimeters/sec	miles/min	3.728×10^{-4}
centimeters/sec/sec	feet/sec/sec	0.03281
centimeters/sec/sec	kms/hr/sec	0.036
centimeters/sec/sec	meters/sec/sec	0.01
centimeters/sec/sec	miles/hr/sec	0.02237
chain	inches	792.00
chain	meters	20.12
chains (surveyors' or Gunter's)	yards	22.00
circular mils	sq cms	5.067×10^{-6}
circular mils	sq mils	0.7854
circular mils	sq inches	7.854×10^{-7}
circumference	radians	6.283
cords	cord feet	8.0
cord feet	cu feet	16.0
coulomb	statcoulombs	2.998×10^{9}
coulombs	faradays	1.036×10^{-5}
coulombs/sq cm	coulombs/sq in	64.52
coulombs/sq cm	coulombs/sq meter	1×10^{4}
coulombs/sq in	coulombs/sq cm	0.1550
coulombs/sq in	coulombs/sq meter	1,550.0
coulombs/sq meter	coulombs/sq cm	1×10^{-4}
coulombs/sq meter	coulombs/sq in	6.452×10^{-4}
cubic centimeters	cu feet	3.531×10^{-5}
cubic centimeters	cu inches	0.06102
cubic centimeters	cu meters	1×10^{-6}
cubic centimeters	cu yards	1.308×10^{-6}
cubic centimeters	gallons (U.S. liq.)	2.642×10^{-4}
cubic centimeters	liters	0.001
cubic centimeters	pints (U.S. liq.)	2.113×10^{-3}
cubic centimeters	quarts (U.S. liq.)	1.057×10^{-3}
cubic feet	bushels (dry)	0.8036
cubic feet	cu cms	28,320.0
cubic feet	cu inches	1,728.0
cubic feet	cu meters	0.02832
cubic feet	cu yards	0.03704
cubic feet	gallons (U.S. liq.)	7.48052
cubic feet	liters	28.32
cubic feet	pints (U.S. liq.)	59.84
cubic feet	quarts (U.S. liq.)	29.92
cubic feet/min	cu cms/sec	472.0
cubic feet/min	gallons/sec	0.1247
cubic feet/min	liters/sec	0.4720
cubic feet/min	pounds of water/min	62.43
cubic feet/sec	million gals/day	0.646317
cubic feet/sec	gallons/min	448.831
cubic inches	cu cms	16.39
cubic inches	cu feet	5.787×10^{-4}
cubic inches	cu meters	1.639×10^{-5}
cubic inches	cu yards	2.143×10^{-5}
cubic inches	gallons	4.329×10^{-3}
cubic inches	liters	0.01639
cubic inches	mil-feet	1.061×10^{5}
cubic inches	pints (U.S. liq.)	0.03463
cubic inches	quarts (U.S. liq.)	0.01732
cubic meters	bushels (dry)	28.38
cubic meters	cu cms	1×10^{6}
cubic meters	cu feet	35.31
cubic meters	cu inches	61,023.0
cubic meters	cu yards	1.308
cubic meters	gallons (U.S. liq.)	264.2
cubic meters	liters	1,000.0
cubic meters	pints (U.S. liq.)	2,113.0
cubic meters	quarts (U.S. liq.)	1,057.0
cubic yards	cu cms	7.646×10^{5}
cubic yards	cu feet	27.0
cubic yards	cu inches	46,656.0
cubic yards	cu meters	0.7646
cubic yards	gallons (U.S. liq.)	202.0
cubic yards	liters	764.6
cubic yards	pints (U.S. liq.)	1,615.9
cubic yards	quarts (U.S. liq.)	807.9
cubic yards/min	cubic ft/sec	0.45
cubic yards/min	gallons/sec	3.367
cubic yards/min	liters/sec	12.74

D

To Convert	Into	Multiply by
days	seconds	86,400.0
decigrams	grams	0.1
deciliters	liters	0.1
decimeters	meters	0.1
degrees (angle)	quadrants	0.01111
degrees (angle)	radians	0.01745
degrees (angle)	seconds	3,600.0

To Convert	Into	Multiply by
degrees/sec	radians/sec	0.01745
degrees/sec	revolutions/min	0.1667
degrees/sec	revolutions/sec	2.778×10^{-3}
dekagrams	grams	10.0
dekaliters	liters	10.0
dekameters	meters	10.0
drams (apothecaries' or troy)	ounces (avoirdupois)	0.1371429
drams (apothacaries' or troy)	ounces (troy)	0.125
drams (U.S., fluid or apothecaries')	cubic cm	3.6967
drams	grams	1.7718
drams	grains	27.3437
drams	ounces	0.0625
dyne/cm	erg/sq millimeter	0.01
dyne/sq cm	atmospheres	9.869×10^{-7}
dyne/sq cm	inch of mercury at 0° C	2.953×10^{-5}
dyne/sq cm	inch of water at 4° C	4.015×10^{-4}
dynes	grams	1.020×10^{-3}
dynes	joules/cm	1×10^{-7}
dynes	joules/meter (newtons)	1×10^{-5}
dynes	kilograms	1.020×10^{-6}
dynes	poundals	7.233×10^{-5}
dynes	pounds	2.248×10^{-6}
dynes/sq cm	bars	1×10^{-6}

E

To Convert	Into	Multiply by
ell	cm	114.30
ell	inches	45.0
em, pica	inch	0.167
em, pica	cm	0.4233
erg/sec	dyne-cm/sec	1.000
ergs	Btu	9.480×10^{-11}
ergs	dyne-centimeters	1.0
ergs	foot-pounds	7.3670×10^{-8}
ergs	gram-calories	0.2389×10^{-7}
ergs	grams-cms	1.020×10^{-3}
ergs	horsepower-hrs	3.7250×10^{-14}
ergs	joules	1×10^{-7}
ergs	kg-calories	2.389×10^{-11}
ergs	kg-meters	1.020×10^{-8}
ergs	kilowatt-hrs	0.2778×10^{-13}
ergs	watt-hours	0.2778×10^{-10}
ergs/sec	Btu/min	$5,688 \times 10^{-9}$
ergs/sec	ft-lbs/min	4.427×10^{-6}
ergs/sec	ft-lbs/sec	7.3756×10^{-8}
ergs/sec	horsepower	1.341×10^{-10}
ergs/sec	kg-calories/min	1.433×10^{-9}
ergs/sec	kilowatts	1×10^{-10}

F

To Convert	Into	Multiply by
farads	microfarads	1×10^{6}
faraday/sec	ampere (absolute)	9.6500×10^{4}
faradays	ampere-hours	26.80
faradays	coulombs	9.649×10^{4}
fathoms	meter	1.828804
fathoms	feet	6.0
feet	centimeters	30.48
feet	kilometers	3.048×10^{-4}
feet	meters	0.3048
feet	miles (naut.)	1.645×10^{-4}
feet	miles (stat.)	1.894×10^{-4}
feet	millimeters	304.8
feet	mils	1.2×10^{4}
feet of water	atmospheres	0.02950
feet of water	in of mercury	0.8826
feet of water	kgs/sq cm	0.03048
feet of water	kgs/sq meter	304.8
feet of water	pounds/sq ft	62.43
feet of water	pounds/sq in	0.4335
feet/min	cms/sec	0.5080
feet/min	feet/sec	0.01667
feet/min	kms/hr	0.01829
feet/min	meters/min	0.3048
feet/min	miles/hr	0.01136
feet/sec	cms/sec	30.48
feet/sec	kms/hr	1.097
feet/sec	knots	0.5921
feet/sec	meters/min	18.29
feet/sec	miles/hr	0.6818
feet/sec	miles/min	0.01136
feet/sec/sec	cms/sec/sec	30.48
feet/sec/sec	kms/hr/sec	1.097

To Convert	Into	Multiply by
feet/sec/sec	meters/sec/sec	0.3048
feet/sec/sec	miles/hr/sec	0.6818
feet/100 feet	per cent grade	1.0
foot-candle	lumen/sq meter	10.764
foot-pounds	Btu	1.286×10^{-3}
foot-pounds	ergs	1.356×10^{7}
foot-pounds	gram-calories	0.3238
foot-pounds	hp-hrs	5.050×10^{-7}
foot-pounds	joules	1.356
foot-pounds	kg-calories	3.24×10^{-4}
foot-pounds	kg-meters	0.1383
foot-pounds	kilowatt-hrs	3.766×10^{-7}
foot-pounds/min	Btu/min	1.286×10^{-3}
foot-pounds/min	foot-pounds/sec	0.01667
foot-pounds/min	horsepower	3.030×10^{-5}
foot-pounds/min	kg-calories/min	3.24×10^{-4}
foot-pounds/min	kilowatts	2.260×10^{-5}
foot-pounds/sec	Btu/hr	4.6263
foot-pounds/sec	Btu/min	0.07717
foot-pounds/sec	horsepower	0.818×10^{-3}
foot-pounds/sec	kg-calories/min	1.01945
foot-pounds/sec	kilowatts	1.356×10^{-3}
furlongs	miles (U.S.)	0.125
furlongs	rods	40.0
furlongs	feet	660.0

G

To Convert	Into	Multiply by
gallons	cu cms	3,785.0
gallons	cu feet	0.1337
gallons	cu inches	231.0
gallons	cu meters	3.785×10^{-3}
gallons	cu yards	4.951×10^{-3}
gallons	liters	3.785
gallons (liq. British imp.)	gallons (U.S. liq.)	1.20095
gallons (U.S.)	gallons (imp.)	0.83267
gallons of water	pounds of water	8.3453
gallons/min	cu ft/sec	2.228×10^{-3}
gallons/min	liters/sec	0.06308
gallons/min	cu ft/hr	8.0208
gausses	lines/sq in	6.452
gausses	webers/sq cm	1×10^{-8}
gausses	webers/sq in	6.452×10^{-8}
gausses	webers/sq meter	1×10^{-4}
gilberts	ampere-turns	0.7958
gilberts/cm	amp-turns/cm	0.7958
gilberts/cm	amp-turns/in	2.021
gilberts/cm	amp-turns/meter	79.5810
gills (British)	cubic cm	142.07
gills	liters	0.1183
gills	pints (liq.)	0.25
grains	drams (avoirdupois)	0.03657143
grains (troy)	grains (avoirdupois)	1.0
grains (troy)	grams	0.06480
grains (troy)	ounces (avoirdupois)	2.0833×10^{-3}
grains (troy)	pennyweight (troy)	0.04167
grains/U.S. gal	parts/million	17.118
grains/U.S. gal	pounds/million gal	142.86
grains/imp gal	parts/million	14.286
grams	dynes	980.7
grams	grains	15.43
grams	joules/cm	9.807×10^{-5}
grams	joules/meter (newtons)	9.807×10^{-3}
grams	kilograms	0.001
grams	milligrams	1,000.0
grams	ounces (avoirdupois)	0.03527
grams	ounces (troy)	0.03215
grams	poundals	0.07093
grams	pounds	2.205×10^{-3}
grams/cm	pounds/inch	5.600×10^{-3}
grams/cu cm	pounds/cu ft	62.43
grams/cu cm	pounds/cu in	0.03613
grams/cu cm	pounds/mil-foot	3.405×10^{-7}
grams/liter	grains/gal	58.417
grams/liter	pounds/1,000 gal	8.345
grams/liter	pounds/cu ft	0.062427
grams/liter	parts/million	1,000.0
grams/sq cm	pounds/sq ft	2.0481
gram-calories	Btu	3.9683×10^{-3}
gram-calories	ergs	4.1868×10^{7}
gram-calories	foot-pounds	3.0880
gram-calories	horsepower-hrs	1.5596×10^{-6}
gram-calories	kilowatt-hrs	1.1630×10^{-6}
gram-calories	watt-hrs	1.1630×10^{-3}
gram-calories/sec	Btu/hr	14.286
gram-centimeters	Btu	9.297×10^{-8}

To Convert	Into	Multiply by
gram-centimeters	ergs	980.7
gram-centimeters	joules	9.807×10^{-5}
gram-centimeters	kg-cal	2.343×10^{-8}
gram-centimeters	kg-meters	1×10^{-5}

H

To Convert	Into	Multiply by
hand	cm	10.16
hectares	acres	2.471
hectares	sq feet	1.076×10^{5}
hectograms	grams	100.0
hectoliters	liters	100.0
hectometers	meters	100.0
hectowatts	watts	100.0
henries	millihenries	1,000.0
hogsheads (British)	cubic ft	10.114
hogsheads (U.S.)	cubic ft	8.42184
hogsheads (U.S.)	gallons (U.S.)	63.0
horsepower	Btu/min	42.44
horsepower	foot-lbs/min	33,000.0
horsepower	foot-lbs/sec	550.0
horsepower (metric) (542.5 ft lb/sec)	horsepower (550 ft lb/sec)	0.9863
horsepower (550 ft lb/sec)	horsepower (metric) (542.5 ft lb/sec)	1.014
horsepower	kg-calories/min	10.68
horsepower	kilowatts	0.7457
horsepower	watts	745.7
horsepower (boiler)	Btu/hr	33,479.0
horsepower (boiler)	kilowatts	9.803
horsepower-hrs	Btu	2,547.0
horsepower-hrs	ergs	2.6845×10^{13}
horsepower-hrs	foot-lbs	1.98×10^{6}
horsepower-hrs	gram-calories	641,190.0
horsepower-hrs	joules	2.684×10^{6}
horsepower-hrs	kg-calories	641.1
horsepower-hrs	kg-meters	2.737×10^{5}
horsepower-hrs	kilowatt-hrs	0.7457
hours	days	4.167×10^{-2}
hours	weeks	5.952×10^{-3}
hundredweights (long)	pounds	112.0
hundredweights (long)	tons (long)	0.05
hundredweights (short)	ounces (avoirdupois)	1,600.0
hundredweights (short)	pounds	100.0
hundredweights (short)	tons (metric)	0.0453592
hundredweights (short)	tons (long)	0.0446429

I

To Convert	Into	Multiply by
inches	centimeters	2.540
inches	meters	2.540×10^{-2}
inches	miles	1.578×10^{-5}
inches	millimeters	25.40
inches	mils	1,000.0
inches	yards	2.778×10^{-2}
inches of mercury	atmospheres	0.03342
inches of mercury	feet of water	1.133
inches of mercury	kgs/sq cm	0.03453
inches of mercury	kgs/sq meter	345.3
inches of mercury	pounds/sq ft	70.73
inches of mercury	pounds/sq in	0.4912
inches of water (at 4° C)	atmospheres	2.458×10^{-3}
inches of water (at 4° C)	inches of mercury	0.07355
inches of water (at 4° C)	kgs/sq cm	2.540×10^{-3}
inches of water (at 4° C)	ounces/sq in	0.5781
inches of water (at 4° C)	pounds/sq ft	5.204
inches of water (at 4° C)	pounds/sq in	0.03613
international ampere	ampere (absolute)	0.9998
international volt	volts (absolute)	1.0003
international volt	joules (absolute)	1.593×10^{-19}
international volt	joules	9.654×10^{4}

J

To Convert	Into	Multiply by
joules	Btu	9.480×10^{-4}
joules	ergs	1×10^{7}
joules	foot-pounds	0.7376
joules	kg-calories	2.389×10^{-4}
joules	kg-meters	0.1020
joules	watt-hrs	2.778×10^{-4}
joules/cm	grams	1.020×10^{4}
joules/cm	dynes	1×10^{7}
joules/cm	joules/meter (newtons)	100.0
joules/cm	poundals	723.3
joules/cm	pounds	22.48

To Convert	Into	Multiply by
K		
kilograms	dynes	980,665.0
kilograms	grams	1,000.0
kilograms	joules/cm	0.09807
kilograms	joules/meter (newtons)	9.807
kilograms	poundals	70.93
kilograms	pounds	2.205
kilograms	tons (long)	9.842×10^{-4}
kilograms	tons (short)	1.102×10^{-3}
kilograms/cu meter	grams/cu cm	0.001
kilograms/cu meter	pounds/cu ft	0.06243
kilograms/cu meter	pounds/cu in	3.613×10^{-5}
kilograms/cu meter	pounds/mil-foot	3.405×10^{-10}
kilograms/meter	pounds/ft	0.6720
kilograms/sq cm	dynes	980,665.0
kilograms/sq cm	atmospheres	0.9678
kilograms/sq cm	feet of water	32.81
kilograms/sq cm	inches of mercury	28.96
kilograms/sq cm	pounds/sq ft	2,048.0
kilograms/sq cm	pounds/sq in	14.22
kilograms/sq meter	atmospheres	9.678×10^{-5}
kilograms/sq meter	bars	98.07×10^{-6}
kilograms/sq meter	feet of water	3.281×10^{-3}
kilograms/sq meter	inches of mercury	2.896×10^{-3}
kilograms/sq meter	pounds/sq ft	0.2048
kilograms/sq meter	pounds/sq in	1.422×10^{-3}
kilograms/sq mm	kgs/sq meter	1×10^{6}
kilogram-calories	Btu	3.968
kilogram-calories	foot-pounds	3,088.0
kilogram-calories	hp-hrs	1.560×10^{-3}
kilogram-calories	joules	4,186.0
kilogram-calories	kg-meters	426.9
kilogram-calories	kilojoules	4.186
kilogram-calories	kilowatt-hrs	1.163×10^{-3}
kilogram-meters	Btu	9.294×10^{-3}
kilogram-meters	ergs	9.804×10^{7}
kilogram-meters	foot-pounds	7.233
kilogram-meters	joules	9.804
kilogram-meters	kg-calories	2.342×10^{-3}
kilogram-meters	kilowatt-hrs	2.723×10^{-6}
kilolines	maxwells	1,000.0
kiloliters	liters	1,000.0
kilometers	centimeters	1×10^{5}
kilometers	feet	3,281.0
kilometers	inches	3.937×10^{4}
kilometers	meters	1,000.0
kilometers	miles	0.6214
kilometers	millimeters	1×10^{6}
kilometers	yards	1,094.0
kilometers/hr	cms/sec	27.78
kilometers/hr	feet/min	54.68
kilometers/hr	feet/sec	0.9113
kilometers/hr	knots	0.5396
kilometers/hr	meters/min	16.67
kilometers/hr	miles/hr	0.6214
kilometers/hr/sec	cms/sec/sec	27.78
kilometers/hr/sec	ft/sec/sec	0.9113
kilometers/hr/sec	meters/sec/sec	0.2778
kilometers/hr/sec	miles/hr/sec	0.6214
kilowatts	Btu/min	56.92
kilowatts	foot-lbs/min	4.426×10^{4}
kilowatts	foot-lbs/sec	737.6
kilowatts	horsepower	1.341
kilowatts	kg-calories/min	14.34
kilowatts	watts	1,000.0
kilowatt-hrs	Btu	3,413.0
kilowatt-hrs	ergs	3.600×10^{13}
kilowatt-hrs	foot-lbs	2.655×10^{6}
kilowatt-hrs	gram-calories	859,850.0
kilowatt-hrs	horsepower-hrs	1.341
kilowatt-hrs	joules	3.6×10^{6}
kilowatt-hrs	kg-calories	860.5
kilowatt-hrs	kg-meters	3.671×10^{5}
kilowatt-hrs	pounds of water evaporated from and at 212° F	3.53
kilowatt-hrs	pounds of water raised from 62° to 212° F	22.75
knots	feet/hr	6,080.0
knots	kilometers/hr	1.8532
knots	nautical miles/hr	1.0
knots	statute miles/hr	1.151
knots	yards/hr	2,027.0
knots	feet/sec	1.689

To Convert	Into	Multiply by
L		
league	miles (approx)	3.0
light-year	miles	5.9×10^{12}
light-year	kilometers	9.46091×10^{12}
lines/sq cm	gausses	1.0
lines/sq in	gausses	0.1550
lines/sq in	webers/sq cm	1.550×10^{-9}
lines/sq in	webers/sq in	1×10^{-8}
lines/sq in	webers/sq meter	1.550×10^{-5}
links (engineer's)	inches	12.0
links (surveyor's)	inches	7.92
liters	bushels (U.S. dry)	0.02838
liters	cu cm	1,000.0
liters	cu feet	0.03531
liters	cu inches	61.02
liters	cu meters	0.001
liters	cu yards	1.308×10^{-3}
liters	gallons (U.S. liq.)	0.2642
liters	pints (U.S. liq.)	2.113
liters	quarts (U.S. liq.)	1.057
liters/min	cu ft/sec	5.886×10^{-4}
liters/min	gals/sec	4.403×10^{-3}
lumen	spherical candle power	0.07958
lumen	watt	0.001496
lumens/sq ft	foot-candles	1.0
lumens/sq ft	lumen/sq meter	10.76
lux	foot-candles	0.0929
M		
maxwells	kilolines	0.001
maxwells	webers	1×10^{-8}
megalines	maxwells	1×10^{6}
megohms	microhms	1×10^{12}
megohms	ohms	1×10^{6}
meters	centimeters	100.0
meters	feet	3.281
meters	inches	39.37
meters	kilometers	0.001
meters	miles (nautical)	5.396×10^{-4}
meters	miles (statute)	6.214×10^{-4}
meters	millimeters	1,000.0
meters	yards	1.094
meters/min	cms/sec	1.667
meters/min	feet/min	3.281
meters/min	feet/sec	0.05468
meters/min	kms/hr	0.06
meters/min	knots	0.03238
meters/min	miles/hr	0.03728
meters/sec	feet/min	196.8
meters/sec	feet/sec	3.281
meters/sec	kilometers/hr	3.6
meters/sec	kilometers/min	0.06
meters/sec	miles/hr	2.237
meters/sec	miles/min	0.03728
meters/sec/sec	cms/sec/sec	100.0
meters/sec/sec	ft/sec/sec	3.281
meters/sec/sec	kms/hr/sec	3.6
meters/sec/sec	miles/hr/sec	2.237
meter-kilograms	cm-dynes	9.807×10^{7}
meter-kilograms	cm-grams	1×10^{5}
meter-kilograms	pound-feet	7.233
microfarad	farads	1×10^{-6}
micrograms	grams	1×10^{-6}
microhms	megohms	1×10^{-12}
microhms	ohms	1×10^{-6}
microliters	liters	1×10^{-6}
microns	meters	1×10^{-6}
miles (nautical)	feet	6,080.27
miles (nautical)	kilometers	1.853
miles (nautical)	meters	1,853.0
miles (nautical)	miles (statute)	1.1516
miles (nautical)	yards	2,027.0
miles (statute)	centimeters	1.609×10^{5}
miles (statute)	feet	5,280.0
miles (statute)	inches	6.336×10^{4}
miles (statute)	kilometers	1.609
miles (statute)	meters	1,609.0
miles (statute)	miles (nautical)	0.8684
miles (statute)	yards	1,760.0
miles/hr	cms/sec	44.70
miles/hr	feet/min	88.0
miles/hr	feet/sec	1.467
miles/hr	kms/hr	1.609
miles/hr	kms/min	0.02682

To Convert	Into	Multiply by
miles/hr	knots	0.8684
miles/hr	meters/min	26.82
miles/hr	miles/min	0.1667
miles/hr/sec	cms/sec/sec	44.70
miles/hr/sec	feet/sec/sec	1.467
miles/hr/sec	kms/hr/sec	1.609
miles/hr/sec	meters/sec/sec	0.4470
miles/min	cms/sec	2,682.0
miles/min	feet/sec	88.0
miles/min	kms/min	1.609
miles/min	knots/min	0.8684
miles/min	miles/hr	60.0
mil-feet	cu inches	9.425×10^{-6}
milliers	kilograms	1,000.0
millimicrons	meters	1×10^{-9}
milligrams	grains	0.01543236
milligrams	grams	0.001
milligrams/liter	parts/million	1.0
millihenries	henries	0.001
milliliters	liters	0.001
millimeters	centimeters	0.1
millimeters	feet	3.281×10^{-3}
millimeters	inches	0.03937
millimeters	kilometers	1×10^{-6}
millimeters	meters	0.001
millimeters	miles	6.214×10^{-7}
millimeters	mils	39.37
millimeters	yards	1.094×10^{-3}
million gals/day	cu ft/sec	1.54723
mils	centimeters	2.540×10^{-3}
mils	feet	8.333×10^{-5}
mils	inches	0.001
mils	kilometers	2.540×10^{-3}
mils	yards	2.778×10^{-5}
minims (British)	cubic cm	0.059192
minims (U.S., fluid)	cubic cm	0.061612
minutes (angles)	degrees	0.01667
minutes (angles)	quadrants	1.852×10^{-4}
minutes (angles)	radians	2.909×10^{-4}
minutes (angles)	seconds	60.0

N

To Convert	Into	Multiply by
nepers	decibals	8.686
newton	dynes	1×10^{5}

O

To Convert	Into	Multiply by
ohm (international)	ohm (absolute)	1.0005
ohms	megohms	1×10^{-6}
ohms	microhms	1×10^{6}
ounces	drams	16.0
ounces	grains	437.5
ounces	grams	28.349527
ounces	pounds	0.0625
ounces	ounces (troy)	0.9115
ounces	tons (long)	2.790×10^{-5}
ounces	tons (metric)	2.835×10^{-5}
ounces (fluid)	cu inches	1.805
ounces (fluid)	liters	0.02957
ounces (troy)	grains	480.0
ounces (troy)	grams	31.103481
ounces (troy)	ounces (avoirdupois)	1.09714
ounces (troy)	pennyweights (troy)	20.0
ounces (troy)	pounds (troy)	0.08333
ounce/sq inch	dynes/sq cm	4,309.0
ounces/sq inch	pounds/sq in	0.0625

P

To Convert	Into	Multiply by
parsec	miles	19×10^{12}
parsec	kilometers	3.084×10^{13}
parts/million	grains/U.S. gal	0.0584
parts/million	grains/imperial gal	0.07016
parts/million	pounds/million gal	8.345
pecks (British)	cubic inches	554.6
pecks (British)	liters	9.091901
pecks (U.S.)	bushels	0.25
pecks (U.S)	cubic inches	537.605
pecks (U.S.)	liters	8.809582
pecks (U.S.)	quarts (dry)	8.0
pennyweights (troy)	grains	24.0
pennyweights (troy)	ounces (troy)	0.05
pennyweights (troy)	grams	1.55517
pennyweights (troy)	pounds (troy)	4.1667×10^{-3}
pints (dry)	cu inches	33.60

To Convert	Into	Multiply by
pints (liquid)	cu cm	473.2
pints (liquid)	cu feet	0.01671
pints (liquid)	cu inches	28.87
pints (liquid)	cu meters	4.732×10^{-4}
pints (liquid)	cu yards	6.189×10^{-4}
pints (liquid)	gallons	0.125
pints (liquid)	liters	0.4732
pints (liquid)	quarts (liquid)	0.5
Planck's quantum	erg-second	6.624×10^{-27}
poise	gram/cm sec	1.00
pounds (avoirdupois)	ounces (troy)	14.5833
poundals	dynes	13,826.0
poundals	grams	14.10
poundals	joules/cm	1.383×10^{-3}
poundals	joules/meter (newtons)	0.1383
poundals	kilograms	0.01410
poundals	pounds	0.03108
pounds	drams	256.0
pounds	dynes	44.4823×10^{4}
pounds	grains	7,000.0
pounds	grams	453.5924
pounds	joules/cm	0.04448
pounds	joules/meter (newtons)	4.448
pounds	kilograms	0.4536
pounds	ounces	16.0
pounds	ounces (troy)	14.5833
pounds	poundals	32.17
pounds	pounds (troy)	1.21528
pounds	tons (short)	0.0005
pounds (troy)	grains	5,760.0
pounds (troy)	grams	373.24177
pounds (troy)	ounces (avoirdupois)	13.1657
pounds (troy)	ounces (troy)	12.0
pounds (troy)	pennyweights (troy)	240.0
pounds (troy)	pounds (avoirdupois)	0.822857
pounds (troy)	tons (long)	3.6735×10^{-4}
pounds (troy)	tons (metric)	3.7324×10^{-4}
pounds (troy)	tons (short)	4.1143×10^{-4}
pounds of water	cu feet	0.01602
pounds of water	cu inches	27.68
pounds of water	gallons	0.1198
pounds of water/min	cu ft/sec	2.670×10^{-4}
pound-feet	cm-dynes	1.356×10^{7}
pound-feet	cm-grams	13,825.0
pound-feet	meter-kgs	0.1383
pounds/cu ft	grams/cu cm	0.01602
pounds/cu ft	kgs/cu meter	16.02
pounds/cu ft	pounds/cu in	5.787×10^{-4}
pounds/cu ft	pounds/mil-foot	5.456×10^{-9}
pounds/cu in	gms/cu cm	27.68
pounds/cu in	kgs/cu meter	2.768×10^{4}
pounds/cu in	pounds/cu ft	1,728.0
pounds/cu in	pounds/mil-foot	9.425×10^{-6}
pounds/ft	kgs/meter	1.488
pounds/in	gms/cm	178.6
pounds/mil-foot	gms/cu cm	2.306×10^{6}
pounds/sq ft	atmospheres	4.725×10^{-4}
pounds/sq ft	feet of water	0.01602
pounds/sq ft	inches of mercury	0.01414
pounds/sq ft	kgs/sq meter	4.882
pounds/sq ft	pounds/sq in	6.944×10^{-3}
pounds/sq in	atmospheres	0.06804
pounds/sq in	feet of water	2.307
pounds/sq in	inches of mercury	2.036
pounds/sq in	kgs/sq meter	703.1
pounds/sq in	pounds/sq ft	144.0

Q

To Convert	Into	Multiply by
quadrants (angle)	degrees	90.0
quadrants (angle)	minutes	5,400.0
quadrants (angle)	radians	1.571
quadrants (angle)	seconds	3.24×10^{5}
quarts (dry)	cu inches	67.20
quarts (liquid)	cu cms	946.4
quarts (liquid)	cu feet	0.03342
quarts (liquid)	cu inches	57.75
quarts (liquid)	cu meters	9.464×10^{-4}
quarts (liquid)	cu yards	1.238×10^{-3}
quarts (liquid)	gallons	0.25
quarts (liquid)	liters	0.9463

R

To Convert	Into	Multiply by
radians	degrees	57.30

To Convert	Into	Multiply by
radians	minutes	3,438.0
radians	quadrants	0.6366
radians	seconds	2.063×10^5
radians/sec	degrees/sec	57.30
radians/sec	revolutions/min	9.549
radians/sec	revolutions/sec	0.1592
radians/sec/sec	revs/min/min	573.0
radians/sec/sec	revs/min/sec	9.549
radians/sec/sec	revs/sec/sec	0.1592
revolutions	degrees	360.0
revolutions	quadrants	4.0
revolutions	radians	6.283
revolutions/min	degrees/sec	6.0
revolutions/min	radians/sec	0.1047
revolutions/min	revs/sec	0.01667
revolutions/min/min	radians/sec/sec	1.745×10^{-3}
revolutions/min/min	revs/min/sec	0.01667
revolutions/min/min	revs/sec/sec	2.778×10^{-4}
revolutions/sec	degrees/sec	360.0
revolutions/sec	radians/sec	6.283
revolutions/sec	revs/min	60.0
revolutions/sec/sec	radians/sec/sec	6.283
revolutions/sec/sec	revs/min/min	3,600.0
revolutions/sec/sec	revs/min/sec	60.0
rod	chain (Gunter's)	0.25
rod	meters	5.029
rods (surveyor's meas.)	yards	5.5
rods	feet	16.5

S

To Convert	Into	Multiply by
scruples	grains	20.0
seconds (angle)	degrees	2.778×10^{-4}
seconds (angle)	minutes	0.01667
seconds (angle)	quadrants	3.087×10^{-6}
seconds (angle)	radians	4.848×10^{-6}
slug	kilogram	14.59
slug	pounds	32.17
sphere	steradians	12.57
square centimeters	circular mils	1.973×10^5
square centimeters	square feet	1.076×10^{-3}
square centimeters	square inches	0.1550
square centimeters	square meters	0.0001
square centimeters	sq miles	3.861×10^{-11}
square centimeters	sq millimeters	100.0
square centimeters	sq yards	1.196×10^{-4}
square feet	acres	2.296×10^{-5}
square feet	circular mils	1.833×10^8
square feet	sq cms	929.0
square feet	sq inches	144.0
square feet	sq meters	0.09290
square feet	sq miles	3.587×10^{-8}
square feet	sq millimeters	9.290×10^4
square feet	sq yards	0.1111
square inches	circular mils	1.273×10^6
square inches	sq cms	6.452
square inches	sq feet	6.944×10^{-3}
square inches	sq millimeters	645.2
square inches	sq mils	1×10^6
square inches	sq yards	7.716×10^{-4}
square kilometers	acres	247.1
square kilometers	sq cms	1×10^{10}
square kilometers	sq ft	10.76×10^6
square kilometers	sq inches	1.550×10^9
square kilometers	sq meters	1×10^6
square kilometers	sq miles	0.3861
square kilometers	sq yards	1.196×10^6
square meters	acres	2.471×10^{-4}
square meters	sq cms	1×10^4
square meters	sq feet	10.76
square meters	sq inches	1,550.0
square meters	sq miles	3.861×10^{-7}
square meters	sq millimeters	1×10^6
square meters	sq yards	1.196
square miles	acres	640.0
square miles	sq feet	27.88×10^6
square miles	sq kms	2.590
square miles	sq meters	2.590×10^6
square miles	sq yards	3.098×10^6
square millimeters	circular mils	1,973.0
square millimeters	sq cms	0.01
square millimeters	sq feet	1.076×10^{-5}
square millimeters	sq inches	1.550×10^{-3}
square mils	circular mils	1.273
square mils	sq cms	6.452×10^{-6}

To Convert	Into	Multiply by
square mils	sq inches	1×10^{-6}
square yards	acres	2.066×10^{-4}
square yards	sq cms	8,361.0
square yards	sq feet	9.0
square yards	sq inches	1,296.0
square yards	sq meters	0.8361
square yards	sq miles	3.228×10^{-7}
square yards	sq millimeters	8.361×10^5

T

To Convert	Into	Multiply by
temperature (°C) + 273	absolute temperature (°C)	1.0
temperature (°C) + 17.78	temperature (°F)	1.8
temperature (°F) + 460	absolute temperature (°F)	1.0
temperature (°F) − 32	temperature (°C)	5/9
tons (long)	kilograms	1,016.0
tons (long)	pounds	2,240.0
tons (long)	tons (short)	1.120
tons (metric)	kilograms	1,000.0
tons (metric)	pounds	2,205.0
tons (short)	kilograms	907.1848
tons (short)	ounces	32,000.0
tons (short)	ounces (troy)	29,166.66
tons (short)	pounds	2,000.0
tons (short)	pounds (troy)	2,430.56
tons (short)	tons (long)	0.89287
tons (short)	tons (metric)	0.9078
tons (short)/sq ft	kgs/sq meter	9,765.0
tons (short)/sq ft	pounds/sq in	2,000.0
tons of water/24 hrs	pounds of water/hr	83.333
tons of water/24 hrs	gallons/min	0.16643
tons of water/24 hrs	cu ft/hr	1.3349

V

To Convert	Into	Multiply by
volt inch	volt/cm	0.39370
volt (absolute)	statvolts	0.003336

W

To Convert	Into	Multiply by
watts	Btu/hr	3.4129
watts	Btu/min	0.05688
watts	ergs/sec	107.0
watts	foot-lbs/min	44.27
watts	foot-lbs/sec	0.7378
watts	horsepower	1.341×10^{-3}
watts	horsepower (metric)	1.360×10^{-3}
watts	kg-calories/min	0.01433
watts	kilowatts	0.001
watts (absolute)	Btu (mean)/min	0.056884
watts (absolute)	joules/sec	1.0
watt-hours	Btu	3.413
watt-hours	ergs	3.60×10^{10}
watt-hours	foot-pounds	2,656.0
watt-hours	gram-calories	859.85
watt-hours	horsepower-hrs	1.341×10^{-3}
watt-hours	kilogram-calories	0.8605
watt-hours	kilogram-meters	367.2
watt-hours	kilowatt-hrs	0.001
watt (international)	watt (absolute)	1.0002
webers	maxwells	1×10^8
webers	kilolines	1×10^5
webers/sq in	gausses	1.550×10^7
webers/sq in	lines/sq in	1×10^8
webers/sq in	webers/sq cm	0.1550
webers/sq in	webers/sq meter	1,550.0
webers/sq meter	gausses	1×10^4
webers/sq meter	lines/sq in	6.452×10^4
webers/sq meter	webers/sq cm	1×10^{-4}
webers/sq meter	webers/sq in	6.452×10^{-4}

Y

To Convert	Into	Multiply by
yards	centimeters	91.44
yards	kilometers	9.144×10^{-4}
yards	meters	0.9144
yards	miles (nautical)	4.934×10^{-4}
yards	miles (statute)	5.682×10^{-4}
yards	millimeters	914.4

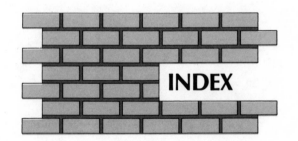

INDEX

ABS, 418
Absorber, shock, 378
Absorption field, 386, 445
Absorption system, 479
Absorptive cooling, 510
AC, 286
Accenting, color, 21
Access hole, circuit box hook-up, 327
Accessories, drill, 121-122
Accessories, ladder, 47
Acid, muriatic, 159, 219, 255, 267
Acid pitch-base roof coating, 210
Acoustic tile, 26
Acoustical tile, 138
Acrylic plastic, 146
Acrylonitrile butadiene styrene (ABS), 418
Adapters, 408
Adhesives
mastic, 98
vinyl, 74, 75, 80
Adjustable jack, 250
Adjustable wrenches, 116, 202, 389-390
Aerosols, 163
Aggregate concrete, 266
AHAM, 514, 518
Air chamber, 378
Air conditioner, wattage, 295
Air economizer, 543
Air-entrainment, 259, 261
Air filters, 504
Air temperature, exterior painting, 62, 228
Aircraft snips, 491, 492
Alcohol, 34, 69
Alkali-resistant primer, 25
Alkyd enamel, 227
Alligatoring, 67-70, 233-234
Alloy steel wrench, 202
Alternating current, 286
Aluminum casement windows, 144, 537
Aluminum fins, 500
Aluminum ladders, 41
Aluminum paints, 25, 37, 66, 96, 226, 236
Aluminum spring stripping, 150-152
Aluminum windows, 239, 244, 246, 537
Aluminum wiring, 305
American Gas Association, 483
American National Standards

Institute (ANSI), 40, 41, 46, 47
American Wire Gauge (AWG), 305
Amperage, 288, 294, 295
Ampere (amp), 286
Analogous harmony, 16
Analogy of electricity and water, 287-289
Angle of sunlight, exterior painting, 62
Angle valve, 408
ANSI, 40, 41, 46, 47
Anthracite coal, 485
Anti-rust priming coat, 23
Appliance plugs, 345-346
Appliances, 294, 295
Appliances, power consumption chart, 295
Applicator, 35
Arbor adaptor, 203
Area heater, 466
Armature, 362, 365, 369
Armored cable, 306, 323
Asbestos-cement shingles, 212-214, 224, 227
Asbestos sheeting, 500
Ash, fly, 485
Asphalt cement, 208, 209, 248, 256
Asphalt roofing, 207-210
Association of Home Appliance Manufacturers (AHAM), 514, 518
Atomizer, 545
Atomizing home burner, 482
Attic insulation, 151-152, 522, 527
Attic ventilation, 548
Auger, 173, 183, 388, 454-455, 459
Aviation snips, 304
AWG, 305
Awl, 197

B

Backing materials, paneling, 96
Backing materials, wallpaper, 75-76
Backsaw, 100
Backsplash, 428

Baffle, 495-496
Bakelite, 308
Ball faucet, Fuller, 413
Ball peen hammer, 160, 196, 218, 396
Ball-type noncompression faucet (diagram), 412
Ballast, fluorescent fixtures, 350
Ballcock, 450, 452 (Fluidmaster)
Baluster, 250-251
Base, solvent, 23, 25
Baseboard
outlet, 469
radiator, 472
Basement
dampness, 530
entry door, 242
heating, 495, 496, 500
insulation, 530
paneling, 100-101
Basin wrench, 391
Batch feed disposer, 429
Bathroom fixtures, 380
Batts, 151, 152, 161, 522, 524, 529, 531
Belt-drive blowers, 505
Bends
closet, 419
eight, 419
long, 419
quarter, 419
reducing, 419
Bearings, motor, 364
Bell-and-spigot pipe, 414
Belt sander, 38
Bending springs, 400
Better Business Bureau, 162
Bidet, 442
Bimetallic switches, 355
Bits
carbide-tipped, 121
carbon steel, 121
drill, 116, 121-122
screwdriving, 203
spade, 121, 203
tungsten carbide, 203
twist, 121, 203
wood screw pilot, 121, 124
Bituminous coal, 485
Bituminous roof coating, 209, 531
Blackout, 338
Blacktop, 264-265
Blade alignment, electric fan (diagram), 364

Blade scraper, 38
Blank stock, 72, 75, 76
Blanket insulation, 522, 534, 529, 530, 531
Bleach, 183
Bleaching oils, 64-65
Bleaching powder, 184
Bleeding, 69
    creosote, 235-236
Bleeding paint, exteriors, 235
Bleeding radiators, 505
Blenders, 365-366
    wattage, 295
Blistering paint, 67, 232-233
Blister-resistant, 24
Blower, 468, 504, 508, 510, 529, 540
Blown fuses, 339
Blown-in insulation, 526, 528
Blowtorch, 170, 396
Board, gypsum, 50, 96
Boiler, 471-474, 503, 540, 551
Bonnet, 491
Bonnet, hair dryer, 371
Booster pump, 472
Bottled gas, 482, 484
Box wrench, 201, 389
Boxes
    electrical, 307-308, 314-315, 335-336
    breaker, 326-327
    outdoor, 328
Braided cotton electric cord, 346
Brass piping, 402
Breaker, 287, 289, 311
    circuit, 175
    screw-in, 311-312
    toggle, 312
    tripped, 339, 520
Breaker boxes, 326-327
Breathing mask, 524
"Breathing" paint, 232
Brick masonry, 24
Brick patio, 268-270
Bristles, 33
British thermal unit (Btu), 480-481
Broad knife, 51
Broiler, 366-367
Broken glass, 245
Bromine, 272
Bronze spring stripping, 150-151
Brooming (concrete), 263
Brush bearings, 370
Brushes, 32, 33-35, 61, 362,

368, 369
    calcimine, 33, 79
    smoothing, 78, 83, 87
    varnish, 26, 55, 96
Brush-type motors, 362-363
Bucket shelf, 44
Bucket shelf ladders, 42
Buckled seams, roofing, 209
Built-up roofing, 210
Bull float, 261
Burlap, 75
Burner, atomizing, 482
Burner care, 506
Burrs, 393
Bushings, 309, 317, 408
Butadiene, acrylonitrile styrene, 418
Butt joints, 84, 131
Butyl calk, 532
Butyl rubber, 273-274
Buying a house, 279-282
Buying tools, 196
"BX" cable, 306, 317

Cable
    AC, 309, 316
    armored, 306, 323,
    "BX", 306, 317
    electric heating, 170
    flexible, 306, 309
    NM, 306, 316
    sheathed, 306, 323
    UF, 307
    USE, 307
CAC, 488
Cadmium sulfide flame detector, 488
Calcimine brushes, 33, 79
Calcium hypochlorite, 183
Calking, 156, 532-539
Calking compound, 58, 217, 532
Calking gun, 38
Calking irons, 396, 418
Calorie, 480
Camouflage, color, 18-19
Can opener, electric, 367-368
Capillary tube, 510
Caps, 408
Carbide-tipped bits, 121, 203

Carbon dioxide test, 506
Carbon steel bits, 121
Carbon steel twist bits, 203
Carbon tetrachloride, 231
Carpenter's level, 201
Carpet roller, 35
Cartridge fuses, 312
Casein paints, 27
Casement hinges, 238
Casement windows, aluminum, 144, 515
Cast iron pipe, 414
Cast iron pipe tools, 396
C-clamp, 119, 148
Cedar, western red, 64
Ceiling boxes, 332, 335-336
Ceiling outlet, 469
Ceiling tile, 138
Cellulose fiber insulation, 522
Cement, asphalt, 208, 209, 248, 256,
    masonry, 270
    Portland, 229, 253, 258
Cement base, 27
Cement, contact, 97
Cement, gypsum, 133
Cement, joint, 51
Cement wall, 219-220
Cement-water paint, 229-230
Central air conditioning, 511, 540, 550
Ceramic tile, 137-138
Cesspool, 244, 378, 381
Chain fixtures, 325
Chain vise, 395
Chain wrench, 201, 391
Chalk line, 79, 83, 86, 138
Chalking, 67
Chalking paint, 233
Chalk-resistant, 23, 67
Chamber, air, 378
Channel-lock pliers, 392
Charcoal, 184
Check valve, 411
Checking, exterior paint surfaces, 233-234
Checkups, 540
Chicken ladder, 211
Chimes, 178, 350-351
Chimney flue, 182
Chimney, prefabricated, 502
Chisels, 38, 91, 118-119, 126, 129, 142, 145, 160, 200-201, 303,
    cold, 201, 396,

paring, 119, 201,
  socket, 118,200-201,
  tang, 118,
  wood, 118-119, 145, 303
Chisel-shaped brushes, 33
Chlordane, 165
Chloride, polyvinyl, 403, 418
Chlorinated polyvinyl chloride
  (CPVC), 403
Chlorine, 272
Choosing exterior paints, 227
Chuck, 202
Chuck size, 120
Circline tubes, 350
Circuit breaker, 175, 287, 289,
  312
Circuit-capacity formula, 313
Circuits, 287, 295, 298, 313-314
Circular saw, 204
Circulating pump, 472
Circulator heater, 466
Clamp fittings, 405
Clamp, pipe sleeve, 414
Clapboard siding, 221
Claw hammer, 91, 196
Clay tile roofing, 211-212
Cleanable filter, 504
Cleaners, drain, 388, 455
Cleaning panels, 101
Clean-up, painting, 54
Clear finishes (exterior), 23
Clear finishes (interior), 27
Cleanout plug, 381, 420
Clik-N-Seal compression fittings,
  398, 400, 403, 405
Clock, wattage, 295
Clock thermostat, 504
Clogged bathtubs, 457-458
Clogged drains, 173
Clogged sewer, 458
Clogged sinks, 456
Clogged toilet, 454-455
Closed hot-water system, 472
Closet auger, 388, 455
Closet bends (see Long Bends)
Closet furnace, 470
Closet spud wrench, 389
Cloth, grass, 76
Clothes dryers, 158
Clothes washer, wattage, 295
Coal
  anthracite, 485
  bituminous, 485
Coal heating, 484-485
Coatings, exterior painting, 62

Cockroaches, 164
Code, National Electric, 174,
  292, 294, 301, 305, 306, 315,
  318, 323, 328
Code, National Plumbing, 384,
  386, 397
Coffee-maker, 356-358
Coffee percolator, wattage, 295
Coil, condenser, 468, 512, 519,
  520
Coil, heating, 474
Coil, nichrome, 354
Cold air return, 469, 497, 551
Cold chisel, 201, 396
Cold water main line, 377
Color-accenting, 21
Color-coding, 306, 319, 320
Color harmony, 16
Color reflectance chart, 18
Color wheel, 16
Colors, intermediate, 16
Combination vise, 395
Combustion air, 530
Comer, circuitry, 331
Commutator, 362, 363
Comparison chart, painting
  tools, 32
Compass, 92
Compass saw, 91, 199
Compass saw blades, 118
Complementary harmony, 16
Compost heat, 486
Compound
  calking, 58, 217
  epoxy, 254, 266
  glazing, 145, 146, 245
  pipe joint, 402
  spackling, 133
  vinyl patching, 254, 266
Compression faucet, 411
Compression fittings, 398, 400,
  403, 405 (Clik-N-Seal)
Compressor, 510
Concealed condensation, 156
Concealed deck faucet, 426
Concrete, 60, 253, 256, 258-260
Concrete, exposed aggregate,
  266
Concrete floors, 127-128, 130
Concrete hoe, 260
Concrete, pouring method,
  256-260
Concrete sealer paint, 127
Condensation, 153-156
Condensation pump, 474

Condensation test, walls, 158
Condensing unit, 512, 539
Condensor coil, 468, 512, 519,
  520
Conductors, 288, 289
Conduit, 307, 317-320
Conduit bender, 304, 318
Connection, cross, 382-383
Connectors, 309
Contact cement, 97
Continuous air circulation (CAC),
  488
Continuous feed disposers, 429
Contractor, 162
Contracting for painting, 57
Control joints, 262-263
Controls, air temperature, 479,
  518
Convector, 471-472
Conversion gas burner, 483
Conversion, water to vapor,
  153-154
Cooling capacity, 513
Cooling coils, 468, 512, 519, 520
Coping saw, 91, 97, 199
Copper napthenate, 226
Copper piping, 397, 499
Copper tubing, flexible, 399
Copper wiring, 305
Cord, sash, 144
Cork, 75
Corner roller, 35
Corners, wallpaper, 85
Corrosion, 288
Counterflow furnace, 470
Countertop surface wiring, 310
Couplings, 406, 419
Cove molding, 138
Covering, protective, 53, 79
Cornell University, 435
CPVC, 403
Cracked flooring, 125-126
Cracking, 67-68
Cracking paint, 234
Crawl-space ventilation, 70-71,
  469-470, 529-530, 541
Crawling paint, exteriors,
  234-235
Crayon, wax patching, 125
Creosote bleeding, 235-236
Cross, 420
Cross connection, 382-383
Cross tee, 406
Crosscut saw, 91, 118, 199
Crown molding, 138

Curing, concrete, 264
Current, 286-287
Curving cuts, 199
Cutter
   glass, 137, 145, 245
   pipe, 392-393
   tube, 393
Cutting-in roller, 35
Cycle, 287

D

Dado-and-rabbet joint, 131
Dado joint, 131
Damper, 468, 493
DC, 286
Decorating scheme, colors, 18-19
Defective mortar joint, 218-219
Dehumidification, 156, 159, 511, 546-548
Designer planks, 90
Detector, flame, 488
Diameter, pipes (charts), 394-398
Diazinon, 164
Die stocks, 394
Dielectric connectors, 402, 410
Dies, 394
Diffuser, 505
Dimmer switches, 309
Direct current (DC), 287
Disc, sanding, 203
Discoloration, 236-237
Dishwasher, wattage, 295
Disposable filter, 504
Disposer, batch feed, 429
Distribution box, 445
Diverter, 434
Door channel, interlocking, 535
Door locks, 238
Door shoe, 535
Door sweep, 535
Doorbells, 178-179, 350, 351
Doorbell transformers, 350
Double bend, 419
Double complementary harmony, 16
Double-headed nail, 258
Double-hub pipe, 415
Double shingles, 214

Double-track storm window, 538
Double Y, 420
Downspouts, 162, 214, 216
Draft test, 506
Drain
   bathtub, 434-437
   fixture, 380, 419
   house, 381
   pop-up, 431, 435, 436
   trip-lever, 435
Drain auger, 388, 454
Drain cleaners, 388, 455
Drain line, vertical, 416
Drain tile, 531
Drainable valves, 410
Drainage, 378 (See also DWV)
Drainage system (diagram), 379, 383
Drainage trench, 216
Draining procedure, 383
Drains, clogged, 173
Drill, 91, 303
   hand, 115-116
   push style, 116
   rotary, 116
   variable-speed, 121, 202
Drill bits, 116, 121-122
Drill chuck, 116, 120
Drinking water, safety, 182-183
Driveway, 253-255
Driving a screw, 198
Dropcloth, 53, 79
Drum fittings, 380
Dryer, hair, 371-372
Drying times, 62
Drywall, 206
Drywall nails, 51
Drywall tape, 51
Drywells, 216, 531
DWV, 378, 380, 386
DWV fittings, 419

E

Eaves, 214
Edging, 262
Edging rollers, 35-36
"Edison" base, 311
EER, 517
Efflorescence, 219, 230
Eight-point crosscut saw, 199

Eighth bend, 419
Elastometric calks, 532
Elbows, 406, 493
Electric auger, 459
Electric baseboard units, 476, 501
Electric blanket, wattage, 295
Electric can opener, 367-368
Electric drill, 120-121, 202-204
Electric eye control, 488
Electric fan, 363-365
Electric frying pan, 358-359
Electric heating, 475, 484, 501
Electric heating cable, 170
Electric loop system, 458
Electric paint softener, 38
Electric knife, 368-369
Electric sander, 204
Electrical boxes, 307-308, 314-315, 335-336
Electrical code, 174, 292, 294, 301, 305, 306, 315, 318, 323, 328
Electrical metallic tubing (EMT), 307
Electrician's screwdriver, 302
Electricity failure, 338
Electromotive force (EMF), 286
Electronic air cleaning, 468, 549
Emery cloth, 137, 404, 508
Emery paper, 324
EMF, 286
EMT, 307
Emulsion paints, 23, 229, 230
Enamel, alkyd, 227
Enamel brushes, 33
Enamels, silicone, 227
Energy Efficiency Ratio (EER), 517
Entrainment, air, 259
Entrance panel, 310
Epoxy patching compound, 254, 266, 530
Epoxy resin, 161
Epoxycrete, 274
Evaporative cooling, 510
Evaporative-plate humidifier, 545
Evaporator, 545
Expansion tank, 472, 474
Exposed-aggregate concrete, 266
Exposed deck faucet, 426
Extension ladders, 45-47
Extension trestle ladders, 44

Exterior clear finishes, 23
Exterior masonry paints, 24, (chart) 25
Exterior metal paints, 24, (chart) 25
Exterior metalwork paint, 231
Exterior paneling, 221-224
Exterior paints, 22-25
Exterior trim paints, 24

F

Face-to-face measuring, 398
Factory primer, 62
Fading paint, 69, exteriors, 235
Fall season (painting), 15
Fallen power lines, 278
Fan, 468, 518, 548
Fan, electric, 363-365
Fan control, 488
Fan (portable), wattage, 295
Fatty acid pitch-base roof coating, 210
Faucet
    compression, 411
    (diagram), 167
    ground key, 413
    hose, 413
    kitchen, 426-428
    lavatory, 431
    noncompression, 412, 426
    mixer type compression, 412, 426, 428,
    repairs, 447-449
    types, 411-413
"Feathered" concrete patching compound, 253-254
Federal Energy and Research Administration, 486
"Feeding" (swimming pool), 275
Feed disposers, continuous, 429
Feed-in, circuit, 326
Feed sprayer, 36-37
Felt, roofing, 207
Female faucet, 428
Ferrule, 33
Fiber brushings, 309, 317
Fiberglass, 51, reinforced polyester (FRP), 437

Fiberglass insulation, 522
Fiberglass roof gutters, 214
Field, 362, absorption, 18, 77, 386, 445, leaching, 381
File, 137, 393
Fill test, static, 384
Filter, 468, 503-508, 511, 518-519
Finish, semigloss, 25, 52
Finished floor, 123, 124
Fin clusters, 500
Fins, aluminum, 500
Fire, 192
Firebrats, 165
Fireplace, 501-502
Fish tape, 304, 319, 332, 334-336
Fishtail, 34
Fittings
    clamp, 405
    compression, 398, 400, 403, 405
    drum, 380
    DWV, 419
    flared, 400
    pipe, 406-408
    shower, 437-438
Fixtures, 378, 386, 422,
    bathroom, 380,
    drain, 380, 419,
    pull chain, 325,
    replacement, 341-342,
    shallow box, 336
Fixture supply line, 378
Flagstone patio, 270-271
Flaking paint, 67-68
Flame detector, 488
Flared fittings, 400
Flaring, 400
Flaring tools, 395
Flashings, 210
Flat brushes, 33
Flat finishes, 25
Flat-tip screwdriver, 115
Flexible armored cable (Type AC or "BX"), 306, 309
Flexible copper tubing, 399
Flies (pests), 164
Float ball, 171, 451
Floating, 261
Floatless ballcock, 452
Flocks, 77, 81, 94
Floor register, 468
Flooring, tongue-and-groove, 251

Floors
    board removal, 126
    concrete, 127-130
    cracked, 125-126
    finishing, 123-124
    sagging, 126-127
    squeaking, 123-125
    tiles, 128-131
Flow, gravity, 378-379
Fluorescent fixtures, 348
Flush mechanism, 450, 453
Flush mount lavatory, 432
Flush valve, 171, 452
Flux, 398
Fly ash, 485
Foam insulation, 522, 528
Foils, 75
Folding rule, 117, 119-200
Food waste disposer, 429
Force cup, 119-120, 173
Force pump, 455
Forced-air heating, 476
Forced hot-water system, 472
Fortified primer, 261
Foundation defects, 107-110
Four-way switches, 309
Framing square, 250
Free-chalking paint, 23
Freezer, wattage, 295
Freon, 510
Fresh water, 382
Frost penetration, 458
Frozen pipes, 170, 459
FRP polyester bathtub, 437
Fryer, wattage, 295
Frying pan, electric (diagram), 358
Fuel cost comparison, 480, 507
Fuel oil grades, 482
Fuels, 480
Fuller ball faucet, 413
Fume-resistant, 23
Fungus, 187, 226
Furnace
    closet, 470
    counterflow, 470
    horizontal, 469
    pipeless, 466
Furnace failure, 191
Furring strips, 95, 100, 136, 138
Fuse, 175-176, 287-289, 310-312, 339-340, 389
    blown, 339, 520
    cartridge, 312
    plug type, 311

S type, 312
time delay, 311, 340
Fuse Boxes, 327
Future fuels, 485

G

Gable ends, roofs, 214
Galvanized gutters, 214
Galvanized pipe, 401-402, 418
Galvanized steel, 60
Ganged electric boxes, 315
Garbage disposer, wattage, 295
Gas, bottled, 482, 484
Gas burner, 482, 486
Gas burner maintenance, 540
Gas heating, 482-483
Gas logs, 502
Gas torch, 38
Gases, 378
Gate valve, 408, 449
Gauge, See American Wire
   Gauge
GFCI, 328
Glass cutter, 137, 145, 245
Glass fiber insulation, 522
Glass, installation, 145-147
Glass, laminated, 146
Glass, wire, 146
Glazier's points, 145, 146
Glazing compound, 145, 146,
   245
Globe valve, 167, 408, 409
Gloss finish, 25, 48
Grained wood paneling, 89-90
Graphite, 238
Grass cloth, 76
Gravity flow, 379
Gravity hot-water heating, 467,
   472
Grease trap, 445
Grilles, air-conditioning, 519
Grips, ladder, 47
Groove flooring, 251
Groover, 260
Ground Fault Current
   Interruption (GFCI), 328
Ground key faucet, 413

Ground key valve, 410, 450
Ground wire, 306, 323
Grounding, 323
Gunite swimming pool, 273
Gun-type oil burner, 482
Gutters, 162,
   galvanized, 214
   hanger and guard, 215
Gypsum cement, 133
Gypsum wallboard, 133-136
Gypsumboard, 50, 96

H

Hacksaw, 199, 303, 332, 392
Hacksaw blade, 132
Hair dryer, 371
Hairline joints, 84
Hammer
   ball peen, 38, 160, 196, 218,
      396
   claw, 196
   jackhammer, 255
   mason's, 196
   nail, 115
   sledgehammer, 115, 255, 396
   tack, 196
   water, 169-170, 378
Hand drill, 115-116
Hand shower, 434
Hand-held hair dryer, 371
Handsaw, 118
Hangers, surface wiring, 310
Hanging tools, 195
Hard coal, 485
Hard water, 356, 362
Hardboard, 89
Hardboard, perforated, 195
Hardboard plywood, 90
Harmony
   analogous, 16
   complementary, 16
   monochromatic, 16
   triad, 18
Hatchet, 143
Heat, compost, 486
Heat lamp, wattage, 295
Heat loss calculation, 490

Heat pump, 476, 481, 543
Heat values table, 481
Heater, circulator, 466
Heater, wattage, 295
Heater wells, 356
Heating, coal, 484-485
Heating coils, 474
Heating elements, 354, 358,
   366, 371
Heating equipment, 109, 465
Heating system capacity, 490
Heating systems, 465
Heating unit efficiency, 481
Heat-resistant rubber (RH)
   insulation, 305
Heaved sidewalk sections, 255
Hemp, 75
"Hickey"
   (fitting), 342
   (tool), 307, 318
High-voltage lines, 297, 298,
   299, 300, 327
Hinges
   casement windows, 238-239
   doors, 141-142, 239-240
Hoe, concrete, 260
Hog bristle, 33
Holes, ceiling and roof, 206-207
Holesaw, 204
Hood-type hair dryer, 371
Hook scraper, 38
Horsepower (hp), 286
Horizontal furnace, 469
Hose faucets, 413
Hose, spray, 425
Hot water heating, 471
Hot-water system, closed, 472
Hot-water system, extension,
   499
"Hot" wire, 306, 320
Hotplate, wattage, 295
Hot-water main line, 377
House circuitry (diagram),
   296-297
House drain, 381
House painting sequence, 61
House shape (painting), 21
Houseflies, 164
Hubless pipe, 396, 414
Humidification, 544
Humidifier, 468, 545
Humidities, relative, 156
Hydration, 264
Hydrogen peroxide, 236-237
Hypochlorite, calcium, 183

I

Icy walks, 278
Immersibility, 358
Inadequate wiring, 300-301
Inner diameter, pipes (charts), 394, 398
Inspection services, house, 282
Inspections, 298-301
Installing glass, 145-147
Institute of Boiler and Radiator Manufacturers (IBR), 471
Insulation, 70, 101, 151-152, 491, 521-531, 551-552
Insulation, exterior walls, 152
Insulator
 batt, 151-152, 161
 heat resistant rubber (RH) 305
 latex rubber (RU), 305
 loose-fill, 151-152
 moisture resistant (RHW) 305
 moisture and heat resistant thermoplastic (THW), 305
 moisture resistant thermoplastic (TW), 305
 rubber (R), 305
 thermoplastic (T), 305
Insurance policy restrictions, 292
Intake (float) valve, 171
Interior clear finishes, 27
Interior paints, 25-27 (chart) 27
Interlocking door channel, 535
Interlocking threshold, 536
Intermediate colors, 16
Interrupter, current, 328
Interval, coats of paint, 62
Invar, 355, 487
Iodine, 183, 272
Ironer, wattage, 295
Iron-oxide paint, 231
Irons, 361-362
 calking, 396, 418
 yarning, 396
Isolation joints, 258

J

J bends, 425-426
Jack, 250
Jackhammer, 255
Jaws, wrench, 202
Jigsaw (saber saw), 91
Joint
 butt, 131
 dado-and-rabbet, 131
 hairline, 84
 lap, 84
 sweated, 398
Joint cement, 51
Joint runners, 396
Joint, sweating, 500
Joist, 250, 500
"Jumper," 322

K

Key, street, 377
Keyhole saw, 199, 303, 332
Keyhole saw blades, 118, 135, 159
Kilowatt hour (KWH), 287, 310
Knife
 broad, 51
 electric, 368-369
Knife sharpener, 368
Knockouts, 308
Knot sealer, 59
Knot, underwriter's, 177
Knots, wood, 226
KWH, 287, 310

L

Lacquer thinner, 34

Ladder
 aluminum, 41
 metal, 41, 42, 48
Ladder codes, 41, 46, 57
Ladder, locking device, 43
Ladder shoes, 47
Ladder, trestle, 44
Ladder wall grips, 47
Lamb's wool rollers, 37
Laminated glass, 146
Lamp cord replacement, 343
Lamp repairs, 177-178, 346-348
Lap joints, 84
Latch stile, doors, 141
Latch striker plate, 242
Latex calk, 532
Latex paints, 23, 50, 62, 63, 67, 227, 232
Latex primer, 227
Latex rubber (RU) insulation, 305
Lathe strips, circuitry, 332
Lathing, 133
Lavatories, 431-433
Lavatory faucets, 431
Leaching field, 381
Leaded-joint procedure, 417-418
Leaf skimmer, swimming pool, 273
Leaks, 160-161
 pipes and tanks, 168-189, 460
 roof, 209, 277
Level (tool), 91, 95, 117, 126, 138, 172, 201
Lever-type flush mechanism, 453
Liftout tray, 195
Light reflectance of various colors (chart), 18
Lighting breakers, 326
Lighting fixtures, 325
Lightning, 286
Limit control, heating, 488
Line level, 201
Lineman's pliers, 303
Linoleum, 129, 130
Linseed oil, 146
Linseed oil base, 23
Liquefied petroleum gas (LPG), 481-482
Liquid wood preservative, 226-227
Locking pliers, 392
Logs, gas, 502
Long bend, 419

Long tee, 420
Long-nap roller, 35
Loop, perimeter, 471
Loop system, electric, 458
Loose-fill insulation, 151-152, 522, 524
Loose wires, 340
LPG (liquefied petroleum gas), 481-482

M

Magmas, 486
Magnesium ladders, 41
Mahogany, Philippine, 64
Malathion, 164, 165
Male faucet, 428
Mallet, rubber, 91
Main lighting breakers, 326
Main shutoff valve, 377
Main stack, 380, 381
Main switch, 326
Main water line, 377
Maintenance, ladders, 47-48
Maintenance, panels, 101-102
Manufactured gas, 482
Markings, insulation and cable, 305-306
Mash hammer, 159
Masonry cement, 270
Masonry paints (exterior) (chart) 25, 67, 229-230
Masonry paints (interior), 26 (chart), 27
Masonry panels, 90
Masonry surfaces, painting, 60
Mason's hammer, 196
Mastic, 128
Mastic-type adhesives, 98
Materials, ladders, 41
Measuring, face to face, 398
Measuring instruments, 117, 199-200
Melting pot, 396
Mercuric compound, 237
Mercury switches, 309
Metal conduit, 307
Metal ladders, 41, 42, 48
Metal paints (exterior), 24 (chart)
Metal paints (interior), 26 (chart)
Metal primer, 27

Metal surfaces, painting, 60
Metalwork paint, exteriors, 231
Meter, 310, 377
Mice, 165-166
Mildew, 69, 185, 187, 546
Mildew discoloration, 236-237
Mildew-resistant, 23, 69, 74, 75
Mineral fiber insulation, 522
Mineral spirits, 34, 50, 60, 231
Mineral-surfaced roofing, 207, 208
Miter box, 100
Mixer, 365
Mixer-type compression faucet, 412, 426, 428
Mixing valve, 489
Mohair rollers, 35
Moisture, painting, 24-25, 66-71
Moisture- and heat-resistant rubber (RHW) insulation, 305
Moisture- and heat-resistant thermoplastic (THW) insulation, 305
Moisture-resistant rubber (RW) insulation, 305
Moisture-resistant thermo-plastic (TW) insulation, 305
Mold, 185-187
Molding, 100, 138
Molten lead, 416-418
Mood suggestion, colors, 18-19
Monochromatic harmony, 16
Mortar, 218
Mortar box, 260
Mortar joint, 218-219
Motor bearings, 364
Motor
    series-wound, 362
    synchronous, 362, 367
Motors, wattage, 295
Mounting boxes, 314-315, 335-336
Mud, 181, 184
Muriatic acid, 159, 219, 255, 267
Mutual complements, 16

N

Nail hammer, 115

Nail ripper, 212
Nails
    drywall, 51
    double-headed, 258
    zinc-coated, 213
Nailset, 38, 91
Naphtha, 34
Naphthenate, 226
National Bureau of Standards (NBS), 536
National Electrical Code, 174, 292, 294, 301, 305, 306, 315, 318, 323, 328
National Fire Protection Association, 292
National Plumbing Code, 384
National Sanitation Foundation, 403
National Swimming Pool Institute, 275
Natural finishes, 64-65
Natural gas, 482
Needle-nose pliers, 303, 346
Neoprene pipe sleeve, 414
Nested saw, 118
"Neutral" wire, 306, 320, 323
New space heating, 490
Nichrome coils, 354
Nipple, fixtures, 342
Nipples, 406
NM, 306, 323
Noncompression faucets, 412, 426
Nonconductors, 288
Nonimmersible frying pans, 358
Nonmetallic sheathed cable (Type NM or "Romex"), 306, 323
Nontamperable (Type S) fuse, 312
Nuclear fuel, 486
Number two Phillips screwdriver, 197
Nut socket wrench, 389
Nylon jacket electric cord, 346

"O" ring, 168
Oakum, 417, 533

Odor, gas, 191-192
Odors, 184
Offsets, 420
Ogee scraper, 38
Ohms, 286
Oil base, 23, 25, 50, 58, 63
Oil base linseed, 23, 146
Oil burner, 482, 506
Oil burner controls, 488
Oil burner maintenance, 540
Oil grades, 482
Oil heating, 482
Oil primer, 227
Oil-base paint, 227
Oils, bleaching, 64-65
One-pipe hot-water system, 472, 474
One-pipe steam system, 474
Open-end wrench, 201, 389
Open hot-water system, 472
Oscillators, mechanical, 363
Outdoor boxes, 328
Outdoor wiring, 327-328
Outflow pipe, 445
Outlet, 287, 295, 331, 469
Oven, 366-367
Oven, wattage, 295
Overflow tube, 451
Overheating, 542
Overload, 287, 340

P

P trap, 380, 419, 420, 425, 546
Packing nut, 168, 536
Packing nut socket wrench, 389
Pad applicators, 35
Paint
    aluminum, 25, 37, 66, 96, 156, 226, 236
    casein, 27
    cement-water, 229-230
    concrete-sealer, 127
    iron-oxide, 231
    latex, 227, 232
    oil-base, 227
    red-lead, 231
    resin emulsion, 229, 230
    self-cleaning, 23
    solution, 237
Paint application, 53-54, 61-63

Paint problems
    blistering, 232-233
    chalking, 233
    cracking, 234
    peeling, 237
Paint quantity (area charts), 29-31
Paint types (chart), 24
Panel heating, radiant, 474-475
Panel number chart, 93
Panel siding, exteriors, 211
Paneling, 136-137
    plywood, 90
    solid-wood, 90
    wood-grain, 89
Paneling materials, 88-90
Paper, emery, 324
Paperhanging tools, 77-79
Paraffin, 143
Parapet walls, roof, 210
Paring chisel, 119, 201
Paste, wallpaper, 82
Paste wheat, 74
Pasting table, 76
Patching compound, 254, 266
Patio, 266-271
PE, 403
Peeling paint, 68, exteriors, 237
Pegboard, 195
Pein hammer, 396
Penetrating stain, 65
Pentachlorophenol, 96, 226
Percolation rate, 386
Percolation test, 385-386
Perforated hardboard, 195
Perimeter heating system, 469
Perimeter loop, 471
Perlite, 522
Peroxide, 236-237
Pesticide safety, 166
Pests, 164
Petroleum, liquefied, 481
Phenyl mercuric compound, 237
Philippine mahogany, 64
Phillips screwdriver, 115, 197
Phosphate, trisodium, 69, 79, 185, 236
Pilot bit, 203-204
Pilot light, 482
Pipe
    brass, 402
    cast iron, 414
    copper, 397, 499
    galvanized, 401-402, 418

hubless, 396, 414
    plastic, 403-405, 418
    rigid copper, 398
Pipe, bell and spigot, 414
Pipe cutters, 392-393
Pipe diameter and thread length (chart), 394
Pipe, DWV, 418
Pipe fittings, 406-408
Pipe joint compound, 402
Pipe, sweating, 459
Pipe wrench, 390
Pipeless furnace, 466
Piping, 384, 389
Pit, seepage, 445
Pitch-base roof coating, 210
Plane, 91
Plane, wood, 142
Planing doors, 241
Planks, designer, 90
Plaster repairs, 133
Plaster walls, 50, 52
Plasterboard, see Gypsum wallboard
Plastic, acrylic, 146
Plastic DWV pipe, 418
Plastic pipe, 403-405
Plastic sheeting, 537
Plates, 93
Platform ladder, 44
Plenum, 467, 491
Pliers, 116, 198, 302, 346, 378, 392
    channel-lock, 392
    lineman's, 303
    locking, 392
    needle-nose, 303, 346
    slip-joint, 116, 198
    small-nosed, 378-379
Plug, cleanout, 381, 420
Plugs, 345-346, 408
Plug-type fuse, 311
Plumb bob, 78
Plumb line, 83, 91, 95
Plumber's furnace, 417
"Plumbers helper," see Force cup
Plumbing codes, 384, 386, 397
Plumbing system, 190, 372, 376 (diagram)
Plumbing shut-down (diagram), 190
Plungers, 388, 454
Plywood paneling, 90
Points, galzier's, 145-146

Polishing disc, 203
Polyester, fiberglass reinforced, 437
Polyester (FRP) bathtub, 437
Polyethylene (PE), 403
Polyethylene plastic sheet, 524, 529
Polyurethane, 27
Polyvinyl chloride (PVC), 403, 418
"Ponding," 264
Popped nails, 50-51
Pop-up drains, 431, 435, 456
Porch, 249-250
Portland cement, 229, 253, 258
Pot-type oil burner, 482
Pouring concrete, 256-260
Powder, bleaching, 184
Power consumption chart, 295
Power failures, 338
Power line, fallen, 278
Power plant, 288
Power saw, 91
Power-out, 338
Prefabricated fireplace, 502
Prepainting, 37
Prepasted wallpaper, 77
Preservatives, water repellant, 64
Preservatives, wood, 226-227
Pressure-feed sprayer, 36, 37
Pressure flush valves, 410
Pressure test, 384
Pressure-type oil burner, 482
Primary colors, 16
Primers, 23, 26, 50, 62, 227, 231, 261
    alkali-resistant, 25
    fortified, 26
    latex, 227
    oil, 227
Professional house inspection services, 282
Propane heating, 482
Propane torch, 38, 396, 398
"Pull boxes," 318
Pull-chain fixtures, 325
Pulley, extension ladder, 46
Pump, booster, 472
Pump check valves, 356
Pump, circulating, 472
Pump, condensation, 474
Pump control, 488
Pump, heat, 476, 481, 543
Pump heater wells, 356

Purchasing tools, 195
Purification, water, 182-183
Push-style hand drill, 116
Putty, 145, 146
Putty knife, 28, 51, 118, 128, 133, 145, 148, 200, 208
PVC, 403, 418

Quarter bend, 419
Quantity of paint (area charts), 29-31

R insulation, 305
Radiant panel heating, 474
Radiator, 471, 540
Radiators, bleeding, 505
Radiator cabinet, 472
Radial saw, 91
Radio, wattage, 295
Rafters, 206-207
Range, wattage, 295
Rapid starters, 348
Rasp, 252
Ratchet wrench, 201
Rate, percolation, 386
Rats, 166
Razor-blade scraper, 38
Ream-cut conduit, 318
Reamers, 393
Receptacles, 308
Red cedar shingles, 213
Red-lead paint, 231
Reducing bend, 419
Reducing tee, 420
Reducing Y, 420
Redwood, 64
Reflectance chart, 18
Refrigerant, 510
Refrigerated air conditioning, 510
Refrigerator, wattage, 295
Register, 468, 496, 505, 510
Reinforcing tape, wallboard, 134
Relative humidities, 156
Removing floor boards, 166
Repairing holes in wallboard, 135
Replacing floor tile, 128, 129
Replacing worn washers, 168
Resin compound, 161

Resin-emulsion paint, 229, 230
Resistance, 287, 288
Resistance heater, 477, 481
Resistance to fumes, 23
Return grille, 505
Revents, 379, 380
Reverse trap toilet, 439
RH insulation, 305
Rheostat, 287
RHW insulation, 305
Rigid copper piping, 398
Ripsaw, 91, 118, 199
Riser, 131, 472, 493, 551
Roaster, wattage, 295
Rock salt, 278
Rock wool insulation, 522, 528
Roll roofing, 207, 209
Rolled vinyl, 535
Rollers, 32, 35-36, 53, 61, 71, 79
"Romex" cable, 306, 316
Ronnel, 164, 165
Roof leak, 277
Roofing
    asphalt, 207-210
    bituminous, 209
    built-up, 210
    mineral-surfaced, 207, 210
    roll, 207, 209
    tile, 211-212
Roofing felt, 207
Room air conditioner, 512, 552
Rosin-core solder, 304
Rotary cranking hand drill, 116
Rotary oil burner, 482
Rotisserie oven/broiler, 366-367
Rotors, 362-363
Round sand brushes, 73
RPM, drill, 202
RU insulation, 305
Rubber, butyl, 273-274
Rubber mallet, 91
Rubber (R) insulation, 305
Rung lock, ladders, 46
Runners, joint, 396
Rust-inhibitive pigments, 231
R-value, 523

S fuse, 312

S trap, 425
Saber saw, 91, 204
Safety codes, ladders, 41, 46, 57
Safety glass, 247
Safety glazing material, 146
Safety, ladders, 48-49
Safety, painting, 57
Safety, pesticide, 166
Safety, roofwork, 206-207
Safety shoe, ladders, 47
Sagging floors, 126-127
Sail stack, 380
Salt, 278
Sander, belt, 38
Sander, electric, 204
Sanding disc, 203
Sandpaper, 38, 52, 59, 75
Sash brushes, 33
Sash cord, 144, 244
Sash pulleys, 238-239
Saw
   circular, 204
   compass, 118, 199
   coping, 91, 97, 199
   crosscut, 91, 118, 199
   hacksaw, 204
   holesaw, 204
   keyhole, 118, 135, 159, 199
      303, 332
   nested, 118
   ripsaw, 118, 199
   saber, 204
SBI, 471
Scrapers, 38
Screeding, 261
Screen doors, 242, 247-248
Screens, 147-148
Screwdriver, 155, 197-198, 302
   electrician's, 302
   flat-tip, 115
   Phillip's, 115, 197
   slots, 197
Screw-driving bit, 122, 203
Screw-in breaker, 311-312
Screw-type jack, 126, 127
Sealer, knots, 59
Seam rollers, 77, 79
Seams, wallpaper, 84
Seasonal checklist, house
   maintenance, 111-113
Seat, 411
Seat repairs, 448
Seat-dressing tool, 168, 387, 448
Secondary colors, 16
Seeding, 267-268

Seepage, 157-158
Seepage pit, 445
Seepage test, wall, 158
Self-cleaning paint, 23
Self-rimming lavatory, 432
Semigloss finish, 25, 52
Semitransparent stain, 65
Septic distribution box, 445
Septic tank, 378, 381, 445
Series-wound universal motor,
   362
Service, 287, 288, 309, 320-321
Service entrance (Type SE)
   cable, 307
Sewers, 378, 458
Sewing machine, wattage, 295
Shadow line, 99
Shale tile roofing, 211-212
Shallow-box fixture, 336
Sharpener, 368
Sheathed cable, 306, 323
Sheet copper, 211
Sheet vinyl, 139
Sheetrock, see Gypsum
   wallboard
Shelf, bucket, 44
Shellac, 27, 55, 96
Shelves, 89
Shim, 93, 141, 240
Shimming, 124, 138, 141
Shingle siding, 221
Shingles
   asbestos-cement, 212-214,
      224, 227
   strip, 207
   wood, 213
Shock absorber, 378
Shoe, door, 535
Shoes, ladder, 47
Short tee, 420
Short-circuit, 339
Shower fittings, 434
Shower stalls, 437-438
Shrinkage cracks, ceramic tile,
   137
Shutoff valve, 377, 378
Sidewalk, 255-258
Siding, 221-224
Silicone alkyd enamels, 227
Silverfish, 165
Single-pole switches, 320
Single-speed drill, 202
Sink, 430-431
Sink strainer, 428-429
Sink tailpiece, 425

Siphon jet toilet, 439
Siphon vortex toilet, 439
Sizing, 75, 80
Skylight, 210
Slate roofings, 210-211
Sledgehammer, 255-396
Sleeve clamp, 414
Sliding windows, 144
Slip-joint pliers, 116, 198
Slump, 267
Small-nosed pliers, 278, 369
Smooth-faced roll roofing,
   207-209
Smoothing brush, 79, 83, 87
Snake, 173, 183, 388, 454-455,
   459
Snips, aviation, 304, 491
Snow line, 328
Socket chisel, 118, 200-201
Softener, 377
Softener, electric, 38
Soil stack, 380
Solar heating, 477-479
Soldering, 324, 396, 398-399
Solderless connectors, 309, 320,
   323, 326
Soleplate, electric iron, 361
Solid-wood stain, 65
Solid-wood paneling, 90
Solution paints, 23
Solvent base, 23, 25
Solvents, 403-405
"Sounding," 334
Space heating units, 466
Space sprays, 163
Spackle, 51, 52, 79
Spackling compound, 133
Spade bit, 121, 203
Spar-varnish, 235
Spigot, bell pipe, 414
Spindle, 411
Spirits, 231
Spirits, mineral, 34, 50, 66
Splicing, 323-324
Spline, 148
Split-complementary harmony,
   16
Spray hose, 425
Sprayers, 32, 36-37, 61
Sprays, 163
Spring season, painting, 15
Spring stripping, 150-152
Springs, bending, 400
Squeaking floors, 123-125
Squeaking stairs, 131

Squeegee, 75, 77
Stack, main, 380-381
Stain, penetrating, 65
Stain problems, 69
Stairs, 131-132
Stalls, shower, 437-438
Standards, American National Institute, 40, 41, 46, 47
Staples, surface wiring, 310, insulated, 351
Starters, 348, 349
Starting screws, 197
Static electricity, 286
Static-fill test, 384
Stator, fan, 363
Steam iron, 362
Steel bathtub, 436
Steel Boiler Institute (SBI), 471
Steel casement windows, 145
Steel, galvanized, 60
Steel pipe clamp, 414
Steel tape, 200
Steel windows, 239, 246
Steel wool, 52
Steep roof, 206-207
Stepladders, 42-44
Steps, 252
Stereo, wattage, 295
Sticking doors, 140-143
Stillson wrench, 390
Stippling, 56
Stock, blank, 72, 75, 76
Stocks, die, 394
Stoker-fired coal burner controls, 489
Storage
    ladders, 48,
    tools, 195-196
Storm debris, 180-181
Storm sash, 536-539
Storm sewers, 162, 214
Straight ladder, 41
Straight tubes (fluorescent), 350
Straightedge, 260, 262
Strainer, downspout, 215
Strainer, sink, 428-429
Strap wrench, 391
Straps, surface wiring, 310
Street elbow, 406
Street key, 377
Street valve, 377
Striker plate, latch, 242
Striking-off, 261
Stringer, 131
Strip shingles, 207

Striping, 56
Stripping
    aluminum, 150-152
    bronze, 150-151
    tension, 144
    weather, 149-151
    wire, 302, 316, 343
Strips, furring, 95, 100, 136, 138
Stucco, 219-220
Stud finder, 331
Studs, 93, 133, 135
Styrene, acrylonitrile butadiene, 418
Subflooring, 123, 124, 500
Subpanels, 337
Suction-feed sprayers, 36
Sulfide discoloration, 236-237
Sulfide flame detector, 488
Summer, painting, 15
Sump pump, 181
Sun lamp, wattage, 295
Sunlight, exterior painting, 62, 228
Supply line, 377
Supply shop valve, 423, 424-425
Surface sprays, 163
Surface wiring, 310, 336
Sweated joint, 398, 500
Sweating pipes, 459
Sweeps, 472, 535
Swelling doors, 140-143
Swimming pool, 272-275
Swirling, concrete, 263
Switches, 287, 288, 308-309, 320-323, 326, 348, 355
    bimetallic, 355
    dimmer, 309
    fluorescent fixture, 348
    four-way, 309
    main, 326
    single-pole, 320
    three-way, 309, 321-323
    push button, 308
Symbols, electrical (chart), 299
Synchronous motor, 362, 367
Synthetic bristles, 33

T

Tack hammer, 196

Tailpiece, sink, 425
Tamper, concrete pouring, 256
Tamping, blacktop, 265
Tang chisel, 118, 200
Tank, septic, 378, 381, 445
Tank vacuum cleaner, 369
Tap splice, 324
Tape
    drywall, 51
    reinforcing, 134
    teflon, 402
Tape measure, 117
Tar paper, 71
Tees, 406, 420, 472,
    cross, 406,
    long, 420,
    short, 420,
    reducing, 420
Teflon tape, 402
Television set, wattage, 295
Temperature, painting, 62
Temperature-pressure relief valve, 411, 444
Tempered glass, 146
Tempered steel screwdriver blade, 197
Template, 331
Ten-point crosscut saw, 199
Tension stripping, 144
Terminal connections, 320
Termite damage, 181
Termites, 181, 226
Terrazzo, 266
Tertiary colors, 16
Test
    percolation, 385-386
    static-fill, 384
Tester, 304-305, 354-355
Tetrachloride, carbon, 231
Textured paint, 55
Thermoplastic (T) insulation, 305
Thermal unit (Btu), 480
Thermostats, 355, 358, 359, 380, 381, 386, 392, 487, 504
Thread length, pipes (chart), 394
Threshold, interlocking, 536
THW insulation, 305
Thinner, 34
Thin-walled conduit, 307, 317
Threaders, 394
Three-way switches, 309, 321-323
Three wire-cable, 321
Three-wire service, 294

Tile
  acoustic, 26
  ceiling, 138
  ceramic, 137-138
  drain, 531
  floor, 128-131
  roofing, 211-212
Time delay fuse, 311, 340
Tincture of iodine, 183
Toaster, 355-356
Toaster, wattage, 295
Toggle bolt, 169
Toggle breaker, 312
Toggle switches, 309
Toilet, 170-173, 438-442,
  450-455,
  siphon jet, 439,
  siphon vortex, 439
Tongue-and-groove flooring, 251
Tool storage, 195-196
Toolbox, 195
Tools, plumbing, 387-396
Torch, propane, 38, 396, 398
Torpedo level, 201
Toxic calk, 532
Trade Commission, 45
Transformer, doorbell, 350
Transparent stain, 65
Trap, 379-380, 419-420, 425,
  445, 546
Trap toilet, reverse, 439
Trash compactor, wattage, 295
Tread, 131
Trestle ladder, 44
Triad harmony, 18
Trim, exterior painting, 24
Trim, paneling, 100
Trim undercoats, 25
Trim, wallpaper, 74
Trimming wheels, 79, 84
Trip-lever drain, 435
Tripped breaker, 339
Trisodium phosphate (TSP), 69,
  79, 185, 236
Trowel, 260-262
Try square, 117
TSP, 69, 79
Tube, capillary, 510
Tube cutter, 393
Tube, overflow, 451
Tubes, fluorescent, 349-350
Tub-shower fittings, 433-434
Tubing, electrical, 307
Tungsten carbide bits, 203
Turnbuckle, 147

Turpentine, 34, 52, 54
TW insulation, 305
Twist bit, 121, 203
Two-speed drill, 202
Two-twenty/two-forty (220-240
  lines), 297, 298, 299, 300, 327
TY, 420
Type AC cable, 309, 316
Type K pipe, 397-398 (chart)
Type L pipe, 397-398 (chart)
Type M pipe, 397-398 (chart)
Type NM cable, 306, 316
Type S fuse, 312
Type SE cable, 307
Type USE cable, 307

U

UL, 40, 46, 47, 292-293
Undercoats, trim, 25
Under-counter lavatory, 432
Underground circuits, 328
Underground fused (UF) cable,
  307
Underground service entrance
  (Type USE) cable, 307, 328
Underwriter's knot, 177, 344
Underwriter's Laboratories (UL),
  40, 46, 47, 292-293
Union, 406
Unit efficiency, heating, 481
United States Pharmocopeia
  (USP), 183
United States Public Health
  Service, 184
Universal motors, 362, 368, 369
Unusual paint effects, 55-56
Upright vacuum cleaner, 369
Ureaformaldehyde, 522
Utility knife, 118, 200

V

Vacuum cleaner, 369-371
Valance, wallpapering, 73
Values table, heat, 481

Valve
  angle, 408
  check, 411
  drainable, 410,
  flush, 452
  gate, 408, 449
  globe, 408, 449
  ground key, 410, 450
  main shutoff, 377
  pressure flush, 410
  pump check, 356
  street, 377
  supply, 423-425
Vapor barrier, 70, 93, 101, 154,
  155, 156
Vaporizing burners, 482
Variable-speed drill, 121, 202
Varnish, 26, 55, 96, 235
Varnish brushes, 33
V-edged rollers, 36
Vent, 378, 379, 380
Ventilation, crawl-space, 70-71
Verticle drain line, 416
Vinyl adhesives, 74, 75, 80
Vinyl bulb, 536
Vinyl patching-compound, 254,
  266
Vinyl, sheet, 129
Vinyl wallpaper, 75
Vises, 394-395
Visible condensation, 155-156
Volt, 286
Voltage, 288
Voltage lines, 297-300, 327

W

Waffle iron, 359-361,
  wattage, 295
Walks, concrete, 253-256
Wall boxes, 308
Wall grips, ladder, 47
Wall scrapers, 38
Wallboard, 50
Wallboard, gypsum, 133-136
Wall-hung lavatory, 432
Wallpaper
  colors, 72-73
  estimate (chart), 74
  hanging, 82-87
  paste, 82

prepasted, 77
trim, 74
vinyl, 75
Walls, plaster, 50-52
Washdown toilet, 439
Washer, 168, 411, 448
Washing machine, wattage, 295
Waste disposal unit, 429
Waste water, 382
Water
bases, 23, 25, 58, 63
faucets, 167
hammer, 169-170, 378
hard, 356, 362
heater, 386, 442-444
heater (diagram), 377
heater recovery rate, 443
waste, 382
Water-repellant preservatives
(WRP), 64
Water-pump pliers, 392
Watt, 287
Wattage, 288, 295, 313,
(formula), 330
Wattage, house appliances
(chart), 295
Wax, 27
Wax patching crayon, 125
Weatherstripping, 149-151,
532-539
Western red cedar, 64
Wheat paste, 74
Wheel, color, 16
Wheels, trimming, 79, 84
Windows
aluminum, 239, 244, 246, 537,

casement, 515
sliding, 144
steel, 145, 239, 246
stuck, 143-145
Winterizing, swimming pool, 275
Wire
electric, 305
ground, 306, 323
neutral, 306, 320, 323
surface, 310, 326
Wire brushes, 38, 67
Wire glass, 146
Wire nuts, 309
Wire size and capacity
(chart), 306
Wire stripping, 302, 316, 343
Wiring, 288, 332
Wiring, aluminum, 305
Wiring, inadequate, 300-301
Wiring symbols, 299, 352 (chart)
Wood
chisels, 118-119, 145, 201-
202, 303
heating, 485
ladders, 41, 47, 48
paint (exterior), 24
paint (exterior chart), 25,
61-62
paint (interior chart), 26
painting surfaces, 59
pane, 142
preservatives, 226, 227
screw pilot bit, 121, 124
shingles, 213
wasps, 226
Wood-grain paneling, 89-90

Woodwork preparation, painting,
52-53
Wool
insulation, 522, 528
rollers, 35
Workbench, 196
Worn washers, 168
Wrenches
adjustable, 116, 202, 389-390
basin, 391
box, 201, 389
chain, 201, 391
open-end, 201, 389
pipe, 201, 390
ratchet, 201, 390
stillson, 390
strap, 391
Wrinkling paint, exteriors, 236
WRP, 64

Y, 420
Yardstick, 117
Yarning iron, 396
Yoke vise, 394

Zinc-coated nails, 213
Zinc napthenate, 226